T3-BNL-211

THE COST OF LIVING IN AMERICA

Since the late nineteenth century, the "cost of living" has been a prominent part of debates about American political economy. By the early twentieth century, that prominence had taken a quantitative turn, as businessmen, unions, economists, and politicians all turned to cost-of-living statistics in their struggle to control and reshape the American economy. Today, the continuing power of these statistics is exemplified by the U.S. Consumer Price Index, whose fluctuations have enormous consequences for economic policy and the federal budget (including the allocation of hundreds of billions of dollars annually through cost-of-living escalator clauses in programs such as Social Security). In this book, Thomas A. Stapleford interweaves economic theory with political history to create a novel account of this quantitative knowledge. Demonstrating that statistical calculations inevitably require political judgments, he reveals what choices were made in constructing and using cost-of-living statistics and why those choices matter, both for our understanding of American history and for contemporary political and economic life.

Thomas A. Stapleford is an assistant professor in the Program of Liberal Studies at the University of Notre Dame, where he also teaches in the Graduate Program in the History and Philosophy of Science. He has published related work in the *Journal of American History, Labor History*, and *Labor: Studies in the Working-Class History of the Americas*. Research for this book was supported by the National Science Foundation, the Notre Dame Faculty Research Program, and the Harvard Center for American Political Studies.

MONTGOMERY COLLEGE
GERMANTOWN CAMPUS LIBRARY
GERMANTOWN, MARYLAND

The Cost of Living in America

A Political History of Economic Statistics, 1880–2000

THOMAS A. STAPLEFORD

University of Notre Dame

CAMBRIDGE
UNIVERSITY PRESS

10300092

DEC 1 0 2010

CAMBRIDGE UNIVERSITY PRESS
Cambridge, New York, Melbourne, Madrid, Cape Town, Singapore,
São Paulo, Delhi, Dubai, Tokyo

Cambridge University Press
32 Avenue of the Americas, New York, NY 10013–2473, USA

www.cambridge.org
Information on this title: www.cambridge.org/9780521719247

© Thomas A. Stapleford 2009

This publication is in copyright. Subject to statutory exception
and to the provisions of relevant collective licensing agreements,
no reproduction of any part may take place without the written
permission of Cambridge University Press.

First published 2009

Printed in the United States of America

A catalog record for this publication is available from the British Library.

Library of Congress Cataloging in Publication data
Stapleford, Thomas A., 1974–
The Cost of Living in America : a political history of economic statistics,
1880–2000/Thomas A. Stapleford.
p.   cm.
Includes bibliographical references and indexes.
ISBN 978-0-521-89501-9 (hardback) – ISBN 978-0-521-71924-7 (pbk.)
1. Cost and standard of living–United States–History. I. Title.
HD6983.S664 2009
339.4′209730904–dc22   2009022050

ISBN 978-0-521-89501-9 Hardback
ISBN 978-0-521-71924-7 Paperback

Cambridge University Press has no responsibility for the persistence or
accuracy of URLs for external or third-party Internet Web sites referred to in
this publication and does not guarantee that any content on such Web sites is,
or will remain, accurate or appropriate.

To Cathy, who made this book possible

Here in this group we are colleagues who can speak with candor. Let us therefore candidly recognize that statistical truths, like the other truths about man's social life, are created rather than discovered.... [W]hen it comes to unemployment or poverty or price inflation or mental disease, we are dealing with social phenomena. It is man who invents and defines these categories. It is man who selects a few dimensions which are capable of measurement and uses them to characterize complex social conditions and relationships. It is man who decides how much effort should be expended in measuring these dimensions or others which might be selected.[1]

> – Arthur M. Ross, Commissioner of the U.S. Bureau of Labor Statistics,
> Speech before the Washington Statistical Society, January 1966

[1] Published in Arthur M. Ross, "Living with Symbols," *The American Statistician*, vol. 20, no. 3 (1966): 16.

Contents

List of Figures, Charts, and Tables

FIGURES

CHARTS

TABLES

Acknowledgments

Over the many years that I have worked on this project, I have accumulated an enormous debt to colleagues, friends, and family. As a graduate student in the history of science at Harvard University, I benefited from the unwavering support and guidance of Anne Harrington, who remains a model teacher and scholar for me. Peter Buck provided both incisive criticism and regular encouragement, and his good-humored skepticism has improved my work immensely. Lizabeth Cohen generously reached across department lines to serve on my committee, and I gained valuable insights into historical analysis and the writing process through her dissertation working group. The graduate students in the Department of the History of Science were an amazing group; I am fortunate to have them as colleagues and friends.

I am grateful to everyone who read all or part of the manuscript and shared their comments, criticisms, and suggestions. Margo Anderson and Spencer Banzhaf gave me extensive comments on every aspect of the book and greatly improved the final version. Peter Buck heroically served double-duty, not only slogging through the dissertation multiple times but returning to read the penultimate manuscript and, as usual, providing crucial advice. My four anonymous readers for Cambridge University Press helped me to think through the larger structure of the book, key components of my arguments, and even the details of my prose. Many others critiqued chapters or large sections at various stages, including Franklin Fisher, Bernd Goehring, Claudia Goldin, Michael Gordin, Meg Jacobs, Eric Kupferberg, Liz Lee, Kevin Mongrain, Jessica Murdoch, Pierpaolo Polzonetti, Pat Spacks, Matt Stanley, and Jack Triplett. Through conversations and correspondence, an even larger number of colleagues have shaped my perspective, helped me to refine my ideas, and shared their own expertise, including Alain Desrosières, Emmanuel Didier, Mary Furner, Phil Mirowski, Mary Morgan,

Sharrona Pearl, Ted Porter, Marshall Reinsdorf, Grace Shen, and Rob Van Horn. At Cambridge University Press, I am grateful for the diligent work of the editorial staff, and especially for Scott Parris's constant enthusiasm and commitment to the project.

Faculty and students in the Program of Liberal Studies at the University of Notre Dame have made South Bend an exciting and stimulating place to work, while the Dean's office and the Office of Research have provided generous financial support for research travel and leave time. Throughout my research and writing, I have been supported by a variety of fellowships and grants, including a grant from the National Science Foundation (no. 0522433), a Packard Dissertation Completion Fellowship, a dissertation fellowship from the Harvard Center for American Political Studies, a summer research grant from the Charles Warren Center, and a research grant from the Faculty Research Program at the University of Notre Dame. While revising the final manuscript, I had the pleasure of being a Visiting Scholar at the American Academy of Arts and Sciences, which gave me the time and resources to complete the project.

Equally valuable was the extensive help I received from archival staff across the country. Without the aid of numerous archivists at the National Archives, I would have never been able to locate the necessary records within the largely unprocessed collection of the Bureau of Labor Statistics. At the George Meany Memorial Archives, Bob Reynolds shared his extensive insight into the history of the AFL research department and its manuscript collections. Judson MacLaury and Linda Stinson at the Historical Office in the U.S. Department of Labor helped me to find and use their rich oral history collections. Staff at Columbia University's Rare Book and Manuscript Library, the Franklin D. Roosevelt Library in Hyde Park, the Walter P. Reuther Library at Wayne State University, the Wisconsin Historical Society, the Special Collections Research Center at George Washington University, and the Special Collections Library at Penn State University all helped to make my research enjoyable and hassle-free. Closer to home, Erik Peterson spent numerous hours compiling valuable data from the early history of the U.S. cost-of-living index.

I have been blessed with a wonderful group of family and friends who are too numerous to thank individually. I'm especially grateful to my immediate family, whose care and company have carried me through. Dick and Judy Boeckenstedt have given me love and support for nearly two decades. My parents, John and Linda, encouraged my intellectual pursuits throughout my life, but more importantly, they have been shining examples of love and service. Any of the character strengths that I have are due to their inspiration. My sister Liza's humor and joyful spirit have entertained me since we were young; I've been lucky to have her as a sibling.

I can never fully express my debt and gratitude to my wife, Cathy, who made this project possible. She dealt with long hours, listened patiently as I worked through problems, arranged vacations around archival trips, and provided a much-needed voice of good sense, wisdom, and support. Most of all, she has been a wonderful mother to our two children, Jane and Will. The love and laughter that the three of them share with me brighten my days and remind me of what matters most in my life. And yes, Jane, Daddy's book is finally done.

Abbreviations

ORGANIZATIONS AND TITLES

AARP	American Association of Retired Persons
ACSL	Advisory Committee to the Secretary of Labor
ACW	Amalgamated Clothing Workers
AFDC	Aid to Families with Dependent Children
AFL	American Federation of Labor
ASA	American Statistical Association
BAE	U.S. Bureau of Agricultural Economics
BHE	U.S. Bureau of Home Economics
BLS	U.S. Bureau of Labor Statistics
BRAC	Business Research Advisory Council
CEA	U.S. Council of Economic Advisers
CIO	Congress of Industrial Organizations
CIR	U.S. Committee on Industrial Relations
COGSIS	Committee on Government Statistics and Information Services
COLA	cost-of-living adjustment
CPI	U.S. Consumer Price Index
CRIW	Conference on Research in Income and Wealth
EFC	Emergency Fleet Corporation
FESAC	Federal Statistics Advisory Committee
GM	General Motors
GNP	Gross National Product
JEC	U.S. Congress, Joint Economic Committee
LRAC	Labor Research Advisory Council
NBER	National Bureau of Economic Research
NCF	National Civic Federation

NCL	National Consumer League
NICB	National Industrial Conference Board
NRC	National Resources Committee
NWLB	National War Labor Board
OEO	U.S. Office of Economic Opportunity
OPA	U.S. Office of Price Administration
OAA	Old-Age Assistance
OASDI	Old-Age, Survivors', and Disability Insurance
OASI	Old-Age and Survivors' Insurance
SLAB	Shipbuilding Labor Adjustment Board
UAW	United Auto Workers
UE	United Electrical, Radio, and Machine Workers
USWA	United Steelworkers of America

PERIODICAL LITERATURE AND BOOK SERIES

AER	*American Economic Review*
BLS Bulletin	Bulletin of the U.S. Bureau of Labor Statistics
HOPE	*History of Political Economy*
ILR	*International Labour Review*
JAH	*Journal of American History*
JASA	*Journal of the American Statistical Association*
JPE	*Journal of Political Economy*
MLR	*Monthly Labor Review*
NABL	Proceedings of the annual convention of officials from state bureaus of labor statistics. The titles of both the organization and its proceedings changed several times; in the notes, the latter is abbreviated as *NABL* (the most common later title being "National Association of Officials of Bureaus of Labor Statistics").
NYT	*New York Times*
PASA	*Publications of the American Statistical Association*
QJE	*Quarterly Journal of Economics*
SIW	Studies in Income and Wealth

ABBREVIATED ARCHIVES AND LIBRARIES

FDR Library	Franklin D. Roosevelt Library, Hyde Park, New York
NARA	U.S. National Archives II, College Park, Maryland

RBML	Rare Book and Manuscript Library, Columbia University, New York, New York
WRL	Walter Reuther Library, Wayne State University, Detroit, Michigan
WSHS	Wisconsin State Historical Society, Madison, Wisconsin

ABBREVIATED MANUSCRIPT COLLECTIONS (INDENTED ABBREVIATIONS ARE SERIES TITLES FROM WITHIN AN ARCHIVAL COLLECTION)

BLS	Bureau of Labor Statistics, RG 257, NARA
ACF 1941–62	Records of the Commissioner of Labor Statistics, Advisory Committee Files, 1941–62
GCS 1934–50	General Correspondence and Subject File, 1934–1950
GCS 1946–72	General Correspondence and Subject File, 1936–1972
LRAC	Records of the Labor Research Advisory Council
PFAC	Program Files of the Office of the Associate Commissioner, Office of Prices and Living Conditions, 1946–1979
RCL-PPF 1950–1975	Records of the Commissioner of Labor Statistics, Program and Policy Files, 1950–1975
Wickens correspondence	Correspondence of Deputy Commissioner Aryness J. Wickens, 1939–1950
DOL	Department of Labor, RG 174, NARA
Ida Merriam papers	Papers of Ida Merriam, George Washington University, Washington, D.C.
Lubin papers	Papers of Isador Lubin, FDR Library
NRPB	National Resources Planning Board, RG 187, NARA
NWLB	National War Labor Board, RG 2, NARA
OHC-CU	Oral History Collection, RBML
OMB	Office of Management and the Budget, RG 51, NARA

CSB-ACSL   Central Statistical Board, Records
                            of Cooperating Agencies, Advisory
                            Committee to the Secretary of Labor
CSB-General Records   Central Statistical Board, General Records
SR 1940–68   Statistical Records Relating to Particular
                            Subject Areas, 1940–1968
Perkins papers   Papers of Frances Perkins, RBML
Stewart papers   Papers of Ethelbert Stewart, Southern
                            Historical Collection, University of North
                            Carolina, Chapel Hill
U.S. Shipping Board   U.S. Shipping Board, RG 32, NARA

Introduction

All progressive modern nations desire a satisfactory guide to changes in price levels, by which the stability of the monetary unit, the adequacy of wages, the justice of taxation, and the flow of credits can be gauged. But a compilation of "averages," covering an endless variety of goods, objects, and services, which are continuously undergoing changes in character both in their production and consumption, cannot form a wholly reliable basis for judgment. Yet, without some statistical measurement along these lines, we would be without the crudest instruments to direct economic and political actions; and all scientific attempts to trace trends and future developments would practically cease, or become mere guesswork and intuition.
—A. M. Sakolinski, *Commercial and Financial Chronicle*, June 15, 1944

Economic statistics are a mainstay of modern government, but most citizens know little about how these figures are produced. Generally, the latest economic numbers elicit commentary on current trends: productivity is up (good); unemployment is rising (bad). But the origin of the numbers themselves—their creation and calculation—typically remains invisible to those not concerned with statistical work. Still, such comfortable ignorance is highly unstable (especially when the consequences of statistical judgments are extensive), and periodically the constant murmur of scholarly chatter about the methods and goals of statistical calculation erupts into more strident public debates, in turn raising unsettling questions about the foundations of modern governance.

One of the more spectacular recent examples occurred in the mid-1990s during discussions about the U.S. Consumer Price Index (CPI), a measure of consumer price change calculated by the U.S. Bureau of Labor Statistics. In congressional testimony in 1995, the Chairman of the Federal Reserve, Alan Greenspan, remarked that the CPI was probably overestimating

1

consumer inflation by at least one percentage point per year.[1] This was no minor issue: since the CPI was the most common measure of retail price change, Congress had built escalator clauses based on the index into a wide variety of federal programs as a hedge against inflation (a practice known as "indexation"). Tax brackets, Social Security benefits, federal pension plans, even payments to the school lunch program: all would shift upward automatically as the CPI rose. Accordingly, any overstatement in the calculations could have dramatic financial consequences.

Following Greenspan's remarks, the Senate Finance Committee appointed a five-member committee of economists, chaired by Michael Boskin of Stanford University, to review the index. The report concluded that the CPI was roughly 1.1 percentage points higher than the true rate of inflation each year, a "bias" that was threatening to cripple the federal budget. Using data from the Congressional Budget Office, the Boskin commission declared that the overstatement would increase the federal debt by a staggering $691 billion over the next decade through a combination of reduced revenues (due to higher tax brackets), increased expenses, and debt financing. "More remarkably," the commission noted, by 2006 "the upward bias by itself would constitute the fourth largest federal outlay program, behind only Social Security, health care, and defense."[2]

That a statistical miscalculation could produce the fourth largest federal expenditure was shocking. But for budget hawks, it was also fortuitous. Here at last, declared the *New York Times*, was "a rational way to reduce the deficit": adjust either the CPI or the indexation formulas used in federal programs.[3] Unfortunately for the *Times*, the rationale for adjusting the index proved less straightforward than initially hoped. Some critics contested the commission's estimate of an upward bias; others went further and questioned the conceptual framework behind the commission's critique. A 2002 committee from the National Academy of Sciences returned a split verdict on that issue, while most government statistical agencies outside the United States likewise rejected the commission's conceptual claims.[4] Within

---

[1]   "As Parties Skirmish over Budget, Greenspan Offers Painless Cure," *NYT*, 10 January 1995, p. A1.

[2]   Michael J. Boskin et al., *Toward a More Accurate Measure of the Cost of Living: Final Report to the Senate Finance Committee from the Advisory Commission to Study the Consumer Price Index* (Washington, D.C.: U.S. GPO, 1996), 1–11, esp. 10.

[3]   "A Rational Way to Reduce the Deficit," *NYT*, 1 March 1997, p. 22.

[4]   Boskin et al., *Toward a More Accurate Measure of the Cost of Living*, iii, 22–23. For reactions of varying critical intensity from American economists, see Angus Deaton, "Getting Prices Right: What Should Be Done?" *Journal of Economic Perspectives* 12, no. 1 (1998): 37–46; Robert A. Pollak, "The Consumer Price Index: A Research Agenda and Three Proposals,"

a few years it became clear that the Boskin report had given new structure and impetus to discussions about price index theory but had not succeeded in creating a consensus about the alleged bias in the index. The predicament highlighted by the Boskin commission and its aftermath was not novel. On the contrary, the CPI has been a hotbed of theoretical, methodological, and political controversy since its inception during the First World War. Just as in later years, such debates did not stop politicians, economists, union officials, or businessmen from vesting great power in the index. By mid-century, the CPI's extensive role in regulating wage and salary adjustments had led a congressional committee to call it "the most important single statistic issued by the government." Even if overblown, the committee's verdict captured the financial power already held by the index in the early 1950s: the committee estimated that a 0.5 percent change in the CPI would produce $1 billion in related income transfers each year.[5] Still, the occasion for this declaration—a congressional hearing driven by ongoing criticism of the index—illustrates how controversy and power have walked hand in hand throughout the history of the CPI. Of course, the particulars of the debates have changed: both the theoretical foundations and operational methods of price indexes are far more sophisticated today. Yet even as the CPI has been refined, its applications have been extended, so that the influence of the index repeatedly outstrips the ability of experts to agree about its accuracy and thereby tags seemingly arcane technical debates about statistical calculation and economic theory with enormous financial weight.

Though the CPI may represent a more extreme example of this phenomenon, its situation is not unique: every major economic statistic faces similar debates about methods and interpretation. For economists and

Journal of Economic Perspectives 12, no. 1 (1998): 69–78; Dean Baker, *Getting Prices Right: The Debate over the Consumer Price Index* (Armonk: M.E. Sharpe, 1998); Charles L. Schultze and Christopher Mackie, eds., *At What Price? Conceptualizing and Measuring Cost-of-Living and Price Indexes* (Washington, D.C.: National Academy Press, 2002). For a summary of the views of the U.S. Bureau of Labor Statistics, see David S. Johnson, Stephen B. Reed, and Kenneth J. Stewart, "Price Measurement in the United States: A Decade after the Boskin Report," *MLR* 129, no. 5 (2006): 10–19. For a useful overview of professional responses, see Ernst R. Berndt, "The Boskin Commission Report after a Decade: After-Life or Requiem?" *International Productivity Monitor*, no. 12 (2006): 61–73. Jack Triplett's paper in the same symposium as Berndt (2006) provides a short summary of international reactions.

5 "Report on the Consumers' Price Index," p. 39, appended to U.S. Congress. House Committee on Education and Labor. Subcommittee to Study the Consumers' Price Index, *Consumers' Price Index: Hearings before a Subcommittee of the Committee on Education and Labor*, 82nd Cong., 1st sess., 8–11, 14–18, 21, 24, May and 29 June, 1951.

statisticians, these arguments highlight issues in need of further investigation; the financial and political consequences merely make the problems more pressing. Yet the combination of power and uncertainty in economic statistics can also raise other questions: How and why did we come to this strange place, where extraordinary amounts of money change hands based on small movements in a controversial and admittedly ambiguous statistic such as the CPI? What choices have been made in constructing and using American economic statistics, and what have been the consequences of those decisions?

These questions form the central motivation for this book, a historical study of the production and use of American cost-of-living statistics, a label that includes measures such as expenditure surveys, family budgets that delineate "adequate" standards of living, and price indexes, especially the Consumer Price Index and its ancestors. In part it is a technical tale, about how American economists and statisticians have wrestled with conceptual and methodological questions: What is meant by the "cost of living"? How can you define a meaningful standard of living within an economically and socially diverse nation, and how can you track the changing cost of obtaining that standard over time, especially as consumer purchasing habits and goods themselves undergo radical alterations? Yet it is also a story about political economy, about the proposed and actual application of economic theory and knowledge by the state in its attempt to influence the production and distribution of material or financial resources. Cost-of-living statistics have been used to adjudicate wage disputes, to guide economic planning and policy decisions, and to determine both eligibility and compensation levels for government welfare programs. Economic statistics and twentieth-century political economy are thus deeply intertwined and cannot be fully understood independently of one another.

Grounded in this perspective, my study of American cost-of-living statistics is therefore a study of American political economy as seen through a focused lens, a lens trained on the role of state-created, quantitative knowledge about the "cost of living" in policy decisions, government administration, and industrial relations. Why has it proven so hard to reach agreement about the accuracy of cost-of-living statistics? Why did Americans nonetheless come to rely so heavily on these numbers in political economy, a dependence exemplified by the massive financial transactions controlled through indexation? What can we learn about the development of American politics and labor relations by examining the history of these statistics?

* * *

We can begin by considering the motivation behind the most extreme use of economic statistics in political life—indexation. Fundamentally, indexation is an attempt to eliminate political responsibility for certain government operations by treating them as technical, administrative tasks. Politicians need not haggle over the adjustment of tax brackets or poverty thresholds each year; the CPI does that for them. Not only does indexation promise greater administrative efficiency, but it is often portrayed as a superior solution—a rational method free from the messy imperfections of political negotiation. (Indeed, when President Richard M. Nixon first proposed indexing Social Security payments to the CPI, he explained that this step would help "depoliticize" the system.)[6]

Borrowing from the sociologist Max Weber, I describe processes like indexation as attempts to "rationalize" governance by restricting action to allegedly reasonable rules that are grounded in objective, empirical knowledge.[7] Once the system is established, rules replace the judgment of individual administrators. Accordingly, the propriety of the resulting actions depends solely on the propriety of the rules (should Social Security benefits be adjusted according to changes in the national cost of living?) and the accuracy of the empirical knowledge (is the CPI correct?).

In Weber's view, rationalization would necessarily accompany attempts to gather and exploit power in a liberal democracy.[8] In political theory, liberalism assigns high value to individual rights and autonomy, while democracy (in a pure form) gives every citizen equal control over government affairs. Powerful institutions or groups, if unconstrained, could threaten both the liberal and the democratic character of a society. Rationalization promised to ameliorate this threat by limiting actions to a "reasonable" framework of rules or guidelines. The vast sums of money transferred through

---

[6] Richard M. Nixon, "Special Message to the Congress on Social Security, 25 September 1969," in *Public Papers of the Presidents: Richard Nixon, 1969* (Washington, D.C.: U.S. GPO, 1971), 740–745.

[7] Weber's use of "rationalization" is notoriously loose: Alan Sica, "Rationalization and Culture," in *The Cambridge Companion to Weber*, ed. Stephen Turner (New York: Cambridge University Press, 2000). Likewise, many scholars (especially since the Second World War) have employed the term in a variety of ways to describe, analyze, and critique modern institutions and forms of life. My own usage is restricted to the definition given above, which could perhaps be qualified as "bureaucratic rationalization," if that phrase was not overly cumbersome. I have chosen to retain the label "rationalization"—despite its slippery nature—because I have found aspects of the neo-Weberian literature on rationalization valuable, even though my own interests lie in the details of specific rationalized systems rather than in rationalization as an abstract, social process.

[8] Max Weber, *Economy and Society: An Outline of Interpretive Sociology* (New York: Bedminster Press, 1968), 956–1003.

the U.S. Social Security Administration, for example, are not distributed according to the whims of individual bureaucrats but according to complex rules and benefit calculations. The logic of rationalization assumes that once politicians or political appointees define the broad goals of a program (poverty thresholds should rise alongside the cost of living), responsibility for administering the system and creating the empirical knowledge at its base can be entrusted to career civil servants and technical agencies. In this manner, power can be concentrated while remaining, in principle, under democratic control or oversight.

Beyond legitimating collective power (by constraining it), governance through rational rules offers other potential administrative benefits: It can abet centralized control by restricting the authority of subordinates or by easing oversight through standardized reporting; it can reduce labor costs by transforming tacit, expert knowledge into explicit instructions to be followed by less skilled employees or machines; it can aid efficient, large-scale administration by allowing rapid processing of information; it can render actions of the system more predictable (a prime consideration for regulatory regimes); and it can channel and constrain conflict into specific domains (consider the extensive rules that often comprise workplace grievance procedures).[9] Thus, there can be many motives for turning to rationalized governance and a complex set of causes that contribute to the creation of any given rationalized system.

As this list of potential benefits also suggests, the attraction of rationalization was not limited to the state alone. On the contrary, Weber noted that rationalization appeared most seductive to capitalist businessmen, who valued the allure of quick, precise, predictable, and logic-driven action and sought to instill rationalized administration both within the state and within the confines of their own organizations.[10] Adopted by the state and

---

[9] For examples, see Hugh G. J. Aitken, *Scientific Management in Action: Taylorism at the Watertown Arsenal* (Princeton: Princeton University Press, 1985); David Montgomery, *Workers' Control in America: Studies in the History of Work, Technology, and Labor Struggles* (New York: Cambridge University Press, 1980); James R. Beniger, *The Control Revolution: Technological and Economic Origins of the Information Society* (Cambridge: Harvard University Press, 1986); Simon Schaffer, "Astronomers Mark Time: Discipline and the Personal Equation," *Science in Context* 2 (1988): 115–145; John Carson, "Army Alpha, Army Brass, and the Search for Army Intelligence," *Isis* 84, no. 2 (1993): 278–309; James C. Scott, *Seeing Like a State: How Certain Schemes to Improve the Human Condition Have Failed* (New Haven: Yale University Press, 1998); S. M. Amadae, *Rationalizing Capitalist Democracy: The Cold War Origins of Rational Choice Liberalism* (Chicago: University of Chicago Press, 2003), 61–75. Of course the operating reality rarely matched the idealized vision.

[10] Weber, *Economy and Society*, 974–975.

by private companies, rule-governed administration has therefore become a pervasive feature of contemporary life.

Statistics have strong ties to attempts to rationalize governance (in both its public and private forms). First, statistics make aggregate concepts tangible. Reducing "national unemployment," for example, cannot be a target for economic policy until that concept is defined and measured. Statistics thus make it possible to exercise centralized control by purporting to bring order and legibility to an otherwise ungraspable complex of interactions.[11] Second, the modern discipline of statistics is itself a form of rationalized knowledge-making: a collection of reasonable techniques (i.e., formal or informal rules) for compiling aggregate data and judging their reliability. Indeed, as Theodore Porter has argued, the impersonal, rule-governed nature of quantitative calculation has greatly contributed to its popularity in political life (for example, in cost-benefit analysis, risk assessment, or oversight through accounting regulations). Accordingly, statistics have developed hand-in-hand with attempts by the state and private entities to organize and control a broader environment through "rational" means.[12] A history of the ties between cost-of-living statistics and American governance is thus a history of such rationalization projects.

* * *

[11] I would distinguish this view—which emphasizes the constructed nature of economic statistics—from Michel Callon's claims about the "performative" character of economics. Callon's usage expands the meaning of both "performative" and "economics" in ways that undercut their analytic utility. See the critiques of Callon from Philip Mirowski, Edward Nik-Khah, and Emmanuel Didier in *Do Economists Make Markets? On the Performativity of Economics,* ed. Donald MacKenzie, Fabian Muniesa, and Lucia Siu (Princeton: Princeton University Press, 2007).

[12] Theodore M. Porter, *Trust in Numbers: The Pursuit of Objectivity in Science and Public Life* (Princeton: Princeton University Press, 1995). Numerous scholars have illustrated these connections in specific contexts, e.g., Jean-Claude Perrot and Stuart J. Woolf, *State and Statistics in France, 1789–1815* (New York: Harwood Academic Publishers, 1984); William Alonso and Paul Starr, ed., *The Politics of Numbers* (New York: Russell Sage, 1987); Ian Hacking, *The Taming of Chance* (Cambridge: Cambridge University Press, 1990); Mary O. Furner and Barry Supple, *The State and Economic Knowledge: The American and British Experiences* (Cambridge: Cambridge University Press, 1990); Michael J. Lacey and Mary O. Furner, eds., *The State and Social Investigation in Britain and the United States* (Cambridge: Cambridge University Press, 1993); M. Norton Wise, *The Values of Precision* (Princeton: Princeton University Press, 1995); Silvana Patriarca, *Numbers and Nationhood: Writing Statistics in Nineteenth-Century Italy* (Cambridge: Cambridge University Press, 1996); Alain Desrosières, *The Politics of Large Numbers: A History of Statistical Reasoning,* trans. Camille Naish (Cambridge: Harvard University Press, 1998); J. Adam Tooze, *Statistics and the German State, 1900–1945: The Making of Modern Economic Knowledge* (Cambridge: Cambridge University Press, 2001).

The trouble with rationalization, of course, is that it cannot deliver what it promises: an apolitical, neutral form of knowledge and governance. Consider the case of economic statistics. Most economists would agree that the proper method for a given calculation depends on its objective; furthermore, selecting objectives for state-produced economic statistics requires political choices. Rationalization assumes a straightforward operation for this principle: the state or its representatives tell technical experts what they would like to know and experts define how best to produce that knowledge and to assess its accuracy. But the situation is rarely that simple, since the central concepts used to define economic statistics—"unemployment," "inflation," "productivity," etc.—are rife with ambiguities. These ambiguities become recognizable when one seeks to translate the concepts into operational terms—that is, to construct a practical, working measure—especially when faced with challenges from those whose political perspectives or values differ from one's own. In this situation, to choose between possible interpretations is to choose between competing objectives for a given calculation, and thus to make what is necessarily a political choice (i.e., a choice that is properly within the domain of political deliberation, even if political reasoning per se has not factored into the decision).

A history of American cost-of-living statistics illustrates how judgments with political implications have been interwoven into the calculation and use of official statistics. Attention to the cost of living typically has taken one of two forms. First, reform-minded Americans have periodically compared household incomes to the cost of an "adequate" standard of living, thereby providing a means to judge the sufficiency of wages or other income. Second, economists have tried to compare the costs of reaching a given standard of living in two time periods (or, less frequently, two geographic locations). Comparisons of the second sort are expressed as an index number, a ratio between two costs:

$$\text{Cost-of-living index} = \frac{\text{Cost of given standard of living (currently)}}{\text{Cost of same standard of living (in base period)}}$$

Today, economists often describe the CPI as an attempt to calculate such a cost-of-living index.

From the outset, it should be evident that comparisons of the first sort (between income and an adequate standard of living) are necessarily dependent on normative judgments. What constitutes an adequate standard for housing, clothing, food, healthcare, recreation, or other typical components of household expenditure? By contrast, comparisons of the second sort (an index number) may seem free of such hazards. After all, here there is no attempt to judge adequacy; one merely tracks the cost of any given standard of living. But this apparent distinction between the first and second forms is illusory, for ambiguities abound in index numbers as well. How can you account for changes in the quality of goods or in the tastes and purchasing habits of consumers? Should a cost-of-living index focus strictly on price changes (as might be appropriate for monetary policy), or should it encompass a host of other shifts (such as moving to a more expensive location) that might also be construed as altering the cost of maintaining a constant standard of living?

In the abstract, of course, there are no universally valid, "right" answers to these questions (though there may be many wrong ones). Proper answers depend on the uses to which any given cost-of-living index is put, and they may be different for different applications, such as guiding monetary policy, "deflating" consumer expenditures for the national accounts, altering the official federal poverty thresholds, or adjusting Social Security payments. Equally important, selecting one of these applications to guide the design of an official cost-of-living index does not put an end to our troubles, for in designing our methodology to match that application (such as the indexation of tax brackets to account for changes in the cost of living), we will invariably encounter questions for which there can be no apolitical answers. (Exactly how should quality improvements in television sets affect tax brackets?)

Economic theory can help to clarify these issues by drawing distinctions, illuminating relationships, and judging the coherence of existing choices, but it cannot resolve the matter except by appealing (perhaps covertly) to applications where the normative judgments are less obvious, less consequential, or less contentious. To put the matter bluntly, a full specification of the proper methods for a statistical calculation requires a full specification of its objectives down to a high level of detail, which means that judgments with political valences extend all the way through the calculation process. (Examples of this claim are described in Chapters 5–9.)

Unfortunately, this reality runs counter to the motivation behind the widespread incorporation of economic statistics into public life, namely, the attempt to depoliticize large swaths of public and private administration through rationalization. The resulting tension—and the attempts to suppress, avoid, or mitigate it—drives the basic narrative of this book. It makes it possible to write an expressly *political* history of economic statistics— to study the choices made in crafting, stabilizing, and dismantling specific systems of rationalized governance (including their empirical bases) and thereby to incorporate the construction and use of economic statistics into the history of American political economy.

Creating such a history is my primary interest. In that sense, although rationalization provides an important framework for my analysis, this book is not about rationalization per se, considered as a generic process. On its own, the concept of rationalization does not provide a rich or satisfying explanation for a given phenomenon. (To say that the indexation of Social Security is an example of rationalization tells us something, but not very much.) Instead, rationalization serves as a useful heuristic, a tool for recognizing analogous situations and suggesting critical questions or interpretations. The contingent nature of rationalization pushes us to probe the details, to ask why specific forms of rule-governed administration appeared at particular times and places, why they developed in certain ways, why they might have failed (if they did), and what consequences these systems had for political, social, and economic life.

* * *

Statistically based, rationalized governance has been an important political strategy in the United States since the country's founding. During the Revolutionary War, for example, Massachusetts used price statistics to adjust payments to its militia, and the most well-known, American example of rationalized governance through statistics is embedded in the Constitution: the use of census data to distribute congressional seats among the states.[13] Nonetheless, rationalized governance based on national economic statistics emerged largely in the twentieth century as Americans grappled with the changes wrought by industrial capitalism and confronted a series of crises—two world wars and a major depression—that precipitated the expansion of federal power.

The growth of federal ambitions to manage American political economy thus forms a basic theme of my narrative. These projects not only elevated national cost-of-living statistics over the local measures that usually held comparable or greater sway up through the 1920s, but they also helped to change the primary form of those statistics. The most influential studies of the cost of living during the late nineteenth and early twentieth centuries were one-time surveys of family expenditures or prices. The prominence of routine data collection—which permitted the ongoing monitoring

---

[13] On the Massachusetts system, see Willard C. Fisher, "The Tabular Standard in Massachussetts History," *QJE*, no. 3 (1913): 417–454.

of specific economic variables such as the change in retail prices—developed as the federal government assumed managerial responsibility over the economy and thus required regular flows of data to assess, guide, and justify its administration. This demand surfaced explicitly during the First World War but (in the case of cost-of-living statistics) soon receded; only through the crucible of the Great Depression and the Second World War would a more enduring conception of the federal government's managerial role take form.

The second theme of my narrative involves the deep and complicated entanglement of rationalized governance, cost-of-living statistics, and economic reform during the twentieth century. This juncture arose from the efforts of moderate and left-wing reformers to use the cost of living as a justification for improving the living conditions of poor and working-class Americans. Such projects—which dovetailed with broader attempts to reform American capitalism by exploiting the power of middle- and working-class consumption[14]—began in the late nineteenth century, moved to the national level temporarily during the First World War, and found a stable home within the federal government in the New Deal. Indeed, national cost-of-living statistics were an integral—though hitherto unexamined—part of the "rise and fall of the New Deal order," or, more accurately phrased, the rise and fall of what David Plotke has identified as the Democratic political order that began in the early 1930s and lasted through the 1960s.[15] I have therefore structured my account around these efforts: the rise and ambiguous legacy of cost-of-living statistics in the Progressive Era, their incorporation into the heart of New Deal political economy (wherein the CPI became a central element), and transformation of national cost-of-living statistics within the

---

[14] For example, Lizabeth Cohen, *Making a New Deal: Industrial Workers in Chicago, 1919–1939* (Cambridge: Cambridge University Press, 1990); Dana Frank, *Purchasing Power: Consumer Organizing, Gender, and the Seattle Labor Movement, 1919–1929* (Cambridge: Cambridge University Press, 1994); Alan Brinkley, *The End of Reform: New Deal Liberalism in Recession and War* (New York: Vintage Press, 1996); Lawrence B. Glickman, *A Living Wage: American Workers and the Making of Consumer Society* (Ithaca: Cornell University Press, 1997); Landon R. Y. Storrs, *Civilizing Capitalism: The National Consumers' League, Women's Activism, and Labor Standards in the New Deal Era* (Chapel Hill: University of North Carolina Press, 2000); Lizabeth Cohen, *A Consumer's Republic: The Politics of Mass Consumption in Postwar America* (New York: Alfred A. Knopf, 2003); Meg Jacobs, *Pocketbook Politics: Economic Citizenship in Twentieth-Century America* (Princeton: Princeton University Press, 2005).

[15] Steve Fraser and Gary Gerstle, eds., *The Rise and Fall of the New Deal Order, 1930–1980* (Princeton: Princeton University Press, 1989). David Plotke, *Building a Democratic Political Order: Reshaping American Liberalism in the 1930s and 1940s* (New York: Cambridge University Press, 1996).

growth-oriented, welfare state that was a major legacy of mid-century, liberal political economy.

Part I (1880–1930) describes the cost-of-living studies that characterized the reform approach in the long Progressive Era. Attention to the cost of living during this period had strong ties to labor reform (usually as a strategy for demonstrating the inadequacy of wages), a link that also explains the institutional home for these projects in the federal government: the Bureau of Labor Statistics. Early recourse to the cost of living in labor activism rested on an ethical basis: wages should be sufficient to meet the costs of an adequate, "American standard of living" and should (at a minimum) rise alongside increases in the cost of living. The First World War marked the high point of this campaign (and its establishment on a national level), but the normative judgments required to define an "adequate" standard of living hobbled this program once the wartime pressures for rationalization receded, and it floundered ineffectually in the 1920s. Accordingly, a loose coalition of economists and labor activists began formulating a new argument for higher wages that would take center stage amidst the next economic crisis.

Part II (1930–1960) concentrates on a major shift first realized in the New Deal, as normative demands for wage hikes gave way to attempts to link expanded labor organization to growth and economic recovery. In the vision of pro-labor liberals, unions became a mechanism for redistributing income by boosting wages. In turn, this redistribution would expand consumer markets and absorb idle productive capacity, thereby lifting the country out of the Depression and (in the future) saving capitalism from self-destructive cycles of "underconsumption." Under this regime, cost-of-living statistics (and especially the federal cost-of-living index, ancestor of the CPI) developed new roles as tools for macroeconomic analysis. The tension between these functions and the earlier use of cost-of-living statistics to evaluate the adequacy of wages paralleled larger fractures in the New Deal's attempted marriage of labor policy and macroeconomic growth. Ultimately, these tensions could not be sustained, and New Deal labor policy collapsed into something less than any of its protagonists had hoped.

Part III (1960–2000) explores the aftermath of this collapse, as liberal strategies for boosting material living conditions shifted instead to the federal government, especially in its roles as a provider of social welfare benefits and a facilitator of economic growth. In practice, these strategies rested largely on pursuing economic expansion, and cost-of-living statistics now became tools for monitoring that progress and protecting absolute gains while giving minimal attention to distributional equity. Despite the prominence of indexation (which began in earnest in the early 1970s), the divergence in potential goals for CPI (assessing the adequacy of income or aiding macroeconomic analysis?) now began to move further in favor of macroeconomic applications, where the normative judgments required to measure the change in the cost of living proved less contentious.

Rationalization was an essential part of these reform efforts and took multiple forms. Amidst the labor activism of the early twentieth century, for example, it included economic arguments (using government statistics) to justify union organization and wage demands; rules and legal restrictions governing wage adjustments during the Second World War (tied to the federal cost-of-living index); and finally, a privatized regime of rationalized industrial relations that included cost-of-living escalator clauses based on the CPI (the new official name for the older "cost-of-living index"). As left-wing and moderate liberals in the second half of the twentieth century shifted their focus from union organization to the pursuit of economic growth and the expansion of the welfare state, national cost-of-living statistics developed new tasks: guiding, evaluating, and justifying federal economic planning while also providing a rationalized framework for adjusting parameters and payments within social welfare programs (including Social Security).

Though reform-minded liberals provided the initial impetus for attention to the cost of living, they could not construct their rationalized systems unopposed: disruptive effects arose from populist and democratic impulses, from political fragmentation, from the extraordinary economic and social diversity of America, and from the competitive nature and chaotic tendencies of capitalism itself. Nor were left-wing liberals the only Americans who recognized the political power of rationalized governance through cost-of-living statistics. Employers often adopted cost-of-living wage adjustments in order to fend off unionization (by portraying their wage policies as rational and enlightened) or to constrain labor conflict. Likewise, Republican congressmen later turned to indexation as an apolitical mechanism to contain federal spending and control the deficit. Accordingly, government officials, unions, businessmen, and economists of all political leanings struggled throughout the twentieth century to shape administrative rules and statistical methodology in ways that would better fit their own conceptions of political economy and of economic knowledge.

The result of these conflicts was to minimize the role of overt and contentious normative judgments in the construction of official cost-of-living statistics and systems of rationalized governance. Naturally, that tendency also created important constraints on left-liberal efforts to reshape American economic structure, at least insofar as those reform efforts were dependent (as they typically were) on the expansion of rationalized state power. In this respect, my narrative reinforces two common themes in recent historical scholarship: first, the serious obstacles that confronted grand, left-wing visions for economic reform during the 1930s through the 1960s; and second, the dominant tendency of American social scientists (especially after the First World War) to eschew explicitly normative judgments in favor of pursuing a more elusive (and more limited) form of allegedly objective analysis.[16]

Understanding the dynamics of rationalization allows us to connect these two common stories but also to place them in a different interpretive framework. To the extent that social science expertise was incorporated into the expansion of state power (to justify or guide state actions), that union readily led to the pursuit of an ideal of apolitical objectivity as the easiest way to reconcile extensive state power and heavy reliance on elite experts with liberal and democratic values.[17] A binary opposition between "advocacy and objectivity," however aptly it captures the early throes of professionalization and struggles over academic freedom in the late nineteenth century, cannot be taken as an adequate template for understanding twentieth-century social science, wherein (as odd as it may sound) the push for apolitical objectivity was often an effective political strategy.[18] Of course, rationalization constrained both the acceptable forms of social scientific knowledge

---

[16] For accounts of the political obstacles that limited the New Deal and its legacy, see (among others) Fraser and Gerstle, eds., *Rise and Fall of the New Deal Order*; Brinkley, *End of Reform*; Plotke, *Building a Democratic Political Order*; Cohen, *Consumers' Republic*; Jacobs, *Pocketbook Politics*. On American social scientists and their quest for objectivity, see Edward A. Purcell, *The Crisis of Democratic Theory: Scientific Naturalism and the Problem of Value* (Lexington: University of Kentucky Press, 1973); Robert C. Bannister, *Sociology and Scientism: The American Quest for Objectivity, 1880–1940* (Chapel Hill: University of North Carolina Press, 1987); Dorothy Ross, *The Origins of American Social Science* (Cambridge: Cambridge University Press, 1991); Mark C. Smith, *Social Science in the Crucible: The American Debate over Objectivity and Purpose, 1918–1941* (Durham: Duke University Press, 1994).

[17] Social scientists and other American intellectuals regularly wrestled with the tension between expertise and democratic governance in the early twentieth century: Purcell, *Crisis of Democratic Theory*; Barry D. Karl, *Charles E. Merriam and the Study of Politics* (Chicago: University of Chicago Press, 1974); Donald T. Critchlow, *The Brookings Institution, 1916–1952: Expertise and the Public Interest in a Democratic Society* (Dekalb: Northern Illinois University Press, 1985); Leon Fink, *Progressive Intellectuals and the Dilemmas of Democratic Commitment* (Cambridge: Harvard University Press, 1997). Necessarily, this tension grew more intense as social scientific knowledge became more deeply integrated with state power.

[18] Mary O. Furner, *Advocacy & Objectivity: A Crisis in the Professionalization of American Social Science, 1865–1905* (Lexington: University Press of Kentucky, 1975). Stephen Turner

and, insofar as state intervention was dependent on that knowledge and on an equally "objective" bureaucratic system, the actions of the state itself. But those constraints could not have been overcome simply by pressing left-wing social scientists to pursue more overtly normative forms of social scientific knowledge, for such knowledge would have clashed directly with the demands of rationalization and thereby undermined a crucial justification for the expansion of state power. If the "Democratic political order" that began in the 1930s failed to produce radical changes in the structure of the American economy, that failure derived in no small part from the constraints provided by liberal democracy itself and its own ambivalent relationship with collective power, bureaucratic administration, and elite expertise.[19]

Without ignoring that ambivalence, we can nonetheless recognize that rationalization has left a problematic legacy. The trouble is not that political calculation and conservative objections tempered the ambitions of New Deal liberals. (It is difficult to see how matters could have been otherwise.) The trouble is that the demands of rationalization too often produced those compromises through a conceptual framework—the deployment of apolitical, neutral expertise rather than political negotiation and persuasion— that prevented overt political discussion in the past and continues to limit us today. Because so much of rationalized administration—especially its basis in empirical facts—is framed as a set of technical problems devoid of political questions, important issues are obscured or a priori excluded from discussion. Convenience, bureaucratic precedent, a deliberate focus on less contentious applications, the reliance on abstract theoretical models or methodological principles that exclude controversial (but important) issues—all these tactics and others have been the recourse of economists trapped by the impossible task of producing statistics relevant to political life but free of political considerations. In the epilogue, I consider whether we can devise a more forthright way to resolve this dilemma and thereby construct a new relationship between economic statistics and governance.

has made this point for scientific expertise more generally in *Liberal Democracy 3.0: Civil Society in an Age of Experts* (London: Sage Publications, 2003).

[19] In this sense, my analysis of New Deal liberalism returns to the themes of Ellis Hawley's classic account, *The New Deal and the Problem of Monopoly: A Study in Economic Ambivalence* (New York: Fordham University Press, 1995 [1966]).

A Note on Terminology and Technical Theory

An account that encompasses a long stretch of time and that addresses several distinct academic fields (e.g., economic theory, political history) will necessarily encounter troublesome issues with terminology. I have tried to remain as accurate as possible while keeping the narrative readily accessible to a wider audience. Most terms and concepts are explained as they occur in the main text; however, I prefer to address several of the largest issues here.

"Liberal" and its derivatives cause endless trouble for political historians. First, liberal can mean something quite different in political theory than in colloquial American political discussions from the mid-twentieth century onward. Moreover, usage has changed over time, and even during a given period, liberal remained a contested term. Generally, I use "liberalism" and "liberal values" to denote a basic spectrum of ideas common to most forms of liberalism in political theory: for example, strong support for individual liberty and political equality, commitment to the rule of law and constraints on government action, concern about the potential coercive power of collective organization, and basic support for market-based economies (with more or less regulatory oversight and intervention). When using liberal to define individuals or groups up through the 1930s, I will typically add other modifiers (e.g., "New Deal liberals," "pro-labor liberals") to indicate the particular subsection that I am considering. For the 1940s onward, however, I follow what had become colloquial American usage, wherein liberal refers to groups or individuals who supported a left-wing version of political liberalism (emphasizing a greater role for the state and concern about positive freedoms – for example, equality of resources,—rather than just negative freedoms – for example, freedom from coercion). These men and women were most commonly associated with the Democratic Party.

The phrase "cost-of-living index" is less slippery than liberal but it may cause even more misunderstanding among contemporary economists

16

unfamiliar with the history of price index theory. For contemporary economists, a cost-of-living index is a measure of the change in minimum expenditure needed to maintain a constant level of "welfare" or "utility" in two different situations (a constant-utility index). But that easy co-identification did not occur until the 1960s; prior to that point, many different forms of index number calculation could be, and were, called cost-of-living indexes. Accordingly, I use cost-of-living index in a strictly nominal sense within this book: anything that claimed to compare the cost of living over time counts as a cost-of-living index. When I need to refer to specific conceptual approaches to cost-of-living indexes, I will use theory-specific terms, such as constant-goods index or constant-utility index.

Finally, although the theory and practice of index number calculation is not the sole focus of this book, we will need to wrestle with those topics. I introduce major concepts and terms as they appear in the text; however, it is often helpful to have a reference that sits outside the narrative and can be more easily consulted as needed. To that end, the book contains a short primer on price index theory (in the appendix) which may be especially beneficial to readers who are unfamiliar with the basic concepts behind cost-of-living indexes and which can (but need not) be read before turning to the main text.

PART I

STATISTICS AND LABOR
REFORM, 1880–1930: CENTRALIZATION
AND ITS DISCONTENTS

From the 1870s into the onset of the Great Depression, many Americans struggled to mitigate the worst excesses of their industrial economy—such as a growing concentration of economic power, intermittently tumultuous labor unrest, and periodic, severe depressions—while nevertheless retaining the basic elements of a liberal democracy. Their reform efforts offered conflicting answers to a variety of key questions: what level of action—local, national, or even international—would allow the most effective intervention; what roles should be played by the state, private businesses, and labor organizations; and, most fundamentally, how could these groups stabilize the economy without simultaneously undermining liberal or republican values? Yet each approach held one element in common: the use, in one form or another, of new empirical knowledge about the industrial economy—labor statistics.

My narrative begins with this novel economic domain and the federal and state bureaus created to explore it during the late nineteenth century (Chapter 1). The features of the nineteenth-century effort stand out best through comparison to what followed. By the mid-twentieth century, American labor statistics were dominated by the federal government, utilized highly standardized methods, and embodied a managerial outlook that emphasized regular data collection in order to monitor a crucial set of economic variables over time. By contrast, the nineteenth-century bureaus were a heterogeneous group that produced discrete, topical studies intended to educate the public and legislatures by exploring a complex network of problems—urbanization, the growth of labor unions, factory work, industrial unrest, immigration, etc.—categorized under the rubric of the "labor question." The first commissioner of the federal bureau, Carroll D. Wright, created an early program of regular data collection on wages and prices at the turn of the century, apparently as his own view of the labor question shifted to a managerial mode in which statistics could reveal slow progress and guide voluntary negotiation and mediation between trade unions and companies. Yet this perspective did not gain a solid hold, threatened both by conservative anti-union campaigns and by a progressive-era emphasis on discrete reform projects.

By 1910, a new tide of rising prices had elevated the "high cost of living" into an urgent political topic, especially as observers linked high prices to growing industrial unrest (Chapter 2). Still, approaches to the problem continued to mirror nineteenth-century tactics, with an emphasis on discrete, local studies intended to galvanize public action. That approach was hindered, however, by interstate competition in many manufacturing sectors, which thwarted attempts at local regulation and control. Consequently, labor activists and progressive reformers began looking toward national oversight for an effective response, and in the mobilization efforts of the First World War, they found a fertile political ground for their ambitions. As left-wing and moderate social scientists streamed into a new wartime federal bureaucracy, the production demands of mobilization allowed pro-labor liberals to establish new precedents for labor policy and to reengineer wage rates on a broad scale. Here, for the first time, national cost-of-living statistics—including the Bureau of Labor Statistics' new cost-of-living index (ancestor of the CPI)—became crucial tools for rationalized, bureaucratic management of industrial relations, used to guide and justify wartime wage adjustments.

Peace brought the collapse of the wartime economic management system, but it did not herald a return to the prewar situation. For many of those who had been part of the domestic mobilization effort—social scientists, bureaucrats, workers, labor activists, and businessmen alike—the wartime experience had created new possibilities and new problems (Chapter 3). While economists heatedly debated the methods and merits of the cost-of-living indexes that had sprouted worldwide during the war, businessmen and labor activists each sought to produce and use statistics to shape industrial relations and to justify their actions. Union officials who had grasped at cost-of-living escalator clauses to protect wages amidst the stunning price rises during and after the war now found those techniques turned against them. Non-union businesses seeking to quell labor unrest implemented similar clauses to demonstrate their commitment to "rational" wage policies, and (even worse) employers reversed the logic to justify reducing wages once prices began a rapid descent during the postwar recession.

In response, a cluster of prominent labor activists turned to another wartime tool—normative family budgets designed to embody a "living wage"— which they used to argue for wage hikes both in public propaganda and in arbitration hearings. However, the difficulty of establishing an objective, minimum standard of living allowed conservatives to thwart these efforts. Only in the latter half of the 1920s did labor activists hit upon a strategy with greater purchase: arguing that low wages left American consumer markets unable to absorb the high volume of goods produced by the nation's manufacturers. This analysis of "underconsumption" brought labor activists into an unsteady allegiance with self-proclaimed "institutional" economists (dedicated to the empirical study of the American economy, including markets and labor conditions) and a group of powerful mass producers and mass retailers seeking to strengthen markets for their goods. The shift also returned attention to price indexes for consumer goods, but now in a different context. From being a means to judge the adequacy of wage adjustments for specific groups of workers, retail price indexes became tools for comparing prices, incomes, and productivity on a national scale in order to sustain economic growth. With that transformation, the path was prepared for cost-of-living statistics to find a prominent role in left-wing and moderate reactions to the Depression amidst a permanent shift away from late nineteenth-century political economy.

1

Before There Were Indexes: The "Labor Question" and Labor Statistics, 1880–1910

To popularize statistics, to put them before the masses in a way which shall attract, and yet not deceive, is a work every government which cares for its future stability should encourage and enlarge.[1]

—Carroll D. Wright, Commissioner of the Massachusetts Bureau of Statistics of Labor, 1877

At the next desk was a very quiet and harmless old gentleman, who slept most of the time.... It was said that this old gentleman was a veteran of the civil war, that he had been picked up on the battlefield, that he was unable to tell who he was or to what regiment he belonged, and so he was eventually sent to the Bureau of Labor [Statistics].[2]

—Thomas Robinson Dawley, Jr., 1912

Since government statistics reflect the political structure and concerns of their day, we should expect to find a substantial gap between the labor statistics of the nineteenth century and those of our own time. There are, of course, lines of continuity: the opening epigraph from Carroll Wright—suggesting that government stability may depend on statistical calculation—clearly has its contemporary adherents, at least if the statistical output of most national governments is any guide. Yet, as the second epigraph reminds us, official rhetoric did not always match the underlying reality. More generally, equal praise for the value of statistics did not imply a similar consensus about why those statistics were useful or what they should accomplish.

Today, the primary function of the U.S. Bureau of Labor Statistics (BLS) is to produce data series: monthly or quarterly measures on a variety of topics

[1] Massachusetts Bureau of Statistics of Labor, *Eighth Annual Report* (Boston: Albert J. Wright, 1877), vii–viii.
[2] Thomas Robinson Dawley, Jr., *The Child That Toileth Not: The Story of a Government Investigation That Was Suppressed*, 2nd ed. (New York: Gracia Publishing Company, 1912), 281–282.

such as price changes, earnings, productivity, unemployment, and occupational safety. Though the agency does conduct isolated, one-time studies when requested by Congress or the White House, these special projects are dwarfed by routine data collection. Furthermore, the federal bureau clearly dominates American labor statistics: even when state agencies collect basic data on major topics (such as wages), they typically do so using BLS funds and following federal standards.

These features are congruent with a centralized, managerial orientation toward economic knowledge in which federal agencies monitor changes in specific, aggregate variables from within a stable conceptual framework. Routine data collection allows policymakers and the public to gauge the success of government policies even as the data provide a guide for administrative decisions (including rule-governed operations, such as the indexation of federal programs). That perspective may seem natural today, when the federal government has eclipsed state or municipal control and has adopted a wide range of managerial responsibilities for the economy. Yet it was not the only vision for labor statistics and by no means the dominant one in the nineteenth century.

In the decentralized, federalist structure of nineteenth-century American politics, state bureaus held much larger roles. State legislatures created the first bureaus of labor statistics in the late nineteenth century in order to study the "labor question"—a nebulous confluence of concerns about industrialization, income disparity, immigration, socialism, and class conflict which seemed to grow worse as the century progressed. Nineteenth-century labor reformers viewed this crisis as a set of interlocking problems that might be ameliorated if properly understood. Accordingly, labor statistics served to educate the public and legislators, preparing the ground for voluntary action or government regulation (typically on the state level). Thus, whereas the present-day BLS is asked to monitor a particular dimension of the national economy (macroeconomic variables related to labor), its nineteenth-century counterparts were called upon to study the causes, consequences, and faults of an economic and social upheaval, often in a local or regional context.

Predictably, early bureaus responded by pursuing a wide range of one-time, special investigations rather than devoting themselves to regular data collection on limited topics. Large surveys were expensive (especially on the national level), and routine data collection in labor statistics had no clear ties to reform legislation that might justify the necessary funds. By the turn of the century, some Americans (including the first commissioner of the BLS, Carroll Wright) began to see a greater role for federal, bureaucratic monitoring and oversight of labor relations, a task in which national data series such as price or wage indexes might have important functions. Yet this view remained a minority position; ultimately, it would take the tumult of war (Chapter 2) to sweep away the nineteenth-century political order and establish a new context for labor statistics.

THE MANY FORMS OF LABOR STATISTICS

The branch of knowledge that we now recognize as statistics emerged from multiple, competing traditions, each linked to specific political conditions. Thus in Germany, where Gottfried Achenwall first promoted the term "statistics" at the University of Göttingen in the mid-eighteenth century, this knowledge was largely qualitative and descriptive, intended to characterize the heterogeneous collection of tiny states that composed the fractured empire. By contrast, the quantitative techniques of British political arithmetic arose primarily outside the state (becoming a form of private oversight). Likewise, the British administrative statistics that appeared in the nineteenth century were, like the British political system as a whole, far more decentralized than those of post–Napoleonic France.[3]

Such diversity is hardly surprising: like all empirical knowledge, statistics were intended to answer certain questions; naturally those questions varied among societies with different conditions, goals, and needs. The more puzzling problem is why such diversity began to disappear. In part, the drive for unified methodology arose from the universalizing ideals of nineteenth-century science (reflected, for instance, in the international congresses of statisticians from the mid-nineteenth century onward). Yet government statistics, as a state activity, also require a compelling political reason to enforce or adopt standardized forms of knowledge. Here, the development of national labor statistics in late nineteenth-century America, a country wrestling with the balance of state and federal power, illustrates the pressures operating from both directions.

Labor Reform and Labor Statistics

Basic demographic and trade statistics became a mainstay of state administration in Europe and the United States during the nineteenth century, linked to the development of the nation-state, the rise of capitalism, and the

---

[3] Peter Buck, "People Who Counted: Political Arithmetic in the Eighteenth Century," *Isis* 73, no. 1 (1982): 28–45; Ian Hacking, *The Taming of Chance* (Cambridge: Cambridge University Press, 1990), 16–80; Alain Desrosières, *The Politics of Large Numbers: A History of Statistical Reasoning*, trans. Camille Naish (Cambridge: Harvard University Press, 1998), 16–44, 147–177.

growth of liberalism (wherein statistics promised to reveal to the public the conditions of their society). Picking up great headway between 1820 and 1840, an "avalanche of numbers" poured forth from newly constituted government bureaus, private fact-gathering associations (such as the Statistical Society of London), and individual investigators. Though some of these projects considered workers and industrialization, dedicated study of labor statistics by governments lagged these efforts, awaiting a perceived administrative need for such information.[4]

Bureaus of labor statistics appeared first in America, arising on the state level amidst the proliferation of the localized private and public reform efforts that characterized the American response to the social and economic crises of the Gilded Age. Between 1870 and 1900, the nation grappled with the changes wrought to America's social, economic, and political structure by emerging economic integration, growing urbanization, and the transition from a largely agrarian society to a wage-based, industrial economy with a rapidly rising, increasingly diverse population. Over those thirty years, the nation's population nearly doubled as immigration continued at a rapid clip and soon included large numbers of eastern and southern Europeans. Meanwhile, the economy underwent a major shift. Rail mileage rose by sevenfold and thereby created a distribution network that pulled a patchwork of local and regional economies into a larger whole and fueled the rise of financial speculation, heavily capitalized national corporations, and greater urbanization. Not surprisingly, the structure of the workforce shifted as well. Already by 1870, nearly 70 percent of working Americans were wage-earners or salaried workers of some sort, and that percentage increased as the nation's economic center continued to move from agriculture toward industry and services. In 1870, the agricultural and nonagricultural workforces were roughly equal; by 1900, nonagricultural employment outpaced agricultural work by roughly 3:2. Much of that growth came in sectors that would provide the future core of the labor movement: total employment in mining, manufacturing, and construction nearly tripled over the period, for example.[5]

---

[4]   Michael J. Cullen, *The Statistical Movement in Early Victorian Britain: The Foundations of Empirical Social Research* (New York: Barnes & Noble, 1975); Hacking, *Taming of Chance*; Desrosières, *Politics of Large Numbers*, 147–209; Silvana Patriarca, *Numbers and Nationhood: Writing Statistics in Nineteenth-Century Italy* (Cambridge: Cambridge University Press, 1996); J. Adam Tooze, *Statistics and the German State, 1900–1945: The Making of Modern Economic Knowledge* (Cambridge: Cambridge University Press, 2001), 1–11. The phrase "avalanche of numbers" comes from Hacking, *Taming of Chance*, 2–3.

[5]   U.S. Bureau of the Census, *The Statistical History of the United States, from Colonial Times to the Present* (New York: Basic Books, 1976), 11–12, 14, 127, 138, 728, 731.

Labor struggles were endemic to the age and were only made worse by the three severe depressions that battered the country at regular intervals (1873–1877, 1883–1885, and 1893–1897). Some of America's most violent, bitter, and well-known conflicts occurred during this stretch—the Great Strikes of 1877, the Haymarket bombing in 1886, and the struggles at Homestead and Pullman in the early 1890s—but these were only the larger renditions of similar dramas that occurred repeatedly on smaller scales at shops and factories across the country, with official records showing nearly ten thousand strikes or stoppages during the 1880s alone. If the great 1893 World's Columbian Exposition in Chicago symbolized the potential power and grandeur of American industrial might, the "labor question" was its roiling and threatening underbelly. "It seemed," as one observer put it during the 1877 strikes, "as if the whole social and political structure was on the very brink of ruin."[6]

Bureaus of labor statistics were one response to this threat and usually followed grassroots agitation by workers' organizations and labor reformers. Massachusetts, an especially productive source of regulatory and investigative agencies, created the first "Bureau of Statistics of Labor" in 1869 as an attempt to quell labor unrest by meeting an (apparently) innocuous demand by activists. Labor reformers and leaders in other locations soon pressed for similar actions, and within a decade ten more bureaus of labor statistics had been established.[7] U.S. congressional leaders got a firsthand view of popular predilection for labor statistics when the Senate Committee on Education and Labor launched its own investigation into the "labor question" in 1883 by collecting testimony from labor leaders, union members, businessmen, and social reformers. One of the more striking findings, according to committee chairman and labor sympathizer Henry Blair (R-New Hampshire), was that within the morass of conflicting proposals and claims there existed at least one area of "singular unanimity": "all thought that the establishment of a bureau [of labor statistics] … would contribute largely to their welfare

---

[6] David Montgomery, *Beyond Equality: Labor and the Radical Republicans* (New York: Knopf, 1967), 29–30; Eric Arnesen, "American Workers and the Labor Movement in the Late Nineteenth Century," in *The Gilded Age: Essays on the Origins of Modern America*, ed. Charles W. Calhoun (Wilmington, Del.: SR Books, 1996), 39–61. *New York Tribune*, 25 July 1877, as quoted in Arnesen, "American Workers," p. 40.

[7] On the state bureaus, see Wendell D. MacDonald, "The Early History of Labor Statistics in the United States," *Labor History* 13, no. 2 (1972): 267–278; James Leiby, *Carroll Wright and Labor Reform: The Origin of Labor Statistics* (Cambridge: Harvard University Press, 1960), 47–62; Carroll D. Wright, "Presidential Address, American Statistical Association," *PASA* 11, no. 81 (1908): 12–13; William R. Brock, *Investigation and Responsibility: Public Responsibility in the United States, 1865–1900* (Cambridge: Cambridge University Press, 1984), 149–156, 255–256.

and their happiness."[8] More surprising than this "unanimity" were the hopes that union members attached to their request, calling it "the greatest benefit that could be conferred upon us" or "one of the primary objects of our organization."[9] Reformers associated with management gave the drive a similar prominence: Charles Lentz, editor of the New York paper *Capital and Labor*, told the senators it was "the most important measure and the first legislative act required."[10]

How can we account for such astonishing enthusiasm for labor statistics, especially among working-class organizations? At its core, it reflected the common nineteenth-century conviction that ignorance was a fundamental cause of the deepening social crisis: the public's ignorance of working conditions or company exploitation; workers' ignorance of their own situation; legislators' ignorance of remedies. Much of nineteenth-century labor activism was rooted in republican values that looked to education (of both the public and workers) as the best path for resolving the troubling "labor question." Democratic analysis of economic and social facts would provide the rational basis for government regulation or voluntary change and thereby enable collective responses to social problems without sacrificing liberal or democratic ideals.[11] Bureaus of labor statistics, of course, fit neatly into this vision, and the Knights of Labor (who strongly favored such an approach) later provided the most consistent and active support for a national bureau.[12] Proponents reiterated the value that such knowledge

---

[8] *Congressional Record* (48th Cong., 1st sess.), 1884, p. 4153.

[9] U.S. Senate, Committee on Education and Labor, *Report of the Committee of the Senate Upon the Relations between Labor and Capital* (Washington, D.C.: U.S. GPO, 1885), 87, 1142. Numerous union officials mentioned the national bureau, including prominent figures like Samuel Gompers, who made it one of the three "remedies" he proposed to the committee (v. 1, p. 382).

[10] U.S. Senate, Committee on Education and Labor, *Relations between Labor and Capital*, 245.

[11] James T. Kloppenberg, *Uncertain Victory: Social Democracy and Progressivism in European and American Thought, 1870–1920* (New York: Oxford University Press, 1986); Mary O. Furner, "Knowing Capitalism: Public Investigation and the Labor Question in the Long Progressive Era," in *The State and Economic Knowledge: The American and British Experiences*, ed. Mary O. Furner and Barry Supple (Cambridge: Cambridge University Press, 1990), 241–286; Mary O. Furner, "The Republican Tradition and the New Liberalism: Social Investigation, State-Building, and Social Learning in the Gilded Age," in *The State and Social Investigation in Britain and the United States*, ed. Michael J. Lacey and Mary O. Furner (New York: Cambridge University Press, 1993), 171–241; Michael J. Lacey, "The World of the Bureaus: Government and the Positivist Project in the Late Nineteenth Century," ibid., 127–170.

[12] On the politics of the Knights of Labor, see Leon Fink, *Workingmen's Democracy: The Knights of Labor and American Politics* (Urbana: University of Illinois Press, 1985), esp. 3–27. On the Knights of Labor and a national bureau, see Jonathan Grossman and Judson MacLaury, "The Creation of the Bureau of Labor Statistics," *MLR* 98, no. 2 (1975): 27, 30;

would provide both to the public and to workers themselves, who would better understand their own position and needs. Only in light of this drive can we understand the Senate testimony of one union member, who asked for "a national bureau of labor statistics for the encouragement and the education ... of the laboring classes."[13]

If this ideology accounts in part for the widespread support for bureaus of labor statistics, it is nevertheless not sufficient to explain the rapid institutional replication of these agencies, especially not for the establishment of a national bureau. The latter implied a belief that local investigation and action needed to be complemented by national action, no small issue for a country traditionally and structurally committed to the supremacy of local government. Yet the economic transformations of the post-bellum era, especially the streamlining of national and international distribution networks alongside the rise of large corporations in certain sectors, necessarily challenged the localist view, compelling many Americans to recognize how actions in distant regions could dramatically affect local life. In rural politics, this led to the logical (though unstable) combination of grassroots organization and national ambitions that characterized late nineteenth-century populism. For the labor question, it provided concrete evidence that national policies were needed, at least in some industries.

The railroad, source of extraordinary wealth for a small subset of Americans and visible network linking the country together, served as both an icon and a material support for the new economy, and thus it was fitting that it exemplify the need for national consideration of labor unrest. Responding to a four-year-old depression in 1877, American railroad companies slashed their employees' wages, thereby sparking a series of intense strikes across the United States. Resentment of wealthy railroad owners and the ongoing economic depression gave the wage cuts a resonance that stretched beyond the railroad workers themselves, and many strikes blossomed into broader working-class protests and mob action. In turn, military interventions by state and federal officials provoked a series of violent clashes. When state militia arrived to break a strike in Pittsburgh, the ensuing weekend of "riot and anarchy" (as the *New York Times* put it) left twenty-four people dead and caused an estimated $3–5 million in damages, with almost eighty railroad buildings burned and over two thousand railroad

Judson MacLaury, "The Selection of the First U.S. Commissioner of Labor," *MLR* 98, no. 4 (1975): 16–17.
[13] U.S. Senate, Committee on Education and Labor, *Relations between Labor and Capital*, 13.

cars destroyed.[14] Such violence underscored the urgency of addressing the labor question, but equally important, it suggested that local approaches to the new industrial crisis might not be sufficient. The 1877 railroad strikes had spread across the country following company and rail lines; state militias had proved inadequate to the task set them (quelling the riots); and only federal troops had been sufficient. As the only unquestionably national industry, the railroads remained the center of federal intervention into industrial unrest through the early twentieth century and, as we will see, served as a key industry for the federal bureau of labor statistics.

If railroads thus exemplified the need for national consideration of labor issues, they were not the only such prompts: even when companies did not stretch across state lines, workers themselves had begun to recognize a common cause, reflected in the growth of national trade unions and broader working-class associations such as the Knights of Labor (which did not limit its membership to specific trades or skilled workers). These new working-class organizations transferred many elements of existing local demands, including the establishment of bureaus of labor statistics, onto the national level. At its first national meeting in 1878, the Knights of Labor called for the federal government to establish a bureau of labor statistics; in 1881, the newly formed Federation of Organized Trades (the future American Federation of Labor) raised a similar demand. Reflecting these desires and in lieu of a full-fledged bureau, the 1880 U.S. Census included (for the first and last time) surveys on union membership, strikes, and lockouts. By 1883, a national bureau of labor statistics was firmly entrenched in the standard litany of suggested labor reforms, and it soon appeared on both political parties' campaign platforms.[15]

Economic integration thus prompted the push for a national bureau (as local strategies were projected onto the national level), but it did not provide a similarly unified conception of what this agency would actually do. Though the bureaus of labor statistics had a general mandate to investigate the "labor question," there was no concrete plan for how to translate that into practical work, nor did existing demographic or trade statistics provide much of a guide. On the contrary, as the first chief of the Massachusetts

[14] A Sunday of Riot and Anarchy, *NYT*, p. 1, 23 July 1877; Melvyn Dubofsky, *The State & Labor in Modern America* (Chapel Hill: University of North Carolina Press, 1994), 8–10; Robert V. Bruce, *1877: Year of Violence* (Indianapolis: Bobbs-Merrill, 1959).

[15] Joseph P. Goldberg and William T. Moye, *The First Hundred Years of the Bureau of Labor Statistics* (Washington, D.C.: U.S. Bureau of Labor Statistics, 1985), 2; Grossman and MacLaury, "The Creation of the Bureau of Labor Statistics"; William F. Micarelli, "Evolution of the United States Economic Censuses: The Nineteenth and Twentieth Centuries," *Government Information Quarterly* 15, no. 3 (1998): 343.

bureau described, early labor statisticians confronted a perplexing unknown: "Here we found ourselves in a field to us entirely new and unexplored, the boundaries of which we could not then (nor can we now) perceive by any telescopic power at our command. Nor was there any path or landmark, nor any precedent of former explorer here, at home, to guide us." Wrapped in "doubt" and "sometimes bewildered by diversity of counsel," the pioneers had to "tentaculate our way, step by step."[16] Not surprisingly, such novelty left room for a range of approaches, an ambiguity that undoubtedly helped further ensure widespread support for "labor statistics," but which would also hinder any easy consolidation.

Framed against the expansive background of the labor question, the domain of labor statistics could encompass any topic conceivably relevant to social unrest or industrial economics, including not only the workplace itself but also other aspects of working-class life, such as living conditions. Throughout the latter half of the nineteenth century, for instance, a consumption-based labor movement advocated reforms by demanding economic and social justice for workers, described in loose phrases like a "living wage" that would allow workers to meet the "American Standard of Living."[17] The common mandate of many state bureaus to collect information on "the commercial, industrial, social, education and sanitary conditions of the laboring classes" reflected elements of this agenda. Not surprisingly, two early champions of the consumerist reform effort, Ira Steward and George McNeill, contributed to the growth and work of the first state bureau of labor statistics in Massachusetts, and studies of working-class life (especially family expenditures) became a staple of labor statistics.[18]

Yet this was not the only vision for the national bureau. Other union members portrayed its main task as investigating employers, forcing them to disclose their costs, profits, and wages.[19] Furthermore, as exemplified by the

[16] Massachusetts Bureau of Statistics of Labor, *Report of the Bureau of Statistics of Labor [First Annual Report]* (Boston: Wright & Potter, 1870), 6.

[17] Lawrence B. Glickman, *A Living Wage: American Workers and the Making of Consumer Society* (Ithaca: Cornell University Press, 1997); Roseanne Currarino, "The Politics of 'More': The Labor Question and the Idea of Economic Liberty in Industrial American," *JAH* 93, no. 1 (2006): 17–36.

[18] Many early agency charters appear in *NABL* 1 (1883). Ira Steward, "Poverty," in *Fourth Annual Report of the Bureau of Statistics of Labor [Massachusetts]* (Boston: Wright & Potter, State Printers, 1873), 411–439; Leiby, *Carroll Wright*, 55. On Steward and McNeill, see Lawrence Glickman, "Workers of the World, Consume: Ira Steward and the Origins of Labor Consumerism," *International Labor and Working Class History* 52 (1997): 72–86.

[19] U.S. Senate, Committee on Education and Labor, *Relations between Labor and Capital*, 1142.

diversity among the state bureaus, the national agency could potentially serve multiple roles: a source of reform proposals, a government representative of union or worker interests, a regulatory or oversight agency, or simply an investigative body.[20] In general, as the congressional debates over the founding of the national bureau made clear, "labor statistics" was an ideal component for a political platform, since it could be defined to appeal to almost anyone. Legislators described a variety of social groups beyond workers who could use such statistics, from "moralists, social philosophers, and churchmen [who] would advance morality, social and individual virtue" to "political economists and to social economists and to writers and speculators upon economic questions." Moreover, they hoped the bureau could shed light on some of Congress's own regulatory functions, such as setting tariff rates.

Not surprisingly, the initial bill to establish the national bureau in 1884 was staggeringly broad in scale. The House version listed no less than seventy-three separate mandates for the new agency, prompting one senator to embark on a mocking, line-by-line exposé elucidating its gargantuan scope. Others echoed his sarcasm, and in the end, the Senate deleted the list of headings and opted for a less specific (though still broad) authorization. The bureau would "collect information upon the subject of labor, its relations to capital, the hours of labor, and the earnings of laboring men and women, and the means of promoting their material, social, intellectual, and moral prosperity."[21] This sounded grand, but it hardly gave the agency any coherent direction (and in fact neatly straddled the vexed question about whether the bureau should merely describe problems or should recommend specific legislation).

The task of turning this expansive objective into a practical agenda would rest with the agency's first leader, and thus a critical step toward narrowing the focus of the bureau was made with the appointment of its commissioner. Labor organizations signaled their hope that the agency would become a direct vehicle for reform by pushing the candidacy of two labor activists: Terence Powderly, head of the Knights of Labor, and a Republican candidate from the Federation of Organized Trades and Labor Unions, John Jarret. After an extended period of equivocation, President Chester A. Arthur eventually settled on a politically moderate choice: the head of the Massachusetts Bureau of Statistics of Labor, Carroll Wright.[22] Since

---

[20] Brock, *Investigation and Responsibility*, 148–184.
[21] *Congressional Record* (48th Cong., 1st sess.), 1884, pp. 3148, 4155. On tariffs, ibid., 3139, 3142, 3147–3148, 3152. On the bill's scope, ibid., 4282–4283. For the final version, ibid., 4429.
[22] MacLaury, "Selection of the First U.S. Commissioner," 16–19.

the Massachusetts bureau had been the model for other state bureaus and Wright was the most experienced commissioner, he seemed like an obvious candidate. But Wright had no ties to labor organizations, and Arthur's indecision illustrated the lack of consensus over the relationship between a "bureau of labor statistics" and workers themselves, a problem that would continue to plague the new agency for years to come.

Wright, a former military officer and state legislator, had no statistical experience prior to taking over the Massachusetts bureau; his chief qualities were political moderation and a gift for administration. Still, both served him well in the contentious and confused world of nineteenth-century statistics, and having turned to "statistical science," Wright threw himself into the work. From the beginning of his tenure in Massachusetts in the 1870s, he built support for the bureau, expanded its scope, and undertook several extensive surveys, becoming in the process one of "the foremost statisticians of the world."[23] A description of the ideal government statistician written by Charles F. Pidgin, Wright's chief clerk at the Massachusetts bureau, provides perhaps the best summary of Wright's approach to labor statistics:

[He] must be expert in the use of figures, but such aptitude is only the mere alphabet of his work; he must know the tendencies of the times and select such topics for investigation as will answer the public demand; he must frame inquiries, draft schedules, write instructions for those filling in or answering inquiries, examine the returns, at the same time correcting errors and supplying omissions, adopt and supervise the application of the most improved methods of tabulation, prepare the material for expressive and concise presentation in print, and give therewith such careful explanation and exhaustive analyses that all parties will agree that the truth was his object, that he has found it, and that progressive action may be safely based upon the results presented.[24]

The labor statistician was thus the investigative arm of a reform-minded public, seeking only "the truth" in areas conducive to "progressive action," and conducting studies that reflected the "tendencies of the times" and met "public demand" (but not, one should note, agitating for specific reform measures).

This system had served Wright well in Massachusetts, but his move to Washington raised a new question: could approaches that succeeded on the state level be directly and easily transplanted into the federal government?

---

[23] Leiby, *Carroll Wright*, 63–69, esp. 66.

[24] Charles Felton Pidgin, *Practical Statistics: A Handbook for the Use of the Statistician at Work, Students in Colleges and Academies, Agents, Census Enumerators, Etc.* (Boston: William E. Smythe Co., 1888), v.

The sheer scale of Wright's new assignment and the diversity of his constituents suggested potential problems. Moreover, Congress had handed Wright a broad mission but little guidance, and even worse, limited funds.[25] To appreciate the extent of Wright's dilemma, we need to examine the practical side of nineteenth-century labor statistics.

Practical Difficulties and Practical Statisticians

Designing, collecting, tabulating, and publishing large volumes of information was not an easy task. American statisticians in the nineteenth century—especially those who had worked under Carroll Wright—frequently talked about "practical statistics," a phrase that carried several connotations, but generally referred to the conduct of statistical investigations by official government agencies. In the eyes of its proponents, "practical statistics" was analogous to laboratory work for a chemist or clinical work for a physician.[26] It was the experimental branch of social science, producing the basic "facts" and having its own peculiar "practical" problems, of which the theorist might know very little. The most sustained attempt to describe this art came from Wright's aforementioned chief clerk, Charles F. Pidgin, who in 1888 produced a handbook aptly titled *Practical Statistics*.

Unlike existing treatments of statistics, Pidgin explained that his book covered "the practical part of statistical work," and the guide clearly reveals the immense difficulty of gathering statistics in the late nineteenth century. First there were the basic administrative hurdles faced by anyone running a large clerical operation, but beyond bureaucratic trivia, collecting information was itself a bewildering and frustrating enterprise. The most common method was to mail or distribute surveys, but these faced two formidable obstacles: inaccurate or incomplete responses ("Persons show an absolute genius in misunderstanding questions," Pidgin complained) and a truly dismal rate of return. Though these problems could be mitigated by careful survey design and public education, many statisticians eschewed mailings in favor of direct interviews by bureau representatives. Of course, this second method brought its own complications: field agents needed to be trained and monitored, and their salaries expanded the project costs enormously. For both mailed surveys and interviews, bureaus also faced resistance from recalcitrant workers and businessmen reluctant to disclose information,

---

[25] The Bureau's initial budget was $25,000, an absurdly small amount which rapidly expanded to about $170,000; Goldberg and Moye, *First Hundred Years*, 22.

[26] Cf. Pidgin, *Practical Statistics*, 187.

plus the expense of tabulation (done by hand or with the aid of adding machines) and the costs of inevitable overruns in time and budget. To further complicate matters, the bureaus usually pursued novel topics whose intricacies only became apparent later. For instance, Wright described the difficulties one investigator had encountered when trying to break down the cost of production of a commodity (to show how much of the price came from the production, transportation, and retail processes). Having started by studying the cost of transportation, the investigator was led to consider what might be a "reasonable freight rate," which then pushed him to study the "cost of roads," in turn leading to a host of other issues, with the net result that, as Wright put it, "he got all wound up, and is wound up now." Labor statisticians who attended the annual national conventions repeatedly bemoaned the difficulty of gathering economic and social information (especially with their meager allocations), and the commissioner of the California bureau lyrically captured the common disillusionment greeting new administrators: "The agents, full of energy, entered upon their work with buoyant spirits, and I, full of hope, awaited the result. They are still working, but their buoyancy of spirit is gone. I am still waiting, but hope has lost its brilliancy."[27]

In the end, bringing a statistical study to a successful conclusion required time, experience, and especially money. For the federal bureau, whose activities were supposed to span the entire nation, the cost of undertaking broad surveys using field agents—Wright's favored method—meant that only one or (at best) two major projects could be undertaken at any time. The state bureaus were an obvious place to look for potential collaboration, but this proved far more difficult than Wright had hoped, and indeed it revealed the difficulty of trying to build a national statistical system on top of a federalist political structure.

The Struggle to Unite the State Bureaus

One of the major sticking points during the debate over the federal bureau had been why the country needed a national bureau of labor statistics at all. Many states already had such bureaus, and more were appearing each year—why should the federal government duplicate their efforts? In an era

[27] Ibid., esp. v, 1. Carroll Wright, *NABL* 20 (1904): 95. George W. Walts, *NABL* 9 (1892): 192. On the similar problems early statisticians faced in Britain, see Roger Davidson, *Whitehall and the Labour Problem in Late-Victorian and Edwardian Britain: A Study in Official Statistics and Social Control* (London: Croom Helm, 1985), 169–214.

when the country was struggling mightily over the proper balance between state and federal power, this was no idle issue. For the bill's supporters, though, such statistical proliferation only highlighted the need for a national bureau. The work of the state bureaus was not "collected or brought into one body," noted Rep. John King (D-Louisiana). As things stood now, the individual actions of the states would only lead to hopeless confusion and massive tomes of uncoordinated data. "Not only will State interests interfere and lack of united action present an insurmountable obstacle," argued Rep. Charles O'Neill (D-Missouri), "but the difference in methods, the variety of means used, and the lack of compilation under one management would diminish the usefulness and the value of the statistics."[28]

This "difference in methods" was more than a mere irritation; it prevented statistics from serving their main purpose: providing a solid foundation for reformers to address the labor question. Without one centralized source of statistics, warned Rep. James Hopkins (D-Pennsylvania), legislators would find themselves falling into endless debate; to create useful information, the nation needed one bureau using one set of methods. In the vision of the bureau's primary sponsor, Senator Henry Blair, the vista opened up by the bureau could dwarf all other work and turn criticism about statistical duplication upside-down: "If I were to do anything, I would make this bill broader in its scope, and all these other statisticians and all these other bureaus having to do with statistics should revolve around this as the grand center."[29] A national bureau devoted to studying a dominant segment of American society would form the center of all federal investigative agencies and produce unified, comprehensive statistics.

These comments illustrate a recurring theme: to be effective, statistics require standardized methods and categories. Thus, if statistics abet centralized control, they require the deployment of centralized (or centralizing) power to create and maintain this standardization.[30] Unfortunately for Wright, the federalist nature of American political structure inhibited such national action. Wright had neither the funds to produce comprehensive national statistics nor the direct power to control state agencies, but he nevertheless strove to muster the "great chain of bureaus" stretched out across the states into a unified statistic instrument, calling on his colleagues at the state

[28] *Congressional Record* (48th Cong., 1st sess.), 1884, pp. 3157, 3142.

[29] Ibid., pp. 3139, 1676.

[30] Cf. Eric Brian, "Statistique Administrative et Internationalisme Statisque Pendant la Second Moitié du XIXe Siècle," *Histoire et Mesure* 4 (1989): 201–224; Marie-Noëlle Bourguet, *Déchiffrer la France: La Statistique Départementale à l'Époque Napoléonienne* (Paris: Éditions des Archives Contemporaines, 1988).

level "to simplify and unify methods, to eliminate faulty presentations, and to dignify, as well as popularize, the labor statistics of the country."[31] When he addressed the convention of state bureaus in 1885 as the commissioner of the new federal Bureau of Labor, Wright outlined a grand plan for nationwide statistical cooperation. He hoped to make the state bureaus "associates" of the federal bureau (effectively serving as local agents of the bureau when necessary), to send funds their way as they participated in federally sponsored programs, and to compile and disseminate their studies.[32] In 1891, recognizing that state and federal studies sometimes overlapped, he called for "some plan or harmonious cooperation, to avoid duplication of effort."[33] Yet pursuing "harmonious cooperation" required sharing common objectives and methods, and here many of the state agencies were still quite far apart.

As William Brock has demonstrated, although the Massachusetts bureau often served as a model and inspiration for the other states, each bureau developed among its own peculiar set of circumstances and constraints.[34] Most basically, state bureaus often had different responsibilities and goals. In Massachusetts, Wright and his successors emphasized the agency's place as an impartial investigator of the facts, pursuing issues and questions raised by the legislature, and educating the public about the condition of the laboring class, but not setting or recommending policies.[35] Other bureaus, such as those in Maryland and Ohio, set an explicitly reformist agenda and saw themselves as fact-gathering allies of labor, not merely neutral observers.[36] Moving in the opposite direction came those like the Missouri and Maine bureaus, whose broad construal of labor statistics included producing commercial data about trade and tourism (often to the consternation of their reform-minded colleagues).[37] Moreover, many agencies had mandates to undertake other time-consuming tasks, such as inspecting factories or gathering agricultural statistics.[38]

These diverse goals combined with varying levels of financial support to produce a broad methodological variance among the bureaus. At the deepest

---

[31] Carroll D. Wright, "The Growth and Purposes of Bureaus of Statistics of Labor," *Journal of Social Science*, no. 25 (1888): 13, 7.

[32] Carroll D. Wright: "The Work of the United States Bureau of Labor," *NABL* 3 (1885): 130–131, 133–134.

[33] U.S. Commissioner of Labor, *Seventh Annual Report*, 2 vols. (Washington, DC: U.S. GPO, 1891), 5.

[34] Brock, *Investigation and Responsibility*, 148–184.

[35] *NABL* 3 (1885): 125–126; Leiby, *Carroll Wright*, 63, 100, 145–148.

[36] *NABL* 13 (1897): 57; Brock, *Investigation and Responsibility*, 158–159, 163–164.

[37] *NABL* 9 (1892): 29–35, 40–43; *NABL* 14 (1898): 44–46.

[38] *NABL* 11 (1895): 8.

level, the state agencies reflected a long-standing split in statistics between those who valued extensive written descriptions and those who favored numerical tables.[39] Under Wright, the Massachusetts bureau emphasized quantitative results, eschewing projects where quantification would be difficult or impossible, while stretching the bounds of mathematical rationalization.[40] But others took a different approach. For instance, state politics and funding limitations in New York hindered that bureau's ability to collect extensive data, giving its reports (in William Brock's words) an "impressionistic" flavor that had more in common with "investigative journalism."[41] Generally speaking, such accounts had a stronger connection to reform than did Wright's preferred tables of statistics, because evocative narrative more readily lent itself to rousing public emotion than did what Wright described as admittedly "cold," "quiet," and "unlovely" numbers. Even among the like-minded, deciding how to compile such numbers could lead to other discrepancies. Bureaus with smaller budgets resisted Wright's preference for field agents and interviews, insisting that mailed questionnaires were far less expensive and could be accurate when used properly.[42] Beyond such basic debates, crafting a comprehensive statistical system required the acceptance of standardized categories, variables of interest, and survey forms, and the state bureaus never came close to reaching such detailed agreement.

The inability to agree on common goals or a common methodology plagued statistics worldwide. At the 1903 convention, Wright described several European and international efforts (including the recent formation of the International Statistical Institute) to standardize statistical approaches, noting that "so far ... nothing has been accomplished." Undeterred by this poor track record, Wright suggested that the state bureaus now had an opportunity to solidify America's pioneering work in labor statistics by creating a unified approach.[43] The association dutifully responded with several attempts at creating a comprehensive methodology, including a 1904 proposal to create a "uniform schedule ... [showing] what constitutes the cost of living."[44] This was ceremoniously sent to a committee for further study, but the designated group never reported. After a prolonged discussion the following year, one association member declared the topic to be a

[39] Desrosières, *Politics of Large Numbers*, 18–25, 40–44.
[40] Leiby, *Carroll Wright*, 64.
[41] Brock, *Investigation and Responsibility*, 161.
[42] Wright, "Presidential Address," 15. For an early methodological debate, see *NABL* 6 (1888) 30–34.
[43] *NABL* 19 (1903): 66.
[44] *NABL* 20 (1904): 96.

"complicated" and "confusing" one, subject to "infinite ramifications," and concluded that "it appears to be one of those interesting subjects that the more it is discussed, the less we know about it."[45]

Overall, state bureaus argued incessantly about the proper methods of data collection and indeed the very nature of a "bureau of labor statistics." Time failed to bring a resolution to these questions; if anything, the differences grew worse: the 1905 annual meeting of labor statisticians featured a rather raucous discussion about the purpose of state bureaus and the convention itself. Each agency functioned independently, accountable only to its legislature, and bound by its own specific charter, funding level, and staff limitations. Trying to craft these diverse agencies into a unified statistical community was a losing proposition, as centralizing enthusiasts learned time and again. The most determined effort came in 1903–04, when Simon Newcomb Dexter (S.N.D.) North tried to organize cooperation between the states and the federal Census Bureau to conduct a census of manufacturing. Despite high hopes, the plan soon foundered on administrative difficulties and federal-state bickering, and slowly collapsed. Without prospects for serious interstate cooperation, participation at the annual meetings of labor bureaus dwindled, and in 1911 the beleaguered remainder merged with an association of factory inspectors, effectively marking the end to Wright's dream of a "great chain" of statistical production. Not until after the Second World War, under a more powerful federal government which could send substantial funds to the state agencies, would the state bureaus be crafted into more effective collaborators. In his memorial to Wright before the American Statistical Association, a frustrated S.N.D. North threw one last dig at the early state bureaus, whose "contributions to our statistical literature," he told the audience, "[have] been much greater in bulk than in value."[46]

THE FEDERAL BUREAU AND THE "LABOR QUESTION"

Without state help, the federal bureau was left to create national labor statistics on its own. Facing difficult obstacles, supplied with limited funds,

---

[45] *NABL* 21 (1905): 46. A second committee made a new effort in 1907, producing a "tentative report, subject to further criticism and consideration," that was then circulated to the state bureaus. The association could not reach a final resolution, however, and the matter was dropped. *NABL* 24 (1908): 100.

[46] Ibid., 67–81. Leiby, *Carroll Wright*, 86–88; *NABL* 25 (1909): 29–48. S.N.D. North, "The Life and Work of Carroll Davidson Wright: Fifth President of the American Statistical Association," *PASA* 11, no. 86 (1909): 452. Extensive federal–state collaboration began with employment statistics in the late 1940s: Goldberg and Moye, *First Hundred Years*, 186–188.

and lacking a clear focus, Wright responded by producing discrete, topical studies. Only by the turn of the century, with the growing prominence of unions, would Wright find a new center for his work: producing data relevant to organized labor or for use in collective bargaining. Yet even here, the weakness and limited scale of trade unions, combined with the federal government's lack of involvement in labor relations, made it difficult to justify the expense of regular, extensive data collection on specific subjects like the "cost of living."

The Federal Bureau and Special Investigations

While in Massachusetts, Wright had developed a twofold approach to statistical research. First, he ran a number of "special investigations," one-time studies focused on particular topics such as female laborers, the connection between poverty and crime, and wages in certain industries or locations. These reflected his overall view that the social and economic strife wrought by industrialization could not be eliminated through any single grand program: "There is no panacea," he remarked early in his tenure in Massachusetts, "The Bureau cannot solve the labor question, for it is not solvable." But while bureaus of labor statistics could not bring social salvation, they could nevertheless reduce specific, egregious faults and illuminate more limited problems. Along with these special investigations, Wright promoted regular study of economic and social conditions via the state census, which soon came under his control.[47]

When Wright moved to the federal bureau, however, he focused almost exclusively on topic-oriented studies rather than regular collection of economic data like prices, wages, or hours of labor. Although Wright never gave an explicit explanation for the change, the main problem appears to have been a lack of resources.[48] Wright did try to repeat his Massachusetts experience by leveraging the power of the national census, which had repeatedly expanded its coverage of economic issues and surveys of particular

---

[47] Leiby, *Carroll Wright*, 65–68, 222–224. The term "special investigation" is Leiby's, e.g., p. 122. Massachusetts Bureau of Statistics of Labor, *Eighth Annual Report*, vi.

[48] Leiby suggests that Wright believed routine data collection was the province of a census office and that bureaus of labor should stick to special investigations (Leiby, *Carroll Wright*, 121–123). But this thesis has several problems. First, Wright started background work for new indexes (1900) just as Congress was moving toward a permanent Census Bureau, and he continued the indexes after it had been established. Moreover, although the Census conducted regular investigations, they were each separated by a decade, whereas Wright published his indexes on a much more frequent basis (annually). In short, as argued below, I suspect Wright was dissuaded from starting major data series largely by a lack of funds.

industries since 1810. Wright joined the campaign for a permanent census bureau, and several attempts were made either to place the Bureau of Labor within a larger census agency or to place the census under Wright's control. Yet bureaucratic infighting repeatedly stymied the quest for a central statistical agency, and although others (including Herbert Hoover) would make similar efforts in later years, the two remained separate.[49]

Without state cooperation or extensive funding, gathering comprehensive economic data on production, wages, prices, hours of labor, employment, and so forth was simply out of the question. Indeed, even for Wright to have committed himself to regular data collection on one or two of these topics would have severely curtailed his ability to study other subjects. Once the bureau did start gathering information on retail prices and wages in the early part of the twentieth century, Wright's successor stated that merely collecting the data occupied "the entire force of field agents from six to seven months" each year (because of the reliance on personal interviews), and that tabulation "required a large part of the office force for four or possibly five months."[50]

Committing to regular data collection, therefore, would necessarily limit the bureau's ability to work on other projects. What topic could justify such extended attention? Single-minded devotion to one issue did not fit Wright's conception of the labor question as a complex of interlocking problems, nor did he receive any concrete guidance from Congress or the public at large, who held similarly diverse views of what a bureau of labor statistics ought to be doing. Without any clear focus to the bureau's work, it slipped from project to project, naturally precluding any systematic, long-term study of the nation's economy. What the agency did produce in spades were individual investigations of limited scope, often focused on select groups of workers in specific geographic locations or on specific topics.

Taken as a whole, the reports were an eclectic bunch, reflecting the diversity of those who could lay claim to labor statistics. The topics ranged widely, including things like "Industrial Depressions," records of strikes, the wages of various workers, studies of particular communities, the effects of increasing mechanization, the "Liquor Problem," industrial education, studies of public and private utility companies, and compilations of foreign or

---

[49] Margo J. Anderson, *The American Census: A Social History* (New Haven: Yale University Press, 1988), 104–106, 118–123; Micarelli, "Evolution of the United States Economic Censuses," 335–344; Leiby, *Carroll Wright*, 124–126. On Hoover's efforts, see Goldberg and Moye, *First Hundred Years*, 121–122.

[50] Testimony of Charles P. O'Neill, "Original Transcript," 27 March 1913, pp. 46–47, Folder 18/3, Box 59, General Records, 1907–1942, Chief Clerk's Files, DOL.

state labor statistics, as well as more peculiar subjects like "The Attitude of Women's Clubs and Associations Toward Social Economics," "Public Baths in Europe," and "A Report on the Statistics of and Relating to Marriage and Divorce."[51] (Facing some criticism over the latter, Wright defended himself by arguing that "if there is any subject in which labor should be actively interested, and which concerns the happiness of the workingman, it is the sacredness and permanency of home relations.")[52] If individual studies were sometimes enlightening, it was difficult to discern any overriding purpose to the set. Such was the inevitable result, in an age when statistics were both ambiguous and novel, of producing statistics without any clearly defined application or audience, and it led to a predictable tendency to conflate value with detail.[53]

In light of this context, the truly curious question is why Wright ever initiated regular data series on retail prices and wages data at all. Indeed, the question becomes more salient when we consider Wright's first foray into national statistics on wages and prices: the Aldrich reports of 1892–93.

The Aldrich Reports: Statistics and Tariffs

A basic problem plaguing the federal bureau was the nature of the federal government itself. In the late nineteenth century, progressive reform was largely local, and states usually had far more regulatory power than the national government. The federal government thus had a limited scope of action and a correspondingly limited use for statistics; indeed, the bureau's work prior to 1900 had minimal impact on legislation. Significantly, when Wright wrote an article on the "Value and Influence of Labor Statistics" in 1893 (revised and republished in 1904), most of his focus was on the efforts and efficacy of the state bureaus.[54]

---

[51] Leiby, *Carroll Wright*, 107–112; Furner, "Knowing Capitalism," 246–268. The reports on industrial depressions, the liquor problem, mechanization, strikes, and industrial education appear in the bureau's first, twelfth, thirteenth, third (as well as tenth and sixteenth), and eighth annual reports, respectively. The studies on attitudes of women's groups and on public baths come from the *BLS Bulletin*, nos. 23 and 11; the study of marriage was the bureau's first "special report," issued in 1889.

[52] Carroll D. Wright, "The Working of the U.S. Bureau of Labor Statistics," *Bulletin of the Bureau of Labor*, no. 54 (1904): 983.

[53] Wright repeatedly assessed the quality of government statistics in terms of the amount of information produced, e.g., Carroll D. Wright, "Presidential Address of Carroll D. Wright to the American Statistical Association," *PASA* 11, no. 81 (1908): 8, 10–11, 14.

[54] Carroll D. Wright, "The Value and Influence of Labor Statistics," *Bulletin of the Bureau of Labor*, no. 54 (1904): 1087–1096; Leiby, *Carroll Wright*, 89, 102–103, 107.

There was, however, one area in which national politicians expected the bureau's research to have direct relevance to legislation: tariffs. Setting tariff rates was one of the most critical (and contentious) economic activities of the federal government, and debates often hinged on national and international data about prices and wages. For instance, pro-tariff legislators (largely Republicans and northern Democrats) argued that if European manufacturers exploited their workers, only high tariffs could prevent American companies from being forced to drive down costs by cutting wages. During the debate over the founding of the Bureau of Labor, Rep. Martin Foran (D-Ohio) claimed that no "just standard" for reform of the tariff laws could be created without data on "the comparative difference between the wages and the cost of living in the manufacturing centers of Europe." Yet no such data existed, and thus, as one legislator opined, the country could not move beyond "fine-spun theories or dogmatic utterances based on unreliable facts." Other congressmen agreed, repeatedly invoking the contentious tariff debates of 1883 to justify the creation of the new bureau. To set national policy, legislators needed national statistics.[55]

The first direct push in this direction came alongside the 1888 act that transformed the federal bureau into a "Department of Labor." (The new label was a clear attempt to mollify union demands for federal representation without actually ceding any real authority: the department lacked Cabinet status and retained the bureau's exclusive focus on statistical studies.) Beyond pulling the bureau from the Department of the Interior, the act also charged Wright's new agency with studying the cost of producing "dutiable" items in Europe and America, plus investigating the "comparative cost of living, and the kind of living" for workers in associated trades. Wright responded by examining costs and wages in key industries (iron, steel, coal, glass, and textiles) while also conducting a detailed survey of household expenditures covering roughly 8,500 families of workers in these industries spread across the United States and Europe (primarily in Great Britain).[56] As Wright was completing this project in 1891, the Senate Committee on Finance asked for data to assess how the 1890 McKinley tariff—which raised overall duties to a new high—had affected prices. In turn, Wright

[55] *Congressional Record* (48th Cong., 1st sess.), 1884, 3147–3148, 3141, 3142; cf. pp. 3139, 3142, 3147–3148, 3152. For the political resonance and power of the tariff issue in this time period, see Joanne Reitano, *The Tariff Question in the Gilded Age: The Great Debate of 1888* (University Park: Pennsylvania State University Press, 1994).

[56] Goldberg and Moye, *First Hundred Years*, 14–15. U.S. Commissioner of Labor, *Sixth Annual Report* (Washington, D.C.: U.S. GPO, 1890), 3; U.S. Commissioner of Labor, *Seventh Annual Report*.

expanded his existing work both chronologically and in breadth (including additional wholesale commodities plus retail prices for consumer goods). The results were then analyzed by Roland P. Falkner (an economist at the University of Pennsylvania), who compiled the data into index numbers for retail prices between 1889 and 1891, and wages and wholesale prices from 1840 to 1891.[57]

Price indexes were not a new statistical technique: they had been proposed and occasionally calculated by various authors since the late eighteenth century and published on a regular basis by commercial periodicals such as the *Economist*, *The Commercial and Financial Chronicle*, and the *Statist* since the late 1860s.[58] But they were new for Wright's federal bureau, which had only published average prices for goods over a range of years during its 1888–90 studies of wholesale prices. By contrast, an index number compared prices in two specific periods by turning them into a ratio (known as a "price relative"). For example, if p_{iron}^{1840} represents the average price of iron in 1840, then

$$\frac{p_{iron}^{1890}}{p_{iron}^{1840}}$$

would be a price relative comparing prices for iron in 1890 with those in 1840. By keeping the denominator constant and changing the numerator to reflect prices in different years (1891, 1892, etc.), one could construct a data series showing the average price in each subsequent year as a percentage of the average price in the base period (1840, in this example). Accordingly, index numbers made it much easier to spot trends in price changes. Moreover, a set of "price relatives" could be combined into an overall index showing the average change in price for a set of commodities, like iron, wheat, and corn:

$$\text{Price Index}_{1840-1890} = \left(\frac{p_{iron}^{1890}}{p_{iron}^{1840}} + \frac{p_{wheat}^{1890}}{p_{wheat}^{1840}} + \frac{p_{corn}^{1890}}{p_{corn}^{1840}} \right) \times \frac{1}{3}$$

[57] Edward S. Kaplan and Thomas W. Ryley, *Prelude to Trade Wars: American Tariff Policy, 1890–1922* (Westport: Greenwood Press, 1994), 1–9. Goldberg and Moye, *First Hundred Years*, 34–36. U.S. Congress, Senate, Committee on Finance, *Retail Prices and Wages* (Washington, D.C.: U.S. GPO, 1892), and *Wholesale Prices, Wages and Transportation* (Washington, D.C.: U.S. GPO, 1893).

[58] Wesley C. Mitchell, *The Making and Using of Index Numbers*, BLS Bulletin, no. 173 (Washington, D.C.: U.S. GPO, 1915), 6–8.

By the late nineteenth century, many economists recommended "weighting" the price relatives when combining them into an average, so that the price changes of commodities with greater impact on the economy would have a proportionally greater effect on the overall index:

$$\text{Weighted Price Index}_{1840-1890} = w_{iron} \times \frac{p_{iron}^{1890}}{p_{iron}^{1840}} + w_{wheat} \times \frac{p_{wheat}^{1890}}{p_{wheat}^{1840}}$$

$$+ w_{corn} \times \frac{p_{corn}^{1890}}{p_{corn}^{1840}}$$

where w_{iron} is the weight used for the price relative of iron, and so forth. Typically these weights were based on the proportional expenditure on each commodity in a given year. Thus, if 50 percent of the money in our hypothetical economy of iron, wheat, and corn was spent on wheat, the price relative for wheat would have a weight of 0.5 in the overall index.

When working on the 1892 and 1893 Aldrich reports (named after the chairman of the Senate Finance Committee, Nelson W. Aldrich, R-Rhode Island), Roland P. Falkner used the bureau's newly collected data to create an elaborate set of price indexes covering both "wholesale" commodities (raw materials sold to producers) and retail commodities (goods sold to consumers; see Table 1.1). Falkner hoped that creating a chronology of price changes could illuminate the effects of specific tariff regulations. But the results surely disappointed anyone who had hoped for a decisive end to the tariff debates. Some legislators, including Aldrich himself, still cited other price statistics that gave conflicting results, while both Democrats and Republicans drew on different aspects of the reports to support their positions.[59] Worse, an early, anonymous review of the Aldrich reports argued that historical price statistics could contribute little to the tariff debates because it was impossible to separate out the effects of the tariff from the consequences of other issues, including the "general depression" of 1889–91.[60] Indeed, in 1894, Wright referred back to the tariff debates when he warned about the "Limitations and Difficulties of Statistics," reiterating his position that statistics could elucidate facts about the present situation, but those facts might also carry important caveats and be open to multiple interpretations. As he and others had argued during meetings

[59] See *NYT* editorials from October 15, 17, 22, 26, 28, 30, 31 of 1892, as well as "Proceedings in Detail: Final Speeches and Decisive Vote on the Tariff Bill," *NYT*, 2 February 1894.

[60] Anonymous, "Retail Prices under the McKinley Act," *QJE* 7, no. 1 (1892): 104.

Table 1.1: *The Retail Price Indexes of the Aldrich Reports*

To create retail price indexes for the Senate Committee on Finance in 1891, the bureau gathered prices in 70 cities and towns using a list of 214 items. The list of items was provided by the Committee on Finance after consulting "the persons most familiar with the distribution of articles of general consumption." Unlike most expenditure surveys, the committee drew no distinctions between personal and occupational expenses, which later complicated attempts to combine the price survey with expenditure data. The list was subdivided into eight categories as follows:

Items	Category	Items	Category
60	Food	14	Lumber & Building Materials
61	Cloth & Clothing	7	Drugs & Chemicals
6	Fuel & Lighting	27	House-Furnishing Goods
34	Metals & Implements [tools]	5	Miscellaneous [soap, starch, & 3 kinds of tobacco]

The economist charged with analyzing the data, Roland P. Falkner, recognized that merely combining price relatives for all of these goods into an unweighted average might give inaccurate results, and so he sought to weight the price relatives by proportionate consumption among working-class families. However, the only relevant expenditure data came from an earlier study by the bureau which did not use the same set of goods as the committee. Accordingly, Falkner struggled to assign his price data to different expenditure categories: thus, to take the worst case, prices for "metals and implements," "lumber and building materials," and "drugs and chemicals" were all slotted to the catch-all category of "expenditures for other purposes" (which comprised roughly 22% of average family expenditures). On the other side, one important category from the expenditure surveys (rent) had no corresponding prices. In the end—following a common pattern for early price indexes (see Chapter 3)—the complications hardly seemed to matter: Falkner's weighted index showed that prices had fallen about 0.5% between June 1889 and September 1891, while the unweighted index showed a decline of 0.7%.

Source: U.S. Senate. Committee on Finance, *Retail Prices and Wages*, 32nd Congress, 1st Session, 1892, pp. i–l.

of the association of state bureaus, statistics were primarily descriptive: they could reveal problems but not necessarily what one member called the "deeper and more profound underlying causes," much less the appropriate solutions.[61] Repeatedly over the next century, others would learn a similar lesson: economic statistics rarely ended political debate—they proved at once too flexible (open to multiple interpretations) and too unstable (open to direct challenge through methodological critiques or indirect challenge through the citation of competing and conflicting figures).

[61] Carroll D. Wright, "The Limitations and Difficulties of Statistics," *Yale Review* 3 (1895): 121–143. *NABL* 8 (1891): 13–51; *NABL* 11 (1895): 89–97.

Despite these limitations, Wright had a clear sense of the value of labor statistics. First, they could have direct effects whenever merely illuminating the darker corners of industrial life (like hazardous working conditions) was sufficient to rouse the public into taking ameliorative action. More generally, Wright insisted that statistics educated the public and thereby informed, if they did not resolve, public debate.[62] His emphasis on the historical role of statistics reflected a vague but optimistic hope that however perplexing and limited current compilations might be, they might prove of great value to future scholars able to divine an order beneath the empirical relics.[63]

For now, however, labor statisticians received only lukewarm encouragement from political economists. Though Wright had a relatively high reputation among the newly forming social science professions, academic social scientists had a rocky relationship with their "practical" colleagues in public statistical agencies. "The course of study [in American universities]," complained Wright's colleague, Charles Pidgin, "seems to teach the manner of criticizing the work done by others, rather than a way of doing the work."[64] Indeed, academic critiques of government statistics were a routine occurrence. After reviewing the reports of many state bureaus, Richmond Mayo-Smith (Columbia University) concluded that "very few ... are doing any strictly scientific statistical work." Similarly, a series of reviews by the American Economics Association in the early 1900s complained that it took "the time of Methuselah" and "the patience of Job" to make sense of state statistics.[65]

As an academic economist working on a government project, Roland P. Falkner had hoped to use the Aldrich reports to bridge the "wide divergence between the theoretical, professorial treatment of the subject and the views of practical statisticians."[66] Unfortunately, though many commentators praised parts of Falkner's work, the overall results were deemed seriously inadequate (on the wage statistics, one economist declared that the "insufficiency of the data is truly startling").[67] Finding himself in the

[62] Wright, "Value and Influence." Cf. *NABL* 16 (1900): 115–116.

[63] *NABL* 10 (1894): 11, 78; *NABL* 11 (1895): 15; Wright, "Presidential Address," 15.

[64] Pidgin, *Practical Statistics*, 180.

[65] Richmond Mayo-Smith, "Reports of Bureaus of Statistics of Labor (Review)," *PASA* 1, no. 4 (1888): 164. The quotations from the American Economics Association are given in Leiby, *Carroll Wright*, 85.

[66] Roland P. Falkner, "The Theory and Practice of Price Statistics," *PASA* 3, no. 18/19 (1892): 119.

[67] For some critical commentary on the original reports and Falkner's later revisions, see H. L. Bliss, "Eccentric Official Statistics. V," *American Journal of Sociology* 6, no. 1

same position as many previous government statisticians and having seen firsthand the difficulty of collecting and compiling large amounts of data, Falkner had little patience with his critics. "If practice differs from theory," he argued, "it is only because practical necessity has forced us into short cuts to reach approximately the same results as would be obtained by the more cumbersome procedure which theory demands."[68]

Thus, the Aldrich reports had failed to resolve the tariff debates, while the criticisms from political economists emphasized the great difficulty of collecting reliable data, especially when trying to say something meaningful about the nation as a whole. In both regards, they provided no incentive for the bureau to continue the work. The research had taken a tremendous amount of time and effort, and there were many other aspects of the "labor question" left to study, along with new calls from Congress for other surveys that would severely stretch Wright's resources during the 1890s.[69]

A New Program for the Bureau: Prices, Wages, and the Cost of Living

Given this context, it seems remarkable that Wright ever returned to price and wage statistics, much less did so on a regular basis. Yet several years later, he committed a substantial portion of the bureau's limited resources to ongoing studies of wages and prices (including a wholesale price index and a retail price index for select foods). Although methods developed during the Aldrich reports provided some of the framework for these studies, the impetus came from transformations in the American labor movement and political ideology, which created a new role for bureaus of labor statistics.

When Wright first started his work as a statistician, the "labor question" was a vague mixture of concerns about industrialization and economic inequity. The most successful labor organization of the 1880s was the Knights of Labor, which admitted any worker as a member and which advocated a variety of social and economic remedies. Staunch business resistance (strengthened by state and local governments) undercut the Knight's efforts, however, and the organization was further weakened by internal dissension,

---

(1900): 2105–2113; Charles J. Bullock, "Contributions to the History of Wage Statistics," *PASA* 6, no. 45 (1899): 187–218; Arthur L. Bowley, "Comparison of the Rates of Increase of Wages in the United States and in Great Britain, 1860–1891," *Economic Journal* 5, no. 19 (1895): 369–383, esp. 216; Charles B. Spahr, *An Essay on the Present Distribution of Wealth in the United States* (New York: T.Y. Crowell & Co., 1896), 103–113.

[68] Roland P. Falkner, "Wage Statistics in Theory and Practice," *PASA* 6, no. 46 (1899): 278.

[69] On Wright's funding troubles, see Goldberg and Moye, *First Hundred Years*, 22–23.

the defection of skilled workers, and anti-labor sentiment that followed the 1886 Haymarket bombing. The 1893–1897 depression further sapped the strength of the labor movement, undermining most trade unions except those in the strongest economic positions, namely, skilled craft workers. By 1900, the labor movement was dominated by the American Federation of Labor (AFL) under Samuel Gompers, who focused primarily on organizing skilled workers to seek improved wages, hours, and working conditions.[70]

Gompers eschewed wider, class-based political organization and activism in favor of a trade unionism characterized by narrow goals, and his approach complemented the aims of political moderates, represented by politicians such as Theodore Roosevelt and organizations such as the National Civic Federation (NCF), of which Gompers was a member. Founded in 1900 by Ralph M. Easley, the NCF promoted a voluntary approach to industrial relations based upon conciliation between unions and companies, including collective bargaining (primarily focused on wages and hours) and limited improvements in working conditions, in order to prevent overt class conflict. If many workers (including those in AFL unions) retained more radical goals rooted in broader working-class solidarity (rather than trade and craft loyalties), the hostility of conservatives toward working-class movements and the support of moderate businessmen and politicians for union leaders like Gompers left trade unions as the politically acceptable face of the labor movement.[71] This consolidation of the "labor question" was consequently reflected in the shape of labor statistics toward the turn of the century.

On the state level, bureaus of labor increasingly took on regulatory and administrative functions, and much of their research was directed toward the pragmatic needs of trade unions. Wright, who had been indifferent or hostile to unions early in his career, gradually placed much of his hope

---

[70] Louis Schultz Reed, *The Labor Philosophy of Samuel Gompers* (Port Washington: Kennikat Press, 1966 [1930]); Arnesen, "American Workers and the Labor Movement in the Late Nineteenth Century," 49–58; Foster Rhea Dulles and Melvyn Dubofsky, *Labor in America, a History*, fifth ed. (Wheeling: Harlan Davidson, 1993), 120–156.

[71] David Montgomery, *The Fall of the House of Labor: The Workplace, the State, and American Labor Activism, 1865–1925* (Cambridge: Cambridge University Press, 1987), 4–6, 257–264; James Weinstein, *The Corporate Ideal in the Liberal State, 1900–1918* (Westport: Greenwood Press, 1981); Clarence E. Wunderlin, *Visions of a New Industrial Order: Social Science and Labor Theory in America's Progressive Era* (New York: Columbia University Press, 1992), 27–45; Furner, "The Republican Tradition and the New Liberalism," 214–218, 228–230. For a more sympathetic view of the NCF, see Christopher J. Cyphers, *The National Civic Federation and the Making of a New Liberalism, 1900–1915* (Westport: Praeger, 2002).

for industrial stability in the voluntary collective bargaining promoted by Gompers, a view that was greatly strengthened by his post hoc investigation of the 1894 Pullman strike. In a widely publicized report, Wright condemned the intransigence of the railroad employers and documented the hardships of Pullman workers but nonetheless criticized the decision to strike (which had paralyzed rail traffic) and praised the AFL for resisting the railroad union's call for a more general strike. Equally important, he argued that trade unions had a legitimate and necessary place in an industrial economy, though he also insisted that unions should be constrained to working in the public interest (a point on which the railway unions had failed).[72] Paralleling Wright's new attention to the merits of trade unions, the federal Bureau of Labor increasingly focused its efforts during the 1890s on topics relevant to skilled, male workers, such as studies of technology and de-skilling, the effects of female, child, or immigrant workers on wages, and more mundane subjects such as records of strikes and compilations of labor legislation. Wright's decision in 1900 to begin annual publication of extensive wage and price data, broken down by geographical location and, in the case of wages, by occupation, must be seen as part of this trend: a simultaneous narrowing of the field and a growing sense that the bureau's primary role lay in monitoring and facilitating industrial relations. Significantly, Wright started his indexes just as trade unions were expanding rapidly (from roughly 450,000 to 2 million workers over 1897–1903), during a brief lull in violent strikes and repression (1898–1903), and shortly after the creation of the NCF.[73]

Wright had ample reason to believe that wage and price data could play an important role in easing labor negotiations and rooting out exploitation. Under Gompers, the AFL had adopted consumption-based arguments for higher wages, including advocating a "living wage."[74] Though Gompers eschewed attempts to fix the numerical value of a just minimum wage, Wright was less reticent: In 1875, while commissioner of the Massachusetts bureau, he had (unsuccessfully) proposed establishing a rather generous minimum wage based on his recent survey of working-class incomes and

---

[72] Leiby, *Carroll Wright*, 152–180; Furner, "Knowing Capitalism," 252–261, 267–268; Dubofsky, *The State & Labor in Modern America*, 31–32; Nancy Cohen, *The Reconstruction of American Liberalism, 1865–1914* (Chapel Hill: University of North Carolina Press, 2002), 195–202.

[73] Leiby, *Carroll Wright*, 111–112. Leo Wolman, *Ebb and Flow in Trade Unionism* (New York: NBER, 1936), 16; Dubofsky, *The State & Labor in Modern America*, 38.

[74] Samuel Gompers, "A Minimum Living Wage," *American Federationist* (1898): 25–30. Currarino, "The Politics of 'More.'"

expenditures. Now, at the turn of the century, he tried a different tack: not defining a minimum rate but adjusting existing wages based on price movements. In 1902, as part of a federal commission arbitrating a bitter anthracite coal strike, he awarded a pay raise based on bureau statistics about food prices over the previous three years. The latter intervention, prompted by President Roosevelt's fears of "socialist action" if the dispute was not resolved, illustrated a direct connection between economic data and the resolution of industrial conflict.[75]

The Aldrich reports had provided a crucial innovation that made Wright's price indexes even more attractive: the creation of a "wage index" that showed the average change in wages over time.[76] Setting a wage index next to a price index appeared to offer an easy way to compare changes in wages with changes in the cost of living, thereby showing the general progress (or regress) of workers. Following the example of the Aldrich reports, the bureau presented the new statistical series in 1904, placing its two indexes side by side to create a measure of worker "purchasing power." This, the staff was pleased to note, had increased by 5.4 percent in 1903 over the average in the last decade of the nineteenth century (in fact, a healthy 9.2 percent since 1891).[77] The apparent industrial progress validated what historian Eric Rauchway has aptly characterized as Wright's "Panglossian ... social Darwinism," his unwavering belief that time and virtue would alleviate the labor-capital conflict while retaining that "divine discontent ... which gives us whatever civilization now exists."[78]

Thus, by the turn of the century, it seemed that Wright had stabilized the bureau and set it on its future path. Over the next thirty years, the one-time,

---

[75] On Wright's 1875 study, see Massachusetts Bureau of Statistics of Labor, *Sixth Annual Report* (Boston: Wright & Potter, 1875), 193, 358–359, 380, 447–450; John F. McClymer, "How to Read Wright: The Equity of the Wage System and the Morality of Spending," *Hayes Historical Journal* 8, no. 2 (1989): 37–43; Margo Anderson, "Standards, Statuses, and Statistics: Carroll Wright and the American Standard of Living," *Advancing the Consumer Interest* 9, no. 1 (1997): 4–12. On the coal arbitration, see Jonathan Grossman, "The Coal Strike of 1902—Turning Point in U.S. Policy," *MLR* 98, no. 10 (1975): 24–26; Sanford M. Jacoby, "The Development of Cost-of-Living Escalators in the United States," *Labor History* 28, no. 4 (1987): 520; U.S. Bureau of Labor Statistics, "Report of the Anthracite Coal Commission," *Bulletin of the Department of Labor*, no. 46 (1903): 477, 625–626.

[76] Falkner, "Wage Statistics in Theory and Practice," 287. Falkner credited British statistician Robert Giffen as being the first to suggest creating a wage index to compare to a price index.

[77] U.S. Bureau of Labor Statistics, "Wages and Cost of Living," *Bulletin of the Bureau of Labor* 53 (1904): 723.

[78] Eric Rauchway, "The High Cost of Living in the Progressives' Economy," *JAH* 88, no. 3 (2001): 901. *NABL* 13 (1897): 10–13. North, "The Life and Work of Carroll Davidson Wright," 464.

special investigations that he had produced early in his career would gradually be supplanted by statistical series: index numbers of wages and prices, studies of employment and hours, and so forth. Yet though the strategy succeeded in the long term, Wright had in fact overestimated the desire for the indexes, and they proved to be far less attractive during the first decade of the twentieth century than he had anticipated. The problem was less a lack of general interest (many people apparently enjoyed hearing proclamations about the progress of workers) than the lack of a compelling interest, one that could justify the huge effort needed to keep the series going. Industrial relations would be the key to the bureau's future, but in 1905, the role that regular statistical data collection would play in that future was far from clear.

An Ambiguous Ending

Arriving at the happy conclusion about wage and price changes since the 1890s had been an arduous task, one more testimony to the difficulty of creating labor statistics on a national scale. In order to create the various index numbers, the bureau gathered a great deal of basic information, including a study of the income and expenditures of over 25,000 families and the compilation of price quotations for thirty-three food items stretching back to 1890 (see Table 1.2).[79] Wright had initially planned to complete the survey in 1901, but "the great labor involved in the collection and compilation of the data and the comparatively small force available for the work" had pushed the end date back into 1902 and then 1903; the full report was not available until 1904.[80]

Sadly, this last delay proved disastrous. By 1904, the nation was slipping into an economic downturn. As a result, the bureau's reports presented a rosier picture of working-class economics than many workers were inclined to believe. Several union papers criticized the methodology, especially with regard to the index of wages, and in *Political Science Quarterly*, Ernest Howard declared that the report "cannot be accepted as representative of the general labor experience."[81] To make matters worse, 1904 was a presidential election year, and both Democrats and many labor officials accused Wright of subordinating the integrity of his work to party politics. The chairman

---

[79] U.S. Bureau of Labor Statistics, *Cost of Living and Retail Prices of Food: Eighteenth Annual Report of the Commissioner of Labor* (Washington, D.C.: Department of Commerce and Labor, 1904).

[80] U.S. Bureau of Labor Statistics, "Wages and Cost of Living," 703.

[81] Goldberg and Moye, *First Hundred Years*, 38.

For the index of food prices first published in 1904, the bureau gathered prices for 30 items from 811 merchants in 33 states across the country, with representation roughly proportional to the extent of manufacturing employment. As appropriate for a statistical report in a federalist era, states rather than cities formed the primary geographic unit of analysis; it is unclear how price collection was distributed within states. Few of the merchants supplied prices for every item; e.g., evaporated apples had only 36 prices in 1903.

Bureau staff calculated simple (unweighted) averages of price relatives for each food item (e.g., wheat bread, molasses, etc.). These item indexes were combined into two different overall indexes: a simple total index and a weighted total index. The weights were derived from the average proportionate expenditure of 2,567 families, namely, those among the 25,440 families who participated in the 1901–1902 survey who were willing to provide detailed data about their annual expenditures. According to the bureau, field agents found these families "somewhat more intelligent and better educated than the average family canvassed," and they were also larger (5.31 persons vs. 4.88) and had higher average incomes ($827 / year vs. $768). Participation was limited to "families of wage workers and persons on salaries not exceeding $1,200 per year." These included "native" and "foreign-born" families, a small number of which were led by single parents (of both sexes). The staff reported gathering data from "quite a number of colored families," but this information was not distinguished in the tables (though presumably included under "native" families).

As with the Aldrich reports of 1892, the expenditure categories were broader than the list of items priced, requiring some consolidation:

Expenditure Category	Food Items	Weight	Expenditure Category	Food Items	Weight
Fresh Beef	Roast & Stew Meat	16%	Lard	Lard	3%
	Steaks		Bread	Bread (wheat)	4%
Salt Beef	Salt Beef	2%	Flour & Meal	Flour, Wheat, Corn Meal	5%
Fresh Hog Products	Pork, Fresh	5%	Rice	Rice	1%
			Potatoes	Potatoes, Irish	4%
Salt Hog Products	Bacon Dry/Pickled Pork Salt Ham	5%	Fruit	Apples, evap. Prunes	5%
Other Meat	Mutton & Lamb Veal	3%	Vinegar, Pickles, & Condiments	Vinegar	1%
Poultry	Chickens	3%	Teas	Tea	2%
Fish	Fresh Fish Salted Fish	3%	Coffee	Coffee	4%
Eggs	Eggs	5%	Sugar	Sugar	5%
Milk	Milk	7%	Molasses	Molasses	1%
Butter	Butter	9%	Other Food	All items (including beans) except meat	6%
Cheese	Cheese	1%			

Source: BLS, *Cost of Living and Retail Prices of Food* (Washington, D.C., 1904).

of the Democratic Party called the report "unscientific and partisan," and claimed that it was issued "for the special use of the Republican Campaign Committee."[82] For a man who had built his career on a dedication to impartial fact-gathering, these were harsh charges. Even more charitable reactions to the 1904 report were damning in their assessment of the place of labor statistics in political life. The National Civic Federation concluded that though the bureau's work was not exactly wrong, and might in fact have some historical value, it was nevertheless irrelevant to the "immediate present," a "fault, perhaps inevitable, of all government statistics."[83]

The attacks on the 1904 report were only the latest in a series of setbacks for Wright. The association of state bureaus was still mired in disagreement, and S.N.D. North's recent failed attempt to organize the census of manufactures had illustrated that the "great chain" was simply a series of uncooperative links. Moreover, in early 1903, Wright's "Department of Labor" had been reduced back to bureau status within Roosevelt's new Department of Commerce and Labor. Frustrated and tired of Washington politics, Wright resigned in January 1905, and left the association of state bureaus shortly thereafter. Both his personal reputation and his optimism about the benefits of national statistics remained high, though, and he spent the four remaining years of his life serving as an elder statesman in statistics (for instance, as president of the American Statistical Association), where he preached the virtues of impartial, quantitative facts.

Following Wright's resignation, Roosevelt appointed Charles P. O'Neill as the second commissioner of the Bureau of Labor. A political economist at Catholic University, O'Neill shared the conviction (common to both Wright and most liberal progressives of the time) that the labor problem could be best addressed by investigating specific problems, creating targeted reform regulations, and encouraging voluntary negotiations between employers and organized workers. However, unlike Wright (who had been heavily involved with the Massachusetts census), O'Neill had no particular enthusiasm for large-scale data collection efforts, nor was it obvious how such projects would further the progressive reform agenda.[84] As Roosevelt

---

[82] "[Cowherd] Calls Wright's Report Part Manipulation," *NYT*, 8 October 1904; "Republican Tariff Figures Assailed," *NYT*, 16 October 1904.

[83] Goldberg and Moye, *First Hundred Years*, 37–38.

[84] On O'Neill's views, see Furner, "Knowing Capitalism," 262–263; Richard G. Balfe, "Charles P. O'Neill and the United States Bureau of Labor: A Study in Progressive Economics, Social Work and Public Administration" (Ph.D. dissertation, University of Notre Dame, 1956). On progressive approaches to labor reform more generally, see Shelton Stromquist, *Reinventing "The People": The Progressive Movement, the Class Problem, and the Origins of Modern Liberalism* (Urbana: University of Illinois Press, 2006).

expanded the power of the executive branch, he also asserted control over the bureau and began to direct it toward popular progressive reform topics, such as studies of sanitation in the meat-packing industry (galvanized by Upton Sinclair's *The Jungle*), immigration, the eight-hour law, child labor, and industrial safety.[85] National wage and price indexes held no similar attraction.

Indeed, the only concrete application that Wright had found for wage and price data had been adjusting wages during his 1902 arbitration of the anthracite coal strike. In the abstract, O'Neill might have encountered a similar conjunction of interests, since resolving labor disputes became one of his most time-consuming activities. Wright's report on the 1894 Pullman strike had led to the Erdman Act of 1898, which authorized voluntary federal mediation in railroad strikes (followed by arbitration as necessary) and assigned the commissioner of the Bureau of Labor leading responsibility for resolving the conflicts. Though the Erdman Act had been little used before 1906, Roosevelt's experience with the anthracite strike led him to exploit the full potential of the law during O'Neill's tenure, sending the commissioner to mediate almost 60 different strikes and effectively turning such work into O'Neill's primary responsibility.[86] Yet the ideology that O'Neill brought to this task limited the relevance of federal wage and price statistics. Like both the NCF and many union leaders, O'Neill preferred to handle labor disputes through conciliation and voluntary negotiations between unions and companies rather than through state arbitration. Therefore, unlike Wright's function in the 1902 anthracite coal strike, O'Neill's job was to persuade each side to compromise, not to search for a "just" settlement.[87] "A mediation decision," as another commentator noted, "is merely an adjustment of the dispute, rather than a judgment on the merits of the case."[88] Such efforts required great diplomatic skill, but not extensive economic data; not until

---

[85] On the general expansion of federal bureaucratic administration under Roosevelt, see Stephen Skowronek, *Building a New American State: The Expansion of National Administrative Capacities, 1877–1920* (Cambridge: Cambridge University Press, 1982), 170–173. On O'Neill's statistical studies, see Goldberg and Moye, *First Hundred Years*, 46–55, 58–61.

[86] On Wright and O'Neill's involvement in labor disputes, see Goldberg and Moye, *First Hundred Years*, 45–47, 56–57; Joseph P. Goldberg and William T. Moye, "The AFL and a National BLS: Labor's Role Is Crystallized," *MLR* 105, no. 3 (1982): 21–29. On the growth of Roosevelt's mediation after the anthracite strikes, see Grossman, "Coal Strike," 21–28. For an overview of Roosevelt's industrial policy, see Dubofsky, *The State & Labor in Modern America*, 39–51. On O'Neill's views, see

[87] Charles P. O'Neill, *Bulletin of the Bureau of Labor Statistics*, no. 98 (1912): 15.

[88] J. Noble Stockett, Jr., *The Arbitral Determination of Railway Wages* (Boston: Houghton Mifflin, 1918), xiii.

after O'Neill's tenure had ended would arbitration take over as the standard practice in railroad labor disputes.[89]

Even as Roosevelt touted mediation and pushed the bureau to pursue special investigations that could aid progressive reform efforts, O'Neill encountered the same funding difficulties that had plagued Wright. Roosevelt's dynamism gave the bureau politically meaningful work, but he had less success in gathering the funding to go along with his plans. To make matters worse, O'Neill was worried about the efficiency and competence of his clerical staff (inherited from Wright) and had "serious doubts as to the integrity of some of the field agents," who sometimes submitted reports full of "gross errors." Both the budget problems and the weakness of his staff led O'Neill to curtail the bureau's activities, and it was only too obvious where to make the cuts. As a good progressive, O'Neill admitted to a predilection for "studies of practical problems" that "would lead to remedial legislation" instead of engaging in "large, general statistical investigations." The latter clearly referred to the wage and retail price indexes, which had never been the impetus for "remedial legislation," and which also consumed a disproportionate amount of time and effort (requiring the collaboration of most of the staff for nearly half a year). Not surprisingly, producing the indexes interfered with any other decent sized project undertaken by the bureau. Moreover, they were politically controversial (witness 1904). In 1905, O'Neill decided to collect and publish the data only in alternate (non-election) years; in 1907, he stopped the indexes altogether, pending reforms of the field staff and a reorganization that would make the system more efficient.[90] The only time-series data published throughout O'Neill's tenure were wholesale prices (i.e., prices of raw materials and bulk commodities), which could be readily and inexpensively gathered from trade journals or by correspondence with major firms and trade organizations. Indeed, the most well-known wholesale price indexes were calculated by independent journals like *The Economist*.[91] With the wage and retail price indexes out of the way, O'Neill could focus on more immediate progressive aims, including a massive, nineteen-volume study of *Woman and Child Wage-Earners*.[92]

---

[89]   Frank H. Dixon, "Public Regulation of Railway Wages," *AER* 5, no. 1 (1915): 257–259; Stockett, *Determination of Railway Wages*, xi–xxv.

[90]   Goldberg and Moye, *First Hundred Years*, 73–77. Testimony of Charles P. O'Neill, "Original Transcript," 27 March 1913, pp. 46–52, folder 18/3, box 59, General Records, 1907–1942, Chief Clerk's Files, DOL.

[91]   Goldberg and Moye, *First Hundred Years*, 72. Mitchell, *Making and Using of Index Numbers*, 6–8, 30–33.

[92]   U.S. Bureau of Labor Statistics, *Report on Condition of Woman and Child Wage Earners*, 19 vols. (Washington, D.C.: U.S. GPO, 1910–1913).

Despite later laments over the elimination of the indexes, O'Neill's decision apparently caused little criticism at the time, one more testimony to the lack of a clear use for the annual data.

LABOR STATISTICS IN THE LATE NINETEENTH CENTURY

We are now in a position to broaden our gaze and assess the trajectory of American labor statistics. Though our story ends in 1910, I have left it under the "nineteenth-century" rubric to emphasize the continuity that existed well past the sharper chronological division. Even as the national progressive reform efforts associated with Roosevelt and other reformers had their roots in the local reform projects of the nineteenth century, so too was O'Neill's Bureau of Labor, even more so than Wright's, effectively a projection of the state bureaus of labor statistics onto the national level. The federal bureau had faced two problems after its creation: disagreement about labor statistics, and (relative to the states) a far weaker connection to any obvious center for political action. Though the former remained unsettled, Roosevelt had mitigated its effects by pressing the federal government to adopt new regulation and oversight responsibilities and by expanding the reach of the presidency, thereby bringing the bureau into the range of a new power. Nineteenth-century proponents conceived the bureau largely as a resource for the legislature; under Roosevelt, it drew closer to the executive and received new direction, giving O'Neill's collection of special investigations a focus and coherence that Wright's had never had. Equally important was the general shift toward trade union issues that occurred on both the state and federal levels beginning in the 1890s and thereby narrowed the potential range of studies.

Pulling back to the international level, it is clear that enthusiasm for labor statistics had spread quickly across the Atlantic as the American bureaus became models for European agencies: Great Britain (1886), Switzerland (1886), France (1891), Germany (1891), and Belgium (1895), followed by many others. Yet the lack of attention to continuous data collection in America at first looks anomalous: if agencies producing labor statistics in European countries also emphasized trade unionism, they seem to have gravitated more quickly to the production of economic, time-series data. But this superficial characterization is misleading. Britain provides a good example. Parliament created a Labour Bureau (and later a better-funded Labour Department) within the Board of Trade in 1886. By 1910, the Labour Department was producing both a wage index and an index of retail food prices, as well as statistics on unemployment. Yet each measure relied upon severely limited data and faced widespread criticism: the wage index represented only selected trades; the index of food prices contained nine items (the U.S. version had thirty) which were priced only in London (and economists doubted its accuracy even for that city); and the unemployment statistics came from union reports and were clearly unrepresentative.[93] The limitations that led to these weaknesses would have been familiar to American statisticians: funding shortfalls and an inability to gain the cooperation of other agencies and organizations who might have aided the department's efforts.[94] Where O'Neill had decided to suspend his data series in the face of similar obstacles, the British Labour Department essentially opted for a cruder set of estimates.

The United States, therefore, was hardly alone in its lack of commitment to most labor-related, time-series data in 1910. Such statistics were exceedingly difficult and expensive to gather, and they had no compelling role in the dominant political order or conception of political economy. If some social scientists and activists clamored for more and better data on national prices and earnings, most ruling governments had neither the inclination nor the popular pressure to enact programs that would require such information. As with the American federal government, the British administration in Whitehall pursued industrial policies rooted in voluntarism, conciliation, and limited arbitration. If anything, Whitehall was more conservative than the American government or its statisticians: many of O'Neill's special investigations were far more expansive and reform-oriented than anything from the British Labour Department, which occasionally even suppressed or repackaged statistics it felt might be incendiary.[95]

Within little over a decade, the situation would change entirely. By the 1920s, every major Western government produced regular data series on a core set of economic topics relevant to labor, such as earnings, employment, labor disputes, and the cost of living. Even in 1910, the industrial strategies pursued in Britain and America were starting to unravel: unions, companies, and labor economists had become disillusioned with conciliation; conservative businesses were driving unions out of their shops even as workers grew more militant and radical; and rising prices were fueling social

---

[93] Davidson, *Whitehall and the Labour Problem*, 152–162; Frances Wood, "The Construction of Index Numbers to Show Changes in the Price of Principal Articles of Food for the Working Classes," *Economic Journal* 23, no. 92 (1913): 619–620; Goldberg and Moye, *First Hundred Years*, 37; Arthur L. Bowley, *Wages and Income in the United Kingdom since 1860* (Cambridge: Cambridge University Press, 1937), 115.

[94] Davidson, *Whitehall and the Labour Problem*, 169–205.

[95] Ibid., 241–273.

unrest and demands for government intervention.[96] But the real source of transformation in national labor statistics was the looming catastrophe that would exhaust or topple the European imperial powers and shape a new political order: war.

[96] Montgomery, *Fall of the House of Labor*, 257–329; Wunderlin, *Visions of a New Industrial Order*, 72–129; Rauchway, "High Cost of Living," 898–924; Meg Jacobs, *Pocketbook Politics: Economic Citizenship in Twentieth-Century America* (Princeton: Princeton University Press, 2005), 39–45.

2

The Cost of Living in Peace and War: Statistics and Economic Management, 1910–1918

War has come to be a conflict of directed masses—of aggregates. Men, money, munitions, food, railways, shipping, raw materials, and manufactured products of great variety are impressed into the service of the nation. The problems of the effective control and use for war purposes of these varied national resources is ultimately dependent upon a knowledge of their quantities, that is, upon statistics.[1]
       —Allyn A. Young, Presidential Address to the American
               Statistical Association, 1917

As Chapter 1 described, nineteenth-century labor statistics served primarily to elucidate diverse aspects of the "labor question," and they exhibited a form and style that matched the prevailing political culture. Early labor statistics were broad in scope, democratic in their orientation (aimed at informing the public or legislature in order to further public deliberation about legislation), and directed toward discrete problems in need of reform. Moreover, they reflected the federalist political structure, with much of the attention and power deriving from the work of state bureaus. Within this statistical web, routine data collection by the federal government held only a minor place. Economic series such as national retail price indexes subsisted on the sidelines of American political and economic life, expensive to produce and lacking any deeply compelling application.

By mid-century, the situation would be radically different, as regular data collection on key topics such as prices, unemployment, and wages became the primary focus for the Bureau of Labor Statistics. Within this new suite of economic numbers, cost-of-living statistics led the way in methodological sophistication and importance, primarily in the form of national retail price indexes. Underlying this shift were three transformations. First, the "cost of living" developed into a critical topic in both American political

[1] Allyn A. Young, "National Statistics in War and Peace," *PASA* 16, no. 121 (1918): 873.

economy and industrial relations (thereby requiring special attention). Second, both the public and most federal officials came to view the national state as a bureaucratic manager, responsible for constantly monitoring the economy and acting to ensure a stable prosperity. In this managerial mode, economic statistics served as both indicators of performance and tools for administrative control and constraint, and in each case, the emphasis on stability required standardized measurements over time: that is, time-based data series of the sort that had been only a minor part of nineteenth-century labor statistics. Finally, conceptual developments in both industrial relations and political economy made retail price indexes the link between these first two transformations: BLS retail price indexes became the appropriate tools for assessing national changes in the cost of living, information that could then be used to guide the national economy and to manage industrial relations.

By 1910, the first of these transformations was well under way, as a trend of rising prices turned the cost of living into a potent political subject. Yet, tellingly, attention to the rising cost of living did not translate into equal interest in national retail price indexes. Economists turned to wholesale prices when analyzing monetary trends. Meanwhile, most reform-oriented studies repeated nineteenth-century patterns, with an emphasis on local, democratically oriented investigations that were rarely repeated. The first chink in this perspective came as the highly localized reform projects that characterized the early progressive era failed to quell economic disruptions, leading many would-be reformers to believe that the complex problems wrought by an industrial market economy—including the rising cost of living itself—necessitated greater centralized control (a regime in which national, economic data series would fulfill crucial functions). Still, it was war that provided the catalyst for this shift. The logistical demands of a large-scale, industrialized, international military venture provided the first impetus that propelled national, bureaucratic management clearly to the forefront. The brief period from 1917–1918 thus saw the emergence of a cluster of agencies and strategies that would provide basic prototypes (and lessons in failure) for future programs in both the New Deal and later war administrations.

Not surprisingly, quantitative knowledge was a central element in the new regime. As the epigraph from Allyn Young suggests, American mobilization created an enormous appetite for statistical knowledge. Within this framework, extensive wartime inflation coupled with federal oversight of the labor market drove the BLS to create national cost-of-living statistics for wartime labor arbitration. By the end of the war, some agencies had even turned to proto-forms of indexation based on BLS statistics, highlighting the ties between bureaucratic management and cost-of-living escalator clauses. Still, the haphazard evolution of the wartime labor system illustrates that the pull toward centralization and rule-governed administration—so critical to the later triumph of a national index and indexation policies—emerged only partially formed, driven by specific pressures and often facing resistance. The trends were promoted equally by two different desires—efficient wartime management and progressive reform—a convergence whose significance and consequences would only become apparent in retrospect.

CONFRONTING THE "COST OF LIVING" IN THE PREWAR ERA

Even before the onset of wartime inflation, high prices had become a potent political topic in America, a remarkable shift from the nineteenth-century world. In 1896, William Jennings Bryan ran an ambitious presidential campaign by rallying Democrats and populists around plans to abandon the gold standard and thereby devalue the dollar (i.e., promote inflation). Though Bryan lost the race, he still got his wish: 1897 began a new trend of rising prices worldwide, documented by international and domestic wholesale price indexes that showed a roughly 30 percent increase between 1897 and 1910, with the BLS wholesale price index rising even faster.[2] Far from being cheered by these developments, however, most Americans were now worried about the new "high cost of living." Although manufacturers and farmers would periodically promote increased prices as a solution to economic woes, these movements never won the widespread popular support that had characterized the free silver campaigns of the late nineteenth century. From 1910 onward, inflation was almost always a foe to be vanquished or a lurking threat to be contained.

What propelled this remarkable transformation? In large part the causes were economic and demographic, namely, the ongoing shift from a rural society composed of small producers and farmers to a more urbanized society dominated by wage-earners and salaried employees. As both producers and consumers, farmers necessarily bore a complex relationship to prices: they wanted low tariffs (reducing the cost of manufactured goods), high crop prices, and generally inflationary policies that could reduce the burden of their debt (especially as agriculture became more capital-intensive). For

---

[2] U.S. Bureau of Labor Statistics, *Wholesale Prices, 1890 to March 1910*, BLS Bulletin, no. 87 (Washington, D.C.: U.S. GPO, 1910), 385; Irving Fisher, "An International Commission on the Cost of Living," *AER* 2, no. 1 (1912): 94–95.

wage-earners and low- to mid-grade salaried employees—who did not own their products and who increasingly depended on the market to supply all their domestic goods—high prices of any sort were damaging. Their income had only an indirect relationship to the prices charged by their employers, and any benefits of general price hikes (for debt reduction) would be far outweighed by the new costs. In 1896, Bryan had built his support from a coalition of traditional Democrats and largely rural populists who would benefit from devaluing the dollar; he still lost the election, however, and the size of such a pro-inflation coalition would only continue to shrink.

Parallel to this demographic shift were transformations in retail practices that encouraged price consciousness among consumers. In the mid-nineteenth century, Americans purchased basic materials to make most of their own clothing, bought few finished goods, and patronized local shopkeepers with whom they built relationships allowing for the extension of credit and negotiation over prices. By the First World War, this world was vanishing quickly. The advent of the railroad and telegraph permitted enterprising businessmen to construct mass distribution systems that complemented the growing mass production of finished goods and ready-to-wear clothing. Department stores such as Macy's, Wanamaker's, Marshall Field's, and Bloomingdale's appeared in major cities beginning in the 1860s and 1870s; mail-order companies such as Montgomery Ward and Sears, Roebuck, & Co. grew rapidly in the 1880s and 1890s to serve rural families and towns; and chain stores proliferated in smaller urban areas after the turn of the century. All the new retail systems shared a common feature: they exploited a high volume of sales to make profits on low-margin transactions. By rapidly turning over large quantities of goods, they could offer lower prices than more traditional, smaller shopkeepers while still making hefty profits. Low prices were thus their competitive advantage, and naturally these companies acted to highlight their strength. They instituted storewide, "one-price" policies that eliminated haggling and traditional bargaining; they advertised prices prominently, had clerks tag individual goods for easy price comparison, and encouraged shoppers to survey stores for the best price (a practice made easier by the rise of national brands). The inflationary rise of the early twentieth century thus occurred among a population more dependent upon market purchases, more embedded in a system of fixed (non-negotiable) prices, and with more information about those prices (through ads, tags, and comparison shopping).[3]

---

[3]   Alfred D. Chandler, Jr., *The Visible Hand: The Managerial Revolution in American Business* (Cambridge: Belknap Press, 1977), 209–239; William Leach, *Land of Desire: Merchants,*

Not surprisingly, therefore, the price increases before the First World War (though modest in comparison with what would follow) precipitated a chorus of laments, complaints, and accusations that had reached a crescendo by 1910, filling newspapers and magazines. Many proposed solutions followed the well-heeled path of individual responsibility. Some commentators insisted that the "high cost of living" was simply a consequence of modern extravagance, with weak-willed families stretching beyond their means or engaging in wasteful spending that increased prices. Even less judgmental observers offered suggestions for reducing expenditures, setting budgets, and maintaining closer control over family finances. Practitioners in the new field of home economics—a turn-of-the-century response to the social and economic changes of the previous decades—published numerous guides promising to help housewives manage money, shop carefully, and make the most of their purchases. Women's magazines and general periodicals like *Harper's Weekly* or *Literary Digest* created advice columns that reviewed readers' household budgets and ran articles describing strategies for thrift and wise management.[4]

But while the high cost of living inspired jeremiads about materialism or resolutions for thrift and economy, these discussions were also framed by broader social and economic changes marking the roughly twenty years between 1896 and America's entry into the First World War. If a minority of Americans blamed extravagance and individual waste for rising prices, a larger number pinpointed structural causes, such as industrial collusion, trusts, railroads, or price-gouging middlemen. These concerns were strengthened by the rapid economic changes over recent years, like the great merger movement of the turn of the century (which raised concerns about monopolistic power) and the push by small businesses and manufacturers to enforce minimum prices through "fair trade" legislation (as a defense against high-volume, mass retailers).[5] Equally important were the perceived secondary effects rising prices had on social stability, as middle-class reformers and union leaders alike blamed the increased cost of living for

---

Power, and the Rise of a New American Culture (New York: Pantheon Books, 1993), 15–150; Meg Jacobs, *Pocketbook Politics: Economic Citizenship in Twentieth-Century America* (Princeton: Princeton University Press, 2005), 15–30.

[4]   Daniel Horowitz, *The Morality of Spending: Attitudes toward the Consumer Society in America, 1875–1940* (Baltimore: Johns Hopkins University Press, 1985), 50–108; Eric Rauchway, "The High Cost of Living in the Progressives' Economy," *JAH* 88, no. 3 (2001): 898–924; Thomas A. Stapleford, " 'Housewife vs. Economist': Gender, Class, and Domestic Economic Knowledge in Twentieth-Century America," *Labor: Studies in Working-Class History of the Americas* 1, no. 2 (2004): 91–97.

[5]   Jacobs, *Pocketbook Politics*, 30–41.

producing urban consumer protests, boycotts, strikes, and growing labor turmoil. The economist Irving Fisher was not alone when he cited rising prices for sparking a "deep-seated unrest which has been expressing itself in many ways: in blame of all sorts of persons and conditions for increasing the cost of living, in resentment against taxation, in strikes, in bread and meat riots, and in socialist agitation."[6]

These concerns drove many academics, public agencies, and reformers to study the cost of living. Yet, remarkably, their efforts had only minimal connections to retail price indexes; indeed, the greatest attention to high prices before the war erupted just in the period from 1907 to 1912 when the nation in fact had no retail price statistics (these having been suspended by BLS commissioner Charles P. O'Neill pending reforms; Chapter 1). Even when O'Neill finally resumed the BLS food price index in 1912, he reduced its scope to lower the cost, dropping the number of items from thirty to fifteen, the cities covered from sixty-eight to thirty-nine, and the number of dealers from whom prices were obtained from 1,000 to 675. More importantly, O'Neill abandoned the bureau's traditional use of field agents to collect prices, instead obtaining food prices from merchants through mailed questionnaires, a switch which he claimed had reduced the cost of gathering data by over two-thirds.[7] Contemporaries recognized how deeply these changes could affect the results. Writing in the *American Economic Review*, I. M. Rubinow decided that the new index was "untrustworthy" because recalculations for 1890–1907 using the more limited set of goods showed a substantial divergence from the original index. Moreover, unlike the old index, the weighted and unweighted versions of the new index were significantly different (see the appendix for a review of these terms).[8] But despite these laments, there is no evidence of popular or official pressure on the BLS to expand or improve its coverage. Instead, prewar investigations relevant to the cost of living followed other directions. Examining the features and goals of these studies helps to explain this divergence and to sharpen the contrast with the system of monitoring and management that would develop during the war.

---

[6] Fisher, "An International Commission on the Cost of Living," 93; Jacobs, *Pocketbook Politics*, 41–52.

[7] Joseph P. Goldberg and William T. Moye, *The First Hundred Years of the Bureau of Labor Statistics* (Washington, D.C.: U.S. GPO, 1985), 70–71; I. M. Rubinow, "The Recent Trend of Real Wages," *AER* 4, no. 4 (1914): 800; Testimony of Charles P. O'Neill, "Original Transcript," 27 March 1913, p. 51, Folder 18/3, Box 59, General Records, 1907–1942, Chief Clerk's Files, DOL.

[8] Rubinow, "The Recent Trend of Real Wages," 800–802.

Cost-of-Living Surveys: Local and Democratic

Today, when most Americans are apt to think of the Consumer Price Index as a basic macroeconomic indicator, it seems surprising that widespread discussions of the high cost of living could be held without recourse to such statistics. But our perspective rests on a series of developments in macroeconomic theory and political economy that would not take hold until the 1930s and 1940s, when consumer "purchasing power" would be identified as a key variable for economic growth and stability. To the extent that rising prices became part of general discussions in the early twentieth century about the economy or government policy, retail price indexes had a minimal role. Economists who blamed increasing gold supplies and other monetary events for the worldwide inflation made their case using wholesale price indexes, which tracked the cost of raw materials and were both easier to obtain (through commodity exchange markets) and thought to be more representative of general economic conditions.[9] Those who cited other structural causes—such as the reformers and politicians who condemned monopolies and trusts, or the conservatives who targeted unions—turned to synchronic studies that tracked the costs of producing and distributing specific commodities, looking for bottlenecks, price-gouging, and inefficiencies.[10] Neither approach gave much attention to the aggregate change in retail prices over time.

When retail price indexes did finally achieve a prominent function during the war, it would not be for economic policy writ large but for adjusting wages to better match price changes. Before the war, many progressive reformers shared a similar concern about the gap between wages and prices, but tellingly investigated this problem via different means. Whereas the wartime system would emphasize maintaining wage-price stability through national statistics and rule-governed administrative action based on quantitative calculation, prewar reformers adopted almost the opposite approach: aiming to alter wage-price relationships through local studies that would prompt voluntary or legislative action. These traits are readily apparent in

[9] Robert W. Dimand, "Interwar Monetary and Business Cycle Theory: Macroeconomics before Keynes," *Research in the History of Economic Thought and Methodology* 21-A (2003): 121–148. On the relative merits of wholesale price indexes, see Irving Fisher, *The Purchasing Power of Money: Its Determination and Relation to Credit Interest and Crises* (New York: MacMillan, 1911), 225–228.

[10] Cf. Massachusetts Commission on the Cost of Living, *Report of the Commission on the Cost of Living* (Boston: Wright & Potter, 1910); U.S. Senate, Select Committee on Wages and Prices of Commodities, *Investigation Relative to Wages and Prices of Commodities* (Washington, D.C.: U.S. GPO, 1911).

considerations of the cost of living within the archetypical form of reform-oriented, quantitative study in the progressive era: the social survey.

The period between 1900 and 1930 was the golden age of social surveys, conceived not in the narrow, contemporary sense (questionnaires and opinion polls) but as a much broader vision common to the early twentieth century: the empirical, at least partially quantitative, study of specific aspects of a community with an eye toward political action or social reform. These surveys could emanate from government offices but were more regularly the product of a common Progressive-era combination: wealthy donors supporting middle-class legwork and reform organizations (ranging from settlement houses to charitable institutions). A 1930 bibliography compiled by Allen Eaton and Shelby Harrison for the Russell Sage Foundation (a major sponsor of such projects) listed 2,775 surveys "made as a basis for social action" between 1907 and 1928 (primarily in the United States).[11] That same year, a separate bibliography of "studies of costs and standards of living" included over two hundred entries, the bulk of which dated from 1900 onward.[12]

The early, privately sponsored surveys had a range of origins and ambitions, from the tightly focused study of Chicago's nineteenth ward in the *Hull-House Maps & Papers* (created by residents of Jane Addams's settlement house in 1895) to Robert Chapin's 1907 study of "the standard of living among workingmen's families" in New York City (organized by the New York State Conference of Charities and Corrections) to the six-volume, multifaceted Pittsburgh Survey of 1907–1908 (led by Paul Kellogg and heavily subsidized by the Russell Sage Foundation) that launched a social-survey frenzy thanks to continued support from Russell Sage.[13] Nevertheless, we can recognize several trends. Consideration of the cost of living in the survey tradition primarily meant studying family expenditures and living conditions—in other words, research that showed how families were adapting to existing prices. Moreover, the studies were intended to be aids to democratic deliberation, not tools for bureaucratic administration or academic reflection. They aimed to inform and prod the public into action, an objective

[11] Allen Eaton and Shelby M. Harrison, *A Bibliography of Social Surveys* (New York: Russell Sage Foundation, 1930).

[12] Faith M. Williams, *Bibliography on Studies of Costs and Standards of Living in the United States* (Washington, D.C.: U.S. Department of Agriculture, 1930).

[13] On early social surveys, see Jean M. Converse, *Survey Research in the United States: Roots and Emergence, 1890–1960* (Berkeley: University of California Press, 1987), 11–53; Martin Bulmer, Kevin Bales, and Kathryn Kish Sklar, eds., *The Social Survey in Historical Perspective, 1880–1940* (Cambridge: Cambridge University Press, 1991); Maurine W. Greenwald and Margo Anderson, eds., *Pittsburgh Surveyed: Social Science and Social Reform in the Early Twentieth Century* (Pittsburgh: University of Pittsburgh Press, 1996).

naturally reflected in their methodology and style. In general, survey authors utilized quantitative statistics but regularly embedded the numbers in a larger web of verbal description, photographs, anecdotes, and graphic illustrations. Even topics like family expenditures were buttressed with other forms of evidence and explanation. Describing the expenses of garment trade workers (developed for the *Maps & Papers*), Isabel Eaton combined numerical survey results with quotations from employers and union members, copies of clothing advertisements, and descriptions of housing arrangements—all intended to illustrate the quality of items purchased.[14] As part of the 1907 Pittsburgh Survey, Margaret Byington produced an analysis of family expenses in Homestead replete with photographs, detailed descriptions of living conditions, and sample case studies.[15]

Undoubtedly most authors of these projects would have agreed with the European statisticians who claimed that focused explication of a few samples added "the blood, the flesh and the muscles to the skeleton built from general statistics."[16] "Embodying" numbers had an obvious pragmatic attraction for anyone seeking to rally the public to alleviate the ills documented in their reports. Like reform-oriented labor statisticians from the nineteenth century, survey authors recognized that untrained eyes needed help recapturing the life behind statistical tables. Indeed, those with greater commitment to reaching the public, notably Kellogg and his followers, exerted correspondingly greater effort to augment any numerical data with "flesh and blood" examples.[17] Government agencies and committees who

---

[14] Isabel Eaton, "Receipts and Expenditures of Certain Wage-Earners in the Garment Trades," *PASA* 4, no. 30 (1895): 135–180.

[15] Margaret F. Byington, *Homestead: The Households of a Mill Town* (New York: Charities Publication Committee, 1910). Other authors associated with Kellogg distinguished their work from the highly quantified version of statistics. For instance, Shelby Harrison excluded census results and most BLS reports from his 1930 bibliography of social surveys, describing them as simply "statistical compilations." Eaton and Harrison, *A Bibliography of Social Surveys*, xxxviii; cf. Stephen Turner, "The Pittsburgh Survey and the Survey Movement," in *Pittsburgh Surveyed: Social Science and Social Reform in the Early Twentieth Century*, ed. Maurine W. Greenwald and Margo Anderson (Pittsburgh: University of Pittsburgh Press, 1996), 46.

[16] M. Bodio, as quoted by A. N. Kiaer in the *Bulletin de l'Institut International de Statistique* (1897): 182–183, translated and excerpted in Alain Desrosières, "The Part in Relation to the Whole: How to Generalise? The Prehistory of Representative Sampling," in *The Social Survey in Historical Perspective, 1880–1940*, ed. Martin Bulmer, Kevin Bales, and Kathryn Kish Sklar (Cambridge: Cambridge University Press, 1991), 236. More generally, see the rest of this essay and Alain Desrosières, *The Politics of Large Numbers: A History of Statistical Reasoning*, trans. Camille Naish (Cambridge: Harvard University Press, 1998).

[17] For Kellogg's devotion to public presentation of the survey results, see essays in Greenwald and Anderson, eds., *Pittsburgh Surveyed*. Or again, compare Robert Chapin's written

maintained a reformist zeal likewise enlivened their publications with similar details: the report of the Massachusetts Commission on Minimum Wage
Boards included an appendix proffering examples of "The Human Story"
evincing the need for a "living wage."[18] Similarly, when the BLS examined
the living conditions of cotton-mill workers during an anti–child labor campaign, the authors opted for a 250-page study of thirty-five "thoroughly representative" families, thereby providing a set of "concrete examples" which
they insisted would "give a much clearer picture of prevailing standards of
living than could be obtained from masses of statistics." The report made a
remarkable contrast with Carroll Wright's 1901–1902 survey of prices and
family expenditures across 25,000 wage-earning families, but it was perfectly in keeping with Charles P. O'Neill's progressive tendencies and desire
to promote "remedial" legislation.[19]

As the tight geographic limitations on the majority of the surveys further
indicate, the mode of action underlying the projects was not only democratic, it was highly local. Settlement house workers wanted to build and
publicize "an intimate and personal neighborhood study" of their poor,
urban environment; municipal charity organizations wanted to better
understand their patrons; while Kellogg portrayed surveys as a rich source
of communal self-knowledge for cities and towns.[20] Most expenditure surveys from the period aimed to delineate the costs and "standards of living"
of a specific set of working-class families in a given city or small region,
graphically illustrating the "two sides of the vise, wages and prices," that
were squeezing working-class families, and thereby (hopefully) inspiring
public pressure on local employers, support for local minimum wage laws
and other welfare provisions, or at least greater sympathy for workers.[21]

report (relying on extensive tabular data) with the detailed descriptions of living condi-
tions included in a presentation of the results to a reform-oriented organization: Robert C.
Chapin, *The Standard of Living among Workingmen's Families in New York City* (New York:
Russell Sage Foundation, 1909), 263–284.

[18] Massachusetts Commission on Minimum Wage Boards, *Report of the Commission on
Minimum Wage Boards* (Boston: Wright & Potter, 1912), 186–189. The main text also
included substantial textual description.

[19] Wood F. Worcester and Daisy Worthington Worcester, *Family Budgets of Typical Cotton-
Mill Workers* (Washington, D.C.: U.S. GPO, 1911), 9, 20–21.

[20] Quotation from Louise Bolard More, *Wage-Earners' Budgets: A Study of Standards and
Cost of Living in New York City* (New York: Henry Holt, 1907), 1.

[21] Chapin, *The Standard of Living*, 250. Lawrence B. Glickman, *A Living Wage: American
Workers and the Making of Consumer Society* (Ithaca: Cornell University Press, 1997). The
concentration of cost-of-living studies on working-class families is readily documented in
Williams, *Bibliography on Studies of Costs and Standards of Living*.

Alongside this narrow geographic focus, early studies also paid close attention to the variation in income and expenditures across different groups of workers as defined by nationality (or race) and gender. That attention derived in part from the common belief that racial and gender differences led female and non–Anglo-American workers to accept lower wages, either because these were sufficient to meet their more restricted needs and desires or because power inequities prevented these groups from bargaining as effectively as organized, Anglo-American, male workers.[22] Here, too, the emphasis remained on examining the links between standards of living and wages while using the former to press for changes in the latter.

In principle, retail price indexes could complement this political agenda for expenditure surveys by tracking the cost of a given standard over time. But, as with bureaus of labor statistics in the nineteenth century, limited resources and other priorities pushed price indexes aside. Given the low wages of most unskilled workers, price monitoring paled in comparison to the larger (and primary) task of reaching the basic standard in the first place. Moreover, as Charles P. O'Neill could testify, tracking retail prices with any sophistication was expensive—not an attractive proposition for the philanthropies, state or local governments, and charitable organizations that funded most surveys and had many other goals to meet. Like nineteenth-century labor statistics, where "special investigations" had predominated, most prewar cost-of-living studies were one-time affairs. Local, democratic, singular studies that were rarely repeated: these features characterized the survey tradition—and created the problems it faced as the twentieth century progressed.

Centralizing and Bureaucratic Impulses

In emphasizing local reform projects, survey authors were following nineteenth-century trajectories as well as more general Progressive-era tendencies. But they also confronted the same obstacles. Just as liberal elites encountered fierce resistance when they sought to demolish urban political machines or reshape rural life, Paul Kellogg and his allies soon realized that city officials and citizens resented outsiders highlighting the flaws and corruption of their hometown—the massive Pittsburgh Survey,

---

[22]   Glickman, *A Living Wage*, 78–91; Thomas C. Leonard, "Protecting Family and Race: The Progressive Case for Regulating Women's Work," *American Journal of Economics and Sociology* 64, no. 3 (2005): 757–791; Marilyn Power, "Parasitic-Industries Analysis and Arguments for a Living Wage for Women in the Early Twentieth-Century United States," *Feminist Economics* 5, no. 1 (1999): 61–78.

for instance, had little effect on the city's politics.[23] Or again, state and local efforts to support labor unions and enact regulatory and welfare provisions, inspired by accounts of working-class hardship, were frequently declared unconstitutional by conservative federal courts—for example, judicial rulings led states to limit minimum-wage laws to women and minors, and even these were struck down by the courts in 1923.[24] More generally, effective local action against the social and economic ills produced by the growth of industrial market capitalism could be confounded by the very reach of the new economic systems. When unions in midwestern and northeastern cities organized a meat boycott in the early months of 1910 to protest high prices, they successfully forced local butchers to slash prices so that they could unload stock before spoilage, but the large networks of packers and producers simply curtailed production or redirected shipments to other locales.[25] The disjuncture between the limited reach of local politics and the power of national markets became most apparent when states (particularly in the north) tried to enact regulatory legislation: industries that faced national competition from less stringent states fought the measures bitterly and sought to limit or evade them wherever possible.[26]

These pressures increasingly drove both labor unions (even the AFL) and middle-class reformers to look toward national politics to overcome the constraints on local solutions, whether by ensuring uniform action at the state level or turning directly to the federal government. But interstate cooperation largely failed because local companies in more lax states benefited from existing asymmetries. Likewise, a parallel dynamic in Congress (comprised of regional representatives) hindered effective national legislation, while congressional hearings on complex economic problems typically echoed a discordant national conversation. Meanwhile, a comparatively weak

[23] Margo Anderson and Maurine W. Greenwald, "The Pittsburgh Survey in Historical Perspective," in *Pittsburgh Surveyed*, 8–9; Turner, "The Pittsburgh Survey," 35–49.

[24] On the courts and unions in this period, see Melvyn Dubofsky, *The State & Labor in Modern America* (Chapel Hill: University of North Carolina Press, 1994), 37–60. On early minimum wage laws in America, see Dorothy W. Douglas, "American Minimum Wage Laws at Work," *AER* 9, no. 4 (1919): 701–738.

[25] "The Meat Boycott," *Review of Reviews* (March 1910): 274; "Meat prices higher ...," *NYT*, 23 March 1910.

[26] Edward D. Berkowitz and Kim McQuaid, *Creating the Welfare State: The Political Economy of Twentieth-Century Reform*, 2nd ed. (New York: Praeger, 1988), 39–47. For a synthetic analysis of the consequences of economic competition within a federalist system, see Colin Gordon, *New Deals: Business, Labor, and Politics in America, 1920–1935* (Cambridge: Cambridge University Press, 1994), 14–29.

executive branch coupled with a court system scrupulous about constitutional limits on federal power kept bureaucratic national action constrained to a few domains of interstate commerce, particularly railroads. Altogether, the still-strong federalism of the early twentieth century replicated national diversity and thereby blunted attempts to overcome the disjuncture between reach of economic integration and the boundaries of political power. In turn, those rankled by the political fragmentation (liberal activists and businessmen alike) sought new solutions, such as reshaping constitutional interpretation or promoting the authority of "nonpartisan" experts who could guide policy, construct effective and just systems of bureaucratic oversight, and adjudicate disputes.[27]

Retail price indexes themselves had little part in these efforts prior to the war, mirroring their general irrelevance to critical economic discussions during the period. But two of the prewar initiatives eventually shaped how price statistics would be deployed in the wartime arbitration system.

The first, stemming from Yale economist Irving Fisher's campaign to restore price stability by adjusting the gold standard, exemplifies the link between price indexes and bureaucratic, economic management. Fisher's

---

[27] On the unions and nationalization, see Christopher L. Tomlins, *The State and the Unions: Labor Relations Law, and the Organized Labor Movement in America, 1880–1960* (Cambridge: Cambridge University Press, 1985), 68–91; Dubofsky, *The State & Labor in Modern America*, 37–60; David Montgomery, *The Fall of the House of Labor: The Workplace, the State, and American Labor Activism, 1865–1925* (Cambridge: Cambridge University Press, 1987), 356–369. On (largely unsuccessful) progressive attempts to overcome the limits of federalism via interstate cooperation, see William Graebner, "Federalism in the Progressive Era: A Structural Interpretation of Reform," *JAH* 64, no. 2 (1977): 331–357; Berkowitz and McQuaid, *Creating the Welfare State*, 49–51. Again, my perspective is shaped by Gordon, *New Deals*. An excellent example of the sectional response to national investigations is the controversy over the BLS study of *Women and Child Wage-Earners* in 1912: Daniel J. B. Mitchell, "A Furor over Working Children and the Bureau of Labor," *MLR* 98, no. 10 (1975): 34–36; Judson MacLaury, "A Senator's Reaction to Report on Working Women and Children," *MLR* 98, no. 10 (1975): 36–38. On the struggles of liberal intellectuals to overcome perceived deficiencies in the American political system, see David W. Eakins, "The Origins of Corporate Liberal Policy Research, 1916–1922: The Political-Economic Expert and the Decline of Public Debate," in *Building the Organizational Society: Essays on Associational Activities in Modern America*, ed. Jerry Israel (New York: Free Press, 1972), 163–179; Edward A. Purcell, *The Crisis of Democratic Theory; Scientific Naturalism & the Problem of Value* (Lexington: University Press of Kentucky, 1973), 74–80; Donald T. Critchlow, *The Brookings Institution, 1916–1952: Expertise and the Public Interest in a Democratic Society* (DeKalb: Northern Illinois University Press, 1985), 1–40; Clarence E. Wunderlin, *Visions of a New Industrial Order: Social Science and Labor Theory in America's Progressive Era* (New York: Columbia University Press, 1992), 95–125; Leon Fink, *Progressive Intellectuals and the Dilemmas of Democratic Commitment* (Cambridge: Harvard University Press, 1997).

work built on long-standing debates among economists about the quantity theory of money, the deductive principle that (*ceteris paribus*) the value of money (reflected in the general level of prices) varied in inverse proportion to the quantity of money in circulation. (Thus, as the supply of money increased, its value would fall, leading to higher prices.) In 1863, the British economist William Stanley Jevons had reinvigorated this discussion by constructing a price index and comparing its fluctuations to changes in the supply of gold. (Since Britain, like the United States and most countries, utilized the gold standard for currency—with a basic unit of national currency exchangeable for a fixed weight of gold—gold was in effect the underlying currency.)[28] After the turn of the century, Fisher took up Jevons's project, creating a more precise formulation of the quantity theory and using historical statistics to argue that the rising cost of living since 1896 derived primarily from the increase in the gold supply.[29] Both then and now critics had difficulty reconciling Fisher's analysis with other aspects of economic theory and complained about the simplifications made in his treatment.[30] But informed commentators accepted the dominant influence of rising gold supplies for a simple reason: worldwide price indexes all showed comparable rises over the same period.[31] If prices were following similar patterns worldwide, logic dictated a search for a more universal underlying cause, of which the gold supply was an obvious choice.

Naturally, this presented a serious problem for local political action: how could states or even nations react effectively to a worldwide phenomenon? The 1911 report by the Massachusetts Commission on the Cost of Living exemplified this dilemma: having identified the increased gold supply as the "primary cause" of rising prices, the commission could then offer only a comparatively feeble set of recommendations, such as making Boston markets more efficient, improving freight transportation, and devising "more intelligible and more serviceable" state statistics.[32] More than anyone else,

---

[28] Jevons explored these questions in three publications reprinted in W. Stanley Jevons, *Investigations in Currency and Finance* (London, 1884). Jevons's work on index numbers is discussed in different contexts by several authors in Judy L. Klein and Mary S. Morgan, eds., *The Age of Economic Measurement*, Annual Supplement to HOPE (Durham: Duke University Press, 2001).

[29] Fisher, *Purchasing Power of Money*, 311–318.

[30] Robert L. Allen, *Irving Fisher: A Biography* (Cambridge: Blackwell, 1993), 118–125; Daniel Pope, "American Economists and the High Cost of Living: The Late Progressive Era," *Journal of the History of the Behavioral Sciences* 17, no. 1 (1981): 76–78.

[31] Cf. Fisher, "An International Commission on the Cost of Living," 92–101.

[32] Massachusetts Commission on the Cost of Living, *Report*, 529–533.

Fisher saw clearly how global financial connections and new theoretical approaches in economics were complicating traditional solutions:

It might seem at first glance that local investigations and local efforts were sufficient to cope with these problems. But further consideration shows it to be otherwise, for the reason that the problem is essentially international and not local; that the facts as to the rise in the cost of living are extremely similar in different countries; and that remedies which go to the root of the matter, if any remedies are available, must be of an international character. It is almost as absurd for any one particular locality or state, on the basis of its own experience, to grapple with the problem of the world-wide rise in the cost of living as it would be for villagers on the Bay of Fundy to attempt to prevent the rise of the tides. They experience this rise, but its causes lie far beyond their vision or control.[33]

Fisher aimed to attack the problem at its root—the fixed gold standard—and thereby to ease the widespread economic and social disruptions stemming from price fluctuations that he claimed were "daily adding to the ranks of socialists."[34] His basic idea, first raised tentatively in 1911, was to vary the gold-exchange ratio of the dollar and other currencies based on changes in an international price index (developed from an average of wholesale price indexes).[35] As the index number rose (indicating a fall in the value of the dollar), each dollar would be exchangeable for more gold, thereby making it more valuable and hopefully leading to a fall in prices. The process would be reversed as the index number fell, in principle making the index fluctuate within a narrow range and thus (in Fisher's view) stabilizing the dollar.

Two features of this proposal are worth highlighting. First, recognizing the growing interconnection of capitalist markets, Fisher concluded that effective economic regulation demanded an equally far-reaching power. However, he also perceived that consolidating control within the state meant that such "power might be abused," permitting "manipulation of the currency by Government officials." Like others on both sides of the political spectrum, Fisher hoped to neutralize the dangers of centralized power by relying on empirical, expert-sanctioned facts—in this case, price statistics—that could be safely embedded in a rule-governed, administrative mechanism. The combination of rules and facts would thereby produce

---

[33] Fisher, "An International Commission on the Cost of Living," 93.

[34] Irving Fisher, "A Remedy for the Rising Cost of Living: Standardizing the Dollar," *AER* 3, no. 1 (1913): 27.

[35] Fisher, *Purchasing Power of Money*, 337–347; Irving Fisher, "A More Stable Gold Standard," *Economic Journal* 22, no. 88 (1912): 570–576; Irving Fisher, "A Compensated Dollar," *QJE* 27, no. 2 (1913): 213–235; Fisher, "A Remedy for the Rising Cost of Living: Standardizing the Dollar," 20–28.

efficient action insulated (in theory) from partisan aims. Thus, to counter fears of "manipulation," Fisher insisted that his solution required "purely clerical" adjustments in gold-exchange rates determined by shifts in objective measurements.[36] It was a strategy that others would pursue repeatedly during the twentieth century—and it remains a central attraction of cost-of-living-escalator clauses—but it was not without potential weaknesses: one perceptive opponent warned that the extensive "financial consequences" of currency adjustment would prevent statistical calculation from being "the simple matter of clerical routine which Professor Fisher assumes it to be."[37]

The validity of this prediction was never directly tested. Fisher was an unflagging crusader in a host of reform projects, and he promoted his plan incessantly through lectures and in print, but although he gathered supporters, he found the overall project stymied at nearly every turn: critics doubted its feasibility and wisdom; political leaders (including Woodrow Wilson) made enthusiastic gestures but dropped the idea in favor of more familiar strategies (such as creating the Federal Reserve System); the general public proved willing to listen but hardly agitated about an indexed dollar; and conservative financial interests denounced any tinkering with the hoary gold standard. Perhaps the greatest pragmatic obstacle, however, was Fisher's own recognition that the plan would require international cooperation, a prospect supported by an "impressive array of world leaders" in principle but derailed by lack of funding to even discuss the idea and effectively ended by war in Europe.[38]

Fisher's struggle and failure illustrate some of the factors that blocked centralized administrative management before the war, including both entrenched interests and a suspicion of concentrated bureaucratic power. Moreover, his attention to international cooperation reminds us that the increasing consolidation of economic control and management at the national level through much of the twentieth century was not necessarily predicated on a similarly constrained economy; the latter had extensive

---

[36] Fisher, "A Compensated Dollar," 216–217; Fisher, *Purchasing Power of Money*, 343, 345–346.

[37] Willard C. Fisher in "Standardizing the Dollar—Discussion," *AER* 3, no. 1 (1913): 40. Willard Fisher had good grounds for his skepticism, having produced a definitive history of Massachusetts' experiment with using index numbers for paying troops during the Revolutionary War: Willard C. Fisher, "The Tabular Standard in Massachussetts History," *QJE* 27, no. 3 (1913): 417–454.

[38] Allen, *Irving Fisher*, 100, 121–129; William J. Barber, "Irving Fisher as a Policy Advocate," in *The Economic Mind in America: Essays in the History of American Economics*, ed. Malcolm Rutherford (London: Routledge, 1998), 31–42; Pope, "American Economists and the High Cost of Living," 75–78. For a sample of early objections to Fisher's plan, see comments in the *AER* in 1913 and 1919.

global dimensions by 1914.[39] Rather, it reflected the limits of political possibilities, which replicated on an international scale a more extreme version of the problems (and benefits) of American federalism. Though Fisher
never abandoned his dream, he responded to these barriers by pursuing
action where he could: rather than adjusting currency, he later began to use
an index number to shift the salaries of employees in his small business, one
of the first modern versions of a cost-of-living escalation clause. During the
war, with the advent of national labor management for mobilization, Fisher
would press the federal government to adopt a similar scheme.

Our second example of the unfulfilled movement toward centralized,
bureaucratic power for economic oversight takes us back to the prewar history of industrial relations. When we left detailed consideration of the labor
question at the end of Chapter 1, the voluntary, conciliatory approach of
the National Civic Federation had captured the hopes of many moderates,
including prominent union leaders such as Samuel Gompers and the commissioner of the BLS, Charles P. O'Neill. However, outside of railroads—
subject to federal oversight and source of constant mediation work for
O'Neill—the NCF's model collapsed almost before it began. Using open-
shop regulations, private police forces, anti-labor local politicians, and a
conservative judiciary, businessmen smashed existing unions and staved
off new organizing drives during the first decade of the twentieth century.
In turn, however, they bred growing anger and radicalism, exemplified by
the expansion of groups who openly advocated direct force and revolution,
such as the Industrial Workers of the World (the "Wobblies"). Violence and
rioting flared sporadically in cities and industrial towns across the country,
repressed by state intervention but never ceasing and mounting in severity as the years progressed. The symbolic culmination came in the fall of
1910, when several union leaders dynamited the offices of the virulently
anti-labor *Los Angeles Times*, killing twenty men.[40]

The bombing catalyzed action by progressive intellectuals—including
many involved with the social survey movement such as Paul Kellogg—who
now called for a national investigative commission that would unveil the

---

[39] For a valuable survey, see Kevin H. O'Rourke and Jeffrey G. Williamson, *Globalization and History: The Evolution of a Nineteenth-Century Atlantic Economy* (Cambridge: MIT Press, 1999), as well as the extended review by C. Knick Harley, "A Review of O'Rourke and Williamson's 'Globalization and History: The Evolution of a Nineteenth Century Atlantic Economy,'" *Journal of Economic Literature* 38, no. 4 (2000): 926–935.

[40] Montgomery, *Fall of the House of Labor*, 257–329; Wunderlin, *Visions of a New Industrial Order*, 72–94; Dubofsky, *The State & Labor in Modern America*, 38–51. For several detailed case studies, see Graham Adams, Jr., *Age of Industrial Violence, 1910–1915* (New York: Columbia University Press, 1966).

exploitation presumably fueling working-class unrest and promote solutions. President William H. Taft proposed a tripartite council (labor, business, and "public" representatives) stocked with moderates and conservatives near the close of his administration, but the newly elected Democratic Congress refused to confirm his choices. In 1913, Woodrow Wilson nominated a far more left-wing slate, including fateful choices as two of the three public members: Wisconsin labor economist John R. Commons and a lesser-known Catholic politician and attorney from Kansas City, Frank Walsh. The full story of the resulting U.S. Committee on Industrial Relations (CIR, 1913–1915) has been well-told and analyzed in other places; what concerns us here is the split that developed between Commons and Walsh.[41]

Initially, the two men led apparently complementary strands of the investigation. Commons, along with his deputy Charles McCarthy and a small army of former students and associates, directed the research division for the commission: conducting interviews, making preliminary investigations, gathering statistics, writing reports, and even drafting proposed legislation. Meanwhile, Walsh chaired the committee meetings and ran the public hearings conducted at sites across the country. Inspired by European corporatism and experience with the Wisconsin Industrial Commission, Commons and McCarthy envisioned their work as the foundation for similar administrative programs on the federal level in which experts could use empirical research to guide tripartite regulatory and investigative councils. By contrast, Walsh's instincts were democratic and populist; he strove to bend both the research and public hearings toward a single aim: full, detailed revelation of capitalist abuses and working-class suffering which would hopefully inspire radical legislation. The split embodied the tensions that had suffused social and economic investigations since the late nineteenth century. It was not, as the division would sometimes be misread, ideologically neutral "objectivity" versus explicitly committed reform—both Commons and Walsh had obvious political agendas—nor was it corporate-friendly action versus radical transformations—both men lay far to the left of where the NCF and major business leaders were willing to go. Instead, it was the tension between expert

---

[41] Alongside specific notes, the following paragraphs rely on useful narratives and analysis from Adams, *Age of Industrial Violence*; Leon Fink, "Expert Advice: Progressive Intellectuals and the Unraveling of Labor Reform, 1912–1915," in *Intellectuals and Public Life: Between Radicalism and Reform*, ed. Leon Fink, Stephen T. Leonard, and Donald M. Reid (Ithaca: Cornell University Press, 1996), 183–213; Wunderlin, *Visions of a New Industrial Order*; James Weinstein, *The Corporate Ideal in the Liberal State, 1900–1918* (Westport: Greenwood Press, 1981); Mary O. Furner, "Social Scientists and the State: Constructing the Knowledge Base for Public Policy, 1880–1920," in *Intellectuals and Public Life*, 177–181.

knowledge coupled with bureaucratic, expert power and populist knowledge bound to deeply democratic action. Idealism attracted reform-oriented liberals to the latter; pragmatism drove them to the former.[42] For months, the CIR rolled forward along both tracks; by the end, it had fractured. The conflict had multiple roots but it came to a climax in the aftermath of the "Ludlow massacre" of 1914, when National Guard troops attacked a tent colony of armed, striking miners in Colorado. Reporters quickly traced 40 percent ownership of the area's dominant and obviously exploitative mining company to the Rockefeller family, thereby framing the episode as a perfect exemplar of class conflict, pitting wealthy capitalists against struggling workers. Subsequent events—including secret correspondence between McCarthy and his old college friend, John D. Rockefeller, Jr., plus the Rockefeller Foundation's ill-judged announcement of a plan to fund studies of industrial relations—convinced Walsh that the "Wisconsin idea" promoted by Commons and McCarthy relied too heavily on corporate cooperation and bureaucratic action that could be manipulated against working-class interests. Instead, Walsh demonstrated his own preferred approach by mercilessly cross-examining John D. Rockefeller, Jr., in CIR hearings over several days in May 1915, a spectacle that brought cheers from working-class observers and censure from social and political elites.[43] The CIR *Final Report* split in three directions: one version from Walsh and the labor members, a second from Commons and the other "public" representative, Florence Harriman (a wealthy heiress and socialite turned reformer), and a third from the three business members. Walsh's version (full of "incendiary and revolutionary" rhetoric, according to Harriman) won him the devotion of union leaders and working-class radicals alike, but he had less success implementing his recommendations, such as a high inheritance tax, various constitutional amendments designed to protect striking workers, condemnations of the open shop, and guaranteeing the right to organize.[44] If Walsh's strategy illustrated the popular appeal of revealing economic exploitation, it also demonstrated the limitations on democratic action.

As a whole, the CIR provided a fitting dénouement to prewar attempts to construct empirical knowledge for ameliorating economic problems. Like

---

[42] Leon Fink has made a similar argument about the CIR in Fink, "Expert Advice." On Commons's views and the CIR, see Wunderlin, *Visions of a New Industrial Order*, 113–129.

[43] Adams, *Age of Industrial Violence*, 164–163; Fink, "Expert Advice," 200–209; Weinstein, *Corporate Ideal in the Liberal State*, 189–199.

[44] Adams, *Age of Industrial Violence*, 204–226; Florence Harriman, *From Pinafores to Politics* (New York: Henry Holt, 1923), 174–175.

so many of the early survey projects, it proved more effective at document-ing industrial ills than eliminating them. At the same time, its investiga-tions confirmed the recent conclusions of other reformers, revealing the extensive local obstacles to labor reforms and supporting the perceived need for federal intervention. Indeed, by simply lifting local problems onto a national stage, the CIR also exemplified how federal action could prove beneficial to labor interests, and it helped cement the growing links between organized labor and the Democratic Party.[45] Finally, although the CIR had minimal direct effect on legislation or regulation, its research division had gathered, funded, and developed a cluster of social scientists such as Selig Perlman, William Leierson, Sumner Slichter, W. Jett Lauck, David Saposs, and Francis H. Bird who would form the core of a new class of industrial relations specialists.[46] Prewar failures had not dampened the enthusiasm of progressive social scientists for the reformist potential of empirical eco-nomic investigation; what they needed was a more effective political and bureaucratic context for their work.

WAR MOBILIZATION AND COST-OF-LIVING STATISTICS

In December 1918, the economist Wesley C. Mitchell delivered his pres-idential address to the American Statistical Association (ASA), using the occasion to reflect on the effects of the war. "Since the American Statistical Association was founded in 1839," he told his colleagues, "no year has brought such stirring changes in American statistics as the year now clos-ing." First among these changes was "a rapid expansion in the scope of fed-eral statistics and the creation of new statistical agencies.... Probably there are few professional societies which have had so considerable a portion of their membership engaged in war work as this Association." If Mitchell had been asked to name a second professional organization linked to the war, no doubt he would have chosen the American Economics Association (many of whose members were, like Mitchell himself, also participants in the ASA).[47] The explosion of federal bureaucracy during the war attracted

[45] On labor's new alliance with the Democratic Party and Frank Walsh's supporting role, see Montgomery, *Fall of the House of Labor*, 360–365; Joseph A. McCartin, *Labor's Great War: The Struggle for Industrial Democracy and the Origins of Modern American Labor Relations, 1912–1921* (Chapel Hill: University of North Carolina Press, 1997), 33–37.

[46] Furner, "Social Scientists and the State," 178–181.

[47] Wesley C. Mitchell, "Statistics and Government," *PASA* 16, no. 125 (1919): 223. On econo-mists and the war, see Michael Bernstein, *A Perilous Progress: Economists and Public Purpose in Twentieth-Century America* (Princeton: Princeton University Press, 2001), 31–38.

droves of social scientists anxious to demonstrate the value of their expertise, especially those who saw in new government powers what John Dewey
(unironically) described as the "social possibilities" of the war.[48] Yet the
proliferation of federal agencies and oversight was propelled less by statist
ideology than by the demands of mobilization. The Wilson administration
reluctantly turned to bureaucratic solutions for logistics, production planning, and economic management only when the failures of voluntary, ad
hoc approaches became abundantly clear. Those who wished to control mass
production and distribution in an industrialized economy were invariably
forced to develop centralized, bureaucratic strategies—along with a requisite compendium of statistics for monitoring and managing vast numbers
of people, commodities, production facilities, and financial transactions.
The "dollar-a-year" businessmen who shaped and guided wartime political
economy recognized this in practice, however much they touted the virtues
of voluntary cooperation.[49]

War did not simply mean more statistics, however: it shaped the structure and objectives of quantitative knowledge, even when pursuing popular
prewar topics such as the cost of living. Wartime labor arbitration fostered
the development of a national, rationalized approach to industrial relations,
one that necessarily entailed new empirical approaches. It was *national* in
that it favored standardization, conglomeration by regions and industry,
and negotiations with national union leaders. It was *rationalized* in that it
sought to control and stabilize labor relations by binding them in a rule-
governed bureaucratic system staffed by its own class of professional experts.
Correspondingly, in contrast to the local, democratic, public-oriented form
of empirical knowledge that characterized prewar statistics in the survey
tradition, wartime policies promoted the construction of national statistics
to be embedded in bureaucratic systems where they would ideally function
with minimal public debate. It was the first, fitful and disjointed incarnation
of the national administrative state, and it arose directly from the demands

---

[48] Dewey, quoted in David M. Kennedy, *Over Here: The First World War and American
Society* (London: Oxford University Press, 1980), 50. For a polemical assessment of this
trend, see Murray N. Rothbard, "World War I as Fulfillment: Power and the Intellectuals,"
Journal of Libertarian Studies 9, no. 1 (1989): 81–125.

[49] Robert D. Cuff, "American Mobilization for War, 1917–1945: Political Culture vs.
Bureaucratic Adminstration," in *Mobilization for Total War: The Canadian, American
and British Experience, 1914–1918, 1939–1945*, ed. N. F. Dreisziger (Waterloo, Canada:
Wilfrid Laurier University Press, 1981), 71–86; Robert D. Cuff, *The War Industries Board:
Business-Government Relations During World War I* (Baltimore: Johns Hopkins University
Press, 1973); Paul A. C. Koistinen, *Mobilizing for Modern War: The Political Economy of
American Warfare, 1865–1919* (Lawrence: University Press of Kansas, 1997), 105–299.

of mobilization as interpreted and guided by the left-wing progressives and moderates who staffed federal agencies.

Labor Crises and Federal Intervention

Nothing epitomized the extent and complexities of America's mobilization task like the shipbuilding industry. U.S. participation in a European war necessitated bringing troops and supplies across the Atlantic, a process hampered by insufficient shipping capacity and the very trigger that had finally dragged the Americans into the fight: submarine warfare. From 1914 to 1917, Allied shipping capacity had sustained a net loss of 7.5 million tons, and rapid mobilization would require far more than the Allies' original capabilities. To meet this need, the United States quickly expanded its shipbuilding production using the newly established Emergency Fleet Corporation (EFC) to fund and oversee private construction on an astonishing scale: from April 1917 to October 1918, the number of major shipyards quadrupled, while the related workforce ballooned from 95,000 to 375,000. Building an industry from scratch at such great speed and under immense pressure led to predictable complications, including a flood of inexperienced workers and speculators lured to shipbuilding by federal contracts.[50]

Not surprisingly, both companies and workers sought to exploit the upheaval in the industry. Existing shipyard owners leveraged the influx of new workers to rationalize their production process and loosen the control of older employees. Unions strove to build membership rolls using the incoming laborers and to exploit the shortage of skilled workers in critical trades for dramatic wage increases. In earlier years, violent repressions or lockouts might have crippled the union cause, but with a tight labor market and intense production pressures, workers were no longer overmatched. As in other industries, strikes plagued the shipyards during the summer of 1917—over 6 million workdays were lost in industries nationwide between April and October—and when workers did not form organized walkouts, they simply left: annual turnover rates in shipyards ranged from 60 percent to an extraordinary 688 percent. By August 1917, the industry was descending into chaos, and the EFC responded like most other federal war agencies: it established an arbitration system (previously seldom used on the national level outside of the railroad industry) and fashioned alliances

---

[50] Paul H. Douglas and F. E. Wolfe, "Labor Administration in the Shipbuilding Industry During Wartime, I," *JPE* 27, no. 3 (1919): 145–149.

with moderate union leaders (especially Samuel Gompers and the AFL) wherein war agencies traded federal protection and union representation on the arbitration boards for help in suppressing more radical groups such as the Wobblies. The EFC's version was the Shipbuilding Labor Adjustment Board (SLAB), led by wealthy oil and petroleum heir V. Everitt Macy, which began by handling labor disputes and eventually exercised de facto control over most of the industry.[51]

Overall, labor management strategies mirrored the rest of Wilson's wartime policies, emerging in an uncoordinated fashion among a host of agencies defined by departmental or economic boundaries, such as the War Department, Railroad Administration, and Fuel Administration. Although each developed distinctive approaches, several common threads appeared by early 1918. First, wage adjustments to meet the rising "cost of living" became a widely accepted practice. Retrospective price indexes would document the familiar wartime phenomenon of dramatic price rises from 1916 to 1920, but most consumers did not need official statistics to tell them prices were spiraling upward, especially for food. In early 1917, working- and middle-class housewives in cities across the United States united to protest rising prices with boycotts, demonstrations, rallies, and the formation of new consumer cooperatives. Wilson responded by establishing the Food Administration under Herbert Hoover, in which the future president sought to control prices through exhortation, efforts toward conservation and efficiency, community vigilance by housewives, and limited direct action. It was in many respects the institutionalization of Progressive-era crusades against middlemen and trusts, with Hoover targeting waste and profiteering. Despite his best efforts, he was (as Irving Fisher had predicted about similar proposals five years before) unable to stem the rising tide, much less turn it back. With workers demanding wage hikes to meet the new costs and organizing powerful strikes when employers balked, war production agencies took matters into their own hands, granting repeated wage hikes linked to the rising cost of living.[52]

---

[51] Bernard Mergen, "The Government as Manager: Emergency Fleet Shipbuilding, 1917–1919," in *Business and Its Environment: Essays for Thomas C. Cochran*, ed. Harold Issadore Sharlin (Westport: Greenwood Press, 1983), 49–80; Montgomery, *Fall of the House of Labor*, 370–375; Dubofsky, *The State & Labor in Modern America*, 61–71; Willard E. Hotchkiss and Henry R. Seager, *History of the Shipbuilding Labor Adjustment Board, 1917–1919*, BLS Bulletin, no. 283 (Washington, D.C.: U.S. GPO, 1921), 7–11.

[52] Jacobs, *Pocketbook Politics*, 53–66; Koistinen, *Mobilizing for Modern War*, 255–256; W. Jett Lauck, *The New Industrial Revolution and Wages* (New York: Funk & Wagnalls, 1929), 43–45; Elma B. Carr, *The Use of Cost-of-Living Figures in Wage Adjustments*, BLS Bulletin, no. 369 (Washington, D.C.: U.S. GPO, 1925).

But as the shipbuilding agency, SLAB, learned with its first award (covering the Pacific coast), cost-of-living increases alone would not be sufficient to solve its labor troubles. In a November ruling, SLAB offered Pacific-coast workers a cost-of-living increase over the wage rates in existence on June 1, 1916. However, the decision infuriated local labor leaders, who insisted that 1916 rates in many communities were inadequate and who noted that well-organized workers in Seattle (especially those employed in yards with more favorable contracts) had already obtained wages roughly 20 percent above the award level. This reaction coupled with similar events in other regions pushed the board to make two changes in December. First, rather than applying cost-of-living increases to actual prewar wages in all communities, it now intended to use base rates that were "admitted to be equitable."[53] Second, the Emergency Fleet Corporation reorganized SLAB to eliminate local representation (by both employers and employees) in favor of a streamlined national board. The restructuring presaged SLAB's growing commitment to standardizing wages and working conditions, at first regionally and eventually nationally. Standardization reduced the turnover problem by eliminating wage differentials between shipyards, thereby preventing inter-yard competition for skilled workers. But it also made SLAB's operations more efficient by reducing the number of rulings, and it allowed the board to deal with national AFL officials, who were typically less radical than local leaders. Moreover, standardization had strong support from workers. In practice (as prewar experience in the railroad industry had demonstrated), standardized rates typically approached or matched the highest existing base rate, a benefit that most workers willingly grasped in exchange for ceding greater control to national officials. Indeed, shipyard workers from districts with less favorable initial awards repeatedly demanded that SLAB grant similar pay for similar work.[54] All told, standardization was the exemplary marriage of national, managerial efficiency by the wartime state and long-standing progressive aims thwarted by local obstacles.

Standardization thus joined "equitable" basic wages and cost-of-living increases in a general policy common to wartime arbitration across multiple

---

[53] U.S. Bureau of Labor Statistics, "Adjustment of Shipbuilding Disputes on the Pacific Coast," *MLR* 6, no. 3 (1918): 68–69; Hotchkiss and Seager, *History of the Shipbuilding Labor Adjustment Board*, 8–31; Douglas and Wolfe, "Labor Administration in the Shipbuilding Industry," 156–158. Lauck to Macy, Seager, and Blackman, 30 November 1917, box 1, Records–Cost of Living, U.S. Shipping Board.

[54] Douglas and Wolfe, "Labor Administration in the Shipbuilding Industry," 152–153, 156, 162–165; Hotchkiss and Seager, *History of the Shipbuilding Labor Adjustment Board*, 24, 34, 44–45; J. Noble Stockett, Jr., *The Arbitral Determination of Railway Wages* (Boston: Houghton Mifflin, 1918), 1–53.

agencies by mid-1918: wage rates should be standardized at an equitable level and then raised alongside the cost of living during the war.[55] But what did this mean in practice? How did boards define adequate wages or determine the change in the cost of living confronting workers? Given the scope of arbitration decisions, quantified knowledge inevitably became a critical part of the process. Two of the most active boards were also key contributors to the expansion of BLS cost-of-living statistics: SLAB and the National War Labor Board (NWLB), established by Wilson in April 1918 to craft a more unified approach to labor policies and chaired jointly by Frank Walsh and former president William H. Taft. Considering the work of these agencies in more detail sheds useful light on the place of statistics in the wartime order.

Cost-of-Living Statistics and Wartime Arbitration

Labor arbitration can invite cynical judgment. When, as often happens, the tie-breaking "public" representatives on tripartite boards have links to big business—as did SLAB's chairman, V. Everitt Macy—it is hard not to see arbitration as a smokescreen protecting vested corporate interests.[56] Yet early twentieth-century labor activists did not always share that same perspective, even when they recognized the limits of arbitration. For one, labor supporters sometimes managed to place their cases before sympathetic judges or boards, and occasionally presumed conservatives startled friends and foes alike by labor-friendly decisions, as happened with Taft and the NWLB.[57] More generally, though, arbitration changed the dynamics of labor disputes. Employers could not simply crush unions with scabs, open-shop requirements, and yellow-dog contracts that banned union membership; they had to explain why their wages and working conditions were just, reasonable, or necessary—arguments that could then be criticized, countered, or refuted. Arbitration placed employers and workers' representatives on a more equal footing (even if not before a neutral judge) and offered labor activists a chance to articulate an alternative vision of industrial relations. It could change public opinion, influence other employers, and maybe even lead to direct improvements. For unions that had been suppressed legally

---

[55] Lauck, *New Industrial Revolution*, 43–50.

[56] E.g., Weinstein, *Corporate Ideal in the Liberal State*, 252–253.

[57] For a detailed consideration of Taft's surprisingly moderate leadership of the NWLB (emphasizing Frank Walsh's role), see Valerie Jean Conner, *The National War Labor Board: Stability, Social Justice, and the Voluntary State in World War I* (Chapel Hill: University of North Carolina Press, 1983).

(thanks to conservative courts) or through criminal violence overlooked by business-friendly politicians, these were not small victories.[58]

The attraction was even stronger when pro-labor progressives and union officials had the opportunity to help build a massive arbitration system from the ground up, one that would need leaders but also a small army of support staff to provide technical advice, conduct field investigations, and handle paperwork. Small wonder, then, that wartime labor agencies were filled with moderate or left-wing academics. Henry Seager, a Columbia University economist and supporter of the minimum wage, became the executive secretary for SLAB and then hired W. Jett Lauck (former researcher for the CIR and adviser to railroad unions) as lead statistician. Lauck in turn asked William F. Ogburn (then a young social scientist at the University of Washington) to direct the agency's first cost-of-living investigations, and when Lauck moved to the NWLB as its executive secretary, he brought Ogburn with him. Through this work, Ogburn would become a leading expert on working-class expenditures and a prominent advocate of an empirically based living wage. Meanwhile, Lauck and Frank Walsh proceeded to hire a host of union-friendly subordinates as field staff for the NWLB—including former labor officials, union members, and CIR researchers—making it, as one historian described, "the most left-leaning government agency that Washington had ever seen."[59]

If wartime arbitration offered opportunities to reshape American industrial relations, however, it also constrained and channeled that action toward national, rationalized strategies, a trajectory that affected not only the resulting policies but also the knowledge used to justify and guide arbitration rulings themselves. Most notably, wartime needs favored national statistics. Efficiency prompted labor boards to standardize wages, a move that also required national statistics constructed on a uniform basis. Nothing prevented boards from gathering their own information about topics such as the "cost of living"—indeed, some, including the Railroad Commission, did just that—but others recognized the benefits of handing this task to a federal agency already charged with collecting such data. In November 1917, Everitt Macy asked the BLS to study changes in the "cost of

---

[58] See the opening reflection on arbitration by an experienced labor activist in George Soule, *Wage Arbitration: Selected Cases, 1920–1924* (New York: MacMillan, 1928).

[59] On the NWLB, see Conner, *The National War Labor Board*; Robert P. Reeder, *The National War Labor Board: A History of Its Formation and Activities*, BLS Bulletin, no. 287 (Washington, D.C.: U.S. GPO, 1922); Dubofsky, *The State & Labor in Modern America*, 70–72; Koistinen, *Mobilizing for Modern War*, 260–261; Montgomery, *Fall of the House of Labor*, 353–355. Quotation from McCartin, *Labor's Great War*, 90–91.

living" in eighteen major shipbuilding centers for use by SLAB. The following summer, the NWLB called on the bureau to conduct a major, national
survey of prices and working-class expenditures in ninety-two cities and
towns across the United States. War provided both the impetus and the
means for the new work: over roughly a one-year span, the BLS received
approximately $375,000 in special funding from Wilson to complete these
two studies, a sum more than 50 percent greater than the bureau's regular
annual budget. Altogether, defense supplements provided about $650,000
to the bureau from 1917 to 1919.[60] War had finally propelled the federal
government toward the goal envisioned by early sponsors of the BLS: a uniform system of national, quantitative knowledge about American workers.

The drive for standardization also propelled a narrower and more homo-
geneous characterization of American workers. The bureau's last national
expenditure survey (under Carroll Wright in 1901–1902) had classified
families by the "nativity of [the] head of the family"—that is, the country
in which the husband had been born (typically a European nation or the
United States). As in most other prewar expenditure surveys, Wright had
treated nativity as an important category, producing eleaborate tables in
which average family composition, earnings, and expenditures were shown
for each relevant nationality.[61] By contrast, the bureau's wartime studies
did not gather data on nationality and specifically excluded "non-English
speaking families who have been less than five years in the United States."
Field agents collected information from a small number of "colored" families, but these data were not included in the final report nor used in the
official cost-of-living index. Alongside other eligibility requirements that
were intended to restrict the survey sample to "families dependent for support … upon the earnings of the husband," these rules had the net effect of
simultaneously narrowing the scope of cost-of-living statistics and effacing
categories once deemed important. Official, wartime cost-of-living statistics referred to families where "white," male wage-earners and low-salaried
clerks provided the bulk of family income.[62] Intentionally or not, this characterization also fit many union officials' conception of their membership.

[60] Macy to Meeker, 10 November 1917 [folder 1919], box 2, Selected General Correspondence
of the Bureau, 1908–1939, BLS. The regular annual budgets in 1918–1919 (the years of the
expenditure survey) were $213,000 and $243,000, respectively. Goldberg and Moye, *First
Hundred Years*, 104, 109.

[61] U.S. Bureau of Labor, *Cost of Living and Retail Prices of Food: Eighteenth Annual Report
of the Commissioner of Labor* (Washington, D.C.: Department of Commerce and Labor,
1904).

[62] U.S. Bureau of Labor Statistics, *The Cost of Living in the United States*, BLS Bulletin, no. 357
(Washington, D.C.: U.S. GPO, 1924), 2, 64; National Industrial Conference Board, *The Cost*

Alongside national standardization, wartime pressures prompted other tendencies. Especially in war production areas such as shipbuilding, stability and productivity remained the ultimate justification for federal intervention and hence the ultimate goal. Stability demanded quick resolution of disputes, a process eased by mutual agreement on the basic facts at issue. In turn, this promoted "black-boxing" statistics such as cost-of-living measurements: turning them into non- or minimally disputable items used by the board in its judgments. Arbitration boards learned the value of such steps quickly. When SLAB held its first hearings on the Pacific coast in the fall of 1917, employers, unions, and SLAB staff (led by Ogburn) each presented their own estimate of wartime price changes, complicating any decision. Macy hoped that by having the BLS collect statistics, he could reduce this problem in the future, explaining to the BLS commissioner that "your figures will be accepted without question by both sides, while investigations carried on by our Board might be subject to the suspicion that we were trying to make facts fit with our decisions." Yet despite Macy's expectation, unions continued to contest BLS statistics in later hearings by offering their own figures, finally leading SLAB to designate the BLS as its sole "authority" for information on the cost of living.[63]

Making an acceptable numerical fact required more than specifying a source for the statistical data. Self-aware researchers recognized that measuring changes in the cost of living was not a straightforward process, and even when they trusted their own results, they knew that others could critique their methods and assumptions, requiring time-consuming debates and extra work that would slow the desired resolution. Therefore, access to the inner-workings of their calculations had to be carefully screened. In November 1917, a SLAB statistician (almost certainly Lauck) explained the methods behind the team's cost-of-living calculations to Macy and SLAB economist Henry Seager, but warned them not to share the details with "union executives" since "certain technicalities might be used as a basis of unnecessary controversy."[64] It was a quiet acknowledgment of the practical

---

of Living in the United States (New York: National Industrial Conference Board, 1925), 70, n. 2.

[63] Macy to Meeker, 10 November 1917, folder 1919, box 2, Selected General Correspondence of the Bureau, 1908–1939, BLS. U.S. Bureau of Labor Statistics, "Recent Awards of the Shipbuilding Labor Adjustment Board," *MLR* 6, no. 5 (1918): 1184–1185; U.S. Bureau of Labor Statistics, "New Wage Adjustment in the Shipbuilding Industry," *MLR* 7, no. 6 (1918): 1682.

[64] Unsigned letter to Macy, Seager, and Blackman, 30 November 1917, box 1, Records–Cost of Living, U.S. Shipping Board. Given the topic and context, Lauck was almost certainly the author.

quandaries faced by those who recognized both the production demands of mobilization and the ambiguity of cost-of-living statistics.

The man most familiar with retail price statistics, the new BLS commissioner, had some of the gravest doubts about their significance and also the most complicated public position. In 1913, Charles P. O'Neill had resigned from his low-paying post as commissioner to take a more lucrative job in the railroad industry, and Woodrow Wilson appointed a fellow Princetonian, economist Royal Meeker, as O'Neill's successor. Meeker, who had studied under E.R.A. Seligman while working toward his Ph.D. from Columbia University, was a more accomplished economist than O'Neill but he shared his predecessor's anxieties about the bureau's retail price index.[65] "Long before I took charge of the Bureau of Labor Statistics," Meeker told a group of economists and statisticians in 1915, "I had become very suspicious of the Bureau's index numbers, especially its retail price index." Familiarity had not eased his concerns, but only buried him deeper into a morass of complexity and headache. "Some people here present will no doubt recall that I was wont to have fun with the Bureau's index numbers," he continued. "I no longer have fun with them—they have fun with me."[66] Meeker had not despaired, however, and continued attention to rising prices coupled with the war in Europe only strengthened his resolve. With the advice of Irving Fisher and Wesley C. Mitchell, he revised the index over several years, most visibly by expanding its scope. By 1917, he had increased the number of food items in the index from fifteen to twenty-seven and broadened the geographical coverage from thirty-nine cities to forty-five.[67]

Still, the retail price index remained limited to food. Meeker knew that European countries had begun constructing full cost-of-living indexes (usually covering food, rent, clothing, fuel, and other major items from working-class budgets) to help manage wartime labor disputes. In a similar vein, he began publishing semiannual, average prices for domestic gas, several kinds of coal, and eight different fabrics. But these remained separate from the food index, and Meeker made no moves toward a more comprehensive measure of retail price change. He was not alone in his hesitation. Like his predecessor and countless economists after him, Meeker worried about how, in a dynamic consumer market, he could find stable goods whose prices

---

[65] Goldberg and Moye, *First Hundred Years*, 78, 81–86.

[66] Walter F. Wilcox et al., "The Statistical Work of the United States Government," *AER* 5, no. 1 (1915): 174.

[67] Meeker began his revisions (including some methodological changes discussed in Chapter 3) in 1914; see Royal Meeker, "Some Features of the Statistical Work of the Bureau of Labor Statistics," *PASA* 14, no. 109 (1915): 433–441.

could be compared month after month. For wholesale commodities, food, and perhaps rent he felt reasonably confident that agents could obtain more or less comparable items, but clothing and "miscellaneous" expenses were more troublesome. Styles, materials, and quality changed rapidly and often without explicit notice, making it hard to set specifications. As he explained in a private meeting about wages and index numbers in March 1918, "I can with certain mental reservations hold up my hand and swear that I have the retail prices [of food], that we are getting them as trustworthy as it is possible to get them, but when it comes to the rising cost of ladies' hats that is a different matter."[68]

Meeker spoke frankly and with good humor when discussing the limitations of cost-of-living statistics, including at professional meetings before and after the war. But official BLS presentations looked rather different during 1917–1918. Even as Meeker confessed his skepticism in March, the bureau was already collecting prices for ladies' hats alongside a host of other figures used to document wartime changes in the cost of living within shipbuilding centers. Privately, Meeker declared that such efforts demanded "great heroism in making assumptions," and with a touch of earnest concern he joked that the "awful holes" in bureau cost-of-living studies "simply [keep] me awake at night sometimes." Only a faint glimmer of these anxieties appeared in official bureau publications, however, which contained tables showing calculated changes with little commentary. Indeed, outside economists later complained about the opacity of the bureau's cost-of-living calculations.[69]

The reticence of Lauck and Meeker reflected a pragmatic paternalism of the sort that develops naturally in bureaucratic cultures where efficiency becomes a primary concern. Both men were pro-labor in their sympathies and both felt that their calculations were reasonable. But both also recognized that union and company representatives would critique the inevitable

---

[68] Transcript of meeting between Louis Post, Meeker, Henry Seager, and Irving Fisher, 19 March 1918, Dept. of Labor, box 3, General Records, U.S. Shipping Board. Charles P. O'Neill expressed similar concerns about obtaining retail prices beyond food: U.S. Senate, Select Committee on Wages and Prices of Commodities, *Investigation Relative to Wages and Prices of Commodities*, vol. 4 (Washington, D.C.: U.S. GPO, 1911), 215–216.

[69] Transcript of meeting between Post, Meeker, Seager, and Fisher, 19 March 1918. On the obscurity of BLS methods, see George E. Barnett, "Index Numbers of the Total Cost of Living," *QJE* 35, no. 2 (1921): 262. Significantly, both before and after the war, BLS officials more readily discussed the complications of retail price comparisons. Cf. U.S. Bureau of Labor Statistics, "Retail Prices of Bread," *MLR* 3, no. 4 (1916): 439–440; Royal Meeker, "The Possibility of Compiling an Index Number of the Cost of Living," *AER* 9, no. 1 (1919): 108–117; U.S. Bureau of Labor Statistics, *Retail Prices, 1913 to December, 1919*, BLS Bulletin, no. 270 (1921).

assumptions and limitations inherent in the analysis, thereby destabilizing the statistics, complicating the arbitration process, and hampering war production. The minimal discussion of methodology was accompanied by a similar retreat from the "flesh and blood" details that had peppered prewar social surveys and even many BLS reports (under both O'Neill and Meeker). Overall, the contrast between prewar treatments of the cost of living within the survey tradition and the stark, terse briefs issued by the Bureau of Labor Statistics during 1917–1918 was sharp and revealing.[70] The latter aimed not to provoke public discussion but to eliminate it. Such was the price of participation in the wartime system.

Designating a source for data, protecting its perceived reliability—one further step anchored a statistically based administrative mechanism, turning it (in Irving Fisher's terms) into a "clerical" operation: establishing strict rules to govern the application of quantitative knowledge. The last step existed in embryonic form since the beginning of wartime labor arbitration, but it had to evolve into more regimented guidelines. Like most arbitration boards, both SLAB and the NWLB proclaimed a preliminary set of principles, but these were vague and in some cases contradictory. (The NWLB, for instance, promised to respect existing "standards, wage scales, and other conditions" but also affirmed the "right ... to a living wage.")[71] Crafting more specific guidelines required time and experience. In the case of cost-of-living adjustments, for example, SLAB's initial statement promised merely that the board would "keep itself fully informed" about "living costs" in relevant districts. Within a year officials had explicitly defined events that would trigger cost-of-living adjustments: a 10 percent or more change in BLS cost-of-living statistics during specified six-month intervals.[72]

A few recognized quite early on the logical culmination of this process: automatic cost-of-living adjustments. Irving Fisher had quickly realized his plan for a "compensated dollar" could be adapted to wage policies, and in May 1917, he wrote Assistant Secretary of Labor Louis Post proposing that

---

[70]   E.g., U.S. Bureau of Labor Statistics, "Cost of Living in Philadelphia," *MLR* 6, no. 3 (1918): 604. By contrast, consider public reports about the bureau's investigation of the cost of living in Washington, D.C., completed in the first half of 1917 and intended for congressional debate about local conditions rather than for use by an arbitration board. These studies contained long descriptions about living conditions, the quality of goods purchased, and their adequacy—all much closer to the style of prewar, cost-of-living surveys. See articles in the *MLR*, October 1917–April 1918.

[71]   U.S. Bureau of Labor Statistics, "National War Labor Board: Its Purpose and Functions," *MLR* 6, no. 5 (1918): 1105; Conner, *The National War Labor Board*, vii.

[72]   U.S. Bureau of Labor Statistics, "Plans for Adjustment of Disputes in Shipyards and in Loading and Unloading Ships," *MLR* 5, no. 10 (1917): 666; Carr, *Use of Cost-of-Living Figures*, 56.

wages could be adjusted at half the rise in the BLS index of food prices (assuming that food prices rose twice as fast as other components of working-class budgets). Meeker expressed some doubts and the Emergency Fleet Corporation apparently had little interest, but neither opposition nor apathy daunted Fisher. By February 1918, he was campaigning in full force, contacting Post, officials in labor arbitration agencies, and private companies who had adopted some form of index-based wage adjustments. Meeker supported indexation in principle, but wanted to use the food price index (based on his doubts about broader cost-of-living measurements); SLAB economist Henry Seager felt that food prices alone would be insufficient. This placed them at an impasse, but Post had been captivated by Fisher and in March he asked Meeker and Seager to consult further with Fisher about implementing a plan to index wages. Soon Americans learned that European labor policies were following a similar trajectory: in April, the BLS *Monthly Labor Review* reported that British garment trades had adopted a sliding scale of wages tied to the Board of Trade's cost-of-living index, described as the "first attempt on a large scale to adopt a scientific method of regulating earnings according to the cost of living." That August, Secretary of Labor William B. Wilson told the president he supported automatic wage increases at fixed increments based on BLS statistics. Several months later, the *Monthly Labor Review* opened with an article by Fisher describing various private plans that linked employee compensation to price indexes, including one by Fisher's own company, Index Visible, Inc. (manufacturer of an index-card filing system).[73]

Still, the progression toward administrative management of wages was neither uniform nor absolute. In the early fall of 1918, Woodrow Wilson called a conference of "National Labor Adjustment Agencies" to hammer out a more uniform set of arbitration policies. Although the recommendations were rendered irrelevant by the November armistice, they nevertheless illustrate how numerous officials balked at leaving wage rates solely to the statistical calculations of an administrative system. "[T]he broad principle of maintaining standards of living," declared the final report, "cannot be reduced to a mathematical formula, but must follow the dictates of reason and justice." The latter included establishing "a fair and equitable wage" where necessary while allowing employers to give higher-paid workers

[73] Transcript of meeting between Post, Meeker, Seager, and Fisher, 19 March 1918; U.S. Bureau of Labor Statistics, "Regulation of War Wages by Cost of Living in Great Britain," *MLR* 6, no. 4 (1918): 920–921; Goldberg and Moye, *First Hundred Years*, 102–103; Meeker, "Index Number of the Cost of Living," 110–114; Irving Fisher, "Adjusting Wages to the Cost of Living," *MLR* 7, no. 5 (1918): 1151–1155.

something less than the "full force" of cost-of-living adjustments (following the common principle that war required national sacrifice).[74] Undoubtedly many disagreed with these conclusions, but the recognition of "reason and justice" as ideals and their placement in contrast to a "mathematical formula" indicated the limits of strictly administrative governance even at the culmination of wartime management.

Equally telling were the contrasting approaches to "equitable" wages developed by SLAB and the NWLB. Whereas SLAB effectively defined an "equitable" basic wage by using prewar union rates, Frank Walsh pushed the NWLB to confront the concept of a living wage directly, employing a style of empirical reasoning with close ties to the prewar survey tradition and his earlier experience in the CIR. Statistics did not provide complete answers; they were starting points for further discussion and bargaining. Walsh began NWLB hearings on living wage with a presentation from William Ogburn, who had culled a variety of sources to compile estimates for a "minimum subsistence" budget (about $1,300 per year, intended for unskilled workers) and a "minimum comfort" budget ($1,750, for skilled workers). As in most standard budgets used to evaluate men's wages during this period, both of Ogburn's budgets were predicated on a "family wage" concept—that is, the income needed for a male worker to support a wife and dependent children (three, in this case). Within the NWLB, Ogburn's work proved only a springboard for a long series of debates. Walsh proposed the "minimum comfort" level as a national minimum wage (a rate that would nearly double the existing average for unskilled labor); labor representatives (citing personal experience) insisted that Ogburn's figures were too low for many cities; stunned employers, already resisting the very idea of a minimum wage, claimed that no universal, living wage could apply to workers who lived in different locations and had widely varying spending habits and numbers of family dependents. After tumultuous arguments spanning several days, the board abandoned the quest for a fixed, national standard and agreed to consider each case individually. But Walsh had scored a victory by making Ogburn's "minimum subsistence" budget appear like a reasonable compromise, and the unskilled rates in wage schedules produced by the board typically approached Ogburn's lower level. Moreover, in a rare move for a wartime labor board, he had Ogburn's report published almost immediately, positioning it as an official NWLB document on the "minimum wage."[75]

---

[74] Hotchkiss and Seager, *History of the Shipbuilding Labor Adjustment Board*, 43, 101.
[75] William F. Ogburn, *Memorandum on the Minimum Wage and Increased Cost of Living* (Washington, D.C.: U.S. GPO, 1918); Conner, *The National War Labor Board*, 50–67.

For all of Walsh's predilections, however, the NWLB remained a national, bureaucratic agency embedded in a war mobilization system. The private, closed-door discussions of the living wage were a far cry from Walsh's public cross-examination of John D. Rockefeller, Jr., at the end of the CIR. Over time, the sheer volume of cases handled by the NWLB forced it to adopt even more administrative features, such as assigning staff to prepare digests of petitions rather than holding full hearings. Furthermore, the narrow range of awards for unskilled labor suggests that the board had tacitly adopted its own set of informal guidelines—a necessity given the huge number of cases it tackled in a short period (roughly 500 rulings over sixteen months).[76] Finally, pro-labor members of the NWLB found themselves hobbled by mobilization demands, such as pressures to allow a wage differential for shipbuilding (to maintain a high workforce), which made SLAB award levels de facto constraints.[77] In the end, despite its more left-wing leadership, NWLB actions resembled those of other federal arbitration agencies: they raised wages for workers (especially unskilled laborers) in low-paying industries or regions but had less (or no) effect on rates for skilled, organized trades.[78] It was not an ideal outcome for pro-labor liberals, but here was the hard truth recognized even by populists like Walsh: it was better than what the past three decades could have led them to expect from regulatory legislation or strictly "voluntarist" union action. In an economically and regionally diverse nation, moving outside the boundaries of democratic politics had its advantages.

DECEMBER 1918

At the annual meeting of the American Economics Association in December, Royal Meeker confessed to an intellectual conversion. Since the summer, the BLS had been gathering data on family expenditures in ninety-two cities and towns for use by the NWLB. Alongside the continuing compilation of data for SLAB, this experience had convinced Meeker that although compiling a cost-of-living index remained "a task of enormous

---

NWLB Executive minutes, 10, 24, 25, 26 July 1918, boxes 1–2, NWLB. The details of most wartime cost-of-living studies were only published after the war, if at all.

[76] Reeder, *The National War Labor Board*, 12–23. Valerie Conner indicates that the NWLB "generally" set rates for unskilled labor at 40–42 cents per hour: Conner, *The National War Labor Board*, 67.

[77] NWLB Executive Minutes, 10 July 1918, pp. 30–35, box 1, NWLB.

[78] Conner, *The National War Labor Board*, 67. Compare the trends in hourly earnings for union workers versus unskilled labor during the war: Paul H. Douglas, *Real Wages in the United States, 1890–1926* (Boston: Houghton Mifflin, 1930), 138–139, 182–183.

difficulty and of endless and infinite detail," it was nevertheless possible to create such a series embodying tolerable assumptions. Pragmatic daring had been the defining characteristic of wartime statistics overall; as Wesley Mitchell explained during his presidential address to the American Statistical Association, the urgency of war had pressed even cautious statisticians to rush past all obstacles. For Meeker, the experience had eased his previous doubts: a national cost-of-living index was not only a "theoretical possibility," he announced to the audience, "but ... a practical fact in process of coming into being."[79]

The new cost-of-living index exemplified the transformations that had occurred in labor statistics over the previous fifty years. Both the state bureaus and "special investigations" were fading before regular monitoring of specific aspects of the national economy. The institutional dominance of the BLS (especially supported by wartime funding) likewise narrowed the methodological diversity that had characterized earlier labor statistics. The narratives, detailed focus on salient examples, and "flesh and blood" descriptions that featured prominently in the work of some state bureaus and much of the prewar survey tradition had no place in the BLS wartime cost-of-living statistics. Rather, the new index reflected the function of statistics in federal labor management: dependent on extensive wartime funding, national in scope, and embedded in bureaucratic systems designed to ensure labor stability and efficient production.

The latter features suggest about wartime labor policies what historians have recognized about wartime political economy as a whole: they promoted stability and growth through business-government cooperation, and in doing so, handed the greatest benefits to larger corporations already well-positioned in militarily relevant industries. Nevertheless, it was not primarily the offspring of what historians have labeled "corporate liberalism": a more or less conscious attempt by big business to offer token improvements to workers in return for maintaining control and maximizing profits. Employer representation on the NWLB, for instance, came from the conservative National Industrial Conference Board, who, along with most of the business community, gradually grew to hate the NWLB and attacked it bitterly by the end of the war. SLAB, although led by wealthy heir V. Everitt Macy, was primarily a tool for the federal government to negotiate with national unions; shipyard employers had no representation on the board, and indeed were not sufficiently organized to participate effectively.

---

[79] Meeker, "Index Number of the Cost of Living," 110–114; Mitchell, "Statistics and Government," 26.

Overall, an organized business community was a product of the war, not its controlling master.[80]

Construction of the wartime labor arbitration system, especially our salient examples of SLAB and the NWLB, came instead from an alliance between the Wilson administration and those pro-labor liberals and union leaders who rejected the revolutionary strategies of radicals such as the Wobblies. It was an opportunity to bypass the local obstacles and federal courts that had thwarted labor reform, working-class progress, and union growth. But it was not and could not be a full triumph. Clinging to the wartime state meant conforming to its objectives and accepting its allies. It meant compromise with private industry and business leaders, the very men whom reformers and unions had battled up to and through 1917. Stable cooperation could not be founded on widespread trust between individual employees and owners. Rather, it came through centralization of power (in the boards and their "representative" members), imposition of discipline on constituents, the proliferation of procedural rules and guidelines, and the deployment of black-boxed statistics to create aggregate, conceptual entities ("the cost of living in Philadelphia") for use as administrative tools. Modern American labor statistics, understood as aids for monitoring and managing a national economy rather than "special investigations" into social problems, were co-created in war alongside the national, bureaucratic American state.

Still, it was a fragile birth. The wartime system had been sustained by an uneasy coalition of moderate businessmen, pro-labor liberal elites, trade unions, and the Wilson administration itself, which had wielded patriotic rhetoric, an occasional iron fist, and the trump card of wartime emergency just deftly enough to hold it all together. Once the European battles ended, domestic fissures rapidly reappeared. No longer facing the threat of government takeover, conservative employers openly defied the NWLB.[81] Meanwhile, in Seattle a strike by shipyard workers in late January sparked a general citywide strike, potentially heralding a wider working-class revolt.[82] Moreover, even progressives who had participated in the wartime arbitration

---

[80] Koistinen, *Mobilizing for Modern War*, 263–267; Conner, *The National War Labor Board*; Hotchkiss and Seager, *History of the Shipbuilding Labor Adjustment Board*, 91–92; Mergen, "The Government as Manager," 68. For accounts that give greater priority to business control, see Weinstein, *Corporate Ideal in the Liberal State*; R. Jeffrey Lustig, *Corporate Liberalism: The Origins of Modern American Political Theory, 1890–1920* (Berkeley: University of California Press, 1982); Cuff, *The War Industries Board*.

[81] Conner, *The National War Labor Board*, 126–141, 158–172.

[82] Dana Frank, *Purchasing Power: Consumer Organizing, Gender, and the Seattle Labor Movement, 1919–1929* (Cambridge: Cambridge University Press, 1994), 15–39.

system could not agree about how to proceed during peace. Naturally, these threats to the wartime management apparatus also encompassed its statistical supports. After opening his 1918 ASA presidential address by praising the wartime effort of statisticians, Wesley Mitchell fretted over the potentially fleeting nature of their recent gains, already endangered by conservatives seeking budget cuts.[83] Back at the Bureau of Labor Statistics, Royal Meeker was mulling over similar concerns. The studies for the cost-of-living index had been financed through Wilson's special wartime fund, which was no longer available. "Much larger appropriations to the Bureau of Labor Statistics will be necessary," he told his professional colleagues, "to enable the retail prices to be collected and tabulated rapidly enough and frequently enough for the purposes of a usable index number of the cost of living."[84] The war had transformed the federal government and federal labor statistics, but the durability and nature of its legacy remained in doubt.

[83] Mitchell, "Statistics and Government," 227.
[84] Meeker, "Index Number of the Cost of Living," 115.

3

Searching for Normalcy: Cost-of-Living
Statistics and Industrial Relations in the 1920s

One aspect of the problem of index numbers may be unanimously admitted. It is the problem of referring back, in a period of confusion caused by the war and economic and psychological upheavals, to the standard of earlier conditions. Index numbers have a deeper significance than that of an economic symptom or tool; they are the symbol of a shattered civilisation which seeks to escape from the chaos and instability of a relativist age by finding a settled standard of measurement.[1]
  —Felix Klezl, Austrian Statistical Office, 1924

After all is said and done, what do we mean by 'cost of living?' Whose living? Living how? Living for what—to develop another government clerk? What is living?[2]
  —Ethelbert Stewart,
  Commissioner of the Bureau of Labor Statistics, 1920–1932

For Europeans, the war had been a patriotic jaunt that grew slowly and painfully into a horrific, grinding nightmare. For Americans on the home-front, mobilization was an intense but brief spasm that ended before it had reached any real rhythm or stability. Like military officers perusing a recent campaign, federal officials and the country itself began the post-war era trying to figure out what they had done, whether it had worked, and what portents it might hold for the future. Some Americans no doubt hoped to turn the clock back to 1916, or even 1913, an attitude symbolized by Warren G. Harding's call for "normalcy." But others, even while cheering the dismantling of the wartime administration, saw important peacetime lessons in its actions, including the possibility of sustaining the high economic productivity that had accompanied mobilization. "Normalcy," insisted the Republican Secretary of Commerce Herbert Hoover in 1923, "is a vastly higher and more comfortable standard than 1913." From this

---

[1] Felix Klezl, "Methods of Calculating Index Numbers," *ILR* 10, no. 2 (1924): 262.
[2] Ethelbert Stewart, "Cost of living for what?" [n.d., early 1930s], 4–5, Part I, B, Stewart papers.

perspective, the postwar pursuit of "normal" activity demanded not a return to the past but the search for a new kind of peacetime order, one that avoided the extensive federal controls of mobilization while retaining some of its benefits.[3]

Of course, different groups saw different predicaments and opportunities in the reconversion process, a generalization that includes those affected by wartime industrial relations. For economists who studied price index theory, the widespread use of cost-of-living indexes had thrust their subject into the spotlight but also made them acutely aware of the theoretical and practical weaknesses of current methods. For unions, mobilization had swollen their ranks, but the return of peace offered both relief—such as an end to wartime restrictions on strikes—and threatening developments, including the end of government protection. For businessmen, the puzzle was how to deal with a resurgent labor movement while retaining some of the productivity and profit gains from the war.

Most of these deliberations occurred in isolation. Few index number theorists had direct experience with labor disputes or deep knowledge of industrial relations; even fewer union officials or businessmen knew much about price index theory. And of course unions and most businessmen clashed on so many fundamental principles in this period that collaboration between the two was nearly impossible—as illustrated by the impotence and collapse of Wilson's two grand postwar Industrial Conferences.[4] But some saw in cost-of-living statistics a thread that wove its way through industrial relations and bound an abstruse technical subject to the social and economic crises of the age. For Felix Klezl, manning his statistical bureau in war-ravaged Austria, the link was almost existential, with the careful calculations and neatly printed tables of the statistician forming a bulwark of order amidst a roiling upheaval. For those Americans lured by the political potency of the "cost of living," the concerns were more pragmatic, a sense that in the aggregative power and structured rules of statistical analysis there lay a key that could bring stability and even some justice to industrial relations.

[3] Herbert Hoover, Department of Commerce press release, 8 May 1923, as quoted in W. Jett Lauck, *The New Industrial Revolution and Wages* (New York: Funk & Wagnalls, 1929), 80. William J. Barber, *From New Era to New Deal: Herbert Hoover, the Economists, and American Economic Policy, 1921–1933* (Cambridge: Cambridge University Press, 1985), 1–4. My perspective owes much to the work of Ellis Hawley on this period, synthesized in Ellis W. Hawley, *The Great War and the Search for a Modern Order: A History of the American People and Their Institutions, 1917–1944* (New York: St. Martin's Press, 1979).

[4] Melvyn Dubofsky, *The State & Labor in Modern America* (Chapel Hill: University of North Carolina Press, 1994), 79–80.

In practice, that vision proved difficult to realize. Theoretical and methodological debates over cost-of-living statistics prevented technical consensus about proper measurements. Moreover, whereas wartime pressures had sustained statistically based, national systems for labor management, the postwar situation took a different turn. Political decentralization, economic variation, and capitalist competition now produced fragmented industrial relations and and an equally diverse set of methods and applications for cost-of-living statistics. Furthermore, as the decade progressed and union militancy faded in many sectors, the strictures of rule-governed wage calculations often apppeared unnecessary altogether. Still, neither the attraction of quantitative rationality nor the political power of the "cost of living" disappeared entirely, and some employers (seeking to stabilize their workforce) as well as many embattled unions (struggling for any foothold of influence) pursued new strategies to exploit this potential. The general search for "normalcy" during the 1920s thus encompassed a smaller quest to construct a rationalized, rule-governed, empirically grounded framework for labor relations, one whose potential outlines would only become clear near the end of the decade.

This chapter follows the postwar quest for rationalized labor relations through two initially distinct narratives about cost-of-living statistics. First, I consider the main theoretical frameworks for cost-of-living indexes that emerged among economists in the wake of the war, describing both the problems that threatened to undermine the significance of these statistics and the dominant approach utilized by government statisticians. That framework, supported in America by self-described "institutional economists," emphasized the objective nature of cost-of-living indexes, insisting that one could (and must) measure price changes by following the cost of a fixed collection of goods and services. The second section takes up a different narrative, examining the use of cost-of-living statistics to govern wage adjustments. Here, I explore the fragmentation of the wartime labor system and the concomitant devaluation of the national retail price indexes created by the BLS in favor of a highly pluralistic approach to cost-of-living measurements. Finally, the concluding section draws elements of these two threads together, describing how growing attention to "purchasing power" in the late 1920s (especially among institutional economists) laid the groundwork for a new interest in national retail price indexes (seen as objective measures of price changes) and thereby reinvigorated the ties between cost-of-living indexes and hopes for progressive reform of industrial relations.

INDEX NUMBERS IN THEORY AND PRACTICE

Government officials worldwide had used retail price statistics to stabilize wartime labor relations by grounding wage adjustments in a putatively neutral and reliable fact: the change in the cost of living. Amidst the pressures of war, these measures had escaped serious critical scrutiny from academic theorists. With the return of peace, however, economists and statisticians began to question the significance of their creations, and as the opening epigraphs suggest, their concern focused on the fundamental issue that continues to plague index-number theory: how to define a stable standard in a dynamic economy. The radical economic transformations of the war forced economists to confront this problem, their own variant of the larger puzzle about postwar normalcy: if cost-of-living indexes measured the changing cost of a "normal" (typical) standard of living (usually drawn from working-class families), how should these indexes be adjusted when consumption patterns changed dramatically? When normalcy had a new meaning, how could one compare two different time periods?

By the early 1930s, respondents to this question could be roughly divided into two groups, each of which identified an alternative standard that could be held constant in a changing environment. The first group—composed mainly of European (and especially British) neoclassical economists such as A. C. Pigou, Arthur Bowley, R. G. D. Allen, Alexander Konüs, Gottfried Haberler, and Hans Staehle—insisted that a cost-of-living index ought to measure the changing cost of obtaining a fixed level of "utility," "satisfaction," or "welfare."[5] In this vision, "normal" (typical) consumption might provide an initial base level of utility, but there was no guarantee that normal consumption in future years would correspond to the same utility level. I will refer to this approach as a "constant-utility index."

The second group, supported in the United States primarily by institutional economists, argued that cost-of-living indexes could successfully measure average changes in retail prices without recourse to amorphous, subjective concepts like satisfaction. In turn, they supported what we will call a "constant-goods index," which tracked the changing cost of a fixed collection of goods and services. Here, "normal" (typical) working-class consumption patterns defined the goods included in the index, but the prices of those goods (and not the cost of any welfare that they provided) were the objects of interest.

[5] Hans Staehle, *International Comparison of Food Costs* (Geneva: International Labour Office, 1934), 74–92; Ragnar Frisch, "Annual Survey of General Economic Theory: The Problem of Index Numbers," *Econometrica* 4, no. 1 (1936): 10–12.

Although the neoclassical perspective now dominates contemporary economics (such that the phrase "cost-of-living index" is virtually synonymous with "constant-utility index"), the situation was quite different during the 1920s, when most government statisticians sided with the institutionalist analysis. Considering the theoretical debates during the 1920s allows us to see the problems facing cost-of-living indexes, the reasons for the success of the institutionalist perspective, and the techniques statisticians used to confront the practical difficulties of measuring the cost of living. Moreover, the institutionalist success shaped both the function of cost-of-living indexes in political economy (as we will see in the concluding section) and the framework for debates about the validity of BLS retail price statistics for the next fifty years.

War and Price Index Theory

The theoretical literature treating price indexes prior to the First World War is a rich realm of arcane economic debate, complete with bitter feuds, constant miscommunication, and occasional cries of despair. Amidst this cacophony, one theme stands out: prewar discussions supplied a plethora of conflicting methods for calculating index numbers, a controversy whose significance was somewhat deflated (in practical, if not theoretical terms) by widespread recognition that most reasonable approaches gave substantially similar results. Methodological discussions coalesced on three major issues: how many (and which) commodities to include in an index; what form of average (arithmetic mean, geometric, median) should be used to combine the price changes of each into an overall result; and whether (and how) the price changes of different commodities should be "weighted" within the calculations. (For a review of these concepts, see Chapter 1 or the appendix.) Weaving through these debates were theoretical presumptions about central economic concepts—such as the "value of money" or a "standard of living"—and the (multiple?) objectives of price indexes themselves.[6] But

---

[6] Maurice Kendall, "The Early History of Index Numbers," *Revue de l'Institut International de Statistique* 37 (1969): 1–12; Robert A. Horváth, "The Rise of Macroeconomic Calculations in Economic Statistics," in *The Probabilistic Revolution, Volume 2: Ideas in the Sciences*, ed. Lorenz Krüger, Gerd Gigerenzer, and Mary S. Morgan (Cambridge: MIT Press, 1987), 147–169; John Aldrich, "Probability and Depreciation: A History of the Stochastic Approach to Index Numbers," *HOPE* 24, no. 3 (1992): 657–687; W. Erwin Diewert, "The Early History of Price Index Research," in *Essays in Index Number Theory, Vol 1*, ed. W. Erwin Diewert and Alice O. Nakamura (Amsterdam: Elsevier Science Publishers, 1993), 33–65; Joseph Persky, "Retrospectives: Price Indexes and General Exchange Values," *Journal of Economic Perspectives* 12, no. 1 (1998): 197–202; Stephen M. Stigler, *Statistics on*

the happy accompaniment to this chaos was the common assertion that it hardly mattered: provided that one included a substantial number of commodities, most basic formulae gave generally the same results when used with real-world data, irrespective of the type of average chosen or the system of weighting employed; moreover, these minor variations had no significant practical consequences.[7] Then came 1914.

"The war," declared Irving Fisher in 1920, "has caused the greatest upheaval of prices the world has ever seen."[8] In combination with the general economic tumult and the demands of mobilization, these dizzying transformations jolted the staid domain of price index theory. Concern over rising prices during and after the war fueled a proliferation of price indexes worldwide, including cost-of-living indexes that (as in America) sprouted routinely to aid government management of labor disputes. The results reinforced a sense that prices were out of control: between 1914 and 1918, cost-of-living indexes showed a rise of 52 percent in the United States, 103 percent in Britain, and over 280 percent in parts of Italy. Retrospective calculations during the early postwar years in the most ravaged countries portrayed extraordinary shifts: 800 percent in Germany and 24,000 percent in Poland by 1921. Austria, the home of our epigraph-author Felix Klezl, produced an index showing an unfathomable 53,000 percent rise between 1914 and December 1921.[9]

Shocking as these numbers may be, contemporary theorists also recognized that they were highly problematic. To create official indexes, government statisticians had produced price relatives for a subset of goods purchased by working-class families and then calculated the average of these ratios (either an unweighted average or one with fixed weights, typically based on proportional family expenditures during some time period).[10] Since both the items and weights remained fixed for each index, these calculations were effectively "constant-goods" indexes, that is, ratios of the cost

the Table: The History of Statistical Concepts and Methods (Cambridge: Harvard University Press, 1999), 69–76; Thomas A. Stapleford, "The 'Most Important Single Statistic': The Consumer Price Index and American Political Economy, 1880–1955" (Ph.D. dissertation, Harvard University, 2003), 85–102, 110–115; Harro Maas, *William Stanley Jevons and the Making of Modern Economics* (Cambridge: Cambridge University Press, 2005), 265–270.

7 F. Y. Edgeworth, "Recent Writings on Index Numbers," *Economic Journal* 4, no. 13 (1894): 158–159; A. W. Flux, "Modes of Constructing Index Numbers," *QJE* 21, no. 4 (1907): 613; Henry Rogers Seager, *Economics: Briefer Course* (New York: Henry Holt, 1909), 281; F. W. Taussig, *Principles of Economics*, 2nd ed. (New York: Macmillan, 1915), 294–295.

8 Irving Fisher, *Stabilizing the Dollar: A Plan to Stabilize the General Price Level without Fixing Individual Prices* (New York: MacMillan, 1920), vii.

9 "Cost of Living and Retail Prices," *ILR* 6, no. 1 (1922): 54–55.

10 International Labour Office, "Prices and Cost of Living," *ILR* 10, no. 1 (1924): 171–178.

to purchase a fixed collection of goods and services (the "market basket") in two different time periods:

$$\text{Constant-goods index} = \frac{\text{Cost of fixed market basket (currently)}}{\text{Cost of fixed market basket (in base period)}}$$

(Table 3.1 describes the market basket used in the BLS cost-of-living index.) Invariably, therefore, each index crashed headlong into the central problem with such statistics: how could you decide which goods to place in the market basket?

During the nineteenth century, political economists had argued that the basket should reflect an existing consumption pattern, perhaps the purchases of a certain social class or the expenditures of an entire nation.[11] But they also recognized that these consumption patterns could change over time, thereby introducing some ambiguity: what consumption pattern should define the market basket? The names of two German economists working in the 1860s and 1870s, Ernst Laspeyres and Hermann Paasche, are now commonly associated with the two basic alternatives: deriving the market basket from average consumption in the base time period (Laspeyres) or the current time period (Paasche).[12] But neither choice was altogether satisfying, because both ignored the central problem: the change in consumption patterns. Some theorists tried to solve this dilemma by averaging the two sets of goods, while others devised even more complicated alternatives.[13] Still, no solution gained consensus approval prior to 1914, a stalemate that, as with index numbers in general, appeared theoretically irritating but practically irrelevant.

Just as the war upended so much of European culture, however, it likewise destroyed any peaceful indifference to cost-of-living index theory. On the one hand, the common link between cost-of-living statistics and wages that had developed in both Europe and America during the war (whether through arbitration or collective bargaining agreements) now meant that the figures tumbling forth from government offices could have serious

---

[11] cf. Joseph Lowe, *The Present State of England in Regard to Agriculture, Trade, and Finance; with a Comparison of the Prospects of England and France* (New York: E. Bliss & E. White, 1824), esp. 298–304 and appendix, 96–98.

[12] E. Laspeyres, "Die Berechung einer mittleren Waarenpreissteigerung," *Jahrbücher für Nationalökonomie und Statistik* (1871) 296–314. H. Paasche, "Über die Preisentwicklung der letzen Jahre nach den Hamburger Börsenentwicklungen," *Jahrbücher für Nationalökonomie und Statistik* (1871): 168–178.

[13] Correa M. Walsh, *The Measurement of General Exchange-Value* (New York: MacMillan, 1901), 98–99.

Table 3.1: *The 1917–1919 Market Basket for the BLS Cost-of-Living Index*

During 1918 and 1919, the BLS conducted a large survey of family expenditures as part of its work for war mobilization agencies (Chapter 2). That survey provided the basis for the market basket used in the BLS cost-of-living index. The six major components of the full index are described below. (Note that only food prices were collected monthly; other components were calculated either quarterly or semiannually throughout the decade.)

Food: The bureau collected prices for 43 items each month from 51 cities by mailed questionnaires. Most fresh fruits and vegetables were excluded due to seasonal quality and price variations.

Clothing: Field agents gathered prices for 71 articles of clothing chosen to represent typical purchases for an adult male, an adult female, a boy (age 12), and girl (age 6). The weights for each item corresponded to average purchases for that item recorded during the survey.

Housing: A sample of rents secured in each city, ideally for the same apartments in each period.

Fuel and Light: Included coal, wood, gas, electricity, and kerosene.

Furniture and furnishings: A sample of 22 items, primarily furniture and linens, but also including flooring (e.g., carpets, linoleum), stoves, brooms, sewing machines, and ice refrigerators (not modern electric refrigerators).

Miscellaneous: The general grab-bag: movies, street-car fare, newspapers, medicine and healthcare (physician, hospital care, dental care, eyeglasses), laundry, cleaning supplies, toiletry supplies and services, telephone, and tobacco. Alcohol was not included, either here or in the food category.

	Proportional Weight (1917–1919)
Food	38.2%
Clothing	16.6%
Rent	13.4%
Fuel and Light	5.3%
Furniture & Furnishings	5.1%
Miscellaneous	21.3%

Sources: National Industrial Conference Board. *The Cost of Living in the United States* (New York: National Industrial Conference Board, Inc., 1925), 65–88. This NICB report is the most useful source for a general overview of the BLS index during the 1920s.

financial effects.[14] At the same time, wartime economic transformations, especially in Europe, had made the constant-goods assumption nearly impossible to uphold. Rationing and shortages limited many goods, while

[14] International Labour Office, "The Adjustment of Wages to the Cost of Living," *ILR* 3 (1921): 152–165.

others disappeared entirely; the quality of manufactured items (especially clothing) often declined; and both incomes and prices changed dramatically and at different rates, driving consumers to make substitutions and purchase new items. In sum, it was abundantly clear that prewar and postwar consumption patterns were entirely different. How to incorporate those changes into a statistical calculation was less obvious. "All the difficulties [of price index theory] are at their maximum when we deal with the problems of cost of living," warned British statistician and economist Arthur L. Bowley. "Here indeed statisticians may fear to tread, however bold the representatives of labour."[15] Bowley argued that wartime changes had rendered the British Board of Trade's cost-of-living index "purely academic" because it was based on a prewar market basket; the necessary caveats and limitations accompanying the calculation demonstrated "that the measurement has no practical importance." But, unlike in the prewar era, these failings now had serious financial effects. Bowley, for instance, argued that adjustments in working-class consumption habits had made the true inflationary rise smaller than official numbers, and that use of the Board's data in setting railway wages was unnecessarily costing the British government several million pounds per year.[16]

As of 1919, however, neither Bowley nor anyone else had a clear mechanism for saving the government from its apparent folly. How could you measure the change in the cost of living when consumption itself was changing? The problems raised by the war reinvigorated debate about index numbers in general and cost-of-living indexes in particular. The best bibliography of index-number literature lists twenty-four entries in the decade before 1914; for the 1920s, it includes 121, most of which cover price indexes.[17] While much of this literature superficially resembled the prewar discussions—filled with conflicting formulas, ideals, accusations, and angry retorts—many economists now focused more clearly and determinedly on the theoretical foundations of price indexes: exactly what were they trying to measure? And if consensus still proved elusive, it nevertheless became possible to distinguish more readily the roots of continuing disagreements.

Among European neoclassical economists, especially those in Britain, the wartime experience prompted a return to their theoretical origins. The label "neoclassical" is necessarily a loose descriptor—both then and now—but

[15] Arthur L. Bowley, "The Measurement of Changes in the Cost of Living," *Journal of the Royal Statistical Society* 82, no. 3 (1919): 346.

[16] Bowley, "Measurement of Changes in the Cost of Living," 347–348.

[17] W. F. Maunder, ed., *Bibliography of Index Numbers: An International Team Project* (London: University of London, 1970), 2–7.

a blunt categorization will serve our purposes. Particularly in Britain and America, the term "neoclassical" signified a turn away from classical political economists who based economic value in productive work. Instead, neoclassical economists declared, along with British economist William Stanley Jevons, that "value depends entirely on utility"—the value of a good, in other words, derives from the "satisfaction" or "welfare" that a consumer receives from it.[18] A standard of living was thus defined not by a particular collection of goods (which might deliver different amounts of satisfaction to different people or to the same person at different times and places) but rather by a particular level of utility (which likewise could be reached just as readily by purchasing alternative sets of goods). From this perspective, one could envision a consumption-based index number that tried to track the minimum cost of obtaining a fixed level of utility, an objective that many prewar economists recognized but only began to label as a "cost-of-living index" after those statistics sprouted across the globe:[19]

$$\text{Constant-utility index} = \frac{\text{Cost of a fixed level of utility (currently)}}{\text{Cost of the same level of utility (in base period)}}$$

Wartime economic upheaval drove British neoclassical theorists to pursue the constant-utility approach more deliberately than they had before.[20]

---

[18] Maurice Dobb, *Theories of Value and Distribution since Adam Smith: Ideology and Economic Theory* (Cambridge: Cambridge University Press, 1973). William Stanley Jevons, *The Theory of Political Economy*, 3rd ed. (London: Macmillan, 1888), 1.

[19] Both British and American economists discussed utility-based consumption standards for measuring the changing value of money, for example: Lucius S. Merrian, "The Theory of Final Utility in Its Relation to Money and the Standard of Deferred Payments," *Annals of the American Academy of Political and Social Science* (1893): 483–501; Edgeworth, "Recent Writings on Index Numbers," 161–162; Frank Fetter, "The Exploitation of Theories of Value in the Discussion of the Standard of Deferred Payments," *Annals of the American Academy of Political and Social Science* (1895): 882–896; Henry Sidgwick, *The Principles of Political Economy*, 3rd ed. (London: MacMillan, 1901), 72–73, 84–85; Thomas S. Adams, "Index Numbers and the Standard of Value, Parts I & II," *JPE* 10, no. 1 and 2 (1901): 1–31, 193–213; A. C. Pigou, *Wealth and Welfare* (London: MacMillan, 1912), 41–51. See also discussion of the "Consumption Standard" in Edgeworth's papers for the *British Association for the Advancement of Science* (1887–1889), reprinted in Francis Ysidro Edgeworth, *Papers Relating to Political Economy*, vol. 1 (London: MacMillan, 1925), 208–211, esp. n. 1 on p. 210. During the 1920s, British economists led the exposition of constant-utility indexes; American economists did not return to the subject in earnest until the 1940s.

[20] Contrast Edgeworth's prewar entry for "Index Numbers" in *Palgrave's Dictionary of Political Economy* (pp. 384–387; 1926 edition) with his postwar updates (pp. 895–896; 1926 edition).

(Only one leading American neoclassical economist, Irving Fisher, wrote about cost-of-living indexes in the 1920s, and Fisher, as we will see, was a special case.) In their eyes, widespread shortages, changes in income, and dramatic (but uneven) price rises had highlighted deep theoretical flaws in the constant-goods approach; what sense could be derived from calculating the cost of a fixed collection of goods when both the markets and consumers had changed so greatly? A proper solution could only come by returning to first principles (value rooted in utility) and building an accurate measurement focused on those objectives. As Arthur Bowley put it tentatively in 1919 and more forcefully a decade later, a cost-of-living index should reveal the "change in expenditure [that] is necessary after a change in price to obtain the same satisfaction as before."[21]

Defining that goal was one thing, however; reaching it was another. Even the most thoughtful prewar theorists who adopted the utility perspective had been thwarted by the enormous difficulty of averaging and comparing a nebulous and subjective concept like "satisfaction": such efforts were necessarily "indefinite," concluded Henry Sidgwick, or subject to "very rough methods," according to Alfred Marshall.[22] Extensive use of cost-of-living indexes for wage adjustments had greatly magnified the consequences of such ambiguity but had not made it easier to eliminate. Bowley, for instance, attacked the problem on three occasions between 1919 and 1928, ending with a different solution each time.[23] Reiterating the central importance of utility but also its resolutely amorphous nature, Francis Ysidro Edgeworth, the looming giant of British statistical economics and a formidable if eccentric intellect, urged his colleagues in 1925 to accept the reality that "index numbers for cost of living ... have not the objective character of nautical tables or reports of yesterday's weather."[24]

For many economists, however, such conclusions were unacceptable; indeed, they pointed to a fundamental weakness in orthodox theory: the concept of utility itself. How valuable was a theoretical construct that proved so elusive to empirical observation and measurement? Such questions stretched beyond the problems of price indexes alone; rather, they

---

[21] Arthur L. Bowley, "Notes on Index Numbers," *Economic Journal* 38, no. 150 (1928): 223. Cf. Bowley, "Measurement of Changes in the Cost of Living," 343, 351.

[22] Sidgwick, *The Principles of Political Economy*, 72; Alfred Marshall, "Remedies for Fluctuations of General Prices," *Contemporary Review*, no. 51 (1887): 372.

[23] Bowley, "Measurement of Changes in the Cost of Living"; Arthur L. Bowley, "Cost of Living and Wage Determination," *Economic Journal* 30, no. 117 (1920); Bowley, "Notes on Index Numbers."

[24] F. Y. Edgeworth, "The Plurality of Index-Numbers," *Economic Journal* 35, no. 139 (1925): 381–382.

swept them into a larger set of fractures among economists that appeared with greatest visibility during the interwar era, a debate over methods and goals whose fluctuating battle lines would shape American cost-of-living statistics for the rest of the twentieth century.

Institutional Economics and Price Indexes

In interwar America, the most vociferous challenge to neoclassical analysis came from "institutional" economists, a self-description first applied publicly at the 1918 meeting of the American Economics Association.[25] Prior to the 1950s and 1960s, American economics was far too diverse to be neatly categorized into a few competing schools of thought; nevertheless, the institutionalist label has proven to be a valuable category for denoting a subset of American economists linked by common interests, methods, training, and (of course) institutional ties (particularly at Columbia and Wisconsin, alongside several research organizations founded during the 1920s, such as the National Bureau of Economic Research and the Brookings Institution). Traditionally, Thorstein Veblen is cited as the founder of institutionalism, with John R. Commons and Wesley Mitchell rounding out the triumvirate. Yet as Malcolm Rutherford has argued, Veblen served as more of an inspiration than a direct founder, Commons was a latecomer (with a distinct viewpoint), and thus the early years of institutionalism owed more to Mitchell, Walton Hamilton, and John M. Clark. With their colleagues, these three pushed for a new form of economics, one that was more sensitive to institutional (hence the name) and social influences, grounded in empirical, quantitative studies, coherent with contemporary ideas from other social sciences (especially psychology), and more directly connected to applied economic analysis.[26] In the institutionalist depiction, traditional economists appeared as the archetypical armchair theorists: taking an unrealistic,

---

[25] Walton H. Hamilton, "The Institutional Approach to Economic Theory," *AER* 9, no. 1 (1919): 309–318. The full session also included papers by William Ogburn and John M. Clark.

[26] On interwar American economics, see Mary S. Morgan and Malcolm Rutherford, eds., *From Interwar Pluralism to Postwar Neoclassicism* (Durham: Duke University Press, 1998). On institutional economics, see Michael E. Starr, "The Political Economy of American Institutionalism" (Ph.D. dissertation, University of Wisconsin, Madison, 1983); Dorothy Ross, *The Origins of American Social Science* (New York: Cambridge University Press, 1991), 407–420; Yuval P. Yonay, *The Struggle over the Soul of Economics: Institutionalist and Neoclassical Economists in America between the Wars* (Princeton: Princeton University Press, 1998); Malcolm Rutherford, "Understanding Institutional Economics: 1918–1929," *Journal of the History of Economic Thought* 22, no. 3 (2000): 277–308.

ahistorical, a priori theory of human behavior and constructing deductive, abstract, untenable systems of economic thought. Increasingly, institutionalists insisted, this left economic theory isolated from the problems and tasks facing both businessmen and governments. Institutional economists aimed to bridge this division by constructing new, historically aware (and necessarily contingent) theories through the empirical study of human behavior and economic life within its dynamic context (including legal systems, technology, institutions, social and cultural norms, and so forth).[27]

The institutionalist agenda had several consequences for American cost-of-living statistics. First, institutionalist devotion to empirical study led them (and particularly Mitchell and his associates) to take great interest in improving, producing, and using statistical data. In a related vein, their commitment to applied analysis (almost always coupled with liberal-progressive political views) drew them to cooperation with—or service within—government agencies, an attraction reinforced by the greater opportunity afforded by state resources to compile extensive quantitative knowledge. Especially after the First World War, these two characteristics combined to create a close bond between institutional economists and federal statistical agencies, a connection that was, in the case of BLS price indexes, exemplified by the influence of Mitchell himself.

Mitchell's interest in price statistics had grown hand-in-hand with his early projects on monetary theory and business cycles, which he began as a doctoral student at Chicago near the turn of the century and continued throughout his career (spent largely at Columbia University). Though Mitchell only worked briefly in the federal government, he was a constant consultant on issues that interested him, including price statistics. Shortly after Royal Meeker became commissioner of the BLS in 1913, he sent out a plea to his colleagues for help in revising the bureau's price indexes; he received only two responses—one from Mitchell and one from Irving Fisher.[28] Although today Fisher may be the better-known index-number theorist, Mitchell had a far greater impact on the BLS. In 1915, the bureau published a major commentary by Mitchell on *The Making and Using of Index Numbers* (emphasizing wholesale prices indexes); a revised version appeared in 1921 and a substantial reprint in 1938, both testimony to the

---

[27] Rutherford, "Understanding Institutional Economics," 289–297; Jeff Biddle, "Social Science and the Making of Social Policy: Wesley Mitchell's Vision," in *The Economic Mind in America: Essays in the History of American Economics*, ed. Malcolm Rutherford (New York: Routledge, 1998), 43–79; Yonay, *Struggle over the Soul of Economics*, 77–99.

[28] Walter F. Wilcox et al., "The Statistical Work of the United States Government," *AER* 5, no. 1 (1915): 175.

text's continued influence on the agency.[29] Mitchell's closer ties to BLS work were abetted by his own pragmatic orientation and background. If Fisher was an unflagging social crusader and superb mathematical economist, he had limited experience producing statistical data on a large scale. By contrast, Mitchell had worked briefly in the Census Bureau after graduate school, and during the war he returned to government to lead the Price Section of the War Industries Board, an internship he capped by spending nearly a year after the armistice directing the compilation of a massive, fifty-seven-volume, *History of Prices During the War*.[30] These activities had given Mitchell a clear sense of the difficulties and possibilities surrounding federal statistical research and helped him build numerous contacts with economists who shared a similar commitment to gathering quantitative data and who would later serve in the government, including future commissioner of the BLS, Isador Lubin.

Mitchell's approach to price indexes followed directly from the weaknesses that insitutionalists saw besetting traditional economics. Attention to contemporary psychology led institutional economists to reject the neoclassical framework for economic motivation and decision making, namely the theory of marginal utility (wherein individuals made decisions based upon the net utility they anticipated deriving from each action) and hedonistic psychology (effectively Jeremy Bentham's conception of individuals as seeking pleasure and avoiding pain). Instead, following trends in the other social sciences, institutionalists such as Mitchell highlighted the effects of habit, instinct, and social and cultural influences on both consumer desires and behavior. In the institutionalist perspective, traditional economists had been led astray by their tendency to leap beyond observable facts about human action and thus to create concepts with no empirical significance. Correcting these flaws required recognizing the limits of available knowledge and restricting oneself from speculating about interior states, a theme that Mitchell emphasized in his presidential address to the American Economics Association in 1924.[31]

---

[29] Wesley C. Mitchell, *The Making and Using of Index Numbers*, BLS Bulletin, no. 173 (Washington, D.C.: U.S. GPO, 1915).

[30] Lucy Sprague Mitchell, *Two Lives: The Story of Wesley Clair Mitchell and Myself* (New York: Simon & Schuster, 1953), 95–97, 296–305, 331–332.

[31] Wesley C. Mitchell, "Quantitative Analysis in Economic Theory," *AER* 15, no. 1 (1925): 3–7. Cf. Wesley C. Mitchell, "The Backward Art of Spending Money," *AER* 2, no. 2 (1912): 269–281; John M. Clark, "Economics and Modern Psychology, Parts I & II," *JPE* 26, no. 1–2 (1918): 1–30, 136–166; Biddle, "Social Science and the Making of Social Policy," 43–58; Rutherford, "Understanding Institutional Economics," 295–297.

It should now be apparent how institutionalists would reinterpret neo-classical struggles with the constant-utility index. The subjectivity of utility was its fatal weakness, rendering it incapable of measurement and hence unsuitable for employment within an empirically minded science. The inability of neoclassical economists to construct a straightforward, constant-utility index was a sign that they were heading down a false path, chasing an ephemeral wind. A proper methodology could be derived only by avoiding the quest for elusive, subjective entities and focusing on the central observable phenomena within cost-of-living statistics: prices. In Mitchell's eyes, the measurement of price changes was akin to measuring "the weight of the atmosphere, the velocity of sound, fluctuations of temperature, and the precession of the equinoxes."[32] There was no need to develop an elaborate theory to measure price changes; rather, like their physical analogues, price changes would be the raw data upon which theory could be constructed.

From this perspective, a price index was simply an average of individual measurements, namely the "price relatives" that comprised the index, each showing the price change in a specific commodity over the period of the index. Recall, for example, the basic formula used to calculate a price index (here shown with three commodities—apples, bread, and lettuce):

$$\text{Weighted Price Index}_{1900-1915} = w_{apples} \times \frac{p_{apples}^{1915}}{p_{apples}^{1900}} + w_{bread} \times \frac{p_{bread}^{1915}}{p_{bread}^{1900}}$$

$$+ w_{lettuce} \times \frac{p_{lettuce}^{1915}}{p_{lettuce}^{1900}}$$

On an abstract level, a weighted average of price relatives looked quite different than a constant-goods, cost-of-living index. However, if the weights for the price relatives were derived from proportional expenditures on each item in the base period (as was common practice), then the situation changed. In that case, the calculation became mathematically equivalent to a constant-goods index with a base-period market basket (usually known as a Laspeyres index):[33]

---

[32] Wesley C. Mitchell, *Index Numbers of Wholesale Prices in the United States and Foreign Countries*, BLS Bulletin, no. 284 (Washington, D.C.: U.S. GPO, 1921), 10.

[33] In mathematical terms:

Weighted average of price relatives $= \sum w_n \frac{p^t}{p^0}$, where w_n is the weight for the nth price relative

Laspeyres, constant-goods index

$$= \frac{\text{Current cost of base-period "market basket"}}{\text{Original cost of base-period "market basket"}}$$

Still, if the two calculations (average of price relatives using base-period weights vs. Laspeyres, constant-goods index) gave the same results, the two different formulations highlighted different features and hence promoted different interpretations. The constant-goods formulation, for instance, drew direct attention to the "standard of living" (here defined by the market basket) that was to be held constant across both time periods: the very concept that had led neoclassical economists to adopt the constant-utility framework for cost-of-living indexes. By contrast, using the weighted-average-of-price-relatives formulation made the price relatives the salient features, a perspective that resonated with Mitchell's views.

Treating price indexes as averages of price ratios (whether weighted or not) implied that their construction and first-order interpretation did not require a systematic economic theory, only standard statistical tools and good experimental practice. Thus, for instance, Mitchell put great emphasis on studying the changing distribution of price relatives over time, a topic to which he devoted much of his 1915 treatise on index numbers and which would become a central concern for Mitchell's price-index disciple, Frederick C. Mills.[34] Most critically for our story, Mitchell recognized that the best way to investigate a phenomenon was to isolate it; hence, he aimed to keep a steady background against which the movements of prices could be observed. In turn, this pushed him to reject formulae that combined variables other than prices (such as quantities) and to recommend using a constant set of weights derived from proportionate expenditure in the base period.[35] Because this calculation was equivalent to a constant-goods index with a market basket

Constant-goods index $= \dfrac{\sum q_n p_n^t}{\sum q_n p_n^0}$, where q_n is the quantity of the nth item

With the weights equal to the proportionate expenditure on each item at base period prices, these two forms become equivalent:

$$\text{Index} = \sum_{n=1}^{N} w_n \frac{p_n^t}{p_n^0} = \sum_{n=1}^{N} \left(\frac{q_n p_n^0}{\sum_{n=1}^{N} q_n p_n^0} \right) \frac{p_n^t}{p_n^0} = \frac{\sum_{n=1}^{N} q_n p_n^t}{\sum_{n=1}^{N} q_n p_n^0}$$

[34] Mitchell, *Making and Using of Index Numbers*, 10–24; Frederick C. Mills, *The Behavior of Prices* (New York: National Bureau of Economic Research, 1927).
[35] Mitchell, *Index Numbers of Wholesale Prices*, 113.

drawn from the base period (the Laspeyres index), it reinforced and justified the constant-goods framework for cost-of-living indexes. But by basing his approach on measurements of prices (rather than the cost of a fixed standard of living), Mitchell bypassed the pitfalls that had led neoclassical economists to incorporate subjective concepts such as utility.

The full significance of Mitchell's view is best seen against the backdrop of Irving Fisher's alternative approach to index numbers. Although Irving Fisher was a leading American neoclassical economist, both he and Mitchell shared several common ideas about price indexes, including doubts about the validity of embedding utility within price statistics. (Pursuing the constant-utility standard, Fisher declared, was "as fatuous a quest as the search for the philosopher's stone.") Likewise, both men developed analogies between measuring price change and measuring physical qualities (like length). Yet Fisher's perspective on index numbers developed from his own work on the quantity theory of money, in which a price index served to measure changes in the general "price level" within the economy. That view indirectly shaped a series of "tests" that Fisher developed to determine the "best" index number formula, first in his 1911 book on *The Purchasing Power of Money* and more extensively in his 1922 magnum opus, *The Making of Index Numbers*.[36] After judging the performance of an extraordinary number of formulae within his tests, Fisher winnowed the field to an "ideal" index number (Formula 353), which was effectively a geometric average of the two basic constant-goods indexes, the Laspeyres and Paasche indexes (where the market baskets were derived from the base period and current period, respectively).[37]

---

[36] Irving Fisher, *The Purchasing Power of Money: Its Determination and Relation to Credit Interest and Crises* (New York: MacMillan, 1911), 220, 222; Irving Fisher, *The Making of Index Numbers: A Study of Their Varieties, Tests, and Reliability* (Boston: Houghton Mifflin, 1922). Robert W. Dimand, "The Quest for an Ideal Index Number: Irving Fisher and the Making of Index Numbers," in *The Economic Mind in America: Essays in the History of American Economics*, ed. Malcolm Rutherford (New York: Routledge, 1998), 128–144; Marcel Boumans, "Fisher's Instrumental Approach to Index Numbers," in *The Age of Economic Measurement*, ed. Judy L. Klein and Mary S. Morgan (Durham: Duke University Press, 2001), 313–244; H. Spencer Banzhaf, "The Form and Function of Price Indexes: A Historical Accounting," *HOPE* 36, no. 4 (2004): 591–603; Stapleford, "The 'Most Important Single Statistic,'" 115–119. Fisher's work was well-received in many circles but (not surprisingly) faced sharp criticism from British commentators for its alleged neglect of theoretical foundations.

[37] Fisher, *Making of Index Numbers*, 220–223:

$$\text{Ideal Index} = \sqrt{\left(\frac{\sum p^t q^0}{\sum p^0 q^0}\right)\left(\frac{\sum p^t q^t}{\sum p^0 q^t}\right)}$$

Mitchell's pragmatism led him to reject Fisher's claim that there could be a single, "best" index number formula suitable for all purposes.[38] But he found an equally important flaw in Fisher's inclusion of two variables: price changes and changes in the market basket. Allowing both prices and the quantities of goods purchased to vary simultaneously within the same calculation would make it difficult to interpret and keep it from being a pure measure of price change. Thus, Mitchell warned that one would be "uncertain what part of the net result is due to price fluctuations and what part to fluctuations in quantities."[39] BLS commissioner Royal Meeker signaled his own allegiance to Mitchell's framework by similarly attacking the confusion he found embedded in Fisher's "best" formula:

We have here an inextricable mixture of changes in prices and changes in quantities of goods. What does this 'ideal index' which has been achieved by so much mathematical labor, represent? Is it an index of price changes? Or is it an index of quantity changes? The answer seems clear that it is both and neither .... The all important fact is that this index does not mean anything that can be clearly grasped.[40]

To achieve clarity, a price index should only measure changes in prices; the statistician's task was to minimize the effect of any quantity changes on the price index. For the next half century, this would be the overriding goal of the Bureau of Labor Statistics' cost-of-living index and the mantra of those, like Mitchell, who supported its approach. A cost-of-living index was quite literally a "price index": ideally, it contained no varying constituents other than prices.

Cost-of-Living Indexes in Practice

The BLS's adherence to the constant-goods index should not be attributed solely to the influence of American institutional economists such as Mitchell. On the contrary, support for the constant-goods approach came pouring forth from government statistical offices worldwide during the 1920s. Thus, when a conference of labor statisticians organized by the International Labour Office considered cost-of-living indexes in 1925, the group declared that "the items in the budget and the weights [in short,

---

[38] See Mitchell's comments in Irving Fisher, "The Best Form of Index Number," *Quarterly PASA* 17, no. 133 (1921): 537. H. Spencer Banzhaf, "The Form and Function of Price Indexes," 591–603.

[39] Mitchell, *Index Numbers of Wholesale Prices*, 93.

[40] Royal Meeker, "On the Best Form of Index Number," *Quarterly PASA* 17, no. 135 (1921): 912.

the market basket] must of course remain unchanged during the whole period covered by the index numbers, for they are the standard by which prices—the variable factor—are measured and reduced to a single term." Likewise, the host of cost-of-living indexes created across the globe during and after the war were based as far as practicable on the constant-goods ideal.[41] The growing ties between institutional economists and the BLS did not, therefore, lead to an overhaul of the agency's orientation; on the contrary, the BLS had been following a constant-goods approach for its retail price indexes since they were first started by Carroll Wright. Rather, Mitchell's analysis helped the bureau clarify and justify its approach, providing an explicit statement of principles and the sanctioning authority of an academic economist, functions that institutional economists continued to fulfill over the next decades.

The parallels between the views of American institutional economics and the practices of government statisticians reflected the deep empiricism common to both, an empiricism that was not (and could not be) merely an abstract ideal. The constant-utility index fell far short of these requirements. Although it won a growing number of adherents among academic theorists from the 1930s on, the inability to translate the theoretical objective into functioning statistics beyond highly implausible special cases rendered the constant-utility ideal largely irrelevant to actual price indexes. Thus, even in Britain, where neoclassical economists defended the constant-utility ideal most vociferously during the 1920s and 1930s, the official government retail price index remained a constant-goods index due to the lack of "trust-worthy statistics" that could allow adjustments for changing consumption patterns.[42] Likewise, when Hans Staehle, economist at the International Labour Office and supporter of the constant-utility approach, reviewed the work on utility-based indexes in 1935, his assessment was rather bleak: "It is unfortunately typical of a great deal of present-day work in economics that ... few of the above mentioned authors ... seem to have considered seriously whether the assumptions on which their unquestionably elegant theories were based, were either generally admissible in practice or could in any way be verified."[43] Mounting a serious challenge to the constant-goods

---

[41] International Labour Office, "Second Conference of Labour Statisticians," *ILR* 25, no. 1 (1925): 3, 19; International Labour Office, "Prices and Cost of Living," 171–178.

[42] Ministry of Labour, *The Cost of Living Index Number: Method of Compilation* (London: H. M. Stationery Office, 1931), 3–4.

[43] Hans Staehle, "A Development of the Economic Theory of Price Index Numbers," *Review of Economic Studies* 2, no. 3 (1935): 170. Of course, previous failures did not stop Staehle from pursuing his own (ultimately unsuccessful) resolution.

approach would require overcoming these obstacles and building a tighter connection to practical calculations. Consequently, the constant-utility index remained a solely academic topic until well into the latter half of the twentieth century; how and under what conditions neoclassical economists returned to active participation in the debates over actual cost-of-living statistics will be discussed in Chapter 8.

Still, if government statisticians were freed from substantial debate with neoclassical theorists, they could less easily escape the problems—like quality changes and shifts in consumption patterns—that had revitalized discussion of the constant-utility index in the first place. Recognizing these issues, government officials and their allies did not reinvent their conceptual premises but rather adopted methodological solutions consistent with the constant-goods framework. For instance, since financial and practical considerations made it impossible to track the prices of all goods purchased by working-class families, cost-of-living indexes typically excluded items where quality change was frequent and significant, such as fresh produce.[44] For highly variable goods that also attracted a high proportion of expenditures—notably clothing, house furnishings, and (in the diet of the times) potatoes—scrupulous statisticians recognized that exclusion was not a viable option and had to confront the problem head-on, often aware that they had only partial answers. For clothing and house furnishings, for example, the BLS tried to maintain a reasonable continuity in the index by instituting what would later be known as "specification pricing," in which field agents visited participating stores and used past descriptions to guide the selection of similar items for pricing from one time period to the next.[45]

For the more general problem of changes in the market basket, approaches varied. In Austria, confronting the dramatic shifts in consumption during the war, Felix Klezl sidestepped the issue by basing the official cost-of-living index on a theoretical market basket that included those "principal articles of necessity" still available in the 1920s. On the other hand (while admittedly facing a less devastated economy), the British Ministry of Labor rejected the "arbitrary" nature of "minimum of subsistence" estimates, choosing instead to stick with a prewar market basket as the only empirically grounded approach (despite the difficulty of interpreting the significance

---

[44] Cf. Ugo Giusti, "Methods of Recording Retail Prices and Measuring the Cost of Living in Italy," *ILR* 4, no. 2 (1921): 267; Ministry of Labour, *The Cost of Living Index Number*, 4. U.S. Bureau of Labor Statistics, *Methods of Procuring and Computing Statistical Information of the Bureau of Labor Statistics*, BLS Bulletin, no. 326 (Washington, D.C.: U.S. GPO, 1923), 22–23.

[45] U.S. Bureau of Labor Statistics, *Methods of Procuring and Computing*, 15.

of this measure after dramatic changes in consumption). Meanwhile, the American bureau followed what would later become a common procedure worldwide: using a "chain index" to shift market baskets over time (a method first proposed by British economist Alfred Marshall, and later supported by Wesley Mitchell).[46]

The chain index developed from the recognition that a constant-goods index could be re-described as the product of a series of smaller indexes, all using the same market basket but covering subsets of the original time period. For example, an index, I, describing price changes from 1920 to 1923, could be re-written as:[47]

$$I_{1920-1923} = (I_{1920-21}) \times (I_{1921-22}) \times (I_{1922-23})$$

One could thus view any index number as a string of smaller indexes, and then imagine replacing some of the "links" with price indexes based on altered market baskets. For instance, to return to our previous example, one could switch from market basket A to market basket B in 1922 as follows:

$$I_{1920-1923} = (I_{1920-21,\ Basket\ A}) \times (I_{1921-22,\ Basket\ A}) \times (I_{1922-23,\ Basket\ B})$$

Effectively, the chain index spliced together different constant-goods indexes. During the 1920s, the BLS used this procedure primarily for expansions or contractions of coverage (such as when it began pricing 42 rather than 22 food items in 1921) and when it was forced to make substitutions as items disappeared from shelves, stores closed, and so forth. Later, the technique would become standard procedure for major changes as well.

Of course none of these strategies offered complete solutions. Defining adequate specifications for pricing was a tricky business, and it left untouched the larger difficulty about what to do when no comparable items could be found or when new goods appeared. Chain indexes incorporating multiple market baskets could handle such changes and many others,

---

[46] On Austria and Britain, see International Labour Office, "Prices and Cost of Living," 173; International Labour Office, "Second Conference of Labour Statisticians," 4; Ministry of Labour, *The Cost of Living Index Number*, 4. Mitchell, *Making and Using of Index Numbers*, 114; Marshall, "Remedies for Fluctuations of General Prices," 373–375.

[47] The mathematical equivalence is easy to see in algebraic terms:

$$I_{1920-1923} = I_{1920-1921} \times I_{1921-1922} \times I_{1922-1923}$$

$$= \frac{\Sigma q_n p_n^{1921}}{\Sigma q_n p_n^{1920}} \times \frac{\Sigma q_n p_n^{1922}}{\Sigma q_n p_n^{1921}} \times \frac{\Sigma q_n p_n^{1923}}{\Sigma q_n p_n^{1922}} = \frac{\Sigma q_n p_n^{1923}}{\Sigma q_n p_n^{1920}}$$

but only by sacrificing the straightforward interpretation that had made the constant-goods index so attractive in the first place: while the meaning of any individual "link" might be clear, it was harder to grasp the significance of the larger composite result.[48]

Over time, critiques of the working solutions developed in the 1920s would prompt economists to reconsider the conceptual basis for official cost-of-living indexes. For most government statisticians during the interwar period, however, theoretical worries were dwarfed by more pressing practical concerns, such as gathering and compiling reliable price data quickly and efficiently, or maintaining a sufficient and representative sample of goods and stores. Having spent time in government offices, Mitchell recognized that "field work is not only fundamental, it is also laborious, expensive, and perplexing beyond any other part of the whole investigation." Naturally, "practical makers of index numbers … seldom troubled themselves greatly about theoretical refinements of method." Moreover, the institutional context for existing cost-of-living statistics—created on the fly during times of economic upheaval and usually operating under substantial financial constraints—meant that few indexes could approach the simplicity envisioned in abstract discussions. Even the BLS cost-of-living index— established after the most extensive and detailed expenditure survey in any country, operating in a wealthy nation minimally affected by the war, and containing by far the most comprehensive list of items for pricing—still reflected the messy complexity of its ad hoc, wartime origins.[49] Though the BLS made 1913 the base period for its cost-of-living index (to show prewar comparisons), price data prior to 1917 was spotty at best, many cities were spliced into the index at later dates, and the expenditure survey that set the market basket occurred not in 1913 (the base period) but in 1918–1919. These inconsistencies led many critics to complain that the index had an upward bias because it overemphasized the importance of those goods that had become most expensive during the war.[50]

---

[48] In 1921, Mitchell himself expressed doubts about the wisdom of compiling long chains of index numbers with different baskets: Mitchell, *Index Numbers of Wholesale Prices*, 113.

[49] Mitchell, *Making and Using of Index Numbers*, 27, 80–81. For the comparative strength of the U.S. index, see International Labour Office, "Prices and Cost of Living," 171–178. On German struggles to create a national index, see J. Adam Tooze, *Statistics and the German State, 1900–1945: The Making of Modern Economic Knowledge* (Cambridge: Cambridge University Press, 2001), 90–96.

[50] Paul H. Douglas, *Real Wages in the United States, 1890–1926* (Boston: Houghton Mifflin, 1930), 44–46; National Industrial Conference Board, *The Cost of Living in the United States* (New York: National Industrial Conference Board, 1925), 65–66. George E. Barnett, "Index Numbers of the Total Cost of Living," *QJE* 35, no. 2 (1921): 249–250.

Overall, the war had prompted the rapid development of cost-of-living indexes but likewise highlighted the obstacles facing constant-goods indexes. Nevertheless, insofar as debates about these problems affected actual statistics, they were addressed at a methodological level rather than a conceptual level, framed by the constant-goods ideal. Indeed, the inability to create a practical constant-utility index made the dominance of the constant-goods approach inevitable. To note this working consensus is not to minimize the serious questions raised about cost-of-living indexes in this period; as the examples above and others below will illustrate, skeptics found plenty of reasons to critique the significance of BLS price statistics. But it does help us to understand why the conceptual arguments about cost-of-living indexes that appeared in professional journals rarely affected the methodology of actual statistics and failed to intersect with the more salient and critical debate about the relevance of cost-of-living figures to wages. It is to those discussions that we now turn.

WAGE ADJUSTMENTS AND COST-OF-LIVING STATISTICS

While academic economists debated the theoretical underpinnings of cost-of-living indexes, labor unions, companies, and government officials sought to use these and other statistics to fashion a new "normalcy" in industrial relations. The war had promoted national, managerial oversight of labor relations led by the federal government and embodied in rule-governed arbitration systems increasingly dependent on national economic statistics (notably BLS cost-of-living statistics). When the federal government began dismantling its managerial system after the November peace declaration (with the eager prompting of businessmen and many unions), the struggle to establish a new order began.

Labor unions entered 1919 with militant dreams, exemplified by the general strike in Seattle during the early part of the year and a cascading wave of subsequent strikes that involved roughly 4 million workers nationwide. In the end, of course, the combination of a renewed open-shop campaign by employers, the Red Scare, and especially the 1920–1921 depression crushed these hopes, muting labor activism and rapidly reducing union membership.[51] Nevertheless, the industrial struggles that characterized the early postwar era, though no less bitter than prewar conflict, had a recognizably

---

[51] David Montgomery, *The Fall of the House of Labor: The Workplace, the State, and American Labor Activism, 1865–1925* (Cambridge: Cambridge University Press, 1987), 399–409; Dana Frank, *Purchasing Power: Consumer Organizing, Gender, and the Seattle Labor Movement, 1919–1929* (Cambridge: Cambridge University Press, 1994), 15–107; Dubofsky, *The State & Labor in Modern America*, 78–97.

different form and context. Partially this reflected the legacy of the war-time system of labor management: arbitration boards that survived the armistice (especially in coal and transportation), former wartime officials who became consulting industrial relations experts (including Jett Lauck, William Ogburn, and Paul Douglas), and the logic of the wartime wage decisions themselves. Cost-of-living statistics, for example, had played only a minor role in prewar bargaining and wage disputes; in the aftermath of wartime policies and continuing price volatility, they became far more central to the resolution of industrial conflict in the 1920s.

Perhaps the most critical factor was the growing acceptance of an "associational order" (to borrow Ellis Hawley's phrase) among a broad base of trade unions, pro-labor intellectuals, and moderate businessmen (especially those in large, profitable companies insulated from competition). In the associational vision, efficiency, economic growth, and social justice within an industrialized, mass economy required the organization and collaboration of both workers and businesses. Though this perspective had clear roots in the moderate coporatism of the late nineteenth and early twentieth centuries (exemplified by the National Civic Federation, see Chapter 1), the combination of technical expertise, planning, and collaboration that supporters claimed had spawned the wartime production boom garnered a wider range of converts within the business community and established networks of enthusiastic professionals eager to adopt the methods in a demobilized economy. Whereas the wartime state had structured groups and relationships by fiat, Americans would now be given freer rein to self-organize and cooperate for mutual gain, all with the guidance of experts (from economists, lawyers, management consultants, etc.) and the light hand of an "associative state" (promoted most vigorously by President Warren G. Harding's new Secretary of Commerce, Herbert Hoover). Lubricating this interlocking machine would be flows of neutral, reliable, quantitative information on prices, trade, production, employment, wages, and other critical features of the economy, all of which would allow groups to establish a firm basis for negotiation and action. Social science expertise featured prominently in this model, whether deployed from within government agencies, business associations, or the newly created, private think tanks that formed after the war, most notably the National Bureau of Economic Research led by Wesley Mitchell.[52]

---

[52] Ellis W. Hawley, "Herbert Hoover, the Commerce Secretariat, and the Vision of an 'Associative State,' 1921–1929," *JAH* 61, no. 1 (1974): 116–140; Guy Alchon, *The Invisible Hand of Planning: Capitalism, Social Science, and the State in the 1920s* (Princeton: Princeton

In practice, of course, the associational order proved far more chaotic and unbalanced than idealistic proponents described. Common praise for a "new era" masked substantial disagreement about what it entailed: businessmen formed trade associations and pushed to limit anti-monopoly regulation while seeking to confine worker organization to company "unions"; labor leaders struggled for their independence and formed alliances with consumer groups to battle price-gouging and trusts. The competition endemic to a free-market system undermined any deep collaboration, not only between businesses and workers as collective groups, but even among individual companies and among workers themselves.[53] What emerged, therefore, was not a coordinated system, but a fragmented political economy dominated by individual firms. Meanwhile, labor statistics—and particularly cost-of-living statistics—failed to produce the consensus and rationalized justice that proponents had envisioned. Whereas the war had promoted an increasingly standardized, national system of wage adjustments based on fixed procedures and grounded in federal statistics, the 1920s saw a rise in managerial and bureaucratic discretion resting on pluralistic, conflicting quantitative knowledge. Far from knitting industrial relations together into a cohesive and stable set of wage policies, postwar cost-of-living statistics replicated the fragmentation of the associational order itself.

Wages and Price Statistics in an Associational Order

By the end of the war, key arbitration boards had embedded BLS cost-of-living statistics in proto-indexation clauses that promised to adjust wages (often on a national basis) when prices rose. During the 1950s, similar clauses would become commonplace in industrial relations, and indexation would later develop into a basic administrative tool for the federal government. As the history of industrial relations in the 1920s illustrates, however, the subsequent prominence of national indexation depended upon particular political and economic circumstances that promoted both national standardization and reliance on rule-governed administrative systems. During the 1920s,

University Press, 1985); William Leach, *Land of Desire: Merchants, Power, and the Rise of a New American Culture* (New York: Pantheon Books, 1993), 349–378; Paul A. C. Koistinen, *Mobilizing for Modern War: The Political Economy of American Warfare, 1865–1919* (Lawrence: University Press of Kansas, 1997), 266–267.

53 Montgomery, *Fall of the House of Labor*, 411–464; Colin Gordon, *New Deals: Business, Labor, and Politics in America, 1920–1935* (Cambridge: Cambridge University Press, 1994), 35–165; Meg Jacobs, *Pocketbook Politics: Economic Citizenship in Twentieth-Century America* (Princeton: Princeton University Press, 2005), 86–90.

pressure for the latter existed only in distinct domains—namely within large companies and those few industries (such as printing) that featured relatively strong unions and relatively low competition. National standardization had even less support. Accordingly, the ties linking wages to statistical calculation loosened and BLS cost-of-living statistics lost their dominant place in industrial relations, as companies and federal arbitrators turned to a host of competing measures.[54] Overall, analysis of the cost-of-living adjustments in the 1920s provides a useful foil to the later dominance of national indexation, showing how extensively economic and political circumstances (even leaving aside the course of prices themselves) drove the reliance on automatic cost-of-living escalation based upon national statistics.

At first glance, the trajectory of the BLS cost-of-living index during the 1920s would seem to explain the low interest in escalator clauses in this period. After June 1920, the BLS index dropped precipitously and then varied within a small range (Chart 3.1). Certainly this fall in prices helped eliminate union support for cost-of-living adjustments. Yet price trends alone do not tell the full story, as international comparisons make clear: British wages, for example, had perhaps the greatest dependence on escalator clauses during the 1920s, even though the Ministry of Labour's retail price index showed a similar drop after 1920.[55] Meanwhile, extraordinary postwar inflation prompted both Austria and Germany to experiment with automatic escalation linked to an official index, only to scale back these efforts when the mechanism was deemed inadequate.[56] Moreover, even near the height of the American price fluctuations in the early 1920s, automatic adjustment based on the BLS index was rare. A bureau survey in 1921–1922 found that of the responding firms who considered the "cost of living" when

[54] On the minor place of automatic cost-of-living adjustment clauses in this period, see Henry Lowenstern, "Adjusting Wages to Living Costs: A Historical Note," *MLR* 97, no. 7 (1974): 21–26; Sanford M. Jacoby, "The Development of Cost-of-Living Escalators in the United States," *Labor History* 28, no. 4 (1987): 522–525.

[55] Brian R. Mitchell, *British Historical Statistics* (Cambridge: Cambridge University Press, 1988), 39. International Labour Office, "Adjustment of Wages," 161–162. As the British index fluctuated, so did the number of workers covered by "sliding-scale" agreements, from a high of 3 million in 1922 to 1.25 million in 1933. Nevertheless, even the lower number remained significantly higher than in the United States, both in absolute terms and relative to the total population of non-agricultural workers: Arthur George Pool, *Wage Policy in Relation to Industrial Fluctuations* (London: Macmillan, 1938), 256–258; Rodney Lowe, *Adjusting to Democracy: The Role of the Ministry of Labour, 1911–1939* (Oxford: Oxford University Press, 1986), 100–101.

[56] Carl Forchheimer, "Sliding Wage Scales in Austria," *ILR* 10, no. 1 (1924): 30–47; Fritz Sitzler, "The Adaptation of Wages to the Depreciation of the Currency in Germany," *ILR* 9, no. 5 (1924): 643–666.

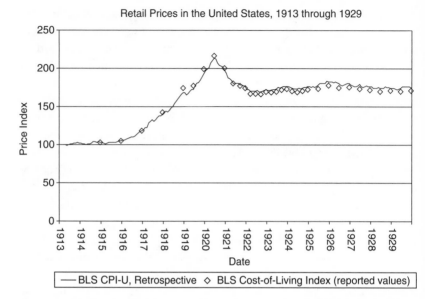

Chart 3.1: Retail Prices in the United States through December 1929. The solid line shows retrospective estimates of national price trends for all consumers as calculated by the BLS in the late twentieth century. Diamond shapes mark actual reported values for the BLS national cost-of-living index during this period.
Sources: BLS, Historical CPI-U (BLS website; updated May 2008); *Monthly Labor Review*, various issues.

adjusting wages, only 3 percent utilized the BLS cost-of-living index in a "definite" (i.e., rule-governed) way.

The minimal role of BLS statistics reflected two interlocking forms of skeptical caution: lack of agreement about a single, authoritative cost-of-living index and a widespread reluctance to commit to a purely mechanical, rule-governed adjustment system. According to the 1921–1922 survey, only about 60 percent of firms making cost-of-living adjustments used one source exclusively for their analysis, and of these, only roughly one-third chose BLS price indexes, with the remaining two-thirds split between wholesale indexes, cost-of-living statistics from various business sources (including individual firms and business associations), and "general information" drawn from the community. Furthermore, just 9 percent of firms making cost-of-living adjustments did so in a "definite" (rule-governed) way, again with roughly two-thirds using non-BLS statistics as the primary basis for their calculations.[57]

---

[57] Elma B. Carr, *The Use of Cost-of-Living Figures in Wage Adjustments*, BLS Bulletin, no. 369 (Washington, D.C.: U.S. GPO, 1925). The figures given above are based on my more detailed analysis of Carr's study in Stapleford, "The 'Most Important Single Statistic'," 197–213.

This combination of managerial discretion and pluralistic statistical calculation was grounded in part on the methodological ambiguities in price
indexes noted above, which became manifest during the 1920s as competing
measures of changes in the cost of living produced different results.[58] An
excellent example was the monthly, national cost-of-living index published
by the National Industrial Conference Board (NICB) beginning in 1918. The
exact divergence between the BLS and NICB calculations varied over time
and occasionally disappeared, but was substantial enough to promote alternately subtle or direct criticism from both sides. BLS statisticians blamed the
split on inconsistencies and unreliable techniques used in the NICB index,
particularly the board's choice to gather price data through questionnaires
mailed to retailers across the United States. For its part, the NICB insisted
that visits by BLS field agents (who gathered data on clothing, house furnishings, and rent) irritated businessmen (which might lead to inaccuracies),
and more importantly, made a timely, comprehensive measure prohibi-
tively expensive.[59] Here the NICB struck its most effective blow. The bureau's
national cost-of-living index only appeared quarterly and was based entirely
on thirty-two industrial cities. The latter reflected the index's wartime origin, containing the original eighteen shipbuilding centers plus Washington,
D.C., and an additional thirteen cities considered important in size or industrial concentration. Together, these cities were home to approximately 20
percent of the population according to the 1920 Census. But it was a relatively homogenous sample, drawn exclusively from urban, industrial areas.[60]
Accordingly, the NICB complained that "the Bureau's so-called index for the
country ... is merely a by-product of these local indexes"; by contrast, questionnaires allowed the board to maintain a much broader coverage, including areas "of varying sizes, geographical location and industrial conditions"
that it insisted had experienced lower price rises than major cities.[61]

---

[58] Cf. Leo Wolman, "The Cost of Living and Wage Cuts," *New Republic*, 27 January 1921, 238.
[59] National Industrial Conference Board, *Family Budgets of American Wage-Earners: A
Critical Analysis* (New York: Century, 1921), 1; Elma B. Carr, "Cost of Living Statistics of
U.S. Bureau of Labor Statistics and the National Industrial Conference Board: Comparison
of Methods," *JASA* 19, no. 148 (1924): 484–507; Virgil Jordan, "The Cost of Living Indices
of the N.I.C.B. and of the B.L.S.," *JASA* 20, no. 150 (1925): 249–253.
[60] The thirteen additional cities were Atlanta, Birmingham, Cincinnati, Denver, Indianapolis,
Kansas City, Memphis, Minneapolis, New Orleans, Pittsburgh, Richmond, St. Louis, and
Scranton. Population data from U.S. Census Bureau, *Statistical Abstract of the United
States, 2001* (Washington, D.C: U.S. GPO, 2001), 8.
[61] Jordan, "The Cost of Living Indices," 252; National Industrial Conference Board, *Cost of
Living in the United States*, 122–123; National Industrial Conference Board, *Family Budgets
of American Wage-Earners*, 1.

Compounding these basic methodological trade-offs—such as inexpensive questionnaires against more controlled and detailed personal interviews—the economic diversity of the United States was itself the greatest spur to competing cost-of-living calculations. As BLS statisticians collected cost-of-living data during the war, they recognized that price fluctuations could vary dramatically from city to city, divergences that did not disappear after the country began to readjust to a peacetime economy: by December 1924, prices in Detroit had risen 65 percent over the previous seven years; at the opposite extreme was Atlanta, where prices were up only 15 percent.[62] Such variance perplexed those forced to make some sort of national judgment. After consulting numerous statistics in 1921, the U.S. Railroad Board declared that "it is practically impossible to find any exact average line of decrease [in the cost of living] for the entire country." Stymied by the inconsistency, the board could only conclude that "there has been a decrease, and the tendency is at present downward."[63] Invariably, such diversity undercut the relevance of national price statistics to wages at specific factories. Even as the NICB faulted the bureau's national index, many arbitrators and firms preferred to use alternative, local information about the cost of living, and in some cases calculated figures for a specific group of employees even when the BLS published a relevant city index. According to the bureau's 1921–1922 survey, roughly 40 percent of the companies making cost-of-living adjustments used non-BLS, local information about prices as their main source, including material from business associations, local governments, nearby universities, individual firms, and newspapers.[64] Just as the state bureaus had given multiple approaches to statistics room to flourish in previous years—thereby impeding easy consolidation—the institutional pluralism of the 1920s' "associational order" mapped onto the economic diversity of the nation to produce a plethora of alternative measures of the cost of living.

[62] National Industrial Conference Board, *Cost of Living in the United States*, 191, 197. Elma B. Carr, "Comparison of Food Costs in 45 Cities, September, 1917, to October, 1918," *MLR* 7, no. 11 (1918): 1252–1253; Hugh S. Hanna, "Summary of Increased Cost of Living, July 1914 to June 1919," *MLR* 9, no. 4 (1919): 991–992.

[63] U.S. Railroad Board, New York Central Railroad Case (1921), quoted in Herbert Feis, *A Collection of Decisions Presenting Principles of Wage Settlement* (New York: H.W. Wilson, 1924), 251.

[64] Carr, *Use of Cost-of-Living Figures*, 355, 434–435; Victor Rosewater, "Wages, Budgets, Cost of Living," *AER* 11, no. 4 (1921): 660. According to Carr's statistics, 11% of responding firms who had made cost-of-living adjustments used non-BLS, local statistics (supplied by local governments, universities, business associations, or the firm itself). An additional 28% relied on "general information" that was primarily local ("newspaper clippings, bank reports, and general observation").

Finally, while regional variance raised questions about the local significance of national cost-of-living figures, economic disparities between industries (and firms) complicated any uniform application of cost-of-living adjustments. A company's profits might not increase at the same rate as a general average of retail prices, whether because of industry-wide conditions or factors specific to an individual firm. Not surprisingly, employers regularly used this reasoning to justify smaller raises or deeper cuts than the cost-of-living statistics alone might suggest, or to explain the irrelevance of cost-of-living arguments altogether. From the opposite side, unions frequently argued that cost-of-living increases alone were insufficient, since earlier wage rates at the company or industry in question had been too low to begin with. In either case, the net effect was the same: to loosen the ties between price indexes and wages and hence complicate any simple, automatic adjustment scheme.[65]

Ambiguous methodology and economic diversity thus created a reasonable groundwork for undercutting the authoritative reach of the BLS cost-of-living index. But neither of these factors was novel: both had existed during the war (when BLS price statistics had been much more influential and been embedded in nearly mechanical systems of wage adjustment) and both could be found in other countries (such as Britain or Belgium) where official government figures nevertheless carried more weight.[66] Rather, the crucial missing feature was a combination of political and economic pressures sufficient to compel adherence to a uniform, rule-governed system to regulate wages. What emerged instead was a fragmented form of industrial relations in which competing groups (businesses, unions, government agencies) tried to use statistics to achieve order and control in their own local context without the standardizing pressures imposed by war mobilization or a well-organized, national economic interest group.

Labor arbitration, which had been the original impetus for the BLS index, provides a good example. With the dismantling of federal, wartime machinery for labor management, significant use of arbitration dwindled to a small number of industries led by traditional craft unions (such as printing) or where critical commercial interest motivated government intervention (such as transportation or coal). Though it remained more prevalent than in prewar days, arbitration nevertheless became less common and less

[65] Feis, *Principles of Wage Settlement*; Carr, *Use of Cost-of-Living Figures*, 430.
[66] Pool, *Wage Policy*, 255–285; Peter Scholliers, "Index-Linked Wages, Purchasing Power and Social Conflict between the Wars: The Belgian Approach (Internationally Compared)," *Journal of European Economic History* 20, no. 2 (1991): 407–439.

dramatic after the 1920–1921 recession sapped the strength of labor unions and compounded failed attempts to nationalize key industries (coal and railroads).[67] With the (not unrelated) fading of these two impulses—heavy federal oversight of labor relations and strong national unions—the push for national wage standardization evaporated rapidly, and with it much of the justification for clinging to a single set of national cost-of-living statistics.[68]

Where arbitration did occur, the removal of wartime mobilization pressures permitted a drift away from the rule-governed mechanisms of the NWLB and especially SLAB, and back toward a quasi-legal model that emphasized a combination of reasoned argument, negotiation, and veiled economic power. As a result, both sides presented their own evidence about economic conditions (including the cost of living), contested opposing or official statistics (including the BLS index), and left arbitrators to muddle their way through. Some boards responded by mounting their own independent studies; others tried to adjudicate between competing claims. Neither solution proved fully satisfying to critics or participants: one commentator dryly noted that students seeking knowledge of index number methodology would "not find the matter well presented in the literature of wage disputes." Faced with conflicting proposals and statistical estimates, many arbitrators simply aimed somewhere down the middle.[69] The enterprise was a testament to the inability of technical expertise to offer more than limited guidance for resolving labor disputes in the absence of sufficient political or economic pressure to force a stable solution, and it tended to magnify rather than reduce differences in statistical methodology and argument.

The influence of price statistics on wages was not confined to arbitration during the 1920s, however, which leads us to two questions: why did some companies voluntarily adopt cost-of-living adjustments, and why did they make those adjustments based on a variety of conflicting methods and sources of information? The initial impetus clearly came in response to labor activism: workers had called incessantly for wage hikes during the rapid price rises of the war and early postwar era. When prices began to

---

[67] On the failures in coal and railroads, see Montgomery, *Fall of the House of Labor*, 385–410; Dubofsky, *The State & Labor in Modern America*, 89–97.

[68] Carr, "Comparison of Food Costs," 1248; Hanna, "Summary of Increased Cost of Living to June 1919," 991–992. Federal arbitration boards made the most consistent use of BLS statistics: Carr, *Use of Cost-of-Living Figures*, 432.

[69] Feis, *Principles of Wage Settlement*, 205, 191–192; George Soule, *Wage Arbitration: Selected Cases, 1920–1924* (New York: MacMillan, 1928), 82, 94; Carr, *Use of Cost-of-Living Figures*, 23–33.

fall, some employers seized the reverse argument for their own ends, now seeking cost-of-living reductions. In either case, however, employer action was driven by concerns about labor: first, the need to make limited wage increases to appease restive employees, and later, the desire to blunt reactions to wage cuts by providing a justification previously advanced by workers themselves.[70]

Individual companies imposed this self-regulation—in which managerial discretion over wages was constrained to greater or lesser degrees by empirical study—in response to a variety of specific business contexts that made it a worthwhile sacrifice. Active labor unions, of course, provided a significant impetus, particularly when (as in printing) employers could obtain long-term contracts in exchange for cost-of-living adjustments.[71] But the direct reach of unions was limited—especially after the 1920–1921 recession and an open-shop campaign dropped union membership from 5 million to 3.6 million and kept organized labor outside most mass-production and heavy industry sectors. Nevertheless, the fear of unionization exerted a broader influence, and while embattled firms in highly competitive, low-skill industries relied on force and job insecurity to maintain an open shop, more prosperous and better-insulated companies could balance their threats with offers to maintain purchasing power in the face of rising prices, one component of the anti-union strategies subsequently dubbed "welfare capitalism." Such techniques, along with their inevitable accompaniment—the company union—were particularly attractive to local-market firms (dependent on local community support) and mass-production enterprises that needed a stable, organized workforce but feared the loss of shop-floor control that could come with an external union. Coupled with these defensive, union-centered motivations were internal desires to rationalize and organize wage and salary procedures, especially within large companies, all part of a broader movement toward centralizing personnel administration within specific bureaucratic units under the leadership of new, industrial-relations experts.[72] Though cost-of-living adjustments were not necessary elements

[70] Wolman, "The Cost of Living and Wage Cuts," 239; Feis, *Principles of Wage Settlement*, 250; Carr, *Use of Cost-of-Living Figures*, 350.

[71] On printing and cost-of-living escalators, see Francis H. Bird, "The Cost of Living as a Factor in Recent Wage Adjustments in the Book and Job Branch of the Chicago Printing Industry," *AER* 11, no. 4 (1921): 622–642; Jacoby, "The Development of Cost-of-Living Escalators," 524–525.

[72] Kim McQuaid, "Corporate Liberalism in the American Business Community, 1920–1940," *Business History Review* 52, no. 3 (1978): 345–349; Sanford M. Jacoby, *Employing Bureaucracy: Managers, Unions, and the Transformation of Work in American Industry* (New York: Columbia University Press, 1985), 13–205; Montgomery, *Fall of the House*

for such systems, they fit easily into them, providing a simple mechanism and rationale for shifting the basic wage rates for large numbers of employees. Significantly, an early issue of the *Bulletin of the Taylor Society* (devoted to rationalizing labor relations and industrial production under the control of enlightened management) contained an article by an open-shop employer praising cost-of-living adjustments for reducing labor agitation.[73] Likewise, during the mid-1930s, large, mass-production companies (such as Standard Oil, General Electric, and U.S. Steel) adopted automatic, cost-of-living clauses as they battled a resurgent industrial unionism.[74]

Employer perspectives on cost-of-living statistics were partially shaped by their defensive posture on the issue. Businesses and trade associations such as the NICB created their own statistics as alternatives to union statistics or those of federal agencies perceived to be unduly sympathetic to labor (namely the BLS). Accordingly, business leaders tended to emphasize the ambiguity of such measures. Thus, when the BLS criticized the NICB cost-of-living index, NICB economist (and future president) Virgil Jordan defended the board's methods but also denied that there could be a single, authoritative measure "in so vague and vast a field." Jordan denounced BLS complaints as a "stone-throwing spree in a village of statistical glass houses," and lamented the "unfortunate implication" that "everything in the Bureau's index ... is based on the tables of scientific law handed down from some statistical Sinai."[75]

These pluralist instincts were reinforced by the dominant position companies held in labor relations during most of the 1920s. Since individual firms were embedded in different economic contexts (geographical regions, financial conditions, labor needs, etc.) with different institutional resources and access to technical knowledge about price statistics, invariably they adopted a host of different sources of information and methods for making adjustments. These factors are illustrated by context-dependent trends that appear in the 1921–1922 BLS survey of cost-of-living wage adjustments, especially those trends linked to a rough measurement of average company size (the ratio of total employees to total firms in each category).[76] Firms

of Labor, 411–457; Frank, *Purchasing Power*, 3; Gordon, *New Deals*, 87–127; Dubofsky, *The State & Labor in Modern America*, 79. Union membership statistics from Jacoby, pp. 171–173.

[73] Leroy D. Williams and Alfred B. Holt, "Cost of Living in Relation to Wage Adjustments," *Bulletin of the Taylor Society* 4, no. 5 (1919): 32–33, 42–43.

[74] Lowenstern, "Adjusting Wages to Living Costs," 22; Jacoby, "The Development of Cost-of-Living Escalators," 525, n. 20.

[75] Jordan, "The Cost of Living Indices," 250–251.

[76] Data from Carr, *Use of Cost-of-Living Figures*, 434–435. Unfortunately, individual returns are not available, making it impossible to calculate a true "average size," much less analyze

relying on "general information" rather than explicit statistics were by far the smallest (640 employees/firm), and companies using multiple sets of statistics were (on average) 50 percent larger than those using one figure only (2,700 vs. 1,850). The highest aggregate employee/firm ratio (approximately 8,000) came from firms who used price statistics in a "definite" (rule-governed) rather than "general" way. Together, these examples illustrate that the ability and desire to rationalize labor relations using quantified data increased with the size of a company, as larger firms sought order and efficient management of their labor force through rule-governed, administrative bureaucracy.

A general dynamic is therefore clear. During the war, federal agencies like SLAB and the NWLB had pushed cost-of-living adjustments toward a single, national set of statistics for the agencies' own operating efficiency. During the 1920s, absent the standardizing pressures of war, the decentralized and combative nature of arbitration prevented clear consolidation around a single set of statistics. Meanwhile, those companies that chose to utilize statistics to rationalize and unify their wage system (whether for administrative benefits or to stave off unionization), adopted a wide-ranging set of cost-of-living measures predicated on their own needs and capacities. Lacking the discipline imposed by a unified and powerful labor movement or a managerial state, companies found no reason to confine themselves to BLS statistics. (Significantly, arbitration boards jointly appointed by companies and unions during the First World War and the 1920s typically used BLS figures, as did union contracts with cost-of-living clauses.)[77] Instead, a pluralistic approach to statistics flourished amidst a fragmented economy dominated by companies subject to diverse conditions and governed by a federalist, associative state.

Labor Unions and the "Cost of Living": A Growing Predicament

Even as the firm-dominated, fragmented nature of the associational order explains the variety of statistics and methods embodied within cost-of-living adjustments in the early 1920s, so too does it help us understand why their use declined after this period. Companies adopted cost-of-living adjustments (limiting their discretion over wages) when pressed by arbitrators, unions, or the disruptive potential of employee turnover. As the

the distribution. Obviously, there are serious caveats to the aggregate method used above, but it supplies a rough estimate.
77 Carr, *Use of Cost-of-Living Figures*, 233–333, 433.

decade progressed, a combination of technological improvements and internal migration toward northern industrial centers contributed to a flush industrial labor market (following on the heels of the early recession), which meant both that unions grew much less militant and that companies worried less about turnover (and hence less about appeasing workers through rationalized wage systems).[78]

Meanwhile, when prices began to collapse in 1920, workers and labor leaders more vehemently rejected wage adjustments based solely on price changes, arguing (as we have heard before) that prior rates were inadequate. Adjustments based on a retail price index remained comparatively stronger in Britain (even under a similar price change) because they were used most extensively within the Trade Boards system, in which individual industries established minimum wages. The Trade Boards themselves, of course, were a product of a stronger labor movement and a less fragmented political system, which forced companies into a more organized and standardized labor system. In the absence of such protection in the United States, where federalism and conservative judicial interpretations constrained and then eliminated any effective political intervention to establish uniform basic rates, labor economists and union leaders proved more leery. They had accepted price-based adjustments reluctantly during the war and postwar, regularly coupling their demands with a call for an adequate "living wage." Once the downward spiral of prices became clear, unions concentrated more fully on the latter and thereby set the stage for the most virulent and most consequential 1920s debate over cost-of-living statistics.

The early 1920s proved the high point of a union living-wage campaign that developed out of the wartime labor system, especially the National War Labor Board. Former NWLB economists Jett Lauck and William Ogburn helped unions develop living-wage arguments for crucial national arbitration hearings in coal and railroads, while the BLS used data from its wartime expenditure surveys (conducted at the behest of the NWLB) to create a "tentative quantity-cost budget" that would sustain a family of five at "a standard of health and decency." (Again, as during the war, the union's living wage was based on a family wage concept.) Shortly thereafter, the Labor Bureau, Inc.—an organization formed in 1920 by Evans Clark, David Saposs, and George Soule to provide technical advice to unions—made the BLS budget a standard component in a host of arbitration hearings. Critically, and in contrast to the prewar "subsistence" budgets developed

---

[78] McQuaid, "American Business Community," 350–352; Jacoby, "The Development of Cost-of-Living Escalators," 522–525; Jacoby, *Employing Bureaucracy*, 167–205.

by reformers and minimum-wage advocates, the unions based their arguments around Ogburn's higher, "minimum comfort" budgets that had been designed for skilled workers. As a result of these efforts, according to *New York Times* journalist James C. Young, the question "What is a living wage?" dominated discussions of labor relations by 1922 and appeared "likely to assume national and economic importance overshadowing almost any other problem of industry."[79]

Unfortunately for the unions, the subjectivity inherent in the topic made it difficult to define a living wage on terms favorable to their members. The BLS, for example, conceded that the phrase "health and decency" was "not entirely precise in meaning," and indeed could never "be wholly satisfactory."[80] Moreover, it never bothered to calculate the actual cost of the worker's budget in any cities, nor did it extend the work into other studies or update it as the decade progressed. Repeatedly over the next half-century, BLS staff would make abortive efforts to create more empirically grounded, objective standard budgets, but the project never reached any long-term stability and was eventually abandoned in the 1970s (Chapter 9).[81] In practice, standard budgets could only be stabilized by social and political consensus, which typically required reducing the specified living conditions to a (comparatively) very low level. Thus, for example, the NICB co-opted the unions' living wage arguments by conducting numerous small studies in which it took a self-defined "fair standard of living" (comparable to Ogburn's lower "minimum subsistence") and adjusted it to meet prevailing local conditions (in some cases rather substantially).[82] In the end, the living wage became largely synonymous with a minimum wage for very low-income, unskilled, unorganized workers, making it useless for most union members.

Overall, the labor movement was in a difficult bind by the mid-1920s. Lacking economic or political power, union officials needed a compelling

---

[79] Thomas A. Stapleford, "Defining a 'Living Wage' in America: Transformations in Union Wage Theories, 1870–1930," *Labor History* 49, no. 1 (2008): 1–22. James C. Young, "What Is a Worker's Living Wage?" *NYT*, 19 November 1922, p. 105.

[80] U.S. Bureau of Labor Statistics, "Minimum Quantity Budget," *MLR* 10, no. 6 (1920): 1307; U.S. Bureau of Labor Statistics, "Tentative Quantity-Cost Budget Necessary to Maintain a Family of Five in Washington, D.C.," *MLR* 9, no. 6 (1919): 1687.

[81] On the bureau's struggles with standard budgets, see Joseph P. Goldberg and William T. Moye, *The First Hundred Years of the Bureau of Labor Statistics* (Washington, D.C.: U.S. GPO, 1985), 105–106, 158–159, 198–199, 233–234.

[82] Cf. National Industrial Conference Board, *The Cost of Living among Wage-Earners: Fall River, Massachusetts, October, 1919* (Boston: National Industrial Conference Board, 1919). In total, the NICB published eight regional and city surveys conducted between 1919 and 1922, all with similar titles.

argument to persuade or coerce employers to raise wages. The rapid fall in prices had made cost-of-living indexes irrelevant or even harmful for such purposes; likewise, by 1923 it was clear that ethically based appeals to living conditions were similarly ineffective, however assiduously these claims might be draped in empirical research. Instead, thoughtful labor activists began to search for alternatives. By the end of the decade, they had found a substitute, a rationale that could appeal to business sensibilities and that also pulled together multiple threads from the story of cost-of-living statistics in the 1920s: institutional economics, price indexes, and the push for higher wages.

PRODUCTIVITY AND "PURCHASING POWER": A NEW FUTURE FOR COST-OF-LIVING STATISTICS

In 1923, an observer might have justly concluded that federal cost-of-living statistics would occupy a minor role in future industrial relations, far from the heady days of the war and early postwar era. Certainly there was little cause for optimism within the BLS. In 1919, the bureau had received $625,000 in special funding—just over 2.5 times its regular operating budget—much of which went toward its cost-of-living work. But these bonuses quickly disappeared, leaving the bureau to struggle along with a regular allocation that had increased far less than the rise shown by its price measurements (roughly 35 percent budget expansion from 1914 to 1921 versus 70 percent rise in the cost-of-living index).[83] Perhaps sensing the inevitable, Royal Meeker resigned in 1920 to become Director of the Statistical Division of the International Labour Office in the League of Nations, leaving his former chief statistician, Ethelbert Stewart, to battle budget-conscious conservatives. In the bureau's official history, the subtitle to the chapter on Stewart's decade-long leadership, "Holding the Fort," nicely illustrates the agency's siege mentality. Stewart called repeatedly for new funding to expand and strengthen the bureau's cost-of-living work, but the minor role of these statistics in America's fragmented industrial relations (especially after the 1920–1921 depression) left him without powerful business allies. Not only was Stewart unable to extend the geographic coverage of the index or update its market basket; in 1925, he was actually forced to shift from a quarterly to a semiannual publication.[84]

---

[83] Goldberg and Moye, *First Hundred Years*, 109, 136–138.

[84] In a curious twist, Meeker later served for seven years (1930–1936) as president of Irving Fisher's "Index Number Institute," responsible for publishing a weekly index of

Even as Stewart retrenched, however, the groundwork was being laid for a revived interest in cost-of-living statistics that would flourish in the 1930s, a substructure built by a loose coalition of moderate businessmen, institutional economists, and labor activists who found common ground in a basic problem rooted in the productive boom of 1920s manufacturing: the need to balance supply and demand for consumer goods. Classical and neoclassical theory predicted that as the supply of goods increased, prices and production patterns would shift to bring markets into a new equilibrium; markets, in short, would take care of themselves. But these orthodoxies were little comfort to those affected by the adjustments: workers hit by wage cuts or unemployment as companies slashed production and costs, or businesses holding glutted inventories and facing sharply reduced profits and even failure. Moreover, institutional economists argued that real-world markets were not nearly as responsive as the idealized constructions of deductive theorists, and thus there was no guarantee that markets would quickly reach a new equilibrium. In either case, critics insisted that the country needed new forms of collaborative planning, empirical monitoring, and action that could prevent imbalances and allow for more rapid adjustments.

For many businessmen and planning advocates, the depression of 1920–1921 exemplified the limitations of existing practices. A sharp plunge in consumer demand caught many major companies by surprise, leaving them awash in red ink, battling to unload excess inventory and sitting on costly excess capacity. The experience prompted a concerted, widespread effort to improve knowledge of consumer markets, dampen cyclical fluctuations, and expand mass consumption. Individual firms such as General Motors worked to streamline distribution channels, increase flexibility, boost market research, raise the level and sophistication of advertising, and pioneer new forms of credit and consumer incentives. On a broader scale, Hoover's Department of Commerce exemplified how the associative state could aid capitalist development, as it won praise from leading businessmen for the torrent of new economic and commercial data pouring forth from its rapidly expanding statistical agencies. The crisis boosted efforts to understand and manage economic fluctuations, including the studies of business cycles pursued by Mitchell's National Bureau of Economic Research (NBER) or

wholesale prices. Goldberg and Moye, *First Hundred Years*, 113, 122. Ethelbert Stewart to E. J. Henning (Asst. Secretary of Labor), 14 August 1923, and Stewart, "Recommendations Regarding the Bureau of Labor Statistics," 13 October 1924, both in folder 1924, box 2, Selected General Correspondence of the Bureau, 1908–1939, BLS.

the plans for countercyclical public spending touted by numerous advocates. Finally, it prompted many businessmen, economists, and labor activists to highlight the critical importance of consumer purchasing power in a
growing, mass-production economy.[85]

Among left-wing economists, the purchasing-power thesis built upon a
long-standing series of arguments about "underconsumption," most notably the work of British economist and socialist John A. Hobson (who linked
inadequate consumer demand to an unequal distribution of income).[86]
American advocates in the postwar era warned that if productivity gains
were not passed on to workers (in the form of lower prices or higher wages),
the economy would falter. Facing surplus production, companies would
hoard profits rather than reinvest them, and a substantial portion of gains
distributed to wealthier Americans (as salaries or dividends) would be
diverted into savings, which would find no easy investment outlet (because
of the production glut). The result would be a vicious downward spiral as
the gains from new productivity were sucked out of the economy rather
than stimulating more consumption. Avoiding this crisis required raising
real wages and keeping them in line with rising productivity.

During the 1920s, institutional economists in America began to adopt
elements of the underconsumptionist analysis as they studied distribution problems in a complex economy. (Hobson in fact lectured for one
year at the Robert Brookings Graduate School, a central forum alongside
Wisconsin and Columbia for the advancement of institutional economics
during the 1920s.) In the midst of the Depression a decade later, institutional economists such as Rexford Tugwell, Mordecai Ezekiel, and Isador
Lubin would elevate underconsumption arguments to a central place in
New Deal political economy.[87] But versions of varying sophistication were
also promoted by a broader range of Americans as the 1920s progressed.

[85] Alfred D. Chandler, Jr., *The Visible Hand: The Managerial Revolution in American Business*
(Cambridge: Belknap Press, 1977), 456–463; Alchon, *The Invisible Hand of Planning*; Barber,
From New Era to New Deal, 15–22, 53–58; Leach, *Land of Desire*, 349–378; Gordon, *New
Deals*, 35–45; Sally Clarke, "Consumers, Information, and Marketing Efficiency at GM,
1921–1940," *Business and Economic History* 25, no. 1 (1996): 186–195; Coleman Harwell
Wells, "Remapping America: Market Research and American Society, 1900–1940" (Ph.D.
dissertation, University of Virginia, 1999), 291–304, 314–335; Jacobs, *Pocketbook Politics*,
84–87.

[86] M. F. Bleaney, *Underconsumption Theories: A History and Critical Analysis* (New York:
International Publishers, 1976); Roger E. Backhouse, "J. A. Hobson as Macroeconomic
Theorist," in *Reappraising J. A. Hobson: Humanism and Welfare*, ed. Michael Freeden
(London: Unwin Hyman, 1990), 126–136.

[87] Joseph Dorfman, *The Economic Mind in American Civilization*, vol. 5 (New York: Viking
Press, 1946), 570–579; Barber, *From New Era to New Deal*, 55–58; Malcolm Rutherford,

For labor unions, the underconsumption thesis offered a seemingly perfect marriage between rising wages and business self-interest. The pro-labor consultants of the Labor Bureau, Inc. (namely Evans Clark, George Soule, David Saposs, and Stuart Chase) promoted an underconsumption analysis in arbitration hearings and public commentaries. Meanwhile, AFL officials adopted the link between productivity and real wages as a basic platform in 1925: "Social inequality, industrial instability and injustice must increase," the convention declared, "unless the workers' real wages … are progressed in proportion to man's increasing power of production." Brookwood Labor College became a central institutional base for the diffusion of the underconsumption framework to labor organizers and sympathetic intellectuals during the 1920s, an effort that would shape the ideology of mass industrial unionism when it rebounded during the 1930s. Linking wages to productivity attracted both the political left (where communist intellectuals saw ties to Marx's theories about the "surplus value" created by labor) and progressive moderates such as the Taylor Society (whose member valued efficiency and an allegedly "scientific" means of determining wages). Most critically, tying higher wages to economic prosperity and the growth of mass markets garnered support from liberal or moderate Republicans such as Herbert Hoover and from businessmen whose companies depended on mass-consumer sales, such as Edward Filene, Henry Ford, and Eugene Grace. Thus, in 1927, a mere five years after the U.S. Railroad Board had declared the living wage a "fallacy" in a major arbitration decision, the chairman of General Electric's board of directors, Owen D. Young, insisted that workers needed not merely a living wage, but a higher "cultural wage" appropriate to American aspirations (and American production).[88]

Young's invocation of the living wage might suggest a misleading continuity between the underconsumption thesis and older traditions of labor activism. To be sure, union leaders had always insisted that a living wage could not be an eternally fixed rate but must rise alongside the general American economy (as Samuel Gompers declared in 1898, "a living wage today may be denounced as a starvation wage in a decade"). Indeed, they

"On the Economic Frontier: Walton Hamilton, Institutional Economics and Education," *HOPE* 35 (2003): 611–653; Jacobs, *Pocketbook Politics*, 95–175.

[88] Marc Linder, *Labor Statistics and Class Struggle* (New York: International Publishers, 1994), 6–24; Barber, *From New Era to New Deal*, 27–30; Jacobs, *Pocketbook Politics*, 74–87; Sanford Jacoby, "Union-Management Cooperation in the United States: Lessons from the 1920s," *Industrial & Labor Relations Review* 37, no. 1 (1983): 23–26. Quotations as cited in Lauck, *New Industrial Revolution*, 176, 122–123.

had even invoked earlier versions of the underconsumption argument.[89] But through the early postwar period, the emphasis remained on ethical grounds: workers *ought* to share in rising productivity; hence the detailed elaboration of what constituted an appropriate "American standard of living" and the primacy given to the expenditure surveys and standard budgets as tools in wage arguments. By contrast, the 1920s purchasing-power advocates began to supplement, even supercede, these ethical justifications with an economic argument that linked higher real wages to continuing growth and business prosperity. As union leader John P. Frey told the American Economics Association at a 1925 roundtable, "Wages have been considered for too long upon the basis of what the wage earner should receive, his standard of living, or an amount sufficient to enable him to save. Industry and commerce, for its own salvation, must see that the wage-earner's capacity to buy keeps pace with the capacity to produce."[90] Accordingly, purchasing-power advocates paid less attention to the description of living conditions among the working class than to the relative movements of prices, wages, and productivity.

Basing industrial relations on underconsumptionist arguments had three important consequences. First, it placed bargaining in a rationalized framework of economic analysis dependent on quantitative knowledge (productivity, real wages), one that in principle excluded or muted both ethical appeals and direct confrontation (strikes, lockouts). Thus, it is no surprise that the Amalgamated Clothing Workers (ACW), one of the unions most committed to the purchasing-power framework and advised by the institutional economist Leo Wolman, was also bound most tightly to economic analysis: as Colin Gordon has noted, ACW contract negotiations in the late 1920s "resembled economic surveys of the industry."[91] These patterns would reappear in the 1940s and 1950s among unions in the Congress of Industrial Organizations, many of whose officials had ties to Brookwood and the purchasing-power logic.

Second, the attention to mass purchasing power altered the relative prominence of functions for cost-of-living statistics. Studies of standards of living

---

[89] Lawrence B. Glickman, *A Living Wage: American Workers and the Making of Consumer Society* (Ithaca: Cornell University Press, 1997); Roseanne Currarino, "The Politics of 'More': The Labor Question and the Idea of Economic Liberty in Industrial American," *JAH* 93, no. 1 (2006): 22–30; Samuel Gompers, "A Minimum Living Wage," *American Federationist* (1898): 25.

[90] Herbert Feis et al., "The Consuming Power of Labor and Business Fluctuations," *AER* 16, no. 1, supplement (1926): 83.

[91] Jacobs, *Pocketbook Politics*, 78–79; Gordon, *New Deals*, 102.

(filled with detailed descriptions of living conditions) would gradually be marginalized, confined mainly to studies of poverty that had limited connections to wage contracts (excepting minimum wage legislation); instead, expenditure surveys would develop new functions as tools for revealing and modeling consumer demand.[92] Cost-of-living indexes would continue to be relevant for industrial relations—as a key tool for transforming nominal wages into measures of real purchasing power—but these no longer had a merely local meaning for workers and their families. In light of an underconsumptionist analysis, cost-of-living indexes now exuded macroeconomic significance (to use an anachronistic term), for they allowed economists to judge whether real wages were keeping pace with productivity.

The effects of this shift are evident in the work of University of Chicago economist Paul Douglas over the decade. Douglas had served as a labor arbitrator for the Emergency Fleet Corporation in Philadelphia, supported the living wage campaign, and wrote the only monograph-length, international analysis of family allowance systems (based on the family wage version of the living wage) for his first major book in 1925. But with no political action forthcoming, Douglas abandoned the topic for the next quarter century. His second book, *Real Wages in the United States, 1890–1926*, had a decidedly different flavor, using price and wage statistics to chart the progress of real purchasing power among workers in different industries—which Douglas then compared (favorably) to productivity gains over a similar period—all conducted without any discussion of adequate standards or a living wage.[93]

Finally, the rise of underconsumption analyses cemented the ties between institutional economics and cost-of-living indexes, thereby solidifying support for the constant-goods approach to price index theory. As noted in the first section of this chapter, institutional economists had the most substantial commitment to large-scale, quantitative empirical analysis among American economists in the interwar period. In the case of prices, leading figures such as Mitchell and his NBER protégé, Frederick C. Mills, focused on wholesale prices for much of the 1920s, but the new attention to mass

---

[92] Thomas A. Stapleford, "Market Visions: Expenditure Surveys, Market Research, and Economic Planning in the New Deal," *JAH* 94, no. 2 (2007): 418–444.

[93] Paul H. Douglas, *Wages and the Family* (Chicago: University of Chicago Press, 1925); Douglas, *Real Wages*; Paul H. Douglas, *In the Fullness of Time: The Memoirs of Paul H. Douglas* (New York: Harcourt Brace Jovanovich, 1971), 66–68. In fact, Douglas insisted that higher productivity led to higher real wages. *Real Wages* was published with support from the Pollack Foundation for Economic Research, established by William Trufant Foster and Waddill Catchings to promote underconsumptionist analysis. Significantly, in relation to the next point, the Pollack Foundation's first publication was Irving Fisher's *The Making of Index Numbers*.

purchasing power increasingly directed their consideration toward retail prices as well. (By the late 1920s, both AFL leader John Frey and Labor Bureau, Inc., consultant George Soule were members of the NBER's board of directors; in fact, Frey was the board chairman.)[94] By the 1930s, as we will see in Chapter 4, institutional economists had joined the federal government and made BLS retail price statistics a central part of their economic analyses, a transformation predicated on the new prominence of purchasing power. In turn, this move reinforced support for the constant-goods approach over the neoclassical constant-utility ideal, both through personnel (as institutional economists filled the BLS) but also because of cognitive affinities. When cost-of-living indexes were understood in the institutionalist mode—as measures of price change relevant to particular groups of consumers (notably working-class families)—they could be readily interpreted as an (inverse) measure of "purchasing power" directly related to productivity: falling prices meant that workers could purchase more goods. By contrast, the statistics had a more ambiguous relationship to productivity when conceived as constant-utility indexes: working-class families might derive greater satisfaction simply by purchasing different goods rather than more goods. The analytical nexus of productivity and purchasing power thus went hand-in-hand with a constant-goods index, which showed how (in a balanced and growing economy) workers could purchase the same set of goods for less money, leaving surplus funds for investment or increased consumption.

It was against this background of the new underconsumption arguments that in 1929 long-time labor economist and union consultant Jett Lauck heralded the arrival of a "New Industrial Revolution" predicated on high wages and high productivity, a gospel that Lauck and his fellow industrial relations experts proclaimed at home and abroad, and one that attracted extensive foreign commentary.[95] That spring, the Committee on Recent Economic Changes (organized by Hoover) released a landmark study of the

---

[94] Consider Mills's growing attention to retail prices, "living costs," and purchasing power in Mills, *The Behavior of Prices*; Frederick C. Mills, "Price Movements and Related Industrial Changes," in *Recent Economic Changes in the United States*, vol. 2, ed. President's Committee on Recent Economic Changes (New York: McGraw-Hill, 1929), 603–656; Frederick C. Mills, *Prices in Recession and Recovery: A Survey of Recent Changes* (New York: National Bureau of Economic Research, 1936).

[95] Lauck, *New Industrial Revolution*. Cf. Herbert Feis, "Recent Development in Industrial Relations in the United States," *ILR* 12, no. 6 (1925): 776–798; J. H. Richardson, "The Doctrine of High Wages," *ILR* 20, no. 6 (1929): 797–815; Committee on Recent Economic Changes, *Recent Economic Changes in the United States*, vol. 1 (New York: McGraw-Hill, 1929), 1–6.

economy from the NBER, in which the committee attributed the rousing successes of recent years to "the maintenance of our economic balance," including "a more marked balance of production-consumption."[96] Thus, it seemed that the postwar search for economic normalcy and ordered industrial relations had reached a stable endpoint. Dismantling the wartime bureaucracy had allowed a fragmented, firm-dominated, pluralistic form of industrial relations to emerge, one in which larger companies might use cost-of-living statistics to help govern their workforce but which left comparatively little need for a federal retail price index. Unions had tried to compensate for political weakness by combining ethical demands and empirical study in their quest for a higher, living wage, but appeals to expert knowledge proved insufficient for that task. Only an argument from underconsumption, it appeared, could grant workers some of their desires by relying on the munificence and self-interest of companies in a business-led associational order.

Aggregate economic statistics both then and since confirmed large parts of this optimistic story, showing substantial gains in real wages, consumer expenditures, and productivity both after 1914 and during the 1920s. But the aggregate figures also masked significant disparities. Income trends varied greatly across different occupations (with some experiencing significant declines) and the largest rises during the 1920s came for skilled workers and salaried employees. Equally troublesome, growing evidence indicated that high wages and productivity had been accompanied by stagnant or falling employment in manufacturing, and there were conflicting claims about whether income distribution was becoming more unequal. Furthermore, arguments about underconsumption had as yet done little to help labor unions: many of the businessmen in mass-production industries who gave vocal support to high wages (e.g., Henry Ford) also used them to block union organizing, while others simply ignored the rationale altogether. Indeed, even while Lauck optimistically praised the new era of industrial relations in public, as adviser to the United Mine Workers he gloomily watched the union shrink dramatically under open-shop competition.[97]

96 Committee on Recent Economic Changes, *Recent Economic Changes in the United States*, xix–xxi.

97 On wages, productivity, unemployment, and national income in the United States during the 1920s, see Douglas, *Real Wages*; Edwin G. Nourse, *America's Capacity to Produce* (Washington, D.C.: Brookings Insitution, 1934); Maurice Leven, Harold G. Moulton, and Clark Warburton, *America's Capacity to Consume* (Washington, D.C.: Brookings Institution, 1934); Frank Stricker, "Affluence for Whom? Another Look at Prosperity and the Working Classes in the 1920s," *Labor History* 24, no. 1 (1983): 5–33; Jacoby, *Employing Bureaucracy*, 167–174. For the fate of underconsumption arguments in the

Subsequent events, of course, would lead left-wing economists and intellectuals to highlight these factors as portents of serious underlying problems rather than minor anomalies. But instead of abandoning the underconsumption thesis, they reevaluated the merits of Hoover's associational order.[98] The struggles of the 1920s thus formed the foundation for the labor-liberal response to the Depression and the revitalized federal government that they crafted over the next two decades, a world in which purchasing power would become a central component of New Deal political economy and the BLS cost-of-living index would develop into a critical economic statistic. But if debates during the 1920s had led many pro-labor liberals to drop normative evaluations of consumption and wages in favor of economic arguments, they had also left behind a series of unanswered questions. How, as academic price index theorists continued to wonder, could you track "real wages" when both prices and purchasing habits were changing? In a diverse nation and complex economy, how meaningful were aggregate statistics (which, after all, had apparently proved misleading in the late 1920s)? Would a general measure of consumer purchasing power necessarily provide appropriate guidance for evaluating wages among specific groups of employees, and if not, what consequences did this have for the attempt to link wages to macroeconomic analyses? As BLS price statistics returned to prominence in later decades, so too would these issues left unresolved from the aftermath of war.

business community, see Gordon, *New Deals*, 37, 45, 95, 119–121. On Lauck, see Leon Fink, *Progressive Intellectuals and the Dilemmas of Democratic Commitment* (Cambridge: Harvard University Press, 1997), 220–224.

[98] Alchon, *The Invisible Hand of Planning*, 152–166; Jacobs, *Pocketbook Politics*, 90–92.

PART II

RATIONALIZING THE DEMOCRATIC POLITICAL ORDER, 1930–1960: COST-OF-LIVING STATISTICS IN THE HEART OF THE NEW DEAL

We are facing fundamental changes in the social order. Laissez faire, in my opinion, is dead forever. … The New Deal represents an attempt to preserve the complexities and hence the standards of our civilization by social control of a mechanism that is no longer self-operating. … The precise forms of future organization are not now visible. But we cannot turn back and I am sure that statistics will be essential in finding the way forward. The industrial era was built upon natural science. The era of social control will rest upon factual information about economic and social structures and processes.[1]
— Stuart A. Rice, Presidential Address to the American Statistical Association, 1933

In the 1920s, a collection of government officials, institutional economists, and corporate leaders in mass-production and distribution industries had argued that economic stability required active intervention to balance production and consumption through either public efforts or coordinated, private actions. Pro-labor liberals and many of their union allies had seized on one version of this analysis, claiming that the nation risked a crisis of underconsumption (due to high productivity and low wages) which could only be rectified by boosting working-class purchasing power. The depression that began in 1929 plus the subsequent election of the first Democratic

---

[1] Stuart A. Rice, "Statistical Opportunities and Responsibilities," *JASA* 29, no. 185 (1934): 1–2.

president in over a decade, Franklin D. Roosevelt, offered a rationale and a means to put this perspective into operation. From that basis grew a left-wing vision of political economy that would shape debates over macroeconomic policy and industrial relations for the "Democratic political order" that lasted until the late 1960s.[2] Of course, justifying and enacting plans for "social control" over the ensuing decades would require a plethora of new economic data, and at the heart of these efforts lay figures on retail prices and family expenditures compiled by the Bureau of Labor Statistics.

In the years after the First World War, the Department of Labor and the Bureau of Labor Statistics had both suffered from financial neglect while the bureau's national cost-of-living statistics had lost ground to competing measures from private sources and local governments. The arrival of the Roosevelt administration transformed both situations. The BLS received an influx of money and new staff, largely economists trained in the tradition of institutional economics. The new arrivals overhauled the bureau's statistics and positioned themselves and their work as central elements within New Deal economic planning (Chapter 4). Sharing a common view of the depression as a problem of underconsumption, top officials such as Commissioner Isador Lubin helped to bind labor policy to macroeconomics by arguing that strong unions would redistribute national income to the working class. In turn, according to Lubin and others, this redistribution would boost mass consumption and thereby pull the country out of the economic crisis. To justify and guide these plans, Lubin turned to the bureau's national cost-of-living statistics, including both price statistics and studies of family expenditures. Though this synthesis appeared to tie pro-union reforms to a consumption-based, liberal political economy (mediated by calculations from the Bureau of Labor Statistics), there were hidden tensions that would soon erupt.

The Second World War provided severe tests for the conceptual and methodological foundations of the national cost-of-living index and for the New Deal's attempted marriage of labor reform to macroeconomic policy. Both were found wanting. Drawing support from the tradition of institutional economics, statisticians in the Bureau of Labor Statistics had designed the cost-of-living index to measure (ideally) the changing cost of a fixed collection of goods and services. But amidst the radical economic transformations brought by the war, that goal became both unreachable and increasingly meaningless. Simultaneously, however, the federal government

[2]   David Plotke, *Building a Democratic Political Order: Reshaping American Liberalism in the 1930s and 1940s* (New York: Cambridge University Press, 1996).

thrust the index into national prominence, using it to measure the success of federal anti-inflation programs and to restrict wage adjustments. Given the methodological problems of the index, it soon became the subject of a major controversy involving national unions, business associations, government agencies, and academic economists. This episode, explored over two chapters (Chapters 5 and 6), forms a rich case study exemplifying two themes at the center of my analysis: the impossibility of excising judgments that carry political valences from the practical construction of economic statistics, and, simultaneously, the strong pressures to treat statistics as politically neutral facts in order to bolster the rationalized frameworks that justify centralized power.

The wartime controversy operated on multiple levels. First and foremost, the controversy was a debate about the proper methods and concepts for cost-of-living indexes, as labor unions—chafing under wage limits that were tied to the BLS index—argued that the bureau's calculations failed to account adequately for the radical changes in goods and consumption patterns created by war mobilization. Yet the conflict was also a struggle over who defined the objectives for federal statistics, since answering the central question—was the BLS cost-of-living index accurate?—first required defining the index's primary function and scope. Bureau economists claimed that right for themselves. They had crafted a self-image of federal statisticians as nonpartisan, technical experts who were devoted to the national interest rather than the goals of particular groups. Yet they were also deeply involved in policy advising for the Roosevelt administration and were now faced with a situation in which the broader community of experts could offer no clear, consensus advice. Meanwhile, national union leaders rejected the bureau's view and insisted that the objectives of a statistical agency in the Department of Labor should be set by labor organizations. Thus, the beginning of the wartime controversy found pro-labor, left-wing government economists battling union officials over both the proper scope of a cost-of-living index and the more general function of labor statistics and statistical agencies in the New Deal political order (Chapter 5).

Unable to sway the BLS, national labor leaders created their own estimate of the wartime rise in the cost of living and thereby exemplified an alternative conception of statistical knowledge (Chapter 6). Union cost-of-living statistics were both deeply populist and overtly political. Labor officials trumpeted the authoritative knowledge of working-class housewives over government economists and appealed to public judgment rather than expert consensus. Whereas BLS statisticians had refused to incorporate admittedly important factors that lacked a sufficiently rigorous quantitative

basis, union economists freely offered estimates, justifying their constructions through (supposedly) common experience. Moreover, they insisted
that statistical calculation could not be separated from political judgments
and political values. Yet the union program was founded on an unstable
tension, for the populism and politicization that labor officials promoted
during debates over the cost of living ran counter to centralizing, bureaucratic trends of the unions themselves and their own commitment to the
rationalization of political economy (as a pro-union strategy). In the end,
the wartime conflict ended inconclusively, with the BLS politically wounded
and national unions unable to achieve their goals.

Though the rationalization of industrial relations had been severely challenged during the war, the postwar era would see its triumph (Chapter 7).
Major industrial unions had resisted tying wages to price statistics during
the early 1940s and had criticized the BLS cost-of-living index (rechristened
the "Consumer Price Index" in 1946). Yet by the mid-1950s, national labor
unions had collaborated with major corporations to make cost-of-living
escalator clauses based on the national CPI a common component of labor
contracts. One factor that eased this shift was the creation of two advisory
boards to the BLS, one for unions and one for businesses, which allowed
both groups some degree of influence over BLS methods. Still, the advisory
boards were not an ideal solution for anyone involved: The boards created
headaches for bureau staff even as they failed to give unions (or businessmen) the degree of control they had desired. Nonetheless, both unions and
corporations remained simultaneously committed to the advisory board
system, to the use of bureau statistics in labor contracts, and to an overall
vision of rationalized industrial relations predicated on economic knowledge. In the Cold War environment, rationalization allowed both corporate
officials and union leaders (for differing reasons) to portray an alternative
view of industrial relations in which reason and calculation (rather than
power and class struggle) characterized worker-employee relationships. Of
course, rationalization did not end labor conflict. But it did constrain it,
and, unfortunately for unions, the final collapse of the attempted New Deal
marriage of labor policy and macroeconomic growth meant that Cold War
rationalization ultimately favored managerial prerogatives.

4

The Nature of a Revolution: The Bureau of Labor Statistics in the New Deal

The modern Leviathan may go the way of his pre-historic predecessors. Then, when men again are living in a state of nature, naked, rude and barbarous, some traveler from New Zealand, standing on the ruins of the Commerce building, may read our epitaph: "Here lies the body of Leviathan, dead of locomotor ataxia, complicated by a plethora of indigestible statistics."[1]

—Frederick C. Mills,
Presidential Address to the American Statistical Association, 1934

The New Deal has long been seen as a watershed in American political history, a perspective that has also been applied to the history of federal statistics. In a well-known, internal history of government statistical research, Joseph Duncan and William Shelton declared 1926–1976 to be a period of "revolution in United States government statistics," a transformation that encompassed four main facets: the advent of probability sampling, the creation of national income and product accounts, the rise of computer tabulation and analysis, and the push for a coordinated federal statistical system. Underlying these developments was what Duncan and Shelton called the "hallmark of the revolution," namely the "professionalization of Federal statistics." Prior to the mid-1920s, many government statistical agencies, including the Bureau of Labor Statistics, were staffed by self-described "practical statisticians," men and women who specialized in the collection of quantitative data but who often had little or no advanced academic training. In the 1920s, a few agencies began hiring larger numbers of social scientists with graduate school credentials; during the New Deal these small streams became a flood as a host of young mathematicians, economists, and other social scientists flocked to government bureaus that were now clamoring

---

[1] Frederick C. Mills, "Statistics and Leviathan," *JASA* 30, no. 189 (1935): 10.

for their services. As Duncan and Shelton stated approvingly, "Government statistics [shifted] from a clerical operation to a professional one."[2]

It was no accident that this "professionalization" reached its peak during the New Deal, for the shift was tightly bound to a view of the state as a bureaucratic manager overseeing the economy. Statistics provided easily aggregated measures of economic factors (which could then be manipulated and combined into overall assessments or predictive models); the numbers could be produced by following formal procedures (abetting centralized control of large-scale operations and reducing costs); and, as we have seen, they could be embedded in rule-governed administrative systems. Economic statistics and economic planning therefore went hand-in-hand: the previous high point for federal production of economic statistics had been the mobilization efforts of the First World War, and the two departments who devoted the most resources to statistics during the 1920s (Commerce and Agriculture) had the strongest (albeit conflicting) commitments to an expertly managed economy.[3] Given both the widespread conviction that only planning of some form could overcome the depression and the common reference back to wartime mobilization as a model for planning success, vastly expanded and improved federal statistics seemed a prerequisite for long-term economic recovery. As Frederick C. Mills bluntly declared to his colleagues in the American Statistical Association in 1934, "Leviathan must develop a central nervous system."[4]

Still, we should be wary of accepting these narratives without closer analysis. Just as scholars have reconsidered the "revolutionary" status of the New Deal in political history by highlighting crucial continuities with earlier decades (including the 1920s' emphasis on "purchasing power" described

[2]   Joseph W. Duncan and William C. Shelton, *Revolution in United States Government Statistics* (Washington, D.C.: U.S. Department of Commerce, 1978), 1–3, 30–31.

[3]   On planning in the 1920s, see Guy Alchon, *The Invisible Hand of Planning: Capitalism, Social Science, and the State in the 1920s* (Princeton: Princeton University Press, 1985); Ellis W. Hawley, "Economic Inquiry and the State in New Era America: Antistatist Corporatism and Positive Statism in Uneasy Coexistence," in *The State and Economic Knowledge: The American and British Experiences*, ed. Mary O. Furner and Barry Supple (Cambridge: Cambridge University Press, 1990), 287–324.

[4]   Mills, "Statistics and Leviathan," 3. Márcia L. Balisciano, "Hope for America: American Notions of Economic Planning between Pluralism and Neoclassicism, 1930–1950," in *From Interwar Pluralism to Postwar Neoclassicism*, ed. Mary S. Morgan and Malcolm Rutherford (Durham: Duke University Press, 1998), 153–178; William E. Leuchtenberg, "The New Deal and the Analogue of War," in *Change and Continuity in Twentieth-Century America*, ed. John Braeman, Robert J. Bremmer, and Everett Walters (Columbus: Ohio State University Press, 1964), 81–143.

in Chapter 3), so too do the dramatic claims about federal statistics during this period require careful scrutiny. Why, for example, did expanding and improving federal statistics require that social scientists replace "practical statisticians" in federal agencies? In what ways did the new staff members change existing statistics, and how did they alter their own agencies and the place of statistics in the federal administrative structure?

For the case of the BLS and its cost-of-living statistics, the answers to these questions are more complicated than one might expect. Many of the methodological changes to the bureau's cost-of-living index, for example, had only tangential connections to the advanced academic training of the new staff and likewise had only marginal effects on the final results. Perhaps the greatest transformations came not in the numbers produced by the bureau but in the functions assumed by its top leaders, most of whom were institutional economists with connections to the labor-liberal analysis of underconsumption that had been developed in the previous decade. Not surprisingly, this background led them to reconstruct the role of the BLS in ways that reinforced aspects of the emerging political economy of the New Deal. By the late 1930s, bureau staff had positioned the agency as a central part of New Deal attempts to craft a new, more statist version of Hoover's associational order. In this vision, the state would help organize certain sectors of the economy (labor, consumers, agriculture) to provide greater balance against corporate power, and then actively coordinate the interactions of these groups to promote stable economic growth and a somewhat nebulous "national interest." At the heart of these adjustments lay the balance between productivity and "purchasing power," a connection that would soon drive the resurgence of the BLS cost-of-living index.

THE ACADEMIC AND PRACTICAL STATISTICIANS

Since both Commerce and Agriculture had already revitalized their statistical services to some extent during the 1920s, it was appropriate that the first push for statistical reform came from Roosevelt's new Secretary of Labor, Frances Perkins. At the onset of the depression, Perkins, then serving as New York State Industrial Commissioner, had been a major participant in a series of controversies over American unemployment statistics in which she and others had complained that the estimates issued by the Hoover administration were far too optimistic. The ensuing controversy led to a review committee composed of various politicians, labor and business representatives, and academic experts that made a number of recommendations

for improving the federal government's work.[5] The experience had soured
Perkins on federal statistics, and according to her own account, nothing she
found on arrival assuaged those concerns.

The Department of Labor as a whole was in a dismal state. As Perkins
later described, it was clear that "there had to be a reorganization of the
Labor Department. I really hate to dignify it by calling it a reorganization.
The Labor Department had very little content." She learned that over the
years, the department had become "the dumping ground of all the people
who were too inadequate" for other agencies but whom fellow bureaucrats
were reluctant to fire. In Perkins's view, the BLS had not been immune to
these trends. Early in her tenure, she stopped by the bureau to evaluate
the staff with an eye to replacing Ethelbert Stewart, who had been released
as a consequence of the unemployment controversy. The results were not
encouraging. Finding Stewart's deputy, Perkins tried to ask him several
questions about the operation, but "I couldn't get anything out of him when
I spoke to him. He either didn't know, or didn't know how to cooperate, or
was frightened to death." In general, the bureau "did not have an adequately
trained staff," in part because "people's relatives had gotten in one way or
another." She decided that Stewart had "kept an awful shop—oh a terrible
shop!—padded with people who didn't do anything and couldn't do anything, and padded with untrained and uneducated people to whom he gave
jobs."[6] Ewan Clague, a young economist and student of John R. Commons
who worked in the bureau during the 1920s, told a similar tale, although in
less harsh terms. According to Clague, the BLS had only one "professional,"
that being a medical doctor named Parker who was in charge of "pencils
and supplies." The bureau, in fact, had refused to give another employee
a leave of absence in order to study for a graduate degree. As Clague concluded, "this was a working organization in which professional stature,
in the modern sense of the term, had no meaning at all."[7] Overall, these
descriptions match Duncan and Shelton's characterization of many federal
statistical agencies prior to the New Deal, a world filled with "rather large
numbers of clerks and clerical supervisors, directed more by administrators
than by professionals."[8]

---

[5]　Joseph P. Goldberg and William T. Moye, *The First Hundred Years of the Bureau of Labor Statistics* (Washington, D.C.: U.S. GPO, 1985), 129–132, 139; Margo J. Anderson, *The American Census: A Social History* (New Haven: Yale University Press, 1988), 161–170.

[6]　Reminiscences of Frances Perkins (1955), OHC-CU, Book IV, pp. 254, 244–245, 242, 132.

[7]　Reminiscences of Ewan Clague (1958), OHC-CU, p. 54. As described below, Clague was incorrect: the BLS had at least two economists with Ph.D.'s on staff in the late 1920s.

[8]　Duncan and Shelton, *Revolution in United States Government Statistics*, 1.

Yet there are contradictory elements throughout these accounts. The low unemployment statistics criticized by Perkins had been issued by the U.S. Employment Service. The BLS had given higher estimates, while Stewart (in Perkins's words) "raised the roof and did his best to get publicity," getting himself fired in the process (a connection widely acknowledged and condemned in editorials of the time).[9] Clague, though lamenting the lack of interest in "professional" training, was nevertheless impressed with the competency of his BLS colleagues in the late 1920s. Indeed, many of the reforms instituted by New Deal staff built upon methodological trends already existing in the bureau, and the changes that the staff introduced often had minimal effects on the final results. In short, the "professionalization" of the BLS was a murky business.

The Rise of the Academic Statisticians

Though Frances Perkins became the most prominent New Deal cabinet member to press for the reform of government research agencies by credentialed social scientists, the transition likely would have occurred without her, especially given the purge mentality of the Roosevelt administration and its affection for academic experts, many of whom were anxious to reshape federal statistics. Institutional economists had left wartime service dazzled by the potential to bend government power in the service of quantitative research, but through the 1920s they made only limited inroads into federal agencies—notably in the Federal Reserve, the Department of Commerce, and the Department of Agriculture—and only in the last of these were they able to conduct any sophisticated analytical work. Instead, the most impressive quantitative studies in economics during the 1920s arose from joint public-private efforts, such as the research into business cycles conducted by the NBER in cooperation with Herbert Hoover. Yet the potential of such projects was limited: economists remained highly dependent on basic data produced by government agencies, which alone (in an era before probability sampling) had the financial resources necessary to run large statistical surveys. But these same federal bureaus were hobbled by low civil-service salaries for leadership positions, making them unattractive career options for ambitious young economists. Instead, social scientists worked largely from the outside, trying (usually unsuccessfully) to leverage the authority of

---

9   Reminiscences of Frances Perkins (1955), OHC-CU, Book IV, p. 132. For reactions to Stewart's firing, see newspaper clippings from July 1932, in Part I, Series 3, Stewart Papers.

their professional societies and the power of foundation funding to control federal agendas. In 1922, for instance, the American Statistical Association (ASA) established a "Committee on Government Labor Statistics" that ran for over a decade under Mary Van Kleeck (Russell Sage Foundation), while the Social Science Research Council (SSRC) repeatedly pushed for improvements in federal social and economic statistics through meetings with government officials and more formal conferences.[10]

Only with the transition to a new administration amidst a deepening economic crisis did these efforts bear substantial fruit. During the late 1920s, a core group of New York–based members from the ASA Committee on Government Labor Statistics had made common cause with the state's Democratic establishment—including Senator Robert F. Wagner, then-governor Franklin D. Roosevelt, and the state Industrial Commissioner, Frances Perkins—as they battled Hoover and tried to reform federal unemployment statistics.[11] After the 1932 election, this alliance became a conduit for change. With the collaboration of Stuart Rice, who was the current president of the ASA and an equally committed reformer, Perkins established an Advisory Committee to the Secretary of Labor (ACSL) that was staffed with former members of the Committee on Government Labor Statistics and included three future members of the BLS: Ewan Clague, Aryness Joy Wickens, and Sidney Wilcox.[12] ACSL sparked interest from other departments, like Agriculture, Commerce, and the Interior, and by June, they helped to establish a broader Committee on Government Statistics and Information Services (COGSIS).[13]

---

[10] Duncan and Shelton, *Revolution in United States Government Statistics*, 10–22, 27; Alchon, *The Invisible Hand of Planning*; Hawley, "Economic Inquiry and the State," 287–324; Michael Bernstein, *A Perilous Progress: Economists and Public Purpose in Twentieth-Century America* (Princeton: Princeton University Press, 2001), 41–61.

[11] Mary van Kleeck, "Report of the Committee on Governmental Labor Statistics [1928]," *JASA* 24, no. 165, supplement (1929): 268–269; Bryce M. Stewart, "Report of the Committee on Governmental Labor Statistics [1930]," *JASA* 26, no. 173, supplement (1931): 276–277.

[12] Stuart A. Rice, *Next Steps in the Development of Social Statistics*, ed. Stuart A. Rice and Florence DuBois (Ann Arbor: Edwards Brothers, 1933). Cf. Anderson, *American Census*, 170–171; Mary Van Kleeck to Stuart Rice, 31 March 1933, folder 1, box 1, CSB-ACSL, OMB; Rice to Van Kleeck, 3 April 1933, ibid. ACSL had nine primary members, of whom five were participants in earlier ASA committee: Bryce Stewart, J. Frederic Dewhurst, Meredith B. Givens, Ralph Hurlin, and Howard B. Meyers. In addition, two other CGLS members collaborated with ACSL: Sidney W. Wilcox and Arthur J. Altmeyer. ACSL, *Interim Report* (April 1934, unpublished), p. 7, folder 3, box 1, CSB-ACSL, OMB.

[13] Perkins to Rice, 15 March 1933, folder 1, box 1, CSB-ACSL, OMB; Duncan and Shelton, *Revolution in United States Government Statistics*, 26–27. Committee on Government

COGSIS functioned as a bridge for social scientists between Hoover's "associational state" and the more nationalistic, more explicitly statist, New Deal.[14] For the first year-and-a-half, COGSIS was funded exclusively by the Rockefeller Foundation and administered by the SSRC. Officially, COGSIS was an SSRC project—the Council recruited members from the American Statistical Association, helped to direct the committee's work, and published the final report. The top members of COGSIS came from a variety of academic, philanthropic, and business posts centered in the northeast, such as Columbia, Harvard, the Rockefeller Foundation, the Twentieth Century Fund, Giannini Foundation for Agricultural Economics, AT&T, and Industrial Relations Counselors, Inc. The Department of Commerce provided the physical space for the consultants, but in all formal respects this was a private effort. Of course, in practice the public-private division frequently blurred, as COGSIS consultants worked individually and informally with various government agencies. Though the committee had no official authority, cabinet secretaries had cooperated in its formation, and therefore COGSIS consultants had no qualms about appealing to top department staff when agency bureaucrats proved recalcitrant.[15]

In combination with the ongoing transition to a new administration, the fuzzy boundaries of the consultants' roles enabled COGSIS to function as a gateway for academic experts to enter federal statistical agencies: of the fifty-seven participants in COGSIS and ACSL, twenty-six became top staff members in different federal bureaus and departments. Three ACSL members would eventually join the BLS: Ewan Clague (who spent roughly a decade at the Social Security Board before becoming the sixth commissioner of the bureau), Aryness Joy Wickens (who became Chief of the Cost of Living and Retail Price Division in the late 1930s), and Sidney Wilcox (who had led the New York Bureau of Labor Statistics under Frances Perkins and was added to ACSL at her request). Besides joining existing agencies, COGSIS members also helped to staff the new Central Statistical Board, an oversight agency created on COGSIS's recommendation that aimed to coordinate, and where possible integrate, all federal statistical research.[16] More generally,

Statistics and Information Services, "Government Statistics," *Bulletin of the Social Science Research Council*, no. 26 (1937): x.

[14] On planning in Hoover's associational state, see Alchon, *The Invisible Hand of Planning*; Kim McQuaid, "Corporate Liberalism in the American Business Community, 1920–1940," *Business History Review* 52, no. 3 (1978); Hawley, "Economic Inquiry and the State."

[15] Duncan and Shelton, *Revolution in United States Government Statistics*, 120–124, esp. 123.

[16] Reminiscences of Ewan Clague (1958), OHC-CU, pp. 126–128; Duncan and Shelton, *Revolution in United States Government Statistics*, 146–151.

COGSIS consultants emphasized the need to upgrade the mathematical and theoretical skills of agency staff in order to implement reforms; ACSL informed Frances Perkins that it was "of little use ... to suggest improvements in statistical methods" until the BLS acquired new, appropriately qualified personnel. Accordingly, as federal statistical bureaus (including the BLS) expanded or replaced staff members during the early New Deal, they drew heavily on the plethora of younger graduate students and former economics majors seeking jobs during the ongoing depression.[17]

For BLS cost-of-living statistics, the most important additions were two female economists with ties to institutional economics. Aryness Joy Wickens, the ACSL and COGSIS member who would lead the bureau's Cost-of-Living and Retail Prices Division by the end of the decade, had studied sociology and economics as an undergraduate at the University of Washington (then home to William Ogburn and the institutional economist Theresa McMahon), had lived with Dorothy and Paul Douglas while studying for her master's degree in economics at Chicago, and had helped Paul Douglas assemble data for his book on *Real Wages*. Below Wickens and in direct charge of cost-of-living projects was Faith Williams, who had pursued her doctorate in economics at the institutionalist Columbia University and conducted the cost-of-living surveys for Robert and Helen Lynd's study of *Middletown*. As these two examples suggest, the influx of economists during the New Deal also accelerated a growing gender shift in the bureau. The BLS had begun as an all-male organization, but women had established a large place in the bureau's work on retail prices and the cost of living by the 1920s. Ida M. Fisher, then the highest ranking woman in the BLS, was serving as the head of the Retail Price Division as early as the First World War, and it is clear that women formed the overwhelming majority of field agents collecting data on retail prices and the cost of living.[18] During the COGSIS and ACSL review work, administrators assigned many female academics to revise the bureau's cost-of-living and retail price statistics, including Margaret Klem, Margaret Hogg, Edna Lonigan, Helen Wright, and Faith Williams.[19] By 1940, the top

[17] Stuart Rice to Frances Perkins, 15 September 1933, folder 5, box 1, CSB-ACSL, OMB. Duncan and Shelton, *Revolution in United States Government Statistics*, 31.

[18] For the breakdown of the bureau's top staff as of 1918, see Royal Meeker to Roger W. Babson, 6 April 1918, box 2, 1916–1924, Selected General Correspondence of the Bureau, 1908–1939, BLS. On the gender of the field staff, see the implicit assumptions in Ethelbert Stewart to Secretary of Labor, 25 November 1927, folder 2, box 1, Correspondence of the Commissioner with the Secretary of Labor and Units of the Labor Department, 1925–1929, BLS.

[19] Stuart Rice to Frances Perkins, 15 September 1933, folder 6, box 1, CSB-ACSL, OMB; ACSL minutes, 3 November 1933, folder 2, ibid.; "Interim Report of ACSL," April 1934, pp. 35–36, folder 3, ibid.

staff supervising the cost-of-living index were entirely female (Wickens, Faith Williams, and Estelle Stewart), and the subordinate staff were also largely women. Indeed, the gender inequity was so complete that the highest ranking man in the branch referred to it as a "matriarchy."[20]

The high concentration of women involved in cost-of-living statistics resulted directly from the long-standing connection between women and domestic consumption. In their quest for greater political and social influence during the late nineteenth and early twentieth centuries, many middle- and upper-class women had used their roles as mothers and managers of the home as resources to create new public positions.[21] For female academics in the early twentieth century, studying domestic consumption allowed their gender to bolster (rather than hinder) their nascent attempts to break into the largely male world of statistics, economics, and academic sociology, and by 1929 they had established productive (if frequently vulnerable) institutional bases at Chicago, Berkeley, the University of Washington, Iowa State, and the Bureau of Home Economics (BHE) in the Department of Agriculture. The interest in consumption among institutional economists helped forge a bond between these women and the institutionalist tradition, while attention to the living wage and then to underconsumption made their work relevant to both labor economics and political economy more generally. The National Consumer League (NCL)—a longtime bastion of female-led labor reform—exemplified these ties, bringing together female labor activists, consumer advocates, and institutional economists to press for labor legislation that would be justified by underconsumption arguments. During the New Deal, NCL members were deeply intertwined with major New Deal programs such as the National Recovery Administration and the Fair Labor Standards Act of 1938, serving both as external activists and within the government itself (most visibly in the persons of Eleanor Roosevelt and Frances Perkins).[22]

---

[20] Oral History with Aryness Joy Wickens, *Women in the Federal Government Project*, Schlessinger Library, p. 57.

[21] On the connection between gender ideology and female-led progressive reform, see John H. Ehrenreich, *The Altruistic Imagination: A History of Social Work and Social Policy in the United States* (Ithaca: Cornell University Press, 1985); Ellen Fitzpatrick, *Endless Crusade: Women Social Scientists and Progressive Reform* (Oxford: Oxford University Press, 1990).

[22] Joseph Dorfman, *The Economic Mind in American Civilization*, vol. 5 (New York: Viking Press, 1946), 570–578; Margaret I. Liston, *History of Family Economics Research: 1862–1962: A Bibliographical, Historical, and Analytical Reference Book* (Ames: Iowa State University Research Foundation, 1993); Nancy Folbre, "'The Sphere of Women' in Early Twentieth-Century Economics," in *Gender and American Social Science: The Formative Years*, ed. Helene Silverberg (Princeton: Princeton University Press, 1998), 35–60; Landon

These ties help to explain the numerical dominance of women in the BLS cost-of-living division during the 1930s and 1940s, yet the effect of their presence on the agency's work is less clear. In the early twentieth century, the segregation that kept female reformers within self-created organizations (such as settlement houses or the NCL) and a subset of government agencies (such as the Children's Bureau) had also allowed and even encouraged them to cultivate their own approaches to social research (just as different institutional bases for labor statistics in the nineteenth century or the early social survey movement had likewise fostered different research traditions).[23] As women slowly began to break down institutional barriers—training alongside men in graduate programs and seeking to establish themselves in traditional disciplines—they necessarily lost (and sometimes deliberately shed) gender-based distinctions in methodology. However much gender affected the personal careers of the female economists who entered the BLS in the 1930s, it is less obvious that it gave them a distinct perspective on cost-of-living statistics—all of these women, in fact, had trained in traditional academic departments, typically with leanings toward institutional economics. Indeed, as we will see during consideration of the 1940s controversy over the BLS cost-of-living index (Chapter 6), the status of female BLS economists as technical experts had created a perceived split between them and the traditional "housewife."

For the history of the bureau's cost-of-living statistics, therefore, the most critical trait of the new staff members was not their gender but their training as institutional economists. By the mid-1930s, the BLS (previously nearly devoid of "professionals") was now filled with economists at multiple levels

---

R. Y. Storrs, *Civilizing Capitalism: The National Consumers' League, Women's Activism, and Labor Standards in the New Deal Era* (Chapel Hill: University of North Carolina Press, 2000); Thomas A. Stapleford, "'Housewife vs. Economist': Gender, Class, and Domestic Economic Knowledge in Twentieth-Century America," *Labor: Studies in Working-Class History of the Americas* 1, no. 2 (2004): 89–112; Thomas A. Stapleford, "Market Visions: Expenditure Surveys, Market Research, and Economic Planning in the New Deal," *JAH* 94, no. 2 (2007): 422–423, 429.

[23] On female reformers and institutional segregation in the early twentieth century, see Judith Sealander, *As Minority Becomes Majority: Federal Reaction to the Phenomenon of Women in the Work Force, 1920–1963* (Westport: Greenwood Press, 1983); Judith Ann Trolander, *Professionalism and Social Change: From the Settlement House Movement to Neighborhood Centers, 1886 to the Present* (New York: Columbia University Press, 1987); Fitzpatrick, *Endless Crusade*; Robyn Muncy, *Creating a Female Dominion in American Reform, 1890–1935* (Oxford: Oxford University Press, 1991); Kathryn Kish Sklar, "Hull-House Maps and Papers: Social Science as Women's Work in the 1890s," in *The Social Survey in Historical Perspective, 1880–1940*, ed. Martin Bulmer, Kevin Bales, and Kathryn Kish Sklar (Cambridge: Cambridge University Press, 1991), 111–147.

down into its hierarchy. Coming into service alongside a host of colleagues during a time of national change and full of idealistic self-assurance, the whole set enjoyed, as Duncan and Shelton put it, "a heartening fraternal cohesion and interchange of ideas."[24] However, understanding the nature of the transition within the BLS requires a closer look not only at the reforms that the social scientists instituted but at the men whom they replaced.

The Last of the Practical Statisticians

If academics had been searching for a clear contrast between their version of government statistics and the "non-professional" version, they could have hardly picked a better person than the 1920s' BLS commissioner, Ethelbert Stewart. Even more than Carroll Wright, Stewart epitomized the practical statistician, and, having been born in 1857, he was quite literally a throwback to the nineteenth century. Whereas both Meeker and Charles P. O'Neill had earned doctoral degrees, Stewart had almost no formal education because a severe stammer had kept him out of local schools. He was also the only commissioner to have been a member of the working class as an adult, working in an Illinois coffin factory for several years before being blacklisted for his labor activism. Stewart started his career in labor statistics with the Illinois Bureau of Labor Statistics in 1885; joined the federal bureau as a temporary field agent in 1887; and worked his way up to become Chief Statistician in 1913 under Royal Meeker. By the time he became commissioner in 1920, he was sixty-three years old; his release after the unemployment controversy was thereby eased, since by 1932 he was well past the mandatory retirement age.[25] Even Stewart's appearance invoked overtones of an earlier time; as Clague put it, Stewart was the "living image of Mark Twain ... and apparently he was rather proud of this connection, because he did nothing to discourage the analogy."[26]

Given Stewart's own career path, his attitude toward the development of BLS staff is not surprising. His Chief Statistician, Jesse C. Bowen, might have been Stewart himself a decade or so before. As Clague described, Bowen

---

[24] Duncan and Shelton, *Revolution in United States Government Statistics*, 2.

[25] Goldberg and Moye, *First Hundred Years*, 115–117; Chester McArthur Destler, "A Coffin Worker and the Labor Problem: Ethelbert Stewart and Henry," *Labor History* 12, no. 3 (1971): 409–434.

[26] Reminiscences of Ewan Clague (1958), OHC-CU, p. 44. Goldberg and Moye, *First Hundred Years*, 115–117. Journalists regularly noted how Stewart's appearance and mannerisms recalled Mark Twain, e.g.: Richard Barry, "'Human Cussedness' Causes Labor Disputes," 6 August 1916, *NYT Magazine*, 9.

had received no "more than home-made statistical training in the Bureau itself. He'd just come up through its own operations, and those operations were not highly theoretical. They were the practical collection and processing of statistics." Below Bowen was a former butcher who "began his career as a killer in the slaughterhouse floor" and specialized in "wage studies in slaughtering and meat packing." Now the butcher was "some sort of statistical guide … training other people in methods." Generally, according to Clague, higher-level BLS staff members "were operators who had come up as statistical collectors. A man began by doing some field work, under somebody's supervision, and he worked his way up."[27] In truth, this was not completely accurate: as of 1931, at least three BLS staff members (Hugh Hanna, Boris Stern, and Witt Bowden) had doctoral degrees. But none of these men had control over major survey programs, which lay in the hands of Stewart, Bowen, and their deputies (like the former butcher).[28]

Despite Clague's obvious bewilderment over the bureau's attitude toward formal statistical training, he was less inclined than Perkins to make broad judgments about the staff's intellectual capability. Bowen, according to Clague, was "very much interested in intellectual ideas," and the butcher probably had "good brains for [statistical methods]."[29] Likewise, although Stewart lacked formal education, he read broadly, was well-versed in classical political economy (which he disdained), wrote short stories, and was apt to pepper his detailed discussions of industrial relations (built on over forty years of experience) with wide-ranging quotations and allusions to ancient history. He could hold informed (if idiosyncratic) discussions on topics from monetary policy to wage theory, always tempered by abiding concern about the limits and misuse of quantitative knowledge. ("In many lines," he declared near the end of his life, "the statistical average, like patriotism, is the last refuge of the scoundrel.")[30] All told, Stewart resembled

---

27 Reminiscences of Ewan Clague (1958), OHC-CU, pp. 47, 54, 53.
28 A personnel list from the spring of 1933 (before Isador Lubin became commissioner) lists 20 staff members in the higher, "P" grade categorization for civil service salaries. "List of data available for ACSL," 9 June 1933, folder 2, box 1, CSB-ACSL, OMB. Of these, I only have evidence of three men receiving doctoral degrees. Hugh Hanna (Johns Hopkins University, 1906) served as editor of the *MLR* from 1926 to 1944. After graduate school, Boris Stern (Columbia University, 1925) joined the BLS, where he gathered data on industrial relations and served as the bureau's liaison to unions. Witt Bowden (University of Pennsylvania, 1919) wrote his dissertation on economic history, taught history for a decade at Penn, and began work at the BLS in 1931 on projects about technology and employment. Both Stern and Bowden stayed with the BLS until the early 1950s.
29 Reminiscences of Ewan Clague (1958), OHC-CU, pp. 47, 54.
30 See "Crumbling the Walls of Jericho" and "Cost of Living for What?" both written in the 1930s and appearing in Part I, B, Series 2, Stewart papers. Ethelbert Stewart, "A Family Wage-Rate vs. a Family Social Endowment Fund," *Social Forces* 6, no. 1 (1927): 120–125.

his contemporary and mentor, Carroll Wright, who had likewise been self-trained and nevertheless gained a reputation as a leading statistician.

As Clague and others recognized, however, neither Stewart nor his top staff had a firm grasp on current sampling theory, and they lacked the advanced mathematical skills increasingly essential to statistical analysis. Stewart's inattention to topics like data distribution, variance, or regression analysis was not unique among statisticians or the academic economists of his generation; even when a larger group of social scientists adopted some of these techniques in the 1920s, sophisticated mathematical treatments remained a minor theme in the larger community for several more decades.[31] Moreover, Stewart had been trained in an era when the ideal practical statistician avoided complicated theory precisely because it slowed tabulation and made statistics less clear to their intended audience: the public. Thus, Carroll Wright had championed a "simple and direct method, leaving out of consideration the mathematical expressions which have to be studied to be comprehended"; moreover, he had doubted the value of British statistician Arthur Bowley's more complex treatments, telling his colleagues that "there is nothing in that line of work for us as commissioners of labor statistics to follow."[32] By the late 1920s, however, the economists most committed to quantitative research took a very different view, finding more advanced mathematics (like regression techniques) and statistical theory (such as analyses of distribution) essential not only for interpreting published results, but for designing survey samples and tabulating the "raw" data.[33]

[31] Patti W. Hunter, "Drawing the Boundaries: Mathematical Statistics in 20th-Century America," *Historia Mathematica* 23 (1996): 7–30; Jeff Biddle, "Statistical Economics, 1900–1950," *HOPE* 31, no. 4 (1999): 607–651.

[32] *NABL* (1900): 113–114. Wright apparently had a more favorable view of advanced mathematical analysis early in his career, cf. Carroll D. Wright, "The Study of Statistics in Colleges," *Publications of the American Economic Association* 3, no. 1 (1888): 19–20. By 1900, however, he had decided that "every attempt to apply algebraic expression to statistical data has been a failure, except with the man who makes it" *NABL* (1900): 113. This was not an idiosyncratic preference; in Britain, for instance, the Board of Trade also refused to use new sampling and correlation techniques when creating labor statistics, despite having top theorists such as Arthur Bowley and G. Udny Yule on the staff: Roger Davidson, *Whitehall and the Labour Problem in Late-Victorian and Edwardian Britain: A Study in Official Statistics and Social Control* (London: Croom Helm, 1985), 220–229. Moreover, even a century later, public resistance to probability sampling techniques in the United States is quite strong for politically critical investigations such as the population census.

[33] An excellent, early example of the contrast is William Ogburn's analysis of the dissaggregated data from the BLS survey of family expenditures in Washington, D.C. during 1916: William F. Ogburn, "Analysis of the Standard of Living in the District of Columbia in 1916," *Publications of the American Statistcal Association* 16, no. 126 (1919): 374–389.

This comparison allows us to clarify the distinction between the New Deal staff and its predecessors. As Carroll Wright had argued in the nineteenth century, and as academic economists such as Roland Falkner or Wesley Mitchell had discovered when they worked for government bureaus, being a "practical statistician" required substantial judgment and skill—far more so than most academic social scientists appreciated. Stewart and his colleagues were not mere clerks engaged in mindless and naïve tabulation; they understood the complexities of selecting topics and designing appropriate survey forms, had faced the myriad difficulties accompanying field work, and laced their interpretations of results with one eye fixed on the perceived needs of the public and a second on the limitations of statistical surveys.

Nevertheless, the heyday of the practical statisticians had come prior to the First World War, a time when sampling theory was in its infancy and analytic methods (like correlations, regressions, etc.) had little connection to the practical compilation of government statistics. As statistical theory developed and drew greater attention to sampling strategies and data distribution, academic social scientists began to view complex mathematical analysis as a necessary component of reliable data production. The cleavage that developed between the practical statisticians and their academic counterparts was exacerbated in the BLS because of low funding (which made it an unattractive career path for economists), civil service rules (which protected older employees), and the long tenure of Stewart (who regarded many of the complex, proposed changes to BLS methods as "juggling" the figures).[34] Significantly, those federal agencies that employed substantial numbers of economists during the 1920s and made greater use of analytic techniques were either recent creations (such as the Bureau of Agricultural Economics and the Federal Reserve) or greatly expanded organizations (such as the Bureau of Foreign and Domestic Commerce under Hoover).[35]

Social scientists interested in mathematical analysis of sampling comprised a high percentage of COGSIS staff, including those who worked with the BLS, such as Margaret Hogg: Frederick F. Stephan, "History of the Uses of Modern Sampling Procedures," *JASA* 43, no. 241 (1948): 23, 28.

[34] ACSL members concluded that the BLS paid lower salaries than those granted by other federal agencies for similar positions: ACSL minutes, 6 April 1934, pp. 4–5, Advisory Committee Reports, box 80, Frances Perkins–General Subject File, DOL. On Stewart's attitude toward more complex analysis, see Reminiscences of Ewan Clague (1958), OHC-CU, pp. 47–48; Oral History with Aryness Joy Wickens, *Women in the Federal Government Project*, Schlesinger Library, p. 30.

[35] Duncan and Shelton, *Revolution in United States Government Statistics*, 10–11, 18, 21–22; Hawley, "Economic Inquiry and the State," 287–324; William Leach, *Land of*

Even after the 1930s reforms, some drift over time was natural between two sets of institutions (government agencies and university departments) that had significantly different constraints, objectives, and values. Indeed, the disjuncture that separated many government statisticians from their academic peers during the late 1920s did not prove unique: instead, the distinct institutional contexts for the groups fostered a cyclical pattern of slowly growing independence followed by periodic recalibration. Stewart may have felt vindicated to know that younger economists in the early 1970s echoed his successors' critiques from the 1930s, lamenting the lack of "creative thinking" in the bureau and worrying that it had "taken on the character of a production outfit, concerned almost entirely with the creation of numbers."[36]

The Nature of Academic Reform

If retrospective, participant accounts have mischaracterized the transition in federal statistical agencies from 1920 to 1935 as sophisticated "professionals" replacing backwards "clerks," so too have they misunderstood the nature of reforms instituted in that period, attributing much to the effects of the new academically certified staff.[37] In truth, many New Deal accomplishments within the BLS were built upon preexisting strategies (such as extending bureaucratic control over lower-level staff) or commonly voiced desires (such as expanding coverage and standardizing procedures) that now succeeded because of increased funding and the administrative flexibility engendered by a new administration facing a major national crisis. To be sure, the academics brought an influx of fresh ideas and approaches, but only some of these drew upon their more sophisticated mathematical background, and the legacy of the whole set is less clear-cut than contemporary accounts might lead one to expect.

The revisions to the BLS cost-of-living index provide an excellent example. Frances Perkins made reforming the index a top priority for ACSL, and the committee's initial review confirmed the pressing need for changes, finding the index "thoroughly inadequate for its purpose."[38] Although the

Desire: Merchants, Power, and the Rise of a New American Culture (New York: Pantheon Books, 1993), 358–368.

[36] "CPI Division: Year End Stock Tacking," 18 January 1971, Historical CPI, box 15, PFAC, BLS.

[37] Cf. Duncan and Shelton, *Revolution in United States Government Statistics*, 2–3.

[38] ACSL minutes, 9 June 1933, and Frances Perkins to Bryce Stewart, 3 April 1934, both in folder 2, box 1, CSB-ACSL, OMB; Frances Perkins to Stuart Rice, 13 September 1933, Advisory Committee Reports, box 80, Perkins–General Subject File, DOL. Stuart Rice to Frances Perkins, 15 September 1933, folder 6, box 1, CSB-ACSL, OMB.

full committee joined in reviews and recommendations, the largest influences came first from Helen Wright (a well-respected institutional economist and statistician at the University of Chicago's School of Social Service Administration) and then Margaret Hogg (a British statistician who had worked with Arthur Bowley at the London School of Economics before joining the Russell Sage Foundation). With Wright's return to teaching at Chicago in late 1933 and Hogg's severe illness in the summer of 1934, leadership fell to Faith Williams (now at the BLS) and ACSL member Ewan Clague.[39]

Two of the reforms instituted by ACSL were novel, in that earlier staff members neither desired nor contemplated these changes. First, like critics a decade earlier, Hogg argued that the bureau's use of expenditure data from 1917–1918 to weight an index based in 1913 had skewed the results, notably overemphasizing the importance of food. Moreover, through a clever set of simple mathematical steps, she demonstrated both the extent of the problem and how to compensate for it within the constant-goods framework.[40] In 1935, the BLS revised the weights of the six main component indexes (food, clothing, rent, house furnishings, fuel and light, and miscellaneous) based on Hogg's analysis and recalculated the index from 1913 onward.[41] The agency also followed a second, novel suggestion from Hogg that led it to alter the weights of individual items in the market basket.[42] Prior to 1935, the bureau assigned each item a weight based on its prominence in the family budget. But the staff did not have the time or money to collect prices on all items purchased by the average family; as a result, they gathered prices covering only about two-thirds of the family budget. If the prices of the remaining portion moved in a similar fashion, there was no problem. However, the New Deal staff argued that this was

---

[39] Wright devoted about six weeks to the project in late 1933; Hogg joined in November of that year, but did little after the following summer and died in 1935. Williams became involved as a consultant on expenditure surveys, and she joined the BLS in the fall of 1934. Clague's participation stemmed from his membership in COGSIS and ACSL. "Interim Report of the ACSL," April 1934, folder 3, box 1, CSB-ACSL, OMB; Faith Williams to Morris Copeland, 26 December 1934, folder F123, box 57, CSB-General Records, OMB; Ralph G. Hurlin, "Margaret Hope Hogg," *JASA* 30, no. 192 (1935): 753–754. For early comments and changes, see papers by Wright, Hogg, Williams, Clague, Jacob Perlman, and Hugh S. Hanna in *JASA*, 29 no. 185, supplement (1934): 24–32, 118–134; Faith M. Williams, Margaret H. Hogg, and Ewan Clague, "Revision of Index of Cost of Goods Purchased by Wage Earners and Lower-Salaried Workers," *MLR* 41, no. 3 (1935): 819–837.

[40] Margaret H. Hogg, "A Distortion in the Cost-of-Living Index," *JASA* 26, no. 173 (1931): 52–57.

[41] Williams, Hogg, and Clague, "Revision of Index," 825–827.

[42] Margaret H. Hogg, "Revising the Wage-Earners' Cost-of-Living Index," *JASA* 29, no. 185, Supplement (1934): 123.

unlikely, because there were systematic biases in the categories of goods left unpriced. (Recall, for example, that the 1920s staff had severely limited coverage of fresh produce since its quality could vary so dramatically.) To overcome this discrepancy, BLS staff developed the policy of price "imputation," whereby prices of a larger, unpriced set of goods were assumed to move in concert with a smaller, representative set that was then weighted to reflect expenditures on the full group. (For example, the weight for carrot prices reflected the proportional expenditure on carrots, beets, and turnips combined.)[43] Thus, although a substantial proportion of the budget remained unpriced, the groups were more fairly represented.

Both of these changes (the revision of group index weights and the policy of imputation) were probably improvements that the old staff would not have made on its own. At the same time, it would be a mistake to assume that the old staff was insensitive to weighting and sampling problems. In 1931, the BLS responded to the growing popularity of chain stores by weighting its price calculations using sales figures from the 1930 Census of Retail Distribution, thereby giving a more appropriate balance to prices from chain stores versus from independent retailers.[44] Likewise, most other 1930s alterations followed lines promoted by Ethelbert Stewart but which he had been forced to abandon because of insufficient funding. The most obvious example was a new national survey of working-class expenditures conducted by the BLS during 1934–1936 in order to update the market basket for the index (see Table 4.1), a project that Stewart had requested numerous times.[45] The BLS also used new funds to expand the coverage of the index, for example by boosting the number of foods priced in the index from forty-two to eighty-four. Finally, the agency added regional population weights to the city indexes when calculating the overall, national index in order to reflect population distributions. Again, Stewart had tried to expand geographical coverage to make the national index more representative of population distributions, although his concerns lay more with the absence of smaller cities in the index (an imbalance that also troubled Hogg).[46]

---

[43] Stella Stewart and Faith M. Williams, *Retail Prices of Food, 1923–1936*, BLS Bulletin, no. 635 (Washington, D.C.: U.S. GPO, 1937), 164–165; Williams, Hogg, and Clague, "Revision of Index," 821–825.

[44] Stewart and Williams, *Retail Prices of Food, 1923–1936*, 166–167.

[45] For one example, see Ethelbert Stewart to James J. Davis (Secretary of Labor), 21 July 1927, enclosure, "Report of the United States Commissioner of Labor Statistics for the Fiscal Year Ending June 30, 1927," box 1, Correspondence of the Commissioner with the Secretary of Labor and Units of the Labor Department, 1925–1929, BLS.

[46] Williams, Hogg, and Clague, "Revision of Index," 820–821, 828–830. Ethelbert Stewart to E. J. Henning (Asst. Secretary of Labor), 14 August 1923, box 2, 1916–1924, Selected General

Table 4.1 : *The 1934–1936 Market Basket*

The new market basket for the bureau's cost-of-living index was based on its 1934–36 expenditure survey (discussed later in the chapter). The number of items included in the index rose from 165 to 198, with most of the increase coming in the "Miscellaneous" category. Qualitative changes to the basket are described below by major category and illustrate the dramatic shifts that occurred in urban, lower-income consumption during the 1920s.

Food: Staff began pricing more fresh fruit and vegetables, while overall family expenditures on fruits and vegetables rose, largely at the expense of cereals and bakery products.

Clothing: The bureau actually reduced the number of items priced, and proportional expenditure in this category fell substantially (as did proportional expenditure on another staple: food).

Fuel, Electricity, and Ice: Expenditure on gas fell in favor of a large rise in electricity; coal also fell as other forms of fuel and energy were substituted for heating and cooking. Ice was added to the index.

House furnishings: Here, a critical new set of appliances appeared, indicating a major change in material living conditions: radios, washing machines, vacuum cleaners, electric and gas refrigerators, and light bulbs. The bureau likewise highlighted the rise in installment purchases that made these acquisitions possible and created new purchasing habits, such as buying matched sets of furniture.

Miscellaneous: The bureau added numerous items (often by expanding previous subcategories), but the largest change came in "Transportation," which showed substantial new expenditures for automobiles and auto care.

	Old Weight (1917–1919)	New Weight (1934–36)
Food	38.2%	33.9%
Clothing	16.6%	10.5%
Rent	13.4%	18.1%
Fuel (+ electricity, ice)	5.3%	6.4%
House furnishings	5.1%	4.2%
Miscellaneous	21.3%	26.9%

Sources: U.S. Bureau of Labor Statistics, "The Bureau of Labor Statistics' New Index of Cost of Living," *Monthly Labor Review* 51, no. 2 (August 1940): 367–404; National Industrial Conference Board. *The Cost of Living in the United States* (New York: National Industrial Conference Board, 1925), 87.

The most dramatic changes occurred in the administrative operation of the bureau, where New Deal leaders increased their oversight of field

Correspondence of the Bureau, 1908–1939, BLS. Stewart, "Recommendations Regarding the Bureau of Labor Statistics," 13 October 1924, p. 2, box 2, 1916–1924, Selected General Correspondence of the Bureau, 1908–1939, BLS. Hogg, "A Distortion," 57, note 1.

workers and tabulating staff, expanded administrative and technical documentation enormously, and tightened, formalized, and standardized operating procedures wherever possible. The nature of these reforms, however, owed far more to bureaucratic rationalization than to technical training in economics or statistics. Moreover, as with the continuity in methodology, these steps continued a centralizing trend that had been under way since at least the tenure of Charles P. O'Neill, if not before. Indeed, attempts over the years to gather more extensive and detailed statistics, which required more numerous and more elaborate instructions for field workers and tabulating staff, had proceeded hand-in-hand with the growth of bureaucratic oversight. Formalized rules and standardized procedures allowed for greater centralized control by top agency staff members, but also reduced costs by permitting the BLS to hire large numbers of temporary, low-skill employees (typically workers from relief roles during the 1930s). As with other areas, the New Deal accelerated the bureau's path along this trajectory, but it was not a fundamentally new shift.[47]

Further undermining any clear correlation between academic training and the statistical reforms of the early 1930s, discussions revealed that experts often did not speak with one voice and that "reforms" from one period might be discarded in the next. For instance, in 1940 the staff decided that the cost of the expanded food index outweighed its benefits, and they reduced the coverage from eighty-four to fifty-four items.[48] Or again, in 1931, Margaret Hogg criticized Paul Douglas for weighting city indexes by population (thereby overemphasizing the large cities that already dominated the index); in 1935, the BLS added population weights and made the situation more confusing by including extra weights for the population of "adjacent metropolitan areas where prices are considered to move in a similar fashion." ("Adjacent," as Figure 4.1 illustrates, had a loose meaning.)[49] More fundamentally, Hogg, Helen Wright, and Royal Meeker had all

---

[47] Thomas A. Stapleford, "The 'Most Important Single Statistic': The Consumer Price Index and American Political Economy, 1880–1955" (Ph.D. dissertation, Harvard University, 2003), 322–358. O'Neill's concerns and actions are described in "Original Transcript," 27 March 1913, folder 18/3, box 59, General Records, 1907–1942, Chief Clerk's Files, DOL. The growth of procedural rules even at an early stage is readily apparent by comparing the instructions for the 1901–1902 BLS expenditure survey and the 1917–1919 survey, reprinted in Helen Humes Lamale, *Methodology of the Survey of Consumer Expenditures in 1950* (Philadelphia: University of Pennsylvania, 1959), 186–188, 193–196.

[48] U.S. Bureau of Labor Statistics, "The Bureau of Labor Statistics' New Index of Cost of Living," *MLR* 51, no. 2 (1940): 372.

[49] Hogg, "A Distortion," 57, note 1. U.S. Bureau of Labor Statistics, "New Index of Cost of Living," 828.

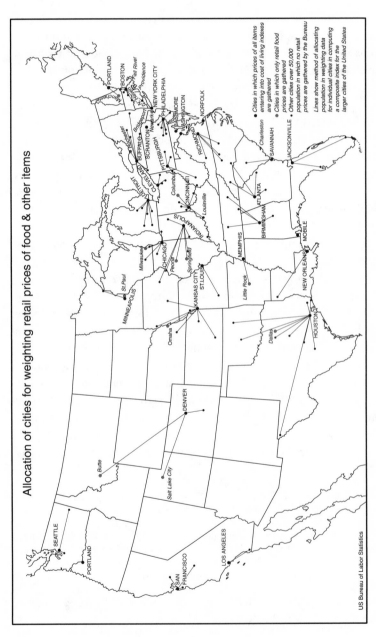

Allocation of cities for weighting retail prices of food & other items

- Cities in which prices of all items entering into cost of living indexes are gathered
- Cities in which only retail food prices are gathered
- Other cities over 50,000 population in which no retail prices are gathered by the Bureau

Lines show method of allocating population in weighting data for individual cities in computing a composite index for the larger cities of the United States

US Bureau of Labor Statistics

Figure 4.1: Regional Population Weighting for Cities in the Food Index, 1935. Notice the broad spread for cities like Denver and Houston.

Source: Williams, Hogg, and Clague, "Cost of Living," *Monthly Labor Review* 31, no. 3 (1935): 829.

insisted that the BLS delay plans for a new expenditure study because the depression made family purchases unrepresentative of regular economic activity.[50] Although BLS staff also worried about the abnormal nature of the mid-1930s, political opportunity still drove the schedule for changing economic statistics, just as it had during the war. Following the lead of numerous federal statisticians, Isador Lubin bypassed Congress and treated the 1934–1936 survey as a work-relief program for white-collar workers, thereby securing the several million dollars required for the project from the Works Progress Administration.[51]

Overall, the simple story about statistical reforms (academic credentials yields dramatic, novel transformations in procedures) does not withstand close scrutiny. What about the results of New Deal innovations? Here, too, the sharp condemnation of the existing index ("thoroughly inadequate for its purpose") faded to a murkier reality as the changes offset one another and produced only a minor net difference. For example, the increased emphasis on fresh fruits and vegetables (due to imputation) raised the food price index, but using estimated 1913 weights (rather than the weights from the 1917–1918 survey) reduced the importance of food relative to more stable expenses like rent. By 1935, the revised and original cost-of-living indexes were virtually identical (Chart 4.1). Likewise, despite widespread angst about the out-of-date market basket, a second revision in 1940 that incorporated results from the 1934–1936 expenditure survey also resulted in only slight deviations from the original (Chart 4.2).

In fact, this minor difference was not surprising and had been predicted by Royal Meeker. In the constant-goods framework, changing the market basket simply meant changing the weights assigned to different price shifts, and economists knew that in practice (absent some kind of systematic bias) such alterations usually had minimal effects.[52] Of course, there was a substantial difference between the total cost of the old market basket at 1935 prices and the cost of the new basket, which included additional expensive items such as automobiles, radios, and electric appliances that had become more common among working-class families since the war.[53] But

---

[50] Hogg, "Revising the Cost-of-Living Index," 122; Helen Wright, "Memorandum #1 on 'Cost of Living' Work," 16 October 1933, folder 6, CSB-ACSL, OMB; Meeker to Stuart Rice, 4 April 1933, p. 7, folder 4, box 1, CSB-ACSL.

[51] On the WPA, see Duncan and Shelton, *Revolution in United States Government Statistics*, 26. On the funding for the survey, see Reminiscences of Isador Lubin (1957), OHC-CU, pp. 101–102; William E. Leonard to Milton C. Forester, 10 March 1938, Appendix A, folder C58, box 27, CSB-General Records, OMB.

[52] Meeker to Stuart Rice, 4 April 1933, p. 7, folder 4, box 1, CSB-ACSL, OMB.

[53] U.S. Bureau of Labor Statistics, "New Index of Cost of Living," 367–404.

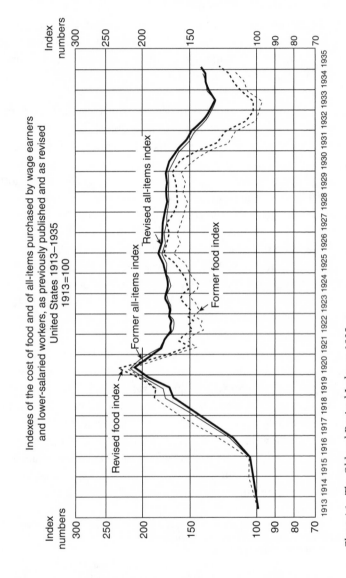

Chart 4.1: The Old and Revised Indexes, 1935.

Source: Williams, Hogg, and Clague, "Cost of Living," *Monthly Labor Review* 31, no. 3 (1935): 831.

Chart 4.2: The New and Original Cost-of-Living Indexes, 1940. The "new" index used data from the 1934–1936 expenditure survey for its market basket.

Source: U.S. Bureau of Labor Statistics, "The Bureau of Labor Statistics' New Index of Cost of Living," *Monthly Labor Review* 51, no. 2 (1940): 390.

the constant-goods approach, focused exclusively on measuring changes in prices rather than changes in total costs, demanded that this absolute cost difference be excluded from the index. Accordingly, the bureau "linked" the new (post-1935) index to the old index (used through January 1935) to form a chain index (see Chapter 3):

$$I_{1913-1940} = (I_{1913-1935, \, Original \, basket}) \times (I_{1935-1940, \, New \, basket})$$

As a result, the addition of new expenses into the post-1935 basket (automobiles, radios, etc.) did not affect the results.

What to make of such a revolution? We might be tempted to dismiss the academics' claims as self-important rhetoric and borrow Roland Falkner's response after critics dissected his wage statistics for the Aldrich reports in the late nineteenth century: "If practice differs from theory," Falkner had complained, "it is only because practical necessity has forced us into short cuts to reach approximately the same results as ... the more cumbersome procedure which theory demands."[54] This overlooks substantial elements of the 1930s story, however. First, the effects of limitations in earlier methods were unknown until the reformers pursued their changes. At any time, of course, statisticians face a trade-off between the unknown errors created by

---

[54] Roland P. Falkner, "Wage Statistics in Theory and Practice," *Publications of the American Statistical Association* 6, no. 46 (1899): 278.

the assumptions and approximations inherent in their methods and the costs of pursuing more sophisticated and extensive techniques. By 1933, the costs of inaction were steep. The unemployment controversy had cast doubt on federal economic statistics as a whole; the cost-of-living index became a specific problem when the Economy Act (March 1933) allowed reductions in federal salaries of up to 15 percent based on movements in the index. Naturally, federal employees and their unions attacked the measure and, with the aid of recently ousted commissioner Ethelbert Stewart, drew attention to the out-of-date market basket used by the BLS.[55] ACSL chairman Bryce Stewart told the committee that Frances Perkins felt unable to "justify the use of the present index," and indeed, both Perkins and Roosevelt used the formation of ACSL to demonstrate their commitment to providing accurate data on the cost of living.[56] A major aim of ACSL was thus to restore public confidence in federal labor statistics, and the academic social scientists itching to reshape federal agencies proved a convenient vehicle for accomplishing this task.

Moreover, though I have deliberately emphasized lines of continuity to this point, the BLS did change quite abruptly in at least two ways during the early New Deal. The first reflects the primary distinction between the old and new staff members: the greater interest in advanced mathematical and theoretical analysis among the latter. While the New Deal staff wrestled with the same kinds of problems and questions as their predecessors, they now approached many of these discussions (especially about sampling) through mathematical analysis. In doing so, they paved the way for the advent of probability sampling in government statistics, an innovation that would drastically reduce the cost of surveys. In this respect, Duncan and Shelton are quite correct to see the personnel changes of the late 1920s and 1930s as a necessary prerequisite for major transformations in statistical practice that would occur during the 1940s and 1950s.[57]

The second shift was equally dramatic but has received far less attention, for it involved not the technical content of federal labor statistics but the role of BLS statisticians. In the years following Roosevelt's inauguration, the BLS became a radically different organization, a transition that reflected

---

[55] "Federal Cuts Will Be Aired at Labor Meeting," *Washington Post*, 3 October 1933, p. 2; "U.S Budget Cut Stirs Workers to Plan Appeal," *Washington Post*, 20 November 1933, p. 1; Ethelbert Stewart, "Cost of Living Statistics and Wage Cuts," *The Union Postal Clerk*, November 1933, p. 18.

[56] "New Board Named to Fix Living Cost," *Washington Post*, 15 April 1933, p. 2; "Roosevelt Asks Revision of Cost of Living Index," *NYT*, 16 September 1933, p. 2.

[57] Stephan, "History of the Uses of Modern Sampling," 23–28; Duncan and Shelton, *Revolution in United States Government Statistics*, 32–73; Anderson, *American Census*, 176–190.

the return to a Democratic administration more sympathetic to labor but also the rapid expansion of bureaucratic power in the federal government and the new functions of economists within this political order. It is here that the real revolution in 1930s labor statistics can be found.

THE BUREAU OF LABOR STATISTICS IN
THE NEW DEAL ORDER

Historians have largely demolished the myth of the New Deal as a *de novo* creation that represented a radical and abrupt rupture with past American political history. Not only was much of the New Deal founded upon ideas that had germinated and ripened in the 1920s (including the underconsumption theories discussed in Chapter 3), but Herbert Hoover had already adopted a more active role for the government in economic management and championed actions (such as countercyclical public spending) that would be widely associated with Roosevelt's recovery program. Nevertheless, we can still recognize several critical distinctions that proved particularly relevant for the BLS.

First, in keeping with the vision of an "associative state," Hoover had promoted a "microeconomic approach to macroeconomic coordination" (in historian Guy Alchon's words), in which the federal government facilitated the dispersal of expert economic analysis (often created by independent organizations like the NBER) to guide the voluntary collaboration of individual firms, local governments, and trade associations in efforts to mitigate swings in the business cycle. By contrast, economic management in the New Deal increasingly occurred on the national level—led by federal officials, predicated on the deployment of federal power, and grounded more readily on federal (rather than private) planning and statistical analysis. The National Recovery Administration—whose corporatist representatives set industry-specific minimum wages and prices—is a perfect example, but one could easily cite the public works projects, agricultural policies, or proto-Keynesian fiscal policies that continued in later years.

Second, institutional economists had a central role in constructing the strategies adopted by the federal government in the 1930s, exemplified most visibly in "brain trust" member Rexford Tugwell, but extending down deeply into the federal substructure through influential figures like Mordecai Ezekiel, Gardiner Means, and a host of other economists. (The economists involved in COGSIS, for example, had strong ties to the institutionalist tradition, including Winfield Reifler, Morris Copeland, Willard Thorp, Lewis Douglas, and Ewan Clague.) Moreover, whereas economists in

Hoover's New Era had largely been excluded from federal power—housed in less prominent areas like the Department of Agriculture, confined to data collection in the Department of Commerce, or offering Hoover advice from within private organizations such as the NBER or SSRC—institutional economists now had direct access to the mechanisms of planning. In turn, many of these men maintained underconsumption and "purchasing power" as central themes throughout the New Deal, battling opponents who took the opposite tack and blamed overproduction. That view—the inverse of the underconsumption analysis—had adherents both in industry (especially among manufacturers with high fixed costs, such as those in steel, auto, electrical products, and petroleum) and in the New Deal itself (where production controls became the cornerstones of both the National Recovery Administration and federal agricultural policy).

Third, the Roosevelt administration gave much greater attention to workers and organized labor, and thus the Department of Labor—a marginal institution during most of the 1920s—once again became a powerful player in Washington politics. This change resonated with the emphasis on underconsumption, as pro-labor, New Deal liberals blamed the depression in part on rising income inequality and falling real wages. One response was to attack the price side of the equation, for example by strengthening consumer organizations or busting monopolies. But a second approach emphasized the inadequacy of common wages, a failure produced (so advocates claimed) by the weak labor movement. Accordingly, many pro-labor, New Deal liberals argued for protecting and expanding labor organizations to build and maintain mass purchasing power and thereby linked left-wing labor policy to macroeconomic recovery.[58]

[58] My comparison of the new era and New Deal in these three paragraphs is drawn from Ellis W. Hawley, *The New Deal and the Problem of Monopoly: A Study in Economic Ambivalence* (New York: Fordham University Press, 1995 [1966]); Ellis W. Hawley, "Herbert Hoover, the Commerce Secretariat, and the Vision of an 'Associative State,' 1921–1929," *JAH* 61, no. 1 (1974); Alchon, *The Invisible Hand of Planning*; William J. Barber, *From New Era to New Deal: Herbert Hoover, the Economists, and American Economic Policy, 1921–1933* (Cambridge: Cambridge University Press, 1985); Michael Bernstein, *The Great Depression: Delayed Recovery and Economic Change in America, 1929–1939* (Cambridge: Cambridge University Press, 1987); Colin Gordon, *New Deals: Business, Labor, and Politics in America, 1920–1935* (Cambridge: Cambridge University Press, 1994); William J. Barber, *Designs within Disorder: Franklin D. Roosevelt, the Economists, and the Shaping of American Economic Policy, 1933–1945* (Cambridge: Cambridge University Press, 1996); Alan Brinkley, *The End of Reform: New Deal Liberalism in Recession and War* (New York: Vintage Press, 1996); Meg Jacobs, *Pocketbook Politics: Economic Citizenship in Twentieth-Century America* (Princeton: Princeton University Press, 2005). Quotation from Alchon, *The Invisible Hand of Planning*, 4.

The effect of this context on the Bureau of Labor Statistics was both predictable and dramatic. According to minutes of an early ACSL meeting, Frances Perkins told the committee that she intended "to make the Department a vigorous and energetic organization for the promotion of labor's interests" and that a revitalized BLS would provide the technical grounding and economic analysis for this role (a position enthusiastically endorsed by Roosevelt, who was seeking to reduce the prominence of the Republican-dominated Commerce Department in producing economic data).[59] Perkins's choice for BLS commissioner, Isador Lubin, had strong ties to institutional economics, having trained under Thorstein Veblen, worked in various federal agencies during the First World War with both Veblen and Mitchell, and spent much of the 1920s affiliated with the Brookings Institution. Moreover, Lubin was a strong supporter of underconsumption analyses and an advocate of federally led economic planning to promote recovery. Since 1929, Lubin had been an economic adviser to Senators Robert Wagner and Robert La Follette, facilitating contacts between both men and institutional economists while spreading the purchasing-power gospel. A high point in this process came in the late fall of 1931, when Lubin gathered a host of "outstanding bankers, industrialists, engineers, economists, statisticians, trade-association executives and labor leaders" for three months of Senate hearings to consider whether "the consumptive power of our citizens [could] be raised to the point where it would equal our productive capacity." As this objective suggests, the hearings were the brainchild of purchasing-power progressives such as Harlow Persons (Taylor Society), George Soule, John M. Clark, and Sidney Hillman (Amalgamated Clothing Workers), and the hearings featured a heavy dose of sympathetic institutional economists.[60] After Roosevelt's election, Wagner recommended Lubin for the position of BLS commissioner. Having accepted the job, Lubin positioned the agency (with its studies of wages and retail prices) as the primary source for federal information on mass purchasing power, thereby making it an indispensable component of critical recovery programs. (Thus, to take one example, the BLS supplied much of the basic data on industry wages, prices, and hours used to set codes for the National Recovery Administration.) Moreover, Lubin soon built on his Washington connections and background in

59 "Report of the [ACSL] Meeting with Secretary Perkins," 12 September 1933, pp. 7–8, folder 5, box 1, CSB-ACSL, OMB. On Roosevelt's attitude toward the BLS, see Oral History with A. Ford Hinrichs (1978), DOL Historical Office, pp. 3–6.

60 Isador Lubin, "The New Lead from Capitol Hill," *The Survey* 67, no. 11 (1932): 573ff.; Lewis Lansky, "Isador Lubin: The Ideas and Career of a New Deal Labor Economist" (Ph.D. dissertation, Case Western Reserve University, 1976), 71–102.

economic planning in order to engage the web of federal agencies crafting and implementing federal economic policy.[61] Much of Lubin's influence on New Deal political economy evolved from his work with the National Resources Committee (NRC). In the period between the dismantling of the National Recovery Administration in 1935 and the start of war preparations at the end of the decade, the NRC's "Industrial Committee" was the only federal entity deeply engaged in economic planning across all sectors. During this stretch, some of the most well-known New Deal economists interested in consumer purchasing power participated in the Industrial Committee, including Lubin, Gardiner Means, Leon Henderson, Lauchlin Currie, Mordecai Ezekiel, and "consulting member" Alvin Hansen, all alongside less prominent but influential research staff such as Henry D. White (Treasury), Louis Bean (Agriculture), and Thomas Blaisdell (Social Security Board). Accordingly, the Industrial Committee played a crucial role in shifting the Roosevelt administration from the concern with restricting production (characteristic of the National Recovery Administration) toward an emphasis on boosting mass consumption. The committee directed its attention to the production-consumption balance, conducting numerous studies designed to aid planning, including investigations into national consumption. In 1935, the committee began a mammoth "Study of Consumer Purchases" that gathered income data from 300,000 families across the country, with 60,000 of those families also supplying information about annual expenditures (subdivided into more than 500 categories). Administered by the BLS and BHE, and funded largely by the Works Progress Administration, the project was a direct descendant of a proposal first discussed by the SSRC in 1929 but which had proven impossible to conduct within the framework of the "associative state" because of its great expense. Now a reality thanks to New Deal money, Industrial Committee members hoped to use the study's data to guide federal economic planning by forecasting how consumption patterns would shift with changes in the distribution and amount of national income.[62]

[61] Lansky, "Isador Lubin," 129; Goldberg and Moye, *First Hundred Years*, 160, 171, 173–174; Joseph P. Goldberg, "Frances Perkins, Isador Lubin, and the Bureau of Labor Statistics," *MLR* 103, no. 4 (1980): 25–26, 28–29.

[62] Frederic S. Lee, "From Multi-Industry Planning to Keynesian Planning: Gardiner Means, the American Keynesians, and National Economic Planning at the National Resources Committee," *Journal of Policy History* 2, no. 2 (1990): 186–212; Brinkley, *End of Reform*, 94–105, 134–141; Stapleford, "Market Visions," 425–437. Membership drawn from the minutes of the Industrial Committee, boxes 301–302, Central Office Records, NRPB.

In the end, the committee's goals proved too ambitious, but conversations among its members nevertheless helped to shape New Deal plans that linked fiscal policy, consumption, and economic recovery—all later formalized in Keynesian terms. In 1939, Isador Lubin used data from the Study of Consumer Purchases in his opening testimony before the Temporary National Economic Committee, a joint congressional-executive committee created by Roosevelt that became a key vehicle for introducing an "Americanized" Keynesianism into federal economic strategies. Serving as the representative of the Department of Labor, Lubin deployed BLS statistics (including the survey data) to emphasize the need to raise mass-purchasing power, and later joined Lauchlin Currie (alongside several other Industrial Committee members) as an advocate of Keynesian approaches (a path increasingly pushed by the successor to the NRC, the National Resources Planning Board). Lubin's growing influence over federal economic policy was exemplified by the leave of absence he began in 1940 to devote his energies full-time to war mobilization planning, eventually becoming a direct adviser to the president.[63]

The contrast between Lubin's power and that of his predecessors is sharp. None of the previous commissioners had been shy about voicing their own views, but aside from their function in settling certain labor disputes, they had minimal effects on federal economic policy. In large part, of course, this was because federal intervention into the economy prior to the New Deal was confined mainly to areas dominated by congressional politics—such as tariffs and regulatory functions—or was controlled within insulated agencies such as the Federal Reserve. On those few occasions that saw broader, bureaucratic federal action—namely during the war or under Hoover—businessmen or civil servants in other departments had taken the lead, occasionally (in later years) with advice from private social science organizations like the NBER. There is no evidence, for example, that Royal Meeker made any substantial contribution to economic policy (or even labor policy) during the First World War, and Ethelbert Stewart certainly never had Hoover's ear.

The revitalization of the Department of Labor, the expansion of federal economic management during the 1930s, and the perceived connections between working-class purchasing power and macroeconomic growth all contributed to a new prominence for the BLS, of which Lubin's influence was but one sign. Between 1934 and 1939 (a period in which the BLS

---

[63] Brinkley, *End of Reform*, 124–131, 246–258; Barber, *Designs within Disorder*, 108–131; Goldberg, "Frances Perkins, Isador Lubin, and the Bureau of Labor Statistics," 29.

cost-of-living index rose barely 4 percent), the bureau's regular budget nearly doubled, while its total budget (including appropriations for special projects like the expenditure surveys) more than quadrupled, as did the size of its regular staff.[64] The agency's new leaders—who had studied political economy in graduate school, who cherished their ability to interpret quantitative results through the lens of economic theory, and who had arrived in the midst of an unresolved economic crisis—likewise shaped an administrative culture attuned to broader themes in economic policy beyond traditional "labor" matters. An excellent example is Lubin's deputy, A. (Albert) Ford Hinrichs. Although Hinrichs wrote his dissertation at Columbia University on labor unions in the coal industry, he built his early reputation as an expert on national economic planning. Having made several trips to Europe to study planning in action, Hinrichs was recruited by the National Planning Board (predecessor of the NRC) to co-write a book on national planning with the institutional economist Lewis Lorwin (who had been friends with Lubin since their days at the Brookings Institute). On Lorwin's recommendation, Hinrichs joined the BLS as Chief Economist, where he served as Lubin's alternate to both the Industrial Committee of the NRC and the Temporary National Economic Committee. When Hinrichs became Acting Commissioner in Lubin's absence, he also continued Lubin's role as a central economic policy adviser to Frances Perkins.[65]

This new, broader focus for the BLS reflected an equally new position of labor policy within much of New Deal thought. By the late 1930s, federal labor policy was no longer merely a matter of resolving labor disputes, defining the legal status of unions and their activities, setting workplace regulations, and occasionally guiding the labor market itself (during war, for instance, or by restricting immigration). With the attention to underconsumption, later refined within the framework of American Keynesianism, labor policy had been linked to a larger perspective on economic management. As Senator Robert Wagner argued while promoting the 1935 National Labor Relations Act (with the help of institutional labor economists as advisers), a strong labor movement could force companies

[64]   Goldberg and Moye, *First Hundred Years*, 171; Goldberg, "Frances Perkins, Isador Lubin, and the Bureau of Labor Statistics," 25.

[65]   A. Ford Hinrichs, *The United Mine Workers of America, and the Non-Union Coal Fields* (New York: Columbia University Press, 1923); Lewis L. Lorwin and Albert Ford Hinrichs, *National Economic and Social Planning: Theory and Practice with Special Reference to the United States* (Washington, D.C.: National Resources Board, 1935). Oral History with A. Ford Hinrichs (1978), p. 2. For examples of Hinrich's role as policy adviser to Perkins, see his memos on wage control policy during 1943–1944 in box 34, Perkins papers.

to pay higher wages and thus facilitate an adequate distribution of consuming power.[66] Proper labor policy could therefore prompt an economic recovery and help to sustain stability or growth. In turn, just as labor itself had a new place in political economy, so too did formerly narrow "labor statistics." Most notably, BLS data about prices and wages now had a crucial significance for macroeconomic analysis, and the institutional economists who filled the federal bureau positioned themselves as vital and even powerful participants in a burgeoning system of bureaucratic, federal oversight of the economy. From a marginal agency in the 1920s, the BLS had been transformed into a central bulwark of the New Deal order.

Yet there were unresolved tensions lurking within this system. On the level of political economy itself, the link between underconsumption and labor policy had serious potential weaknesses. Theoretically, underconsumption could be ameliorated through a broad rise in national consumer purchasing power that would balance increased productivity. Wages, however, had specific microeconomic determinants, such as the financial status of particular companies and industries. It was unclear whether industry-specific changes in productivity could permit wage hikes sufficiently broad enough to offset the new goods. (Rising productivity in the auto industry might allow auto companies to raise wages, for example, but there was no guarantee that this would create a market sufficient to absorb new production or that other economic sectors could carry the slack.) This mismatch made it tempting to look toward broad fiscal policy (which might affect larger numbers of consumers) or toward the other determinate of purchasing power: not income, but prices. If rising productivity led to reduced prices, that alone would permit increased consumption that could balance the greater output. These advantages led many underconsumption advocates in the 1930s, including moderates such as Harold Moulton and statist planners such as Gardiner C. Means, to focus on the price side of the equation, looking for the sources of artificially high prices and for potential solutions.[67] Even those who gave greater attention to low wages recognized that if wage increases merely translated into higher prices, there would be

[66] Jacobs, *Pocketbook Politics*, 138–149.

[67] On Moulton's views, see Harold G. Moulton, "The Trouble with Capitalism Is the Capitalists," Fortune, November 1935, 77ff.; Donald T. Critchlow, *The Brookings Institution, 1916–1952: Expertise and the Public Interest in a Democratic Society* (DeKalb: Northern Illinois University Press, 1985), 122–124. On Means, see Gardiner C. Means, "Industrial Prices and Their Relative Inflexibility," U.S. Senate Document 13, 74th Congress, 1st sess. (Washington, D.C.: U.S. GPO, 1935); Barber, *Designs within Disorder*, 60–64, 126–127; Lee, "From Multi-Industry Planning to Keynesian Planning," 186–212.

no net gain. Preventing companies from setting or maintaining artificially high prices therefore was a central component of any economic strategy built on underconsumption.

In traditional economic theory, of course, market mechanisms automatically shifted prices to the most efficient levels for existing production costs and demand, making excessively high prices impossible. During the 1930s, however, critics both inside and outside the New Deal had argued that many sectors of the economy no longer operated as true free markets; rather, the concentration of economic power through trade associations or market dominance created "sticky" prices that were higher than free competition would produce. The price side of the underconsumption problem thus derived from monopoly practices. What to do about that conclusion was unclear, however. Classical liberal theory required breaking up concentrated power to permit increased competition. But a large and ultimately more influential group of New Deal liberals argued that full destruction of concentrated power was impractical in a capital-intensive, industrial economy and unwise because it would eliminate economies of scale. Once business proved incapable of self-regulation in the early years of the National Recovery Administration, the remaining solution appeared to be closer state management of highly concentrated industries, a position advocated most forcefully within the Roosevelt administration in the latter half of the 1930s by former associates of Rexford Tugwell, such as Gardiner Means and Mordecai Ezekiel. Unfortunately for these statist planners, their objectives proved no more practical or politically viable than did a wide-ranging antitrust campaign announced with great fanfare by Thurman Arnold in 1938 in which Arnold targeted price-inflating, anti-competitive practices. By the end of the 1930s, the monopoly problem remained unresolved, and it would resurface to plague the legacy of New Deal political economy after the coming war.[68]

The statistical corollary to the unstable link between labor policy and underconsumption appeared in the objectives of the bureau's cost-of-living index: could one statistic guide wage adjustments for particular groups of workers and provide a general measure of consumer purchasing power? The economists advising the BLS recognized one component of this problem, namely defining appropriate market baskets: in an early memo for ACSL, Helen Wright had recommended using at least seven indexes to cover different socioeconomic groups until statisticians could judge the significance

---

[68] Hawley, *The New Deal and the Problem of Monopoly*; Brinkley, *End of Reform*; Barber, *Designs within Disorder*, esp. 23–79, 112–128.

of any variations between these statistics.[69] In principle, this was a relatively trivial problem amenable to empirical study. In practice, however, the costs of gathering and tabulating data limited the bureau to a single index, and a combination of tradition and practical constraints kept the focus of the BLS index rather narrow.

The market basket for the bureau's original index had reflected its wartime use in labor arbitration, giving priority to the white, relatively skilled workers who comprised many unions. During the 1917–1919 survey, BLS agents conducted interviews with 12,837 families of wage-earners and salaried workers making less than $2,000 per year. However, the data for the 741 "colored" families in this sample were not incorporated into the bureau's cost-of-living index. Likewise, "slum" and "charity" families were excluded, as were "non-English speaking families who have been less than five years in the United States." Furthermore, "at least seventy-five percent of the family income" had to come from "the principal breadwinner or others who contribute all earnings to the family fund," while no boarders were permitted and only a maximum of three lodgers. On this last point, Royal Meeker conceded that the focus on "normal natural families" obscured "the almost universal practice of taking in lodgers during the housing shortage of the war period." Nevertheless, traditional ideals about working-class family life and the economics of wage-earning necessitated the narrow focus: "The object in making the [income, lodging, and boarding] exclusions," explained one BLS report, "was to secure families dependent for support, as largely as possible, on the earnings of the husband."[70]

The bureau's 1934–1936 expenditure survey continued the same emphasis on wage workers and low-salaried clerks; consequently, the revised index still only covered a subset of even the lower-income, urban population, not to mention all "consumers." The 1934–1936 eligibility requirements mixed income and occupation: both high-salaried employees and managerial supervisors of any kind were excluded, but so too were the self-employed (regardless of income) or those who worked on commission (including what the bureau dubbed "street trades" such as "selling on the street, delivering newspapers, [or] shining shoes"). Equally critical, given the timing

[69]   Helen Wright, "Cost of Living Memorandum No. 1," December 1933, p. 10, folder 6, box 1, CSB-ACSL, OMB.
[70]   Lamale, *Methodology of the Survey of Consumer Expenditures*, 197; Royal Meeker, "What Is the American Standard of Living?" *MLR* 9, no. 1 (1919): 7; U.S. Bureau of Labor Statistics, "Cost of Living in the United States–Family Incomes," *MLR* 9, no. 6 (1919): 30; National Industrial Conference Board, *The Cost of Living in the United States* (New York: National Industrial Conference Board, 1925), 70, n. 2.

of the survey, it excluded any families who had received "relief" during the year—whether from private sources or government programs such as the Works Progress Administration—and those with annual income below $500. Finally, to simplify data collection and analysis, staff continued to exclude single individuals, families with boarders or numerous lodgers, and certain workers who might receive substantial non-monetary support (e.g., domestic servants, who might live in their workplace or receive meals).[71]

These restrictions had gender and racial consequences that undercut other efforts by the New Deal staff to make the survey and the cost-of-living index more inclusive. For example, the staff abandoned the 1917–1919 survey's emphasis on families "dependent ... upon the earnings of the husband" and also began including data from black families when creating the market basket for the index. But the elimination of domestic servants and single individuals nevertheless cut out a large swath of the female workforce. Similarly, the occupational restrictions and the no-relief policy likewise greatly reduced the size and influence of the sample of black families, so that national averages that included black families showed only a "negligible difference" from those for whites alone (despite racially distinct purchasing habits).[72] Thus, the expenditure survey, the cost-of-living index, and indeed the bureau as a whole tended to maintain their long-standing emphases on white families of employed males who worked as wage-earners or low-salaried clerks.

Beyond population coverage, equally troubling theoretical questions loomed. The tension between collecting data for wage adjustments and data for measuring "consumer purchasing power" threatened to intersect the conceptual problems interwoven into cost-of-living statistics. ACSL's first memo on the bureau's index declared that "the 'cost of living' is not a single phenomenon, but a composite one involving all the economic and social forces influencing family incomes and consumption habits," and conceded that "it is not now possible to construct an 'index' of the cost of living."[73] Instead, BLS statisticians had tried to isolate one component of

[71] "Plan for Tabulating Data on Family Expenditures of Employed Wage Earners and Lower-Salaried Workers," 25 April 1935, p. 4, 1934–36 Wage Earner Study–Tabulation Instructions–Rev. & Old, box 1, Records of the Consumer Expenditure Survey Program and Predecessors, BLS. Lamale, *Methodology of the Survey of Consumer Expenditures*, 209–210.

[72] Faith M. Williams and Alice Hanson, *Money Disbursements of Wage Earners and Clerical Workers, 1934–36, Summary Volume*, BLS Bulletin, no. 638 (Washington, D.C.: U.S. GPO, 1941), 366–367, 371.

[73] "The index of the cost of living," 9 August 1933, folder 6, box 1, CSB-ACSL, OMB. No author is listed, but it may have been written by Edna Lonigan.

this phenomenon, price changes, that they also linked to macroeconomic considerations such as purchasing power. But did this narrower concept match the notion of the cost of living as commonly understood by labor unions, and if not, what should be done about that disjuncture?

The answers to that question depended upon a larger issue: who set the agenda for the BLS and its investigations? ASA president Stuart Rice reported that Perkins wanted the BLS to be "a service organization to labor particularly, as well as the public"—but that was an ambiguous statement, as Rice realized, and it left aside the bureau's relationship both to the rest of the federal government and to the community of economists and statisticians who now supplied its leadership and were supposed to sanction its work.[74] The tensions among these potential roles became apparent when the BLS and ACSL members convened a meeting of statisticians associated with labor unions in the spring of 1934 to discuss changes to BLS statistics. In the combined context of falling prices, the Economy Act (which linked federal wages to the BLS index), and the depression more generally, union representatives revived the living-wage ideal and pressed the bureau to disavow the use of its existing index to adjust wages. Indeed, half of the attendees felt the BLS should actually abandon its current index, and a substantial majority favored the creation of a new "health and decency" budget to provide a substitute measure of the "cost of living."[75] Although both Royal Meeker and Helen Wright had also recommended updating the bureau's old standard budget, the BLS ignored these requests, and not without reason—as we saw in Chapter 3, such a task was inevitably subjective and fraught with political risk.[76]

The compromise fell along the same lines as it had in the 1920s. In 1936, Margaret Stecker (former economist for the National Industrial Conference Board) published two standard budgets for the Works Progress Administration: a "maintenance level" that met "average minimum requirements for industrial service" and an "emergency level" that was not sufficient for long-term health. Though Stecker insisted that her maintenance level surpassed the older minimum of subsistence, she also conceded it did not meet the previously defined standard of "health and decency." In practice, even these reduced budgets proved too generous for administrative

---

[74] Stuart Rice to Joseph B. Willits, 5 April 1933, pp. 1–2, folder 5, box 1, CSB-ACSL, OMB.

[75] Minutes of the Meeting of Labor Unions' Statisticians (Washington, D.C.), 18 May 1934, pp. 6–9, folder 2, box 1, CSB-ACSL, OMB.

[76] Helen Wright, "Memorandum #1 on 'Cost of Living' Work," 16 October 1933, folder 6, box 1; Royal Meeker to Stuart Rice, 4 April 1933, p. 7, folder 4, box 1, both in CSB-ACSL, OMB.

use. When New Deal liberals pressed for national minimum wage regulation in the mid-1930s, many Southern businessmen (who benefited from regional wage differentials) and their congressional supporters bitterly attacked the proposal. The final legislation, the Fair Labor Standards Act of 1938, set a mandatory wage floor for a limited set of industries at 25 cents per hour, adjustable by industry boards to a maximum of 40 cents per hour. At 40 hours per week, this *maximum* wage floor translated to about $800 per year, which was still 10 percent less than the average income needed to meet Stecker's lower, emergency level and provided only about 60 percent of her maintenance level.[77]

In such a political environment, it is unsurprising that the BLS declined to create new versions of its own, more generous "health and decency" budgets from the 1920s and instead confined itself to updating the costs of Stecker's budgets intermittently until 1943. In contrast to the agency's tepid commitment to standard budgets, the BLS gathered huge sums of money to update its cost-of-living index and to undertake the large Study of Consumer Purchases, both of which had connections to urgent questions about mass purchasing power and appeared to avoid the obvious normative judgments that plagued standard budget projects. Reasonable as these choices were, they did not satisfy most unions, who wanted the Department of Labor (in the form of the BLS) to endorse a more generous standard budget for adequate wages.[78]

This episode illustrates how the bureau's staff, like most New Deal liberals, viewed themselves as independent agents rather than as representatives of particular economic groups amidst a fully corporatist political economy. It is true, as I suggested earlier, that New Deal liberals actively worked to organize certain economic sectors (farmers, unions, consumers) to provide a counterweight to established corporate power. Yet they envisioned the federal government as a semi-independent entity alongside these interest groups, an institution supporting something more than the sum of group demands. The Department of Labor might become, as Perkins put it, "a vigorous and energetic organization for the promotion of labor's interests," but its policies would not be dictated by union officials. The distinction was

---

[77] Margaret Loomis Stecker, *Intercity Differences in Costs of Living in March 1935, 59 Cities* (Washington, D.C.: U.S. GPO, 1937), xii–xiv, xix; George E. Paulsen, *A Living Wage for the Forgotten Man: The Quest for Fair Labor Standards, 1933–1941* (Selinsgrove: Susquehanna University Press, 1996).

[78] Goldberg and Moye, *First Hundred Years*, 158. For union interest in more generous standard budgets, see proceedings of BLS conferences with union research directors, 1941: 44, 57–60, Labor Research Directors Conference, box 1, ACF 1941–62, BLS.

similarly captured in Perkins's description of the BLS as "a service organization to labor particularly, *and the public*" (emphasis added). What did the latter mean?

We can gain some insight from the book on "planning" created in 1935 for the National Planning Board (the forerunner of the NRC and other New Deal planning agencies) by Isador Lubin's friend Lewis Lorwin and BLS Chief Economist Ford Hinrichs. Having surveyed "planning" in a variety of national contexts, in the final chapter Lorwin insisted that democratic planning required resolving conflicts not by fiat (totalitarianism) or sheer compromise (the "parliamentary system") but rather "by working out long range national objectives and by the use of research and scientific analysis." The trick was to ensure that political conflict between groups would be "kept within bounds and given a rational form." Within this system, government agents would serve to regulate the discussion and ultimately represent "the people as a whole." This in turn would require "a new class of civil servants," distinguished by their devotion to the "national interest" and their technical expertise.[79]

In its general orientation, Lorwin's perspective matched that of Carroll Wright, who had rejected calls from labor activists to be (in his view) a partisan advocate and had insisted that bureaus of labor statistics existed to serve the public by providing accurate, informed, and nonpartisan empirical information on relevant topics. As Wright had discovered, however, producing statistics for the public was a tricky endeavor, for it was not clear how to discern public desires, nor that such discernment would produce a clear and coherent agenda, nor even that these goals would match what the practical statistician believed to be possible, much less valuable. Wright had found himself pulled this way and that, relying on a combination of congressional mandates and direct petitions, all sifted by his own judgment. The bureau's activities took on a definite direction only as Wright began to focus on skilled workers and unions, and again as the executive branch became a stronger institutional force, especially amidst the First World War. There, under the sway of an extensive and powerful bureaucracy aiming to guide economic activity, it was easy to conflate the "public" with the "state"—not in an abstract sense, but rather as the specific needs of colleagues and immediate superiors, all filtered through one's training within a particular disciplinary community. This did not mean manipulating or falsifying results—there is no evidence that BLS staff ever even considered such a step—but these allegiances could shape what topics the

---

[79] Lorwin and Hinrichs, *National Economic and Social Planning*, 453–454, 448.

agency pursued, what methods it used, what questions it asked, and how it presented the results. Hence, Royal Meeker had kept his concerns about the bureau's cost-of-living statistics largely private during the war and produced the information anyway, while former union consultant Jett Lauck had warned the Shipbuilding Labor Adjustment Board not to share details of the calculations with "union executives." Such a conflation between "public" and "state" proved equally tempting for New Deal liberals, convinced that workers' interests and the general public interest (both rightly construed) largely lay along the same path, and that Roosevelt was committed to pursuing both as best he could. The question was whether these assumptions would hold true.

DELINEATING THE REVOLUTION

The transformation of BLS statistics and staff during the 1930s constituted a particularly dramatic example of a cyclical process in which government agencies achieved (temporarily) greater coordination with academic experts. The context made this particular realignment seem more radical that it actually was: greatly improved funding, a general shift in federal personnel as an ambitious Democratic regime ended a decade-long Republican dominance, generational and intellectual gaps between the young social scientists and the "practical statisticians" (especially concerning the importance of advanced mathematics), and the previous continuity in the bureau (anchored by Stewart's leadership)—all led the new staff to perceive a sharp difference between themselves and their predecessors, a fissure that they attributed indirectly (and misleadingly) to their own "professional" orientation. In practice, at least for cost-of-living statistics, many of their reforms continued existing trends and the improvements had little immediate effect on final results, serving rather to restore public confidence in federal labor statistics and pave the way for future developments in sampling theory.

Yet this strictly internal perspective—looking primarily at the figures produced by the BLS and the methods advocated by its staff—does not exhaust our modes of analysis. If we consider the function of the Bureau of Labor Statistics and its top staff, we can see a sharper break occurring in the years surrounding 1932. As New Dealers abandoned the voluntarist, microeconomic "planning" of Hoover's New Era to experiment with federal economic management on a scale not seen since the First World War, they necessarily required tools for monitoring and assessing national economic performance, in other words, reliable national economic statistics. Under a Democratic administration and supported by the left-wing, underconsumption explanation for the depression, the BLS (and especially its statistics on wages and prices) quickly became a critical part of the federal planning apparatus. Meanwhile, the new staff members—trained in economics and often holding deep interests in economic policy—readily integrated themselves in to the policymaking process within the Roosevelt administration.

As Ford Hinrichs described in an interview decades later, it was a "very exciting" time to work at the bureau, when the top staff could not only design statistical measures but help "put the figures to use," for—unlike during the 1920s—many of the key "users" were now fellow bureaucrats in the federal government.[80] But if it was an exciting time, it was also built on a shaky foundation, one that would soon collapse and bring Hinrichs down with it. As we have seen, the cost of living was an elusive concept with several possible meanings, an ambiguity not eliminated by turning it into an index number. At the same time, the loyalties of the bureau were likewise split, between the labor movement and "the public" (however that might be defined). In the context of the 1930s, alongside a newly awakening labor movement and a deflationary depression economy, these fissures had been easily ignored. In the wartime environment they would reinforce one another and thereby foment a stark challenge to the cost-of-living index, the staff's understanding of its function in the government, and the New Deal order itself.

[80] Oral History with A. Ford Hinrichs (1978), pp. 5–7, 33–34.

5

Tracking an Elusive Home-Front "Enemy": Price
Indexes and Wage Adjustment

It has seemed to us all a very simple matter to draw up a table with which to show the movements of general prices and of the value of money. But this is because, as it were, we economists have been allowed to amuse ourselves in this task. Since no practical consequences were to follow, nobody has felt moved to object to any particular table which anybody has thought fit to prepare. But we may be very sure that just as soon as it appears that a table of general prices is to have important financial consequences for men in various relations, just so soon a multitude of influences, some shrewdly intelligent and some not, will be set to work to shape the table this way and that.[1]

—Willard C. Fisher,
Conference of the American Economics Association, 1912

Throughout this book we have encountered a series of unresolved questions that confronted Americans as they sought to manage the disruptions accompanying industrial capitalism while harnessing its productive power. The narrowest set concerned cost-of-living statistics: Were aggregate measures of retail price change the best tools for adjusting wages to meet a rising "cost of living"? What did that phrase mean anyway? How could you track the cost of a fixed standard of living in a dynamic economic environment where prices, purchasing habits, and goods were all changing at once? Superimposed upon these debates we have found more general questions about the function of federal labor statistics in American political economy: Who determined the agenda for the Bureau of Labor Statistics? How did the staff resolve their myriad of loyalties—to their superiors and colleagues within the government, to the larger professional community of technical experts, and to the demands of unions? Finally and most broadly, how could statistics help restrain conflict and ease adjustments within an industrial economy?

[1]   "Standardizing the Dollar–Discussion." *AER* 3, no. 1 (1913): 40.

All of these themes collided in a major controversy over the BLS cost-of-living index during the Second World War, a struggle that we will follow in detail over the next two chapters. The multiple sources of this conflict are not hard to recognize in light of previous events. For the BLS, the Second World War repeated many elements of the first. Once again, government officials turned to economic statistics to help manage the economy, and the bureau's data, including its cost-of-living index, found a central place in labor arbitration hearings. Like twenty years earlier, the wartime economy also complicated these calculations: shortages, rationing, quality changes, shifts in consumer behavior, and widespread economic transformations all highlighted the problem of using a fixed market basket to track the cost of living.

Still, these parallels appeared in a markedly different context, creating a new dynamic. By 1940, the BLS was both substantially larger and more prominent, led by liberal, institutional economists who positioned the agency as a central part of an expanded system of federal economic management (Chapter 4). For Lubin, Hinrichs, and many New Deal economists, economic statistics both justified and maintained this new order: providing the documentation that federal action was necessary, guiding any intervention, and permitting the negotiation of fair compromises between competing groups. Technical expertise and quantitative facts would limit the threat posed by the consolidation of power, making both a stronger central government and a quasi-industrial corporatism (dominated by large corporations and a growing base of industrial unions) safe for democracy. But what if the facts themselves were under dispute?

Indeed, external developments over the interwar period had placed labor statistics in a more precarious position. By the 1920s, larger companies and trade associations had begun hiring their own technical experts, using them for internal purposes and to sway public debate. (Recall, for example, how the NICB produced expenditure surveys and its own national cost of living index after the First World War—Chapter 3.) During the mid- to late 1930s, these groups worked hard to dismantle the statistical arguments of New Deal programs deemed to be anti-business.[2] Meanwhile, as unions expanded rapidly under the 1935 National Labor Relations Act (which protected the right to organize and gave the National Labor Relations Board legal oversight of industrial relations), they too added research staff.

[2]   E.g., John Scoville and Noel Sargent, eds., *Fact and Fancy in the T.N.E.C. Monographs: Reviews of the 43 Monographs Issued by the Temporary National Economic Committee* (New York: National Association of Manufacturers, 1942).

Nowhere was this more evident than within the newly formed Congress of Industrial Organizations (CIO), an umbrella organization that was more centralized, more disciplined, and more committed to technical, intellectual expertise than the older AFL. Had Carroll Wright and Ethelbert Stewart still been alive, they might have warned the 1940s bureau of the potential danger posed by these separate institutional bases for statistical research, where, like the state bureaus in the nineteenth century or various private associations in the early twentieth, different research traditions could promote distinct visions of statistical work. Sure enough, shortly after the bureau's cost-of-living index became the centerpiece of wage-control efforts, unions began to complain about inaccuracies; in early 1944, the CIO and AFL released their own set of cost-of-living statistics showing a wartime increase nearly double that of the BLS figures.[3]

The result was a bitter public feud that raged intensely for six months and lingered for many years, leaving a legacy of heated rhetoric rarely encountered by government statisticians. (The CIO and AFL, for instance, labeled one BLS report on the cost of living "the most insulting document to organized labor that has emanated from the Department of Labor since its creation.")[4] And if the immediate effects of the controversy have dissipated, it nevertheless retains its intellectual power. Evaluations of the wartime civilian economy, and especially the effectiveness of wartime price controls and other anti-inflationary programs, depend upon equally contentious evaluations of the validity of cost-of-living statistics.[5] The wartime debates have also become a salient example of several central theoretical problems for cost-of-living indexes (most notably how to account for quality

---

[3]   George Meany and R. J. Thomas, *Cost of Living: Recommended Report for the Presidential Committee on the Cost of Living* (Washington, D.C.: Congress of Industrial Organizations, 1944); Philip Murray and R. J. Thomas, *Living Costs in World War II, 1941–1944* (Washington, D.C.: Congress of Industrial Organizations, 1944).

[4]   "AFL-CIO ask Poll of Housewives on War Increases in Cost of Living," 29 February 1944, *AFL Weekly News.*

[5]   Hugh Rockoff, *Drastic Measures: A History of Wage and Price Controls in the United States* (Cambridge: Cambridge University Press, 1984), 127–176; Milton Friedman and Anna Jacobson Schwartz, *A Monetary History of the United States, 1867–1960* (Princeton: Princeton University Press, 1963), 557–558; Hugh Rockoff, "The United States: From Ploughshares to Swords," in *The Economics of World War II: Six Great Powers in International Comparison*, ed. Mark Harrison (Cambridge: Cambridge University Press, 1998), 81–121; Robert Higgs, "Wartime Prosperity? A Reassessment of the U.S. Economy in the 1940s," *Journal of Economic History* 52, no. 1 (1992): 49–53; Geofrey Mills and Hugh Rockoff, "Compliance with Price Controls in the United States and the United Kingdom During World War II," *Journal of Economic History* 47, no. 1 (1987): 197–213.

changes).[6] Moreover, considered within the political history of statistics, the controversy unveiled the contours of a larger struggle over the nature of statistics and their place in American political economy. How could you define the "cost of living"? What was the function of government statistics and statistical agencies? To whom should the BLS be accountable? Who got to define the goals and methodology of federal statistics? Raised into prominence by the government's wartime labor and economic policies, the BLS index became a central focus for these debates, in which labor unions challenged both BLS statistics and the function of technical expertise in the American political order.

THE INDEX IN WARTIME POLITICAL ECONOMY

Inflation as the Enemy

During the Second World War, the U.S. government mobilized both soldiers and the country itself; though civilians were not fighting the Germans or Japanese directly, the government assured them that other critical duties waited at home. Judging from the effort expended to control inflation—what the Office of War Information dubbed the home-front "Enemy"—rising prices loomed as the most dangerous of domestic foes. Fears of inflation spurred many of the most dramatic domestic wartime policies: controversial wage limits, heavy taxes, patriotic bond drives, widespread rationing, and the creation of the Office of Price Administration (OPA)—a massive organization that historian Meg Jacobs has called "one of the strongest manifestations of the interventionist New Deal regulatory state."[7]

America was not alone in devoting substantial resources to controlling inflation; every major, combatant state aggressively (though not always

---

6   H. Spencer Banzhaf, "Quality-Adjusted Prices: Theory, History, and Application to Air Quality" (Ph.D. dissertation, Duke University, 2001), 212–249; Marshall Reinsdorf and Jack E. Triplett, "A Review of Reviews: Ninety Years of Professional Thinking About the Consumer Price Index," in *Price Index Concepts and Measurement*, ed. W. Erwin Diewert, John S. Greenlees, and Charles Hulten (Chicago: University of Chicago Press, forthcoming).

7   Richard R. Lingeman, *Don't You Know There's a War On? The American Home Front, 1941–1945* (New York: Putnam, 1970); John Morton Blum, *V Was for Victory: Politics and American Culture During World War II* (New York: Harcourt Brace Jovanovich, 1976). Office of War Information, *Battle Stations for All. The Story of the Fight to Control Living Costs* (Washington, D.C.: U.S. GPO, 1943). Meg Jacobs, "'How About Some Meat?': The Office of Price Administration, Consumption Politics, and State Building from the Bottom Up, 1941–1946," *JAH* 84, no. 3 (1997): 911.

successfully) tried to contain wartime price rises. In part these efforts reflected a common public fear of inflation, fed by memories of the disastrous hyperinflation (especially in Europe) at the end of the First World War. More generally, though, the unpredictability of wartime inflation was the true danger. Uncertainty would keep unions pressing for larger and more frequent cost-of-living adjustments, while the value of savings and fixed-income payments would inevitably suffer. This could lead to social unrest (witness the widespread protests in 1917–1919), and even undermine national unity by pitting different groups against one another. Moreover, uncertainty could wreak havoc on war production: schedules would slip as prices spiraled, costs would be nearly impossible to predict, and thus uncontrolled inflation could cripple wartime mobilization. Significantly, the main agency established to control the cost of living in wartime America was called the Office of Economic *Stabilization*—if the economy could not be normal, at least it could be kept predictable, and hence manageable.[8]

The BLS cost-of-living index served two functions in the struggle against this domestic foe: a gauge of the inflationary rise and a means for its control. This curious double role arose from the two-pronged nature of Roosevelt's anti-inflation crusade, which reflected the two components of purchasing power—prices and wages. Wartime policies included price controls (a direct intervention to prevent rising prices) and programs to reduce spendable income (such as taxes, the promotion of savings and bonds, and wage and salary regulation—all of which would reduce the money in circulation and hence lower inflationary pressures). On the prices side, the index became the main measure of the OPA's success in controlling prices; simultaneously, the tripartite National War Labor Board (NWLB) used the index to establish a ceiling for wage increases.

By virtue of this dual role, the index aptly illustrated the tensions in the New Deal strategy of linking labor empowerment to macroeconomic policy. Both the OPA and the NWLB had strong ties to purchasing-power liberalism. The OPA, led initially by purchasing-power advocate Leon

---

[8] Office of War Information, *Battle Stations for All*. On anti-inflationary efforts in major combatant countries, see Alan S. Milward, *War, Economy, and Society* (Berkeley: University of California Press, 1977), 99–109; Geofrey T. Mills and Hugh Rockoff, *The Sinews of War: Essays on the Economic History of World War II* (Ames: Iowa State University Press, 1993); Mark Harrison, ed., *The Economics of World War II: Six Great Powers in International Comparison* (Cambridge: Cambridge University Press, 1998). On the United States in particular, see Harold G. Vatter, *The U.S. Economy in World War II* (New York: Columbia University Press, 1985), 89–112; Rockoff, *Drastic Measures*, 85–126; Paul A. C. Koistinen, *Arsenal of World War II: The Political Economy of American Warfare, 1940–1945* (Lawrence: University Press of Kansas, 2004), 419–433.

Henderson, can be seen as a direct outgrowth of New Deal concerns about excessive profits, corporate power, and high prices.[9] Likewise, the NWLB owed less to its namesake from the First World War than to the precedents created by the 1935 National Labor Relations Act. New Deal liberals such as Senator Robert Wagner had justified the legislation partly through arguments about underconsumption, insisting that strong unions were necessary to raise mass purchasing power (by raising wages), thereby building a foundation for sustainable growth (Chapter 4). Whether or not the macroeconomic side of this plan succeeded, it had boosted union membership enormously (from less than 3 million in 1933 to 10.5 million in 1941), had promoted centralizing and nationalizing tendencies in unions (especially the new industrial unions), and had codified the federal government's ultimate authority over collective bargaining. In this context, it is hardly surprising that the patchwork of agencies that had governed labor relations in 1917–1918 was replaced in the new war by a solitary body, the NWLB, whose labor members represented the CIO and AFL.[10]

Yet, if left-wing members of the Roosevelt administration had been seeking to boost mass-purchasing power through wage hikes in the 1930s, the booming wartime economy now called for the opposite action (in order to restrain inflation) and thereby brought macroeconomic policy into conflict with union demands. As the NWLB faced its first major case that spring—commonly known as "Little Steel" because it involved all the major steel companies outside of the giant U.S. Steel Corporation—the board chairman and purchasing-power liberal William H. Davis was searching for an acceptable way to impose wage limits on workers. His solution was to offer unions "maintenance of membership" clauses that preserved unionized shops (meeting a key labor demand) while also providing for limited wage increases to compensate for inflation. To that end, the board announced that steel wages could be raised a maximum of 15 percent above their levels in January 1941, a judgment drawn directly from the changes in the BLS cost-of-living index over a similar period. The Little Steel "formula" effectively became a universal policy after Roosevelt granted the NWLB oversight of all wage increases (not just those involving labor disputes) in October and

[9] Meg Jacobs, *Pocketbook Politics: Economic Citizenship in Twentieth-Century America* (Princeton: Princeton University Press, 2005), 164–197.

[10] Christopher L. Tomlins, *The State and the Unions: Labor Relations Law, and the Organized Labor Movement in America, 1880–1960* (Cambridge: Cambridge University Press, 1985), 252–254; Melvyn Dubofsky, *The State & Labor in Modern America* (Chapel Hill: University of North Carolina Press, 1994), 182–186; Alan Brinkley, *The End of Reform: New Deal Liberalism in Recession and War* (New York: Vintage Press, 1996), 201.

then ordered federal agencies to "Hold the Line" against all wage and price increases in April 1943.[11]

The Little Steel decision only linked the cap on wage increases to the rise in the cost of living as a temporary measure, one that would ameliorate the increased costs that workers faced by the late spring of 1942. But what would happen if the cost of living kept rising well beyond 15 percent? Though William Davis insisted that the formula was a one-time accommodation, the board also hinted on occasion that it might be revised if the OPA did not keep prices under control.[12] By January 1944, the BLS index was at 23.4 percent, and yet the formula had not been altered from 15 percent. Clearly, an eight-point difference was not enough of a gap—what would be? The board majority provided no clear answer and deliberately avoided addressing the question. For labor unions, though, this ambiguity raised a potential opening: if they could demonstrate a dramatic rise in the cost of living, they could perhaps break the 15 percent cap.

National Labor Organizations during the War

As the Little Steel decision became entrenched in administration policy, union opposition grew more vociferous. Not only did Little Steel directly affect workers' income, but it also aggravated other difficulties for national labor organizations. As a consequence of the national and corporatist labor policies of the late New Deal, the labor movement was slowly undergoing a process of centralization and consolidation, one greatly complicated by wartime changes. The result was increasing tension between national labor organizations (the AFL, CIO, and some of the major industrial unions) and their local affiliates. The AFL and CIO had announced patriotic "no-strike" pledges shortly after Pearl Harbor, a move that helped them to gain positions on the NWLB (just as alliances twenty years before had brought the AFL into the wartime arbitration system). But this move also committed the unions to arbitration rather than strikes, and the Little Steel decision

[11] Kathryn Smul Arnow, *The Attack on the Cost-of-Living Index* (Washington, D.C.: Committee on Public Administration Cases, 1951), 12–26; Vatter, *U.S. Economy in World War II*, 89–101; Brinkley, *End of Reform*, 209–212; Koistinen, *Arsenal of World War II*, 402–418, 422–427. Frances Perkins, William H. Davis, and Leon Henderson (then head of the OPA) all joined in recommending that Roosevelt extend wage controls beyond arbitration. Perkins, Davis, Henderson, and McNutt to Roosevelt, "Wage Stabilization," 21 May 1942, War Labor Board (World War II), box 77, Perkins papers.

[12] Arnow, *Attack on the Cost-of-Living Index*, 18–19, 56, 76; Joseph C. Goulden, *Meany* (New York: Atheneum, 1972), 103–104.

had subsequently blocked the possibility of significant wage gains through arbitration.[13]

The logjam became more disturbing as a host of other pressures piled on. Rank-and-file members were far less committed to the no-strike pledge than were national leaders, and wage issues plus shop-floor concerns led to a series of "wildcat" strikes throughout the war, nearly 14,000 involving 7 million workers between 1942 and September 1945. The strikes angered much of the public (at least according to Gallup poll results), and national leaders found themselves squeezed between the demands of union members and the potentially devastating damage to organized labor's tenuous reputation. The ability of renegade unions, especially John L. Lewis's United Mine Workers, to use strikes to obtain wage increases over the Little Steel limit raised the stakes even higher. As the final complication, unions were rapidly expanding because of defense production and the "maintenance of membership" provisions granted by the NWLB in exchange for accepting wage limits under Little Steel. These provisions virtually guaranteed full union membership in workplaces operating under collective bargaining, and since war production was expanding in union industries, greater military production translated into greater union membership.[14]

Among the industrial unions that formed the core of the CIO, the growth was phenomenal. The United Steelworkers of America (USWA) tripled its membership during the war, topping 700,000. The United Electrical, Radio and Machine Workers (UE) increased eightfold, to over 430,000. The United Auto Workers (UAW) grew from 165,000 in 1939 to a staggering 1 million by 1944. While the soaring union rolls provided good news in one sense, most new members were women, agricultural workers (including many African Americans), or former white-collar workers with little or no union experience. They typically joined the big unions merely as a by-product of taking their job, and initially had little sense of or commitment to the union cause (especially since older white male members frequently fought to exclude women and blacks). Moreover, women in particular often viewed (or were forced to view) their war work as a temporary activity rather than a long-term career. Though some new members soon grew more militant, capturing the loyalty and commitment of the expanded rank-and-file remained an ongoing concern. One UAW official described the disappointing attitudes

[13]   Robert H. Zieger, *The CIO, 1935–1955* (Chapel Hill: University of North Carolina Press, 1995), 147–163, 167–175; Nelson Lichtenstein, *Labor's War at Home: The CIO in World War II* (Cambridge: Cambridge University Press, 1982), 67–81, 157–202; Goulden, *Meany*, 98–115.

[14]   Zieger, *The CIO, 1935–1955*, 145–147, 150–152.

of new workers at a major aircraft facility: "They have no understanding at all of the union and are probably a little mystified as to how they ever got into it." The problem was especially acute for the national organizations, whose distance from local environments and tendency to suppress (rather than support) shopfloor activism made it hard for many new workers to see their benefits. National labor leaders thus found themselves trapped in relative impotence just when they most needed to demonstrate their relevance. The campaign to break the Little Steel formula therefore became a central focus for large labor organizations, and when the BLS index appeared as a vulnerable link, national headquarters eagerly promoted any criticism.[15]

Union Researchers and Cost of Living, 1940–June 1943

To lead this challenge, labor officials drew upon the skills of new staff members: union statisticians and economists. Union "research" had once meant (as it did for AFL Research Director Florence Thorne) gathering and disseminating reports or newspaper clippings, not analyzing economic data. Although larger unions in industries such as railroads, mining, textiles, and printing had employed economists earlier, technical research groups appeared in force during the 1930s. Their emergence corresponded to a growing need for aggregate analysis and technical expertise in industrial relations, in turn predicated on the rationalized, national corporatism promoted by New Deal liberals in which labor policy became linked to economic analysis and business prosperity. At first, researchers worked as individuals (perhaps with a small staff) in major unions and national labor organizations, but formal research divisions were established by the CIO in 1940 and the AFL in 1944.[16] The relative tardiness of the AFL was no coincidence, for the prominence of CIO research staff reflected the CIO's stronger alliance with purchasing-power liberals in the federal government (exemplified by the National Labor Relations Board); its greater engagement with large, rationalized corporations; and its concomitant reliance on technical, economic arguments to justify union demands and promote union policies.

15 Lichtenstein, *Labor's War at Home*, 72–81; Ruth Milkman, *Gender at Work: The Dynamics of Job Segregation by Sex During World War II* (Urbana: University of Illinois Press, 1987), 84–98; Zieger, *The CIO, 1935–1955*, 145, 147–150, esp. 150.

16 On union researchers, see Arnow, *Attack on the Cost-of-Living Index*, 48–50, and "Agency History," Finding Aid, Research Department, Boris Shishkin Papers, RG 13–001, GMMA." Arnow's account is filtered through the bureau's post-controversy view of the labor researchers. See also the oral histories with Katherin Pollack Ellickson and Nat Weinberg (WRL), and with Solomon Barkin (WSHS).

(Ford Hinrichs reported that some new CIO unions "set up a research department before they have any members.") Many CIO research staff members had trained at Brookwood Labor College (alongside sophisticated and experienced labor economists such as Jett Lauck and David Saposs) and had worked in New Deal agencies. Accordingly, the CIO tended to be far more aggressive in deploying expertise to challenge both businesses and federal agencies.[17] Given the CIO's activist stance and greater membership pressures, it is no coincidence that the three union researchers who made the most contributions to labor's two major reports on the index in 1944 came from the three largest CIO unions: the UAW (Lincoln Fairley), the USWA (Harold Ruttenberg), and the UE (Russ Nixon).[18]

Recognizing the growth of labor research groups and the importance of keeping in contact with this core constituency, in 1940 the BLS began a series of multi-day annual conferences with union researchers where bureau staff presented their current work and received extensive feedback. From the inception of these meetings, the BLS cost-of-living index drew frequent criticism, and after 1941, researchers complained that it inadequately reflected wartime economic transformations. Unlike the First World War, when U.S. mobilization peaked just as the war ended, Americans during the 1940s experienced a substantially longer war effort, in which economic effects had greater time to spread. War production precipitated a shift in U.S. manufacturing from civilian to military materials and led to widespread rationing, shortages, or even the disappearance of certain goods. Moreover, consumers complained that merchants and manufacturers were lowering quality (on clothing, house furnishings, and even food), eliminating low-end product lines, and reducing special discounts to avoid or minimize the effect of price controls set by the OPA.[19] Besides changing market goods, war production

[17] Hinrichs to Perkins [n.d., probably January 1945], History of Union Research Directors' Conference, box 2, ACF 1941–62, BLS. "Agency History," Boris Shishkin Papers, GMMA. Robert D. Reynolds, Jr., "A Career at Labor Headquarters: The Papers of Boris Shishkin," *Labor's Heritage* 1, no. 4 (1989): 58–75. On the ties between CIO staff and the New Deal, see Harold Ruttenberg, *Verbatim Transcript of Meetings: The President's Committee on the Cost of Living* (unpublished transcript housed in Langdell Law Library, Harvard University), 25 January 1944, p. 12, as well as the Oral History with Katherine P. Ellickson (WRL) and Nelson Lichtenstein, *The Most Dangerous Man in Detroit: Walter Reuther and the Fate of American Labor* (New York: Basic Books, 1995), 222–224.

[18] A. J. Wickens, "Notes on conversation of 5/19/50 between Mrs. Wickens and Mrs. Arnow," p. 2, Committee for Public Administration, box 3, Wickens correspondence, BLS.

[19] On shortages and rationing, see Lingeman, *Don't You Know?* 234–270; D'Ann Campbell, *Women at War with America: Private Lives in a Patriotic Era* (Cambridge: Harvard University Press, 1984), 166–186; Barbara McLean Ward, *Produce and Conserve, Share and Play Fair: The Home Front Battlefield During World War II* (Portsmouth, NH: Strawbery

altered daily life and common purchasing habits. Men worked longer hours and often ate meals away from home. Women joined the workforce, and consequently had less time to shop, clean, cook dinners, or watch children. As a result, families bought more convenience items, shopped at local, more expensive stores, ate more meals in restaurants, and incurred added expenses for childcare.[20] Furthermore, war production created a wealth of new jobs, but often in new professions and almost always in new locations.

Although national economic statistics create the impression of an overall economic boom, wartime growth was uneven and highly regional. Defense contracts funneled money across the country in large chunks, with major industrial corporations collecting the bulk of the funds and setting out to build a defense industry almost from scratch. Some factories were converted, but most companies opted to plop down giant plants in the middle of heretofore less populated areas of the Southeast, West (almost 10 percent of the war contracts went to California alone), and Midwest (especially the suburbs of Detroit). As hundreds of thousands of jobs opened up within several months, workers streamed into sleepy counties that were suddenly bursting at the seams, since the influx of workers was not accompanied immediately by an equal jump in available housing, retail services, or public infrastructure. An estimated 13 million Americans migrated through the country during the Second World War, and most ended their journeys as wage workers or clerical workers in densely populated areas.[21]

In the eyes of labor critics, the bureau's index (following the constant-goods ideal) did not sufficiently address these dramatic shifts, missing the effects of quality deterioration, changing retail practices, new consumption patterns, and widespread variation in the wartime price changes.[22] Unknowingly resurrecting older debates about index numbers, union officials lamented the narrow scope of the bureau's index: "it is unrealistic to say that there is just one way of measuring [the] cost of living"; "it doesn't really measure the cost of living, and many workers are misled by it"; the index

---

Banke, 1993). On the OPA and production problems, see Jacobs, *Pocketbook Politics*, 209–220.

[20] For union assessments, see Murray and Thomas, *Living Costs in World War II*, 64–65, 71–73, 141. For historians' perspectives, see Blum, *V Was for Victory*; Campbell, *Women at War with America*, 11–118; Lingeman, *Don't You Know?* 85–87.

[21] Lingeman, *Don't You Know?* 67–69; Vatter, *U.S. Economy in World War II*, 145–170; Gerald Nash, *World War II and the West: Reshaping the Economy* (Lincoln: University of Nebraska Press, 1990).

[22] See proceedings of BLS conferences with union research directors: 1940: 6–8; 1941: 55, 60; 1942: 38–44, 51–55; 1943: 14–21, Labor Research Directors Conference, box 1, ACF 1941–62, BLS.

"will not reflect the actual increases [in costs] that will be taking place."[23] Just as in the early 1920s, war was prompting a new look at the meaning and methods of cost-of-living indexes.

Despite this rash of criticism, however, BLS staff encouraged union researchers to speak their minds during the annual meetings (established in 1940) and appeared quite happy to listen to complaints. For their part, union economists likewise praised "the cooperative attitude that has been taken by the Bureau."[24] That cooperation, however, was threatened by two troubling developments: public criticism of the BLS by union leadership as part of the anti–Little Steel campaign, and a growing tendency for labor unions to provide their own alternative statistics to support these pronouncements. Initially, unions confined their efforts to double-checking BLS work, conducting scattered price surveys in individual cities during 1941–1942. By late 1942 (after the Little Steel decision), these surveys "were frequent, usually well-publicized, and were receiving increasing attention."[25] In early 1943, national leaders of the AFL and CIO cited the data while disparaging the index in testimony before Congress and in conversations with the president. That spring, the AFL magazine the *American Federationist* ran a series of articles (including several by Secretary-Treasurer George Meany) that attacked the economic stabilization program, criticized the BLS index, and cited AFL surveys reporting increases in excess of 75 percent.[26]

Creating alternative statistics proved controversial even among the unions themselves. George Meany, who was using the Little Steel fight to solidify his own leadership position in the AFL, would be the only major AFL figure to offer strident public denunciations of the BLS based on union statistics. Many union researchers also disliked this new development, an attitude best exemplified by Lazare Teper (International Ladies' Garment Workers' Union, AFL). Teper had been one of the most vocal and detailed

[23] Proceedings of BLS conferences with union research directors: Horace B. Davis (United Shoe Workers), 1942: 53; David Kaplan (Int'l Assoc. of Machinists), and Harold Ruttenberg (Steelworkers Organizing Committee), 1940: 7, 8 (respectively), Labor Research Directors Conference, box 1, ACF 1941–62, BLS.

[24] Proceedings of the BLS conferences with union research directors: 1941: 68; 1942: 50; 1943: 63, 19, Labor Research Directors Conference, box 1, ACF, 1941–62, BLS.

[25] See Goulden, *Meany*, 111–114; Archie Robinson, *George Meany and His Times: A Biography* (New York: Simon & Schuster, 1981), 114–116; George Martin, *Madame Secretary: Frances Perkins* (Boston: Houghton Mifflin, 1976), 452–455; Arnow, *Attack on the Cost-of-Living Index*, esp. 56–78.

[26] Boris Shishkin, "Inflation Crisis," *American Federationist*, April 1943, pp. 3–6; George Meany, "War Production and Food Prices," *American Federationist*, May 1943, pp. 3–5; *American Federationist*, June 1943, pp. 9–11. Arnow, *Attack on the Cost-of-Living Index*, 59–60; Goulden, *Meany*, 111.

critics of the cost-of-living index during the annual meetings, and at the 1943 conference, he read excerpts from a comprehensive critique, subsequently published in the *Journal of the American Statistical Association.* There, Teper raised many issues later echoed by the official CIO-AFL cost-of-living reports that appeared in 1944: quality deterioration, lack of representative sampling, decrease in "special" sales, the price of restaurant meals, taxes, and ambiguity over the meaning of "cost of living." Despite these parallels, union researchers such as Teper and future authors of the labor reports such as Harold Ruttenberg maintained very different views on the role and nature of union statistical research. Teper had been concerned by the rash of union-directed price surveys, which he and several others considered both technically deficient and politically foolish (better to have a "nonpartisan" agency collect data used in industrial relations). Rather than duplicating BLS work, Teper argued that the union researchers should be active critics, seeking to modify bureau procedures through dialogue.[27]

Teper's perspective matched that of the bureau staff. Aryness Joy Wickens (now Chief of the Prices and Cost-of-Living Branch) recalled that the bureau considered his article "not as part of a controversy, but as a quite justifiable criticism of the index." Acting Commissioner Ford Hinrichs likewise separated the older tradition of union advice and criticism (exemplified by Teper) from what he saw as new, flawed, and politically motivated union statistics.[28] In general, the bureau staff and many New Deal economists shared an understanding of statistics and their place in the modern political order that esteemed expertise and sought to insulate technical judgments from overt political pressure. Hinrichs made a sensible response to the unions based on that framework: he asserted the neutrality of the bureau; he emphasized the staff's technical sophistication; and he called in the experts, in this case a review committee from the American Statistical Association (ASA). He hoped that these efforts and the committee's favorable report (October 1943) would quell dissent. He was wrong—it got worse.[29]

[27] Lazare Teper, proceedings of BLS conferences with union research directors, 1941: 55; 1942: 43, in Labor Research Directors Conference, box 1, ACF 1941–62, BLS. Lazare Teper, "Observations on the Cost-of-Living Index of the Bureau of Labor Statistics," *JASA* 38, no. 223 (1943): 271–286. Lazare Teper and Virgil Case, proceedings of BLS conference with union research directors, 1943: 15, 22.

[28] Wickens, "Notes on a conversation of 5/19/1950," p. 3; Faith Williams, "Comments on 'The Dispute over the Cost-of-Living Index, 1942–1944,'" Committee for Public Administration, box 3, Wickens correspondence, BLS. On Hinrichs, see Arnow, *Attack on the Cost-of-Living Index,* 66–67.

[29] Frederick C. Mills et al., "An Appraisal of the U.S. Bureau of Labor Statistics Cost-of-Living Index," *JASA* 38, no. 224 (1943): 387–405. Arnow, *Attack on the Cost-of-Living Index,* 84–86.

THE SPLIT OVER THE COST-OF-LIVING INDEX

Hinrichs's hopes foundered on two problems. First, some data which ought to have been included in the index calculations (even under the bureau's methodological framework) simply were not available. How, for example, should the bureau quantify the effects of widely acknowledged quality deterioration in goods and services? As we will see in Chapter 6, union economists decided to estimate the price equivalents of quality deterioration when they calculated their own cost-of-living figures during the winter and spring of 1944, which in turn prompted a sharp critique from the BLS that challenged the assumptions and methods behind union calculations. But a more fundamental division between bureau staff and the unions occurred earlier and created bitter feelings on both sides.

Hinrichs, along with fellow institutional economists, defined a cost-of-living index as a measure of price changes. However, when the NWLB tied wages (temporarily) to the rise in the "cost of living," it inadvertently prompted a broader discussion of this concept. National labor officials, it soon became clear, did not share the institutionalist definition; instead, they insisted that the war had created many additional expenses for workers aside from price increases (e.g., relocation costs, increased childcare, etc.) that ought to be considered when making wage adjustments. BLS economists argued that these "changes in the manner of living" (effectively, changes in the market basket) should not be reflected in a cost-of-living index. Moreover, BLS staff members had an alternate application for the index—judging the effectiveness of OPA price controls—that fit more readily with their preferred methodology. The resulting clash, which erupted dramatically during the fall of 1943, therefore focused on two central questions that could not be resolved by appeals to expert opinions alone: what was the proper scope of a cost-of-living index and what was the proper role of a statistical agency in the Department of Labor?

The Formation of the President's Committee on the Cost of Living

Two committees shaped the debate over the index during the fall of 1943 and simultaneously illustrated the intertwining of "technical" and "political" problems: the ASA committee convened by the BLS and a subsequent President's Committee on the Cost of Living drawn from the NWLB. The institutional economist Frederick C. Mills—the NBER's price statistician—led the ASA committee. Although other members had more varied backgrounds, they nevertheless supported the bureau's constant-goods methodology, concluding that "within the limitations established for it, the cost-of-living index provides a trustworthy measure of changes in the prices."[30] Overall, institutionalist perspectives dominated external reviews of the bureau's work throughout the 1940s controversy, a tendency that reflected the distribution of the economics community. As we have seen, institutional economists had shown the most interest in empirical work, forged the tightest connections to government agencies, and produced numerous quantitative studies. Thus, when the BLS or other administrators went looking for external experts, they repeatedly recruited from institutionalist agencies such as the NBER.

The ASA committee released its report in the fall of 1943, only to see it eclipsed almost immediately. With the CIO preparing for a major challenge to the Little Steel decision, in which a critique of the index would almost certainly play a part, Roosevelt wanted to end the controversy conclusively. In November, he asked the chairman of the NWLB, William H. Davis, to head a tripartite committee that would examine the "controversy and dispute as to what the cost of living is." Including George Meany and R. J. Thomas (Vice President, CIO) as the labor representatives, the President's Committee on the Cost of Living met intermittently over the following year and generated extensive commentary on the index. The CIO and AFL produced their two cost-of-living reports for this committee, and two other major reports had a similar origin: one written by the National Industrial Conference Board (supporting the industry members) and the other created by a second external "technical committee" whom Davis appointed as his advisers in 1944. (As with the ASA committee, institutional economists dominated Davis's technical committee, which was led by Wesley Mitchell himself, alongside fellow NBER economist Simon Kuznets and former ASA committee member Margaret Reid.) The President's Committee's summary report in November 1944 contained separate comments by Davis, the industry members, and labor representatives, along with a host of supporting documents. Nevertheless, when the committee first convened, most members thought

---

[30] Mills et al., "An Appraisal," 388. Other committee members included E. Wight Bakke (Yale University), Reavis Cox (University of Pennsylvania), Margaret G. Reid (Iowa State), Theodore W. Schultz (University of Chicago), and Samuel S. Stratton (Harvard University). Dorothy Brady (U.S. Bureau of Home Economics) and Solomon Fabricant (NBER) served as research staff. From the main committee, both Reid and Shultz had significant training under institutional economists (Reid under Hazel Kyrk at the University of Chicago; Schultz at the University of Wisconsin).

it would take only a month or two to resolve the contentious problems and issue a unanimous recommendation.[31]

Far from being discouraged by the ASA report, labor officials enthusiastically supported many of its conclusions. For example, both groups agreed that the BLS's index did not encompass all aspects of a worker's economic experience. The ASA committee articulated this problem as a distinction between tracking *expenditures* and tracking *prices*:

> The phrase "cost of living" is ambiguous. … In every-day speech families are apt to think of their cost of living as the total amount they spend for consumer goods and services. Several different factors may cause such expenditures to change. Thus, they may change because the unit prices of goods and services rise or fall. Again, they may change because families are forced by circumstances beyond their control to alter their manner of living, as when the exigencies of war make some goods unavailable. Yet again, they may change because families have experienced an increase in income and can afford to buy more goods or better goods. … As used in technical statistical parlance, the term "cost of living" has applied only to the first of the factors which determine family expenditures, that is, to unit prices.

This, of course, was the standard institutionalist line: cost-of-living indexes only measured price changes. According to the ASA committee, however, the wartime economy had exacerbated the distinction between measuring changes in prices and measuring changes in expenditures, and thereby had widened the gap between popular perceptions of the "cost of living" and expert calculations:

> The difference between the movements of prices and changes in actual expenditures is significant in times of great mobility, changes in the pattern of living, commodity and housing shortages, quality deterioration, and increased taxes and bond purchases. Since a price index cannot reflect completely these facts of consumers' experience, it cannot fully measure what workers mean by changes in their cost of living.

Though these limitations did not invalidate the index, the committee implied that they should be recognized when utilizing the index to adjust wages.[32]

[31] Franklin D. Roosevelt to William H. Davis, quoted in Joseph P. Goldberg and William T. Moye, *The First Hundred Years of the Bureau of Labor Statistics* (Washington, D.C.: U.S. GPO, 1985), 155. The reports include: Meany and Thomas, *Cost of Living*; National Industrial Conference Board, *A Critical Analysis of the Meany-Thomas Report on the Cost of Living* (New York: NICB, 1944); Murray and Thomas, *Living Costs in World War II*; William H. Davis, ed., *Report of the President's Committee on the Cost of Living* (Washington, D.C.: U.S. GPO, 1945). For a discussion of the initial plans of the committee, see *Verbatim Transcript*, 6 January 1944, pp. 8–9.

[32] Mills et al., "An Appraisal," 389, 402.

With such statements in hand, labor officials believed that they had found common ground with the statisticians. George Meany declared that the President's Committee ought not "to fight with the Department of Labor ... but to cooperate with them." He was sure that there were limitations to the index, and thought that he had support from critiques like Teper's, the assessment by the American Statistical Association, and Hinrichs's own comments. A meeting between the President's Committee and two BLS representatives (Hinrichs and Aryness Joy Wickens) was scheduled for November 23, and labor officials arrived ready to join forces with the bureau. Meany wanted close the gap (as described by the ASA report) between the cost-of-living index and "what workers mean by changes in their cost of living." "If the index is a retail price index and not actually a cost-of-living index," he told Hinrichs, "we have no particular interest in what the index has done in the past. ... My attitude is ... let's go into partnership and see what we can do together—this committee and your department—to make the index do the thing that it has not done."[33]

Immediately, problems arose. Hinrichs appeared unenthusiastic about this prospect, and sidestepped Meany's requests. In the bureau's view, the limitations described by the ASA committee were inherent in all cost-of-living indexes. By definition, a "cost-of-living index" was a constant-goods index (focused upon retail prices), and therefore it could not include new expenses arising solely from changes in the quantities or kinds of goods purchased. From labor's perspective, this was either hypocrisy or downright deceit. The BLS described the index as a "price barometer" and concurred with the ASA that it did not "fully measure what workers mean by changes in their cost of living."[34] Nevertheless, the agency still labeled the measure a cost-of-living index. Meany was convinced that bureau staff was unfairly trying to capitalize on the political power of the cost of living without fully committing to the concept. "You persist in calling your index a cost-of-living index," he complained, "and then when you discuss it, you insist on discussing it as an index of prices."[35]

[33] See William H. Davis's recollection of George Meany's comments (affirmed by Meany), *Verbatim Transcript*, 6 January 1944, p. 5. Meany, *Verbatim Transcript*, 23 November 1943, pp. 3–5. Cf. UAW-CIO Research Dept., "Memorandum on the cost of living," 15 November 1943 and CIO Dept. of Education and Research, "Limitations of use of U.S. BLS cost of living index in determination of wage rates", [November 1943] in folder 29, box 8, UAW Research Dept. Collection, WRL.

[34] The "price barometer" label comes from Wickens to W. H. Davis, 16 November 1943, encl. "The Cost-of-Living Index of the Bureau of Labor Statistics," p. 1, Published Materials on the BLS Cost-of-Living Index, box 17, GCS 1934–50, BLS.

[35] *Verbatim Transcript*, 23 November 1943, p. 26.

As the President's Committee meeting progressed, all participants agreed that many important factors were left out of the index and that additional studies were needed. Hinrichs, however, refused to accept labor's position that these studies should be incorporated into the index.[36] He tried to articulate his view of a proper "cost-of-living index," but this only resulted in further clashes. Meany grew more irritated, and the meeting ended without resolution. Unable to understand the bureau's stubbornness, labor leaders walked away suspecting that the BLS was stonewalling in order to support administration wage controls, and they developed a deep personal resentment toward Hinrichs.

Underlying Hinrichs's intransigence, of course, was the institutionalist commitment to the constant-goods framework, in which an unchanging market basket allowed one to isolate price changes. Admittedly, the consumer's world was not a static place, but the proper response was to follow the methodological ideal while recognizing its limitations.[37] Frederick C. Mills conceded to USWA statistician Harold Ruttenberg that economists faced a fundamental dilemma:

> The problem is, in a very real sense, unsolvable. You can measure changing unit prices of commodities and services under a fixed standard of living, but to the extent that modes of living are changing the pure price measure loses in significance. You can measure the cost of living in the sense of total family expenditure, but here you combine in a single index the effects of unit price changes and of all the shifts that have occurred in the quantity, quality and character of goods purchased.[38]

Implicitly, Mills adopted the methodological premises that had guided Wesley Mitchell: a good statistical measure had only a single variable (prices, in this case). Allowing other factors ("shifts … in the quantity, quality and character of goods purchased") to change and thereby to affect the calculation would muddle its meaning; at any rate, it would no longer be a *price* index. Still, as Mills admitted, the value of a constant-goods price index declined as "modes of living" changed dramatically. How would this limitation affect the propriety of using such a measure for wartime wage adjustments?

Wages, War, and the Cost of Living

When the government took de facto control of union wages via the NWLB, it necessarily made wage adjustments a political question. To understand

[36] Cf. *Verbatim Transcript*, 23 November 1943, pp. 47–48.
[37] Cf. Mills et al., "An Appraisal," 388–389.
[38] Mills to Harold Ruttenberg, pp. 1–2, encl. in Mills to Hinrichs, June 19, 1944, Cost of Living Materials, box 17, GCS 1934–50, BLS.

the adoption of cost-of-living arguments in this context therefore requires understanding the politics of the wartime economy. War production represented a welcome economic expansion after a long and dismal depression, but no one was eager to portray themselves as a war profiteer. Consequently, talk about how to divide the benefits of the economic boom was couched in terms of sacrifice and equity. Nothing so dominated discussions of federal economic management as questions about whether a policy was "unfair" to this group or another, or whether one group was being forced to make an unreasonable "sacrifice" (or no sacrifice at all).[39] The OPA regulated corporate income (prices), so companies claimed that, to be fair, the government ought to regulate corporate costs (wages) as well. Roosevelt urged the farm bloc to accept regulation of agricultural prices by balancing them against wage controls for industrial workers and reminding farmers that "war demands sacrifice." In battling the Little Steel formula on behalf of workers, George Meany complained that "everyone else is not making equal sacrifices." On the other hand, Harold Fleming of the *Christian Science Monitor* decided that labor's quest to adjust the Little Steel formula "ignores any argument built around the word 'sacrifice.'"[40]

The Little Steel case proved how tricky it could be to apply this analytical framework in practice. Despite the anti-inflationary rhetoric surrounding the decision, the formula was not effective in holding down the total earnings of workers. Although it limited wage rates, employers and workers found numerous other ways to negotiate increased pay: overtime, longer shifts, premium payments, various bonuses, and so on. Labor unions focused on increasing basic rates for the same reason employers opposed this: it would be harder to drop rates than to eliminate overtime and other extra payments during the postwar readjustment. The contest over rates took on gendered dimensions as well. Both male and female union members complained that managers were downgrading rates in specific occupations by explicitly or

---

[39] See Mark H. Leff, "The Politics of Sacrifice on the American Home Front in World War II," *JAH* 77, no. 4 (1991): 1298–1306. Leff argues that in the United States, rhetoric about an "equality of sacrifice" proved less effective than patriotic appeals to consumerism and postwar abundance. However, discussions of wage and price controls in the Unites States suggest that this rhetoric remained powerful in America, at least in relation to workers.

[40] Franklin D. Roosevelt [Sept. 7, 1942], quoted in Jacobs, "'How About Some Meat?'": 917. George Meany, quoted in an AP story from the *Baltimore Sun*, Feb. 20, 1944, excerpted in "Cost of Living," National War Labor Board, Division of Public Information, Press Digest, 21 Feb. 1944, 3(44): 1; Harold Fleming, "More Pay, Less Tax Arguments Seen Same," *Christian Science Monitor*, undated clipping. Both articles can be found in box 17, GCS 1934–50, BLS. Unless a full citation is given, other newspaper articles quoted in this chapter can also be found in these folders.

implicitly classifying them as "women's work" so that they could pay lower rates.[41] Meanwhile, the Roosevelt administration had its own interest in wage rates beyond general concerns about inflation. When establishing production contracts with a number of major companies, the government agreed to escalator clauses based on labor costs as measured by BLS data on average hourly earnings (i.e., wage rates). As Acting Commissioner Ford Hinrichs explained in 1941, any wage hike in war industries would "substantially raise the cost of executing the defense program."[42]

Wage rates, therefore, not total earnings, were the real objects of contention during the cost-of-living controversy, and the "sacrifice" arguments had to be adjusted accordingly. Labor officials never seriously tried to argue that wartime price rises pushed workers into destitution. Indeed, the NWLB permitted increases over the Little Steel limits for wages deemed to be substandard, though the system was slow, heavily criticized by unions, and tended to reify regional differences (in contrast to the national standardization promoted during the First World War). More generally, a tight labor market along with plentiful overtime and bonuses meant that working-class families as a whole were making more money, even when considering national labor's own estimated cost-of-living increase of 45 percent (this did not include increased taxes, however).[43] But labor officials argued that much of this increase was due to longer hours or to women taking jobs. A "fair" cost-of-living adjustment would raise basic wage rates, and not merely allow working-class families to meet the rising cost of living by working more.[44] Thus, though it was rarely articulated clearly, the

[41] Arnow, *Attack on the Cost-of-Living Index*, 23; Milkman, *Gender at Work*, 56–83.

[42] Hinrichs to Frances Perkins, "Earnings in Steel Industry," 7 April 1941, Hinrichs folder, box 34, Perkins papers. Perkins drew two emphasis lines in the margin next to this paragraph.

[43] Lichtenstein, *Labor's War at Home*, 116–117. Arnow, *Attack on the Cost-of-Living Index*, 23. (Arnow relies upon BLS earnings data to make her argument.) Earnings calculations can be quite complex, but it seems clear that earnings significantly outpaced the BLS index when overtime and other incentives are included. As some economic historians have argued, moreover, overall per capita civilian consumption remained quite high during the war, certainly higher than during the Depression. Harold Vatter, "The Material Status of the U.S. Civilian Consumer in World War II: The Question of Guns or Butter," in *The Sinews of War: Essays on the Economic History of World War II*, ed. Geofrey T. Mills and Hugh Rockoff (Ames: Iowa State University Press, 1993); Rockoff, "The United States: From Ploughshares to Swords," 90–94. But how this consumption was distributed among the population is more difficult to ascertain—for a nuanced attempt to analyze wartime prosperity, see Koistinen, *Arsenal of World War II*, 433–439.

[44] For a near contemporary view on wages and wage policy from an economist and ex-OPA official, see Seymour E. Harris, *Inflation and the American Economy* (New York: McGraw-Hill, 1945), 301–339. As an example of union arguments in action, see the careful focus on

"sacrifice" question for Little Steel reduced in part to this: were total earnings or wage rates the proper vehicle for compensation due to the rising cost of living? Furthermore, how much compensation should workers expect and how should the expense be distributed among businesses and the state (ultimately taxpayers)?

Analyzing the rising cost of living itself in terms of "sacrifice" was similarly complex. Frederick Mills had divided changes in family expenditures into two components: price changes and other factors (changes in the "quantity, quality, and character of goods purchased"). As the ASA committee noted, however, popular usage of the phrase "cost of living" encompassed a range of factors beyond "unit prices." When a group of non-economists (the NWLB) agreed to adjust wages according to "changes in the cost of living", what did they mean? In practice, this question produced a different binary division: those factors affecting family expenditures that should, and should not, lead to wage adjustments. There was no guarantee that these two ways of dividing expenditure changes would produce identical categorizations.

In fact, the political demands of a wartime economy had already driven the BLS to stretch the constant-goods methodology. The application of the constant-goods ideal to cost-of-living indexes had always involved a conflation of two different objectives: measuring average price changes for a specific set of goods (those purchased by urban working-class families) and measuring "the changing cost of a fixed standard of living" (in Ford Hinrichs's description).[45] What held these two goals together was the assumption that a constant market basket supplied a "fixed standard of living," and indeed was the only way to reliably define such a standard (given the inaccessibility of subjective concepts such as utility). Both the "prices" perspective and the "standard of living" perspective therefore mandated retaining a constant market basket. Both could also be used (under certain circumstances) to justify linking two indexes together in order to change the market basket:

$$I_{Total} = \left(I_{Through\ Link\ Date,\ Basket\ A}\right) \times \left(I_{After\ Link\ Date,\ Basket\ B}\right)$$

Under the "prices" perspective, one could claim (as the BLS did when adding about twenty items to the food index in the early 1920s) that the price

wage rates (rather than earnings) in the UAW's submission to the NWLB on 29 September 1944, folder 16, box 75, USWA Research Dept., Penn State University.

[45] Ford Hinrichs, draft of letter to Frances Perkins [Feb. 1945?], handwritten mss., p. 5, Cost of Living—New Name for the Cost-of-Living Index, box 18, GCS 1934–50, BLS.

changes of the new basket roughly matched (or would have matched) the price changes of the old basket over previous years.[46] Alternatively, one could argue that when the new basket was more expensive than the older version for the same time period (as with the updated market basket adopted for the BLS index in the 1930s), the absolute cost difference represented the cost of reaching a higher standard of living and therefore could be justly excluded from an index tracking the cost of a "fixed standard of living."[47]

For certain wartime changes, such as the substitution of margarine for butter or the disappearance of goods such as new automobiles and most household appliances, this rationale and method continued to function. But other developments forced the BLS to adapt its approach to comply with political and social expectations. Thus, for example, the bureau reduced its market basket to match rationing regulations, even when larger quantities of the original items could be purchased on the black market. That choice was affirmed by the external review committees (the ASA committee and the Mitchell committee), who insisted that illegal purchases should be omitted from an "official index."[48] Or again, when lower-priced goods vanished from store shelves and left only higher-priced substitutes, the BLS included the full cost difference within the index regardless of whether the substitutes were higher-quality items. For such "forced uptrading," the BLS abandoned linking (which would have excluded the cost difference) and turned to a direct comparison:

$$I = \frac{\text{Cost of higher-quality substitute in current month}}{\text{Cost of original item in the base period}}$$

The implicit justification for the BLS formula, of course, was that consumers had no other options but to purchase the available substitute. But

[46] U.S. Bureau of Labor Statistics, *Retail Prices, 1890–1927*, BLS Bulletin, no. 464 (Washington, D.C.: U.S. GPO, 1928), 16.

[47] Cf. Wesley C. Mitchell, Simon Kuznets, and Margaret Reid, "Report of the Technical Committee Appointed by the Chairman of the President's Committee on the Cost of Living, June 15, 1944," in *Report of the President's Committee on the Cost of Living*, ed. William H. Davis (Washington, D.C.: Office of Economic Stabilization, 1945), 272. Note how the Mitchell committee used "utility" as synonymous with "serviceability" and "usefulness"—a pragmatic orientation that differs from the strictly subjective neoclassical concept. For a detailed and slightly different interpretation of Mitchell's treatment of quality change, see H. Spencer Banzhaf, "Quantifying the Qualitative: Quality-Adjusted Price Indexes in the United States, 1915–1961," in *The Age of Economic Measurement*, ed. Judy L. Klein and Mary S. Morgan (Durham: Duke University Press, 2001), 252–258.

[48] Mills et al., "An Appraisal," 394; Mitchell, Kuznets, and Reid, "Report of the Technical Committee," 289.

Table 5.1: *Alternative Ways of Categorizing Factors that*
Affect Family Expenditures

Items in bold are those that should be properly included in a cost-of-living index according to each group.

Frederick Mills	BLS Wartime Practice	National Labor Officials
1. Price changes	**1. Price changes**	**1. Price changes**
2. "Shifts … in the quantity, quality, and character of goods purchased."	**2. "Forced uptrading"** (treated as a price change)	**2. New expenses caused by war economy** (includes forced uptrading plus other factors)
	3. Other changes in expenses	3. Voluntary increases in workers' real standards of living

it nevertheless deviated from the constant-goods ideal: strictly following either the "prices" perspective or the "fixed standard of living" perspective would have led the BLS to use linking, not direct comparisons.[49]

These changes to BLS practice arose from (implicit) political judgments about wartime "sacrifice": workers would not be compensated for extra costs associated with the black market, but they would for the disappearance of low-end price lines. National labor officials agreed with the spirit, if not the execution, of these changes, but they further argued that "forced" expenses included extra costs that union officials claimed were associated with many war jobs. These included items beyond price changes per se, such as relocation to high-cost areas, transportation to new war-production factories, eating out more frequently due to overtime work, and shopping at local stores or incurring greater childcare expenses as women entered the workforce and had less time for other tasks. As George Meany told the President's Committee, a cost-of-living index ought to encompass these "compulsory changes" brought on by participation in a war economy. Effectively, union officials had divided the change in total family expenditures into three categories (see Table 5.1): price changes, other "compulsory" new expenses, and voluntary increases in standards of living (which union leaders implied were minimal).[50]

The BLS response to union arguments took two tacks. First, the bureau described most non-price changes as voluntary additional expenditures: if

[49]　Mitchell, Kuznets, and Reid, "Report of the Technical Committee," 262, 264, n. 1.
[50]　For union views, see *Verbatim Transcript*, 23 November 1943, 5–6, 13, 25–26, 80–81.

a worker chose to take a new job with extra expenses, the increased income would presumably offset the new costs. Such voluntary changes in the "manner of living," the bureau insisted, had no place in a cost-of-living index—they represented a rise in the standard of living predicated on increased income.[51] Adjudicating between the BLS and unions thus depended upon how one differentiated between "forced" and "voluntary" changes. For example, USWA statistician Harold Ruttenberg claimed that workers faced a palpable "social pressure" to take a job that supported the war effort. Furthermore, he noted that changes in the war economy often necessitated abandoning a prior profession: "With prices rising so rapidly workers *must* take war jobs or suffer a declining standard of living." But these new jobs might not outlast the war, and so workers needed to "provide for possible future unemployment."[52] Though Ruttenberg spoke only of "workers," his comments had subtle gendered overtones: women had been actively recruited into war production jobs and were expected to leave those positions at the end of the war; meanwhile, management was using the civilian-military production shift plus the influx of new employees to downgrade wage rates to levels that might remain low in the postwar as well. Against this background, concern about "changes in the manner of living" took on another dimension.[53] Moreover, even among men, the uneven wartime economic expansion forced many male workers to relocate to crowded, higher-cost, war production centers when they lost their prior jobs or faced stagnating wages.[54]

Most statisticians acknowledged these complications, and in fact the bureau's second line of defense was more fundamental: how could a statistician decide what constituted "compulsory" new expenses? Unlike new retail practices (such as the disappearance of low-end price lines), changes in the manner of living involved shifts in both family expenditures and family income simultaneously. In turn, this made it difficult to discover the net effect on families simply by collecting prices from local stores. From

---

[51] Cf. U.S. Bureau of Labor Statistics, "The Cost-of-Living Index of the Bureau of Labor Statistics: A Review and Appraisal of the 'Cost of Living' Report by George Meany and R. J. Thomas," in *Report of the President's Committee on the Cost of Living*, ed. William H. Davis (Washington, D.C.: U.S. GPO, 1945), 166. The disjuncture between the BLS and union officials is apparent in *Verbatim Transcript*, 23 November 1943, e.g., 14–16. The phrase "manner of living" was frequently used during the controversy to denote the purchasing habits of families (e.g., Davis, ed., *Report of the President's Committee*, 5).

[52] Harold Ruttenberg, "Comments on the June 15, 1944, Report of the Mitchell Committee," in Davis, ed., *Report of the President's Committee*, 399.

[53] On women's employment during the war, see Milkman, *Gender at Work*, 49–127.

[54] For a similarly skeptical analysis of the wartime boom, see Higgs, "Wartime Prosperity? A Reassessment of the U.S. Economy in the 1940s," 52–53.

the bureau's perspective, the key question was not whether workers were "forced" into new lifestyles with increased costs but how one could construct reliable statistics that revealed the extent and consequences of such developments.

This distinction became clear when Hinrichs and Meany discussed a hypothetical construction worker who lost his job in New York and took a war production job in more expensive Seattle. Hinrichs began offering the traditional "voluntarist" analysis: "There is a fair presumption, since there was no element of compulsion involved, that the man, in moving from New York to Seattle, thought that his situation was going to be better, or he wouldn't have gone." George Meany quickly jumped on this response: "Well, you see, that is where you are right off the dock in your theory or guesswork. You say there is no compulsion. You mean he can starve to death in New York?" Hinrichs, though, was not worrying about motivation or environmental circumstances, and he implicitly accepted Meany's arguments about the compulsory nature of the change. The real problem was that comparing the cost of two different market baskets (the worker's purchases in Seattle vs. in New York) might just reflect changes in income (rather than prices), and therefore could give a misleading impression. "I say [this increased expense] is so bound up with changes in family income," Hinrichs told Meany, "that you can't get a clear picture of it unless you consider both things simultaneously."[55] If income and expenses were both rising, how could you judge whether or not a worker was making an unfair sacrifice? How could changes in the cost of living be isolated from changes in the standard of living? BLS and labor officials were in fact hashing through the same issues that had troubled economists after the First World War, but doing so in a tense political environment, where extensive financial consequences rested on the outcome.

Expenditure Surveys and the Proper Role of the Index

To solve the dilemma, the BLS planned to use expenditure surveys that would reveal the incomes and expenses of working-class families. These studies could not be combined into an index (because they encompassed too many changing variables), but would instead provide snapshots of American living conditions. "The only way in which you can measure the

---

[55] *Verbatim Transcript*, 23 November 1943, pp. 15–16, 14. Cf. the Mitchell Committee's judgments on the same issue: Mitchell, Kuznets, and Reid, "Report of the Technical Committee," 262, 292–293.

well-being of a family [with changing income and expenses]," Hinrichs told labor officials at the November meeting, "is to make at periodic intervals a study of the incomes they were receiving and the goods that they were buying. What are they getting currently? How are they living?"[56] The surveys would document any hardships faced by workers, while the cost-of-living index itself would retain its focus on measuring retail price changes (including the "price changes" caused by the disappearance of low-end goods).

The BLS had strong theoretical reasons for not altering its index, including traditional statistical practice and the difficulties the staff foresaw in trying to untangle expenditures and income changes: "To think that the key to this problem lies in manipulating the cost-of-living index is nonsense," complained Aryness Joy Wickens in 1942.[57] But the agency also had a pressing practical reason not to change the cost-of-living index, namely its use by the Office of Price Administration. Because price controls and wage controls each had a different bureaucratic home (the OPA and the NWLB), the policies tended to be executed independently. At times this provided an easy way for harassed administrators to bracket off problems and pass responsibility. For instance, when the cost-of-living index pushed past the Little Steel level of 15 percent, NWLB government members could conveniently point the finger at the OPA. This was a price control problem, not a wage control problem, and so there was no need to revise the formula. The split also encouraged administration officials to view price stabilization and wage stabilization as related—but nonetheless distinct—goals. In keeping with the broader interest in economic management that BLS officials had adopted during the New Deal, bureau staff saw their index as a tool for the OPA. Not only was the OPA a much larger federal agency, but its programs touched all consumers, not merely workers, and the index was the main measure of the OPA's success.[58] Reflecting back on the controversy, Wickens recalled that BLS officials had been most concerned about the effect that union attacks would have on public confidence in the OPA, and thus the entire economic stabilization project.[59] Price controls, not wage adjustment, shaped the bureau's view of its index.

---

[56] *Verbatim Transcript*, 23 November 1943, pp. 14–15.

[57] Wickens to Lubin, Nov. 18, 1942, pp. 1–2, Cost of Living Materials, box 17, GCS 1934–50, BLS.

[58] Arnow, *Attack on the Cost-of-Living Index*, 75–76. On the size of OPA, see Ira Katznelson and Bruce Pietrykowski, "Rebuilding the American State: Evidence from the 1940s," *Studies in American Political Development* 5, no. 2 (1991): 322–323.

[59] Wickens, "Notes on a conversation of 5/19/1950", p. 1. See also the prominence of the OPA in a proposed press release: Isador Lubin to Roosevelt, 17 November 1944, Published Materials on the BLS Cost-of-Living Index, box 17, GCS 1934–50, BLS.

Considering the cost-of-living index in light of the OPA rather than Little Steel had critical consequences. It reinforced the bureau's decision to treat the disappearance of low-end goods (often used to evade OPA price limits) as a "price change" within the index. At the same time, it also reinforced the exclusion of those changing consumption patterns that labor unions insisted were "forced" alterations. Whatever the proper relationship between changes in the manner of living and wage rates, those transformations often held less relevance for evaluating price controls. If workers had to commute longer distances to new factories, the added cost might justifiably be considered in comparison to their wages, but how did those expenses relate to a mandate to "freeze" prices? Or if Rosie the Riveter was no longer around to cook dinner and the family now spent more time eating out, did these new costs represent a failure by the OPA? The simplest answer was no. The OPA wanted to keep an eye on retail prices; the BLS said it had a measure of retail prices; and questions about changing market baskets conveniently slipped to the wayside.

Indeed, despite the relevance of price indexes to the OPA, numerous statisticians acknowledged that such figures might be insufficient when considering wages. Ironically, many high-level BLS staff members opposed the Little Steel decision. Hinrichs, for instance, felt that a national index did not offer the best tool for making decisions about wage rates in widely varying locales and industries, and in 1943, he privately told union research directors that this weakness could be exploited by the unions in their challenge. Moreover, Hinrichs repeatedly noted that the index did not cover several critical factors affecting household income, most notably taxes, and so was not the most useful measure for setting wage rates.[60] The American Statistical Association committee reached similar conclusions. As part of its analysis, the ASA committee evaluated the index's validity for three policy applications: a measure of inflation, a gauge of retail price controls, and a basis for wage adjustment. While the committee had some brief caveats for the first two cases, its treatment of wage adjustment took close to two pages. The committee concluded that the index was "not satisfactory" for giving "an indication of the pressure placed upon present wage rates by workers'

---

[60] Hinrichs to Harvey W. Brown, International Association of Machinists, 16 May 1946, Micro 07, Reel 8, U.S. Government Agencies, Office of the President, RG 1, GMMA. Hinrichs, [1943] typescript outline for discussing the index [probably with the President's Committee], Cost of Living Materials, box 17, GCS 1934–50, BLS. During late 1943–early 1944, Hinrichs proposed a plan to "bury the Little Steel formula" while still blocking wage "increases in higher wage industries" by expanding the bracket system: Hinrichs to Frances Perkins, 12 Dec. 1943, 1 Jan. 1944, and 12 Jan. 1944, box 34, Perkins papers.

experience in meeting the rising cost of living."[61] In effect, the ASA committee agreed with union officials: some non-price-related changes in expenditures were relevant to wage rates.

The bureau, though, viewed these problems (and their solution) through its existing framework and priorities. The government would treat the index as a measure of retail price inflation, thereby making it a useful tool for the OPA. Expenditure studies would capture all of the messy problems surrounding changes in the manner of living, and unions could then use this information in presentations before the NWLB. Moreover, because statisticians could separate the expenditure data based on income levels, regions, or industries, these studies might reflect more of the individual variations that Hinrichs felt were missed by the Little Steel formula. But the bureau's determination to see the index only as a tool for the OPA underscores the changes that had occurred in the staff over the previous twenty years and reflected the agency's new role in macroeconomic planning. An index that originally had been established to adjust wage rates in wartime was now seen primarily as a measure of retail price inflation, and only secondarily in relation to wages. "This thing [the index] has its uses," Wickens told labor leaders at the end of the November President's Committee meeting. "They are limited, they may not be what you want for this purpose [wage rates], but for the OPA and for like purposes … they are very good."[62]

The Role of a "Statistical Bureau"

Unfortunately, labor officials did not take the same view. Although they had no quarrel with expenditure studies (as in previous years, union researchers had vigorously advocated both expenditure surveys and the pricing of new standard budgets), they wanted this research to be incorporated into the index.[63] After all, the index, and not some hypothetical expenditure survey, formed the basis for the Little Steel formula. Hinrichs, however, refused to alter the index or prepare a supplementary version for setting wage limits; instead, he steadfastly maintained that changes in the manner of living should not be directly incorporated into a price index. Moreover, Hinrichs

---

[61] Mills et al., "An Appraisal," 402.

[62] *Verbatim Transcript*, 23 November 1943, p. 87.

[63] On union interest in expenditure surveys and analyses of "adequate" budgets, see proceedings of BLS conference with union research directors, 1942: 51–55; and minutes of the Standing Committee of Research Directors for 18 February 1941, 18 September 1941, 18 December 1942, and 26 July 1943, all in Labor Research Directors Conference, box 1, ACF 1941–62," BLS.

avoided making any explicit criticism of the Little Steel decision, even though both he and Wickens doubted the index's relevance to wage rates. Hinrichs's actions reveal how BLS officials understood the function of federal statistical agencies, in effect answering a key question we considered near the end of Chapter 4: how would the staff navigate its responsibilities to the larger community of economists, to unions, and to other members of the administration? It is clear that the influence of the latter dominated (particularly in the person of Frances Perkins), though that influence was alternately constrained and aided by Hinrichs's sense of professional integrity. From the beginning of his tenure as acting commissioner in 1940, for example, Hinrichs refused to criticize administration policy in public (regardless of what he felt privately). As the index became a central part of the economic stabilization program, it too needed to be handled carefully. When a critic at the 1943 union researchers' conference asked Hinrichs "to tell the War Labor Board that the index does not exactly and adequately reflect the real increase in the cost of living," Hinrichs claimed that such a direct step was beyond his authority as a government statistician. The BLS had not been "invited" to discuss the index with the NWLB, though he insisted that if such an opportunity came, he would not "avoid the question of any shortcomings." Hinrichs's disavowal of responsibility reflected his belief that, though he might privately discuss policy with Perkins and others, the bureau had to maintain a public position as a strictly fact-gathering agency serving higher entities in the government who made policy decisions (the Department of Labor, the NWLB). Of course, Hinrichs would not give outright false information, but neither would he publicly critique the Little Steel decision.[64]

At first glance, Hinrichs's testimony before the President's Committee appears to meet the criterion he laid out during the 1943 meeting: a formal request to evaluate the index in relation to workers and wages. However, ambiguity about the purpose of the committee provided a way for supporters of the stabilization program to avoid confrontation. Although it was composed entirely of members from the NWLB (including the board's chairman, William Davis), the President's Committee was not an official part of the board. During the November meeting, William Waldron (secretary for the

[64] Russ Nixon, Paul Pinsky, and A. F. Hinrichs, proceedings of BLS conferences with union research directors, 1943: 19, 20–21, 64 (respectively), Labor Research Directors Conference, box 1, ACF 1941–62, BLS. On Little Steel, see Hinrichs to Lubin, 4 May 1943, pp. 8, 11–12, 1943–White House–Lubin, box 71, GCS 1934–50, BLS. On Hinrichs's reluctance to jeopardize the administration's use of the index, see Arnow, *Attack on the Cost-of-Living Index*, 54–55.

absent William Davis) reminded everyone that "wage policy ... is a question for the War Labor Board," and not for the committee, a view with which labor members initially concurred.[65] This left the role of the committee somewhat nebulous, however. When William Davis later wrote a draft of his official report, he alternated between two different goals. On page six, he emphasized the connection between the committee and Little Steel: "The issue is ... whether [the index] gives a close enough approximation of changes in living costs to be useful as a guide to wage policy in wartime." By page nine, however, he had eliminated "wage policy" from consideration: "The question of whether the index is accurate enough to be put to the uses that have been made of it by the War Labor Board is one for the Board to decide."[66]

The distinction proved extremely important. As the ASA report demonstrated, the index could be accurate for some purposes (such as evaluating price controls) but less useful for setting wage rates. "Accuracy," therefore, depended on the role of the index. If the application of the index was left outside the scope of the committee, Hinrichs could quite easily discuss the merits of the index without contradicting his own views on the flaws of the Little Steel formula, and thus avoid any public conflict with the NWLB. During the November meeting, Hinrichs maneuvered along a fine line: the index had limitations (but these were inherent in price indexes); expenditure studies could address some of the problems (but the Little Steel formula was not mentioned).

Even if labor members had followed Hinrichs's suggestions, it is unlikely that expenditure studies would have effectively combated Little Steel. Although expenditure surveys may have resulted in some individual adjustments, labor would have needed extensive studies to break the formula, consuming time, manpower, and funds that simply were not available. The bureau's 1934–1936 national study took two years to complete (and another three before publication) and relied on workers and massive funding from the Works Progress Administration. By contrast, the 1940s bureau was already stretched far beyond its means, struggling with a lack of adequately trained staff in a tight labor market and caught between numerous demands from war agencies and a conservative Congress intent on cutting all non-essential budget items. Expenditure studies apparently landed on the non-essential side. The BLS had completed a small-scale survey of

---

[65] *Verbatim Transcript*, 23 November 1943, pp. 77, 59. Labor members later realized the bitter consequences of this separation: R. J. Thomas, "Comments on the Chairman's Report," in Davis, ed., *Report of the President's Committee*, 29.

[66] "Rough Draft" [apparently of the final report by William Davis], 6 Sept. 1944, Published Materials on the BLS Cost-of-Living Index, box 17, GCS 1934–50, BLS.

"Family Spending and Saving in Wartime" in early 1942, but Congress had on three occasions denied requests to extend that to a larger study.[67] A more dramatic showdown over the expenditure studies never occurred, however, because labor representatives rejected the bureau's position at the November 1943 meeting. While Hinrichs refused to comment on the Little Steel decision in order to avoid blending policy and statistics, labor members accused the bureau of having made just that error. As described above, they rejected Hinrichs's attempts keep income-related changes in the manner of living from affecting the index. Moreover, they found such a decision to be outside the purview of a mere statistician. Conceding that the differentiation between "voluntary" and "compulsory" expenditures might be a difficult or impossible task for a politically neutral statistician, they nonetheless insisted that certain war-related changes in expenditures (e.g., relocation costs) ought to be included in the index. Rather than relying on the bureau to make these judgments, differentiating between voluntary and compulsory expenditures would be the responsibility of a policy board, namely the NWLB. Three of the labor representatives in attendance, Donald Montgomery (former Consumer Counsel for the Agricultural Adjustment Administration, now with the UAW), George Meany, and CIO Research Director Raymond Walsh, made this quite clear to Hinrichs:

Montgomery: I don't follow you on whether [a new expense] is voluntary or compulsory. I don't quite get the relationship between that and what is happening to the cost of living. If the cost of living rises, that is a question that I can understand, unrelated to what causes it to rise.

Meany: That is the point in all of Mr. Hinrichs' explanations and discussion here this morning that I don't get either. If it is your job to go out and measure something, that is your job.

Montgomery: That is right.

Walsh: Yes, that is right.

Meany: And not to try to find out why.[68]

"Finding out why" involved interpretation, not data collection, and interpretation was not the bureau's proper function.

---

[67] Reminiscences of Isador Lubin (1957), OHC-CU, pp. 101–102. On the strain on the BLS in the 1940s, see Hinrichs to Perkins, 17 March 1943, Hinrichs, box 127, Correspondence of the Labor Commissioner, 1933–43, BLS. The "Survey of Spending and Saving in Wartime" was subsequently published in 1945 as BLS Bulletin, no. 822. On BLS attempts to secure funding for additional surveys, see *Verbatim Transcript,* 23 November 1943, p. 17.

[68] *Verbatim Transcript,* 23 November 1943, 57–58.

By laying out the framework in this way, the labor officials got some support from William Waldron:

Waldron: Isn't this the fundamental difference between you [Hinrichs] and Mr. Meany? You say you can collect these data which will show changes in spending habits of groups of people [who have relocated for war production jobs]. Now, you are going to say, when you submit these data, some of these changes are forced on people and some of them are voluntary because their incomes are greater.

Mr. Meany is going to say, "I am not willing to recognize that distinction, it is all a change in habits and therefore it is an increase in the cost of living."

Now I don't see why, as long as we recognize that difference, you as a statistician, submitting the data, can't say that these data are subject to two interpretations. ... But that second question [i.e., which interpretation] goes to the question of policy: what is the Board going to do with the data once they get them?

Meany: That is their business.

Waldron: That is right. I don't see why you have to discuss that, really.[69]

On the surface, this position matched with relationship described by Hinrichs: the BLS would produce statistics and the board would decide what to do with them. But there were two additional issues: the constant-goods ideal and the use of the index by the OPA. The BLS had the support of American institutionalist economists and most government statisticians worldwide in arguing that cost-of-living indexes should only include price changes; moreover, the staff had a reason (the OPA) to adhere to that definition. Consequently, the BLS could resist labor's arguments by using the institutionalist concept of cost-of-living indexes, and (in the end) William Davis could use the same justification to support the index and avoid altering the Little Steel formula.

For their part, labor officials rejected the bureau's decision not to include changes in the manner of living and were infuriated by Hinrichs's refusal to alter the index. They argued that a statistical bureau ought to be responsive to the needs of its constituents, especially when other professional statisticians (like the ASA committee) had already pointed to obvious limitations in the index. As the November President's Committee meeting cycled repeatedly over the same issues, Meany became convinced that Hinrichs

[69]   Ibid., 77–78.

was either unbearably stubborn or acting in bad faith: "We didn't get any cooperation from him," Meany later told William Davis. "In fact, we couldn't get a decent answer out of him for three hours."[70] Indeed, the lack of "cooperation" from the bureau (predicated on the constant-goods ideal) propelled the two sides into a more explicit public split.

Toward the end of the meeting, Meany vented his growing frustrations in a long monologue. Though it revealed his suspicions about the adequacy of the index, it was also an offer to compromise, if Hinrichs would bend a bit in labor's direction:

We don't say that this index doesn't truly reflect prices, we haven't said that officially, although privately I think that is so. I think you could do a much better job than what you are doing. ... I don't agree with the limited sampling that you take; I don't agree with the limited cities that you take; I don't agree with your method of getting prices. ... However, I am not talking about any of those things; I am not talking about any criticism of what you have done within the limitations that you have established for yourselves. What I am saying is that you should remove some of those limitations and try to take in some of these things that are annoying our people, that we say [are not reflected] in this.

Once again, Meany reiterated his views on the proper role of the bureau, pleading with Hinrichs to take some action:

I think you are under an obligation to either tell us that you will do this, or give us some definite reason why it can't be done, because if you don't do it, I don't know who is going to do it. You have got this statistical bureau, and a statistical bureau to me means a bureau that makes a measurement of a certain condition or set of conditions. Now all we are asking for is your cooperation to find out these things.[71]

In Meany's view, the role of the BLS was simply to gather data requested by their constituents, in this case, the labor unions. When Hinrichs did not "cooperate," labor officials took this as a sign that the bureau had abandoned the proper role of a statistical agency, and thus someone else would have to step in to make the needed measurements. The other members of the President's Committee (perhaps unwittingly) encouraged this view by asking the labor members to collect evidence that illustrated troubling issues.[72]

As union officials gathered materials in December, they became convinced that the index had widespread deficiencies. What began as a quest to

---

[70] *Verbatim Transcript*, 6 January 1944, p. 10.
[71] *Verbatim Transcript*, 23 November 1943, pp. 73–74.
[72] *Verbatim Transcript*, 13 December 1943, pp. 9–11.

create a statistical supplement grew into a wholesale indictment. "The more we have dug into this thing, " R. J. Thomas reported in early January, "the more my research people feel there have been some hellish discrepancies in the Department of Labor figures and we are digging into it more; we are finding more all the time."[73] This burgeoning mass of statistical compilations provided the basis for the joint CIO-AFL report on the cost of living, which in turn would solidify the split between labor officials and the BLS. The heated arguments that built during the meeting of the President's Committee in November became the opening skirmish of a struggle that would challenge the New Deal conception of statistical expertise and its function in industrial relations.

PRICE INDEXES AND POLITICS

In 1925, labor economist and union consultant Evans Clark praised the AFL for discarding the "double-edged" strategy of linking wage adjustments to price changes and heralded the arrival of the underconsumptionist, "purchasing-power" arguments that justified wage increases through macroeconomic analysis (keeping pace with productivity) and the promotion of business prosperity.[74] Less than twenty years later, unions were learning that economic policy could also cut both ways: if wage increases might be celebrated for expanding consumer markets, they could likewise be blamed for contributing to rising inflation. But having (pragmatically) justified wage increases and union power by insisting these would benefit the general economy, union officials also recognized the danger in cutting those ties—as illustrated by the public condemnation and anti-labor legislation that followed maverick, wartime strikes by mineworkers and others. Rather than abandon the NWLB, leaders from the AFL and CIO challenged the statistical measure that now bound workers' wages, hoping to increase that official limit and thereby win wage hikes without violating the bargain that committed them to general economic welfare. The same logic that had driven unions to embrace macroeconomic analysis now pressed them to critique the quantitative measures that lay at its heart.

If union criticism of the BLS cost-of-living index had a pragmatic motivation, though, that critique was made possible by the limitations of statistical analysis itself. Institutional economists had defined cost-of-living indexes in

---

[73] R. J. Thomas, *Verbatim Transcript*, 6 January 1944, pp. 2–3. Cf. Meany, *Verbatim Transcript*, 6 January 1944, pp. 20–21.

[74] Evans Clark, "Union Labor Takes New View of Wages," *NYT*, 18 October 1925.

abstract terms: measures of retail price change based on a constant market basket. But adapting this ideal to a practical, politically meaningful measure within a dynamic economic environment required judgments about goals and methods that had clear political overtones. What was the primary objective for the index: gauging the success of OPA or adjusting wages? What kinds of "sacrifices" should workers (or consumers) be expected to endure under the wartime regime? Furthermore, even when the goals were identified, could one devise a straightforward set of quantitative techniques that would measure the desired phenomena?

BLS staff had anticipated these problems; the limitations of the index under wartime conditions could come as no surprise to anyone familiar with cost-of-living statistics. What they had not expected, however, was that union leaders would not only reject bureau solutions but even the agency's authority to make those choices. The bureau had hoped to manage debates about the index according to the top staff's own view of how federal statistics should function in American political order: produced by nonpartisan agencies; designed by qualified experts; subject to critique via private channels and academic journals; directed and used as the governing administration best saw fit. National labor leaders rejected this perspective, questioning the control of government statistics, the function of federal statistical agencies, and soon the very nature of statistical knowledge itself. In the end, the fruitless outcome of the early meetings between labor officials and the bureau staff led the AFL and CIO to create their own comprehensive, fully articulated alternative to the BLS index. In the process, as Chapter 6 describes, they brought an entirely different vision of statistics and statistical agencies into explicit view and challenged the New Deal economists' conception of their own role in regulating a corporatist economy.

6

Statistics from the Bottom Up: Union Research
on the Cost of Living

> Just by way of friendly advice to statesmen skating on thin ice, we would suggest: "Gentlemen, beware of index numbers."
> —"Indexes are Inedible," *The Chicago Sun*, October 20, 1943

At the close of the December meeting of the President's Committee on the Cost of Living, the public and industry representatives had encouraged George Meany (Secretary-Treasurer, AFL) and R. J. Thomas (Vice President, CIO) to gather evidence supporting their critique of the BLS cost-of-living index. In early January, the two labor officials returned with some preliminary materials, which they supplemented several weeks later. Before the committee had discussed the report, however, Meany and Thomas cited its conclusions during a congressional hearing, proclaiming a 43.5 percent rise in the cost of living since January 1941 (versus a 24 percent increase in the BLS index). As the BLS and industry representatives scrambled to prepare comprehensive replies to the union report, Meany and Thomas waited impatiently for three weeks before ratcheting the pressure upward once again, this time by sending a sharply worded letter to the president (subsequently released to the press). In light of alleged deficiencies in the index, Meany and Thomas declared that the bureau's willingness to let its statistics "be used as a basis for measuring the rise in the cost of living" was "the gravest type of injustice that could possibly be perpetrated by it upon the American people." Accordingly, the agency should face "an intensive investigation" that would reveal why it had "distort[ed] the basic facts of our war-time living costs." Roughly one week later (February 25), the BLS issued its official response, justifying its index and detailing the flaws that staff members found in labor's statistics. Meany and Thomas, however, were not swayed; if anything, they became angrier: "No group of government bureaucrats," the two men declared, "[has] ever before had the audacity to insult America's

219

millions of housewives by telling them that their experiences are all wrong and that they should instead try to live on BLS statistics."[1]

This brief window into the second stage of the cost-of-living controversy captures key elements of union tactics after the unproductive meeting of President's Committee with BLS staff in November. National labor officials such as Meany and Thomas appealed to the public through press releases, articles in labor periodicals, and speeches, while also positioning the debate as a political struggle, complete with polemical rhetoric. Fundamentally, they accused the BLS of failing to capture the purchasing experiences of working-class families, here and elsewhere symbolized by the figure of the housewife. But the unions went beyond critiquing BLS work: they claimed to have created a more accurate statistical measure that met their own criteria. We can characterize the union approach as "bottom-up" statistics, combining elements of the social survey tradition (including some of its methods and its democratic appeal) with two additional principles: (1) labor statistics should reflect workers' (or their wives') self-understanding of their economic condition, and (2) statistics inevitably embodied political judgments and hence could legitimately be shaped by political pressure and negotiation.

BLS leaders rejected each of these positions. They argued that detailed exposition of salient examples (typical of the survey tradition) could not compensate for a lack of adequate, aggregate statistics. They warned about the dangers of subjective, individual experience and insisted that credentialed experts, not public opinion, should supply the ultimate assessment of economic conditions. They recognized that constructing statistical measures required judgments, but they rejected union accusations of partisan manipulation, resented the public, inflammatory attacks on the bureau,

---

[1] *Verbatim Transcript of Meetings: The President's Committee on the Cost of Living* (unpublished transcript housed in Langdell Law Library, Harvard University), 13 December 1943, 2 January 1944, 25 January 1944. "Living Costs and Wages," *NYT*, 31 January 1944; "Labor Charge of 43.5% jump in Cost of Living is Disputed," *Washington Post*, 31 January 1944. George Meany and R. J. Thomas, *Cost of Living: Recommended Report for the Presidential Committee on the Cost of Living* (Washington, D.C.: Congress of Industrial Organizations, 1944). George Meany and R. J. Thomas to Franklin Roosevelt, 17 February 1944, Cost of living—1943–44, box 1, Official File 238, FDR Library; "Up Wages, Reduce Prices," Meany Counsels Roosevelt," *AFL Weekly News*, 23 February 1944. U.S. Bureau of Labor Statistics, "The Cost-of-Living Index of the Bureau of Labor Statistics: A Review and Appraisal of the 'Cost of Living' Report by George Meany and R. J. Thomas," in *Report of the President's Committee on the Cost of Living*, ed. William H. Davis (Washington, D.C.: U.S. GPO, 1945), 139–241. (Originally released on February 25, 1944.. "AFL-CIO asks poll of housewives on war increases in cost of living," *AFL Weekly News*, 29 February 1944. Kathryn Smul Arnow, *The Attack on the Cost-of-Living Index* (Washington, D.C.: Committee on Public Administration Cases, 1951), 112–125.

and defended their ability to act in the "national interest" (to borrow Lewis Lorwin's words), constrained by the strictures of accepted practice among their professional peers. The outcome of the clash did not offer a full victory to either side. The extent, bitterness, and consequences of the controversy illustrated to BLS staff that they could not insulate themselves or their statistics from the political pressures that originated from both within and outside the state. The postwar era would thus find the staff struggling more explicitly to manage these pressures while retaining some measure of independent judgment. On the other side, national labor officials found themselves stymied by a paradox arising from their use of "bottom-up" statistics: the contradiction between appealing to individual experience and democratic judgment while simultaneously seeking to consolidate their own power, suppress internal dissent from local unions, and support a national, bureaucratic, administrative approach to industrial relations (the NWLB). The episode revealed both the fractures within New Deal corporatism and the incompatibility between a deeply populist approach to quantitative knowledge and the requirements of bureaucratic centralization. Though the conflict ended largely unresolved, it would set the stage for more effective postwar attempts to craft an ordered, constrained system of industrial relations bounded by economic statistics.

STATISTICS FROM THE BOTTOM UP

Statistics as Populist Discourse

Labor's first report on the cost of living (alleging a 43.5 percent wartime increase) appeared at the end of January 1944. Attributed to George Meany and R. J. Thomas (and hence often called the Meany-Thomas report), it was based primarily on the work of CIO statisticians, especially Harold Ruttenberg (USWA).[2] After the BLS criticized the union efforts, the CIO issued an updated report in June 1944 (attributed to CIO president Philip Murray and R. J. Thomas and known as the Murray-Thomas report), that added 1.5 percent more to the January estimate. Both reports highlighted limitations in the BLS index that had been noted by other union researchers.

---

[2] Arnow, *Attack on the Cost-of-Living Index*, 107–108. Although the two reports relied on research from numerous unions, Ruttenberg usually presented the results at major meetings and later took the lead in replying to the Mitchell Committee. See *Verbatim Transcripts* for Jan. 6, Jan. 25, Feb. 2, and Oct. 30, 1944, as well as *Proceedings of CIO Executive Board*, Jan. 27–28, 1944, pp. 22–32, and June 16–18, 1944, pp. 183–189, GMMA.

They claimed that the index took insufficient account of widespread quality deterioration, shortages, the disappearance of low-end price lines, and a reduction in "special and week-end sales." Further, since men were working longer hours and many women had taken war production jobs, labor statisticians argued that families were being forced to shop at more expensive, local stores, to eat out more frequently in restaurants, and to buy more convenience items. They charged that the bureau's index did not provide adequate coverage of congested war production cities and did not reflect the skyrocketing housing costs of most migrating workers (because it excluded rent payments in boardinghouses, furnished rooms, and trailers). Finally, labor officials took issue with the bureau's practice of price "imputation" (whereby the price change of a specific item was assumed to be representative of a larger group of goods; Chapter 4), insinuating that the Office of Price Administration focused its efforts on items in the index, allowing the prices of other goods to rise more rapidly.[3]

In the abstract, these themes echoed criticism that the BLS had heard from other sources, and if the unions' calculations reported a much greater rise than the bureau's index, the practice of devising alternative cost-of-living measures was hardly new or disreputable (consider the cost-of-living index created by the NICB in 1918—Chapter 3). But the form, content, and presentation of the CIO-AFL efforts distinguished them from previous projects. Instead of pursuing private consultation or criticism in professional forums, Meany and Thomas deliberately fostered a public debate about both the accuracy of the index and the integrity of the bureau: issuing press releases, making speeches, touting their findings in congressional hearings, and promoting the reports vigorously through articles in labor periodicals, including a four-page "Cost of Living Supplement" issued by *The CIO News* (complete with cartoons; see Figure 6.1).

Most critically, as the conflict wore on without resolution, labor officials adopted increasingly polemical rhetoric that moved from criticism to accusations of partisan manipulation and finally descended to the level of personal insults, as when Harold Ruttenberg called Hinrichs a "nervous little man" who was "the personification of a statistic."[4] Based on interviews with

---

[3]   Meany and Thomas, *Cost of Living*, 4–6; Philip Murray and R. J. Thomas, *Living Costs in World War II, 1941–1944* (Washington, D.C.: Congress of Industrial Organizations, 1944), 3, 64–65, 71–73.

[4]   Both the *AFL Weekly News* and *The CIO News* carried numerous lead articles on the cost-of-living controversy from late 1943 through 1944. The original Meany-Thomas report never accused the BLS of improper action, though it made suggestive comments in one appendix (pp. 85–89). These charges first took a central place in the letter that the two

Figure 6.1. Pummeled by the Cost of Living.
Source: "Special Cost-of-Living Supplement" in the *CIO News*, February 1944.

BLS staff in the 1950s, Kathryn Smul Arnow reported that many members were "deeply outraged" and saw the unions' tactics as "hitting below the belt." Other observers also perceived a clear distinction between statistics and politics, and felt that Meany and Thomas had crossed an important line. "These are strong words to use in a scientific controversy," wrote labor economist Leo Wolman (a former member of the NBER) after reading labor's open letter to the president. "They would seem to be designed not to clarify technical issues, but to intimidate the Bureau."[5]

If the forum and tone of the union analysis differed from statistical debates in professional journals, so too did its methodology. In some cases,

officials sent to Roosevelt in mid-February: Meany and Thomas to Roosevelt, 17 February 1944. Harold Ruttenberg, "BLS Cost of Living Index to Be Thorny Rose by Another Name," *The Guild Reporter* (American Newspaper Guild), 1 Feb. 1945.

[5] Arnow, *Attack on the Cost-of-Living Index*, 117–118. Leo Wolman, "Pressure Politics Put to Work in Attacking Labor Statistics Unit," *Washington Post*, 5 March 1944.

the union researchers used methods familiar to BLS staff: to prove the limits of price imputation, for example, unions conducted price surveys that mimicked the bureau's own work (albeit with a different set of goods). Generally, though, union researchers were attempting to make arguments that stretched beyond immediately available quantitative data or standard statistical practice. How, for example, could one quantify the results of quality deterioration on a wide array of consumer goods? In the absence of comprehensive studies, union officials relied heavily on detailed exposition of selected examples: to support allegations of quality deterioration in restaurant meals, for instance, union representatives in Pittsburgh visited lunch rooms in nearby steel towns and noted that, along with general price rises, the daily "specials" no longer included appetizers or desserts, and customers now had to pay extra for bread and butter.[6] Unable to create national studies that could capture such rich detail, lead author Harold Ruttenberg used limited surveys to illustrate general trends and bolstered union analysis with comments drawn from newspaper articles, trade associations, consumer groups, and other government agencies (all presented in a series of seven "exhibits" at the end of the Meany-Thomas report, later expanded to forty-two exhibits in the Murray-Thomas report).[7] Buttressed by this evidence, Ruttenberg estimated the total effects of each issue on specific categories, and then combined the results with the BLS index.

Not surprisingly, BLS statisticians condemned the Meany-Thomas report as a hodgepodge of evidence, thrown together without careful examination of the sources and providing insufficient grounds for any numerical estimates. In its official reply to labor's cost-of-living report (February 1944), the BLS accused the unions of conducting poorly planned surveys and of relying on "unrepresentative data." Bureau staff insisted that union researchers had misconstrued or misunderstood many of their sources while overlooking evidence that contradicted their claims; the entire report, the BLS complained, was "replete with errors," including "mistakes of fact" and "distortion of the facts." Ruttenberg's descriptions of the minutiae of economic life, such as restaurant meals in Pittsburgh or the quality of women's skirts in Maryland, were ignored or dismissed as unrepresentative, and labor's attempt to quantify effects such as quality deterioration was discarded as a "guess."[8]

---

6   Meany and Thomas, *Cost of Living*, 25.
7   Ibid., 75–104; Murray and Thomas, *Living Costs in World War II*, 3–76 (appendix).
8   Arnow, *Attack on the Cost-of-Living Index*, 125–127; U.S. Bureau of Labor Statistics, *The Cost-of-Living Index of the Bureau of Labor Statistics: A Review and Appraisal of the 'Cost of Living' by George Meany and R. J. Thomas*, typescript ed. (Washington, D.C.: U.S. GPO, 1944), i, 3, 31–32, 48–49, 27. (N.B.: As described in a later note, the version of the BLS

In a few cases, Ruttenberg acknowledged the limitations in the first union report, but overall, he continued to rely on individual testimonies and small-scale studies.[9] No doubt this procedure reflected the financial and time constraints that limited union research, combined with the difficulty of quantifying effects like "quality." Yet, Ruttenberg and his union allies also shared a view of statistics in which individual experiences could ground, and to a certain extent supplant, sweeping (but necessarily more limited) quantitative calculations. In contrast to the BLS, union officials remained impressed by the persuasive power of detailed, individual descriptions. At a meeting of the CIO Executive Council, President Philip Murray shared the story of one steel worker, Charlie Moore of Calumet, Illinois. Giving an item-by-item breakdown of Moore's household budget over three months, Murray showed how wartime price increases combined with wage freezes had left Moore $69 in debt (with a $718 income), and concluded that "it is an affront to Americans, under those circumstances, to be confronted all the time with these perfectly stupid, wholly unreliable figures submitted by the Bureau of Labor Statistics."[10] The board members were deeply moved. One participant suggested that Murray's remarks "be put on paper," thereby giving the CIO "a very concrete and a good story for the average worker." Another complimented Murray on his "very humane method" and proclaimed that examples like Charlie Moore would have "a more convincing effect upon the average American than any other sort of tables and statistics we can produce."[11]

The CIO board was not spurning statistics; on the contrary, members agreed that "we certainly need all the statistics we can get," and hoped to find "ten thousand or a million" examples like Charlie Moore to present to the public. Rather than avoiding numerical research, the board envisioned a form of statistics that would somehow combine the personal impact of Murray's "very humane" individual method and the power of quantification.[12] In the board's skepticism about the effectiveness of "tables and statistics" we can see echoes of the reform-minded social survey tradition of the early twentieth century (with its attention to "flesh and blood" examples)

analysis published in the final report on the President's Committee by William Davis is slightly different than the original. Whenever the two are equivalent, I will cite the more readily accessible version from the President's Committee report: U.S. Bureau of Labor Statistics, "The Cost-of-Living Index: A Review and Appraisal," 139–241.)

9 Murray and Thomas, *Living Costs in World War II*, 57. Examples of individual testimonies and small studies on page 79 and in exhibit 24.
10 *Proceedings of CIO Executive Board*, Jan. 27–28, 1944, p. 50, GMMA.
11 *Proceedings of CIO Executive Board*, Jan. 27–28, 1944, pp. 55–56, 72, GMMA. The *CIO News* did run Murray's story in its "Supplement on the Cost of Living" in February.
12 *Proceedings of CIO Executive Board*, Jan. 27–28, 1944, p. 72, GMMA.

and of the journalistic style of statistical analysis practiced by some of the state bureaus. As earlier reformers knew well, blending numerical calculations with detailed personal accounts proved a more effective technique for reaching a general audience, and not surprisingly, this form of statistical knowledge lived on in other public forums, such as congressional hearings and arbitration proceedings. (Indeed, Ruttenberg's placement of evidence in "exhibits" mirrored the common format for these events, and he drew several of his concrete examples from congressional hearings.) In a similar vein, a press release from a Senate subcommittee examining the cost of living of white-collar workers in January 1944 gave pride of place to the testimony of individual workers, who "convincingly depicted" the struggles of their entire class. "Stenographers, clerks, professional men and women and government girls, in turn showed dollar by dollar and sometimes penny by penny ... the climb in price of life necessities." The only formal statistics cited were a range of cost-of-living index estimates, bounded by Hinrichs's estimate at the bottom and Murray's at the top.[13]

The stylistic parallels between arguments in these different forums (the survey tradition, public hearings, the union reports) resulted from a common objective (persuasion of non-experts) coupled with belief that mere "tables and statistics" were oversimplified abstractions readily prone to error. "We are too often compelled to contend with too much theory [in] life," Philip Murray complained, "and the sort of study that we have made ... is therefore not a theoretical study, not by any means."[14] But if extensive quantitative data and expert analysis were unavailable or flawed, and if full comprehension of the rising cost of living could only be obtained through detailed stories like that of Charlie Moore, how could union researchers answer the charges that their examples were "unrepresentative," skewed to one extreme and ignoring countervailing factors?

Experience

In the bureau's view, they could not; indeed, the evidence suggested to BLS staff that the union approach to statistics was seriously flawed. Although the two union reports ended with roughly similar conclusions (a price rise of about 43–45 percent), they derived these final results in different ways. For instance, the Meany-Thomas report (January) called for a

[13] Joint Statement by Senator Elbert D. Thomas and Senator Claude Pepper, 31 January 1944, Labor Statistics—1944–Cost of Living, box 148, Perkins—General Subject File, DOL.
[14] *Proceedings of CIO Executive Board,* Jan. 27–28, 1944, pp. 44–45, GMMA.

13 percentage-point increase in the food index due to imputation issues, while the Murray-Thomas report (June) reduced this to 6 points and increased the adjustment for the disappearance of "special sales" from 4 to 8 points. In an August 1944 letter (after the release of the review from Wesley C. Mitchell's "technical committee"), union researcher Harold Ruttenberg placed the greatest emphasis on the "distinction between the retail-price factor in the cost of living and the total cost of living" (in other words, price changes only vs. prices plus other factors).[15] Alongside the apparently scattershot nature of union evidence, such mutability reinforced convictions that unions had built their statistical house on shifting sands and validated underlying suspicions that the labor leaders had started with a conclusion (the index is faulty) and were now scrambling to find supporting data.[16] In the eyes of BLS staff, this violated proper scientific procedure and demonstrated the partisan nature of union critiques. A statistician should begin by defining an appropriate methodology and then follow the results wherever they might lead (recognizing, of course, the inevitable limitations); only in this way could one preserve a measure of objectivity.

Union leaders saw the situation in a different light. They had indeed started with the belief that the index was out of line, but this was a solid experiential fact, not mere opinion. Both publicly and privately, union officials insisted that the BLS index did not match workers' experience, and hence could not be trusted. As William Green (President, AFL) explained to the Senate in the spring of 1943, "prices are running away ... [and] official statistics fail to tell the truth. ... [W]orkers and their families do not eat statistics."[17] Since the BLS refused to change its approach, labor unions had been forced to do the work themselves, and the union reports represented their continuing attempt to bring quantitative estimates in line with (supposedly) common experience. "The Meany-Thomas Report," argued one union

---

[15] For a comparison of the union calculations, see Horace B. Horton and George K. Batt, "Wartime Cost of Living: Report of the Industrial Members of the Presidential Committee on the Cost of Living," reprinted in William H. Davis, ed., *Report of the President's Committee on the Cost of Living* (Washington, D.C.: U.S. GPO, 1945), 67–68. Cf. A. J. Wickens to A. F. Hinrichs, Sept. 22, 1944, Cost of Living Materials, box 17, GCS 1934–50, BLS. Harold Ruttenberg to William H. Davis, 24 August 1944, reprinted in Davis, ed., *Report of the President's Committee*, 87.

[16] E.g., Reminiscences of Isador Lubin (1957), OHC-CU, p. 103; Reminiscences of Aryness Joy Wickens (1957), OHC-CU, pp. 37–41; Oral History with A. Ford Hinrichs (1978), DOL Historical Office, pp. 26–27.

[17] William Green, testimony before the Special (Senate) Committee Investigating the National Defense Program, March 1943, as quoted in Arnow, *Attack on the Cost-of-Living Index*, 60.

official, "expressed in statistical terminology the deficiencies of the Index which the man in the street had obliquely defined as 'something wrong.'" CIO President Philip Murray took a similar view: "I knew there was something wrong," he told the CIO Executive Board in January 1944. "I didn't know what it was, but with the help of all these research people I think we have finally got it nailed down."[18]

Throughout the controversy over the cost of living, one figure served as a central icon for this "bottom-up" knowledge about prices and consumption championed by union officials: the American housewife. As Chapter 4 described, most Americans perceived women as possessing detailed knowledge of local prices, goods, and markets by virtue of their common role as the main purchasers of household goods and food. Through the 1920s and 1930s, consumer advocates urged women to become vigilant shoppers, on guard against price gouging or misleading retail practices and perspicacious in discerning the quality of available items. This process culminated in the OPA's recruitment of multitudes of female volunteers to monitor compliance with price controls in their local stores, which, as Meg Jacobs has described, "encouraged housewives to see themselves as uniquely qualified advocates."[19] It is hardly surprising, therefore that union officials turned to the "housewife" as their symbol of bottom-up knowledge about inflation, drawing on her authority in speeches, articles, even cartoons (see Figure 6.2).[20]

In the hands of labor officials, the significance of the housewife lay only partly in her gender—both national leaders and union researchers knew that the BLS index was supervised primarily by women (Aryness Joy Wickens, Faith Williams, and Stella Stewart) and compiled from data collected by female price agents. Rather, the housewife served as a symbol for the virtues of daily experience over distant expertise and academic reasoning (both of which disqualified women like Wickens or Williams). These themes ran strong in an impassioned speech Philip Murray gave to the CIO Executive Board about the cost of living:

There is no better way to get the facts about what it is costing the average family to live these days than by visiting the housewife, who budgets those things for herself

---

[18] Edward J. Volz to War Labor Board, 8 September 1944, p. 21, Little Steel, box 36A, GCS 1934–50, BLS. *Proceedings of CIO Executive Board,* Jan. 27–28, 1944, p. 32, GMMA.

[19] Meg Jacobs, *Pocketbook Politics: Economic Citizenship in Twentieth-Century America* (Princeton: Princeton University Press, 2005), 122–134, 186–189, 202–211.

[20] E.g., Boris Shishkin, "Inflation Crisis," *American Federationist,* April 1943, p. 3; "AFL-CIO asks poll of housewives on war increases in cost of living," *AFL Weekly News,* 29 February 1944; various cartoons, "Cost of Living Supplement," *CIO News,* February 1944.

Figure 6.2: The Wisdom of Housewives. Two cartoons included in a "Cost of Living Supplement" in the *CIO News* in February 1944. Both reflect the contrast between the Bureau's index and the daily shopping experience of housewives. The top cartoon refers to the disappearance of low-end goods, while the bottom describes "upgrading" of low-quality goods to higher price lines.

in her own home. There is no academic reasoning there, there is no theorizing with life there; you are not living in the city of Washington, writing up a lot of artificialities. You are visiting a woman who understands these problems, and who has the responsibility of running the house, and the best economist that has ever been developed in the history of mankind has been the housewife.

The detailed, immediate knowledge of the housewife trumped any amount of theoretical expertise. "If I am compelled to take my choice between [Isador] Lubin and some steel worker's wife ...," Murray continued, "my inclinations will naturally run to the facts presented to me by the housewife."[21]

The crux of union arguments, of course, was the claim that most working-class women distrusted the BLS index. Whether or not this was true (and no relevant survey data exist), there is little question that BLS staff believed it to be correct. In his notes for the November meeting of the President's Committee, Ford Hinrichs conceded that "almost every housewife in the country" thought that the cost of living had risen more than BLS statistics; in fact, he noted that his father's housekeeper had come to the same conclusion.[22] Similarly, the BLS liaison with labor unions, Boris Stern, concluded that most workers were "firmly convinced that the Bureau is in the wrong." Articles about the controversy in popular magazines often made the same assumption, an attitude that was reinforced by reactions like that of the consumer advocacy group, Consumers' Union: "What the people want is less statistics as such and a little more frank discussion of actual facts. They are tired of being told they are boobs because they insist, on the basis of their own experience, that the cost of living has gone up way beyond what the statisticians claim."[23] In October 1943, Frances Perkins acknowledged the discrepancies between common opinion and the BLS index, joking that Ford Hinrichs's wife "sometimes hurls the price of a head of cabbage at him—the price, not the cabbage." Though Perkins pointed to expert support for BLS work, the anecdote itself backfired. The Associated Press carried the story under the title "Cost of Living Expert Dodges Wife's Figures" and began with an unflattering lead: "If you don't believe the cost-of-living index accurately reflects the wartime dent in your pocketbook, consider the life of an index man. He hasn't even convinced his wife."[24]

---

[21] *Proceedings of CIO Executive Board*, Jan. 27–28, 1944, pp. 44–45, GMMA. More generally, see Thomas A. Stapleford, "'Housewife vs. Economist': Gender, Class, and Domestic Economic Knowledge in Twentieth-Century America," *Labor: Studies in Working-Class History of the Americas* 1, no. 2 (2004): 89–112.

[22] Hinrichs's handwritten notes for meeting of Pres. Committee [1943], 1944—Committee—Cost of Living, box 16, GCS 1934–50, BLS.

[23] Boris Stern, "Labor Relations for BLS Regional Offices," 21 March 1944, Labor Research Comm., box 2, ACF 1941–62, BLS. Consumers' Union, as quoted in A. J. Wickens to A. F. Hinrichs, 22 April 1944, enclosure, "Reaction of the Labor Press to the Cost of Living controversy [by Boris Stern]", p. 7, 1944—Committee, Cost of Living box 16, GCS 1934–50, BLS.

[24] "Cost of Living Expert Dodges Wife's Figures," AP story in the *Des Moines Register*, 14 Oct. 1943.

Occasionally, the bureau tried to deploy the housewife against labor's statistical analysis, but more generally, the BLS aimed to undermine the authority of bottom-up statistics, warning about the vicissitudes of subjective perception and the dangers of using individual experiences to judge a national average. Thus, in Hinrichs's notes for the President's Committee meeting, he described his reaction to purchasing a few apples at an exorbitant price: "I must say it was an act of faith for me that night to believe that the cost of living had gone up only 23 points. ... For the moment, I was an 'average American housewife.' But," he continued, "as Commissioner of Labor Statistics I had some advantages over the housewife." He proceeded to demonstrate how rational statistical analysis overcame his doubts (for instance, he recalled also buying other items, like bread and eggs, whose price had remained relatively stable).[25] In a similar vein, the ASA committee reported that much dissatisfaction with the index did "not arise from any inaccuracy, but from the fact that it is an average," while a report for the Bureau of the Budget discussing public criticism of the index concluded that "on the whole ... subjective judgments cannot be depended upon in establishing a summary measure of cost of living change."[26] A 1943 script for a government-sponsored radio program designed to reduce complaints about the index exemplified the BLS position. Titled "Housewife vs. Economist," the script featured a discussion between Ford Hinrichs and his wife, in which the acting commissioner gradually convinced his skeptical spouse that the BLS index was as accurate a measure of price rises as could be expected under war conditions. Aryness Joy Wickens and Faith Williams would have heartily approved.[27]

For union officials, however, these arguments missed the point: both research staff and national leaders like Meany understood the concept of an average; they recognized that not all prices rose at the same rate and that inflation could vary from place to place.[28] But they insisted that the divergence between the index and common perception arose from the numerous factors not covered by the index (quality deterioration, "forced uptrading," etc.), factors that were all too evident in the actual purchasing experiences

[25] Hinrichs's handwritten notes for meeting of Pres. Committee [1943], 1944—Committee—Cost of Living, box 16, GCS 1934–50, BLS.

[26] Frederick C. Mills et al., "An Appraisal of the U.S. Bureau of Labor Statistics Cost-of-Living Index," *JASA* 38, no. 224 (1943): 402. Typescript of "Adequacy of Cost of Living Indexes," 14 May 1943, Cost of Living Materials, box 17, GCS 1934–50, BLS.

[27] Robert C. Washburn to Charles G. H. Evans, 29 July 1943, encl. draft of script, Cost of Living—Script for Mr. and Mrs. Hinrichs on the Cost of Living, box 18, GCS 1934–50, BLS.

[28] E.g., see Meany's comments in *Verbatim Transcripts*, 23 November 1943, pp. 75–76.

of working-class families. Since union officials believed that cost-of-living statistics should reflect these experiences, they had no qualms about shifting the controversy over the index from private meetings and academic journals to a larger public forum (where workers could make their voices heard), nor did they hesitate to utilize the tools or rhetoric that they had employed successfully in other public battles. Popular audience, polemical rhetoric, detailed individual examples, the grounding authority of common experience: all of these were interlocking components of a bottom-up approach to statistics.

Bureau staff (and most other economists) regarded labor's efforts as a pernicious development: an unwarranted and dangerous injection of obviously partisan politics into statistical calculation. The union researchers responsible for labor's cost-of-living statistics saw the matter differently. As the next section makes clear, they believed that political judgments and assumptions were inherent in statistical calculation. Bringing political pressure to bear upon these calculations did not violate a sacred distinction; it simply responded to an already existing situation.

THE POLITICS OF MEASURING THE COST OF LIVING

As Secretary of Labor Frances Perkins later described it, the wartime controversy served as a watershed moment for the role of technical, nonpartisan expertise in the federal government:

> [The controversy] centered around the question as to whether or not the determination of policy should be made by Government officials to whom had been delegated responsibility for particular functions, or if such determinations should be based on the desire of one group as against another. The obvious reply, I think, must be the assumption that Government officials, until proven otherwise, are performing their duties at the highest level of impartiality.[29]

Perkins's characterization of the affair matched the self-image of impartial expertise carried by the staff who entered the BLS during the New Deal, a neutrality (grounded in professional practices and guidelines) that would allow them to transcend the pluralistic competition of different social groups. Recall, for instance, that when Ford Hinrichs and Lewis Lorwin outlined a process for democratic economic planning in 1935, the two men promoted expertise rather than "compromise" between "group interests" as

---

[29] Frances Perkins to Kathryn Arnow, 19 Sept. 1950, Committee for Public Administration Cases, box 3, Wickens correspondence, BLS.

the key to setting national policy. Such efforts, they declared, required "a new class of civil servants," distinguished by their devotion to the "national interest" and their technical skill.[30]

By contrast, union researchers such as Harold Ruttenberg were far more skeptical about supposedly neutral experts. When asked by William Davis to suggest an "impartial, non-partisan" economist who could settle the technical questions about the index, Ruttenberg described that as a near impossible task. "I would love to meet an impartial man," he replied. "I am going to live long, I hope, but in my young life I haven't met him yet." Indeed, Ruttenberg freely admitted his own lack of impartiality; when George Meany approvingly called him "thoroughly biased," Ruttenberg wholeheartedly agreed. In his view, the only way to come to a fair decision about the cost of living was to treat economic statistics like other aspects of wartime wage policy: assemble a tripartite board with representatives from labor, business, and the government, and let them hash it out.[31] Statistics, in other words, were simply one more domain for political negotiation.

For the BLS, this was an unacceptable position. It violated both their professional training (which insisted on the possibility of creating objective facts) and a long-standing (if occasionally paradoxical) maxim vigorously promoted by Carroll Wright: the bureau must remain aloof from partisan controversy if it was to be politically effective.[32] Both ideals would be compromised by letting government statistics become the product of corporatist haggling. "I told the meeting of union research directors that they had made a terrible mistake," recalled Aryness Joy Wickens several years later. "I told them that they had attempted to bargain with us about an index, but that we wouldn't bargain about the facts. I told them that they had used the wrong technique; they had used collective bargaining techniques in a technical survey."[33] In the eyes of union researchers, however, Wickens's objections were misguided, referencing a nonexistent ideal in which statistical calculation could be isolated from political judgments. As the debates between the unions and the BLS continued during the spring of 1944, three subjects illustrated to union researchers the impossibility of separating politics and

[30] Lewis L. Lorwin and Albert Ford Hinrichs, *National Economic and Social Planning: Theory and Practice with Special Reference to the United States* (Washington, D.C.: National Resources Board, 1935), 453, 448.

[31] Harold Ruttenberg, *Verbatim Transcripts*, Feb. 2, 1944, pp. 25–26, 30–31.

[32] James Leiby, *Carroll Wright and Labor Reform: The Origin of Labor Statistics* (Cambridge: Harvard University Press, 1960), 63. Cf. *NABL* (1885): 125–126; *NABL* (1886): 68–69.

[33] Aryness Joy Wickens, "Notes on a conversation of 5/19/1950 between Mrs. Wickens and Mrs. Arnow," 19 May 1950, p. 3, Committee for Public Administration Cases, box 3, Wickens correspondence, BLS.

statistics, and in turn reinforced their frustration with the bureau: first, the agency's attitude toward quality deterioration; second, the revelation of an alternative approach to measuring the cost of living pursued by the Bureau of Agricultural Economics in the Department of Agriculture; and finally, the BLS response to union assertions about "forced" trading up.

Quality Deterioration

Quality deterioration was a widely acknowledged occurrence, but there was less agreement about how to treat it in the index.[34] The BLS argued that its price collection procedures did capture the most obvious forms of falling quality: field agents were trained to price similar goods from month to month using uniform specifications and would shift to a more expensive price line if necessary to maintain product equality. Yet several factors hampered this procedure in practice. First, the wide variety of goods available at different stores across the country had forced the BLS to develop specification ranges rather than precise, individual descriptions. Therefore, quality and price could vary substantially within a specification range.[35] Moreover, the bureau admitted that prewar qualities were often no longer available and that quality changes were not always recognized by field agents. But, such deterioration was simply not quantifiable: "With reference to quality deterioration," the agency concluded, "three things may be said: it exists; it cannot be measured statistically; and it cannot be stated in terms of prices."[36]

Other economists supported the bureau's stance, including the "technical committee" of Wesley Mitchell, Simon Kuznets, and Margaret Reid convened by William Davis to adjudicate between the claims of the BLS and the unions. The committee's discussion of "quality" echoed Mitchell's

---

[34] For a discussion of the history of approaches to quality change in price indexes, see H. Spencer Banzhaf, "Quantifying the Qualitative: Quality-Adjusted Price Indexes in the United States, 1915–1961," in *The Age of Economic Measurement*, ed. Judy L. Klein and Mary S. Morgan (Durham: Duke University Press, 2001), 345–370.

[35] In some cases, agents switched to a "higher quality" line almost double the price of the old item while remaining under the original specification. In the abstract, this price jump should have appeared in the index (since the new item remained within specification). But because agents recognized the new item as higher quality than the old version, they "linked" the new item into the index and thereby excluded the price differential from the index. Louis Weiner to A. J. Wickens, 16 July 1943, pp. 2–4, Cost of Living Materials, box 17, GCS 1934–50, BLS. A union review of BLS procedures in the early postwar period came to similar conclusions: Harry Chester to Nat Weinberg, 18 August 1948, pp. 2–3, folder 18, box 6, Research Department, UAW.

[36] U.S. Bureau of Labor Statistics, "The Cost-of-Living Index: A Review and Appraisal," 148, 178–179.

attitude toward utility twenty years earlier: both were disturbingly elusive concepts. Sometimes people valued goods based on pragmatic "serviceability"; in other cases they tried "to get the color, form, flavor, texture, style, or other characteristic that will give the greatest pleasure per dollar spent." How could you measure such a mutable factor? In short, it was impossible: "Because of the various dimensions of quality, the complex interactions among them, and the subjective character of many quality characteristics, there is no objective measure of general quality." Even a seemingly clear-cut trait like serviceability could be nebulous in practice: "There is no directly objective criterion as to when, for example, a pair of shoes is really worn out."[37] In its reply to the Meany-Thomas report, the BLS noted that in 1942 its staff had contacted several federal agencies (including the OPA and the War Production Board) to "help work out a plan for measuring quality deterioration statistically," but to no avail. "These experts reported that one could count on the fingers of one hand the consumers' goods for which there were tests of general serviceability which would yield statistical results and which could be combined with price data."[38]

Without precise, quantified data, the BLS refused to make an adjustment to the index. Ford Hinrichs insisted that there were no measures of quality deterioration "that have any general acceptability or statistical validity"; therefore, the best solution was simply to note that the index took insufficient account of quality. Union officials disagreed: "If all the necessary data are not available," declared the Murray-Thomas report, "it is more accurate to estimate than to ignore the question." Overall, union leaders claimed to be calling the bureau's bluff: "Everybody knows that ... special wartime factors exist. The Bureau of Labor Statistics denies that some of them are important and claims that they cannot be measured. ... The CIO-AFL Cost of Living Study *did measure them* and included them in its realistic statement of the rise in living costs."[39] Of course, union researchers had no more access to "objective" quantitative measurements of quality deterioration than did the bureau: instead, union researchers turned to the detailed examples and limited surveys that BLS staff found unreliable and unrepresentative. For

[37] Wesley C. Mitchell, Simon Kuznets, and Margaret Reid, "Report of the Technical Committee Appointed by the Chairman of the President's Committee on the Cost of Living, June 15, 1944," in *Report of the President's Committee on the Cost of Living*, ed. William H. Davis (Washington, D.C.: Office of Economic Stabilization, 1945), 277.

[38] U.S. Bureau of Labor Statistics, "The Cost-of-Living Index: A Review and Appraisal," 178.

[39] Hinrichs to Harvey W. Brown (International Association of Machinists), 16 May 1946, Micro 07, Reel 8, U.S. Government Agencies, Office of the President, RG 1, GMMA. Murray and Thomas, *Living Costs in World War II*, 45, 11.

statisticians skeptical of the unions' bottom-up approach to statistical calculation, quality deterioration thus presented two undesirable alternatives: give up trying to measure it or make a largely unfounded estimate.

From the bureau's perspective, the solution to this dilemma lay in a different domain: rather than tinkering with the index (which could never accurately track an amorphous trait like quality), unions ought to attack the problem at its source. Even before the controversy, BLS staff viewed quality deterioration and similar issues like shortages or the disappearance of low-end price lines as problems in production. Rather than raising the index to account for these phenomena (and perhaps contributing to inflation), the solution lay in managing production. In a May 1943 memo, Hinrichs told Isador Lubin that "the unions have valid complaints with respect to price stabilization" because of inadequacies of the OPA, including delayed rationing and failure to regulate quality. When he heard about the creation of the President's Committee, Hinrichs suggested to Secretary of Labor Frances Perkins that the group "ought to aim for the production of 'A Joint Report of the W.L.B. and the Dept. of Labor (B.L.S.) on *Production, Consumers Goods, Living Conditions and the Wage Earner in Wartime*.'" The report would have four parts:

I.   War requires more man-hours of work but limits the production of consumer goods.
II.   The very poor must be protected against the hidden taxation of a price rise.
III. Everyone must be assured access to a fair share of available goods.
IV.   Workers in congested areas must be furnished more housing, transportation, etc. *Their problem is not too little income but not enough goods.* [emphasis added]

An appraisal of the BLS index "as a measure of retail prices" would be attached as an appendix.[40]

The bureau drew support for its production-based solutions from the example of other countries, noting how quality standardization and regulated production had eased the political pressure on price controls. In New Zealand, for instance, officials emphasized that the "Government ... took steps to ensure that the standard lines [of shoes] used in the index should be

---

[40] Ford Hinrichs to Isador Lubin, 4 May 1943, "Memorandum on the Cost of Living", box 71, GCS 1934–50, BLS. Hinrichs to Perkins, 23 Oct. 1943, 1944–Committee, Cost of Living, box 16, GCS 1934–50, BLS.

manufactured in adequate quantities."[41] Great Britain, in particular, seemed to be an illustrative case. The weights in the British cost-of-living index had not been updated since 1914, and its accuracy was a "matter of considerable discussion and controversy," according to an official of the British Food Mission. Nonetheless, the index had received little public criticism from unions, a situation which a British labor economist attributed in part (and not, perhaps, correctly) to more effective price control and rationing.[42] In its appraisal of the Meany-Thomas report, the BLS tried to push union officials to focus their efforts on controlling production; likewise, in a letter to a union official in 1946, Hinrichs lamented labor's failure to use "the materials in the Bureau's records for an all-out attack to get standard quality, to get production of low-priced lines, or to get housing. In the fury of the frontal attack on the index itself all the collateral values of the material were lost."[43]

In the view of union officials, however, such suggestions were not part of the bureau's role. During the meeting with the President's Committee, Hinrichs began discussing the relation between housing shortages and high rents: "What you need is additional housing construction for that income group so as to relieve [the] extraordinary pressure under which they are living." But Meany was unsatisfied with this response: "You couldn't measure that as an increase in the cost of living then. In other words, you jump right over it and say 'Here is the way to cure it.' Nobody has asked you how to cure it."[44] It was a common impasse that wove through the entire controversy: the unions were bound by the index and demanded that the BLS alter its calculation to account more fully for factors like quality deterioration or "forced"

---

[41] Faith Williams to ASA Committee, 1 June 1943, "Cost of Living in Great Britain, Sweden, Canada and New Zealand," President's Committee on the Cost of Living, box 10, Wickens correspondence, BLS.

[42] E.M.H. Lloyd, British Food Mission, p. 45, "Proceedings: Bureau of Labor Statistics Third Annual Conference with Research Directors of National and International Unions," 17–18 June 1942, Labor Research Directors Conference, box 1, Records of the Comm. of Labor Statistics, Advisory Comm. Files, 1941–62, BLS. Williams to Wickens, "Status of British Cost of Living Index," 9 February 1944, encl., S. D. Berger to Kezzer, 3 Decemebr 1943, p. 2, unlabeled folder, box 17, GCS 1934–1950, BLS. The BLS never publicly stated Berger's other comments on why the British index did not suffer a similar fate, namely the lack of a rigid wage freeze and severe taxes on profits and luxury goods. For a later comparison that also emphasizes the importance of production controls, see Geofrey Mills and Hugh Rockoff, "Compliance with Price Controls in the United States and the United Kingdom During World War II," *Journal of Economic History* 47, no. 1 (1987): 197–213.

[43] U.S. Bureau of Labor Statistics, "The Cost-of-Living Index: A Review and Appraisal," 148, cf. 145, 178. Hinrichs to Harvey W. Brown, International Association of Machinists, 16 May 1946.

[44] *Verbatim Transcripts*, Nov. 23, 1943, p. 35.

trading up. The BLS refused, arguing that such measures were unreliable, and instead offered alternative solutions that avoided changing the index. The creation of the union cost-of-living reports complicated the situation by purporting to provide valid measurements (thereby forcing the BLS to critique union research and further anger union leaders), but it was also made much worse by a subsequent revelation: not all government agencies shared the bureau's scruples about the proper methods for cost-of-living indexes.

The Role of a Bureau: The Bureau of Agricultural Economics and Its Cost-of-Living Index

Between the creation of the Meany-Thomas report (January 1944) and the Murray-Thomas report (June 1944), union researchers found an alternate, conflicting cost-of-living index published by the government. The Bureau of Agricultural Economics (BAE) in the Department of Agriculture maintained an index for farmers, and its data showed a 45 percent increase between January 1941, and March 1944—virtually equivalent to the estimate in labor's reports. Needless to say, this was a major coup for the unions, and it sent BLS staff scurrying over to the BAE to try and nail down the problem. The result was a joint report analyzing the differences between the two indexes. Although it appeared too late to be part of the Mitchell committee's work, William Davis included the report with his official summary of the President's Committee's conclusions.[45]

The two agencies pointed to several key factors. First, farmers and workers bought different kinds of goods, and the BLS index included items such as rent that tended to stabilize the workers' index. Moreover, farmers bought more lower-quality goods than workers did, and lower-quality goods had experienced a greater price rise. Second, the BAE index was heavily weighted toward the South and rural areas, both of which showed greater price increases than northern, urban areas. Finally, unlike the BLS, the BAE did not try to keep a constant level of quality; instead, it priced the goods "most commonly sold to farmers." Although the BLS-BAE report argued these pricing policies contributed only a "small" effect to the differences, pricing became the focus of union commentary. Because the BAE priced the "most commonly sold" goods, the BAE index had a constantly

---

[45] Dorothy S. Brady and Roger F. Hale, "Comparison of Changes in BLS Cost-of-Living Index and BAE Index of Prices Paid by Farmers for Commodities Used for Family Living: Joint Analysis by the Bureau of Agricultural Economics and the Bureau of Labor Statistics," in Davis, ed., *Report of the President's Committee*, 371–394.

changing market basket where the full price difference from changes in the basket was reflected in the index; thus, the BAE was publishing the same kind of index advocated by labor organizations. The Murray-Thomas report included a chart showing how the BAE and BLS indexes had moved in concert from 1935 to the first quarter of 1941, when the BAE index began rising steeply. Union officials suggested that the BAE index was properly showing the effects of involuntary trading up that were being missed by the BLS.[46]

Regardless of how one judged the BAE index (and it was controversial both before and after the war), it was nevertheless an embarrassment to the BLS.[47] In contrast to the bureau's stalwart commitment to the constant-goods index (price changes only), another government agency was calculating a cost-of-living index that included both changes in prices and changes in goods purchased. Moreover, labor officials pointed out that the BAE figures were "used, by Congressional direction, as one basis for calculating parity prices for farm products. That is, whenever the farmers' living costs go up— as measured by the BAE Index—the prices of farm products likewise rise." The Murray-Thomas report bitterly compared this situation to the "storm of opposition" generated by labor unions' similar approach in trying to break the Little Steel formula.[48] That the Department of Agriculture was publishing this index for farmers while the Department of Labor resisted such a method for workers reinforced union officials' repeated complaints about the relative attitudes of the two departments. For CIO officials, the BAE index was just one more reminder of how the federal government treated farmers and workers differently.[49]

Class Assumptions: The "Overall Index" and Voluntary Trading Up

The bureau's tendency to make policy suggestions and its refusal to act as an advocate for workers frustrated union leaders, but they found the

---

[46] Brady and Hale, "Comparison of Changes in BLS Cost-of-Living Index and BAE Index," 374. Murray and Thomas, *Living Costs in World War II*, 147–149.

[47] In the 1920s, a Commerce Department official had complained to Hoover that Department of Agriculture calculations understated the purchasing power of farmers: William J. Barber, *From New Era to New Deal: Herbert Hoover, the Economists, and American Economic Policy, 1921–1933* (Cambridge: Cambridge University Press, 1985), 53. For a later analysis, see papers in the *Journal of Farm Economics* 38, no. 2 (1956). (Note B. R. Stauber's defense here of pricing strategies for the agriculture index, pp. 371–372.)

[48] Murray and Thomas, *Living Costs in World War II*, 147.

[49] On the CIO's jealousy of the Department of Agriculture's perceived tendency to lobby for farmers, see Arnow, *Attack on the Cost-of-Living Index*, 49–50.

agency's attitude toward "trading up" (buying higher priced goods) to be particularly insulting. Both the BLS and the Mitchell committee insisted that working-class families (and union researchers) often conflated two distinct phenomena: a rise in the cost of a fixed standard of living versus the additional expense of meeting a higher standard made possible by rising real incomes. But in truth neither the BLS nor the Mitchell committee had any reliable, national statistics to demonstrate that working-class standards of living were rapidly increasing. According to the BLS, the best way to assess the current "American standard of living" was through expenditure surveys. But apart from a small study of "Saving and Spending in Wartime" undertaken in 1942, the bureau's funding requests for more surveys had been turned down by Congress. Even without expenditure surveys, one could theoretically assess changes in the standard of living by tracking the parallel shifts in "real" income (i.e., income adjusted for inflation). Unfortunately, as Harold Ruttenberg pointed out, the only relevant measurement of inflation was the BLS cost-of-living index, which thus trapped the statistician in circular reasoning: "The BLS index (assumed to be valid) is used to deflate expenditure figures in order to establish that real income has risen, and therefore that the BLS index (whose validity is under scrutiny) is justified in omitting a large portion of trading up because of its voluntary character."[50]

Ruttenberg tried to avoid this problem by creating an independent check on union calculations. First, he divided data on aggregate food expenditures by estimates of aggregate food production to create a ratio; comparing these ratios from two different time periods produced what Ruttenberg called an "overall" price index for food. He made a similar calculation for clothing, and the results looked much like the union's other estimates.[51] However, the BLS and the Mitchell committee argued that aggregate expenditures were not necessarily representative of working-class purchases. More importantly, they claimed that the increased expenditures were probably associated with higher incomes (as workers purchased higher quality goods and services) and therefore were not "legitimate cost increases for index number purposes."[52] Still, without large expenditure studies or a reliable income deflator, neither the Mitchell committee nor the BLS had a strong statistical basis for asserting that increased expenditures among working-class

---

[50] Harold Ruttenberg, "Comments on the June 15, 1944, Report of the Mitchell Committee," 23 August 1944, in Davis, ed., *Report of the President's Committee*, 397.

[51] Murray and Thomas, *Living Costs in World War II*, 55–56, 74.

[52] U.S. Bureau of Labor Statistics, "The Cost-of-Living Index: A Review and Appraisal," 156, 194–196; Mitchell, Kuznets, and Reid, "Report of the Technical Committee," 298–301.

families were definitely the result of voluntary trading up.[53] The BLS, however, was satisfied to point out the flaws in union research and to suggest alternate explanations. Likewise, the Mitchell committee repeatedly placed the burden of proof on unions rather than on the bureau, and hence the overall index was discarded by the committee.[54]

Not surprisingly, union officials resented this asymmetrical treatment. Ruttenberg pointed to the qualified language used by the Mitchell committee whenever it discussed trading up: "It *seems highly probable* ...;" "We *believe* ...;" "[forced uptrading] is *probably* not important," and so forth.[55] Ruttenberg saw these statements both as evidence of the inadequacy of the pro-bureau argument and as a demonstration that the statisticians were relying on assumptions about working-class life and behavior. "The prevalent belief, apparently shared by the BLS," complained the Murray-Thomas report, "is that we are ... in a silk-shirt—or mink coat—era, the workers vying with millionaires in the purchase of jewels and ermine wraps."[56] George Meany had come to a similar conclusion during the November meeting, when he and Hinrichs had circled round and round the prices/expenditures distinction. "You see," Meany exclaimed at one point, "you come right back to the one thing which has been predetermined in your mind, that the rise in the cost of living is due to the fact that the workers get more money."[57] Unfortunately, some injudicious comments in the BLS appraisal of the Meany-Thomas report reinforced this perspective.

"The BLS reply," declared the Murray-Thomas report, "... is replete with sarcasm, contempt, and arrogance—frequently expressed in 'telling phrases,' some of which ... show a lack of elementary respect for American workingmen."[58] For instance, when the BLS tried to downplay the significance of quality deterioration in meats by noting that lower grade meats

---

[53] The limited basis upon which the Mitchell committee justified its assumption about voluntary trading up is quite remarkable: Mitchell, Kuznets, and Reid, "Report of the Technical Committee," 300, 330. At one point, the committee simply asserts that working-class families "have had an increase in purchasing power" (based on unspecified "evidence") and therefore that these families "probably" used the extra real income to purchase higher grades of goods. Mitchell, Kuznets, and Reid, "Report of the Technical Committee," 335.

[54] Mitchell, Kuznets, and Reid, "Report of the Technical Committee," 301.

[55] Ruttenberg, "Comments on the June 15, 1944, Report of the Mitchell Committee," 398 (emphasis added by Ruttenberg).

[56] Murray and Thomas, *Living Costs in World War II*, 33.

[57] *Verbatim Transcripts*, 23 November 1943, p. 69.

[58] Murray and Thomas, *Living Costs in World War II*, 46. In fact, the final version of the BLS appraisal of the Meany-Thomas report (included in William Davis's report for the President's Committee) deleted or modified some of the harshest assessments. For example, compare U.S. Bureau of Labor Statistics, *The Cost-of-Living Index: A Review and*

contained more protein and less fat, union researchers branded the statement as "on a par with the famous advice to workers: 'Let them eat cake.' ... Market qualities," they continued, "... reflect desirability as established by custom and experience," and not by abstract "nutritional difference."[59] The bureau's dismissal of Department of Commerce figures on food expenditures because those statistics included liquor sales drew particular ire: "The cost of living," proclaimed the CIO report, "is the cost of items that people actually buy, not the cost of items that some Government statisticians think that they need."[60] More generally, having grounded their critique of the BLS index in the subjective experience of working-class families, union officials could portray the bureau's refusal to alter the index as a dismissal of workers themselves. One labor journal epitomized this position in a bitter editorial about the BLS response to the Meany-Thomas report, once again turning to the image of the housewife:

The American housewife and worker are presumably exaggerating when they state the shoddy clothing they buy at higher prices wears half as long as better clothing bought at lower prices before the war. The American housewife is presumably wrong when she reports purchasing grade B eggs at grade A prices. She presumably lies about the lack of service the landlord provides; about the ersatz furniture for which she pays quality prices; and about the five and ten-cent hamburgers for which she pays a quarter. No other inference from Hinrichs' complete disregard for the experience of the American worker and housewife is possible.[61]

From the perspective of national labor officials involved in the controversy, the political failure of the BLS was evident. The bureau had refused to make measurements requested by union leaders (even though the BAE had taken a similar approach for farmers) and had maintained (without any solid empirical evidence) that working-class discontent with the index was misplaced and was based on unreliable, subjective perceptions or on the greater cost of reaching a new, higher standard of living. By June, with this material in hand, George Meany and R. J. Thomas were ready to press for a final resolution.

Appraisal, (Typescript, 25 February 1944), 4; U.S. Bureau of Labor Statistics, "The Cost-of-Living Index: A Review and Appraisal," 145.

[59] U.S. Bureau of Labor Statistics, "The Cost-of-Living Index: A Review and Appraisal," 163; Murray and Thomas, *Living Costs in World War II*, 64.

[60] U.S. Bureau of Labor Statistics, "The Cost-of-Living Index: A Review and Appraisal," 195; Murray and Thomas, *Living Costs in World War II*, 56.

[61] *Proceedings of CIO Executive Board*, Jan. 27–28, 1944, pp. 45–46, GMMA, "Labor Statistics Bureau Refutes AFL Figures in Cost of Living Survey," *Beach Cities Labor Journal*, Santa Monica, Calif., 24 March 1944, box 17, GCS 1934–50, BLS.

ENDGAME

The Failure of Compromise

On June 8, 1944, the BLS held its fifth annual conference with union researchers. But the meeting had hardly started before George Meany arrived unannounced and took the floor for a long monologue. His bitter speech, which was simultaneously released to the press, denounced the BLS for meddling in policy and labeled both the bureau and the Department of Labor as friends of anti-union officials. "The Secretary of Labor," Meany proclaimed, "does not represent the views of labor in the Cabinet." Hinrichs was "a bureaucratic monkey on a stick who moves up and down in conformity with the dictates of administrative wage policy." The BLS had "prostituted its research functions" and "obsequiously acquiesced" to administrative demands to hold down wages using the index; in turn, it was "no longer a free agency of statistical research."[62]

Notes scribbled back and forth between Wickens and Faith Williams during Meany's harangue illustrate the growing frustration of the staff, ending with a wistful comment: "This needs Lubin's touch."[63] After Meany finished, other anti-bureau researchers spoke up, including Harold Ruttenberg, who reiterated old criticisms and offered new evidence from the forthcoming Murray-Thomas report. But the exercise was surely pro forma, intended simply as a public rebuke to the BLS; by this point, neither Meany nor Ruttenberg could have legitimately hoped that the BLS would be receptive to their complaints. During lunch, the agency staff regrouped, and Wickens was given permission to present a carefully worded response to the union representatives, outlining the bureau's arguments but avoiding any direct confrontation. In this way, Wickens aimed to "appeal to the reasonable group at the meeting," whom she felt had been "very much chagrined" by Meany's hostility. Most of her presentation covered old ground: she reiterated the need for expenditure studies ("the only way to answer most of these questions") and pointed out that no available data existed for many factors that unions wanted included in the index.[64] Overall, she continued to insist on the bureau's long-standing, central claim: according to traditional,

[62] "Meany Berates Labor Department for Unrealistic Living Cost Index," *AFL Weekly News*, 13 June 1944. Arnow, *Attack on the Cost-of-Living Index*, 131–132.

[63] "Miss Joy's notes for meeting of Labor Research Directors, June 8, 1944," Labor Research Directors Conference, box 1, ACF 1941–62, BLS.

[64] "Notes on a conversation of 5/19/1950 between Mrs. Wickens and Mrs. Arnow," 19 May 1950, p. 3. "Miss Joy's notes for meeting of Labor Research Directors, June 8, 1944," handwritten notes, p. 3 (see also 4–6 for her general remarks), Labor Research Directors

accepted statistical practice worldwide, "cost-of-living" indexes should be constant-goods indexes that measured changes in prices.[65]

On June 22, the technical committee headed by Wesley C. Mitchell released its final report. Generally, the Mitchell committee supported the BLS, but it did differ from the staff's position in two respects. First, the committee decided to estimate the effect of several factors that the bureau had claimed were unmeasurable, in the end adding three to four percentage points to the index to account for issues such as quality deterioration. However, the committee noted that this supplementary figure was a "guess" and supported the separation of such estimates from the main index.[66] Perhaps more importantly, the Mitchell committee also stated that in light of the ambiguous meaning, the phrase "cost of living," the title of the BLS index, "invited misunderstanding" and the committee suggested that it "be given a less misleading name."[67]

Subsequent accounts have tended to see the Mitchell report largely as a full vindication of the BLS index; at the time, however, the union researchers leading the assault on the index had a different reaction. Beginning in July, the BLS began including a short note about the limitations of the index in its publications, acknowledging that it did "not show the full wartime effect on the cost of living of such factors as lowered quality, disappearance of low-priced goods and forced changes in housing and eating away from home." Equally important, the Mitchell committee (unlike the BLS) had agreed to estimate the effects of these issues, and it had conceded that the subsequent calculations were often based on "crude guesses," apparently leaving space (in the union view) for future negotiation over the final result.[68] In June, Harold Ruttenberg told the CIO Executive Board that he hoped to convince Mitchell to "jack up that figure" and that they could probably reach a compromise between the original CIO and BLS estimates (roughly 45 percent and 24 percent) landing "somewhere in the 30s." But it soon became clear just how deeply Ruttenberg had misjudged the ethos of most statisticians, who, like Aryness Joy Wickens, balked at any suggestion that they negotiate over final results. Having made what it felt was its best judgment, the

Conference, box 1, ACF 1941–62, BLS. Arnow, *Attack on the Cost-of-Living Index*, 133–134.

[65] "Miss Joy's notes for meeting of Labor Research Directors, June 8, 1944," typed notes, pp. 15–16, handwritten p. 7, typed p. 1.

[66] Mitchell, Kuznets, and Reid, "Report of the Technical Committee," 260, 262.

[67] Ibid., 254, 263.

[68] U.S. Bureau of Labor Statistics, "Cost of Living in Large Cities, May 1944," *MLR* 59, no. 1 (July 1944): 180. Mitchell, Kuznets, and Reid, "Report of the Technical Committee," 295.

Mitchell committee stood firm.[69] Later economic historians would often treat Mitchell's estimate as a lower bound to the true rate of inflation (at the high end, Harold Vatter has suggested a rise of 36 percent between 1941 and 1944, based on the estimates of Milton Friedman and Anna Schwartz).[70] In 1944, however, the Mitchell estimate was the only independent calculation. Not surprisingly, William Davis happily followed Mitchell's lead when writing his final report (pleased to have cover for leaving both the index and the Little Steel formula unchanged), while the industry members offered a concurring opinion and the union members, a frustrated dissent. The President's Committee had failed to produce the unanimous report Davis had hoped for in the early months, and the unions continued to present their own cost-of-living statistics in public and in presentations before the National War Labor Board.[71]

The Limits of Bottom-Up Statistics

In truth, the Mitchell committee's rejection of union arguments should have shocked no one: since the release of the Meany-Thomas report, national labor leaders had repeatedly challenged the professional norms shared by most statisticians by appealing to public judgment over expert decrees, making generalizations from clusters of individual examples, attacking the integrity of BLS staff, and so forth. The public, not economists with tight

---

[69] Harold Ruttenberg, *Minutes of the CIO Executive Board*, 18 June 1944, p. 186, microfilm 2, roll 3, GMMA. On Ruttenberg's efforts to reach a compromise, see Arnow, *Attack on the Cost-of-Living Index*, 142–147.

[70] Harold Vatter, "The Material Status of the U.S. Civilian Consumer in World War II: The Question of Guns or Butter," in *The Sinews of War: Essays on the Economic History of World War II*, ed. Geofrey T. Mills and Hugh Rockoff (Ames: Iowa State University Press, 1993), 221–222; Milton Friedman and Anna J. Schwartz, *Monetary Trends in the United States and United Kingdom, Their Relation to Income, Prices, and Interest Rates, 1867–1975* (Chicago: University of Chicago Press, 1982), 101–104, 125. Note that Friedman and Schwartz include the effects of black-market prices, which the BLS deliberately excluded (and which unions avoided in their estimates as well). Hugh Rockoff's detailed treatments are more sympathetic to the Mitchell committee and establish a reduced upper bound of about 7% additional rise above the BLS index by December 1943 (for a total rise of roughly 31% since January 1941): Hugh Rockoff, "Indirect Price Increases and Real Wages During World War II," *Explorations in Economic History* 15, no. 4 (1978): 407–420; Mills and Rockoff, "Compliance with Price Controls," 197–213. All of these subsequent estimates are for civilian consumers as a whole, not simply wage-earners. Yet, I am not convinced that there is enough reliable evidence to allow us to assign substantially different rates of inflation to different social groups.

[71] The full set of concluding reports appear in Davis, ed., *Report of the President's Committee*. For Davis's hope that the President's Committee could come to a unanimous conclusion, see *Verbatim Transcripts*, 2 February 1944, pp. 3–12.

ties to Washington agencies, was the real audience for bottom-up statistics. How, then, did most Americans react to the unions' efforts? Many of the elite periodicals, at least, were not impressed. *The Nation* called union calculations a "highly partisan report" that "contains glaring discrepancies which make it useless as a scientific document." The *New York Times* approvingly labeled the bureau's response as "a merciless microscopic analysis" that presented "an impressive and convincing array of statistics," while syndicated columnist Ernest Lindley considered it "a pretty thorough job of demolition." One Illinois newspaper rejected labor's experiential knowledge because it relied heavily "on a spot check of housewives, a notoriously unscientific method." Even the *New Republic*, while supporting labor's quest to break the Little Steel formula, called aspects of Ruttenberg's arguments "fallacious" (when they were repeated in an article for the magazine) and judged that the BLS "has a good answer to labor's criticism of its figures."[72]

But not everyone was as ready to jump on the expertise bandwagon. Reflecting on the contradictory testimony given by Philip Murray and Hinrichs before a Senate committee, *America* hinted at the insufficiency of official statistics:

> The statistician will say—and prove by figures—that shoes, stockings, anything you like, have gone up only twenty-five per cent. The housewife, however, may know that for some strange reason the articles are wearing out much faster this year, and she strongly suspects that statistics have not yet taken into account that very important fact. ... We rather suspect that the ordinary housewife, who is only mildly statistical, would be inclined to award the debate to Mr. Murray.

After the release of the Mitchell report, the Philadelphia *Record* concluded that "the President's committee ought to do some more studying, realistically— perhaps with a visit to a grocery store—or step aside for another committee more impressed by fact than theory." Several newspaper editorials, typically from the West, Midwest, or small towns, declared the whole dispute a mess of unresolvable claims. Others had harsher words for the BLS; the Waterville, Maine *Sentinel* derided the cost-of-living index as "one of the greatest fakes put out by official agencies," noting that "everyone ... knows that the cost has gone up tremendously." Comments within several editorials suggest how union officials' bottom-up rhetoric could resonate with those distrustful of "theory"

---

[72] *The Nation*, 19 Feb. 1944, pp. 204–205. *NYT*, 28 Feb. 1944, as quoted in BLS internal document, "Press notice of BLS report on Meany Thomas Report," p. 2, Cost of Living Clippings, box 17, GCS 1934–50, BLS. Ernest Lindley, "Cost of Living Debate," *Register* (Des Moines, Iowa), 6 March 1944. "And Why an Index?" *Star* (Rockford, Ill.), 29 Feb. 1944. "The Big Wage Drive," *The New Republic*, 10 April 1944, p. 488.

and government experts. "The unions … have reasonable foundation for their complaints against BLS," declared the Boise, Idaho *Statesman*. "The matter is simply another demonstration that it is not possible to control national economics from the steps of the White House." Concluding that the best estimate lay between the union and BLS estimates, the Emporia, Kansas *Gazette* added, "at least it is safe to assume the government figure is the minimum."[73]

Generally, union publications supported the stance of their national leaders, some quite vehemently. A response to the bureau's appraisal of the Meany-Thomas report in the *Beach Cities Labor Journal* (Santa Monica, California) demonstrates how bottom-up rhetoric could undermine the bureau's appeal to expertise. The BLS review, complained the journal, was "based almost exclusively on the cheap assertion that the CIO-AFL report does not meet 'the high technical standards which usually have characterized trade union research.' Labor's representatives are thus tossed a sop and begged to discuss the problem like gentlemen over tea and cigars while the working man lives on hominy and grits."[74] As of late February, the most favorable treatment the BLS had received from a union periodical was an editorial in *Minnesota Labor* which decided that labor and the bureau were talking about the cost of living in two different areas (steel mill communities vs. large cities). Of course, it is almost impossible to say exactly how rank-and-file members perceived the campaign by national officials. One anecdote relayed by Ruttenberg, however, suggests that the bottom-up rhetoric could strike a chord with many members. While at a local union meeting, Ruttenberg was explaining the bureau's practice of imputing the price change of a single item to a group of related goods when he was asked what he meant by "imputation":

"It's an assumption," I replied.
"And what the hell is that?" he rejoined. (Laughter)
I replied, "An assumption is a guess."
He shot back, "Who's so darn dumb he has to guess about the cost of living?"
"I take it, brother," I replied, "that you've never been to Washington, D.C." (More laughter)[75]

---

[73] "Cost of Living," *America*, 5 Feb. 1944. "The Inedible Index," *Record* (Philadelphia, Pa.), 27 June 1944. "Cost of Living," *Sentinel* (Waterville, Maine), 8 March 1944. "Statistics that Hurt," *Statesman* (Boise, Idaho), 4 March 1944. "The H. C. of L.," *Gazette* (Emporia, Kans.), 16 March 1944. An internal Bureau memo, "Press notice of BLS report on Meany-Thomas report," lists four editorials (from St. Louis, Spokane, South Bend, and Portland, Maine) describing the whole situation as a "muddle," Cost of Living Clippings, box 17, GCS 1934–50.

[74] "Labor Statistics Bureau Refutes AFL Figures in Cost of Living Survey," *Beach Cities Labor Journal*, (Santa Monica , Calif.) 24 March 1944.

[75] "Both Right, Maybe," *Minnesota Labor*, Feb. 25, 1944. Harold Ruttenberg, "Break the Wage Freeze!" *The New Republic*, 10 April 1944, p. 491.

Overall, it is clear that bottom-up statistics resonated in many parts of the United States and among workers themselves.

Unfortunately for the CIO, the primary organization behind the two reports, bottom-up statistics resonated in precisely the wrong way. As the quotations above illustrate, the unions' attack struck home among those distrustful of the federal government, of intellectual expertise, and of centralized power. Yet the CIO had committed itself to all three of these things: national leadership wanted (and indeed needed) to work with a powerful federal government; the CIO was heavily dependent on technical analysis to aid rationalized bargaining and its vision of national corporatism; and, as a consequence of their focus on national action, CIO leaders were famously devoted to centralizing power in their mammoth industrial unions. Recall from Chapter 5 that it was precisely national labor officials' need to demonstrate their relevance and effectiveness to rank-and-file members that had prompted the attack on the index in the first place. (Revealingly, a review of union periodicals by the BLS in the spring of 1944 showed that most of the coverage of the index controversy appeared in national CIO or AFL publications, or the periodicals of major industrial unions such as the steelworkers.)[76] But national leaders such as George Meany, Philip Murray, R. J. Thomas, or Walter Reuther (UAW) did not want to encourage ground-up, grassroots activism and protests against the BLS index or Little Steel—the kind of actions that could easily evolve into wildcat strikes and thereby endanger labor unions' precarious standing in public opinion and influence within the administration. Reasonable as this stance might have been in the wartime context—strikes by John L. Lewis's miners had clearly led to anti-union legislation—it nevertheless robbed bottom-up statistics of any real political force.[77]

The self-imposed limits on labor's bottom-up approach became evident when national officials responded to the BLS review of the Meany-Thomas report. After accusing the agency of various nefarious activities, Meany and Thomas challenged the bureau to let housewives decide the dispute in a nationwide poll. "The CIO-AFL report found living costs rose 43.5 percent since January 1941," began the suggested survey question. "The BLS reports that they rose only 23 percent. Which report is most closely confirmed by

---

[76] A. J. Wickens to A. F. Hinrichs, 22 April 1944, enclosure, "Reaction of the Labor Press to the Cost of Living controversy [by Boris Stern]."

[77] I agree with Alan Brinkley's assessment that more "radical" union leadership would have been unlikely to bring any substantial improvement to workers' status during this period: Alan Brinkley, *The End of Reform: New Deal Liberalism in Recession and War* (New York: Vintage Press, 1996), 224–226.

your own experience?"[78] The proposal was a logical extension of bottom-up epistemology: if cost-of-living statistics should reflect the composite of grassroots perceptions, why not judge the controversy through a poll? But the unions never conducted such a survey, nor, despite the frequent references to "housewives," did they ever make a serious effort to rally flesh-and-blood women to support their cause through the kinds of rallies and protests that had been a staple of consumer activism decades before.

Had Meany and Thomas simply challenged the ability of a single number to subsume the messy complexities of local economic experience, they might have won some supporters, even from within the BLS. (As Ford Hinrichs conceded later, "I have absolutely no idea how in the world you compile a valid CPI during a period of price control.")[79] But national unions did not want to undermine the validity of cost-of-living statistics, and by extension undermine the rationalized framework for the NWLB. Instead, they aimed to substitute a different result: a price rise of exactly 43.5 percent. "The BLS has reduced the average urban wage-worker to a mathematical abstraction," claimed the *Boston Herald* in 1944; but, likewise, unions had "attempted to encompass all economic life in a set of digits."[80] To triumph over the BLS, the unions needed either support from economists (which was precluded by the very nature of union methods) or widespread working-class agitation (which ran counter to the overall strategy adopted by national officials). In the end, union officials' bottom-up statistics foundered on a basic conundrum: how could they use populist rhetoric and appeals to local experience to challenge the procedures of an expert-driven, centralized bureaucracy while they were simultaneously trying to suppress grassroots dissent in order to support that same administrative system?

Federal Statistics and Federal Policy

If the unions failed to break the Little Steel formula through their challenge to the index, the controversy did not leave the BLS unscathed, making it hard to sustain the bureau's conception of itself as a fact-finding agency insulated from policy objectives and political and political pressures. The agency's integration into the larger system of federal economic management after the mid-1930s had already made it difficult to draw these lines cleanly, and some

[78] "AFL-CIO asks poll of housewives on war increases in cost of living", *AFL Weekly News*, 29 February 1944.
[79] Oral History with A. Ford Hinrichs (1978), DOL Historical Office, p. 22.
[80] "Statistics and Soup," *Boston Herald*, 1 March 1944.

staff recognized how this hampered attempts to use the division as a defense against union critiques. Just before the annual meeting with union researchers, BLS Chief Statistician, Sidney Wilcox, told Hinrichs that he should acknowledge that "the Bureau stepped out of its role of a research agency [by not highlighting the deficiencies in the index] ... when it was seeking to strengthen the administrative work of the War Labor Board. It refused to step out of its role to say what the unionists wanted for their administrative purposes."[81] In essence, Wilcox suggested, even if the bureau had done nothing technically objectionable, its mode of presenting its results had manifest a loyalty to the Roosevelt administration that was now a liability.

Perhaps the most obvious, and ultimately tragic, example of the bureau's entanglement with larger federal objectives arose through a seemingly trivial issue: the name of the BLS index. The Mitchell committee had concluded that, in light of ambiguous popular definitions of the cost of living, the title of the BLS index "invited misunderstanding," and thus it "should be given a less misleading name."[82] In later accounts, this recommendation often appears as a minor issue, and certainly the change was quite literally nominal—the committee did not recommend any substantial alterations to the index, nor did they suggest that the BLS calculate a different set of statistics to represent the true cost of living. Nevertheless, since a large part of the conflict revolved around the proper definition of a cost-of-living index, the suggestion to abandon the title because it caused popular confusion appears more dramatic—especially in light of the clash between bottom-up and expert statistics. Certainly, participants in the controversy saw the name of the index as a key issue. The economist Alexander Sachs called the Mitchell committee's suggestion "an extraordinary gaffe and intellectual 'howler,'" because it broke the traditional approach to defining cost-of-living indexes as measures of price change only. Hinrichs labeled Mitchell's comments (particularly the term "misleading") "a careless choice of words" and lamented Mitchell's "studied unconsciousness of the political implications of his recommendation." To a great extent, the struggle over the name of the index crystallized the underlying issue of the controversy: who had the authority to define a government statistic? "The existing title has technical meaning that has grown up with years of use in this country and

---

[81] Sidney Wilcox to Ford Hinrichs, 5 June 1944, Labor Research Comm, box 2, ACF 1941–62, BLS. In a similar vein, Hinrichs later suggested that the controversy had led the BLS to withdraw from the extensive role in policy formulation and analysis that it had developed during the 1930s and early 1940s: Oral History with A. Ford Hinrichs (1978), DOL Historical Office, pp. 6–7.

[82] Mitchell, Kuznets, and Reid, "Report of the Technical Committee," 254, 263.

abroad," Hinrichs told Frances Perkins in February 1945. "As it is accurate in this sense, I would not have felt free as a technician to yield to pressure to change the title for political reasons." Nevertheless, the Mitchell committee's suggestion made the title more problematic, especially since William Davis endorsed their comments. Hinrichs warned Perkins that keeping the name "Cost-of-Living Index" might therefore "have undesirable political consequences," whether the change was technically necessary or not.[83]

No doubt Hinrichs's contact with the union representatives had led him to this conclusion, which indeed proved correct. Perkins, however, preferred to ride out the storm. Pointing to widespread use of the phrase "cost-of-living index," she declared that it had "an accumulated meaning and is perfectly clear to all those who wish to use it." She dismissed Hinrichs's suggested title, "Consumer's Price Index for Moderate-Income Families in Large Cities," calling it "entirely unsatisfactory," "very long and clumsy," and "very misleading," since "nobody knows just what 'consumer' means." On a second sheet, she attached an additional note: "The people who object to this index don't object to its name, you know. They object to its shape and size, and it won't be any more comfortable or acceptable under another name."[84] Though BLS officials, including Faith Williams and Hinrichs, were prepared to change the title of the index and had already started discussing potential new names with union representatives, these discussions ended when Perkins refused.[85] Hinrichs had a deep loyalty to Perkins and, absent a pressing technical reason to change the name of the index, readily acquiesced to her decision to leave it alone. The index did not receive a new name until after Perkins had resigned and the war had nearly ended; in July 1945, the new secretary of labor authorized a shift to Hinrichs's original suggestion (later shortened to "Consumer Price Index").

In the bureau's wartime inaction, labor officials found confirmation of their fundamental charge: the BLS had manipulated its published statistics to support anti-labor federal policies. Despite the Mitchell and Davis reports, the BLS stuck with its original, "misleading" name for nearly a year, presumably to capitalize on the political power of the phrase "cost of living." As Ruttenberg argued in a February 1945 publication of the

[83] Alexander Sachs to Frances Perkins, 29 Sept. 1944, p. 2, 1944—Report of the Tech. Committee, box 17, GCS 1934–50, BLS. A. F. Hinrichs, handwritten draft of letter to Frances Perkins, Feb. 1945, pp. 8, 7, Cost of Living—New name for the Cost-of-Living Index, box 18, GCS 1934–50, BLS.

[84] Perkins to Hinrichs, 8 Feb. 1945, CPI—New Unit Bias, box 18, GCS 1934–50, BLS.

[85] Faith Williams to BLS staff, 20 November 1944 and 29 January 1945, both in CPI: New Unit Bias in Rent Index, box 18, GCS 1934–50, BLS.

American Newspaper Guild, this demonstrated the semi-fraudulent nature of the index. Behind the unaltered name, he saw the hand of "Judge [Fred] Vinson, the wage freezer" in the Office of Economic Stabilization, whom Hinrichs had said would have to approve "any change in the presentation of the index." "Why?" Ruttenberg asked. "American workers know the answer, and none of them like it."[86] For union officials, the stalled name change proved to be a final blow against Hinrichs. When Isador Lubin officially resigned as BLS commissioner in January 1946, major union leaders made it clear that they would vociferously oppose Hinrichs's nomination for the post. Despite being inundated with pro-Hinrichs letters from economists and government officials, Frances Perkins's successor as Secretary of Labor, Lewis Schwellenbach, refused to make the controversial move. That July, Hinrichs resigned. It was an unfortunate ending for a man who, ironically, had been highly critical of Little Steel but who had also committed himself to operating within the framework of administration policy.[87]

Such was the outcome of the wartime struggle over the index. Neither side could be satisfied. The unions had failed to alter the index in any meaningful way or to achieve their primary goal: raising wages despite the Little Steel ruling. On the other hand, although the bureau's approach to cost-of-living statistics had been validated by external economists, the agency had also attracted substantial public criticism and been forced to sacrifice its leader. The postwar era would find both the unions and the BLS struggling to find a new framework in which economic statistics could serve, rather than hinder, their respective objectives.

---

[86] Harold Ruttenberg, "BLS Cost of Living Index to Be Thorny Rose by Another Name," *The Guild Reporter* (American Newspaper Guild), 1 Feb. 1945, 1945—Cost of Living Clippings, box 17, GCS 1934–50, BLS. Hinrichs informed Ruttenberg about the need for Vinson's (and Davis's) approval in a letter on 20 Jan. 1945, CPI—New Unit Bias in Rent Index, box 18, GCS 1934–50, BLS.

[87] For Lubin's efforts to help Hinrichs, see letters in folder "Hinrichs," box 52, Lubin papers. Despite having been driven from his job by the unions, Hinrichs later carried remarkably little hostility toward union officials, and indeed had some amount of sympathy. As he put it in a 1978 interview, "I had said before the war that, before the war begins, I'm going to get out of the BLS because there's no way on God's green earth that you can fight a war without gypping labor, and that's not my specialty. I didn't get out soon enough, and I got stuck." Oral History with A. Ford Hinrichs (1978), DOL Historical Office, p. 23.

7

Bounded Conflict: Collective Bargaining and the Consumer Price Index in the Cold War

For those statisticians who had watched the breakup of federal economic planning agencies after the First World War, the bleak outlook for government bureaucracy in late 1946 looked all too familiar. That fall, Republicans captured Congress, and in the spring they launched a wide-ranging fiscal attack, including a 40 percent cut in the budget of the Bureau of Labor Statistics; in 1948, the House made an additional 40 percent reduction, which would have effectively crippled the bureau's regular work. But at that dark hour came what newly appointed BLS Commissioner Ewan Clague called "an industrial relations 'miracle.'"[1]

On May 24, the United Auto Workers (UAW) signed a two-year contract with the General Motors Corporation, a surprising development in postwar labor relations. The year 1946 had produced the greatest strike wave in American history, and despite constraints on union power from the Taft-Hartley Act of 1947, organized labor remained strong in core industries such as steel, electrical products, and auto. Here the 1946 strikes had been especially bitter, and though the UAW had been defeated, continuing shop-floor conflict nonetheless seemed inevitable.[2] The two-year, GM-UAW contract of 1948, which was double the length of typical auto contracts and had been achieved without a strike, apparently heralded the beginning of more peaceful relations. To make the long contract feasible in a time of economic uncertainty, GM and the UAW created two adaptive wage clauses. The first was an "annual improvement factor" that raised wages each year by three cents (roughly 2 percent of the average wage at GM) to account for rising

---

[1] Ewan Clague, *The Bureau of Labor Statistics* (New York: Frederick A. Praeger, 1968), 25–26.

[2] Melvyn Dubofsky, *The State & Labor in Modern America* (Chapel Hill: University of North Carolina Press, 1994), 193–208.

industrial productivity. The second was an automatic cost-of-living adjustment clause (COLA) that shifted wages up and down every three months based on changes in the BLS retail price index, recently rechristened the Consumers' Price Index (CPI).[3] With the CPI at the center of General Motors' new labor strategies, company executives pressed Republican congressmen to join pro-labor Democrats in reversing the bureau's financial trajectory and restoring the threatened funds back to the agency's budget.[4]

Though the 1948 contract initially had few imitators, COLAs later proliferated among major collective bargaining agreements and eventually found a prominent place in federal programs as well. In 1950, General Motors and the UAW signed a similar contract, now extended for an astonishing five years. By the mid-1950s, the so-called Treaty of Detroit had become the model for a long-term upswing in multiyear labor contracts that typically included one or both of its key features: COLAs and "deferred wage increases" (such as the GM-UAW annual improvement factor).[5] Although the form and extent of COLAs varied over time, the clauses never disappeared: coverage by COLAs (as a percentage of workers included in major collective bargaining contracts) ranged from a low of 20 percent in 1966 to a high of just over 60 percent in 1976 (see Chart 7.1). Moreover, responding in part to union pressure, Congress began to embed COLAs into welfare provisions and tax brackets beginning in the late 1960s, a process that soon took on a life of its own (Chapter 9).

The postwar affinity for COLAs makes a remarkable contrast with the 1920s, when interest in rule-governed cost-of-living adjustments based on retail price indexes rapidly declined and nearly disappeared (Chapter 3). Larger macroeconomic factors surely contributed to this contrasting outcome: whereas price indexes remained relatively stable from 1922 to 1930, the CPI has registered a consistent long-term upward trend since the end of the Second World War (driven by both the abandonment of the gold standard and expansive fiscal policies). But the ties between price changes and COLA adoption are complex. The sharpest postwar price rises occurred during the mid- to late 1940s, when General Motors was the only major

---

[3] Henry Lowenstern, "Adjusting Wages to Living Costs: A Historical Note," *MLR* 97, no. 7 (1974): 23.

[4] Reminiscences of Ewan Clague (1958), OHC-CU, 239–241, 288.

[5] On multiyear contracts, see Joseph W. Gabarino, *Wage Policy and Long-Term Contracts* (Washington, D.C.: Brookings Institution, 1962). Such contracts were widely used before the war in sectors with a long history of union activity (e.g., mining, textiles, and printing): Sanford M. Jacoby, "The Development of Cost-of-Living Escalators in the United States," *Labor History* 28, no. 4 (1987): 517.

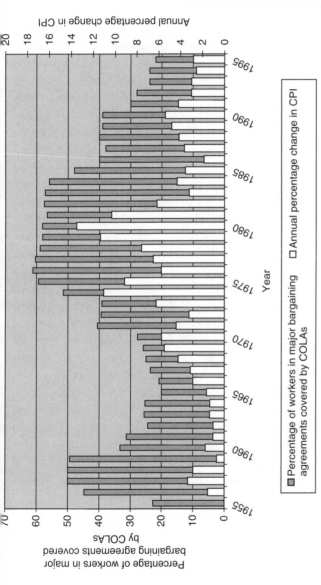

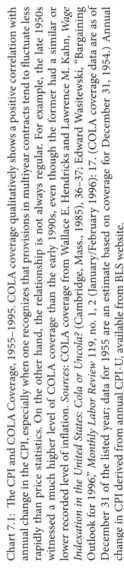

Chart 7.1: The CPI and COLA Coverage, 1955–1995. COLA coverage qualitatively shows a positive correlation with annual change in the CPI, especially when one recognizes that provisions in multiyear contracts tend to fluctuate less rapidly than price statistics. On the other hand, the relationship is not always regular. For example, the late 1950s witnessed a much higher level of COLA coverage than the early 1990s, even though the former had a similar or lower recorded level of inflation. *Sources:* COLA coverage from Wallace E. Hendricks and Lawrence M. Kahn, *Wage Indexation in the United States: Cola or Uncola?* (Cambridge, Mass., 1985), 36–37; Edward Wasitewski, "Bargaining Outlook for 1996," *Monthly Labor Review* 119, no. 1, 2 (January/February 1996): 17. (COLA coverage data are as of December 31 of the listed year; data for 1955 are an estimate based on coverage for December 31, 1954.) Annual change in CPI derived from annual CPI-U, available from BLS website.

255

company to offer a COLA and neither most employers nor most workers sought to follow that example. Although the Korean War prompted a short-term adoption of COLAs, the long-term, peacetime trend toward COLAs first emerged during 1955 and early 1956—a period that followed several years of stable prices and low volatility. Thus, though actual and anticipated inflation has clearly provoked greater use of COLAs, a recent history of high price volatility has not been a sufficient or even entirely necessary cause.[6]

By far the strongest correlation with COLAs over the last fifty years has been union bargaining power. COLAs are almost nonexistent outside of unionized industries, and historically strong union sectors (autoworkers, steel, transportation) have provided the bulk of workers covered by COLAs.[7] The presence of large, strong unions—a distinct difference from the earlier period—also reshaped the statistical basis for cost-of-living adjustments. In the employer-dominated 1920s, firms used a variety of sources to adjust wages beyond the national BLS cost-of-living index: newspaper reports and "general information," state and city statistics, wholesale price indexes, trade association figures (notably the NICB cost-of-living index), and BLS city indexes. This pluralism had derived from the differing economic conditions and expertise of firms, who, in the absence of strong worker organizations, had been able to impose their vision of rationalized labor relations on employees (Chapter 3). The rise of powerful industrial unions prompted two changes: a reliance on government statistics (perceived as a more neutral source) and the growing dominance of national measures. From the 1950s on, government statistics (primarily the CPI) formed the basis for almost all COLAs; indeed, seeing little value for employer-produced measures, the NICB stopped publishing its national cost-of-living index in 1958. Moreover, national statistics took a clear priority over local calculations: roughly 90 percent of COLAs in 1951 used the national CPI, a ratio that has been more or less constant since (with most of the remaining 10 percent relying upon BLS city indexes).[8]

In part the trend toward national statistics reflected the prevalence of large, national firms among those offering COLAs: in the early 1950s, for example, the bulk of workers covered by COLAs came from a small

[6] Gabarino, *Wage Policy and Long-Term Contracts*, 78–79; Jacoby, "The Development of Cost-of-Living Escalators," 525–529.

[7] Wallace E. Hendricks and Lawrence M. Kahn, *Wage Indexation in the United States: Cola or Uncola?* (Cambridge: Ballinger, 1985), 6–7, 66.

[8] Lucy M. Kramer and James Nix, "Wage Escalators and the CPI," *MLR* 72, no. 5 (1951): 509; Beth A. Levin, "Scheduled Wage Increases and Escalator Provisions in 1979," *MLR* 102, no. 1 (1979): 24.

number of corporations with operations stretching across the country, such as General Motors, Ford, Chrysler, United Aircraft, International Harvester, and General Electric.[9] In part it reflected the growing influence of the federal government on industrial relations, exemplified by events such as the Little Steel decision (which had elevated the national index into prominence). To a large degree, however, it was a function of union desires to standardize wage systems both across plants (through centralized negotiations) and within and across industries (through pattern bargaining, wherein a major agreement became a model for subsequent negotiations with other employers). The evidence for such standardization is clear in contract details: not only did the UAW quickly spread the basic elements of the GM contract throughout its jurisdiction (providing roughly half of workers covered by COLAs by early 1951), but it also mimicked the exact indexation formula: a one cent rise for every 1.14 index points. By March 1951, when COLA coverage had risen to 2.6 million workers (with the eventual peak reaching 3.5 million), 45 percent of those covered used the one cent to 1.14 points ratio—even though that formula had been derived from the average wage of GM workers in 1948 and was not necessarily relevant to other firms. (An additional 43 percent of covered workers had contracts with a straight one cent to one point ratio which likewise had no clear basis other than simplicity and past examples.)[10]

The presence of strong unions—and especially the newer unions of the CIO who negotiated with national, industrial corporations—therefore provided the crucial difference between the 1920s and the later postwar era. But this connection only raises more questions. Union leaders had historically opposed COLAs—as recently as 1941, the CIO had passed a resolution condemning the practice.[11] Moreover, major unions (including key COLA supporters like the UAW) had just fought a bitter, largely futile battle over the very measure that sat at the heart of these agreements: the BLS Consumer Price Index. Why would union officials now embrace a statistic and agency that they had vehemently rejected several years before?

According to the postwar commissioner of the BLS, Ewan Clague, the change stemmed from the establishment of two new "advisory councils" on labor statistics (one for unions and one for business groups). Clague believed that the councils had fostered greater communication with the

---

[9] Kramer and Nix, "Wage Escalators and the CPI," 510.

[10] National Industrial Conference Board, *Cost of Living Provisions in Union Contracts* (New York: National Industrial Conference Board, 1951), 1; Kramer and Nix, "Wage Escalators and the CPI," 510.

[11] Jacoby, "The Development of Cost-of-Living Escalators," 526.

agency and thereby boosted the "confidence of both management and labor in the Bureau" such that each side could now comfortably embed BLS statistics in wage agreements.[12] I argue, however, that the causal trajectory ran in the opposite direction: the advisory councils survived and flourished (despite deep divisions) precisely because the constraints of postwar political economy forced unions to justify their wage demands by using economic statistics, especially the Consumer Price Index. Behind that dependence lay a compromise that had been forged in the 1930s and which now unfolded into a fully developed form, shaped in part by the rise of the Cold War: the bureaucratic rationalization of industrial relations. By delineating the bounds of legitimate and illegitimate worker demands (codified in rules and articulated in part through statistical measures of wages, prices, and productivity), pro-labor liberals had captured a recognized place for organized labor within a traditionally hostile political, legal, and economic environment. By the mid-1950s, both the promise and limits of this system were becoming clear, and woven through its fabric were COLAs, the Consumer Price Index, and the underconsumptionist logic articulated several decades before.

CREATING AND OPERATING THE ADVISORY COUNCILS: COLLECTIVE BARGAINING AND STATISTICS

The advisory councils were a direct attempt by the BLS to circumvent the kind of protracted public controversy over its work that had developed during the Second World War. By facilitating private discussions with two major, organized interest groups (unions and corporations), bureau staff hoped to rebuild trust and eliminate the miscommunication that staff members believed had contributed to the wartime conflict. Although the BLS had been consulting union representatives informally since the 1930s and running annual conferences since 1940, these gatherings had an ad hoc attendance and no official status. As a result, they provided little aid to the bureau during the wartime debates, and after George Meany used the June 1944 annual conference to lambaste the BLS for having "prostituted its research functions" in the service of anti-labor administrators (Chapter 6), Frances Perkins responded by disbanding the conference series. Despite Perkins's reservations, bureau staff members were inclined to strengthen formal ties with unions, especially since other government agencies (including the Office of Statistical Standards in the Bureau of Budget) had successfully

---

[12] Clague, *Bureau of Labor Statistics*, 227, 26, 181–184.

created their own advisory systems. Perkins refused, however, and thus the matter was left for her replacement, Lewis Schwellenbach, and his choice for BLS commissioner, Ewan Clague.[13]

Since Clague's time as a member of COGSIS and ACSL (Chapter 4), he had served in different capacities within the Social Security Board, where he had kept in close contact with union representatives. Accordingly, Clague moved quickly to establish a Joint Labor Research Advisory Council (LRAC) comprised of representatives from the three major national labor organizations: eight union statisticians from the AFL, eight from the CIO, and four from the Railway Labor Executives. As a formally structured, publicly recognized entity, LRAC became the official, centralized means of communication between the BLS and labor unions. Both sides committed themselves to working through their differences within the private LRAC meetings, and labor statisticians soon found that they could influence the bureau's work. Recognizing this potential, the National Association of Manufacturers and the U.S. Chamber of Commerce lobbied for their own Business Research Advisory Council (BRAC), which Clague established in October 1947. Each of these councils created smaller subcommittees to handle specific sets of statistics, including groups focused on prices and the cost of living.[14]

Bureau staff had hoped the advisory councils would reduce conflicts with union critics while still allowing the agency to preserve a high level of autonomy, and the operation of the councils reveals both the successes and limits of that strategy. Both the BLS and council members agreed that the latter would not have direct control over bureau statistics: according to minutes from an early LRAC meeting, members "wanted it clearly understood that they had no idea of exercising censorship but merely wanted to be consulted."[15] Yet "consultation" could mean many things. Whereas BLS staff sought to control both the agenda and the formal presentation of the

---

[13] On early BLS-union interaction, see folder 2, box 1, CSB-ACSL, OMB; "Luncheon Club" folder, box 78, Frances Perkins—General Subject File, DOL; and boxes 1–2, ACF 1941–62, BLS. Hinrichs to Perkins, 26 January 1945, Labor Research Comm., 1941–45, box 2, ACF 1941–62, BLS; Hinrichs to Schwellenbach, 5 July 1946, encl. "Annual Report on the Bureau of Labor Statistics", p. 31, Labor Stats—general, 1946, box 16, Lewis Schwellenbach—Subject File, DOL.

[14] Joseph P. Goldberg and William T. Moye, *The First Hundred Years of the Bureau of Labor Statistics* (Washington, D.C.: U.S. GPO, 1985), 179–180; Clague, *Bureau of Labor Statistics*, 181–184. On the formation of LRAC, see David Saposs to Clague, 10 January 1947; and JLRAC minutes, 14 February 1947, JLRAC, 1946–1947, box 2, ACF 1941–62, BLS. On BRAC, see Clague to Cole H. Pilcher, 10 April 1947; and JLRAC minutes, 19 November 1947, JLRAC, 1946–1947, box 2, ACF 1941–62, BLS.

[15] David Saposs to Clague, 25 February 1947, JLRAC, 1946–1947, box 2, ACF 1941–62, BLS.

meetings in order to minimize dissension and restrict the scope of committee authority, LRAC members continually plumbed the details of BLS methodology and challenged its work on every level, from major conceptual questions to the minutiae of data collection procedures. (I have been unable to locate archival records of BRAC meetings, although oral history recollections suggest that they were also fractious.)[16]

Nowhere was this dissension more evident than during discussions of the Consumer Price Index, where the growth of COLAs magnified the consequences of even minor changes in bureau calculations. Consider the GM-UAW contract, with its one-cent wage hike for 250,000 GM workers after every 1.14 point rise in the CPI (a 0.7 percent change overall). For most purposes, such small fluctuations would have been entirely insignificant; now a miniscule increase in the index could raise wage rates by one cent and thereby transfer roughly $5 million annually from GM to unionized auto workers.[17] As similar clauses proliferated in labor contracts during the early 1950s in response to fears about inflation from the Korean War, the effects of the CPI became correspondingly greater. By mid-1952, every index point (0.5 percent change) shifted roughly $70 million annually through COLAs. Even this paled in comparison to the index-based controls set by the Wage Stabilization Board during the same war; Ewan Clague estimated that these developments made every index point "worth about one billion dollars in wages and salaries."[18]

Naturally, these financial consequences dramatically increased the scrutiny of even minor issues in the Consumer Price Index, and there were plenty of problems to go around, including lingering factors from the Second World War (such as a complex system of rent controls); great changes in retail goods, demographics, and consumer purchasing habits since the last major expenditure survey in 1934–1936; and the potential disruptions caused by a new war in Korea. Furthermore, a long-planned revision in the CPI (unfortunately scheduled to begin in 1950, just before the start of the Korean conflict) offered unions a fresh opportunity to press for substantial changes.[19] Accordingly, from the late 1940s through the early

[16] Morris Weisz to Clague, 6 December 1948, JLRAC—1948, box 3, ACF 1941–62, BLS. Reminiscences of Ewan Clague (1958), OHC-CU, pp. 290–291.

[17] The 1.14 points to one cent ratio had been determined by dividing the April 1948 CPI (170) by the average hourly wage of GM workers ($1.491). "Appendix B, Effects of Inequities in the Present GM Escalator Table," folder 19, box 6, UAW Research Department, WRL.

[18] Ewan Clague, "The Use of the Consumers' Price Index in Collective Bargaining," 23 May 1952, Speeches—CPI, box 3, LRAC, BLS.

[19] U.S. House, Committee on Education and Labor, *Consumers' Price Index: Hearings before a Subcommittee of the Committee on Education and Labor*, 82nd Cong., 1st sess.,

1950s, LRAC members offered a constant but accelerating barrage of complaints and suggestions about the index, a campaign led by the union most dependent on the index, the UAW.

Not surprisingly, the UAW critiques held certain conceptual and tactical similarities to union efforts during the 1943–1945 controversy. Shortly after signing its 1948 contract with GM, for example, the UAW's secretary-treasurer informed Clague that the union hoped "to avoid the necessity for a repetition of the attacks we were forced to make on the index during the war years" and, toward that end, demanded that the bureau publish "a simple and candid statement of the present defects of the index."[20] The first concrete issue seized by the UAW—a downward bias in the rent index caused by an outdated housing sample—combined several conceptual problems familiar from the wartime debates, including puzzles about adjusting the market basket to account for new goods (new rental units) and the bureau's studied determination to avoid making judgments about quality when calculating the index.[21]

Union economists presented technical arguments about these and other topics during LRAC meetings, but they were also ready to apply other forms of pressure when the bureau resisted their claims, including issuing press releases denouncing BLS decisions, complaining publicly about the limitations in the index, or having union leaders discuss problems directly with the secretary of labor.[22] Indeed, even bureau staff members often recognized that they lacked an external technical consensus that could provide firm guidance on disputed questions. The rent bias problem again provides a useful example. By spring 1949, the bureau had a rough estimate of the downward bias, though neither the staff nor the advisory councils were happy about the sketchy nature of the data.[23] But what should be done with the result? BRAC urged the bureau to publish the estimate and related

May 8–11, 14–18, 21, 24, and June 29, 1951, 19–24; U.S. Bureau of Labor Statistics, "The Main Features of the Revised Consumer Price Index," *MLR* 76 (1953): 162–165.

[20] Emil Mazey to Ewan Clague, 9 June 1948, folder 1, box 4, UAW Research Dept., WRL.

[21] On the rent index, see Ethel D. Hoover and Bruno Schiro, "Estimate of New Unit Bias in CPI Rent Index," *MLR* 69, no. 1 (1949): 44–49. Lazare Teper to Nat Weinberg, 22 October 1948 and Weinberg to Teper, 28 October 1948, folder 1, box 43, Katherine P. Ellickson, WRL; Weinberg, "Draft memo to Commissioner Ewan Clague," 28 January 1949, folder 1, box 4, UAW Research Dept., WRL.

[22] E.g., Clague to Maurice Tobin, 9 May 1949, CPI—New Unit Bias, box 18, GCS 1934–50, BLS; Walter P. Reuther to Tobin, 9 May 1949, folder 18, box 6, UAW Research Dept., WRL; CIO press release, 5 March 1951, Labor stats—general, box 81, Maurice Tobin—Subject File, DOL.

[23] Clague to Tobin, 9 May 1949, plus enclosure, CPI—New Unit Bias, box 18, GCS 1934–50, BLS.

methodology in a separate article, which would make it more difficult for the UAW to argue that the bias required an adjustment in wage rates. By contrast, LRAC, and especially the UAW, wanted the estimate included in the CPI itself or at the very least in a footnote published with the index. Clague reiterated the typical BLS mantra that "any decisions made with respect to this index should be based purely on good technical grounds" to avoid "suspicion that the index is subject to manipulation."[24] But on which "purely technical grounds" could the BLS decide to place the estimate in a footnote rather than a separate article? Compromise was the inevitable solution: presented with three alternatives, Clague took the middle path and decided to publish a footnote with the April index.

In certain respects, therefore, postwar discussions about the CPI reflected the union perspective on statistics presented in the last chapter. During the struggle over the rent index, UAW officials treated statistics as one more forum in which to press and negotiate their quest for higher wages. Similarly, the debate over how and where to include the estimate reinforced unions' wartime claim that the creation and publication of cost-of-living statistics involved political decisions, not merely a series of well-defined technical problems. Moreover, the advisory council system itself shared parallels with a suggestion that Harold Ruttenberg had made to settle the wartime controversy, namely the appointment of a tripartite board of economists (representing industry, labor, and government) who could create a joint report on the cost of living. Nevertheless, the establishment and operation of the advisory councils did not herald the institutional triumph of labor officials' "bottom-up statistics," much less a new dominance in union control over the Consumer Price Index.

In the first place, the advisory council system had tripartite representation, but it was not a tripartite *board* governing federal labor statistics. The BLS retained full control of its statistical calculations and likewise determined the precise lens through which it would assess committee recommendations. As Clague informed Truman's secretary of labor, Maurice Tobin, "the Bureau cannot yield to pressure to make changes in the index procedure without having confidence that the innovation does not violate the concept of the index, and that the procedures are technically sound, and administratively practicable."[25] As the rent bias case and others

---

[24] Clague to Tobin, 18 May 1949, and Hollander to Clague, 18 May 1949, CPI—New Unit Bias, box 18, GCS 1934–50, BLS.

[25] Clague to Tobin, 25 January 1949, 1949—Labor stats—general, box 14, Maurice Tobin—Subject File, DOL.

demonstrated, these guidelines often provided wide latitude and occasionally proved useless altogether. But nevertheless, the phrases "concept of the index," "technically sound," and "administratively practicable" contained a fairly serious set of constraints. Put bluntly, unions would need to use methods and techniques that were acceptable to a larger technical community (academic economists and statisticians), and even here deference would be given to the bureau's past tradition and the staff's assessment of what was "practicable." There would be no more forceful, radical challenges to the concept of the index, much less to the authority of economists. Gone were appeals to the experience of housewives, alongside the whole paraphernalia of bottom-up statistics, with its "exhibits," newspaper clippings, quotations, and heterogeneous studies, all designed to capture the shifts in elusive traits such as "quality." Instead, the more aggressive union economists, led by the UAW, now sought to exploit existing technical knowledge. During the wartime controversy, union cost-of-living reports made almost no reference to academic literature outside of the report from the American Statistical Association; by the early 1950s, the UAW research staff had compiled a two-page bibliography of recent technical articles and books on price index theory, and they continued to cull new publications for material to use in union arguments.[26]

In a related vein, the emphasis shifted from public, highly politicized debates about BLS statistics (led by top union leaders) to private, closed-door arguments (led by union economists). In the Second World War, the public attack on the BLS and its index had been championed by union presidents and had featured extensive, occasionally vituperative, denunciations of the anti-labor bias of bureau officials. As Ford Hinrichs had anticipated, however, the existence of the advisory councils made it easier for bureau staff to channel all criticism through those forums. When UAW leadership threatened to revive the wartime controversy in 1948 if the bureau did not address its concerns about the index, Clague politely directed them to the price subcommittee of LRAC: here was the proper place to debate statistical methodology.[27] Likewise, Clague made it clear that representation on LRAC was a privilege granted by the BLS, one that was subject to revocation should unions overstep what staff saw as appropriate behavior. In December 1948, for example, the UAW *Ammunition* ran a long article on

[26] Harry Chester to Nat Weinberg, "Review of Hofsten's Price Indexes and Quality Changes," 24 April 1953, CPI—General 1953–61, box 66, UAW Research Dept., WRL; "Bibliography—CPI," ibid.

[27] Emil Mazey to Ewan Clague, 9 June 1948 and Clague to Mazey, 30 June 1948, folder 1, box 4, UAW Research Dept., WRL.

the union research department, explaining that "sometimes ... government information is biased, or even inaccurate," and that with "most wages ... hooked to government statistics," the department worked hard at "keeping them honest." Clague shot off a sharply worded letter to LRAC members lamenting this attack on the "integrity" of BLS staff and warned UAW President Walter Reuther that if this continued, Clauge would be forced to "plan some rearrangement of the relationships between our staff and your Research Department." Reuther disavowed any malicious intent and offered to print a correction to that effect; UAW economists similarly affirmed their trust in the agency's general honesty, if not its specific decisions.[28]

The advisory councils therefore allowed the BLS to control the scope, framework, and forum for union criticism. But they were not the only elements curtailing union ability to influence BLS methodology or policy. Deterred from making broader, conceptual arguments, union economists focused intensely on BLS methods, questioning everything from sampling procedures to the nitty-gritty details of price collection. Understandably, staff members resented external critics probing and dissecting each nook and cranny of their work, and they strove to keep the discussions on higher levels of analysis whenever possible. "It is damned hard to get any factual information from the Bureau," one UAW economist grumpily reported in late 1952, after spending six weeks rooting around bureau offices and quizzing staff about the CPI.[29] A similar bureaucratic inertia extended to actual revisions of the index: it was easy for LRAC members to propose changes; bureau staff had pragmatic concerns (or excuses, depending on one's perspective) about the time and money such alterations might entail or the controversy that they would generate if not firmly based on widely accepted practices.

The nature of the advisory council system reinforced the bureau's ability to resist proposals viewed with skepticism by the staff. Most obviously, LRAC was counterbalanced by the Business Research Advisory Council, which (not surprisingly) often opposed LRAC recommendations and hence offered the BLS ready reason to avoid any complicated or tendentious

[28] "Compiling Facts for Action," UAW *Ammunition* 6, no. 12 (December 1948): 12. Clague to various LRAC members, 21 December 1948; Clague to Reuther, 24 December 1948; Weinberg to Clague, 4 January 1949; Reuther to Clague, 5 January 1949, JLRAC—UAW-CIO Ammunition, box 3, ACF 1941–62, BLS.

[29] Harry Chester to Weinberg, 3 December 1952, CPI—BLS External Memos, box 66, UAW Research Dept., WRL. For a similar complaint, see Weinberg to George Brooks, 27 December 1948, p. 3, folder 18, box 6, UAW Research Dept., WRL. On BLS attempts to keep LRAC discussions away from "details," see Morris Weisz to Clague, 6 December 1948, JLRAC—1948, box 3, ACF 1941–62, BLS.

advice from union members.[30] Furthermore, structural differences between LRAC and the BLS abetted the imbalance in power: the hierarchical (and hence relatively unified) bureau could exploit differences in the democratic LRAC, where philosophical splits between the AFL and CIO aggravated existing divisions between union researchers. As one UAW economist quickly realized, LRAC had to take a united position to achieve anything; otherwise, the bureau would use the lack of consensus "as an excuse for doing nothing."[31] But recognizing this objective was easier than achieving it. During the war, national labor leaders had been able to generate a major controversy because they maintained a public "labor" position. Behind that front, however, lay only a small group of union researchers, whose colleagues may not have always agreed, but who kept their dissent to private channels in the face of vocal union leaders. Most importantly, George Meany's desire to turn the cost-of-living debates into a self-promotional campaign had led to much greater public unity between the CIO and the AFL, from which Meany was the only major figure involved.[32]

Absent the unifying pressures of wartime federal regulation and with union statisticians working as a committee, the situation was quite different: no single statistician had clear authority over the others, and the different needs of their unions combined with their different training to make disagreement inevitable. The largest split came between the CIO and AFL representatives. As noted in Chapter 5, CIO unions relied more heavily on staff economists and showed greater willingness to engage in technically grounded arguments, undoubtedly reflecting the CIO's greater entanglement with the state, its continual interaction with large, modern manufacturing corporations, and its ties to the underconsumptionist justification for wage increases (especially via Brookwood Labor College). The men and women who served as CIO research directors tended to be better trained, more aggressive, and (reflecting CIO philosophy) more committed to organized group action. UAW research director Nat Weinberg—who had an undergraduate degree

---

[30] E.g., Reminiscences of Ewan Clague (1958), OHC-CU, pp. 290–291.

[31] Nat Weinberg to Art Johnstone, "Cost of Living Index," 26 May 1949, p. 6; see also Weinberg to George Brooks, 10 October 1950, folder 18, box 6, UAW Research Dept., WRL.

[32] It is unclear how most labor researchers outside the immediate core of Ruttenberg, Fairley, and Nixon viewed the two cost-of-living reports, though many AFL researchers clearly were not involved. "Notes on conversation of 5/19/50 between Mrs. Wickens and Mrs. Arnow," pp. 2–3, Committee for Public Administration, box 3, Wickens correspondence, 1939–1950, BLS. Most accounts of internal dissent come from BLS sources, who perhaps read more into certain remarks than was warranted and who were actively misled by figures in the AFL about the extent of internal labor opposition to the reports: Joseph C. Goulden, *Meany* (New York: Atheneum, 1972), 113–114.

in economics, had studied and taught at Brookwood, and had served in the federal government (including the BLS)—typified the new breed of CIO economists. Blending a combative nature with statistical acumen, he was, in Clague's description, "very vociferous and very vigorous, [and] extremely able," and like his colleagues, he tended to work in concert with other CIO research directors whenever possible. By contrast, AFL unions were often less dependent on economic or statistical arguments for their contract negotiations and more wary of state entanglement; accordingly, their research staff tended to be less organized and (with some exceptions, such as Lazare Teper) to have weaker technical backgrounds.[33] At the extreme end were the operating unions of the railroad brotherhoods, who had no in-house research staff at all and relied on consultants for technical advice; accordingly, the brotherhoods often gave their LRAC slots to non-operating unions or independent unions such as the Machinists.[34]

Naturally, these distinctions also carried over into LRAC discussions, where research directors whose unions made the least use of BLS statistics could be more sanguine in their attitude toward the bureau's work. Not surprisingly, the UAW's Nat Weinberg (supported by his CIO colleagues) pressed the bureau hardest from within LRAC's price subcommittee, while many AFL members were more cautious. As Weinberg's lieutenant complained in 1952, the AFL members (with the exception of Teper) "don't like our snooping [into BLS methods], don't support our recommendations, and are willing to accept as satisfactory any explanation that the Bureau will give."[35] Perhaps the most dramatic example of LRAC divisions came during the transition to the new, revised CPI in January 1953. Weinberg and the UAW had been hoping to use the introduction of the new index to justify renegotiating the five-year GM-UAW contract signed in 1950, especially elements of its cost-of-living provisions.[36] To this end, the union emphasized the disjuncture

---

[33] Reminiscences of Ewan Clague (1958), OHC-CU, pp. 292–293. For Weinberg's education and job history, see his c.v., circa 1946, folder 20, box 66, UAW Washington Office, WRL. On the contrast between the research directors from the CIO and the AFL, see Hinrichs to Perkins, 26 January 1945, Labor Research Comm., 1941–45, box 2, ACF 1941–1962, BLS; Reminiscences of Ewan Clague (1958), OHC-CU, pp. 303–304.

[34] "The Labor Economists," *Fortune*, December 1948, p. 199. For Machinist involvement, see minutes for 18 September 1947, Working Committee on Prices and Cost of Living, 1947–1950, box 3, ACF 1941–62, BLS.

[35] Chester to Weinberg, 22 July 1952, CPI—BLS External Memos, box 66, UAW Research Dept., WRL.

[36] Weinberg to Donald Montgomery, "Shift to New Price Index," 17 December 1952, folder 28, box 66, UAW Washington Office—Donald Montgomery, WRL; J. A. Livingston, "Reuther Argues for Stop-Loss Against Cost-of-Living Drop," *Washington Post*, 4 February 1953.

between the old and revised indexes and pressed the BLS to avoid making any public comment about how to shift from one to the other. By contrast, many companies, including Ford and GM, wanted to frame the transition process as a mere mathematical operation (due to the change in base period from 1935–1939 to 1947–1949) and asked the bureau to provide appropriate advice.[37] Here the matter might have ended in a business-labor impasse, except that fears of wartime inflation had also driven both AFL unions and the railroad brotherhoods to adopt cost-of-living clauses. Unfortunately, most of these unions lacked the technical staff to argue successfully with their employers and hence also asked the BLS to publish official guidelines for moving from the old index to the new.[38] In the end, not only did the BLS offer transition advice, but the combined lobbying of auto manufacturers, the AFL, and the railroad brotherhoods led the new Eisenhower administration to force the BLS to publish the "old series" CPI alongside the new index through June 1953.[39] The CIO could do little but fume, while the UAW was unable to get a new contract from GM until May.[40]

LRAC was not entirely ineffective, of course; had it been so, CIO economists would have simply left (as they discussed doing after losing one particularly bitter argument in 1951).[41] Indeed, by early 1953, a UAW economist could list ten areas in which LRAC had succeeded in altering bureau procedures or planned updates for the revised index. Though some of these points involved little or no alterations to the actual calculation of the index (e.g., writing an article showing how the inclusion of income tax would affect the CPI), others represented significant methodological changes (for instance, including a closer study of quality in the rent index).[42] Yet it is also

[37] See Weinberg to Clague, 26 May 1952; Weinberg to Clague, 4 June 1953; Clague to Weinberg, 5 June 1952; Weinberg to Clague, 11 June 1952; and Edward Hollander to Weinberg, 17 June 1952, folder 1, box 4, UAW Research Dept., WRL.

[38] "Minutes of Price Subcommittee of L.R.A.C.," 8 September 1952, p. 2, LRAC—Price Subcommittee, box 72, UAW Research Dept., WRL.

[39] "First Labor Issue Put to Eisenhower," *NYT*, 29 January 1953; "'Old' Price Index to Aid Contracts," *NYT*, 31 January 1953; "White House Press Statement," 30 January 1953, CPI—Old Series, box 12, RCL-PPF 1950–1975, BLS. For the CIO response, see "CIO Economist Hits 'Political Pressures' on Consumer Price Index Changes," 5 February 1953, CPI—Revision Misc., box 66, UAW Research Dept., WRL.

[40] "CIO Warns New BLS Consumers' Price Index to Cause Confusion on Labor Scene," 16 January 1953, CPI—Revision, Misc., box 66, UAW Research Dept., WRL; "CIO Economist Hits 'Political Pressures' on Consumer Price Index Changes," 5 February 1953, ibid. UAW press release, 22 May 1953, folder 20, box 43, Katherine P. Ellickson, WRL.

[41] Weinberg to Ellickson, 10 April 1951, folder 14, box 10, UAW Research Dept., WRL.

[42] Chester to Ellickson, 19 February 1953, CPI—BLS External Memos, box 66, UAW Research Dept., WRL.

clear that many union recommendations either went unheeded or appeared in only a limited form, and though research directors reiterated many of the same complaints as during the Second World War, they had a similar lack of success in persuading the bureau to address them.[43]

Why then, despite these constraints, did the CIO remain committed to the advisory councils, when a few years before major CIO unions had led the public charge in attacking the bureau and its cost-of-living index? Undoubtedly the outcome of that earlier struggle shaped their perspective: the unions had been unable to alter the index directly, and the Mitchell committee's "rough guess" of a downward bias (not included in the index itself) had no effect on the Little Steel decision until after the war had ended.[44] If wages were going to be linked to the CPI, then clearly the advisory councils offered a better means (perhaps the only means) for influencing the bureau's work. But this answer only pushes the question to another level. During the war, national labor officials had been forced (under great duress) to accept a link between wages and BLS statistics; from 1948 on, major unions repeatedly adopted these ties voluntarily, often on their own initiative. The advisory councils, therefore, were necessary but not sufficient for numerous unions to commit themselves to wage indexation. Rather, the causal trajectory ran in the opposite direction: reliance on indexation kept the unions committed to the advisory councils. Accordingly, we must widen the scope of our analysis, for the key to the widespread adoption of index-based labor contracts lay not in the new advisory councils, nor in a suddenly heightened confidence in the CPI, but within the political economy of postwar America.

ECONOMIC STATISTICS AND POSTWAR INDUSTRIAL RELATIONS

Like a quarter-century before, the American labor movement and its liberal-left allies exited a major war with grand hopes and a militant attitude; 1946 set a record for work time lost to strikes that has never been surpassed.[45] Yet the later reconversion took place within the legacy of the New Deal, giving it a very different structure. Most obviously, the labor movement now contained large, strong industrial unions thanks to the protection of the

---

[43]   U.S. House, Committee on Education and Labor, *Consumers' Price Index*, 201–262.

[44]   Robert A. Sayre, "Cost of Living: A Five-Year Controversy," *Conference Board Management Record* 8, no. 9 (1946): 293–294.

[45]   George Ruben, "Major Collective Bargaining Developments: A Quarter-Century Review," *Current Wage Developments* (1974): 43.

1935 National Labor Relations Act, unions that were ready to flex their new muscle free of wartime restrictions and which showed no sign of repeating the collapse of two decades earlier. Equally important, the underconsumptionist analysis, which called for raising mass purchasing power to sustain economic growth, now seemed poised to carry New Deal liberals and unions to new heights. The alliance committed both groups to raising wages and restraining prices in an effort to reduce inequities in economic power (sending greater wealth from corporations and investors to the middle and working classes), all justified by the need to balance the nation's productive power with equal consuming capacity. Despite the clear boom in postwar consumption, liberals argued that (as in the 1920s) consumer markets had still not reached the nation's true productive potential, and hence the country risked toppling into another depression (as after the First World War) or at least falling short of full employment.

Unions with the strongest ties to the New Deal and the underconsumptionist logic, notably the CIO in general and the UAW in particular, fulfilled their part by framing their postwar wage drive in underconsumptionist terms: Walter Reuther led the UAW in a major strike against GM under the slogan "Purchasing Power for Prosperity," and demanded a 30-cent wage hike with no corresponding price increases. On a broader front, the CIO commissioned former New Deal economist Robert Nathan (co-developer of the U.S. national accounts) to analyze wage trends and corporate profits, leading to a widely publicized (and controversial) report which claimed that corporations could increase wages without raising prices and still enjoy the same rate of return as they had averaged during 1936–1939. Meanwhile, Congress passed the Employment Act of 1946, committing the nation to "maximum production, maximum employment, and maximum purchasing power"—all slogans of the New Deal planners who had envisioned strong unions and extensive state intervention as prerequisites for economic success. The most visible sign of the New Deal commitment to economic redistribution, however, lay not in abstract policy but in price regulation, where the OPA remained active and enjoyed widespread support well into the spring of 1946.[46]

If the framework for postwar conversion was different in 1945, however, the long-term outcome for the both the labor movement and the more statist members of the political left probably felt depressingly familiar. Neither

---

[46] Robert Nathan and Oscar Gass, *A National Wage Policy for 1947* (Washington, D.C.: Robert R. Nathan Associates, 1946), 11–14; Meg Jacobs, *Pocketbook Politics: Economic Citizenship in Twentieth-Century America* (Princeton: Princeton University Press, 2005), 223–225, 233–235.

extensive state intervention in the economy nor the New Deal's proposed alliance between consumers and unions would long survive. Both steel and auto companies refused to let unions negotiate over managerial decisions about prices, nor would the federal government force the issue. First, steel unions, followed by their automotive colleagues, were forced to settle for an 18.5-cent wage increase that was linked to price hikes (explicitly for steel; de facto for auto). The government's wing of the price-control program fared no better. Under extensive lobbying pressure from businessmen and powerful production boycotts, both the enforcement of stringent price controls and public support for the OPA crumbled through the spring and summer before collapsing in the fall, signaling the end of serious federal efforts to regulate prices directly.[47]

In the November elections, Republicans regained control of Congress and moved aggressively after the other major leg of the New Deal's purchasing-power program: unions. Under the Taft-Hartley Act of 1947, much hated by union officials and the rank-and-file, conservatives succeeded in placing serious restrictions on labor organizing and union actions. These constraints, combined with the traditional obstacles posed by social and economic diversity overlaid on sectional differences that had real political bite, kept unions from expanding much outside their base in the Northeast, Midwest, and West Coast. By the late 1940s, union growth had begun to plateau, and equally important, its strength remained confined to a limited set of industries and channeled largely toward white, male workers. The erection of what Nelson Lichtenstein has called "private welfare states"—high wages and protective benefits achieved by a limited set of strong unions—was symbolized by the common adoption of COLAs within well-organized industries. The latter, by exempting covered workers from price rises that conservatives insisted were caused by artificially high union wages, apparently signaled the end of the broad-based coalition of workers and middle-class consumers that the underconsumptionist analysis had promised and upon which so much of New Deal labor and economic policy had been built. Isolated as a narrow economic interest group bound to a small set of prosperous industries, the labor movement was positioned for failure when these industries began to struggle in the 1970s and 1980s.[48]

[47] Dubofsky, *The State & Labor in Modern America*, 192–195; Nelson Lichtenstein, *The Most Dangerous Man in Detroit: Walter Reuther and the Fate of American Labor* (New York: Basic Books, 1995), 239–246; Jacobs, *Pocketbook Politics*, 225–233.

[48] Nelson Lichtenstein, "From Corporatism to Collective Bargaining: Organized Labor and the Eclipse of Social Democracy in the Postwar Era," in *The Rise and Fall of the New Deal Order, 1930–1980*, ed. Steve Fraser and Gary Gerstle (Princeton: Princeton University Press,

So runs the common postwar narrative. Still, though its basic elements are accurate, it places too much emphasis on the stretch from 1946 to 1948, as though that period represented a novel (subsequently bungled) opportunity for pro-labor liberals to enact major structural change in American political economy. The end of the war indeed marked a high point of left-wing ambitions, but it was not a high point of requisite power. Unions had gathered real strength during the war, but that strength lay in the shop floor, not in boardroom decisions over pricing and production, nor in the government agencies that had controlled wartime mobilization.[49] The radical visions commonly espoused by the political left in the aftermath of war rested on the same shaky foundation as similar versions from the First World War: a mistaken hope that they could eliminate wartime constraints that they disliked (strike restrictions, wage limits) while maintaining or expanding those that they favored (large-scale government intervention into the economy, price controls). But this was a hope, nothing more.

Rather than placing postwar industrial relations against the backdrop of the 1945–1946 strikes (which tends to show a dramatic reversal), they are more accurately viewed within the framework for labor-capital relationships established by the National Labor Relations Act and predicated on economic arguments (underconsumption) developed in the 1920s and 1930s. Here, the continuity is more obvious. Major manufacturing corporations were returning to an economic and political environment which they had only partly addressed before the war: forced to deal with large industrial unions that were protected by the National Labor Relations Board, facing continuing distrust of corporate capitalism and monopoly power, and worried about protecting managerial authority from organized labor and an encroaching state. Meanwhile, unions confronted both an invigorated management community and an increasingly aggressive conservative assault on the prerogatives of organized labor, now construed as "monopoly unionism." Despite the potentially radical implications of postwar demands from many industrial unions, those demands rested on the same moderate rationale (underconsumption) that had justified the growth of industrial

---

1989), 130–145; Dubofsky, *The State & Labor in Modern America*, 199–208; Lichtenstein, *Most Dangerous Man in Detroit*, 296–298; Jacobs, *Pocketbook Politics*, 235–236, 244–245.

[49] On shopfloor conflict during the war, see Howell John Harris, *The Right to Manage: Industrial Relations Policies of American Business in the 1940s* (Madison: University of Wisconsin Press, 1982), 58–67. On the lack of substantive union influence on the political economy of war mobilization, see Alan Brinkley, *The End of Reform: New Deal Liberalism in Recession and War* (New York: Vintage Press, 1996), 203–209; Paul A. C. Koistinen, *Arsenal of World War II: The Political Economy of American Warfare, 1940–1945* (Lawrence: University Press of Kansas, 2004), 402–418.

unions a decade before: the country needed higher wages to maintain prosperity, and hence ceding more power to organized labor would benefit the whole community.[50] But how far could that rationale be pressed?

Given the political configuration of mid-century America, neither side could win a full victory, any more than they had been able to during the late 1930s.[51] The structure of labor-capital relations therefore necessarily involved compromise between two powerful (albeit unequal), competing interests for whom continual, full-bore confrontation would be self-destructive. Mirroring the theme of postwar international engagement, strategies of "containment" took a central place, as postwar industrial relations in unionized industries developed into an exemplary case of rationalized, Weberian bureaucracy: a system guided by an extensive network of rules governing appropriate actions, all of which are putatively reasonable. The rules were spelled out in a multitude of documents: labor legislation, rulings of the National Labor Relations Board, internal union or company regulations, and the increasingly massive labor contracts that covered everything from wage rates to grievance procedures in minute detail. Rationales came from unions and companies as they argued for their desired clauses and from the industrial relations experts (typically lawyers and economists) who sat in judgment over the whole system and offered their own prescriptions.[52] Here, economic statistics could finally fulfill their promise to ease labor-capital struggles (exemplified in features like COLAs), though their bureaucratic function differed substantially from the public-oriented collection of facts for democratic debate that had been initially envisioned nearly three-quarters of a century earlier (Chapter 1).

---

[50] On the continuities between the late 1930s and the postwar era, see Harris, *The Right to Manage*, 37–40.

[51] For a view of American political economy from the late 1930s into the postwar era as a stalemate, see Charles S. Maier, *In Search of Stability: Explorations in Historical Political Economy* (New Rochelle: Cambridge University Press, 1987), 125–128. On the continuity of American political configurations over this period, see David Plotke, *Building a Democratic Political Order: Reshaping American Liberalism in the 1930s and 1940s* (New York: Cambridge University Press, 1996).

[52] David Brody, *Workers in Industrial America: Essays on the 20th Century Struggle* (New York: Oxford University Press, 1980), 200–211; Christopher L. Tomlins, *The State and the Unions: Labor Relations Law, and the Organized Labor Movement in America, 1880–1960* (Cambridge: Cambridge University Press, 1985); Nelson Lichtenstein, "Great Expectations: The Promise of Industrial Jurisprudence and Its Demise, 1930–1960," in *Industrial Democracy: The Ambiguous Promise*, ed. Nelson Lichtenstein and Howell John Harris (Cambridge: Cambridge University Press, 1991), 113–141; Sanford M. Jacoby, *Modern Manors: Welfare Capitalism since the New Deal* (Princeton: Princeton University Press, 1997), 236–242.

In general terms, bureaucratic rationalization fit neatly with New Deal trends: the establishment of "countervailing" organizations which could balance corporate power (unions, consumer groups) and the use of neutral technical experts to constrain conflict and represent the "national interest." Yet, the final form of rationalized industrial relations was significantly more conservative than most pro-labor, left-wing New Dealers had envisioned. Rather than blaming this missed goal on weak Democratic or union leadership, however, I suggest the result reflected the constraints of the New Deal program itself, in particular the hope (born of desire and pragmatic political constraints) that left-wing liberals could undertake a deep transformation of American political economy by using macroeconomic arguments but without challenging the fundamental structure of American capitalism itself.

Rationalizing Industrial Relations

The shape of postwar industrial relations in unionized sectors was not an optimal solution for either management or union leaders; it was a compromise born of external pressures and the political and economic power held on each side. Commitment to legal and bureaucratic strategies for governing labor-management interactions carried severe costs, both in the time and effort devoted to negotiating the tedious minutiae of ever-expanding contracts and in the loss of discretion (for both unions and companies) that the signed agreements imposed.[53] Recognizing the logic behind rationalized wage adjustments like COLAs therefore requires careful consideration of the context for union and company commitments, and here there is no better case study than General Motors and the United Automobile Workers. GM and the UAW were the most ardent advocates in their respective communities of using economic statistics to adjust wages. But they had also been the center of an iconic, widely publicized confrontation in 1945–1946, wherein Reuther's autoworkers had aggressively challenged General Motors' control over prices and profits (by citing underconsumptionist arguments) and had thereby provoked an equally forceful response. Understanding the logic that connected the 1945–1946 strike (when the UAW and GM appeared to embody the heart of postwar political and economic conflict) and the 1948 contract (often seen as a betrayal of an earlier,

---

[53] On the costs of bureaucratic rationalization, see Brody, *Workers in Industrial America*, 203–204; Jacoby, *Modern Manors*, 236–242, 256–258. For a similar dynamic, see Theodore M. Porter, *Trust in Numbers: The Pursuit of Objectivity in Science and Public Life* (Princeton: Princeton University Press, 1995), 89–189.

more radical unionism) reveals much about postwar political economy and about the limitations of the New Deal.

GM's president, Charles E. Wilson, had first sketched the basic parameters for the 1948 contract (COLAs, annual wage increases) back in 1941 (another piece of evidence linking the later postwar era to the waning days of the New Deal). For Wilson, and most corporate leaders who later followed his lead, COLAs and annual wage increases were necessary to secure union agreement to the main management objective: a multiyear contract that would not only reduce the frequency of major strikes but also cut the time and financial costs that accompanied negotiation. Both COLAs and so-called deferred wage increases were strongly correlated with multiyear contracts and proliferated alongside the latter after 1955. The same logic explains a similar correlation between union bargaining power and use of COLAs: where the strike threat was greater and potentially more disruptive, management sought to establish longer contracts and therefore more readily offered COLAs.[54] Still, this trade-off came at a price: commitment to fixed wage increases and ties to macroeconomic statistics like the CPI could cut into profits if industry performance failed to match expectations or keep pace with larger segments of the economy. Steel executives learned this lesson in the late 1950s, when their three-year contract commitments proved less affordable than anticipated, leading them to dilute or eliminate COLA clauses in the early 1960s.[55] Indeed, GM's 1948 two-year contract had few admiring imitators among businessmen, and even the upsurge in escalator clauses during the early 1950s derived primarily from uncertainty after the outbreak of war; not until 1955 would multiyear contracts spread widely.[56]

General Motors' willingness to sacrifice some of its discretion over wage rates rested upon its dominant position in a flourishing, oligopolistic industry. By the late 1940s, GM controlled nearly half of the domestic auto market; in the five years following the war, its profits after taxes increased nearly tenfold, from $87.5 million in 1946 to $834 million in 1950.[57] Such clear market power gave GM both the financial wherewithal to take a calculated

[54] National Industrial Conference Board, *Cost of Living Provisions in Union Contracts*, 1, 18; Hendricks and Kahn, *Wage Indexation in the United States*, 38; Gabarino, *Wage Policy and Long-Term Contracts*, 2, 77–80.

[55] Gabarino, *Wage Policy and Long-Term Contracts*, 92–94.

[56] National Industrial Conference Board, *Cost of Living Provisions in Union Contracts*, 3; Hendricks and Kahn, *Wage Indexation in the United States*, 38–39; Gabarino, *Wage Policy and Long-Term Contracts*, 75–76.

[57] Kathyanne Groehn El-Messidi, "Sure Principles Midst Uncertainties: The Story of the 1948 GM-UAW Contract" (Ph.D. dissertation, University of Oklahoma, 1976), 27; Lawrence J. White, *The Automobile Industry since 1945* (Cambridge: Harvard University Press, 1971), 250.

risk in industrial relations and an increased incentive for avoiding extensive labor conflict that could disrupt production. In part, this incentive was financial: Wilson, for example, estimated that the 1945–1946 strike cost the company almost $1 billion in earnings.[58] But it was also linked to public relations. GM officials recognized that the company's huge profits and market dominance made it a visible target for antitrust investigations and broader public resentment.

Since the anti-monopoly campaigns of the 1930s, GM economists had been fighting a rearguard action against antitrust charges from liberals and left-wing allies of the New Deal (an effort that included arguments about price index theory; see Chapter 8). After a wartime hiatus, this struggle appeared poised to resume, signaled by the successful prosecution of two antitrust cases in oligopolistic industries (Alcoa in 1945, and American Tobacco in 1946). Meanwhile, the UAW opened negotiations in 1945–1946 by calling on the company to boost wages while stabilizing prices, a proposal predicated on GM's "ability to pay" as evidenced by its huge profits and its implied monopoly power. Company officials counterattacked immediately, determined to defend managerial prerogatives over prices and profits against interference by the unions or the state. GM launched a national propaganda campaign promoting a free labor market—rather than company profits—as the ultimate arbiter of wage rates, and when a fact-finding board organized by President Truman insisted on the legitimacy of "ability to pay" arguments, GM representatives walked out of the hearings. In the short term, GM won the struggle, refusing to concede that "ability to pay" was a legitimate factor in wage adjustments. But public opinion polls showed support for UAW arguments, and the decision of the federal fact-finding board threatened to set a precedent that might have more teeth in future confrontations.[59] Thus, GM needed both to stabilize its labor force and to reframe wage discussions in a way that portrayed the company in a more favorable light even as it protected managerial control over prices and profits.

In this context, Charles Wilson resurrected his idea from 1941: obtain a multiyear contract by using COLAs and additional wage increases determined by historical rates of national productivity growth. From a management perspective, it was a brilliant move, incorporating elements of the

---

[58] E. Bruce Geelhoed, "Charles Erwin Wilson," in *The Automobile Industry, 1920–1980*, ed. George S. May (New York: Facts on File, 1989), 486.

[59] Lichtenstein, *Most Dangerous Man in Detroit*, 229–240; Harris, *Right to Manage*, 139–143; White, *The Automobile Industry since 1945*, 10–11, 124–125; John B. Rae, *The American Automobile Industry* (Beverly: Twayne Publishers, 1984), 107; El-Messidi, "Sure Principles Midst Uncertainties," 27.

underconsumptionist analysis of pro-labor, New Deal liberals but within a framework that was relatively innocuous, if not beneficial, to General Motors. As GM officials repeatedly emphasized, the combination of an escalator clause and the "annual improvement factor" met a basic plank of CIO and UAW wage theories (and indeed of the New Deal itself): real wages should rise alongside productivity (Chapters 3–4). UAW officials portrayed this connection as an important management concession—the "big news" of the contract, as one official put it—and later commentators also noted a striking similarity between Wilson's justification of the contract and economic proposals outlined by New Deal moderates such as Alvin Hansen. But there were also important omissions in the GM version. Hansen, for example, suggested coupling a rationalized link between wages and productivity with a "continuous price program [i.e., price regulation] ... designed to give consumers their share ... through lower prices." Likewise, the UAW complained that the contract merely stabilized existing patterns of profit distribution (allowing all to rise equally with productivity), whereas unions insisted that current "wage-price-profit" relationships were "unhealthy," with "prices and profits ... too high and wages too low to maintain prosperity." Of course, this stasis in the wages-prices-profits nexus was precisely the system's virtue in Wilson's eyes: as he declared to more conservative colleagues, the contract wage formula led to the same results as typical union bargaining, but avoided the "friction inherent in the old method," namely strikes and protracted negotiations. In fact, the plan exemplified what Charles Maier has identified as the "politics of productivity" in the postwar era: the deflection of concerns about distribution into a shared consensus about the benefits of increased abundance. Moreover, Wilson was convinced that the company could afford the contract: before offering scheduled wage increases based on economy-wide productivity increases, he confirmed with staff economists that GM's recent and projected productivity gains well outstripped national averages.[60]

All the virtues of rationalization for management were therefore manifest in GM's turn to the COLA/improvement factor formula in 1948. For a small premium in wages and a temporary sacrifice of discretion over

---

[60] Gabarino, *Wage Policy and Long-Term Contracts*, 21–27, esp. 24 (quoting Wilson) and 22 (Hansen); El-Messidi, "Sure Principles Midst Uncertainties", 39–40, 148–150; Maier, *In Search of Stability*, 123–130. For the UAW reaction to the contract, see Donald Montgomery, draft of article for *North American Labor*, 7 June 1948, pp. 1–2; UAW press release, 25 May 1948, pp. 3–4, folder 4, box 72, UAW Washington Office–Donald Montgomery, WRL; Nelson M. Bortz, "Cost-of-Living Wage Clauses and the UAW-GM Pact," *MLR* 71, no. 7 (1948): 2–3.

wage adjustments (easily cushioned by GM's huge profit margin), the company gained virtual amnesty from major strikes. It sidestepped questions about "ability to pay" (thereby keeping profits and prices off the bargaining table), but co-opted other elements of the labor-left program and presented wage rates as natural products of underlying economic factors (price levels, productivity) rather than as contests of power. General Motors had revived the framework of high wages and high productivity which had created limited common ground between unions, labor activists, and some corporate leaders in the mass-production and mass-distribution sectors of the economy in the 1920s (Chapter 3). There was but one important distinction: whereas two decades earlier GM's mass-production counterparts had used the wages-productivity link to ward off labor organization and hence had been able to retain full authority over wage rates, the legacy of New Deal labor law now compelled GM and others to deal with strong unions, thereby leading them to negotiate and codify a precise wage formula. Even the 1950s version presented some anti-union benefits, though, since COLAs created a highly visible correlation between wages and prices, thereby reinforcing management claims about the causal link between the two. Indeed, when the CPI fell several months after the 1948 agreement, GM made a great public show of reducing prices slightly across all its lines, "to pass along to consumers the savings resulting from both downward adjustment of wage and salary payments and the lowered cost of certain materials."[61]

For a company like GM, with a comfortable market position and production-limited sales, trading wage flexibility for labor peace was an attractive move. During the uncertainty of Korea and again after 1955, other major companies facing strong unions would proceed through the same calculus, often leading to the same result, although GM and its followers in the auto industry remained the most consistent supporters of a formula approach to wage adjustments based on COLAs and an "annual improvement factor."[62] Over the long term, of course, GM's strategy would fail in spectacular fashion: after its market dominance eroded, the corporation became trapped by the very labor rules and compensation policies it had once eagerly promoted. Yet that later failure should not be allowed to obscure how logical GM's actions appeared in the 1950s and 1960s, when many observers saw its contract provisions as an appropriate, even savvy, response to its

---

[61] National Industrial Conference Board, *Cost of Living Provisions in Union Contracts*, 6–7.
[62] Gabarino, *Wage Policy and Long-Term Contracts*, 4, 29; Ruben, "Major Collective Bargaining Developments: A Quarter-Century Review," 44–46.

circumstances. "GM may have paid a billion for peace," declared *Fortune* magazine in its analysis of the company's 1950 contract with the UAW, but "it got a bargain."[63]

Fortune's assessment, however, raises questions about the wisdom of the union commitment to COLAs. Indeed, historians have typically viewed the Treaty of Detroit less as a triumph for the labor movement than a capitulation, the symbolic end to radical union efforts to reshape American political economy.[64] Why, then, did most unions accept COLAs, and some, notably the UAW, become avid proponents?

We can begin by considering the larger commitment evidenced by segments of the labor movement, especially the CIO in general and the UAW in particular, to rationalizing labor relations through economic analysis. As we have seen, this commitment had been created by both necessity and opportunism; if General Motors turned to rationalization to defend its existing power against threats posed by union disruption and state intervention, the labor movement had first looked to rationalization from a position of weakness. During the early interwar era, the labor movement had deteriorated under unfavorable economic and legal conditions, and union arguments for higher wages based on ethical demands (e.g., the living wage) had largely failed. Against this background, New Deal labor policy—including the National Labor Relations Act—had taken a different tack. As portrayed by pro-labor, New Deal liberals, strong unions would do more than bring greater justice to industrial relations or create another powerful interest group. Instead, the benefits of union organization extended outward to the middle class and even to most businessmen: by checking corporate greed, organized labor could help ensure the adequate distribution of income needed to keep the economy running smoothly. Despite the chaotic, occasionally violent, grassroots activism that characterized early CIO organizing drives and strikes, the logic of "responsible unionism" would ultimately prevail, for in fact that was what the New Deal framework entailed: working-class power channeled toward public benefit. It shaped the organizational structure of CIO industrial unions and especially the UAW, eventually leading to their combination of massive size, quick mobilization, and centralized, top-down bureaucratic control ready to choke off wildcat action; "power under control," as Nelson Lichtenstein

---

[63] "Treaty of Detroit," *Fortune*, July 1950, p. 53.

[64] Lichtenstein, *Most Dangerous Man in Detroit*, 271–298; Jacobs, *Pocketbook Politics*, 245. Contemporary observers had a similar view: see the commentary in "The U.S. Labor Movement," *Fortune*, February 1951, pp. 93ff.

has described it.[65] It also shaped the ends to which that power would be directed, constraining it to actions justified by economic arguments, and in turn, by statistics. As UAW research director Nat Weinberg explained to the American Statistical Association, quantified knowledge had become a basic tool for the new industrial unions which recognized that they "could make progress only with and not at the expense of the community." Unions were not only part of the national economy, he told the audience, they were essential contributors to its progress: "Statistics are ... instruments for the measurement of the social performance of our economic machine. Labor watches the gauges to discover those parts of the machine which need overhauling and then brings its economic and political strength to bear to secure correction of the defects which it discovers."[66]

If national labor organizations were to sustain this position, they required the services of trained experts, and accordingly the ranks of union research-ers expanded rapidly during the two decades after 1930. Ewan Clague reported that the number of research departments in unions had grown from a scattered few in the 1920s, to thirty or forty in the late 1930s, and then to almost one hundred by 1950.[67] Of course, the quality and func-tion of these departments varied. We have already seen how the CIO relied far more heavily on trained economists, and within the CIO the UAW was clearly at the forefront. As Clague put it, "Reuther's got brains himself, and he hires brainy people."[68] Shortly after Weinberg arrived, he submitted a proposal for overhauling the UAW Research Department, calling for an improved library, hiring professional consultants for certain projects, col-lecting more internal union statistics, and committing to the "technical competence" of research staff. Like the New Deal statisticians, Weinberg envisioned his role as expanding beyond data collection to analysis, pro-duction of "comprehensive reports on current and prospective develop-ments," and "recommendations for policy action."[69] By 1948, Weinberg's

[65] Seth Wigderson, "The UAW in the 1950s (Volumes I & II)" (Ph.D. dissertation, Wayne State University, 1989), 3–5; Lichtenstein, *Most Dangerous Man in Detroit*, 132–153; Steve Fraser, "'The 'Labor Question,'" in *The Rise and Fall of the New Deal Order, 1930–1980*, ed. Steve Fraser and Gary Gerstle (Princeton: Princeton University Press, 1989), 55–84, esp. 67–71, 76–78.

[66] Weinberg, "More Adequate Reports on Industrial Activity," pp. 1–2, folder 20, box 66, UAW Washington Office—Donald Montgomery, WRL.

[67] Ewan Clague, "Use of Labor Statistics in Collective Bargaining," Address before the Regional Conference on Statistical Programs of the Middle Atlantic and New England States, 23 May 1950, pp. 2, Speeches—Uses of Statistics, box 3, RCL-PPF 1950–1975, BLS.

[68] Reminiscences of Ewan Clague (1958), p. 290.

[69] Weinberg to Reuther, "A Program for Strengthening the Research Department," [undated, probably 1947], pp. 3–4, folder 13, box 7, Nat Weinberg, Part II, WRL.

Research Department had a $100,000 budget and included six other economists, twice the number in the CIO national office.[70]

Though some union researchers may have confined themselves to working directly on collective bargaining, the CIO economists crafted a much broader role that included shaping and justifying union policies through economic analyses aimed at the general public; the 1947 Nathan Report was only one of many such efforts.[71] As they developed union wage arguments, CIO economists also provided a direct conduit for the underconsumptionist ideas that had formed the backbone for marriage of economic policy and labor protection in the New Deal. Some, such as Weinberg and CIO associate director of research Katherine Pollack Ellickson, had been at Brookwood Labor College. Many had served in federal agencies under Roosevelt; a 1948 *Fortune* survey of "twenty leading labor economists" [i.e., union economists] found that "three-quarters had worked in government agencies." Donald Montgomery, "one of Reuther's closest and most influential advisors" and the architect of many of Reuther's macroeconomic proposals, had worked for multiple New Deal organizations and became the source for the UAW's postwar, underconsumptionist slogans, such as "purchasing power for prosperity."[72] Thus, as Ewan Clague recognized, both the growth of union research staff and the attention to economic analyses grew organically from New Deal labor policies: Justifying wage demands through economic arguments and statistical calculation was a natural counterpart of the legal constraints established by the National Labor Relations Board that legitimated unions insofar as they protected a broader social welfare. Significantly, the one major union that rejected the board and continued more militant action, John L. Lewis's United Mine Workers, was also the one major, non-railroad union without any research staff and without a representative to LRAC.[73]

The adoption of rationalized, economic justifications for union action helped the UAW to cultivate a reputation for being, in the words of one postwar industrial relations expert, "one of the more 'socially conscious' American unions," one which had committed itself to "a policy of 'progress

[70] "The Labor Economists," *Fortune*, December 1948, p. 193.
[71] For an exemplary discussion, see "Abbreviated Minutes—Meeting of CIO Research Directors," 18 February 1953, folder 25, box 7, Department of Research—Nat Goldfinger, RG 13–003, GMMA.
[72] Katherine P. Ellickson, Oral History, vol. 1, p. 15, WRL. "The Labor Economists," *Fortune*, December 1948, p. 198. Lichtenstein, *Most Dangerous Man in Detroit*, 223.
[73] Ewan Clague, "Use of Labor Statistics in Collective Bargaining," 1–2, 7. "The Labor Economists," *Fortune*, December 1948, p. 199.

with the community.'"[74] Yet this rationalization should not be mistaken for a simple conservatism or a naïve trust in the neutrality of technical expertise. The UAW did not abandon an antagonistic stance toward employers that carried class-based valences: During the 1948 negotiations, for example, union representatives coupled their underconsumptionist analyses with direct attacks on GM's huge net profits ("a monstrous monument to unbridled greed," as one official put it).[75] Likewise, in the deliberations of LRAC, we saw how CIO researchers denied that economic statistics were unproblematic, neutral facts; instead, they treated statistical practice and principles as a framework within which they could construct arguments favorable to unions. Rationalization thus did not eliminate conflict—it constrained it: to grievance procedures, to wildcat strikes based on shopfloor conditions, to economic analyses of wages, prices, and industrial conditions, and to discussions about statistical methodology. Lurking behind this system were economic and political pressures that forced many major manufacturing corporations to deal with unions and that forced unions into a public posture of serving the larger community interest.

If both unions and corporations found themselves pressed to participate in a rationalized system, however, that framework did not offer equal footing to each side. On the most basic level, there was an asymmetry in the financial and professional resources needed to compete successfully within a complex system of rules and rationalized arguments. In the case of economic analysis, we can see this disparity directly in the work of LRAC and BRAC. Initial plans for LRAC had granted the committee twenty members, but unions had been unable to fill all the slots regularly. By 1951, the committee numbered sixteen members and ran five subcommittees. By contrast, BRAC had twenty-seven active members overseeing eight subcommittees.[76]

Yet the problems ran deeper than simply a differential in resources, for the forms of bureaucratic rationalization that were adopted favored corporations, and nowhere was this more evident than in COLAs. If union economic analysis aimed at convincing the larger community that organized labor and higher wages served broader interests, COLAs seemed a

[74] Gabarino, *Wage Policy and Long-Term Contracts*, 104, 95.

[75] El-Messidi, "Sure Principles Midst Uncertainties," 86, 84.

[76] U.S. House, Committee on Education and Labor, *Consumers' Price Index*, 25–27. On the resource advantages held by companies in rationalized grievance procedures, see Brody, *Workers in Industrial America*, 208. For a similar argument about public relations, see Elizabeth A. Fones-Wolf, *Selling Free Enterprise: The Business Assault on Labor and Liberalism, 1945–60* (Urbana: University of Illinois Press, 1994).

disastrous misstep. COLAs not only came to symbolize the "wage-price spiral" that conservatives accused unions of fostering, they also exempted union members from the resulting inflation, nearly driving a stake through the claim that unions were a positive force in the nation's economy and a boon to a much wider swath of middle- and working-class consumers.[77] But herein lies the puzzle, for the union that did the most to promote the wage formula approach, the UAW, was also the union most committed to under-consumptionist arguments in the postwar era and to an image of organized labor as a partner in communal progress. Resolving this paradox can tell us much about the later course of liberal political economy in the "New Deal order," for the paradox arose from the flaws inherent in the attempted marriage of labor policy and macroeconomic policy that began in the 1920s, culminated in the 1930s, and was clearly fragmenting by the 1950s.

The source of the problem was a tension already recognizable during the New Deal: purchasing power—the central concept in an underconsumptionist view of economic activity—was a function of prices and income, requiring action on both fronts (Chapter 4). War had blunted the antitrust side of the underconsumptionist attack on high prices, but it had also offered an opportunity to pursue a new solution: price controls. Unlike the comprehensive planning advocated by statist technocrats such as Gardiner Means, price regulation could avoid direct intervention into production decisions (or so it seemed). Likewise, it required none of the precedent-bound, time-consuming investigations and trials needed for antitrust cases. Small wonder, then, that the OPA was led initially by purchasing-power proponent Leon Henderson, or that so many on the political left enthusiastically envisioned the OPA as a basic part of postwar political economy. But the fate of the agency in 1945–1946 illustrates how unrealistic that hope had been. Major business leaders and powerful manufacturing corporations had (barely) tolerated the OPA during the war, swayed by wage controls to offset costs, high profits in a wartime boom, and the desire to appear as good corporate citizens during war mobilization. When the conflict ended, so did the tolerance. The National Association of Manufacturers launched a full assault on the OPA, while trade associations and corporate executives pleaded for relaxing specific sets of price regulations. But beyond the propaganda campaign lay a real asymmetry of power that left the outcome a foregone conclusion: corporations had control over production.[78]

---

[77] Jacobs, *Pocketbook Politics*, 245, 251–256.

[78] On the difficulties of antitrust investigations, see Ellis W. Hawley, *The New Deal and the Problem of Monopoly: A Study in Economic Ambivalence* (New York: Fordham University Press, 1995 [1966]), 449–453. Jacobs, *Pocketbook Politics*, 179–197, 222–227.

During the war, retailers and manufacturers had done their best to avoid the effects of price controls by using many of the tactics highlighted by unions in their cost-of-living investigations: dropping low-end price lines, substituting lower quality materials or manufacturing techniques, and rapidly changing styles to escape price-control specifications (Chapters 5–6). Now free from patriotic mobilization pressures, they added a new strategy: withholding production altogether. When Congress attempted to reinstitute weakened price controls over agricultural products in the fall of 1946, meatpackers began a boycott that nearly eliminated meat from store shelves and destroyed any remaining public support for the OPA.[79]

The meatpacking episode exemplified the weakness of price regulation alone as a solution to the monopoly problem: even if it did establish efficient prices (and critics doubted that), price regulation left concentrated corporate power over production untouched and hence would ultimately be subject to that power. The failure of price controls as a *media via* solution threw the monopoly problem back onto the polarities of the 1930s—break up concentrated industries or have the state take control—but Truman was no more able to make either choice a viable option than Roosevelt had been. When Truman did propose radical action in 1949—announcing a plan to build state-run steel plants if the industry refused to expand production— he faced insurmountable opposition.[80] The price side of the labor-left underconsumptionist program thereby foundered on the basic dilemma of the New Deal: the difficulty of capturing the productive gains provided by capital-intensive mass-production and distribution systems while controlling the potential abuses of concentrated economic power in private hands but without nationalizing the industries in question (which had never been a realistic political possibility).

The fate of the labor-left agenda was further sealed by the success of an alternate underconsumption perspective that had gained traction in the late 1930s: the fiscal stimulus approach promoted by New Dealers such as Marriner S. Eccles, Lauchlin Currie, and Alvin Hansen, and which would later be categorized as "Keynesianism." Expansive state spending offered a way to boost aggregate demand without intervening directly in corporate decisions about wages and prices. Nor did it necessarily require abandoning reform objectives: as envisioned by New Deal liberals, fiscal stimulus could involve redistributive policies such as progressive tax systems and "enlarged

---

[79] Jacobs, *Pocketbook Politics*, 213–216, 227–230.
[80] Jacobs, *Pocketbook Politics*, 242–243. A later threat to take over the steel industry amidst a labor dispute during the Korean War also ended swiftly in failure: Dubofsky, *The State & Labor in Modern America*, 215.

public outlays for health, education, and welfare." Furthermore, it could be combined with an antitrust campaign, as several New Dealers argued during the hearings of the Temporary National Economic Committee near the end of the 1930s. In these respects, fiscal stimulus offered an opportunity to achieve economic reforms while resuscitating the economy, but without requiring a politically hazardous and probably futile direct assault on managerial prerogatives. The weakness of this plan, even beyond conservative opposition to extensive federal spending, was that while antitrust prosecutions and redistribution policies were compatible with Keynesian-style macroeconomics, they were not necessary; antitrust investigations could be reduced and social programs replaced by defense appropriations without seriously affecting the basic model. But in the mid-1940s, fiscal stimulus glimmered like the key to an achievable reform-oriented political agenda.[81]

Whether or not Walter Reuther grasped the full implications of this analysis, after the events of 1946 he surely knew that price control was dead and that the federal government would make little effort to intervene directly in managerial decisions about pricing or the distribution of earnings among workers, managers, and investors. He responded as best he could. On the one hand, the UAW accepted the best wage offer it could get for its members, for the realities of intra-union politics made this an essential step. On the other hand, Reuther continued to press for broader changes, trying to make the more generous GM-UAW contract of 1950 a model for other companies and industries while also maintaining an extensive publicity campaign (supported by statistics and economic analysis from Weinberg and Montgomery) that championed increasing working-class income and attacked high prices, high profits, and monopoly power in the auto industry. Perhaps predictably, these efforts bore only limited fruit. The auto industry plus a small number of other unionized economic sectors remained isolated arenas of working-class prosperity, primarily for skilled white males. Productivity, far from being the base for working-class wage increases, became the limit—allowing workers to reap the benefits of greater production but not increasing their relative share in the national income. Absent power to force companies to divert some profits toward higher wages, it became a commonplace even among liberals that wage increases that

---

[81] William J. Barber, *Designs within Disorder: Franklin D. Roosevelt, the Economists, and the Shaping of American Economic Policy, 193–1945* (Cambridge: Cambridge University Press, 1996), 85–89, 108–131, 158–170, esp. 130; Brinkley, *End of Reform*, 106–136, 227–264; Jacobs, *Pocketbook Politics*, 243–244; Robert M. Collins, *The Business Response to Keynes, 1929–1964* (New York: Columbia University Press, 1981).

outpaced rising productivity were inflationary and hence illegitimate, a position that the Kennedy administration reiterated numerous times. Even the UAW, while nominally retaining the goal of wage hikes beyond productivity to correct for existing imbalances, largely confined itself to claiming that productivity was growing more rapidly than the annual improvement factor specified in its contracts with GM.[82] The left-wing underconsumptionist arguments pioneered in the 1920s and raised to prominence in the 1930s as a strategy that linked labor organization to the redistribution of national income had now reached their end.

As I have suggested, the source of his demise lay in the unresolved dilemmas that plagued the New Deal as a whole. Having abandoned radical antitrust action as impractical and counterproductive, New Dealers seeking the redistribution of real income faced a choice between direct intervention into traditional managerial prerogatives (wages, prices, profits) or working through indirect means (taxation and spending). The latter was far more politically tenable, but it reduced the role of unions in economic policy, turning them from a central component of economic prosperity (as envisioned in the National Labor Relations Act) into a lobbying arm of the Democratic Party that pushed for greater expansion of social welfare programs. These polarities were evident even in the late 1930s, but the choice between them was made starker and cruder by the political context of postwar America, namely the rising Cold War, lingering fears of totalitarianism, and a conservative propaganda campaign that pitted free enterprise (with managerial control free from state intervention) against a single alternative: communism. Here rationalized industrial relations found its final, crucial support.

Communism and the Consumer Price Index

In the 1930s, economic arguments (based on underconsumptionist theories) had provided a key rationale for promoting organized labor; now they served to delineate the bounds of acceptable union wage demands: at or below changes in retail prices (according to the War Stabilization Board),

---

[82] On the importance of economic security, see Brody, *Workers in Industrial America*, 188–191. On Reuther and the UAW, see Wigderson, "The UAW in the 1950s," 100–102; Fones-Wolf, *Selling Free Enterprise*, 47; Lichtenstein, *Most Dangerous Man in Detroit*, 271–298, 352–353, 360–366. On the limits provided by productivity, see Gabarino, *Wage Policy and Long-Term Contracts*, 27–28; Maier, *In Search of Stability*, 128–131; Marc Linder, *Labor Statistics and Class Struggle* (New York: International Publishers, 1994), 33–40.

or at the level of retail prices supplemented by the growth in national productivity (GM-UAW). In both cases, the goal had been to replace unconstrained bargaining and conflict with a "reasonable" rule-based system for wage adjustments. In the anti-communist context of the late 1940s and early 1950s, and especially when placed against the great strike wave of 1945–1946, it was easy to view this shift as the replacement of a Marxist framework for labor-capital relations (based on power and class struggle) with a more constrained system depending on apparently unyielding economic realities. *Fortune*'s portrayal of the 1950 GM-UAW contract exemplified this attitude: in an article that trumpeted the lack of "working-class consciousness" in the American labor movement (which violated "the so-called 'laws of history'" and "baffle[d] the European intellectual"), the editors praised the autoworkers' agreement as "the first major union contract that explicitly accepts objective economic facts—cost of living and productivity—as determining wages, thus throwing overboard all theories of wages as determined by political power, and of profit as 'surplus value.'"[83]

Indeed, as the editors well knew, the UAW's Walter Reuther had consolidated his control over the union by riding the crest of anticommunism in the labor movement in the late 1940s, and Reuther's commitment to wage arguments grounded in statistics and economic analysis meshed directly with his broader ideological stance: an attempt to justify both strong labor organization and union action by placing them within an American tradition of liberal politics and capitalist economics. In Reuther's hands, the UAW's demands were neither symptomatic of unrelenting class struggle (as depicted by Marxists) nor examples of market-distorting monopoly unionism (as viewed by conservatives); they were attempts to restore fair balance between workers and companies and thereby to promote economic prosperity. In this respect, the UAW of the 1950s shared a deep continuity with a core element of the New Deal: to reform (but not overturn) American capitalism by recognizing the need for collective organization (in existing forms like corporations and new forms like industrial unions and the welfare state) that was rendered more tolerable through extensive bureaucratic rationalization.[84]

The success of this project in industrial relations, however, depended on the inviolability of the statistical calculations that now sat at the heart of this rationalized system and hence wielded enormous power. Here was where

---

[83] "The U.S. Labor Movement," *Fortune*, February 1951, pp. 91–92.

[84] On Reuther and anticommunism, see Lichtenstein, *Most Dangerous Man in Detroit*, 248–270, 327–345. On the core themes of the New Deal (and especially its expression in the National Labor Relations Act), see Plotke, *Building a Democratic Political Order*, 95–101, 113–116. The emphasis on bureaucratic rationalization is mine, not Plotke's.

national unions had stumbled during the Second World War: trying to use grassroots, bottom-up experience for an ill-suited end—not to challenge the validity of aggregate, abstract statistical formulations per se, but to support an alternative calculation that denounced the very kind of purportedly apolitical technical expertise and simplified analysis that the rationalization project demanded. By the early 1950s, most American labor unions had changed their posture, a shift evident in the success of LRAC but which became even clearer during a new controversy over BLS cost-of-living statistics that erupted during the Korean War.

As Americans began to anticipate a lengthy struggle on the Korean peninsula following the intervention of Chinese forces in late 1950, prices began to rise rapidly. Thanks to lobbying from GM and the UAW, however, the new economic controls proposed by Truman permitted wage increases that matched the rise in the CPI. Accordingly, COLAs proliferated across many industries, and the stage appeared set for a repeat of the controversies of the Second World War.

On April 24, 1951, a major union held a press conference to declare the Consumer Price Index a "fraud against labor." At the conference, union representatives distributed a thirty-five-page indictment titled "The Facts about High Living Costs," which documented union charges and provided an alternative estimate of the change in the cost of living since January 1950, one that was roughly double the BLS figure. The union declared that its work "brings up to date the CIO-AFL report prepared in 1944," and indeed in almost every respect it followed the labor arguments from the earlier debates. Prepared in part by Russ Nixon, who had co-authored the 1944 reports, the 1951 edition repeated claims about quality change, BLS substitution policies, new expenses caused by moving to higher cost areas, taxes, unpriced items, and differences with the Bureau of Agricultural Economics' price index.[85] Tactically, the episode was a direct repetition of union strategy from the Second World War: union economists turned the debate over the bureau's statistics into a public, political controversy; they attacked the integrity of BLS staff; they tried to present statistical calculation as interwoven with class-based judgments and political maneuvering; and they offered their own alternative calculation based purportedly on common working-class experience.

Yet if the arguments were the same, neither the context nor the reaction followed 1940s patterns. The union in question—the United Electrical,

---

[85] United Electrical, Radio, and Machine Workers of America (UE) press release, 24 April 1951, p. 1, CPI—UE, box 12, RCL-PPF 1950–1975, BLS. *The Facts About High Living Costs* (New York: UE, 1951), ibid.

Radio, and Machine Workers of America (UE)—acted alone, and AFL and CIO economists quickly distanced themselves from their renegade colleagues. As we have seen, both the AFL and CIO had committed to working through LRAC and avoiding the highly politicized, confrontational tactics employed during the Second World War. This decision was reinforced, however, by the status of the UE: two years before, it had been expelled from the CIO for its perceived connections to the Communist Party, one of the major casualties of the purges of the labor movement prompted by anticommunist clauses in the Taft-Hartley Act of 1947.[86] When called to testify about the CPI during congressional hearings prompted by the UE report, CIO economists reiterated a list of complaints that echoed both the UE report and the 1940s arguments, but they never endorsed the UE statistics and indeed never provided an estimate of the understatement in the CPI. Moreover, whereas the UE accused the BLS of "fraud," the CIO spokesman (Solomon Barkin, Textile Workers) deliberately noted that his colleagues had "the greatest of faith in the technicians of the Bureau," even if they were frustrated with certain policy decisions.[87] Following a typical pattern, the AFL researchers gave high praise to the BLS and generally expressed satisfaction with its response to LRAC suggestions.[88]

The perceived ties between communist connections and politicized attacks on labor statistics received an additional boost later that summer when Clague received an urgent telegram from Isador Lubin, now a delegate to the UN Economic and Social Council. The day before, Soviet diplomats had touted the UE report as evidence that the United States was exploiting its workers in order to maintain its military. Clague made a quick phone call to Rep. Tom Steed, chairman of a House committee holding hearings on the CPI, and cabled back Steed's statement that the "[Russ] Nixon recommendations are irresponsible and will be ignored." Reflecting on the episode, Clague connected it to a worldwide communist plot to undermine war mobilization by subverting economic statistics. "We are seeing signs of Communist attacks in every country … on cost-of-living indexes," he warned Steed two days later. "The 'line,'" he continued, "consists in arguing that the standard of living must not be lowered for the sake of rearmament. This will be supplemented by a 'peace' line also."[89]

---

[86] On the Communist purge in the CIO, see Harvey A. Levenstein, *Communism, Anticommunism, and the CIO* (Westport: Greenwood Press, 1981).

[87] U.S. House, Committee on Education and Labor, *Consumers' Price Index*, 201–262.

[88] Ibid., 353–370, esp. p. 358.

[89] Lubin to Clague, 6 August 1951; Clague to Lubin, 6 August 1951; Clague to Tom Steed, 8 August 1951, Steed Committee, box 3, Wickens correspondence, BLS.

Given that context, it is hardly surprising that the Steed committee's report was a resounding triumph for the BLS and its index. The committee declared the CPI "the most important single statistic issued by the Government," and called it the "Billion Dollar Index" in light of its use by the Wage Stabilization Board.[90] Though the committee recognized numerous difficulties in the computation of the index, these were repeatedly positioned as technical problems divorced from political or normative judgments. Suffusing the report, and indeed the hearings themselves, was a complex endorsement of statistical objectivity. The CIO had proposed establishing a tripartite executive advisory committee (composed of representatives from business, labor, and the American Statistical Association), but unlike Harold Ruttenberg's similar proposal during the Second World War, this group was designated as an advisory committee (not a policy-making board) and justified primarily by its procedural advantages (it was more effective to have all groups meet together) rather than Ruttenberg's claim that it was impossible to find an "objective, impartial" judge of economic statistics. Even this milder version was too radical for BRAC members, who disliked the corporatist overtones of a tripartite council. General Motors economist and BRAC representative Stephen DuBrul argued that a tripartite committee might imply that members were "bargaining with the BLS on technical matters," whereas in fact BRAC members merely discussed problems and made individual suggestions; they did not "bargain," which would be like trying "to bargain on the length of a yard."[91] The committee itself declared that the bureau staff "should be free of interference or control" by outside groups, but nevertheless it "heartily approved the present system of advisory committees." On the tricky problems of quality, forced up-trading, and so forth that had formed the bulk of the UE and CIO objections both now and during the 1940s, the committee recommended "that the bureau … make every effort to develop techniques to take into account these unusual factors," but made no specific suggestions about how to do this, effectively dropping the issues back on the BLS and its advisers.[92]

Overall, the episode exemplified the relationship between statistics, rationalized industrial relations, and the possibilities for collective worker organization within a liberal, capitalist society. As envisioned by a wide swath of

[90] U.S. House, Committee on Education and Labor, *Report on Consumers' Price Index* (Washington, D.C.: U.S. GPO, 1952), 39, 14.

[91] U.S. House, Committee on Education and Labor, *Consumers' Price Index*, 202–203, 381.

[92] "Report on the Consumers' Price Index," pp. 37–38, appended to U.S. House, Committee on Education and Labor, *Consumers' Price Index*.

liberals and pragmatic moderates in the 1950s, American political economy rested on free markets for investment and consumption, but also allowed for powerful forms of collective organization—corporations, unions, the state—whose actions were constrained by systems of rationalized rules. Insofar as these rules rested on "objective economic facts" (as *Fortune* had put it), they could be defended from critics on the right (who feared state encroachment and "monopoly unionism") and on the Marxist left (who insisted on the transcendence of class conflict and the domination of corporations), and even from those remaining "classical" liberals (skeptical of all forms of concentrated power). The rules did not, of course, offer equal benefits to all: with the collapse of the laborite version of the underconsumption program, postwar liberals began to abandon their attempt to seek economic redistribution through the workplace (in the form of reduced profit rates, higher wages, and lower prices) and instead turned increasingly to the welfare state (a project we will consider in Chapter 9). Nevertheless, the political realities of the postwar environment forced even strong unions to accept the basic framework for postwar industrial relations while seeking discrete areas, such as statistical calculation, to press for changes that would benefit their members.

In statistics, unions found fertile, albeit limited ground: numerous (potentially normative) judgments were required to make complex computations of amorphous notions like the "cost of living," especially on a national level. Yet, in a paradox created by the rationalization project, the political value of statistical flexibility was often correlated with the apolitical reputation of the numbers themselves, leading both mainstream labor organizations and corporations to frame their critiques carefully. Of course, it was occasionally to one side's advantage to highlight the political repercussions of particular choices: for example, when the CIO proposed including income taxes in the CPI, conservatives argued that this would effectively exempt many workers from tax increases. But the potential benefits of bureaucratic rationalization led even antagonistic economic groups such as the UAW and GM to insist on the possibility of an accurate, national measure of retail price change and to commit themselves to a specific measurement, the CPI, even while each could list a myriad of complaints about its calculation. Moreover, those benefits also pressed both unions and corporations to emphasize the apolitical nature of statistical calculation in public, even while they were furiously lobbying the BLS to adopt their proposed changes from within closed-door meetings of clearly partisan advisory committees. Thus, when conservatives in 1951 charged that planned alterations to the CPI were "the result of behind-the-scenes collusion between big labor and the Bureau," BRAC members leapt to the defense of the agency.[93] Likewise, major unions never again mounted the kind of highly public, highly politicized attack on the bureau or its statistics that had been the hallmark of the controversy during the 1940s.

These links between liberal capitalism, rationalized industrial relations, and putatively apolitical statistical calculation were well-illustrated by the postwar careers of the three major authors of the CIO reports from the Second World War. One, Russ Nixon, ended up heading the UE's doomed attempt to repeat the wartime struggle, denounced as a communist plot. A second, Lincoln Fairley, was also dogged by associations to the Communist Party.[94] However, the third and perhaps most important author, Harold Ruttenberg, went in the opposite direction. After losing a struggle with Phillip Murray over the future of the U.S. Steel Workers, Ruttenberg joined the management of a Pittsburgh steel firm, eventually becoming CEO of several companies and working as a labor-relations consultant (much to the irritation of his former union colleagues). While at United Steel and Wire during the 1960s, Ruttenberg instituted a plan that tied wages to productivity and thereby aimed to eliminate labor strife through statistics. In Ruttenberg's version, cost increases and savings from capital investment were divided between the firm's profits and workers' wages using a specific formula. The plan, derived from work by the economist Alan Rucker, used historical profit-wage data to define workers' appropriate share of the benefits of increased productivity, which turned out to be precisely 38.93 percent.[95] Harold Ruttenberg had learned the lessons of the Second World War.

[93] George Smith (Secretary, Committee on Business Statistics, Chamber of Commerce of the United States) to Ewan Clague, 21 December 1950, encl. "Figures Don't Lie, But …," *Economic Intelligence*, December 1950, Interim Revision, box 16, GCS 1934–50, BLS.

[94] Reminiscences of Ewan Clague (1981), p. 147.

[95] Harold Ruttenberg, Interview I, Oral History Project, Pennsylvania State University, pp. 27–30; Harold J. Ruttenberg, *My Life in Steel: From CIO to CEO* (Tarentum: Word Association Publishers, 2001), 225–234.

PART III

THE CPI AND THE FEDERAL
GOVERNMENT, 1960–2000:
A "WELFARE" INDEX FOR THE
WELFARE STATE

Economics was once an academic discipline pursued only by theorists. Back in those days, the Consumer Price Index (CPI) was merely a researcher's tool, and the term "price index" was not part of the average American's vocabulary. Today, economics is a household exercise in budgeting and investment, and the CPI is discussed at the dinner table as well as at the conference table.[1]
—U.S. Bureau of Labor Statistics,
The Consumer Price Index: Concepts and Content over the Years, 1978

By 1960, the Consumer Price Index had become a basic tool for labor contracts within unionized industries. To a large extent, the function of the CPI paralleled that of the Bureau of Labor Statistics as a whole: both were intended to monitor industrial relations and to facilitate peaceful and fair resolutions of disputes. On an institutional level, this conception was instantiated by the bureau's two official advisory boards, one for unions and one for business associations.

Yet the tight ties binding both the bureau and the CPI to industrial relations were unraveling. During the 1930s and 1940s, the federal government had begun to manage the national economy more actively. The Employment Act of 1946 formalized that function by committing the nation to pursuing

---

[1] U.S. Bureau of Labor Statistics, *The Consumer Price Index: Concepts and Content over the Years*, Report no. 517 (Washington, D.C.: U.S. GPO, 1978), 1.

"maximum production, maximum employment, and maximum purchasing power" under the guidance of the president's new Council of Economic Advisers and the congressional Joint Economic Committee (whose leadership alternated between the House and Senate).[2] During the New Deal, BLS staff had positioned their agency as an important participant in this expansion of federal economic planning (Chapter 4). Though BLS officials became less involved in policy decisions after the breakup of the Roosevelt administration at the end of the Second World War, the agency's data series on prices, wages, unemployment, and (later) productivity retained their critical roles in policy planning and assessment. There was no guarantee, however, that these two general functions now served by bureau statistics—facilitating industrial relations and guiding macroeconomic analysis—would be fully compatible. In fact, these goals had conflicted during the Second World War, when both union officials and bureau staff had recognized that a cost-of-living index useful for assessing national price controls was not necessarily the best tool for adjusting wage rates (Chapter 5).

The position of the CPI was further complicated during the 1960s and 1970s by the rise of indexation in realms beyond labor contracts. The federal government had first used indexation to help control its budget during the early 1930s, when the Economy Act of 1933 allowed reductions in federal salaries of up to 15 percent based on movements of the BLS cost-of-living index (Chapter 4). The strategy resurfaced during the early 1960s as a technique for making fair and timely adjustments to federal pensions in an environment of creeping inflation. Beginning in the late 1960s, both politicians and agency bureaucrats began circulating plans to tie more federal programs to the CPI. Poverty thresholds came first in 1969, followed by Social Security benefits in 1972, both of which in turn affected a host of other programs that were already or subsequently linked to them, such as food stamps, the school lunch program, and veterans' pensions. By 1981, when Congress tied income tax brackets to the CPI, indexation had become a pervasive part of federal governance: the General Accounting Office calculated that an astonishing 50 percent of the federal budget was directly or indirectly affected by the CPI. In an age of rising prices and soaring deficits, federal indexation dominated discussions about the creation and use of data on consumer prices.[3]

[2] U.S. Congress, Joint Economic Committee, *Employment Act of 1946, as Amended, with Related Laws (Annotated) and Rules of the Joint Economic Committee, Congress of the United States* (Washington, D.C.: U.S. GPO, 1977), 1–4.

[3] U.S. General Accounting Office, *What Can Be Done to Check the Growth of Federal Entitlement and Indexed Spending?* (Washington, D.C.: U.S. GAO, 1981), 16. R. Kent

Alongside these shifts came one less noticed until it erupted publicly in the mid-1990s: a change in the fundamental conception of the index. During the 1920s, academic economists had debated the proper definition for a cost-of-living index (Chapter 3). Should it attempt to measure the changing cost of a fixed level of "satisfaction", "welfare", or "utility" (a constant-utility index)? Or should it hold the contents of its market basket as steady as possible (a constant-goods index)? From the 1920s through the 1950s, government statisticians routinely resolved this question in favor of the constant-goods approach. In 1961, however, a review committee from the National Bureau of Economic Research (led by University of Chicago economist and future Nobel-prize laureate George Stigler) concluded that the BLS should aim to produce a constant-utility index. The verdict was controversial at the time, but it was reiterated three and a half decades later, when the Senate Finance Committee asked Stanford economist Michael Boskin to lead a new major review of the CPI. (As described in the Introduction, the Boskin commission concluded that the CPI ought to be a constant-utility index and that deviations from this model led to an annual, upward "bias" in the index of 1.1 percentage points.) Between those two dates, both broader professional sentiment and the opinions of leading BLS officials had grown to favor the constant-utility framework, so that when responding to the Boskin commission in the late 1990s, bureau economists could report that the agency had been treating a constant-utility index as the proper objective for the CPI for several decades.[4]

No logical necessity connected the transformation in the dominant applications for the CPI with the transformation in its theoretical conception. Indeed, the two shifts are typically discussed independently.[5] Nevertheless, I suggest that they were mutually supporting. As I will argue in the following two chapters, strategies for making a constant-utility index into a viable statistical objective required crucial assumptions that, while reasonable for some applications, proved more contentious for others. But the concept of

Weaver, *Automatic Government: The Politics of Indexation* (Washington, D.C.: Brookings Institution, 1988), 38–66.

[4] BLS, "An Updated Response to the Recommendations of the Advisory Commission to Study the Consumer Price Index," June 1998, p. 4, available on the BLS website: http://stats. bls.gov/cpi/cpi0698a.pdf. For a more detailed argument, see John S. Greenlees, "The U.S. CPI and the Cost-of-Living Objective" (paper presented at the Joint ECE/ILO Meeting on Consumer Price Indexes, Geneva, Switzerland, November 2001).

[5] For example, consider both Weaver, *Automatic Government: The Politics of Indexation*; and W. E. Diewert, "Index Numbers," in *The New Palgrave: A Dictionary of Economics*, vol. II, ed. John Eatwell, Murray Milgate, and Peter Newman (London: MacMillan, 1987), 767–779.

utility—especially when described more colloquially as "welfare"—made it easy to slip between applications without considering the consequences of these assumptions. Holding welfare constant seemed like an appropriate objective for many price index applications: deflating macroeconomic measurements, adjusting fixed-income payments to particular groups to compensate for economic changes, or shifting federal tax brackets. But was the same notion of welfare the proper basis for all these tasks? In Chapter 8, I suggest that the constant-utility perspective found its strongest support in an applied domain—empirical, macroeconomic analysis—where economists could more easily adopt simplifying assumptions. Yet, construed as a universal theory appropriate for any index dealing with consumer welfare and applied to a particular statistic (the CPI) with multiple applications, the constant-utility perspective then grew into a seemingly natural and obvious choice. In the United States, this shift was made far easier by Americans' ambivalence about the most financially consequential application for indexation: the welfare state itself. Thus, as Chapter 9 describes, the structure of the American welfare state and the "welfare" theory of cost-of-living indexes became mutually reinforcing.

8

Accounting for Growth: Macroeconomic Analysis and the Transformation of Price Index Theory

Utility seems to be to economists what the Lord is to theologians. Economists talk about utility all the time, but do not seem to have hope of ever observing it this side of heaven.[1]

—Tom Wansbeek and Arie Kapteyn, 1983

But wait: can't we be reasonable, can't we have one index, one all embracing concept of quality change? Alas, kind hearts, we cannot.[2]

—Thomas W. Gavett, BLS economist, c. 1967

In 1911, no less an authority than the neoclassical economist Irving Fisher had declared that the pursuit of a constant-utility index was "as fatuous a quest as the search for the philosopher's stone."[3] How could one track the changing cost of an elusive entity like utility or its synonyms, welfare and satisfaction? Although such skepticism was common in the 1920s (Chapter 3), by the end of the twentieth century, many economists would disagree with Fisher, and the BLS would adopt the constant-utility ideal as its official objective for the CPI. That decision would have substantial consequences, becoming the primary rationale for claims that the CPI overstated the true rise in the cost of living and the justification for a series of methodological changes designed to reduce this alleged upward bias (Chapter 9). Perhaps surprisingly, in light of the CPI's historical functions,

---

[1] Tom Wansbeek and Arie Kapteyn, "Tackling Hard Questions by Means of Soft Methods: The Use of Individual Welfare Functions in Socio-Economic Policy," *Kyklos* 36, no. 2 (1983): 249.

[2] Thomas W. Gavett, "Some Notes on Quality," [n.d.; c. 1967], 44-page typescript, CPI–Quality Adjustment prior to 1972, box 16, PFAC, BLS. Dates on items in the bibliography suggest it was written after 1966 but probably before 1968, and almost certainly before 1970.

[3] Irving Fisher, *The Purchasing Power of Money: Its Determination and Relation to Credit Interest and Crises* (New York: MacMillan, 1911), 222.

the innovations that made the constant-utility index into a viable and attractive goal for the CPI did not develop from arguments over wages or from careful consideration of how to adjust income and income-based parameters in federal programs. Instead, the greatest support for viewing the CPI through the neoclassical framework of utility came from economists immersed in analyzing the focal point of postwar political economy: the pursuit of economic growth.

"In recent years," wrote economist James Tobin in 1964, "economic growth has come to occupy an exalted position in the hierarchy of goals of government policy ... Growth has become a good word."[4] Tobin, who had served on the Council of Economic Advisers (CEA) for President Kennedy from 1961 to 1962 and then acted as a consultant to Democratic administrations throughout the 1960s, was well-positioned to understand the primacy of growth in postwar politics. Under the leadership of Walter Heller, Kennedy's CEA had designed a massive tax cut that traded short-term deficits for the promise of reducing high unemployment and stimulating growth. The plan's success had established the apparent legitimacy of Keynesian macroeconomics, but its very proposal exemplified the new centrality of growth in postwar liberal political economy. During the New Deal, left-wing and moderate liberals had justified numerous reform projects based on their potential to stimulate growth (e.g., labor organization to overcome underconsumption). By the 1960s, that logic had been reversed: growth would not be the product of reforms in political economy but the condition for their possibility. Growth would directly boost the material living conditions of all Americans and provide rising government revenues that could fund targeted interventions, such as President Lyndon B. Johnson's soon-to-be-announced War on Poverty, or, more darkly, the escalating conflict in southeast Asia. But, of course, growth was not a uniquely liberal priority, nor were all visions of how to pursue growth or share its benefits the same. Rather than unifying all Americans, "the political economy of growth," to borrow Robert Collins's description, "became an important arena for ideological expression and conflict in the postwar era."[5]

[4] James Tobin, "Economic Growth as an Objective of Government Policy," *AER* 54, no. 3 (1964): 1.

[5] Robert M. Collins, *More: The Politics of Economic Growth in Postwar America* (New York: Oxford University Press, 2000), xi. Ibid., 48–53; Julian E. Zelizer, *Taxing America: Wilbur D. Mills, Congress, and the State, 1945–1975* (New York: Cambridge University Press, 1998), 147–176; Michael Bernstein, *A Perilous Progress: Economists and Public Purpose in Twentieth-Century America* (Princeton: Princeton University Press, 2001), 130–138; Alice O'Connor, *Poverty Knowledge: Social Science, Social Policy, and the Poor in Twentieth-Century U.S. History* (Princeton: Princeton University Press, 2001), 139–195; Lizabeth

Not surprisingly, the political dissension over growth had a corollary in debates about the proper statistical measures for quantifying, tracking, and analyzing economic expansion. According to an increasing number of economists from the mid-1950s on, the country's existing statistical framework for assessing macroeconomic growth—a system constructed during depression and war—was ill-suited for the nation's dynamic postwar economy. The problem lay in the country's price indexes, which were used to "deflate" figures on output and expenditures (both measured in current dollars) to a consistent standard which could then be compared over time. As the common argument went, because the indexes failed to account properly for changing consumption patterns and for innovation—including dramatic increases in product quality and entirely new kinds of goods—they systematically overstated consumer inflation and understated the growth of real income. In turn, this statistical miscalculation produced a host of misguided assessments and policy proposals. Here, the concern with measuring growth intersected the constant-utility approach to price indexes: in the eyes of many younger neoclassical economists, a utility-based index could provide a superior analysis while also creating a conceptual link between macroeconomic statistics and the neoclassical theories that had come to dominate American microeconomics after the Second World War.

Still, the new vision for assessing growth had its own critics among an older generation of macroeconomists (many of whom had ties to institutional economics). From their perspective, using utility to assess inflation or growth seemed like reverting to an already-rejected paradigm of analysis laden with subjective judgments and normative evaluations. Indeed, in the view of the older generation, neoclassical economists threatened to subvert the very nature of macroeconomic statistics, creating a system wherein calculations such as Gross National Product or productivity could fluctuate with changing fashions, political norms, and consumer tastes—all independently of the physical output of the nation's economy. In the end, the constant-utility ideal became widely accepted, but only after it had been redefined and reconceptualized to allow it to fit more readily within existing traditions of macroeconomic measurement. Placed on a more robust theoretical base and carefully developed by a core group of economists, the constant-utility approach moved from strength to strength. Nonetheless, despite the tantalizing presence of terms such as "welfare" or "utility" in its definition, it was by no means obvious that a constant-utility index

Cohen, *A Consumer's Republic: The Politics of Mass Consumption in Postwar America* (New York: Alfred A. Knopf, 2003), 112–129.

(especially one geared toward macroeconomic analysis) would provide a proper basis for assessing or adjusting income over time.

My study begins by briefly considering the history of the constant-utility ideal from the 1930s through the 1950s. From there we turn to its intersection with the debates over economic growth in the late 1950s to early 1960s, focusing on a major (and controversial) review of federal price statistics conducted by the National Bureau of Economic Research. The third section examines the subsequent debates about the value of utility as a concept in macroeconomic analysis and the transformation that solidified the standing of the constant-utility ideal in empirical macroeconomics. The final section considers the consequence of this development for the suitability of cost-of-living indexes for income adjustments, a discussion that carries over into Chapter 9.

A THEORETICIAN'S STATISTIC: THE CONSTANT-UTILITY INDEX THROUGH THE 1950s

To begin, we need to take a short step into neoclassical theories of consumer demand. In the neoclassical perspective, consumers act to maximize the utility (satisfaction) that they can derive from their income. Modeling consumer behavior therefore requires delineating the satisfaction or welfare that a given consumer expects to derive from different sets of goods, all of which is collectively referred to as the consumer's "utility function." A utility function starts with a preference map, which indicates how the consumer would rank different sets of goods if forced to choose between them. Presumably, certain sets would be viewed as nearly equivalent; in these situations, economists describe the consumer as being "indifferent" to a choice among the specified sets.[6] Today, most economists would regard a preference map as a complete specification of a utility function. Utility, in this view, is an ordinal value; it denotes a relative preference between two or more options without specifying the magnitude of that preference. For example, an ordinal utility function could show that a consumer prefers A to B and B to C, but it would not tell us that A provides five units more utility than B, or that B provides three units more than C.

By contrast, in the late nineteenth and early twentieth centuries, most neoclassical economists treated utility functions as if they provided cardinal values (i.e., we *can* say that A brings five units more utility than B). From

---

[6] Thus, in typical theoretical parlance, what I am calling a preference map is a set of indifference curves or surfaces.

a cardinal perspective, we could imagine a situation in which relative preferences (the preference map) remain constant while the actual satisfaction derived from some or all of the sets changes (e.g., A now provides seven units more utility than B).

Most historical accounts (and most economists) have ignored the distinction between ordinal and cardinal concepts of utility when discussing the evolution of the constant-utility index. As we will see, though, that distinction had important consequences for price index theory, especially because of how it affected attempts to compare utility both between people and over time. Although the "ordinalist revolution" within neoclassical economics began in earnest in the 1930s, its incorporation into price index theory occurred over two stages, with the most consequential developments only beginning in the late 1960s.[7] Accordingly, readers should consider the early debates over the constant-utility index from the cardinal perspective and be wary of reading past discussions through a subsequent conceptual framework.

Given the neoclassical theories of demand, utility appeared as the natural basis for defining standards of living and, in turn, for defining cost-of-living indexes as the minimum change in expenditure needed to maintain a constant level of utility. Having reached this point, however, early neoclassical price index theorists found themselves stymied. After prices had shifted and the goods available in the market had changed, how could economists determine the minimum expenditure needed to reach the original level of utility or welfare? Under a new set of prices, the original bundle of goods might not be the optimum allocation of expenditures. Even worse, the same bundle of goods might not deliver the same satisfaction in two different situations; indeed, early neoclassical theorists recognized that utility functions depended on environmental conditions and hence would not remain stable over time. For example, the neoclassical economist Francis Edgeworth, the leading figure of British price index theory from the late nineteenth century through the 1920s, noted that the utility derived from commodities depended on the larger social and economic context, such as "National Wealth" or the goods possessed by one's neighbors.[8] (Here is a classic illustration of how a cardinal interpretation affects a constant-utility index: relative preferences might remain the same, but the financial

---

[7] For a more detailed version of this history, see Thomas A. Stapleford, "Aftershocks from a Revolution: Ordinal Utility and Cost-of-Living Indexes," forthcoming in the *Journal of the History of Economic Thought*.

[8] See papers from 1887 and 1894, reprinted in Francis Ysidro Edgeworth, *Papers Relating to Political Economy*, vol. 1 (London: MacMillan, 1925), esp. 210, n. 1; 222–223, 344–350.

improvement of the larger society means that the same goods now provide less satisfaction.)

This puzzle defined the central problem for a cardinal, constant-utility index and exemplified the empirical concerns that had prompted government statisticians and institutional economists to reject it in the 1920s (Chapter 3). How could economists find a new bundle of goods in a subsequent time period that delivered the same "satisfaction" as a consumer's original purchases? One solution (perhaps obvious to us, in an age inundated by opinion polls) was to ask consumers themselves. Indeed, in 1920 the British statistician Arthur Bowley suggested that "instead of measuring the satisfaction by formula, we may recognize that it is subjective and a matter of opinion." Accordingly, he proposed polling housewives to get "a rough measure, perhaps as accurate as any more refined measure, of the change in that vague entity 'the cost of living.'"[9] The widespread use of cost-of-living indexes for wage adjustments, however, suggested pragmatic limitations to such an approach, since asking families of wage-earners whether last year's income continued to bring "the same variety and pleasure" seemed like a recipe for endless wage hikes. In any case, Bowley's suggestion was not followed, and indeed, even he returned to an "algebraic process" eight years later.[10]

The other alternative was easier: make an assumption to eliminate the problem. By assuming that utility functions remained stable over time, economists could simplify their task enormously. In the 1920s, for instance, the Russian economist A. A. Konüs demonstrated that (with stable utility functions) economists could calculate an upper limit to what Konüs called a "true index of the cost of living" (derived from a base-period standard of living).[11]

---

[9] Arthur L. Bowley, "Cost of Living and Wage Determination," *Economic Journal* 30, no. 117 (1920): 117.

[10] Arthur L. Bowley, "Notes on Index Numbers," *Economic Journal* 38, no. 150 (1928). More recently, self-reported "well-being," "satisfaction," and "happiness" have become a serious object of study, though these projects bring their own complications and no one seems prepared to turn them into a price index: Daniel Kahneman, Ed Diener, and Norbert Schwarz, *Well-Being: The Foundations of Hedonic Psychology* (New York: Russell Sage Foundation, 1999). We will return to this issue near the end of the chapter.

[11] A. A. Konüs, "The Problem of the True Index of the Cost of Living," *Econometrica* 7, no. 1 (1939): 10. This upper limit had been recognized earlier, notably in A. C. Pigou, *Wealth and Welfare* (London: MacMillan, 1912), 41–43. However, Konüs more clearly explicated the relationship between a "true cost-of-living index" that used base-period "want-satisfaction" and a second, equally valid index that compared the cost of maintaining the current level of "want-satisfaction" from the base period to the present. Konüs's original paper was published in *The Economic Bulletin of the Institute of Economic Conjecture*, Moscow (September 1924): 64–71. Elements of the paper reached British and American economists via a German economist, and similar ideas were proposed independently by the British economist R.G.D. Allen in the early 1930s. For analyses of how Konüs's work fit

The argument was relatively straightforward. Suppose that consumers optimize their purchases to obtain maximum satisfaction under a given system of prices. Further assume that utility functions do not change but that prices do. Under the new system of prices, a consumer would at least be able to obtain the old standard of living by purchasing the original market basket. The ratio of new expenses to old expenses in this case would be the commonly used, constant-goods index with a base-period market basket (e.g., an index like the CPI). However, because prices have changed, the old market basket is no longer necessarily the optimal set of purchases; by shifting expenditures, the consumer might be able to reach the same level of "want-satisfaction" (Konüs's term) at lower cost. Thus, the true index will always be less than or equal to a constant-goods, base-period index such as the CPI.[12]

However, Konüs's analysis only applies when utility functions remain stable; if they change, the logic of the argument collapses. Under a new utility function, the original market basket might not produce the same satisfaction at later dates, and hence the shift in the cost of that basket would no longer be an upper bound to the "true" index. As Konüs put it, his theorem was "valid only when the habits of consumers, their family compositions, and their environments … do not change."[13]

Subsequent price index theorists recognized the severity of these constraints. As Hans Staehle (an economist at the International Labour Office) explained in a 1935 survey of the constant-utility approach, existing theory "still leaves us bound by the very serious assumption of identical tastes and milieu." When that assumption could not be maintained, he warned, "the method of price index numbers must break down altogether."[14] Nevertheless, the growing acceptance of neoclassical demand theory among economists reinforced the validity of the constant-utility idea: if consumer purchases were motivated by desire for utility, then surely the proper measure of the change in the cost of living was a constant-utility index. In a famous 1936 survey article, for example, the Norwegian neoclassical economist Ragnar

---

with existing theory up through 1939, see Henry Schultz, "A Misunderstanding in Index-Number Theory: The True Konüs Condition on Cost-of-Living Index Numbers and Its Limitations," *Econometrica* 7, no. 1 (1939); Ragnar Frisch, "Annual Survey of General Economic Theory: The Problem of Index Numbers," *Econometrica* 4, no. 1 (1936): 11–12, 17–19.

12 In practice, as we have seen, the CPI does not always use a market basket derived from consumption patterns in its base period. Nevertheless, it is commonly regarded as such an index, and the difference is not essential for what follows.

13 Konüs, "True Index of the Cost of Living," 13.

14 Hans Staehle, "A Development of the Economic Theory of Price Index Numbers," *Review of Economic Studies* 2, no. 3 (1935): 188.

Frisch declared that the constant-utility ideal "seems ... to be the only plausible" definition of a cost-of-living index.[15] Still, changing utility functions remained a serious stumbling block, and the early aftermath of the switch to an ordinal concept of utility only made the situation worse.

The reformulation of utility had begun in the early twentieth century; however, it emerged most forcefully and explicitly in Britain in the 1930s (especially through Lionel Robbins, John R. Hicks, and R.G.D. Allen), after which it gathered adherents through the ensuing decades and eventually persuaded most Anglo-American economists to view utility in ordinal terms.[16] In turn, the ordinal shift prompted a reevaluation of constant-utility indexes. Under a cardinal view, one could imagine attaching a numerical value to the "satisfaction" received by a consumer in the base period and then searching for the least expensive set of goods in a second period that produced the same magnitude of pleasure (hence Arthur Bowley's proposal to poll housewives). Under an ordinal interpretation, such a procedure was impossible; these magnitudes did not exist and were unverifiable—only relative preferences counted. Accordingly, as John R. Hicks explained, the only conceivable way of asserting that a consumer's welfare remained the same in two situations was if relative preferences remained constant (e.g., A over B over C) and the consumer remained on the same preference level (e.g., B in both situations). In essence, stable utility functions were now a *requirement* for the very possibility of constructing a constant-utility index. As Hicks put it, "If this assumption cannot be granted, the question whether [the consumer] is better off in one situation or in the other loses all economic meaning." Likewise, MIT's Paul Samuelson, a leading critic of cardinal utility whose widely used textbooks helped to define economics for a generation of students, reported in 1947 that a constant-utility index could admit "a partial answer" (through bounding techniques such as Konüs's theorems) only "if certain rigid assumptions are fulfilled," including the postulation of stable consumer tastes.[17]

---

[15] Frisch, "Problem of Index Numbers," 12.

[16] For two key British expositions, see Lionel Robbins, *An Essay on the Nature and Significance of Economic Science*, 2nd ed. (London: MacMillan, 1945), 54–56, 136–158; J. R. Hicks and R.G.D. Allen, "A Reconsideration of the Theory of Value. Part I," *Economica* 1, no. 1 (1934): 52–76. For a more general consideration, see Joseph Schumpeter, *History of Economic Analysis* (New York: Oxford University Press, 1954), 1057–1066. On the earlier stages of the ordinalist shift, see Christian E. Weber, "Pareto and the 53 Percent Ordinal Theory of Utility," *HOPE* 33, no. 3 (2001): 541–576.

[17] J. R. Hicks, "The Valuation of the Social Income," *Economica* 7, no. 26 (1940): 107; Paul A. Samuelson, *Foundations of Economic Analysis* (Cambridge: Harvard University Press, 1947), 147. More generally, see Stapleford, "Aftershocks from a Revolution."

To many American economists, these assumptions seemed implausible over any significant length of time. Interwar social scientists had emphasized the malleability of human desires in response to environmental conditions such as advertising and emulation, and these convictions ran especially strong among institutional economists.[18] Under such circumstances, it is unsurprising that the BLS and other statistical agencies worldwide continued to avoid the constant-utility approach, despite recognizing its growing appeal among price index theorists who were free from the working constraints of a statistical office. For instance, when the BLS reviewed the conceptual structure for the CPI during the 1949–1953 revision, a staff economist (probably Edward Hollander) reported that "in theory a fixed standard of living is interpreted as 'constant want satisfaction' or 'equal well-being.'" Nevertheless, he noted that "in practice," an index based on such a concept "virtually defies measurement," in part because "the kinds of goods that ... make up a fixed level [of living] change as new products are placed on the markets and influence the tastes and preferences of the consumer."[19]

Such was the status of the constant-utility index in the mid-1950s: theoretically appealing but highly limited, due in no small part to the perceived problems for comparing consumer satisfaction over time when utility functions changed. Yet three developments would alter the landscape for price index theory over the next fifteen years: the increasing professional dominance of neoclassical microeconomics (with its utility-based analysis of demand), renewed attention to the measurement of economic growth (in which quality change and new products attracted great attention), and a reformulation of the constant-utility index itself that was prompted by a deeper consideration of the ordinalist critique. All three of these factors collided in the 1960s to produce a major change in the professional attitude toward the constant-utility ideal and its relevance to practical measurements.

ECONOMIC GROWTH AND PRICE INDEXES: THE DEBATES OF 1957–1961

For many economists, the Second World War had opened new vistas of possibility for government planning. The development of analytic tools such as the national accounts system and macroeconomic analyses such as Keynes's

---

[18] Malcolm Rutherford, "Understanding Institutional Economics: 1918–1929," *Journal of the History of Economic Thought* 22, no. 3 (2000): 295–297.

[19] BLS, "Uses and Limitations of Consumers' Price Index" (draft), pp. 1–2, 18 January 1951, folder 13, box 43, Ellickson collection, WRL.

General Theory held the promise (apparently verified by the wartime production boom) of allowing the government to engineer growth by proper
manipulation of macroeconomic aggregates. Certainly it appeared that way
to Leon Keyserling, a New Deal stalwart and longtime advocate of underconsumptionist arguments who, while serving on President Truman's Council
of Economic Advisers, became a vociferous and effective campaigner for
expanded efforts to promote growth. Tellingly, Keyserling viewed growth
as a mutable cure that could be adapted to many ends. Economic expansion would "go increasingly to filling in the consumption deficiencies of the
erstwhile poor," the CEA suggested in 1947; yet when the Cold War took a
threatening turn in 1949–1950 with the first test of a Soviet atomic weapon,
the communist revolution in China, and the subsequent invasion of South
Korea, Keyserling was prepared to adapt his agenda: growth could now
provide for a worldwide struggle against communism while permitting the
maintenance of existing domestic standards of living. It was precisely this
flexibility that made economic growth such an attractive policy goal, but it
also avoided a troubling question that we will return to later in the chapter:
was all growth qualitatively the same?[20]

Aggregate statistics suggest that Keyserling had been able to achieve many
of his goals (qualitative aspects of growth notwithstanding), with aggregate
output and wages rising through the postwar years. But domestic expansion
and military intervention in Korea combined to raise an old specter: inflation. According to the CPI, prices shot up by almost 8 percent in 1951, handing Dwight Eisenhower and his Republican colleagues a powerful campaign
issue. The Republican return to power in 1952 signaled a modulation of the
growth agenda: Eisenhower intended to pursue a responsible expansion
that maintained price stability. This shift defined a political dynamic that
continued to resonate over the coming years: Republicans and conservative
businessmen argued that liberal policies (labor organization, expansionist
government intervention) were creating continual "creeping inflation" that
damaged those on fixed incomes and threatened to undermine prosperity.
Meanwhile, liberals responded by accusing conservatives of unnecessarily
restraining growth and by blaming price hikes on oligopolistic industries.[21]

---

[20] U.S. Council of Economic Advisers, *Second Annual Report to the President*, as quoted
in Collins, *More*, 20. Ibid., 18–25; Bernstein, *A Perilous Progress*, 108–114; Meg Jacobs,
Pocketbook Politics: Economic Citizenship in Twentieth-Century America (Princeton:
Princeton University Press, 2005), 143–144, 233–235, 243–244.

[21] Robert Griffith, "Dwight D. Eisenhower and the Corporate Commonwealth," *American
Historical Review* 87, no. 1 (1982): 100–109; Collins, *More*, 42–45; Jacobs, *Pocketbook
Politics*, 246–256.

These debates came to a head in the late 1950s as statistics on aggregate growth (such as Gross National Product, GNP) registered a noticeable slowdown, price indexes began ticking upward, and the entire growth debate took on Cold War overtones. With Democrats back in control of Congress in 1957, Senator Estes Kefauver (D-Tennessee) launched a major, six-year investigation of "administered prices" within the Senate Antitrust and Monopoly Committee that focused on steel (a perennial antitrust target), bread bakeries, automobiles, and (especially) pharmaceuticals. Almost simultaneously, the congressional Joint Economic Committee (JEC)—which was responsible for overseeing attempts to implement the Employment Act of 1946—embarked on a two-year study of economic growth and inflation in which unions and companies traded barbs, the administered prices debate gained a thorough airing, and the JEC pressed economists to tell them how to boost growth. The discussions of slowing growth gained further salience in May 1957 when Soviet premier Nikita Khrushchev touted the (supposedly) extraordinary past and future expansion of the Soviet economy, which (if the claims were accurate) would eventually match and surpass U.S. productive capacity. Khrushchev's boast gathered greater credibility later that fall when the Soviets launched *Sputnik*, sparking widespread concern that the United States was losing its technological superiority.[22]

Much of the congressional hearings rehashed familiar themes about structural imbalances that had been raised during the New Deal years. The economists and legal experts supporting Kefauver's antitrust investigations—John Blair, Gardiner Means, Paul Dixon, and Irene Till (wife of institutional economist and antitrust expert Walton Hamilton)—had been part of antitrust efforts since the 1930s, and in the steel, auto, and pharmaceuticals industries they faced a group of similarly seasoned opponents. Underconsumption was a common subject in both the Kefauver and JEC hearings (raised by New Deal economists such as Keyserling and union officials such as Walter Reuther), and charges of monopolistic abuses came

[22] Collins, *More*, 45–51; Jacobs, *Pocketbook Politics*, 247–258. "NAM Calls Inflation Major Issue; Meany Fears Midyear Downturn," *Washington Post*, 7 February 1957, A2; "Inquiry on Price Increases Set, Kefauver Says," *NYT*, 11 March 1957, p. 24. U.S. Senate, Committee on the Judiciary, *Administered Prices: Hearings before the Subcommittee on Antitrust and Monopoly of the Committee on the Judiciary*, 1957–1963; U.S. Congress, Joint Economic Committee, *Relationship of Prices to Economic Stability and Growth: Hearings before the Joint Economic Committee*, 85th Cong., 2nd sess., 1958; U.S. Congress, Joint Economic Committee, *Employment, Growth, and Price Levels: Hearings before the Joint Economic Committee*, 86th Cong., 1st sess., 1959.

from both liberals (aimed at corporations) and business representatives (targeting unions).[23]

Alongside the standard claims and counterclaims, however, both committees heard a small group of economists—notably including Richard Ruggles (Yale University) and Albert Rees (University of Chicago)—present a novel argument. According to Rees and Ruggles, neither unions nor corporations were to blame for rising prices because the widely lamented inflation was in fact fictitious, a problem of faulty statistics. In truth, the American economy was growing far more rapidly than standard assessments indicated. In political terms, this view had an ambiguous interpretation: it could vindicate either Eisenhower's anti-inflation policies (since growth had proceeded rapidly since 1952 with low inflation) or Democratic calls for greater expansion (since the country had not reached full employment and clearly the economy was not overheated by excess stimulation).[24] In general, the arguments advanced by Rees, Ruggles, and their later allies supported neither Republican nor Democratic positions per se, but rather offered a ringing endorsement of the productive power of late industrial capitalism while sweeping aside concerns about concentrated power (in unions or corporations) as a serious source of price distortions.

As Rees and Ruggles explained (in independent testimonies), the measurement problem arose from the inability of current price indexes to capture a central form of growth in the postwar economy: innovation as reflected in product quality and novel commodities. "In almost every line of production," Ruggles subsequently told the JEC, "food processing, textiles, chemicals, electronics, appliances, building construction, space exploration, and

---

[23] On the Kefauver hearings, see Robert Bud, "Antibiotics, Big Business, and Consumers: The Context of Government Investigations into the Postwar American Drug Industry," *Technology and Culture* 46, no. 2 (2005): 329–349. For underconsumption in the JEC hearings, see U.S. Congress, Joint Economic Committee, *Employment, Growth, and Price Levels*, 93–164. For union complaints, see U.S. Senate, Committee on the Judiciary, *Administered Prices*, 2174–2433. An (understated) view from the auto industry is U.S. Congress, Joint Economic Committee, *The Relationship of Prices to Economic Stability and Growth: Commentaries Submitted by Economists from Labor and Industry* (Washington, D.C.: U.S. GPO, 1958), 121–141, esp. 135.

[24] U.S. Congress, Joint Economic Committee, *The Relationship of Prices to Economic Stability and Growth: Compendium of Papers Submitted by Panelists Appearing before the Joint Economic Committee* (Washington, D.C.: U.S. GPO, 1958), 297–308, 651–663; U.S. Congress, Joint Economic Committee, *Employment, Growth, and Price Levels*, 2270–2272. Other economists who raised similar issues (though less intently) included Martin J. Bailey, Neil Jacoby, and Frederic Weston: U.S. Congress. Joint Economic Committee, *The Relationship of Prices to Economic Stability and Growth: Compendium*, 89–105, 642–643; U.S. Congress, Joint Economic Committee, *Employment, Growth, and Price Levels*, 2295.

military equipment, for example—spectacular improvements in products and totally new products are continually being introduced."[25] Champions of innovation could point to a host of novel products appearing in postwar consumer markets, ranging from the mundane to the revolutionary: frozen foods, television, residential air-conditioning, and new "wonder drugs" such as antibiotics, corticosteroids, antihistamines, and oral contraceptives. Moreover, many existing products had likewise changed greatly since the mid-1930s. Some alterations had been highly visible: according to newspaper accounts, the reintroduction of nylon stockings (first sold in 1940 and then restricted during the war) had caused "stampedes" and "riots" as women battled over limited supplies. Other changes were incremental but no less consequential. In a careful study based on entries from the Sears catalog and reviews by *Consumer Reports*, Robert J. Gordon later compiled variety of improvements in durable goods from the 1930s into the 1960s; for refrigerators, to take an example, the changes included greater energy efficiency, auto-defrost features, better temperature maintenance, and improved quality control. Likewise, during the Kefauver hearings, auto companies detailed the lengthy list of new features in American cars since the late 1930s. Any proper assessment of industrial performance had to recognize these shifts, auto executives argued, since industry cost structures ensured that much intercompany competition occurred through quality and service improvements rather than changes in nominal prices.[26]

Unfortunately, according to Rees and Ruggles, American price indexes had failed this test by inadequately accounting for quality change and novel goods. Because new goods were "linked" into both the CPI and the Wholesale Price Index (via the chain index method), the appearance of novel items did not change the level of these indexes. Furthermore, just as unions had complained about the bureau's failure to capture quality deterioration during the Second World War, skeptical economists now complained that BLS methods missed substantial quality improvements. For macroeconomic assessment, these weaknesses had become increasingly important, since many areas where improvement and new goods were

---

[25] U.S. Congress, Joint Economic Committee, *Government Price Statistics: Hearings before the Subcommittee on Economic Statistics*, 89th Cong., 2nd sess., May 24, 25, and 26, 1966, 237.

[26] Bud, "Antibiotics, Big Business, and Consumers," 329–330, 346. "25,000 Mob Store to Buy Nylon Stockings," *NYT*, 23 January 1945, p. 24; Malvina Lindsay, "The Gentler Sex," *Washington Post*, 16 March 1946, p. 10. Robert J. Gordon, *The Measurement of Durable Goods Prices* (Chicago: University of Chicago Press, 1990), 249–270. For auto executive assessments of competition and quality change, see U.S. Senate, Committee on the Judiciary, *Administered Prices*, 2475, 2646, 2681, 2772.

most prevalent (i.e., durable and semidurable goods) were now attracting an ever-larger share of American consumer expenditures. Within the market basket for the CPI, for example, proportional expenditure on food had fallen from 38 percent in 1917–1919 to 22 percent by 1963. A large chunk of the new spending had gone to housing (especially as homeownership expanded in the postwar era), but much had also been used for items such as radios, televisions, household appliances, and especially automobiles and auto care.[27] In short, more money was flowing to sectors that were making rapid quality improvements and introducing novel products, and as a result (Rees and Ruggles argued), official statistics seriously overstated inflation and understated economic growth. Accordingly, a JEC staff report summarizing the committee's hearings in December 1959 recommended that the government "improve the design of these price indexes so that they would more accurately reflect quality and productivity changes and the introduction of new products."[28]

During the hearings, JEC members also heard (from Stanford economist Kenneth Arrow) the now-standard neoclassical argument that constant-goods indexes such as the CPI overstated the true rise in the cost of living because they missed consumer substitution (Konüs's theorem)—assuming, of course, an "unchanged want structure."[29] Though Arrow argued that the CPI should try to emulate a constant-utility index, the constant-utility framework and the problems with assessing quality change had not yet been fully collapsed into a single issue. Neither Rees nor Ruggles, for example, suggested that price indexes should measure the changing cost of a fixed level of welfare or utility (though this was, perhaps, implicit in their complaints), nor did they discuss quality improvements in utility-based terms. Most critically, no one had a concrete plan to compensate for the defects which they had identified. Indeed, the most comprehensive treatment of quality change to date, a 1952 book by the Swedish economist Erland von Hofsten, had attempted to approach the problem from a neoclassical perspective, only to abandon the struggle as fruitless (in light of the inaccessibility and transience of utility functions) and to return to the kinds of "objective" quality measurements common to institutional economics, such as durability or "performance" (consider the wartime treatments of quality

[27] U.S. Bureau of Labor Statistics, *Handbook of Methods*, BLS Bulletin, no. 1458 (Washington, D.C.: U.S. GPO, 1966), 73–74.
[28] U.S. Congress, Joint Economic Committee, *Staff Report on Employment, Growth, and Price Levels*, 86th Cong., 1st sess., December 24, 1959, 109.
[29] U.S. Congress, Joint Economic Committee, *The Relationship of Prices to Economic Stability and Growth: Compendium*, 77–87.

in Chapter 6).[30] But all of that was about to change, courtesy of a new review of federal price statistics conducted by the National Bureau of Economic Research from 1959 to 1961.

The NBER Review

The creation of the NBER review was one early sign of how the federal government's new focus on macroeconomic policy was transforming the context for the Consumer Price Index. Prior to 1959, there had been four major external reviews of the CPI and its ancestors; all except the wartime Mitchell committee had been requested by the Department of Labor or the BLS, and even the Mitchell committee had adopted a narrow focus on the index and its relationship to consumers.[31] The NBER review, by contrast, was commissioned independently by the Office of Statistical Standards (OSS) in the Bureau of the Budget; indeed, the BLS was neither looking for nor expecting a major review of the CPI.[32] The OSS was the descendant of the Central Statistical Board that had been created by COGSIS in the 1930s (Chapter 4), and it had responsibility for coordinating and overseeing all federal statistics. But it had not convened a major external review of a federal program until 1956, when it asked the NBER to examine the national accounts system (the source of statistics on national output, such as GNP); the price statistics review committee was its second such venture.[33] The choice of topics illustrates how the OSS's role as statistical coordinator had taken on a new dimension with the rise of national economic policy: not merely avoiding duplication or providing basic compatibility but attempting to knit the nation's jumble of economic statistics into a more

---

[30] Erland von Hofsten, *Price Indexes and Quality Changes* (Stockholm: Bokförlaget Forum, 1952). H. Spencer Banzhaf, "Quantifying the Qualitative: Quality-Adjusted Price Indexes in the United States, 1915–1961," in *The Age of Economic Measurement*, ed. Judy L. Klein and Mary S. Morgan (Durham: Duke University Press, 2001), 359–361.

[31] These included the Advisory Committee to the Secretary of Labor (ACSL, Chapter 4), the 1943 American Statistical Association committee chaired by Frederick C. Mills (Chapter 5), the "technical committee" convened by the President's Committee on the Cost of Living and led by Wesley C. Mitchell (Chapter 6), and another American Statistical Association committee created for the 1949–1953 revision under Bruce Mudgett.

[32] [Ewan Clague], "Agenda for meeting with Secretary of Labor," 4 November 1959, pp. 3–5, Proposed revision of the CPI, box 6, RCL-PPF 1950–1975, BLS; "Consumer Price Index Revision Program: Index concept and coverage", January 1960, p. 1, Tech memo #3, box 2, Records Relating to the 1960 Revision of the CPI, BLS.

[33] U.S. Congress, Joint Economic Committee, *The National Economic Accounts of the United States*, 85th Cong., 1st sess., Oct. 29–30, 1957.

coherent macroeconomic portrait.[34] Similar pressure came from the two organizations created by the 1946 Employment Act to pursue expanded growth, productivity, and employment: the CEA and the JEC. Early CEA chairmen such as Edwin Nourse, Keyserling, Arthur Burns (former head of the NBER), and Arthur Okun made the improvement of macroeconomic statistics a major priority.[35] Likewise, the JEC had established a Subcommittee on Economic Statistics that held a stream of hearings on that subject from the late 1950s through the 1960s, including hearings on both of the NBER reports commissioned by the OSS.

By 1959, the NBER itself was no longer the same organization that it had been under Wesley Mitchell during the interwar years. As the larger profession shifted away from institutional economics, the NBER was facing its own struggles and trying to survive by attracting researchers interested in econometric studies of macroeconomic issues (from a largely neoclassical perspective).[36] This transition was evident when the NBER selected University of Chicago economist George Stigler to lead its review of federal price statistics.[37] It was a natural choice—Stigler had written a well-received textbook on price theory and was the most relevant economist on the NBER's research staff—but it would greatly influence the outcome of the study. Stigler's graduate training at Chicago had left him deeply committed to neoclassical utility theory as the basis for microeconomics; indeed, he had included the standard constant-utility analysis of cost-of-living indexes within his price theory textbook.[38] Moreover, Stigler's return to Chicago in 1958 had sparked a transformation in his views on antitrust policy as he quickly became one of the leading critics of antitrust intervention and government regulation. In general terms, Stigler began to argue that competition was irrepressible (except by misguided government policies) and often emerged in ways that were overlooked by traditional theory and missed by conventional empirical studies (including price statistics that purported

---

[34] The NBER price report reflected this consideration, e.g., National Bureau of Economic Research, *The Price Statistics of the Federal Government: Review, Appraisal, and Recommendations* (New York: National Bureau of Economic Research, 1961), 56–58.

[35] Collins, *More*, 32–36; Julius Shiskin, "A New Role for Economic Indicators," *MLR* 100, no. 11 (1977): 3–4.

[36] On the postwar history of the NBER, see Malcolm Rutherford, "'Who's Afraid of Arthur Burns?' the NBER and the Foundations," *Journal of the History of Economic Thought* 27, no. 2 (2005): 109–139.

[37] Raymond T. Bowman, 5 February 1959, Stigler committee, box 217, SR 1940–68, OMB; Bowman to George Stigler, 12 August 1959, ibid.

[38] George J. Stigler, *The Theory of Price*, Rev. ed. (New York: Macmillan, 1952), 87–91.

to show how oligopolistic industries were "administering" prices).[39] Stigler was thereby primed to pursue what would become the two most salient and controversial conclusions of the report: that the CPI should aim to become a "constant-utility" or "welfare index," and that an index based on this framework would have registered a substantially lower inflation rate since the Second World War (due to substitution effects, quality change, and a more appropriate handling of new products).[40] The OSS gave the NBER wide latitude in creating the committee, and, consciously or not, Stigler assembled a group that was likely to (and largely did) support these claims. (For example, the committee included both Albert Rees and Richard Ruggles.)[41]

The committee's report became widely influential, in part because of its detailed staff research papers (running to over four hundred pages)

---

[39] George J. Stigler, *Memoirs of an Unregulated Economist* (New York: Basic Books, 1988), 97–112.

[40] National Bureau of Economic Research, *The Price Statistics of the Federal Government*, 52, 55, 35–39. Stigler presented his views more forcefully in the JEC hearings on the report: e.g., U.S. Congress, Joint Economic Committee, *Government Price Statistics: Hearings before the Subcommittee on Economic Statistics of the Joint Economic Committee*, 87th Cong., 1st sess., May 1–5, 1961, 531–533, esp. 533. He would later use one of the staff reports to attack claims that existing oligopolies were uncompetitive and distorted free-market pricing mechanisms: George J. Stigler, "Administered Prices and Oligopolistic Competition," in *Administered Prices: A Compendium on Public Policy*, ed. U.S. Senate. Committee on the Judiciary (Washington: U.S. GPO, 1963), 262–276, esp. 265–269.

[41] Stigler and Solomon Fabricant proposed the initial committee list. The OSS apparently requested only one replacement, asking that William Cochran (Harvard University) rather than William Kruskal (University of Chicago) be the resident statistician; Cochran was unavailable, so the slot went to Philip McCarthy (Cornell University). The OSS also requested "someone reflecting business needs and uses," which seems to have been Edward Denison, then with the Committee for Economic Development. See Solomon Fabricant to Bowman, 24 September 1959, as well as the notes attached to this letter: Stigler committee, box 217, SR 1940–68, OMB. Of the committee's seven members beyond Stigler, two (Rees and Ruggles) were on record arguing that the CPI overstated inflation. The economist representing expertise in consumer economics, Dorothy Brady, had already expressed support for a utility-based approach and would have been known to Stigler because she was good friends with Stigler's colleagues, Milton and Rose Friedman. Dorothy S. Brady, "Research on the Size Distribution of Income," in *SIW*, vol. 13 (New York: NBER, 1951), 25–27; Milton Friedman and Rose D. Friedman, *Two Lucky People: Memoirs* (Chicago: University of Chicago Press, 1998), 108–110. Irving Kravis and Boris Swerling focused on international trade and agriculture, respectively, and were unlikely to oppose a recommendation about the CPI. The committee did not make a strong endorsement of the "welfare" perspective for the Index of Prices Paid by Farmers (the parallel to the CPI). The final member, Philip McCarthy, was a statistician, not an economist. The tenor of what Kruskal might have added to the report (had he been included per Stigler's wishes) is evident from his 1960 article with Lester Telser, which drew a sharp rebuke from Ewan Clague: William H. Kruskal and Lester G. Telser, "Food Prices and the Bureau of Labor Statistics," *Journal of Business* 33, no. 3 (1960): 258–279 (Clague's commentary follows).

but especially because it exemplified how a neoclassical perspective could provide a consistent framework from which to address a range of issues in price index methodology. (Indeed, many of the report's recommendations would be echoed by the 1996 Boskin commission on the CPI.) For instance, the report argued that for infrequently purchased durable goods (e.g., appliances, furniture, automobiles, homes, etc.), "the welfare of consumers depends upon the flow of services" derived from the items each year. Accordingly, rather than focus on transaction prices (i.e., the sale price of a good), a constant-utility index should attempt to calculate the annual cost to the user of these services. In practice, this perspective became most important for homeownership, where the report suggested that the appropriate "cost" to include in the CPI was not the current price of a home but its estimated rent (what the resident would hypothetically have to pay to live there).[42] When the trajectories of rent and home prices began to diverge substantially in the 1970s, this methodological distinction would become a serious issue, as we will see in Chapter 9.

On new products, the committee argued that the "welfare gain" from innovations such as electric lighting or penicillin should be reflected in a "[constant] welfare index" as a decrease in real prices. Although the committee had no easy way to measure such gains, it suggested that a "minimum estimate" could be approximated by introducing new products into the index at an early date. Since novel goods usually appeared at very high prices which fell substantially by the time the goods became widely purchased (and would typically be included in the index), the early introduction of novel products would tend to lower the index to compensate for their welfare benefits.[43]

Finally, the committee noted the difficulty of accurately assessing quality change from a welfare perspective, but suggested three techniques. First, by selecting a "dominant characteristic" judged to be the most salient variable by consumers, a statistician could develop a quantitative measure of quality change. (In an example unlikely to be repeated today, the committee proposed the length of postoperative recuperation in a hospital as an inverse proxy for quality; shorter stays would yield lower real prices.) Second, the committee proposed "the collection and analysis of consumer appraisals of comparative qualities by means of attitudinal surveys." (Tellingly, this proposal, which highlighted the subjectivity of quality assessment, was never

---

[42] National Bureau of Economic Research, *The Price Statistics of the Federal Government*, 53–54, 46–48, 305–335.
[43] Ibid., 52–53, 37–39.

pursued by either the BLS or academic price index theorists.) Finally, the report presented what would become a focal point for research on quality change for the next four decades: a technique described by staff economist Zvi Griliches for estimating how to make quality-based price adjustments when new varieties of goods (e.g., new models of appliances, cars, etc.) directly replaced older versions.[44]

Griliches approached this problem from a distinct perspective. A survivor of the Holocaust who subsequently emigrated to Palestine and then the United States, Griliches studied agricultural economics at Berkeley before shifting to the University of Chicago for his Ph.D. and his early professorial career. At Chicago, Griliches had been trained in the department's long-standing tradition of neoclassical price theory (based on viewing consumers as utility-maximizing agents). Moreover, in his early work on agriculture economics, he had been struck by the need to account for quality when analyzing both demand for agricultural products (namely fertilizer) and the sources of growth in agricultural production.[45] In the course of his research, he discovered several earlier attempts to wrestle with this problem from a utility-based perspective, including a 1939 paper on "hedonic price indexes" by Andrew Court, an economist for the Automobile Manufacturers Association of America. (Court, not coincidentally, had been trying to illustrate how the dramatic quality increases in cars over the previous decade had created lower real prices for consumers, thereby defending the automobile industry from charges that it suppressed competition.)[46]

Adapting this work for the NBER committee and in several independent papers during the 1960s, Griliches placed Court's hedonic techniques on a firmer theoretical and mathematical basis while using the same case study: automobiles.[47] (It is unclear whether Griliches selected autos because of

[44]   Ibid., 35–37.
[45]   On Griliches' research in agricultural economics, see Zvi Griliches, "Hedonic Price Indexes and the Measurement of Capital and Productivity: Some Historical Reflections," in *Fifty Years of Economic Measurement: The Jubilee of the Conference on Research in Income and Wealth*, ed. Ernst R. Berndt and Jack E Triplett, SIW, vol. 54 (Chicago: Universiy of Chicago Press, 1990), 186–187; Banzhaf, "Quanitfying the Qualitative," 363–365.
[46]   Andrew T. Court, "Hedonic Price Indexes, with Automotive Examples," in *The Dynamics of Automobile Demand*, ed. General Motors Corporation (Detroit: General Motors Corporation, 1939), 98–119. For the context of Court's work, see the subsequent commentary by Louis Bean and the closing paper by General Motors' economist Stephen DuBrul, both in the same volume.
[47]   Zvi Griliches, "Hedonic Price Indexes for Automobiles: An Econometric Analysis of Quality Change," in *The Price Statistics of the Federal Government* (Washington, D.C.: National Bureau of Economic Research, 1961), 173–196; Irma Adelman and Zvi Griliches, "On an Index of Quality Change," *JASA* 56, no. 295 (1961): 535–538; Zvi Griliches, "Notes

the antitrust debates, because this was Court's example, or because of the widely recognized quality changes in cars and the availability of price and specification data for the industry.) The basic goal of hedonic analysis was to estimate prices for goods that were never on the market during a given period; this estimated price could then be compared to the actual price of that item at a later date to generate a price index. As Griliches explained, the hedonic approach began by regarding all commodities as "combination[s] of objectively measurable or rankable traits."[48] Regression analysis then allowed economists to use existing price data (which encompassed a range of combinations of traits) to estimate how much an item with a novel combination of traits would have cost. For example, if 1950 price data showed that each 10-horsepower increase in engine power raised the price of automobiles by 5 percent, economists could calculate hypothetical prices for novel combinations of body styles and engine powers. In this way, when a new version of commodity appeared, economists could estimate how much it might have sold for in an earlier period. Because hedonic techniques relied on market prices to gauge quality and minimized subjective judgments by economists—the fit between the data and the regression equations was the ultimate criterion—they soon became a burgeoning field for research.[49]

Yet, for all this promise, the NBER report still had not resolved the most glaring weakness of the constant-utility approach: potential changes in utility functions. Back when Andrew Court had first used hedonic indexes to highlight quality improvements in the auto industry in the late 1930s, Louis Bean (an economist with the Agriculture Department) had complained that Court had ignored how "consumers' appraisal of values and the nature of their satisfactions tend to change simultaneously with improvements," so that a physically identical car actually delivered less satisfaction over time.[50] Likewise, Griliches conceded that a strictly formulated version of the constant-utility comparison had "neither a unique nor an observable answer," and the NBER report (quietly) admitted that "the line separating taste changes from quality improvements" was hard to discern over longer

on the Measurement of Price and Quality Changes," in *Models of Income Determination*, SIW, vol. 28 (Princeton: Princeton University Press, 1964), 381–404.

[48] Adelman and Griliches, "On an Index of Quality Change," 539.

[49] For an early survey, see Zivi Griliches, "Hedonic Price Indexes Revisited," in *Price Indexes and Quality Change: Studies in New Methods of Measurement*, ed. Zivi Griliches (Cambridge: Harvard University Press, 1971), 3–15.

[50] General Motors Corporation, ed., *The Dynamics of Automobile Demand* (Detroit: General Motors Corporation, 1939), 118.

periods of time.[51] More generally, as the 1961 JEC hearings on the report made clear, the committee had not succeed in convincing most users of the index or government officials that a "constant welfare index" was a viable or useful goal for the CPI. The BLS rejected the idea entirely, and a spokesman for the Federal Statistics Users' Group reported that members were generally "skeptical of the practical usefulness of this concept." The economist-turned-senator Paul Douglas (an accomplished expert on price indexes; Chapter 3) complained that the report ignored "the fact that people themselves change," which thereby made intertemporal comparisons of utility impossible. Perhaps the strongest criticism along these lines came, not surprisingly, from union economists such as Lazare Teper, who excoriated the report for its reliance on unrealistic assumptions about human behavior:

It must be noted that the theoretical discussions underlying the construction of utility cost indexes are based on rigid hypotheses which are not always in accord with situations in the real world. It is held, for example, that over the period of time involved in the measurement, individual consumers or consuming units do not change their habits—that they do not acquire new tastes, do not change their environment, and do not age, and that they are totally resistant to advertising, salesmanship, and emulation of their neighbors.

Overall, the JEC hearings were not a ringing endorsement of what one JEC staff economist called "some esoteric college mathematician's dream of a perfect index number."[52]

In Chapter 9, we will follow the BLS's reaction to the NBER report and the continuing struggle by union economists to oppose the constant-utility approach. But, just as concern about measuring growth had created the practical motivation for binding official price statistics to the constant-utility ideal, so too would studies of growth, productivity, and inflation continue to set the context for subsequent applications of that ideal. As neoclassical economists reflected further on the ordinalist revolution, they redefined the constant-utility index in light of ordinalist critiques. In doing so, they subdued the problems posed by changing utility functions, finally gave the constant-utility ideal a firm foothold in empirical measurement, and crafted a persuasive vision of its value for macroeconomic analysis of specific industries and the economy as a whole. Paradoxically, that happened

precisely because the original idea of a constant-welfare index fit so poorly
with what macroeconomists had long been trying to measure.

WELFARE, GROWTH, AND THE CONSTANT-UTILITY INDEX, 1960–

The key to understanding the history of the constant-utility index after 1960
is recognizing a theme that we have encountered throughout this book: the
desire of many economists to eliminate subjective judgments from economic
measurement, especially when such judgments have potentially normative
ramifications. In part, this desire stemmed from general epistemological
goals, such as making economics more "scientific" in the supposed mold of
the natural sciences. But more generally, it was a function of the growing
ties between economics and policy. If economists were to claim that their
discipline had any claim to neutral, technical knowledge, surely that claim
required them to have neutral, apolitical facts—namely economic statistics.
Certainly Wesley Mitchell had felt that way, and a similar view underlay
Milton Friedman's famous 1953 distinction between positive (descriptive)
and normative (evaluative) economics, a distinction which continues to
govern many economists' conception of their discipline. Moreover, for government statistics in particular, avoiding subjective, potentially normative
judgments appeared essential; to do otherwise, as we have seen, would seem
to undermine the rationalized foundation of modern political economy.[53]

One resource for avoiding subjective judgments was a professional
imperative, that is, a demand by one's colleagues to reason according to
certain principles or methods. For institutional economists, that imperative
frequently took a methodological form: concepts should be operationally
defined (if you cannot measure utility, don't use it); statistics should isolate particular variables (don't combine changing prices and quantities in

---

[53] For an account that emphasizes "historical anxieties" and "disillusion with politics" to
explain economists' attraction to a natural science model, see Dorothy Ross, *The Origins of
American Social Science* (Cambridge, New York: Cambridge University Press, 1991), 390–
427. By contrast, for an analysis that views the objectivity as a response to political pres-
sures, see Theodore M. Porter, *Trust in Numbers: The Pursuit of Objectivity in Science and
Public Life* (Princeton: Princeton University Press, 1995). On Mitchell, see Guy Alchon,
The Invisible Hand of Planning: Capitalism, Social Science, and the State in the 1920s
(Princeton: Princeton University Press, 1985); Jeff Biddle, "Social Science and the Making
of Social Policy: Wesley Mitchell's Vision," in *The Economic Mind in America: Essays in the
History of American Economics*, ed. Malcolm Rutherford (New York: Routledge, 1998),
43–79. For Friedman's views, see Milton Friedman, *Essays in Positive Economics* (Chicago:
University of Chicago Press, 1953).

a single index). Empirically minded neoclassical economists kept modified versions of these methodological commitments (utility need not be measurable but its consequences for behavior should), and added theoretical components, especially a commitment to neoclassical microeconomic theory (consumers as utility maximizers). For cost-of-living indexes, however, these imperatives placed them in a bind: a constant-utility index was surely the proper form for a cost-of-living index, but the idea that one could compare "welfare" in two different contexts without introducing subjective (and probably normative) judgments seemed implausible at best.

As we will see, the solution to this dilemma involved reformulating the constant-utility index in ordinalist terms, which thereby eliminated the normative overtones that comparing welfare implied. Initially, this change resulted from efforts to secure the theoretical foundations of neoclassical price index theory by more narrowly delimiting the objective for cost-of-living indexes. With that goal accomplished, however, it was fortuitous that subsequent attempts to apply the approach occurred primarily among economists working on empirical studies of inflation, productivity, or macroeconomic growth, and not on labor economics, poverty assessment, or the design of social insurance programs. Unlike the use of cost-of-living statistics for wage or income adjustments, no individuals (and no transfers of wealth) were directly affected by macroeconomic calculations, making it far easier for macroeconomists to sustain a more constrained notion of a constant-utility index. Indeed, as we will see later in this chapter, many economists who were committed to the constant-utility ideal had qualms about using such an index for income adjustment. The net effect of this dynamic was to bind the constant-utility index—and, by extension, the CPI—more tightly to macroeconomic analysis, for here was a domain where the utility framework could provide real benefits (consideration of changing quality, new goods, etc.) and where welfare could be discussed in non-normative terms without the paradox of that combination causing serious tension.

Welfare and the National Accounts

We can begin by considering the place of welfare in the basic statistical framework for assessing economic growth: the U.S. national accounts. "National accounts" is the generic name for a statistical system that provides a coherent and consistent way to assess a nation's economic activity, especially its production. These calculations provide the source for commonly cited measurements of economic growth, such as national income, GNP, and Gross Domestic Product (GDP). Although national income accounting has a long history, the current U.S. system was created by the Department of Commerce during the 1940s. Befitting that setting, the accounts assess growth through what the economist Amartya Sen has called "opulence"—in other words, more stuff.[54] As one economist put it in 1945, the accounts were "not trying to measure welfare but the value of production from a business point of view."[55] We have encountered this perspective before, albeit on the consumer side, namely among institutional economists who rejected utility as a basis for economic statistics and who defined standards of living as fixed collections of goods (Chapter 3). It should therefore be no surprise that the national accounts system was devised largely by institutional economists associated with Wesley Mitchell's NBER, nor that they had their own debate about the merits of welfare when measuring economic growth and production.[56]

The most famous early argument about welfare and the national accounts occurred between Simon Kuznets, an NBER economist who had vastly improved estimates of national income during the 1930s, and the economists in the Department of Commerce, notably one of Kuznets's students, Milton Gilbert. Kuznets was steeped in the tradition of institutional economics; nevertheless, when it came to calculating national income and national product, he was convinced that meaningful measures could "be defined only in relation to some end-goal of economic activity."[57] Necessarily, that introduced a normative element, and befitting Kuznets's institutionalist leanings, he felt deep misgivings about his own conclusion. He recognized that "the practical difficulties" facing such a project were "formidable" and, even more troubling, that the resulting estimates would "transcen[d] the limits of objective measurement" and would likely "never be more than reflections of the value judgments of an individual investigator." Still, he

---

54 Amartya Kumar Sen, *The Standard of Living* (New York: Cambridge University Press, 1987), 14–16.

55 Milton Gilbert, quoted in Mark Perlman, "Political Purpose and National Accounts," in *The Politics of Numbers*, ed. William Alonso and Paul Starr (New York: Russell Sage Foundation, 1987), 150.

56 On the early history of the national accounts, see Carol S. Carson, "The History of the United States National Income and Product Accounts: The Development of an Analytical Tool," *Review of Income & Wealth* 21, no. 2 (1975): 153–181; Perlman, "Political Purpose and the National Accounts," 133–151; Mark Perlman and Morgan Marietta, "The Politics of Social Accounting: Public Goals and the Evolution of the National Accounts in Germany, the United Kingdom and the United States," *Review of Political Economy* 17, no. 2 (2005): 211–230.

57 Simon Kuznets, "National Income: A New Version," *The Review of Economics and Statistics* 30, no. 3 (1948): 151.

remained convinced that only measures with normative ends could fit the historical meaning and tradition of national income research.[58]

According to Kuznets, the *National Income and Product Statistics* published by the Department of Commerce in 1947 (the project which finally established the U.S. national accounts) had a very different goal, namely measuring "the total output of the economy, with a proper view of the significant sectors and least duplication" (in other words: how much had been produced, by whom, and where it went).[59] Gilbert and his colleagues concurred with Kuznets's description of the divide: they had aimed to measure "total production at any given time"; Kuznets was searching for "comparisons of economic welfare." But such comparisons could not be made objectively (for they could not be deduced solely from behavior); accordingly, Kuznets's proposals would introduce a "moralistic flavor" that was "not in the tradition of quantitative economics."[60]

By contrast, Gilbert argued, the Department of Commerce's approach sidestepped these "moralistic" judgments. More generally, its focus on "total production" (opulence) meshed easily with political economy during this period: the Depression (with its spectacle of idled plants, desolate farming communities, and impoverished urban families), wartime mobilization (with its single-minded focus on maximum production), and the early postwar era (where, as we have seen with Keyserling, "growth" could equally describe the increased production necessary for raising standards of living among the poor or for funding military expeditions). Of course, it was precisely this flexible ambiguity that bothered Kuznets, who insisted on the need to differentiate between the objectives of peacetime and wartime economies and to construct different accounting systems for each.[61] Yet in the end, the Department of Commerce's view prevailed, since it, after all, was responsible for publishing the calculations.

Predictably, the economists who had helped to develop the national accounts system were less enthusiastic about the 1961 NBER report or the ongoing attempt to base price indexes on ideas such as welfare or utility. Prior to the appearance of the NBER review, Milton Gilbert had already attacked utility-based assessments of quality because of their potential to introduce "non-economic" factors such as "a change in style or taste" into

[58] Ibid., 161–162.
[59] Ibid., 161.
[60] Milton Gilbert et al., "Objectives of National Income Measurement: A Reply to Professor Kuznets," *The Review of Economics and Statistics* 30, no. 3 (1948): 189.
[61] Simon Kuznets, *National Product in Wartime* (New York: NBER, 1945), 1–32; Kuznets, "National Income," 156–157.

"the measures of output and price changes that are useful to the study of economic growth." As Gilbert put it, "economic welfare as a measurable idea must be restricted to telling us if we are better off only by our having more goods."[62] When Griliches published his hedonic study, the two men engaged in a short exchange in which Gilbert insisted that introducing utility into price indexes would destroy their relevance for measuring output. To borrow Gilbert's example, if quality became synonymous with satisfaction,

> it would be equally valid to count the few bits of fabric and elastic of present day bathing attire as equal in output to the costumes of earlier days that fully covered the body as well as the arms and knees—since no modern girl in a bikini would admit to less satisfaction on the beach than was obtained by her fully-clothed grandmother. And should this trend reach its limit of no costumes at all, we would still have to say that swimsuit production had not fallen, even though the industry was out of business.[63]

In a related vein, two other national accounts experts who had participated in the debate with Kuznets, George Jaszi and Edward Denison, argued that Griliches' hedonic techniques were not in fact a full-blown "welfare" interpretation of quality and that this was a good thing, since such interpretations raised numerous problems, required value judgments, and were inherently subjective.[64]

In part, economists overcame the critiques raised by older national accounts experts such as Gilbert or Denison by recognizing that measures of output and measures of input (whether consumer purchases or capital goods for production) required two different frameworks: utility was appropriate for input, but output was better served by resource cost.[65] (To take Gilbert's swimsuit example, output of the swimsuit industry would be adjusted by the cost of resources required for production; if, *ceteris paribus,*

---

[62] Milton Gilbert, "Quality Changes and Index Numbers," *Economic Development and Cultural Change* 9, no. 3 (1961): 287–288.

[63] Milton Gilbert, "Quality Change and Index Numbers: The Reply," *MLR* 85, no. 5 (1962): 545.

[64] See comments in Griliches, "Notes on the Measurement of Price and Quality Changes," 404–418, esp. 410–413, 416. Denison was a member of the NBER review committee, but, perhaps significantly, he was one of only two eventual members not on the initial list proposed by George Stigler (see n. 41 above). To my knowledge, Denison was the only committee member who later criticized Griliches's work on hedonic indexes and its utility framework.

[65] Jack E. Triplett, "Concept of Quality in Input and Output Price Measures: A Resolution of the User-Value Resource-Costs Debate," in *The U.S. National Income and Product Accounts,* ed. M. F. Foss, SIW, vol. 47 (Chicago: University of Chicago Press, 1983).

the resources needed to produce the bathing dress cost five times as much as those for the bikini, it would require five bikinis to equal a single bathing dress.) But this differentiation could not eliminate the whole problem, because the national accounts experts were unhappy with utility even on the consumer side of the balances. Gilbert complained that concepts such as "the level of [consumer] satisfaction" clearly fell "outside the realm of economic measurement." Moreover, introducing these notions would disconnect changes in price and quantity measurements from changes in tangible goods, leading to ambiguous situations: it "would be the same as saying that if someone gives up smoking and gets an equivalent sense of satisfaction from this self-denial, he has maintained his real consumption and benefitted from a price decline."[66]

In Griliches' view, Gilbert's concerns were foolish because they missed the foundation of economic value in the first place: "[I]t should be clear that 'goods' do not mean much independently of a welfare or utility calculus. Nor does it make sense to restrict welfare and 'economic growth' measures to goods-only-based output measures." Indeed, by constraining measures of growth to such a framework, economists would miss many forms of "technological advance" that brought increased welfare to consumers. Moreover, Griliches turned complaints about the subjective judgments supposedly inherent in a utility-based approach back on his critics: the quality adjustment techniques promoted by Commerce Department veterans such as Gilbert, Jaszi, and Denison were, in operational terms, filled with subjective judgments (much like the BLS procedures discussed in Chapter 6). By contrast, hedonic methods provided a strictly empirical means to adjust for quality by estimating prices for novel goods, a procedure that Griliches continued to justify in terms of utility, though he also conceded that the methods did not have "an unambiguous welfare interpretation."[67]

The merits of these arguments aside, it was nevertheless clear that fully embracing a notion of value based on utility (at least in its cardinal form) was incompatible with a statistical system dedicated to measuring "total production." As both Gilbert and Kuznets had recognized, welfare and productive output might not move hand in hand; indeed, as we have seen earlier, within a cardinal utility framework, it was entirely possible that the same set of goods might bring less welfare over time. Yet, Griliches'

[66] Gilbert, "Quality Changes and Index Numbers," 291–294.
[67] Griliches, "Notes on the Measurement of Price and Quality Changes," 402, 414–417. Makoto Ohta and Zivi Griliches, "Automobile Prices Revisited: Extensions of the Hedonic Hypothesis," in *Household Production and Consumption*, ed. Nestor E. Terleckyj, SIW, vol. 40 (New York: Columbia University Press, 1975), 326.

argument was becoming harder and harder to resist: following the end of the Second World War, institutional economics (the standpoint for both Kuznets and Gilbert) increasingly disappeared from American universities, while neoclassical utility theory grew to dominate microeconomics and the theory of demand.[68] Accordingly, if macroeconomic statistics were to be conceptually linked to microeconomics, utility would need to enter the system, at least in analyses of consumer expenditures.

The eventual reconciliation between utility and a model of "total production" was twofold. First, following the lines of hedonic analysis itself, goods were treated as collections of characteristics. Rather than more goods per se, "more" now meant greater numbers (or greater intensities) of desirable characteristics. This simple but elegant transformation cleared away a number of vexing problems surrounding quality adjustment.[69] Second, price index theorists reconsidered how the ordinalist revolution affected their work, a shift that could finally free them from the vagaries of changing utility functions.

Completing the Ordinalist Revolution

For cost-of-living indexes, the first generation of ordinalist economists had largely contented themselves with substituting "preferences" for cardinal concepts of utility. Yet the methodological critique at the heart of the ordinalist revolution would prompt a deeper reformulation of the traditional constant-utility index in the late 1960s and 1970s. To understand its basis, we need to examine the issue where the ordinalist revolution made its first, and clearest, inroads: interpersonal comparison of utilities. Consider two individuals, both of whom prefer A to B, and B to C. Under an ordinalist view, we can state that if both individuals substitute B for C, then they will both be better off. But will they be equally "better off"? Such a question requires cardinal values: for example, Consumer 1 gets five additional units of utility by substituting B for C, while Consumer 2 only receives three units. Naturally, ordinalists struck at this point: how could these magnitudes be verified? How could I compare my experience of satisfaction to

[68] Mary S. Morgan and Malcolm Rutherford, eds., *From Interwar Pluralism to Postwar Neoclassicism* (Durham: Duke University Press, 1998).
[69] Triplett, "Concept of Quality in Input and Output Price Measures," 269–311. The characteristics approach built on Kelvin Lancaster's earlier work in the theory of consumer demand: Kelvin Lancaster, *Consumer Demand: A New Approach* (New York: Columbia University Press, 1971).

yours, which I have never felt? A strict ordinal interpretation necessarily precluded such interpersonal comparisons of utility levels.

By the 1950s, many American economists had absorbed the basic ordinalist critique, but they had yet to make a further leap that would have substantial implications for price index theory: the same logic that denied the viability of inter*personal* comparisons of utility levels also vitiated inter*temporal* comparisons.[70] Suppose the two consumers from our example are not two individuals at the same time but a single individual at two different times. Even if relative preferences remain the same, can we assume (as John R. Hicks had done in 1940) that this person is equally "well off" with B in both situations? (Perhaps, for example, B is still preferred to C, but because it is now consumed in a new environment, it has nevertheless become less useful or desirable than it had been previously.) I may consistently describe steak as my favorite food, but does that mean I derive the same satisfaction from steak when I am fifty as when I am twenty? How could one answer such a question? Observing my choices in the marketplace does not suffice.[71] Likewise, introspection is inadequate, and even if I recorded my impressions and assigned equal ratings to my steak meals at both ages, can we conclude that I experienced the same satisfaction? (It seems probable, for example, that such ratings are contingent on context and previous experience, both of which are constantly changing.)[72] In a strong ordinalist view, the subjective experience of my past self is as inaccessible as that of another person; comparing subjective experiences (whether interpersonally or intertemporally) is simply impossible.

If we now view price indexes through the full ordinalist perspective, we can see the need to reformulate the constant-utility framework. In early presentations, neoclassical economists had proposed finding the amount of money required *today* to make a consumer "as well off" as he or she was

---

[70] Stapleford, "Aftershocks from a Revolution."

[71] Suppose that both prices and my income are the same in both periods but that I spend $100 less on steak at age fifty, reducing my annual consumption by 15 pounds. This change indicates that the marginal (additional) utility that I would derive from the last 15 pounds of steak at age fifty is less than the utility that I derive from $100 of other goods. In turn, we can assert that over the previous three decades the marginal utility provided by the last 15 pounds of steak has declined relative to the marginal utility provided by $100 of the other goods. But we don't know whether I am less satisfied with the 15 pounds of steak by age fifty or whether I am deriving more satisfaction from the other goods than I did three decades ago. Observation of purchasing habits can indicate whether relative preferences have changed between one period and the next, but it does not let us compare the levels of satisfaction (utility) derived from goods during those two times.

[72] For example, see the research on self-reported well-being in Kahneman, Diener, and Schwarz, *Well-Being*.

yesterday.[73] But of course that objective required comparing utility levels in two different time periods. As argued in 1968 by two of the strongest proponents of an ordinalist perspective for index numbers, Franklin M. Fisher and Karl Shell, such questions were simply "unanswerable" and "completely without any operational content whatsoever." Instead, the careful economist would substitute a different question, asking how a given consumer (fixed in time and space and hence with a stable utility function) might regard two hypothetical sets of goods, prices, and incomes. For example, take a consumer with 1960 tastes and a certain income. In theory, an ordinalist cost-of-living index would tell you how much additional money such a consumer would require in order to be equally content shopping among 1975 goods at 1975 prices versus shopping among 1960 goods at 1960s prices. Of course, that might not be the same amount that this consumer would require to feel as "as well off" in 1975 as he or she had in 1960, since the consumer's tastes might have changed dramatically over the interim in response to a very different economic and social environment. But such comparisons were no longer the concern of a true cost-of-living index; after all, (in the ordinalist view) they were impossible anyway.[74]

The ordinalist analysis therefore redefined the objective of constant-utility indexes. No longer did these indexes seek to compare the minimum cost of obtaining the same "wants-satisfaction" (as Konüs had put it) in two time periods. Instead, they permitted economists to evaluate two sets of prices and goods (abstracted from their real environments) from the perspective of a consumer fixed in time and space.

Naturally, this redefinition also altered what counted as the right answer for a "true cost-of-living index," and that shift had important consequences. For example, recall that the agricultural economist Louis Bean had objected to the first use of hedonic indexes in the 1930s by arguing that consumer "satisfactions" and "appraisal of values" for automobiles probably changed

[73] Cf. Frisch, "Problem of Index Numbers," 11–12.

[74] Franklin M. Fisher and Karl Shell, *The Economic Theory of Price Indices* (New York: Academic Press, 1972), 4, 3. The original version of this paper appeared in 1968. For similar views, see Robbins, *Essay on the Nature and Significance of Economic Science*, 59–62; R.G.D. Allen, *Index Numbers in Theory and Practice* (Chicago: Aldine, 1975), 265–266. From 1970 onward, leading neoclassical price index theorists regularly defined cost-of-living indexes in terms compatible with an ordinalist perspective: e.g., W. E. Diewert, "The Theory of the Cost-of-Living Index and the Measurement of Welfare Change," in *Price Level Measurement: Proceedings from a Conference Sponsored by Statistics Canada*, ed. W. E. Diewert and C. Montmarquette (Ottawa: Minister of Supply and Services Canada, 1983), 167–168; Robert A. Pollak, *The Theory of the Cost of Living Index* (New York: Oxford University Press, 1989), 6.

Table 8.1: *Hypothetical Comparison of Automobiles, 1925 vs. 1935.*

We assume here that consumers continue to desire the same relative characteristics in cars (more power, more comfort, more gadgets, etc.) but that the utility which they derive from any given piece of equipment depends upon its relative prevalence in the marketplace. As features become standard, they provide less satisfaction than when originally introduced.

Year	Nominal Price	Features	Consumer Satisfaction
1925	Same	Slower, fewer amenities	Same
1935	Same	More powerful, more amenities	Same

as technological improvements became more widespread, such that a car with standard features from 1925 would bring far less satisfaction in 1935.[75] Push Bean's hypothesis to an extreme by supposing that as manufacturers improved automobiles during 1925–1935, consumer expectations kept pace, so that a standard, 1935 automobile brought the same "satisfaction" to 1935 consumers as the 1925 version had to contemporaries. To further simplify matters, suppose that the nominal price of a car remained constant during this period (see Table 8.1).

Under the original (cardinal) version of the constant-utility approach, a true cost-of-living index would show no change in the real price for automobiles from 1925 to 1935; the same amount of money would deliver the same satisfaction. Assuming stable utility functions (as Andrew Court had done) would thereby give the wrong answer, mistakenly showing a decline in real prices.

But what if we approach this scenario using an ordinalist perspective? Now, Bean's critique is rendered irrelevant, for his hypothesis is unverifiable and a proper cost-of-living index would not compare consumer satisfaction anyway. Rather, it would compare prices and features for 1925 automobiles against prices and features for 1935 automobiles, using either the perspective of a 1925 consumer or a 1935 consumer. Either choice (1925 tastes or 1935 tastes) would show a decline in real prices: both 1925 consumers and 1935 consumers would prefer to own 1935 automobiles, which were more powerful and had more amenities. Bean's concern, of course, was that even when consumers' relative preferences remained stable (they always want more powerful cars), the utility that they derived from any given good

---

[75] General Motors Corporation, ed., *The Dynamics of Automobile Demand*, 118.

might depend greatly on the context.[76] The ordinalist approach bypassed such critiques by avoiding temporal comparisons of utility; accordingly, it excised from cost-of-living calculations the possibility that the standard of living provided by a set of goods might be (in part) relative to the economic and social environment in which those goods were used. Though Bean's hypothetical consumers required the same amount of money to derive the same satisfaction from an automobile purchase in 1935 as they had in 1925, that result would never appear in an ordinalist constant-utility index, which would instead show declining real prices.

The ordinalist reformulation did not eliminate the consequences of altered tastes: economists still had to choose whether to use current tastes, base-period tastes, or something in between. Nor did it make it possible to calculate an exact constant-utility index: the ordinalist version of Konüs's theorem, for example, described how to find an upper limit for a constant-utility index that followed base-period tastes, but the theorem did not provide a lower limit (because the extent of consumer substitution was unknown). Yet major theoretical innovations from the 1970s onward (notably by Erwin Diewert) tightened the bounds on ordinalist constant-utility indexes, while empirical investigations illustrated that consumer substitution (in an ordinalist framework) had only minor effects.[77]

Most crucially, the ordinalist view avoided the pitfalls that had worried traditional macroeconomists such as Milton Gilbert. Recall Gilbert's complaint that a utility-based price index would fall (despite no change in nominal prices) when someone gave up smoking and got "an equivalent sense of satisfaction from this self-denial" at less cost. The ordinalist formulation

---

[76] Note again that Bean's hypothesis cannot be refuted simply by observing prices and consumer expenditures. Say that consumers spend the same proportion of their income on automobiles in 1925 as 1935. This would suggest that relative preferences for automobiles (versus other goods) have not changed. Likewise, we have stipulated that consumers continue to have the same relative preferences for features in automobiles (more power, more gadgets, etc.). Of course, in 1935, cars with standard features from 1925 now sell at a fraction of their 1925 prices. Does this mean that real prices have fallen (the standard, ordinal interpretation)? Or does it mean that cars with 1925 features now provide 1935 consumers with less "satisfaction" relative to other goods, and hence that they will now devote a lower percentage of their income to such vehicles (Bean's hypothesis)?

[77] W. E. Diewert, "Exact and Superlative Index Numbers," *Journal of Econometrics* 4, no. 2 (1976): 115–145; W. E. Diewert, "The Consumer Price Index and Index Number Purpose," *Journal of Economic and Social Measurement* 27 (2001): 169–174, 229–230; Steven D. Braithwaite, "The Substitution Bias of the Laspeyres Price Index: An Analysis Using Estimated Cost-of-Living Indexes," *AER* 70, no. 1 (1980): 64–77; Marilyn E. Manser and Richard J. McDonald, "An Analysis of Substitution Bias in Measuring Inflation, 1959–85," *Econometrica* 56, no. 4 (1988): 909–930.

sidestepped this problem: one would choose either smoking or post-smoking tastes, and either selection would show no change in real prices. The ordinalist approach therefore made a constant-utility index more compatible with existing treatments of national income. More generally, by transforming the goal of a constant-utility index, the ordinalist perspective turned taste change—what had been the most common and debilitating objection to the constant-utility ideal—into a relatively minor issue.

The Union of Price Index Theory with Studies of Growth

The new confidence in constant-utility approaches came none too soon, for it arrived just as macroeconomists were facing a series of crises that would prompt a reevaluation of favorite (and competing) policy doctrines, such as the 1960s, growth-oriented Keynesianism or the strict monetarism advocated by the University of Chicago's Milton Friedman. In 1965, price indexes began to rise, and later that decade measures of aggregate output showed reduced rates of growth. By the early 1970s, a combination of the Vietnam War, rapid increases in spending for social programs, and several external supply shocks (oil, drought) had sent the economy down paths that most economists had hitherto deemed impossible: rising prices and rising unemployment.[78] Equally troubling, productivity statistics indicated much slower expansion than in the previous decade, and neither growth nor productivity rates fully recovered when the recession ended. Debates over the causes of the slowdown captivated macroeconomists (unions? regulation? economic policy? the energy crisis? technological stagnation?). As in the late 1950s, there were some suggestions that the long-term slowdown was a statistical illusion caused in part by failure to adequately account for quality improvements. Although the most searching analyses suggested that statistical errors were unlikely to explain the full problem, the controversy did re-focus attention on the problems of technological change in economic statistics. Here, the microelectronics industry took center stage as electronic calculators and personal computers replaced automobiles as the examples of choice for those wishing to highlight radical transformations in quality.[79]

---

[78] For a near contemporary view of these events and their consequences for macroeconomic theory, see Robert J. Gordon, "Postwar Macroeconomics: The Evolution of Ideas and Events," in *The American Economy in Transition*, ed. Martin Feldstein (Chicago: University of Chicago Press, 1980). For a broader assessment, see Bernstein, *A Perilous Progress*, 148–162.

[79] On the slowdown in general, see Edward F. Denison, *Accounting for Slower Economic Growth: The United States in the 1970* (Washington, D.C.: Brookings Institution, 1979);

As before, attention to quantifying quality improvement had a corollary application in antitrust cases. In 1969, the U.S. government charged IBM with violating the 1890 Sherman Act, beginning a long-running series of litigations that lasted until the government abandoned its case in 1982. As part of its defense, IBM relied on the expert testimony of Franklin Fisher, who used hedonic techniques to illustrate that IBM computers had lower "price/performance" ratios than many of the company's competitors.[80] Undoubtedly, this episode contributed to IBM's willingness to collaborate with the Bureau of Economic Analysis in the Department of Commerce to develop a hedonic price index for computer technology in the mid-1980s, which became the first major, highly visible application of hedonic analysis in the national accounts. The dramatic results showed computer prices falling at an astonishing rate (between 15 percent to 20 percent each year) and had equally important consequences for measures of productivity in the high-tech industry (since output was deflated by the new price index). A 1995 study by Andrew W. Wyckoff illustrated that countries that used hedonic deflators for computer technology showed much greater rates of price declines for relevant industries and correspondingly greater productivity growth. Naturally, these results sparked new interest in hedonic analysis.[81]

The impact of quality adjustments on productivity measures is also a useful reminder, though, that quantifying innovation did not have univocal

John W. Kendrick, *International Comparisons of Productivity and Causes of the Slowdown* (Cambridge: Ballinger, 1984). An early suggestion that faulty statistics were to blame (with computers as the example) is Peter K. Clark, "Inflation and the Productivity Decline," *AER* 72, no. 2 (1982): 152. For more skeptical and searching considerations of computers, statistical methodology, and the slowdown, see Martin Neil Baily and Robert J. Gordon, "The Productivity Slowdown, Measurement Issues, and the Explosion of Computer Power," *Brookings Papers on Economic Activity* 1988, no. 2 (1988): 347–431; Jack E. Triplett, "Economic Statistics, the New Economy, and the Productivity Slowdown," *Business Economics* 34, no. 2 (1999): 13–17.

[80] Franklin M. Fisher, John J. McGowan, and Joen E. Greenwood, *Folded, Spindled, and Mutilated: Economic Analysis and U.S. V. IBM* (Cambridge: MIT Press, 1983), 139–163. Fisher had no strong objections to antitrust prosecutions per se; he would later serve as a government expert in testimony against Microsoft. For his account of the differences between these cases, see Franklin M. Fisher, "The IBM and Microsoft Cases: What's the Difference?" *AER* 90, no. 2 (2000): 180–183.

[81] The national accounts had previously incorporated a hedonic index for deflating investment in houses which had been developed by the U.S. Census Bureau; however, this index did not have the same high visibility or impact. David W. Cartwright, "Improved Deflation of Purchases of Computers," *Survey of Current Business* 66, no. 3 (1986): 7–9; Andrew W. Wyckoff, "The Impact of Computer Prices on International Comparisons of Labour Productivity," *Economics of Innovation and New Technology* 3 (1995): 277–293; Jack E. Triplett, "Hedonic Indexes and Statistical Agencies, Revisited," *Journal of Economic and Social Measurement* 27 (2001): 133–141.

political ramifications. In the mid-1980s, for example, the economic sociologists Fred Block and Gene Burns argued that failures of productivity measures to account properly for quality improvements contributed to the political success of conservative attacks on unions and government regulation from the 1970s into the 1980s, since both unions and state oversight were blamed for stunting growth. (Similarly, when unions sought productivity statistics for the auto industry to use in contract negotiations during the 1950s, auto executives adopted the quality-change problem as an excuse to not cooperate with BLS efforts to produce these estimates.)[82] Rather than resolving political debates, the emphasis on quality change tended to change the focus for arguments and direct discussion toward different areas.

Computers were the most prominent site for the study of quality change and price measurement, but economists pursued research on a range of other goods as well, with attention to quality issues in academic circles far outstripping the implementation of novel techniques in official statistics. (We will return to the latter point in Chapter 9.) Reading through the post-1960 literature on empirical studies of economic growth, productivity, and quality change in price indexes makes it evident how much the last issue owed to the first two. The annual Conference on Research in Income and Wealth (CRIW), created by the NBER in the 1930s to pursue research relevant to national income and accounts, proved to be a central forum for binding these topics together, and indeed a source for some of the most important papers on quality change and price indexes. Academic economists such as Griliches, Dale Jorgenson, Richard Ruggles, Erwin Diewert, Edward Denison, Robert J. Gordon, Charles Hulten, and Ernst Berndt (all of whom would be important contributors to the study of quality change and price index theory) appeared and reappeared in the conference proceedings, weaving through multiple topics: capital formation, national accounts, economic growth, studies of productivity, and, of course, price measurements. Although the CRIW occasionally pursued other topics, such as "equity," "well-being," or poverty research, these gatherings were less likely to feature leading figures from the study of quality change.[83]

The composition of the 1996 Boskin commission on the CPI (convened by the Senate Finance Committee) illustrates this convergence. All five

---

[82] Fred Block and Gene A. Burns, "Productivity as a Social Problem: The Uses and Misuses of Social Indicators," *American Sociological Review* 51, no. 6 (1986): 774–776. On the auto industry and productivity measures, see U.S. Senate, Committee on the Judiciary, *Administered Prices*, 2587, 2653.

[83] My comments abour the CRIW are based on a survey of *Studies in Income and Wealth* (*SIW*, the annual conference proceedings) from vol. 31 (1967) through vol. 62 (2001).

members were CRIW participants, and four of them came to the study of quality change primarily through a broader focus on growth and productivity in technologically innovative contexts. By his own account, Zvi Griliches' attention to hedonic price indexes derived largely from his interest in "the measurement of productivity and technological change," an area that remained his dominant focus throughout his career.[84] Like Griliches, Dale Jorgenson was also a leading researcher in empirical studies of productivity and economic growth, and in fact had collaborated with Griliches to introduce quality change into productivity measurements during the 1960s.[85] Robert J. Gordon had similarly built his reputation through macroeconomic analyses of growth, productivity, and inflation in which accounting for innovation remained a persistent theme.[86] Ellen Dulberger, an IBM economist (and the only representative employed outside academia), had written her dissertation on hedonic price indexes while helping to create the hedonic indexes for computers in the national accounts system.[87] Indeed, the only commission member who had not spent extensive time conducting empirical research on growth, productivity, or technological change was Michael Boskin himself. Not coincidentally, Boskin had also produced little research on price indexes; his appointment as chairman likely reflected his tenure as chairman of the Council of Economic Advisers under George H.W. Bush and his long-standing advocacy of (conservative) Social Security reform.[88] It is small wonder, in these circumstances, that the Boskin commission's official report reiterated the major themes of the NBER review from nearly thirty years before, that it so readily (and with no qualification) embraced the

---

[84] Griliches, "Notes on the Measurement of Price and Quality Changes," 382. For a short survey of Griliches's contributions to economic analysis, see Manuel Trajtenberg and Ernst R. Berndt, "Zvi Griliches (1930–1999)," *Journal of Economic & Social Measurement* 27, no. 3/4 (2001): 93–97.

[85] A good sense of the central roles played by Griliches and Jorgenson in research on productivity measurement can be seen through John W. Kendrick and Beatrice N. Vaccara, "Introduction," in *New Developments in Productivity Measurement and Analysis*, ed. John W. Kendrick and Beatrice N. Vaccara, SIW, vol. 44 (Chicago: University of Chicago Press, 1980), 1–6. Beginning in the mid-1970s, Jorgenson began pursuing research on welfare from a cardinal utility perspective. His original and highly sophisticated approach involved aggregating individual demand functions (characterized by demographic traits) into aggregate functions; nevertheless, it did not escape the constraints of stable utility functions. Dale W. Jorgenson, *Welfare* (Cambridge: MIT Press, 1997).

[86] Gordon, *The Measurement of Durable Goods Prices*. Gordon's macroeconomics text has gone through ten editions since 1978.

[87] Ellen R. Dulberger, "An Hedonic Price Equation for Computers" (Ph.D. dissertation, City College of CUNY, 1986).

[88] For a mid-career summary of his views on Social Security, see Michael J. Boskin, *Too Many Promises: The Uncertain Future of Social Security* (Homewood: Dow Jones-Irwin, 1986).

constant-utility approach as an objective for the CPI, and that it emphasized how quality change and new products led the CPI to overstate inflation.[89]

MACROECONOMIC ANALYSIS, INCOME ADJUSTMENT, AND THE CONSTANT-UTILITY INDEX

The current theoretical and methodological foundations for the constant-utility approach (especially in its ordinalist formulation) are surely more robust and pragmatic than either the original version or the traditional constant-goods index. No doubt they also help (as deflators) to produce a better measure of consumers' material wealth, at least when understood as opulence (more). Yet the historical function of the CPI has been wage and income adjustment, a function that it continues to fulfill on an extraordinary scale today. Since discussions about price index theory and methodology after 1960 were increasingly led by economists focused on other applications, this divergence returns us to a question first considered during the Second World War (Chapters 5 and 6): can a single measure serve both macroeconomic analysis and income adjustment?

Economists have recognized (though not always emphasized) one area where these two functions collide: deciding how to aggregate data across all consumers in the index. Wealthier households spend more money; hence, if the national index is calculated using aggregate data (as is typically the case), the purchases of wealthy households will carry greater weight (a formulation known as a "plutocratic" index). By contrast, one could imagine a national index that is an average of each household's individual cost-of-living index. In this version (a "democratic" index), the far more numerous lower- and middle-income households would have a greater effect on the overall result. Because the use of aggregate expenditure data makes it much easier to compute a plutocratic index, all major consumer price indexes follow this form. Moreover, this is the proper basis for deflating aggregate expenditures in calculations such as the national accounts. Yet it will be less reflective of the experiences of lower-income households, a pattern that would be even worse if (as the NBER committee and the Boskin commission recommended) the new, high-priced goods typically purchased by wealthier families are introduced into the index more rapidly.[90]

[89] Michael J. Boskin et al., *Toward a More Accurate Measure of the Cost of Living: Final Report to the Senate Finance Committee from the Advisory Commission to Study the Consumer Price Index* (Washington, D.C.: U.S. GPO, 1996).

[90] S. J. Prais, "Whose Cost of Living?" *The Review of Economic Studies* 26, no. 2 (1959): 126–134; J. L. Nicholson, "Whose Cost of Living?" *Journal of the Royal Statistical Society* 138,

More fundamentally, some economists have begun to wonder whether the constant-utility objective is even a proper basis for income adjustment. Surprisingly, neoclassical economists devoted little attention to this question during most of the twentieth century, perhaps because few leading theorists spent their time studying applications involving income adjustments, whether labor negotiations or federal entitlement programs. Most seem to have assumed that since a constant-utility index would show the minimum cost to reach the same "standard of living" (utility) under two price situations, it would be the appropriate choice for these tasks. But its suitability is debatable (in both its cardinal and ordinal forms). Indeed, when the 1996 Boskin report and concurrent arguments over Social Security reform (Chapter 9) turned the attention of price index theorists to COLAs and indexation, some of the economists most committed to the constant-utility ideal expressed doubts about its use for income adjustment.

First, economists recognize that "welfare" or "utility" depends on more than market goods; accordingly, important aspects of a standard of living lie outside the scope of typical cost-of-living indexes. Indeed, a reaction against the growth-oriented political economy of the 1960s from social critics and the burgeoning environmental movement forced economists to restate the limitations of the national accounts as a complete measure of economic welfare.[91] Of course, few people have suggested that wage-earners or senior citizens be compensated for declines in social community or penalized for tighter environmental controls that have improved pollution levels.[92] A more complicated issue is government services and taxes, however. The CPI currently includes sales taxes but not income taxes, an asymmetry that is (perhaps) justified by viewing sales taxes as part of the transaction costs for certain goods. A broader assessment of the adequacy of income would surely need to include all taxes, but would likewise need to consider the benefits of government services, such as free or subsidized medical care, public infrastructure, and so on.[93]

no. 4 (1975): 540–542. For a subsequent, more comprehensive treatment, see Pollak, *The Theory of the Cost of Living Index*, chap. 6.

[91] Collins, *More*, 132–139. For a reassessment of the national accounts in light of such criticism, see William D. Nordhaus and James Tobin, "Is Growth Obsolete?" in *The Measurement of Economic and Social Performance*, ed. Milton Moss, SIW, vol. 38 (New York: Columbia University Press, 1973), 509–532. Appropriately enough, Simon Kuznets offered the closing commentary to this gathering.

[92] Although, this has happened in a limited way since the BLS "linked" out the cost of mandated pollution control devices in automobiles during the 1960s and 1970s.

[93] An accessible and useful overview of these issues is Charles L. Schultze and Christopher Mackie, eds., *At What Price? Conceptualizing and Measuring Cost-of-Living and Price*

Even if we accept a market-based scope for cost-of-living adjustments, however, the constant-utility ideal may not match common expectations for income adjustment. For example, strictly adhering to a constant-utility approach based on stable utility functions ensures that those Americans who are heavily dependent on index-adjusted payments will be prevented from benefiting from any economic innovations. Suppose a new drug appears that allows an elderly man, who is living entirely on Social Security payments, to reduce the pain from his arthritis. In order to purchase the drug under his existing income, he redistributes his expenditures (perhaps by spending less on food and clothing). By standard neoclassical reasoning, he has now obtained a higher level of welfare through the same expenditures; otherwise, he would have stuck with his original market basket. Accordingly, following the strict logic of the Boskin report, his Social Security benefits should be reduced to return him to his original level of welfare. A similar outcome may occur through what union economists in the Second World War labeled "forced uptrading." Imagine that procedural advances make an existing cancer treatment twice as successful without changing its cost. By the Boskin report's approach, Social Security benefits should fall even though the cost of treatment has remained the same (since welfare-per-dollar has increased).

More generally, the question is whether welfare, utility, or satisfaction potentially have relative dimensions that would be missed by an ordinal constant-utility index (or by assuming stable, cardinal utility functions). Survey data reinforce what intuition suggests, namely that self-reported well-being and assessments of "adequate" income are highly dependent on social expectations conditioned by the economic status of one's contemporaries. (Indeed, economists as diverse as Adam Smith and Thorstein Veblen had made this point long ago.)[94] Likewise, since people adapt behavior and living conditions to new technologies, some of these relative dimensions may be structural in nature. (The utilities provided by automobiles or air conditioning, for example, are both absolute and relative, since the

Indexes (Washington, D.C.: National Academy Press, 2002), 94–105. The theoretical framework derives from Pollak, *The Theory of the Cost of Living Index*, esp. chap. 2 and chap. 9.

[94] On self-reported well-being, see Kahneman, Diener, and Schwarz, *Well-Being*, esp. essays by Argyle, van Praag and Frijters, and Diener and Suh. On ideas about adequacy over time, see the analysis of Gallup poll data by Denton R. Vaughan, "Exploring the Use of the Public's Views to Set Income Poverty Thresholds and Adjust Them over Time," *Social Security Bulletin* 56, no. 2 (1993): 22–46. Adam Smith, *An Inquiry into the Nature and Causes of the Wealth of Nations* (New York: Clarendon Press 1976), 869–870; Thorstein Veblen, *The Theory of the Leisure Class* (New York: MacMillan, 1899).

spatial patterns of residential housing, retail centers, and work sites in the United States have been adapted to widespread ownership of automobiles and availability of electric cooling.) The issue is most pressing for consideration of product quality: Are evaluations of quality dependent on the social and economic environment, including the relative availability of different goods? One suspects that Louis Bean's 1939 critique of hedonic analysis (namely that technological innovation alters consumer expectations) also applies to contemporary economic sectors with rapid technological change (such as health care and consumer electronics).

Of course, these relative dimensions to consumer welfare would also be missed by the traditional, constant-goods ideal that had been previously promoted by government statisticians. But the supporters of the constant-goods framework had never claimed that they were trying to maintain constant "welfare" or "economic well-being" over time, making it easier to recognize the limitations of their calculations. Strictly speaking, the ordinalist formulation avoided temporal comparisons of welfare as well. In practice, however, many economists reverted to looser descriptions of the constant-utility ideal (especially when writing to a general public) that missed this important distinction and thus (to non-economists) readily implied more expansive claims. For example, although the Boskin commission relied on an ordinalist theoretical foundation, it also stated that a cost-of-living index tells us "how much would we need to increase (or decrease) initial (period 1) expenditure in order to make the consumer as well off as in the subsequent period (period 2)," a formulation that sounds remarkably like the original, cardinal constant-utility objective. In a later section, the commission briefly conceded that it had evaluated the welfare supplied by goods and services from the fixed perspective of a static economic and social environment, but it dismissed the issue as largely irrelevant after a cursory examination. Nor did its report explore the practical ramifications of using a constant-utility model for indexation (though two members, Zvi Griliches and Ellen Dulberger, touched on these issues in individual testimonies).[95]

The limitations of the constant-utility ideal have led some economists, including strong advocates of the constant-utility approach such as Dulberger and Griliches, to argue that a strict constant-utility index is not an appropriate tool for indexing federal benefits or program parameters. Tellingly, though, most continue to insist that a cost-of-living index must be

---

[95] Boskin et al., *Toward a More Accurate Measure of the Cost of Living*, 22–23, 73–77. For Griliches and Dulberger, see the next note.

a constant-utility index and have likewise remained committed to aligning the CPI with that ideal. Rather than develop an alternative definition for a cost-of-living index, they propose other mechanisms for income adjustment, typically indexation by wages, perhaps with a minimum floor for benefits or a maximum cap on redistributions of income from the young to the elderly. Since wages have historically risen faster than the CPI, this change would tend to boost benefit levels over time; moreover, the logic of wage indexation ties benefits to the "average" prosperity of American employees (thereby introducing a measure of relative equity).[96]

Wage indexation would address many of the conundrums created by the constant-utility framework (though one suspects that tracking "average wages" has its own set of thorny conceptual and operational issues). Nonetheless, Americans have repeatedly expressed a willingness and desire to adjust wages and income (perhaps only partially or temporarily) to changes in the "cost of living." That was why the CPI was created, of course, and why it was called a "cost-of-living index" in the first place. Would it be possible to construct a theoretical framework for a cost-of-living index that maintains the basic idea (monitoring the changing cost of a fixed standard of living) but avoids the weaknesses of a constant-utility index when considered as a tool for income adjustment or, more generally, as a means to analyze the changing cost of economic well-being over time? If so, what might the ramifications be of pursuing such an option rather than turning

---

[96] Among the Boskin commission members, Zvi Griliches and Ellen Dulberger both expressed doubts about the suitability of a straight constant-utility index for adjusting income benefits in federal programs; Griliches was especially adamant on this score. U.S. Senate, Committee on Finance, *Consumer Price Index: Hearings before the Committee on Finance*, 104th Cong., 1st sess., March 13, April 6, and June 6, 1995, 85–88, 121, 131; U.S. Senate, Committee on Finance, *Final Report of the Advisory Commission to Study the Consumer Price Index: Hearings before the Committee on Finance*, 105th Congress, 1st sess., January 28, and February 11, 1997, 130–132. Other economists involved with price index theory who have voiced related concerns include Jack E. Triplett, "Escalation Measures: What Is the Answer? What Is the Question?" in *Price Level Measurement: Proceedings from a Conference Sponsored by Statistics Canada*, ed. W. E. Diewert and C. Montmarquette (Ottawa: Minister of Supply and Services, 1983), 472–476; Angus Deaton, "Getting Prices Right: What Should Be Done?" *Journal of Economic Perspectives* 12, no. 1 (1998): 37–46; Robert A. Pollak, "The Consumer Price Index: A Research Agenda and Three Proposals," *Journal of Economic Perspectives* 12, no. 1 (1998): 69–78; Martin Neil Baily, "Policy Implications of the Boskin Commission Report," *International Productivity Monitor*, no. 12 (2006): 78–81. The 2002 panel from the National Research Council of the National Academy of Sciences explored many of the potential criticisms of the constant-utility framework: Schultze and Mackie, eds., *At What Price?* Of the economists listed above, Griliches, Triplett, and Baily all voiced support for some kind of wage indexation, perhaps with limits. The NRC panel likewise showed implicit support for this idea in an extended treatment of its merits and complications: Schultze and Mackie, eds., *At What Price?* 199–206.

to wage indexation? To answer these questions, we must leave a strictly historical analysis (since most price index theorists have not pursued this issue)[97] and consider an alternative mode of defining a standard of living.

A Counterfactual Cost-of-Living Index and a Question: Does Terminology Matter?

My strategy is to borrow the conceptual approach to standards of living developed by Amartya Sen, a Nobel prize–winning economist who has spent much of his career thinking about poverty and the proper basis for comparing welfare. Sen discards both self-reported well-being and "opulence" (the quantity and quality of possessions) as inadequate bases for assessing a standard of living. The former can be too readily divorced from material conditions by "social conditioning," while the latter (goods themselves) provide "no more than means to other ends," and it is the "other ends" that truly define a standard of living. The ultimate solution is to consider these ends, which Sen describes as "functionings" (the realization of particular states or operations) and "capabilities" (the actual, not merely formal, freedom to realize a functioning if so desired). Thus, to take an example, the state of being well-nourished is a functioning; the capability of being well-nourished implies that one has the opportunity and resources to realize that state. (But one may choose to fast for religious reasons, for example, and thus not realize this particular functioning at a certain time.) For Sen, capabilities provide the most appropriate definition of a standard of living, since they imply the potential for functionings but allow the individual the freedom to value different states as he or she chooses.[98]

Critically, Sen argues that the capabilities approach allows us to combine both absolute and relative elements in our conception of a standard of living:

Some capabilities, such as [that of] being well nourished, may have more or less similar demands on commodities (such as food and health services) irrespective

---

[97] Perhaps the closest move came in 1966, when Richard Ruggles distinguished a "cost-of-living index" from an index for assessing changes in real prices (a macroeconomic task). Ruggles's primary concern was what I have described as forced uptrading, which he believed ought to be included in a "cost-of-living index" but could properly be excluded from an assessment of productivity or macroeconomic inflation. See U.S. Congress. Joint Economic Committee, *Government Price Statistics: Hearings (1966)*, 242, 262–263. More recently, attention to a household production model within the theory of a cost-of-living index has opened new possibilities for alternative analyses (see n. 99, below).

[98] A concise overview of Sen's ideas is his 1985 Tanner Lectures, published with critical responses in Sen, *The Standard of Living*. Quotations here are from pp. 8, 15–16.

of the average opulence of the community in which the person lives. Other capabilities … have commodity demands that vary a good deal with average opulence. To lead a life without shame, to be able to visit and entertain one's friends, to keep track of what is going on and what others are talking about, and so on, requires a more expensive bundle of goods and services in a society that is generally richer, and in which most people have, say, means of transport, affluent clothing, radios, or television sets, etc.[99]

Sen's analysis here moves from capabilities to the commodities which enable them: some capabilities may require a more or less stable set of commodities; others may require different commodities depending on the relevant social and economic environment. But we could also run the analysis in the opposite direction: a given commodity may provide some capabilities absolutely (at least in reasonably similar circumstances) but other capabilities only relatively. A computer from 1990 still provides many of its original capabilities: I can still run the same software I had when it was new. But it has lost other capabilities that were dependent on the relative performance of its technology: I can no longer purchase and run the software typically available in stores; I may not be able to read (or even receive) files from colleagues and friends (since both software formats and portable media have changed dramatically); if my work or leisure requires extensive computation, I will be at a time disadvantage relative to my peers, and so on.

We can see here the potential implications for evaluating "quality": one would track neither the cost of goods nor the cost of characteristics of goods (the standard hedonic approach), but the cost of capabilities enabled by goods (via their characteristics).[100] Not only could a focus on capabilities force consideration of the relative dimensions of a standard of living, it also provides a way to incorporate the "changes in the manner of living" that had so troubled union economists during the Second World War. For example,

---

[99] Sen, *The Standard of Living*, 18.

[100] This view shares much in common with attempts to integrate price index theory with Gary Becker's idea of a "household production function" (Gary S. Becker, "A Theory of the Allocation of Time," *Economic Journal* 75, no. 299 (1965): 493–517). Indeed, Griliches recognized the desirability of moving beyond goods to their production functions quite early in his work on hedonic indexes: Griliches, "Notes on the Measurement of Price and Quality Changes," 417, n. 4. For examples of subsequent treatments, see John Muellbauer, "Household Production Theory, Quality, and The 'Hedonic Technique'," *AER* 64, no. 6 (1974): 977–994; Pollak, *The Theory of the Cost of Living Index*, ch. 4; Peter Hill, "Household Production, Consumption, and CPIs," in *Price Index Concepts and Measurement*, ed. W. Erwin Diewert, John S. Greenlees, and Charles Hulten (Chicago: University of Chicago Press, forthcoming). John Muellbauer's comments on Sen's Tanner Lectures note the connection while also contrasting Sen's capabilities with Becker's household production model. See Sen, *The Standard of Living*, 39–41.

changes in family structure and work patterns (especially for women) have made childcare an important and often major expense for many families. Because the CPI "links" these changes into the market basket, the absolute increase in costs never appears in the index. A capabilities approach to a cost-of-living index could treat provision for children as a basic component of a standard of living; such an index would then rise if the proportion of families with two working parents rises or the number of single parents increases.

As this example makes clear, though, the capabilities approach produces a host of difficult, often normative, questions. Incorporating childcare expenses into an index would probably provide a more accurate deflator for household income; its relevance to wage rates or income-based adjustment in federal programs would be more questionable. (Should tax brackets rise because there are more single parents or dual-income families?) Indeed, it should be obvious that a capabilities approach to cost-of-living indexes raises innumerable operational problems (how can one assess social capabilities?) and normative issues. Creating a capabilities-based cost-of-living index for indexation of federal programs would require us to identify a set of capabilities which we desire to maintain over time and to then find some means of assessing those capabilities in two different situations. Neither of these would be easy tasks.

We can, therefore, return to the question that motivated this theoretical digression: why bother? A wage index, though it would not be identical to a capabilities approach, would capture much of the relative dimension to Sen's notion of a standard of living, and the operational issues for wage indexation are much more straightforward (even if still not easy). The attraction of wage indexation now seems stronger: strip economic statistics of as many subjective judgments as possible and allow politicians to use whichever measure they find most appropriate. Ideally, ambiguities are driven out from the operational calculation of government statistics and confined to the interpretation of those figures and the selection among them for a given application. Technical matters are thus cleanly divorced from political judgments, and isn't that what we really want?

In the epilogue, I will consider this question in more detail. For now, let me suggest that the separation of the technical from the political here is more problematic than it first appears. The oversight arises from ignoring how the theoretical framing of a statistic can, and almost assuredly will, shape its political interpretation. Compare our hypothetical capabilities-approach to the analysis of the Boskin commission. We have two approaches to measuring the changes in expenditures required to maintain a "constant standard of living." One approach tells us that defining a standard of living is a difficult task, requiring many judgments about the ends (capabilities) we wish people to be able to maintain. Constructing a statistic based on such a concept will not be easy, will always require normative judgments, and cannot be reduced to an apolitical, technical matter. Moreover, we should recognize that a standard of living contains relative dimensions.

The other approach tells us that defining a stable standard of living over time is a simple matter (in principle, if not in practice) that can be completed without any normative judgments at all, and that, although we may never have a fully accurate measure, we can at least be sure that the cost of maintaining a constant standard of living has risen less rapidly than the CPI in recent years. Of course, for the purposes of income adjustment, looking more carefully at peoples' living conditions and constraints may lead us to choose a different statistic as the basis for indexation (e.g., average wages), a statistic that would rise more rapidly than a "true cost-of-living index," and perhaps more rapidly than the CPI. Of course, by virtue of the theoretical framework that we have established, that decision would serve to *increase*—not merely maintain—the "well being," "welfare," "satisfaction," and "standard of living" of the beneficiaries of indexation.[101]

I submit that the practical ramifications for political economy of the choice between these two approaches are substantial, and, as Chapter 9 will illustrate, never more so than in the American political context.

---

[101] These terms are all used by the Boskin commission report when defining a cost-of-living index: Boskin et al., *Toward a More Accurate Measure of the Cost of Living*, 20.

9

From Workers to the Welfare State:
The Consumer Price Index and the Rise
of Indexation

This is so profoundly important and so politically neutral.[1]
—Senator Daniel P. Moynihan,
Consumer Price Index: Hearings before the Senate Committee on Finance, 1995

In 1962, Congress linked adjustments to civil service retirement benefits to movements in the Consumer Price Index; military retirement benefits followed shortly thereafter. In 1969, a statistical directive from the U.S. Bureau of the Budget tied the official federal poverty thresholds to the CPI, a step which in turn (via the derivative poverty guidelines) soon affected income-eligibility levels in a host of means-tested federal programs, from food stamps to Head Start. In 1972, Congress added an escalator clause based on the CPI to the calculation of Social Security benefits. From then on, indexation remained an integral part of federal bureaucratic governance, especially within the welfare state.[2]

Though federal indexation clearly emulated the use of escalator clauses in labor contracts, the scope and financial scale of the new applications quickly surpassed the older model. By 1975, roughly half of all Americans received income tied to changes in the CPI. That figure included 7.5 million wage-earners, but also a much larger set of 78 million recipients of government payments (See Table 9.1). According to BLS calculations, a 1 percent increase in the index would produce about $1 billion in new federal expenditures.[3]

During this same period, the conceptual basis for CPI shifted from the constant-goods approach to the constant-utility ideal. As we saw in

---

[1] U.S. Senate, Committee on Finance, *Consumer Price Index: Hearings before the Committee on Finance*, 104th Cong., 1st sess., March 13, April 6, and June 6, 1995, 35.
[2] R. Kent Weaver, *Automatic Government: The Politics of Indexation* (Washington, D.C.: Brookings Institution, 1988), 38–56.
[3] "The Search for a Better Measure of Living Costs," *The Nation's Business*, May 1976, p. 67.

Table 9.1: *Persons Receiving Payments Escalated by CPI, 1975*

Escalation Based on Full CPI	
Source	*People*
Labor contracts	7.5 million
Military and Civil Service retirees	2.4 million
Social Security recipients	31.2 million
Escalation Based on CPI Components	
Source	*People*
Food Stamp recipients	19.6 million
Subsidies to school lunch program	25.2 million

Note that these tables do not include people affected by eligibility parameters based on movements in the CPI (such as the poverty guidelines).
Source: U.S. Bureau of Labor Statistics, "The Consumer Price Index and Escalation," 6 June 1975, CPI Escalators, box 16, PFAC, BLS.

Chapter 8, attempts to improve empirical macroeconomic analysis—rather than sustained efforts to think about the proper basis for income escalation to meet the rising "cost of living"—provided the primary pragmatic motivation behind this shift. Confronted with the widespread use of the CPI for income adjustment, many price index theorists suggested that a constant-utility index did not provide a suitable basis for this function. Likewise, there is no evidence that Congress or federal bureaucrats intended to tie federal payments to a constant-utility index (understood in the ordinalist sense), and especially to an index geared toward analysis of macroeconomic trends. (Indeed, insofar as the various architects of federal indexation had any concept consistently in mind, it was the bureau's traditional vision of a constant-goods index.) This chapter explains how this mismatch between application and conceptual basis arose, and why it has proven so difficult to change.

Part of the answer lies in the institutional history of the BLS and its relationships to external advisers. In the mid-1960s, the BLS hired a number of younger economists who were better prepared to switch to the constant-utility ideal. Furthermore, the establishment of a new research division created closer ties between BLS staff and academic price index theorists who were pursuing the study of empirical macroeconomics. Even as the constant-utility ideal gained a greater hold within the bureau, the agency's advisory system did not provide any strong external resistance. Despite the rise of federal indexation, the bureau's advisory committees continued to reflect the needs of postwar industrial relations; those affected by federal indexation lacked any direct representation in BLS decision making or analysis. Meanwhile, although at least one of the two existing advisory committees, LRAC, opposed the constant-utility objective, the union economists were ill-positioned to contest the replacement of the traditional, constant-goods framework and unmotivated to develop an alternative conceptual scheme that might have been more appropriate for federal indexation. Accordingly, BLS staff had a theoretical justification for adopting the constant-utility ideal as the objective for the CPI, professional support for doing so, an application (macroeconomic analysis) that could benefit from the result, and minimal effective resistance from close advisers.

Still, these explanations for the ties between indexation and a constant-utility approach are insufficient on their own. The CPI faced substantial scrutiny from Congress and federal agencies (especially from the late 1970s on); moreover, Congress could have changed the method of indexation by altering the formulas, introducing ad hoc adjustments, or choosing a different statistical basis (such as wage indexation). Yet any challenge to the constant-utility objective would have required attending to distributional equity within federal programs and the economy as a whole. Differentiating between macroeconomic inflation and the cost increases faced by poor or low-income Americans, for example, would require recognizing that the benefits of technological improvements and new products were not distributed equally throughout the population. More fundamentally, contesting the applicability of the constant-utility objective to indexation would necessitate either considering the relative dimensions of a standard of living (e.g., a capabilities approach) or insisting that at least some Americans required adjustments that were greater (or less) than what many economists (including those on the Boskin commission) described as the amount needed to ensure constant "welfare."

Unfortunately, the politics of the American welfare state made such actions highly unlikely. (Here and elsewhere I use the terms "welfare state" and "welfare programs" in their broader sense, including social insurance programs such as public pensions and unemployment compensation.) Left-wing and moderate architects of American welfare programs, such as the 1935 Social Security Act or the War on Poverty of the 1960s, had deliberately minimized attention to distributional equity in order to make their programs more politically palatable. Furthermore, a politically difficult environment, the need for administrative efficiency, and the technical complexity of relevant issues had all combined to create an intensely rationalized policymaking context for both Social Security and anti-poverty efforts. Excluding subjective, normative, and potentially contentious issues (such as distributional equity) from the knowledge used to administer such programs seemed essential. Here, the ordinalist constant-utility ideal—which had a theoretical sanction and which ignored distributional issues—found a congenial setting. Thus, despite the poor fit between the constant-utility approach and income adjustment in the abstract, a constant-utility index has nevertheless been a seamless match with the American welfare state.

THE TRIUMPH OF THEORY: THE BLS AND THE "TRUE COST-OF-LIVING INDEX," 1960–1980

In 1961, the BLS rejected the NBER review committee's recommendation that the CPI aim to become a constant-utility index; however, within a decade, the bureau had unobtrusively adopted that objective. The bureau's eventual acceptance of the constant-utility ideal derived from many of the same factors that attracted academic economists. We have already seen, for example, how attention to macroeconomic analysis increasingly placed the CPI in a new perspective (Chapter 8). Still, such alterations would have been less consequential absent a major transformation in the bureau's leadership. At the top level, the retirement of Ewan Clague in 1965 marked the symbolic end of the hegemony of the economists who had participated in the 1930s overhaul of the bureau. His three successors over the ensuing decade—Arthur M. Ross (1965–1968), Geoffrey Moore (1969–1973), and Julius Shiskin (1973–1978)—brought a distinctly different perspective to the bureau. This was not necessarily a permanent shift; Janet Norwood, who succeeded Shiskin and guided the BLS into the 1990s, seems to have shared an outlook more similar to Ewan Clague. But the transition did affect the bureau from the late 1960s into the late 1970s and likewise produced a change in BLS culture.

Both Moore and Shiskin (who had been college roommates) had ties to the tradition of institutional economics associated with the interwar years of the NBER, but they were second-generation members and had witnessed the economics profession align itself more tightly with neoclassical theory. Indeed, at least in the available written record, Ross expressed more skepticism about the constant-utility framework for price indexes than either Moore or Shiskin.[4] Perhaps more significant, all three contributed

---

[4] Arthur M. Ross, "Living with Symbols," *The American Statistician* 20, no. 3 (1966): 18; U.S. Congress, Joint Economic Committee, *Government Price Statistics: Hearings before the Subcommittee on Economic Statistics*, 89th Cong., 2nd sess., May 24, 25, and 26, 1966,

to expanding the bureau's focus. It appears that Secretary of Labor Willard Wirtz had hired Ross from the University of California specifically for this purpose, frustrated with what he perceived as Clague's lackluster efforts to integrate the bureau into the Johnson administration's focus on poverty and "manpower" (i.e., employment).[5] Likewise, both Moore and Shiskin came to the BLS from roles where they had been primed to view labor statistics as elements of a much larger macroeconomic picture: Moore arrived at the BLS after holding leadership positions in the NBER for many years; Shiskin moved directly from the Office of Management and Budget, where he had overseen efforts to coordinate national statistics. Shiskin in particular was inclined to view the BLS from a wider lens; as his successor, Janet Norwood, put it, he wanted to "move the Bureau away from the Department [of Labor]" in order to emphasize its role as "a national statistical agency."[6]

The most obvious sign of this move came when the bureau pushed to expand the coverage of the CPI in the 1970s to include closer to 80 percent of urban households.[7] The shift would make the index more valuable for broader economic analyses but also less reflective of the "wage earners and low-salaried clerical workers" who had traditionally been its focus. The bureau staff felt that the trade-off was warranted; in the end, labor unions successfully forced the bureau to adopt its current practice of publishing two indexes: the CPI for Urban Wage Earners and Clerical Workers (CPI-W) and the CPI for All Urban Consumers (CPI-U).[8] Yet other changes in attitude were more subtle and more successful. For example, a 1974 staff memo raised the problem of "democratic" versus "plutocratic" weighting for the CPI that we considered at the end of Chapter 8. (Recall that in a plutocratic system, each family's contribution to determining the overall, average index would be proportional to its expenditure: families who spent twice as much would have twice as great of an influence. In a democratic system, each family would contribute equally to the overall index.) As the

---

72–73. On the three commissioners, see Joseph P. Goldberg and William T. Moye, *The First Hundred Years of the Bureau of Labor Statistics* (Washington, D.C.: U.S. GPO, 1985), 216–218; Richard Pearson, "Julius Shiskin, 66, Commissioner of Bureau of Labor Statistics," *Washington Post*, 29 October 1978, B6; Oral History with Geoffrey Moore (1978), DOL Historical Office.

[5] Goldberg and Moye, *First Hundred Years*, 185–186, 254–255. Oral History with Janet Norwood (1980), p. 4, DOL Historical Office; Oral History with Harold Goldstein (1978), pp. 26–29, ibid.

[6] Oral History with Janet Norwood (1980), p. 29.

[7] Carlyle P. Stallings, "Redefinition of the Consumer Price Index Population," July 1971, Div. of Prices and Cost of Living, 1969–71, box 3, RCL-PPF 1950–1975, BLS.

[8] Goldberg and Moye, *First Hundred Years*, 227–229.

memo noted, a democratic system would better reflect the experiences of the larger number of "low and middle income families," whereas the plutocratic system would be a better match for analyses of aggregate expenditures. Having asked which solution would be best for "deflating GNP and component income distribution" for the national accounts, Julius Shiskin went with that option (plutocratic).[9]

For the most part, though, the BLS has not been a top-down organization, and therefore the more consequential institutional changes occurred at a lower level in the bureau. Arthur Ross's first year as commissioner (1966) witnessed a wave of retirements and resignations among senior staff, most of whom were replaced by younger economists. Those leaving included Ethel D. Hoover, Laura Mae Webb, and Sidney Jaffe—all of whom had been closely involved with the Consumer Price Index from the 1950s into the mid-1960s and who provided the last direct link to the older generation of New Deal economists.[10] Meanwhile, as part of a plan to strengthen the analytic side of the bureau, Ross reinvigorated the Division of Price and Index Number Research, a small unit devoted to methodological analysis which had been formed under Ethel Hoover after the NBER review.[11] Over the next two decades, the research division would hire a slew of young economists who would reshape the theory and methods behind the CPI, including Joel Popkin, Thomas Gavett, Robert Gillingham, W. John Layng, Marilyn Manser, Jack Triplett, Steven Braithwait, John Greenlees, and Marshall Reinsdorf.[12]

It is hard to underestimate the effect that the research division had on the CPI from the 1970s onward. Bureau officials used the division to help define the framework and scope for the index and to wrestle with methodological decisions; moreover, in the early 1970s, two research division staff members—Joel Popkin and W. John Layng—became the successive

---

[9] Robert Gillingham to W. John Layng, 15 May 1974, CPI Revision 5, box 10, RCL-PPF 1950–1975, BLS; Julius Shiskin to Janet Norwood and John Layng, 22 August 1974, ibid.

[10] Arthur Ross to Willard Wirtz. 3 October 1966, box 381, LS 1–Summary Plans & Reports, Subject Files of William Wirtz, DOL.

[11] On Ross's desire to strengthen the bureau's analytic work, see Oral History with Harold Goldstein (1978), 26–27. On the reorganization of the research division, see Clement Winston to Raymond T. Bowman, 20 January 1967, Prices–General and misc., box 217, SR 1940–68, OMB.

[12] In 1974, the BLS formed a centralized research division, eventually known as the Office of Research and Evaluation, which lasted until the 1990s. This was a distinct entity from the price research division within the Office of Prices and Living Conditions, but its members were also involved in research projects on price indexes and in recommendations for the CPI. For simplicity's sake, I will refer to both groups as the "research division."

supervisors for the Office of Prices and Living Conditions, where they guided the CPI through its major revision in the 1970s. (Another research division alumnus, John Greenlees, would lead the CPI division from 1995 to 2004, as it responded to the Boskin report.)[13] Furthermore, because the staff had the time and institutional support to conduct empirical and theoretical research (rather than focusing on producing regular statistics), members of the research division were able to build tighter ties to academic economists. For example, the economist Robert Pollak (who served briefly in the bureau during the late 1960s) worked closely with the research division over the next decade as he developed a series of theoretical papers that would later become a standard reference in price index theory.[14] Moreover, research division members were regular participants in the NBER's annual Conference on Research in Income and Wealth—especially during years devoted to prices, productivity, or national accounts—where they interacted with many of the growth-oriented economists discussed in Chapter 8, such as Griliches, Gordon, Jorgenson, and so forth. (Indeed, at one point in the late 1970s, three of the ten members of the CRIW Executive Committee were also current or former members of the BLS research division.)[15]

The research division thus placed the bureau and the CPI in a remarkably strong position: On the one hand, agency staff had regular contact

[13] BLS news release, "John Layng to be Assistant Commissioner for Office of Prices and Living Conditions," 21 October 1973, Prices and COL Division, box 7, Norwood A-Z files, BLS. (Layng, who left the bureau in the 1980s, later returned and is currently Assistant Commissioner for Consumer Prices and Price Indexes.) A 1974 paper by Robert Gillingham is still cited in the BLS *Handbook of Methods* as defining the conceptual basis for the CPI: Gillingham, "A Conceptual Framework for the Revised Consumer Price Index," *1974 Proceedings of the American Statistical Association, Business and Economic Statistics Section,* pp. 46–52. Likewise, Jack Triplett's work on quality change and hedonic price indexes has shaped both BLS approaches and statistical methodology worldwide: e.g., Jack E. Triplett, *Handbook on Hedonic Indexes and Quality Adjustments in Price Indexes* (Paris: Organisation for Economic Co-Operation and Development, 2006).

[14] Robert A. Pollak, *The Theory of the Cost of Living Index* (New York: Oxford University Press, 1989).

[15] The major papers and proceedings of the CRIW appear in the annual *Studies in Income and Wealth.* Popkin was an early participant—see vol. 31, plus (after he left the BLS) vols. 42 and 57—but Jack Triplett has been the most active by far: vols. 40, 42, 47–48, plus (after leaving the BLS) vols. 56–58, 62–63. Several "graduates" of the Division of Prices and Index Number Research, notably Marilyn Manser (who later returned to the BLS Office of Research and Evaluation) and Laurits Christensen, have likewise been heavily involved in the CRIW. Triplett, Popkin (who had left the BLS earlier), and Christensen were all on the CRIW Executive Committee during the late 1970s. The division's most extensive involvement occurred from this period through the early 1980s and again in the early 1990s (when the CRIW held a series of conferences dealing with price measurement, vols. 56–58).

with leading academic specialists plus its own in-house experts. On the other, members of the research division had access to low-level data and knowledge about unpublished methodological details that allowed them to conduct numerous empirical studies on price index methodology that would have been much more difficult, if not impossible, from the outside. Accordingly, as participants in 1995 (pre-Boskin) congressional hearings about the CPI before the Senate Finance Committee repeatedly acknowledged, some of the best critical analyses of the CPI came from within the bureau itself.[16]

Accommodating Stable Utility Functions

Of course, the shift in mid-level staff and the reinvigoration of the research division also helped to ease the bureau's acceptance of the constant-utility ideal, as a quick history makes clear. During the 1961 Joint Economic Committee (JEC) hearings about the recent NBER review of federal price statistics, the BLS emphatically rejected the NBER committee's recommendation that the CPI attempt to emulate a constant-utility index. What bothered BLS commissioner Ewan Clague was not the idea of a welfare index per se, but what he saw as the innumerable obstacles to measuring the "cost of living in this psychological sense."[17] Though BLS staff rarely discussed the constant-utility index formally prior to the early 1960s, there is scattered evidence that similar concerns about the subjective and relative nature of "utility" shaped their attitudes toward the constant-utility ideal. Several staff papers expressed the common belief that the same goods would not bring the same "satisfaction" over time, and in 1951 the BLS explicitly rejected the viability of an index based on "constant want satisfaction," in part because of these problems.[18] Indeed, the degree to which the notion of

[16] U.S. Senate, Committee on Finance, *Consumer Price Index*, 21, 52, 63. For a sample of major work deriving from the research division just prior to the Boskin report, see the articles in the special feature, "The Anatomy of Price Change," *MLR* vol. 116, no. 12 (December 1993): 2–46.

[17] U.S. Congress, Joint Economic Committee, *Government Price Statistics: Hearings before the Subcommittee on Economic Statistics of the Joint Economic Committee*, 87th Cong., 1st sess., May 1–5, 1961, 560, 564.

[18] BLS, "Uses and Limitations of Consumers' Price Index" (draft), pp. 1–2, 18 January 1951, folder 13, box 43, Ellickson collection, WRL. For two other examples, see the discussion of automobiles and movies, respectively, in Miss Rice, "Retail prices in the cost of living index: their use and significance," as excerpted in Laura Mae Webb and Ethel D. Hoover, "The Consumer Price Index: Issues of Concept and Practice," 1 October 1965, Div of Prices & COL, 1965–1968, box 3, RCL-PPF 1950–1975, BLS; Faith M. Williams and Ethel

changing tastes dominated the staff's view of a constant-utility index can be seen in their reaction to the 1961 NBER report: "The major difference between price index and a cost of living index," BLS economist Sidney Jaffe told members of the Labor Research Advisory Council that March, "is the fact that a cost of living index would take into account change of preference patterns by consumers."[19]

Although the 1961 JEC Subcommittee on Economic Statistics was also skeptical of a welfare-based index, it nevertheless recommended that the BLS pursue further research on the subject (a step that Clague had been willing to make).[20] Clague assigned Ethel Hoover to examine issues surrounding quality change from a broad perspective while another "senior staff member" (apparently Laura Mae Webb) was granted a year's leave to study the conceptual and practical basis for a constant-utility index.[21] By 1965, the staff had realized what we already considered in Chapter 8: that to make a constant-utility index into a viable objective, neoclassical economists had introduced what Hoover and Webb characterized as "rather rigid assumptions," including the requirement that "tastes and preferences are fixed." It is clear that the staff viewed these assumptions as serious limitations on the utility (so to speak) of the welfare approach. Sidney Jaffe felt that utility functions were unlikely to remain stable "over long periods" (such as a decade) and that changes in tastes presented major obstacles to implementing a constant-utility index. Similarly pointed remarks came from the new commissioner, Arthur Ross, in his testimony before the JEC Subcommittee on Economic Statistics in the spring of 1966. Ross noted that "some very important restrictions" governed the calculation of a constant-utility index, including the requirement that the consumer's "environment and tastes" remained unchanged. "Unfortunately," he continued drily in a parenthetical commentary, "the persons responsible for calculating actual price index numbers cannot bypass such situations."[22]

D. Hoover, "Measuring Price and Quality of Consumers' Goods," *Journal of Marketing* 10, no. 4 (1946): 361.

[19] Minutes – LRAC, March 21 1961, Seminar on prices, box 2, Records of LRAC, BLS.

[20] U.S. Congress, Joint Economic Committee, *Government Price Statistics: Report of the Subcommittee on Economic Statistics*, 87th Cong., 1st sess., July, 1961, 12; U.S. Congress, Joint Economic Committee, *Government Price Statistics: Hearings (1961)*, 564.

[21] Ethel D. Hoover to Arnold Chase, 13 July 1962, LRAC—Price Committee—Fiscal 1963, box 2, Records of LRAC, BLS; Ewan Clague to Paul F. Krueger, 21 September 1965, pp. 3, 7, Div. of Prices and COL, 1965–68, box 3, RCL-PPF 1950–75, BLS.

[22] Webb and Hoover, "The Consumer Price Index: Issues of Concept and Practice," p. 26. Jaffe to Chase, 10 March 1966, Addendum, p. 2, Div of Prices & COL, 1965–1968, box 3, RCL-PPF 1950–75, BLS. U.S. Congress, Joint Economic Committee, *Government Price*

However, with the retirement of older staff such as Hoover, Webb, and Jaffe later that year and the hiring of younger economists to fill the Division of Price and Index Number Research, the bureau's attitude underwent a subtle change that parallels the adoption of the full ordinalist position in price index theory (Chapter 8). From being a highly restrictive assumption that vitiated the constant-utility index, stable utility functions moved into the very definition of a welfare index itself. In 1967, for example, Thomas Gavett argued that changing tastes *ought* to be excluded from price measurements, even when based on "utility or consumer satisfaction." One year later, in a paper on "A Constant Utility Cost of Living Index," Joel Popkin offered an ordinalist definition of the concept, and subsequent BLS publications took the same stance. The bureau's rapid adoption of the ordinal formulation of the constant-utility index may be partially explained by the research division's close ties to Robert Pollak, a former doctoral student of Franklin M. Fisher in the 1960s whose theoretical work in the 1970s (often presented at the bureau) guided the agency's understanding of the constant-utility approach.[23]

The research division thus allowed the BLS to assimilate theoretical advances quite rapidly. Indeed, discussions of price index theory among research division staff were much like those among the growth-oriented price index theorists of Chapter 8, albeit with one important exception. Close familiarity with BLS procedures led research division staff to recognize that existing methods for quality assessment could sometimes overcompensate for quality improvements and that the bureau was also missing some quality deterioration; in short, there was no guarantee that methodological

---

Statistics: Hearings (1966), 72. Ross noted that the constant-utility ideal "does provide some guidance in the operation of a consumer price index," but he also emphasized the numerous requisite assumptions which he found unrealistic, and he appeared to suggest that approximating a constant-utility index would be a research exercise that was necessarily distinct from the calculation of the CPI (cf. pp. 73–74).

[23] Arthur Ross to Nat Weinberg, 20 September 1967, encl.: Thomas Gavett, "Research on Quality Adjustments in Price Indexes," p. 2, unlabeled folder, box 2, Records of LRAC, BLS. Joel Popkin, "A Constant Utility Cost of Living Index", October 1968, pp. 1–2, CPI Rev—Cost of living index, box 4, Janet Norwood, A–Z Files, BLS. Pollak, *The Theory of the Cost of Living Index*. On the theoretical framework for the CPI, see Robert Gillingham, "A Conceptual Framework for the Revised Consumer Price Index"; BLS, "An Updated Response to the Recommendations of the Advisory Commission to Study the Consumer Price Index," June 1998, p. 5, available on the BLS website: http://stats.bls.gov/cpi/cpi0698a.pdf. Gillingham described three of Pollak's essays (two of which were unpublished seminar papers) as the "foundations" for his 1974 article: Gillingham, "A Conceptual Framework for the Revised Consumer Price Index," 246.

changes for quality analysis (such as hedonic indexes) would substantially lower the CPI.[24]

The Advisory System and the Constant-Utility Index

In principle, critiques from those affected by indexation could have stymied the adoption of the constant-utility ideal or pressed the bureau to adapt that ideal to the purpose of income adjustment. Once the constant-utility approach became a focus for public discussion in the wake of the 1996 Boskin report, for example, the American Association of Retired Persons (AARP) took the latter tack. The AARP hired Joel Popkin, a former member of the BLS research division and former head of the BLS Office of Prices and Living Conditions, to critique the Boskin report, and Popkin responded with a broad vision of a constant-welfare index that raised some of the issues considered at the end of Chapter 8.[25] Yet this effort was two or three decades too late and occurred in a forum unlikely to produce much of an operational effect. (Congress, not the BLS, was Popkin's primary audience, and his main goal was to block easy acceptance of the Boskin commission's conclusions rather than to establish a viable alternative). The failure of the bureau's advisory system to develop beyond its postwar focus on industrial relations left it ill-suited to facilitate communications between the agency and new constituents created by federal indexation. Because groups such as the AARP had no formal connections to the BLS, the organization could not become fully informed about the nuances of price index methodology, could not consider how BLS procedures might affect its members, and could not enter into a sustained dialogue with the bureau. Other groups who were equally affected by the CPI but who lacked powerful lobbying organizations (such as the non-elderly poor) had even less access.

Of the bureau's existing advisory committees from the 1960s into the 1980s, LRAC consistently opposed both the constant-utility ideal and specific issues justified by that approach, such as using hedonic indexes, pricing durable goods through a flow-of-services model rather than through

---

[24] E.g., Jack E. Triplett, "Determining the Effects of Quality Change on the CPI," *MLR* 94, no. 5 (1971): 27–32; Jack E. Triplett, "Does the CPI Exaggerate or Understate Inflation? Some Observations," *MLR* 103, no. 5 (1980): 33–35. Subsequent analysis supported Triplett's predictions: David S. Johnson, Stephen B. Reed, and Kenneth J. Stewart, "Price Measurement in the United States: A Decade after the Boskin Report," *MLR* 129, no. 5 (2006): 14–17.

[25] Popkin, in U.S. Senate, Committee on Finance, *Final Report of the Advisory Commission to Study the Consumer Price Index: Hearings before the Committee on Finance*, 105th Congress, 1st sess., January 28, and February 11, 1997, 96–110.

transaction costs, or claiming that the CPI provided an upper limit to a "true cost-of-living index" because of consumer substitution.[26] (The business community had a mixed reaction to the 1961 NBER report, and several financial analysts continue to criticize certain constant-utility applications today.[27] However, there is insufficient archival evidence to judge the overall attitude of BRAC members.) The unions successfully opposed certain proposals designed to pull the CPI closer to macroeconomic analysis or to approximate a constant-utility objective. As already noted, they forced the bureau to keep publishing the original CPI alongside the new All Urban Consumers version in the 1970s, and, with the help of BRAC members plus other academic and government skeptics, they stalled plans to shift the housing component of the index to a rental-equivalency model. (Recall that the NBER review committee had recommended tracking estimated rental costs for homes rather than actual purchases prices, since rental equivalency fit with a constant-utility framework; see Chapter 8.)[28]

Nevertheless, union economists also managed to fulfill a cliché: having won some battles, they still lost the war. Despite their success on isolated points, the bureau moved inexorably into a closer embrace of the constant-utility ideal. Indeed, nothing better exemplified the unions' marginalization on this central point than the oft-repeated claim, voiced both by outside economists and BLS publications, that a major justification for the constant-utility objective was use of the CPI for wage adjustments—this despite the fact that union economists themselves repeatedly and vehemently rejected that conclusion.[29]

[26] E.g., U.S. Congress, Joint Economic Committee, *Government Price Statistics: Hearings (1961)*, 670–684.; Anne Draper (AFL-CIO), "Owned Housing in the Consumer Price Index," March 1977, esp. 9–11, AFL-CIO, box 12, PFAC, BLS; U.S. House, Committee on the Budget, Task Force on Inflation, *Housing Component of the Consumer Price Index: Hearing before the Task Force on Inflation*, 96th Cong., 1st and 2nd sess., December 14, 1979 and January 24, 1980, 78–79.

[27] Cf. U.S. Congress. Joint Economic Committee, *Government Price Statistics: Hearings (1961)*, 695–702, 708–712, 790–791. Bill Goss, "Haute Con Job" and "Con Job Redux," *Investment Outlook* (Pacific Investment Management Company), October 2004; Peter L. Bernstein, "In a Maze of Indexes, Finding Prices to Live By," *NYT*, 5 August 2007.

[28] Goldberg and Moye, *First Hundred Years*, 226–233. On the final decision and its rationale, see Julius Shiskin, "Treatment of Owner-Occupied Housing in the Revised CPI," 15 April 1977, Letter on Housing in Revised CPI, box 34, PFAC, BLS.

[29] For two union views that bracket the time period under discussion, see U.S. Congress, Joint Economic Committee, *Government Price Statistics: Hearings (1961)*, 682–683; U.S. House, Committee on the Budget, Task Force on Inflation, *Housing Component of the Consumer Price Index: Hearing before the Task Force on Inflation*, 78–83. For claims that wage adjustment demanded a constant-utility approach, see National Bureau of Economic Research, *The Price Statistics of the Federal Government: Review, Appraisal,*

How can we account for this failure? It is tempting to blame the general waning of union political power; certainly, it seems that the heyday of LRAC influence on the CPI came during the 1950s and 1960s. Nevertheless, unions had substantial effects on specific issues through the 1970s. Perhaps a more important factor was the scope of the advisory committees' responsibilities (as conceived both by the bureau and committee members themselves). The bureau consulted LRAC and BRAC primarily for operational decisions about the index, such as determining its coverage or devising general pricing procedures for classes of commodities. Yet through the 1960s and most of the 1970s, the constant-utility ideal had few operational consequences for the CPI. Some older BLS administrators continued to resist new techniques such as hedonic indexes in part because they worried that the technically complex calculations might be difficult to explain to the general public. Moreover, the constant-utility approach made greater demands on survey data. To calculate hedonic indexes that were sufficiently reliable to serve in official calculations, the BLS needed a regularly updated, fairly comprehensive dataset that linked detailed quality specifications with transaction prices. For many commodities, such information was not readily available; eventually the bureau had to conduct special surveys to develop its hedonic indexes.[30] Likewise, accurately estimating the effects of consumer substitution required current data on consumer expenditures, and Congress did not begin funding annual expenditure surveys until the 1980s.[31] Indeed, the

and Recommendations (New York: National Bureau of Economic Research, 1961), 52; Gillingham, "A Conceptual Framework for the Consumer Price Index," p. 1; U.S. Bureau of Labor Statistics, *The Consumer Price Index: Concepts and Content over the Years*, Report no. 517 (Washington, D.C.: U.S. GPO, 1978), 2. (Ironically, from my perspective, the 1978 BLS report also claimed that measuring inflation and deflating national accounts data were best served by a constant-goods index; thus, insofar as my historical analysis is correct, the bureau had the desires of many users exactly backwards.) Jack Triplett was one of the few price index theorists to recognize the discrepancy between union perspectives and theoreticians' claims: Jack E. Triplett, "Escalation Measures: What Is the Answer? What Is the Question?" in *Price Level Measurement: Proceedings from a Conference Sponsored by Statistics Canada*, ed. W. E. Diewert and C. Montmarquette (Ottawa: Minister of Supply and Services, 1983), 474.

30 Jack E. Triplett, "Hedonic Methods in Statistical Agency Environments: An Intellectual Biopsy," in *Fifty Years of Economic Measurement: The Jubilee of the Conference on Research in Income and Wealth*, ed. Ernst R. Berndt and Jack E. Triplett, SIW, vol. 54 (Chicago: University of Chicago Press, 1988), 207–233; Jack E. Triplett, "Hedonic Indexes and Statistical Agencies, Revisted," *Journal of Economic and Social Measurement* 27 (2001): 131–151. Triplett noted the difficulties with data collection for hedonic methods in a personal communication with the author, 17 July 2008.

31 Ana M. Aizcorbe and Patrick C. Jackman, "The Commodity Substitution Effect in CPI Data, 1982–91," *MLR* 116, no. 12 (1993): 25–33. Several empirical analyses of substitution effects were published in the 1980s using consumption data from national accounts.

only major application for the constant-utility approach during the 1970s was the treatment of owner-occupied housing, which was challenged by both LRAC and BRAC.

Behind this dearth of applications, however, the research division had laid a theoretical and conceptual foundation for the index that would eventually flourish in the late 1980s and 1990s, when the BLS began implementing hedonic techniques in a number of index components and altered its basic formulae to account for consumer substitution.[32] At least as the archival evidence is any guide, union economists made little or no contribution to the earlier theoretical discussions. The logic governing the creation of the research division treated its work as a series of technical studies; since this research did not affect the calculation of the index until translated into operational terms, there was no need to involve LRAC or BRAC in these conversations. Research division staff were more likely to look to academic economists for feedback and criticism; union economists had few allies in that domain (at least among price index theorists), and they did not participate in important forums such as the Conference on Research in Income and Wealth.[33] By the time BLS research had advanced to the operational stage, the unions were ill-positioned to combat it: their political influence was waning; their members were no longer the dominant, or even a major, group affected by the CPI; and (perhaps because of the previous two factors) their technical staff lacked the training in price index theory to mount a sophisticated critique of proposed changes.[34]

Most crucially, though, union economists failed to articulate an alternative theoretical foundation for the index that could challenge the primacy of the constant-utility framework. Even during the height of union research on price index methodology, the unions' approach to the CPI was thoroughly pragmatic and shaped by the index's role in labor contracts. Union economists recognized (how could they not?) that the main effect of adopting a constant-utility approach would be to lower the index to adjust for alleged consumer substitution, new kinds of goods, and the quality improvements

[32] Johnson, Reed, and Stewart, "Price Measurement in the United States," 10–19.
[33] According to the lists of contributors included in *Studies in Income and Wealth* (the CRIW proceedings) from the 1975 conference on, no union economists gave a major paper or commentary during that period.
[34] For an illustration of the decline in the sophistication of union analyses of price index theory, compare Lazare Teper's response to the NBER review committee in 1961 with the official AFL-CIO response to the Boskin report: U.S. Congress, Joint Economic Committee, *Government Price Statistics: Hearings (1961)*, 670–684; U.S. Senate, Committee on Finance, *Final Report of the Advisory Commission to Study the Consumer Price Index: Hearings before the Committee on Finance*, 111–113.

that were (supposedly) missed by current methods. They were skeptical of the operational viability of many proposed measurement techniques, but more to the point, they did not accept that factors such as consumer substitution or the benefits of new goods were relevant to wage adjustments. Ewan Clague, who anticipated union opposition, wondered "whether the kinds of adjustments in their living pattern that workers make of their own volition under free-economy conditions [i.e., substitutions], should be a factor in escalation of wage contracts."[35] Indeed, there was a certain perversity to suggesting that becoming a more frugal and careful shopper should cause your income to fall (since you now achieved the same "satisfaction" at less cost), or that the appearance of new and exciting goods should lead to a wage cut. Furthermore, the most problematic issues in quality adjustment surrounded durable goods where new models quickly replaced last season's version (leaving no overlap for linking them into the index), but these cases were prime examples of what union economists deemed forced uptrading. In the union view, escalation clauses simply ensured that workers' wage rates would allow them to purchase the same set of goods and services until the next contract negotiation: if thrifty and creative families could find ways to stretch their budget or obtain more "satisfaction" from the same amount of money, good for them. Thus, the relevant basis for wage escalation, Lazare Teper and others argued, was a constant-goods index.[36]

Unfortunately for union economists, their view of the index had no grounding in economic theory. Indeed, it wasn't really a theory at all but a set of claims (always subject to revision and loaded with normative judgments) about what kinds of things were, and were not, relevant to assessing or adjusting wages. This created all kinds of difficulties. In the first place, union research staff could not raise many concerns in a straightforward manner, since the compromise that led to the creation of LRAC implicitly required treating price index methodology as an apolitical, technical matter (Chapter 7). Thus, to take one example, instead of arguing that forced uptrading was a problem for index-based wage adjustment, union economists claimed it was a problem for measuring "inflation" in general (an ambiguity that left the unions facing a host of growth-oriented economists who disagreed).[37] Furthermore, they had no positive theoretical program of their own to offer, nor any clear foundation for developing one. (They would

[35] U.S. Congress, Joint Economic Committee, *Government Price Statistics: Hearings (1961)*, 580.

[36] Cf. Ibid., 683.

[37] For example, see ibid., 670–684; U.S. Congress, Joint Economic Committee, *Government Price Statistics: Hearings (1966)*, 155–162.

have had little interest, for example, in the capabilities-based welfare index that I proposed in Chapter 8.) Unions carefully protected the prerogatives of wage negotiations: ultimately, real gains in workers' material standards of living would come through organizing power and productivity, not expert-sanctioned theory. But this left them vulnerable to the charge (which was largely true) that the constant-goods index had no basis in economic theory, and that vulnerability had important consequences.[38]

As we have seen in previous chapters, recourse to a professional imperative was the bureau's major defense against allegations of political bias. During the Second World War, staff had clung to the institutionalist vision of "price index" in which prices were the only variables; now, with the rise of neoclassical microeconomics, it was the constant-utility index. Unless union economists could offer an alternative theoretical conception (and they could not), they would be (and were) entirely reduced to negative critiques of the constant-utility approach: this wasn't feasible; that required too many untenable assumptions. It was a recipe for exactly what happened: winning battles on specific operational proposals but losing the war over the entire conceptual framework for the index.

WELFARE IN THE AMERICAN WELFARE STATE

By the 1970s, top BLS staff members had begun treating the constant-utility ideal as the objective for the CPI. Yet that decision alone did not ensure that the federal government would (de facto) tie indexation to the constant-utility approach, a link which even many price index theorists would later regard as problematic. Why did politicians and administrators bind benefit payments, eligibility levels, and income-based parameters in so many programs to the CPI? Why, having made that choice, did it prove so difficult to select another basis for indexation that was more suitable for income adjustment (either a revised CPI or another statistical measure entirely)?

In part, the answer was bureaucratic imitation of escalator clauses in labor contracts: as we will see, Congress gave no serious attention to the conceptual basis for indexation when first linking Social Security payments to the CPI. Still, the years since 1972 have seen substantial congressional, academic, and government scrutiny of indexation; nevertheless, though

---

[38] For an example of this common critique of the constant-goods index, see Marshall Reinsdorf and Jack E. Triplett, "A Review of Reviews: Ninety Years of Professional Thinking About the Consumer Price Index," in *Price Index Concepts and Measurement*, ed. W. Erwin Diewert, John S. Greenlees, and Charles Hulten (Chicago: University of Chicago Press, forthcoming).

problems and inequities of the current system have been raised repeatedly, no substantive changes have been made.[39] If anything, the shifts have been in the opposite direction, as the CPI has moved closer to approximating an ordinalist, constant-utility index suitable for macroeconomic analysis. I suggest that a large part of the mismatch between the goals of indexation and the statistical measure at its base lies in the nature of the American welfare state itself and how its features interact with the constant-utility approach.

As we saw in Chapter 8, adopting an ordinalist view of cost-of-living indexes (or assuming stable utility functions) undercuts any relative components to a standard of living: the welfare delivered by a set of material goods is not judged against a dynamic technological, social, and economic environment but assessed in an abstract manner from a static set of consumer preferences or utility functions. One consequence of this step is to prevent distributional equity from affecting cost-of-living index calculations, since (by definition) assessing distributional equity requires considering the benefits of material goods in relation to their broader economic environment. Of course, as numerous scholars have argued, such deliberate inattention to distributional issues has been a hallmark of the American welfare state. The most generous, least stigmatizing benefits (e.g., Social Security retirement payments) have gone to those with stable employment records in industrial or professional occupations. By contrast, less generous, less reliable, and more tightly controlled benefits have gone to the neediest Americans, and thus the system, despite the absolute benefits it provided, has been less effective at eliminating relative deprivation, especially for many women and minorities who exist outside the regular labor force or on its margins.[40]

The political difficulty of distributional questions in American policy was reinforced by the drive for rationalization. Administering welfare programs

[39] We have already noted the comments about indexation during the hearings on the Boskin report (Chapter 8). Similar points were raised earlier and in later studies, for example: U.S. Congressional Budget Office, _Indexing with the Consumer Price Index: Problems and Alternatives_ (Washington, D.C.: U.S. GPO, 1981); Charles L. Schultze and Christopher Mackie, eds., _At What Price? Conceptualizing and Measuring Cost-of-Living and Price Indexes_ (Washington, D.C.: National Academy Press, 2002).

[40] Jerry R. Cates, _Insuring Inequality: Administrative Leadership in Social Security, 1935–54_ (Ann Arbor: University of Michigan Press, 1983); Linda Gordon, _Pitied but Not Entitled: Single Mothers and Welfare Reform, 1890–1935_ (Cambridge: Harvard University Press, 1994); Gwendolyn Mink, _The Wages of Motherhood: Inequality in the Welfare State, 1917–1942_ (Ithaca: Cornell University Press, 1995); M. B. Katz, _The Price of Citizenship: Redefining the American Welfare State_ (New York: Metropolitan Books, 2001); Deborah E. Ward, _The White Welfare State: The Racialization of U.S. Welfare Policy_ (Ann Arbor: University of Michigan Press, 2005).

on a national scale required a substantial bureaucracy, which of course would only be acceptable if it operated on a rule-governed, rational basis. The political salience and growing fiscal importance of various welfare programs accentuated the drive to "take politics out" of their administration, including both benefit calculations and eligibility parameters. Since distributional issues, alongside larger questions about need or adequate standards of living, are invariably laden with normative judgments, the push for rationalization necessarily involved minimizing these topics. In turn, that reinforced tendencies to avoid forms of cost-of-living statistics that explicitly addressed economic equity.

I will explore this dynamic and its connection to the CPI through two case studies of indexation: the creation and indexation of U.S. poverty thresholds and the indexation of Social Security payments. Despite the substantial differences between anti-poverty programs and Social Security (means-tested vs. an "earned" entitlement; disliked vs. widely popular), they nonetheless share key features. Both were motivated by concern for poor and lower-income Americans; both faced political opposition that led supporters to minimize distributional questions; both touted a rationalized objectivity that masked the difficult political judgments needed to make the systems work appropriately; and both became trapped by this context (the desire to address inequity but the political difficulty of dealing with it) and thus were unable to adapt to changing circumstances. Indexation based on the CPI slid easily into this dynamic but only reinforced the dysfunction rather than challenging it.

I will begin by considering the poverty thresholds and the Social Security system on their own terms, then, in a final section, consider how indexation based on the CPI fits with the existing frameworks for both programs.

Poverty and the Cost of Living

The U.S. poverty thresholds are a perfect example of the paradoxes that attend efforts to address distributional equity through the rationalized framework of the American welfare state. On the one hand, defining "poverty" clearly requires normative judgments, and any attention to poverty at all reflects some concern for economic equity. On the other hand, the constraints of American politics require minimizing consideration of distributional questions, while the imperatives of rationalization demand excluding normative factors. The natural consequence of this dilemma is a failed statistical system that cannot produce the knowledge appropriate for the political tasks it has been set. A consideration of the history of the poverty thresholds illustrates this dynamic at work.

In his first State of the Union address on January 8, 1964, President Lyndon B. Johnson announced plans to wage an "unconditional war on poverty," soon to be spearheaded by the Office of Economic Opportunity (OEO). Having unilaterally declared war, however, the administration needed to assess what one early report called "the strength of the enemy."[41] That would not prove easy. Although New Deal programs such as the Social Security Act of 1935 had targeted specific populations (such as the disabled, low-income children, and the unemployed), poverty as such had not been a major policy focus. Moreover, in most means-tested programs, the states had substantial leeway on eligibility and benefit levels, meaning that there were no uniform standards for what constituted "need." Indeed, states often used this freedom to add extra criteria (such as "suitability" of the family environment) to restrict the ability of black children to receive federal aid.[42]

The initial theoretical framework for the war on poverty arose from President Kennedy's Council of Economic Advisers (CEA), which also provided the administration with its first working definition: the poor were those with annual incomes of $3,000 or less. The derivation of that figure had clearly been ad hoc and laden with political concerns.[43] Despite (or perhaps because of) that approach, the CEA definition actually corresponded quite closely to public conceptions of "poverty," at least as best as those can be ascertained.[44] Nevertheless, it had clear problems (making no adjustment for family size, for example) and its lack of formal justification made it an unsuitable basis for rationalized administration. Thus, over the following year and a half, the Office of Economic Opportunity began searching for an improved statistical measurement of its target population.

The BLS, already under pressure from Secretary of Labor Willard Wirtz for not responding to administration initiatives, quickly tried to leverage its

[41] "Text of Johnson's State of the Union Address," 9 January 1964, *NYT*, p. 16. "The First Step," OEO Congressional Report, April 1965, as quoted in Alice O'Connor, *Poverty Knowledge: Social Science, Social Policy, and the Poor in Twentieth-Century U.S. History* (Princeton: Princeton University Press, 2001), 182.

[42] O'Connor, *Poverty Knowledge*, 139–140. Winifred Bell, *Aid to Dependent Children* (New York: Columbia University Press, 1965); Oscar A. Ornati, *Poverty Amid Affluence* (New York: Twentieth Century Fund, 1966), 22–24; Ward, *White Welfare State*, 110–130.

[43] Anonymous BLS memo [perhaps Arnold Chase], "How the Council of Economic Advisers Derived the Estimate of $3,000," January 1965, Poverty I, box 33, GCS 1946–72, BLS. Gordon M. Fisher, "The Development of the Orshansky Poverty Thresholds and Their Subsequent History as the Official U.S. Poverty Measure," 1997), 13–14, available from http://www.census.gov/hhes/www/povmeas/papers/orshansky.html. Fisher's paper provides by far the most complete analysis of the development of the poverty thresholds.

[44] Denton R. Vaughan, "Exploring the Use of the Public's Views to Set Income Poverty Thresholds and Adjust Them over Time," *Social Security Bulletin* 56, no. 2 (1993): 22–46.

intermittent tradition of publishing standard budgets that defined a "modest but adequate" level of living. (Recall that the BLS had abandoned its standard budgets in the 1920s; Chapter 3. In the late 1940s, it made another effort, again based on the family wage concept, in which the bureau estimated expenses for a male wage-earner supporting a wife and two children.) Staff members envisioned a two-stage process: quick development of an interim measure "available promptly in 1965," and a more involved research program that would require consultation with federal, state, local, and academic experts to create a "'minimum adequate' standard budget, built up from scientifically derived standards." Data from the bureau's 1960–1961 consumer expenditure survey would allow the basic budget to be adjusted for families of different sizes, locations, and compositions (i.e., age and relationships of family members).[45]

Yet the bureau's plan was too ambitious, too optimistic about "scientifically derived standards," and too late. In the Social Security Administration, staff statistician Molly Orshansky had been studying poverty among the elderly and children since 1960. Confronted with the same problems of definition, Orshansky chose to eschew the full standard budget approach (which she knew required "considerable work" and many subjective judgments) in favor of a simpler strategy that might produce roughly the same result. For a 1963 article on "Children of the Poor," Orshansky based her classifications on two food budgets prepared by the Department of Agriculture in 1962: a "low-cost" plan and an even more spartan "economy" plan. Since a recent Department of Agriculture survey showed that the average family spent one-third of its after-tax income on food, Orshansky multiplied the cost data for each standard food budget by a factor of three (later known as the "multiplier") to produce two income levels corresponding to the low-cost and economy standards, respectively. Although Orshansky did not publish a full set of poverty lines in her 1963 paper, she did note that a non-farm, two-parent family of four would require $3,165 per year to meet the economy budget, a figure subsequently cited by the CEA when it announced its $3,000 poverty threshold.[46]

[45] On the bureau's trouble with Wirtz, see Goldberg and Moye, *First Hundred Years*, 185–186, 216–217; Clague to Daniel P. Moynihan [then Assistant Sec. of Labor], 16 December 1963, Poverty I, box 33, GSC 1946–72, BLS. On the standard budgets, see Helen H. Lamale and Margaret S. Stotz, "The Interim City Worker's Family Budget," *MLR* 83, no. 8 (1960): 785. For the bureau's plans to create a new poverty measure, see Helen H. Lamale, "Basic Research needs on the problem of poverty," 19 May 1964, Poverty I, box 33, GSC 1946–72, BLS; Robert J. Meyers to Daniel Moynihan, 1 July 1964, ibid.; Clague to V. S. Hudson, 12 October 1964, ibid.; and BLS, "A Program of Research on Poverty," January 1965, pp. 1–4, ibid.

[46] Fisher, "Development of the Orshansky Poverty Thresholds," 3–14. Mollie Orshansky, "Family Budgets and Fee Schedules of Voluntary Agencies," *Social Security Bulletin* 22,

During 1964, Orshansky began expanding her poverty thresholds to cover other family sizes and compositions. Pre-prints of Orshanky's article began circulating through Washington agencies in the late fall of 1964, attracting considerable interest at the OEO; the article itself appeared in January 1965 and drew explicit attention to how the new thresholds offered a different profile of the poor than the CEA's $3,000 line (basically reducing the number of elderly and raising the number of children). Finally, in May 1965, the OEO designated Orshansky's thresholds as its official definition of poverty.[47]

In many respects, the OEO had an easy decision when opting for Orshansky's thresholds over BLS plans for standard budgets; on pragmatic merits alone, Orshansky's version had the great virtue of already existing. Yet, the choice was less obvious than it may appear. Orshansky herself apparently regarded the 1965 thresholds as a preliminary estimate, akin to the bureau's proposed interim measure of poverty: she called her methods "relatively crude" and briefly described ongoing plans "to develop more refined measures."[48] Furthermore, standard budgets had a long history as tools for assessing financial need (cf. Chapter 2), and they were still widely used on the state level and by private charities for tasks such as determining minimum wage levels, eligibility and benefits for Aid to Families with Dependent Children (AFDC), public housing eligibility, fee schedules, and so forth.[49] Moreover, standard budgets could be readily adapted for geographical variations (for example, by altering the composition of the budget to reflect climate differences and then pricing them in relevant locations).

Nevertheless, standard budgets had other features that made them an unlikely choice for a high-profile policy role or a central component of the rationalized administration of poverty programs. Standard budgets exemplified an interlocking triad of (1) a feminized operational domain requiring (2) normative knowledge and targeted at (3) need-based, protectionist policies designed to help struggling women and children. Most standard budgets were produced by women who worked in highly feminized fields such as home economics or social work. Though a few projects (such as the BLS

no. 4 (1959): 17; Mollie Orshansky, "Children of the Poor," *Social Security Bulletin* 26, no. 7 (1963): 8–9.

[47] Mollie Orshansky, "Counting the Poor: Another Look at the Poverty Profile," *Social Security Bulletin* 28, no. 1 (1965): 3–29. Fisher, "Development of the Orshansky Poverty Thresholds," 14–16, 22.

[48] Orshansky, "Counting the Poor," 3.

[49] BLS, "Report of the Advisory Committee on Standard Budget Research," June 1963, Adequacy—Standard Budgets, 1947–63, box 1, Ida Merriam papers.

City Workers' Family Budget) covered higher material standards ("modest but adequate," in the bureau's terms), most aimed at bare minimum standards—and these were the versions that found common application in administrative roles. The intersection of these three features—feminized, normative, protectionist—was not accidental. Standard budgets inevitably involved normative judgments (as much as compilers tried to evade them), and accordingly (as I argued in Chapter 3), they proved acceptable in administrative roles only at the most minimal level. Both of these factors contributed to the gendering of the research, which lacked the financial and cognitive status of more "objective" social science fields and resonated with the image of women as nurturing and protective.[50]

It was not a good match for the OEO. The organization was pursuing a major, controversial expansion of federal social services; not coincidentally, it was also sitting at a pivot point in the history of poverty research in which "'hard' quantitivative data, econometric modeling techniques, and cost/benefit policy analysis" would take center stage.[51] Of course, any attempt to define poverty necessarily required subjective decisions. Yet Orshansky had taken steps to minimize this vulnerability, such as grounding her thresholds in the one section of household spending where something akin to the natural sciences (nutrition) could be used. Likewise, her decision to multiply the food budget by three to follow average family consumption/income proportions was surely (to borrow Orshansky's characterization) "arbitrary, but not unreasonable," and it had the virtue of relying primarily on empirical observation instead of judgments about adequate housing, clothing, and so forth.[52] Admittedly, the mechanical procedure could sometimes lead to strange results, and subsequent critics found numerous problematic assumptions and important questions that the method failed to address (for example, how to handle taxes, geographical differences, "in-kind" benefits such as public housing, or changes in family work patterns that led

---

[50] For surveys of standard budgets in this period, see Orshansky, "Famliy Budgets and Fee Schedules"; BLS, "Report of the Advisory Committee on Standard Budget Research," June 1963; Ornati, *Poverty Amid Affluence*, 19–26; Judith Eleanor Innes, *Knowledge and Public Policy: The Search for Meaningful Indicators* (New Brunswick: Transaction Publishers, 1990), 145–150, 262–271. The predominance of women in this area is exemplified in the credits for the 1948 version of the BLS City Worker's Family Budget: Lester S. Kellogg and Dorothy S. Brady, "The City Worker's Family Budget," *MLR* 66, no. 2 (1948): 133, 136. On the intersection of gender and protectionist policies, see Theda Skocpol, *Protecting Soldiers and Mothers: The Political Origins of Social Policy in the United States* (Cambridge: Belknap Press, 1992); Gordon, *Pitied but Not Entitled*; Mink, *The Wages of Motherhood*.

[51] O'Connor, *Poverty Knowledge*, 21, 166–195.

[52] Orshansky, "Counting the Poor," 4.

to increased expenditures).[53] But the method had the virtue of mechanical simplicity and at least the appearance of minimal judgments about "adequacy," hence making it more attractive for those seeking an objective measure of poverty for rationalized administration.

The strengths of Orshansky's approach in this regard are best seen when viewed against the later history of the BLS standard budget project. In 1966, BLS commissioner Arthur Ross obtained congressional funding to update the City Worker's Family Budget and to produce a "lower standard budget" that would "represent a minimum of adequacy." The new lower-standard budget appeared in 1969, defining a "minimum" that was well below the bureau's moderate standard but still roughly 50 percent greater than the poverty threshold for a family of four. In the interim, however, Ross had resigned and been replaced by President Nixon's choice, Geoffrey Moore of the NBER. Not surprisingly, given Moore's conservative inclinations, his background in institutional economics, and his longtime work at the NBER, he was leery about embedding clearly normative judgments in statistical calculations. "I do not think the BLS should set itself up as an authority on what is adequate or inadequate, what is a luxury and what is not, etc.," he told Joel Popkin later that year, "no matter how reasonable the position may seem to us."[54] His unease would soon grow. When Nixon announced plans to replace cash benefits to needy Americans (under programs such as AFDC) with a negative income tax, advocates for the poor and minority groups used the bureau's low-standard budget to argue that Nixon's proposal was too stingy. Even worse, after Nixon resurrected wage and price controls in 1971 to combat growing inflation, Congress moved to exempt substandard wages from controls and used the bureau's lower-standard budget to define that level. This provoked a short battle between labor activists (with their congressional allies) and Nixon's Cost of Living

---

[53] For example, since nutritionists believed that women required less food than men, their food budgets were correspondingly smaller. Multiplying everyone's food budget by three meant that female-headed households had a substantially lower poverty threshold than male-headed households of the same composition. The discrepancy never affected eligibility parameters for federal programs, but it remained in official poverty statistics until 1981. Fisher, "Development of the Orshansky Poverty Thresholds," 28–30. For a brief overview of other criticisms of the Orshansky thresholds, see Christopher Jencks, "The Politics of Income Measurement," in *The Politics of Numbers*, ed. William Alonso and Paul Starr (New York: Russell Sage Foundation, 1983), 92–105; Constance F. Citro and Robert T. Michael, eds., *Measuring Poverty: A New Approach* (Washington, D.C.: National Academy Press, 1995), 25–31.

[54] Jean C. Brackett, *Three Standards of Living for an Urban Family of Four Persons, Spring 1967*, BLS Bulletin, nos. 1570–5. (Washington, D.C.: U.S. GPO, 1969). Moore to Popkin, 2 December 1969, as quoted in Goldberg and Moye, *First Hundred Years*, 233.

Council (which had authority over implementing the controls), ending in a judicial decision to force a compromise solution.[55]

These political controversies plus the bureau's inability to find an objective basis for deciding "what is adequate or inadequate" precipitated a decade-long struggle by the BLS to rid itself of authority over the standard budgets. It tried handing responsibility for the budgets to other federal agencies, but no one would take it. It tried suspending publication pending further research and new expenditure data, but administrators in state and private social service agencies (along with congressional supporters) forced the program to continue. Finally, it succeeded in gathering official sanction (in the form of an external review committee) to transform the project, which would now publish average expenditures for families at different income levels rather than estimating adequate standards. And then, perhaps a bright spot amidst an otherwise distressing situation, congressional funding cuts in 1981 allowed the bureau to scuttle the entire program.[56]

Such were the hazards of embedding normative judgments too visibly in federal statistical calculations. But of course it was impossible to avoid choices with political valences when constructing any statistic, which brings us back to the poverty thresholds. Having settled on Orshansky's method, the OEO and the Johnson administration faced another problem: how to update the thresholds over time. There were many options, but one big conceptual choice. Should the thresholds be adjusted only for changes in "prices"? Or did poverty naturally have a relative dimension, meaning that any threshold would necessarily rise alongside overall, material standards of living?

For the specialists in both the BLS and the Social Security Administration, the general decision was clear: poverty was at least partially relative. The BLS had already taken a similar stance on its standard budgets, insisting that "such a budget is not an absolute and unchanging thing," but rather would "vary with the changing values of the community, with the advance of scientific knowledge of human needs, [and] with the productive power of the community."[57] Likewise, a similar relativity appeared in Orshansky's thresholds: not only might the minimum food budget change with new knowledge about nutrition, but the "multiplier" (based upon the ratio of food expenses to after-tax income) logically ought to change as consumption patterns shifted. Indeed, throughout the late 1960s, numerous Social

[55] Innes, *Knowledge and Public Policy*, 150–153, 262–263, 268–269.
[56] Goldberg and Moye, *First Hundred Years*, 233–234.
[57] Kellogg and Brady, "City Worker's Family Budget," 137.

Security Administration officials—including Orshansky, the head of the Division of Research and Statistics (Ida Merriam), and the commissioner (Robert M. Ball)—all assumed that the poverty thresholds would need to be updated periodically to reflect changing community standards.[58]

Other officials throughout the executive branch saw the matter differently, however. When the CEA had prepared the conceptual backdrop for Johnson's war on poverty, officials had decided that only an absolute measure would provide a feasible goal. Defining poverty in absolute terms (e.g., as a fixed material standard) fit the basic strategy for liberal political success in the postwar era: resolve economic deprivation through expanded growth while bypassing stickier issues such as relative inequality. At least in principle, absolute poverty could be eliminated as a by-product of broader economic growth. By contrast, adding a relative dimension would complicate the project. "Probably a politically acceptable program [to combat poverty] must avoid completely any use of the term 'inequality' or of the term '_redistribution_ of income or wealth,'" wrote poverty expert Robert Lampman to CEA chairman Walter Heller in the summer of 1963.[59] Moreover, a relative poverty measure might create a continually advancing goalpost that would thwart the administration's plan to end at least one "war" quickly.

By the time agency economists and statisticians began seriously debating how to update the thresholds in the late 1960s, the deteriorating economic situation made the outcome almost inevitable. The combination of escalating spending on Vietnam, rapid growth in domestic outlays for the Great Society, and a serious crisis in the international monetary system led to a massive run on gold in March 1968 that signaled the end of U.S. dominance in international finance. More visibly on the domestic front, price indexes were registering a disturbing resurgence in inflation while growth was slowing relative to government expenditures. Accordingly, the era of using economic expansion to "avoid extensive debate, harsh conflict, and the necessity of painful choices" (as historian Robert Collins has put it) was now coming to an end. In the fall of 1968, the Bureau of the Budget convened an interagency Poverty Level Review Committee to deliberate on updates to the thresholds; the following spring, it voted to adjust the thresholds annually based on movements in the CPI. That summer, the Bureau of the Budget made the thresholds (linked to the CPI and published by the Census

---

[58] Fisher, "Development of the Orshansky Poverty Thresholds," 17–18.

[59] Lampman to Walter Heller, 3 June 1963, as quoted in O'Connor, _Poverty Knowledge_, 154. See O'Connor, ibid., 183–185; Robert M. Collins, _More: The Politics of Economic Growth in Postwar America_ (New York: Oxford University Press, 2000), 40–67.

Bureau) the official government measure of poverty; a slightly modified version (known as the poverty guidelines and published by the Department of Health, Education, and Welfare) became the working administrative definition of poverty, used to set eligibility criteria and so forth.[60]

Taken as a whole, the attempts to define poverty illustrate the desire to avoid addressing controversial questions within official statistics (what counts as "adequate"?), especially as these questions deal with distributional equity. This strategy did not resolve the underlying issues, however, and the result was thus not a meaningful political compromise but an episode of failed governance, as the post-1969 history of the poverty thresholds makes clear. The poverty thresholds have been notoriously difficult to change, and none of the numerous reform efforts have succeeded. The easy explanations for this phenomenon are inadequate. It cannot simply be the operational difficulties of updating a basic metric for government policies or budgeting: the CPI has equal (if not greater) financial impact and high political visibility, and yet aspects of its methodology have changed repeatedly over the last forty years. It cannot be bureaucratic inertia or political deadlock: Although the Office of Management and Budget has titular control over the thresholds, Congress (and certainly the White House) could force a change or develop an alternative measure if so desired, and politicians have passed far more controversial legislation dealing with the poor (e.g., reform of AFDC in 1996) than merely detailing how to count them. Nor can it be conservative opposition, because conservatives themselves have repeatedly failed to lower the measure by counting noncash benefits against the threshold levels.[61] The poverty measures are a remarkable bureaucratic phenomenon: No one likes them; no one thinks they are adequate; and no one can change them.

I suggest that the poverty thresholds are merely a more extreme example of the tensions embedded in statistical rationalization. As an official statistic produced by a federal agency and widely used for administrative purposes, the poverty level is supposed to be an apolitical, neutral technical fact. Yet when it comes to defining poverty, the normative dimensions are simply too visible. Whenever an attempt is made to alter the definition,

---

[60] Collins, *More*, 59–97. Fisher, "Development of the Orshansky Poverty Thresholds," 17–22.

[61] For an overview of early reform efforts, see Fisher, "Development of the Orshansky Poverty Thresholds," 23–33. On more recent attempts, see Rebecca M. Blank, "How to Improve Poverty Measurement in the United States," *Journal of Policy Analysis and Management* 27, no. 2 (2008): 239–244; Howard Glennerster, "United States Poverty Studies and Poverty Measurement: The Past Twenty-Five Years," *Social Science Review* 76, no. 1 (2002): 83–107.

charges immediately fly that "politics" rather than technical merit are behind the change.[62] And, of course, as a piece of rationalized administration, the thresholds are supposed to be—indeed, even need to be—above partisan manipulation. If an administration, political party, or partisan interest group can reduce (or raise) the number of the "poor" simply by fiat, then the number loses all meaning as a fact that is distinct from the policies it is intended to monitor or implement. The result is paralysis: The thresholds can only be changed by revealing them for what they are not supposed to be.

Already the reader can no doubt see how indexation based on the CPI would fit naturally with such a system. That fit became even closer when the CPI was approached from a constant-utility perspective, which similarly ignores distributional questions, purports to avoid normative judgments, and has recourse to theory (neoclassical microeconomics) to justify its operations. Before pursuing this theme further, however, we will examine the history of Old-Age and Survivors' Insurance (OASI), the component of the 1935 Social Security Act that is, on its own, colloquially known as "Social Security."[63]

Indexing Social Security, Ignoring Inequality

Unlike anti-poverty programs, OASI has been enormously popular with Americans since the mid-1950s. Nevertheless, both share certain features. As with anti-poverty programs, the designers of OASI primarily wanted to help low-income Americans but also deliberately minimized attention to distributional equity in much of the structure and official rhetoric about the program. Whereas the war on poverty accomplished the latter goal by setting low, absolute material standards to define eligibility, OASI accomplished the same aim by giving benefits irrespective of need, and in fact assigning higher benefits (in absolute terms) to those with larger incomes. Because of the program's popularity and because the full costs of benefit increases are only realized years, or even decades, later, rationalization has been an essential feature of the system from the beginning—used in this

---

[62] E.g., "Redefining Poverty," *Chicago Tribune*, 20 April 1982; Joan Beck, "Fleecing the Taxpaying Sheep Again," *Chicago Tribune*, 24 April 1982, A8; Alvin L. Schorr, "Redefining Poverty Levels," *NYT*, 9 May 1984, A27. These issues have even split technical advisory panels; cf. the dissent of John Cogan in Citro and Michael, eds., *Measuring Poverty*, 385–390.

[63] In 1956, Congress added disability insurance to the program and created a separate Disability Insurance trust fund; thus today, the program is known as Old-Age, Survivors, and Disability Insurance (OASDI). Nonetheless, much of the focus remains on the OASI components.

case to restrain Congress from overburdening the program. As we would expect, however, these efforts failed—since political judgments cannot be excluded from rationalized systems—and subsequently the difficulty of squarely confronting the normative issues essential to reforming the program have produced OASI's own version of political paralysis.

A brief consideration illustrates the foundations of these later problems. As Peter Ferrara has argued, OASI suffers from an "inherent contradiction."[64] On the one hand, the program is billed as "insurance": only if workers contribute to the system can they (or surviving family members) claim a benefit, and benefits are partially scaled toward contribution rates (so that workers who pay into the system at higher rates will, in principle, get higher monthly benefits). Social Security taxes are collected independently from general income taxes, and benefits are paid from these funds without recourse to general government revenues. Program administrators have avidly promoted these parallels to private insurance plans and have actively differentiated OASI from means-tested relief programs.[65] Moreover, OASI is funded through a regressive taxation plan: a flat payroll tax that is applied to wage and salary income up to a certain level (the "wage base"), above which the tax rate is zero. Thus, although low-income and wealthy earners contribute at the same rate (and wealthy earners pay more in absolute terms), Social Security taxes consume a much larger percentage of the total earnings of low-income earners than of wealthy earners. In all these respects, OASI does seem roughly like a private insurance plan.

On the other hand, many aspects of OASI violate this model. Both when OASI began and when it expanded, the program paid out full benefits to recent retirees who had made only minimal contributions. Moreover, for many years OASI set a minimum benefit level, and even today lower-income retirees will receive a benefit that provides a higher proportion of their previous income than will wealthier retirees. In these respects, OASI has been a tool for redistributing income, both from younger Americans to older Americans and from wealthier earners to lower-income earners. These dual objectives have contributed greatly to both the popularity and the fiscal problems of OASI, and have likewise shaped its relationship to the Consumer Price Index.

The "contradiction" was built into OASI (and its predecessor, Old-Age Insurance) from the very beginning. In no small part, the insurance-like

---

[64] Peter J. Ferrara, *Social Security: The Inherent Contradiction* (San Francisco, Calif.: Cato Institute, 1980).

[65] Cates, *Insuring Inequality*.

aspects were designed to protect the program. As President Franklin D. Roosevelt put it, "We put those payroll contributions there so as to give the contributors a legal, moral, and political right to collect their pensions and their unemployment benefits. With those taxes in there, no damn politician can ever scrap my social security program." But early program architects, such as Secretary of Labor Frances Perkins, Douglas Brown, Arthur J. Altmeyer, and Roosevelt himself, also disliked means-tested relief programs and argued that extensive relief payments would promote a degrading dependency on the state. Instead of what Perkins called the "dole," she and many other New Deal liberals sought public works programs and a commitment to revitalizing the labor movement (Chapter 4); jobs, not ongoing government financial support, were the ultimate solution to poverty (at least among able-bodied men). The Social Security Act of 1935 was designed to mitigate the hazards of the industrial, capitalist economy but not to replace it or provide a guaranteed income. Moreover, Roosevelt and his allies warned that more generous, popular alternatives to their version of social insurance (such as the Townsend Plan to provide a hefty, flat monthly payment to all non-felon, elderly American citizens) were fiscally irresponsible. It was partially from the fear of such programs that early OASI advocates and later administrators retained a dogged commitment to payroll taxes rather than general revenues as a source for benefits: the former permitted an independent accounting system and kept the link between increased taxes and increased benefits highly visible. The payroll tax system thus served a dual purpose: it turned OASI payments into "earned" benefits (making them harder to eliminate while also fostering a sense of self-reliance), and it would keep Congress from rapidly inflating benefits to levels that would create huge long-term deficits.[66]

For the first thirteen years of its existence (1937–1949), OASI struggled both to supplant its competitors (namely public assistance programs, such as the means-tested Old-Age Assistance, OAA) and to win widespread public support. Finally, a major set of amendments in 1950 succeeded in establishing the centrality of the program within domestic political economy by greatly extending its coverage (adding, for example, agricultural workers and the self-employed) and by dramatically boosting benefit payments.

---

[66] Roosevelt, as quoted in Schlesinger, *Age of Roosevelt: Coming of the New Deal*, 308–309. Edward D. Berkowitz, *America's Welfare State: From Roosevelt to Reagan* (Baltimore: Johns Hopkins University Press, 1991), 16–19, 44–47. Martha Derthick, *Policymaking for Social Security* (Washington, D.C.: Brookings Institution, 1979), 213–227; Cates, *Insuring Inequality*; Julian E. Zelizer, *Taxing America: Wilbur D. Mills, Congress, and the State, 1945–1975* (New York: Cambridge University Press, 1998), 55–81.

Shortly thereafter, the number of benefit claims doubled and average payments rose 80 percent. Later that decade, Congress added disability insurance to the program (with a separate trust fund) and renamed it Old-Age, Survivors, and Disability Insurance (OASDI).[67]

In essence, the 1950 amendments allowed OASDI to take over poverty relief for those elderly Americans who had ties to the regular labor force. In many respects, this proved to be a positive development for many low-income Americans since benefits could be more generous and more equitably administered across the country than under the state-led relief program, OAA. Nevertheless, not only did OASDI still exclude some of the elderly poor (only wage and salaried workers or their families could receive benefits), but it also created a dangerous fiscal dynamic. Following the insurance model, when left-wing advocates and their congressional allies wanted to boost benefits for lower-income elderly, they had to raise benefits for everyone. Such benefit hikes were popular, since huge numbers of active voters benefited. Yet they also had the potential to overrun the budget because the full costs would only become due years later.

The solution to this potential danger was rationalization, a strategy that was both endemic to an insurance-based scheme such as OASDI because of its inherent complexity and a necessary feature to protect the system's long-term solvency. OASDI's convoluted benefit formulas and reliance on actuarial analysis produced the very conditions that Max Weber argued would promote rationalized bureaucracy over democratic governance, namely the need for highly skilled, expert functionaries who could specialize in the arcane details of a system: their assumptions, their rationale, and their consequences.[68] To borrow the characterization of Martha Derthick in her landmark 1979 study, Social Security has been "a hard program to classify, and a very hard program to understand." The system's "extreme technicality" helped to make it "incomprehensible to all but a highly expert few at the proprietary core of policymaking." The initial legislation was largely designed by three academic consultants; administrative control was highly concentrated for roughly the first thirty-five years of the program (when it was led by two men, Arthur J. Altmeyer and Robert M. Ball); actuaries and other experts have been essential to preserving the program's independence;

---

[67] Derthick, *Policymaking for Social Security*, 271–274; Berkowitz, *America's Welfare State*, 55–62; Zelizer, *Taxing America*, 66–79. On the role of the CIO in the 1950 amendments, see Seth Wigderson, "How the CIO Saved Social Security," *Labor History* 44, no. 4 (2003): 483–507.

[68] Max Weber, *Economy and Society: An Outline of Interpretive Sociology* (New York: Bedminster Press, 1968), 948–952.

legislative oversight has been constrained by the technical complexity of the system; and major reforms have been sanctioned and crafted more by periodic formal advisory councils and small, informal policymaking networks than by broader congressional negotiation and legislative debate.[69]

These conditions meshed with the goals of the original architects of the Social Security Act, who, viewing the chaos, corruption, inefficiency, and short-sighted operation of state-level public pensions in 1934, had deliberately sought "to substitute expert administration for political discretion" (in the characterization of historian Edward Berkowitz). Especially because pension plans offered the tantalizing and (in their view) dangerous possibility of trading short-term political gain (benefit boosts) for long-term costs that would only emerge years or even decades later, it was essential to limit congressional or executive control over the system.[70] Technical knowledge was thus a pragmatic requirement for administration but also a tool for curtailing the reach of democratic politics.

Even in Congress, a similar (albeit less rigid) form of rationalized policymaking could occur since the centralized power of key congressional committees through the first two-thirds of the twentieth century—especially the House Ways and Means Committee—allowed a small group of politicians to protect OASDI. Thus, as Julian Zelizer has argued, the long-time chairman of Ways and Means, Rep. Wilbur D. Mills (D-Arkansas), successfully parlayed his own "technocratic expertise" into a tool for asserting personal and committee control over tax policy and Social Security legislation from the 1950s into the early 1970s and thereby protecting the solvency of OASDI. Mills's efforts were reinforced by conservative actuarial assumptions from the Social Security Administration—notably an assumption that wages would remain level over time—which provided him with the accounting authority needed to hold back benefit hikes until (as inevitably happened) wage increases outstripped actuarial predictions and the system developed a suitable surplus. Finally, because benefit hikes occurred only periodically, inflation repeatedly eroded the real costs of the expenditures; thus, to hold down expenses, Congress need do nothing but refrain from voting on increased benefits.[71]

Unfortunately, these rationalized bulwarks all failed simultaneously in the 1970s. Ironically, Republicans sparked the problem by suggesting that

[69] Derthick, *Policymaking for Social Security*, 291, 17–210.
[70] Berkowitz, *America's Welfare State*, 16–18.
[71] Derthick, *Policymaking for Social Security*, 274–280, 342–345; Weaver, *Automatic Government: The Politics of Indexation*, 67–69; Zelizer, *Taxing America*, 78–81, 124–132, 159–165.

benefits be indexed to the "cost of living," a proposal that President Nixon placed before Congress in 1969 in order to "prevent future unfairness" and to help "depoliticize" the program. Since benefit increases had historically (if irregularly) exceeded the rise in the CPI, Republicans saw indexation as a cost-saving move. Yet it was also politically popular among liberals— both Lyndon Johnson and the AFL-CIO had endorsed indexation earlier, for example—because it promised to implement cost-of-living increases more rapidly and regularly than in existing ad hoc procedures; moreover, the higher inflationary trends since 1965 made these adjustments increasingly salient (cf. Chart 7.1). The decision to index OASDI to the CPI never received substantial scrutiny in Congress outside of Ways and Means and the Senate Finance Committee. Although some business groups opposed indexation, fearing that it would be a "means of institutionalizing inflation," the most serious objections came from Wilbur Mills, who worried about the loss of congressional discretion. Aside from Mills, the real battle was over the size of any benefit increase that would be attached to indexation proposals.[72] The previous authority granted (in the abstract) to apolitical, rationalized governance of the system now proved nearly impossible to resist. The principle of adjusting payments to the rising cost of living had been well-established before this period, and both union contracts and earlier experiments with Civil Service Retirement and with the poverty thresholds had established precedents for using the CPI. There is little evidence that Congress gave much serious thought to what members meant by increases in the cost of living or whether the CPI was an appropriate measure for their objective.[73]

In the midst of a brief presidential campaign in early 1972, Mills made a sudden reversal: not only would he support indexation (of both benefits and the wage base), he proposed an extraordinary 20 percent benefit increase with minimal tax adjustments, all justified by a new actuarial assumption that wages would continue to grow at historical rates. With Mills's support, the proposals sailed through on overwhelming majorities

---

[72] Richard M. Nixon, "Special Message to the Congress on Social Security, 25 September 1969," in *Public Papers of the Presidents: Richard Nixon, 1969* (Washington, D.C.: U.S. GPO, 1971), 740, 742. Henry H. Chase (U.S. Chamber of Commerce), as quoted in Weaver, *Automatic Government: The Politics of Indexation*, 72. Derthick, *Policymaking for Social Security*, 349–362; Weaver, *Automatic Government: The Politics of Indexation*, 60–79; Zelizer, *Taxing America*, 312–346.

[73] It is telling, for example, that Ways and Means did not invite anyone from the BLS to discuss the CPI during the committee's hearings on indexing OASI: U.S. House, Committee on Ways and Means, *Social Security and Welfare Proposals: Hearings before the Committee on Ways and Means*, 91st Cong., 1st sess., October 15–November 13, 1969.

in a veto-proof form. Of course, shortly thereafter, America's already surging price indexes recorded the largest annual increases since the late 1940s (over 10 percent in 1974 and 1979–1981), as domestic economic problems were deepened by major external shocks. Courtesy of the recently passed indexation amendments, these price increases translated directly into benefit increases. Meanwhile, wage growth stalled, unemployment rose, and demographic trends began working against the long-term financial health of OASDI. In 1977, the system hit the first of what would be a series of increasingly severe crises over the next six years; only a hard-negotiated compromise in 1983—which raised the retirement age, delayed payment of cost-of-living increases tied to the CPI, and increased taxes (including adding a tax on benefits for high-income recipients)— prevented a serious immediate collapse. Since that time, OASDI has existed amidst a seemingly permanent state of anxiety about the long-term viability of the program.[74]

Unfortunately, the source of OASDI's "inherent contradiction"—the desire to avoid politically hazardous topics such as distributional equity— has made it extraordinarily difficult to reform the program. Left-wing politicians and many advocates for the elderly oppose any across-the-board cuts in the program, recognizing that these will substantially harm low-income seniors. Conservatives, capitalizing on the program's rhetoric and insurance-like features, argue that it is a remarkably poor version of an insurance system and hence advocate various forms of privatization. Meanwhile, much of the public, having repeatedly been told that benefit payments are a right that they have earned through contributions, accordingly resist any tinkering with the system that might reduce those benefits.[75] Trapped by the very features that promoted rationalization in the first place, politicians now desperately need a "rational" (apolitical) means to adjust the program. Naturally, that brings us back to indexation, and to the CPI.

---

[74] On the 1972 bill, see citations above. On subsequent developments, Paul Light, *Artful Work: The Politics of Social Security Reform* (New York: Random House, 1985); Weaver, *Automatic Government: The Politics of Indexation*, 79–82. Of course, the merits of anxiety about OASI are still contested: Dean Baker and Mark Weisbrot, *Social Security: The Phony Crisis* (Chicago: University of Chicago Press, 1999).

[75] Ferrara, *Social Security: The Inherent Contradiction*; Light, *Artful Work*; Olivia S. Mitchell, Robert J. Meyers, and Howard Young, ed., *Prospects for Social Security Reform* (Philadelphia: University of Pennsylvania Press, 1999); Daniel Béland, *Social Security: History and Politics from the New Deal to the Privatization Debate* (Lawrence: University Press of Kansas, 2005); Robert B. Hudson, *The New Politics of Old Age Policy* (Baltimore: Johns Hopkins University Press, 2005).

Rationalized Governance and the Consumer Price Index

In the midst of a political deadlock, what better news than to hear how a "technical" adjustment to statistical methodology can ameliorate your problems? Not surprisingly, with OASDI facing its most serious crisis in the early 1980s, the long-standing neoclassical critiques of constant-goods indexes such as the CPI attracted new interest from budget hawks. In a short span, the CPI came under scrutiny from nearly every relevant government body: the Congressional Budget Office, the General Accounting Office, the Senate's Committee on Governmental Affairs, and two task forces from the House Budget Committee. Most attention went to the CPI's homeownership component, which critics blamed for overstating inflation. To support that charge, neoclassical economists implicitly invoked the constant-utility framework by arguing (just as in the 1961 NBER report) that durable goods should be valued by the annual cost to the user rather than through transaction prices. In practical terms, that meant basing the homeownership component on the estimated rent that would be charged for homes rather than on their current resale values. Since rents were rising more slowly than home values, the change would lower the index. In fact, critics had two rent-based measures to illustrate the potential difference: the housing component of the Commerce Department's Personal Consumer Expenditure deflator (used in the national accounts) and an experimental housing index calculated by the BLS. In 1981, over the objections of LRAC members but with substantial support from the bureau's research division and many external economists, the BLS announced plans to adopt a rental-equivalency approach.[76]

---

[76] Since the 1953 revision, the BLS had included owner-occupied housing costs in the CPI. These encompassed several components, including home prices and mortgage interest costs. Critics argued that rising home prices represented "capital appreciation" for existing homeowners, and hence biased the CPI. Moreover, in calculating the weight for the housing component in the index, the BLS included the full cost of the home and future interest payments for all surveyed families who purchased homes during the base year. Accordingly, the housing component carried a substantial weight (roughly 20%) in the overall index. Furthermore, these weights had not been adjusted downward to reflect the falling sales of homes that had occurred as interest rates rose rapidly in the late 1970s and early 1980s. See U.S. General Accounting Office, *Measurement of Homeownership Costs in the Consumer Price Index Should Be Changed: Report to the Congress* (Washington, D.C.: U.S. GAO, 1981); U.S. Senate, Committee on Governmental Affairs, *Consumer Price Index: Hearings before the Subcommittee on Congressional Operations and Oversight*, 97th Cong., 2nd sess., April 20 and May 13, 1982; U.S. House, Committee on the Budget, Task Force on Inflation, *Housing Component of the Consumer Price Index: Hearing before the Task Force on Inflation*; U.S. House, Committee on the Budget. Task Force on Entitlements, Uncontrollables, and Indexing, *Proposed Changes in the Consumer Price Index: Hearings*

After the bureau changed its treatment of housing costs and inflation rates subsided, congressional scrutiny of the CPI also receded. By the early 1990s, however, concern about growing federal debt and the future solvency of OASDI had returned to the political forefront, especially after Republicans gained control of both the House and Senate in 1994 under a promise to cut the deficit. When Federal Reserve Chairman Alan Greenspan told congressional budget committees the following January that they could save $150 billion over five years by "correcting" the CPI, his technical solution attracted bipartisan interest. The end result was the establishment of the Boskin commission by the Senate Finance Committee and the commission's resounding affirmation of the constant-utility framework.[77]

Tellingly, Greenspan and his congressional allies were unable to reach their original goal: using the findings of the Boskin commission as a technical cover to allow Congress to adjust the indexation formula directly (since Greenspan suspected that changing the CPI would be a long-term project).[78] On a broader scale, this failure is unsurprising: the same deadlock that has rendered large-scale reforms to OASDI impossible has also extended to the mechanism of indexation, which has had only minor changes since 1972.[79] Indeed, Congress has been unable to make a shift with a far greater technical consensus behind it, namely changing the basis for OASDI indexation from the CPI-W (the wage-earner index) to the CPI-U (the "all consumers" index).[80] The political pressures surrounding OASDI are so great that even a putatively technical alteration cannot be implemented from within a resolutely political institution (Congress).

Any change to indexation, therefore, had to come from within the CPI itself. Happily for advocates of budget-cutting-through-statistics, neoclassical economists both within and outside the BLS had been laying the

before the *Task Force on Entitlements, Uncontrollables, and Indexing*, 97th Cong., 1st sess., November 17 and December 3, 1981; U.S. Congressional Budget Office, *Indexing with the Consumer Price Index: Problems and Alternatives*.

77   Adam Clymer, "As Parties Skirmish over Budget, Greenspan Offers Painless Cure," *NYT*, 11 January 1995. Michael J. Boskin et al., *Toward a More Accurate Measure of the Cost of Living: Final Report to the Senate Finance Committee from the Advisory Commission to Study the Consumer Price Index* (Washington, D.C.: U.S. GPO, 1996).

78   Louis Uchitelle, "The Negotiators Forgo a Cut in Inflation Index," *NYT*, 3 May 1997, p. 12.

79   Weaver, *Automatic Government: The Politics of Indexation*, 82–92.

80   This point has been raised repeatedly, even by the BLS; cf. Katharine G. Abraham, "Toward a Cost-of-Living Index: Progress and Prospects," *Journal of Economic Perspectives* 17, no. 1 (2003): 51, n. 6. Bizarrely (or perhaps not, for the conspiracy-minded), the poverty thresholds have been switched to the CPI-U, which is arguably less appropriate than the CPI-W: Fisher, "Development of the Orshansky Poverty Thresholds," 28–29.

foundation for a shift to the constant-utility framework for over three decades. Following the constant-utility ideal, the BLS made numerous important changes to its methods in the years after 1980, including the switch to rental equivalency for homeownership, the greater adoption of hedonic techniques for quality adjustments, faster introduction of new goods and more frequent revisions of the market basket (every two years rather than every ten), and an alteration to lower-level formulae designed to compensate for alleged substitution within individual components of the index. A more radical change remains at the experimental stage: abandoning the traditional Laspeyres, constant-goods formula altogether in favor of an approach that incorporates current expenditure data and thereby provides a closer approximation to an ordinalist, constant-utility index.[81]

Despite the potential benefits of the constant-utility framework for deficit reduction, budget concerns have not driven the bureau's methodological innovations. In fact, some changes—such as the introduction of hedonic techniques for apparel—have actually raised the index, illustrating that the BLS has not been politically pressured into reducing the CPI.[82] Budget hawks have found the bureau's theoretical approach convenient, but Congress has not dictated price index methodology. On the contrary, the methodology has remained flexible in the face of political deadlock precisely because the objectives for the index and the responsibilities of the agency have been assiduously defined to avoid potentially contentious political judgment. The ordinalist version of the constant-utility index provides a professionally sanctioned theory to guide methodological decisions and thereby frees the bureau from making overtly normative choices.

Of course, there is a cost to this freedom, namely a mismatch between the conceptual basis of the CPI and one of its major applications. As we have seen, the adoption of the ordinalist constant-utility ideal for the CPI has been justified primarily by reference to the role of price indexes in macroeconomic analysis. By contrast, it is not obvious that the

---

[81] Johnson, Reed, and Stewart, "Price Measurement in the United States," 10–19. The experimental index, the Chained Consumer Price Index for All Consumers (C-CPI-U), uses a Tornqvist formula, which was identified by Erwin Diewert as one member of a larger set of "superlative" formulas that approximate a ordinalist, constant-utility index: W. E. Diewert, "Exact and Superlative Index Numbers," *Journal of Econometrics* 4, no. 2 (1976): 115–145.

[82] For a summary of more recent changes, see Johnson, Reed, and Stewart, "Price Measurement in the United States," 10–19. According to BLS estimates, the adoption of hedonic techniques has led to little net change in the index. The formula change and rental equivalency have both lowered the index. The BLS also calculates an additional version of the CPI that attempts to compensate for between-component substitution, the C-CPI-U.

constant-utility approach provides a suitable conceptual foundation for income adjustment. For those economists who perceive a mismatch in the latter application, the solution has been to offer an alternative, such as wage indexation. In this way, politics can be cleanly separated from statistical calculation, at least on an operational level. Their attitude is not unlike that of BLS staff members when they faced the National War Labor Board during the Second World War: we can tell you that the index is a reasonably accurate measure of changes in the "cost of living" (as we define that phrase); it is up to you to choose to use it or something else for wage adjustment.

I am sympathetic to this view. The problematic issues are obviously political in nature: about equity, about socially-defined, adequate standards of living in a dynamic economy, about handling topics such as forced uptrading where no straightforward empirical answers exist. Why drag statistical calculation into such a morass? "To think that the key to this problem lies in manipulating the cost-of-living index is nonsense," wrote Aryness Joy Wickens in 1942.[83] Let the politicians and appointed civil servants select whichever measures they find politically appropriate from the range of theoretically sound, objectively calculated, seemingly apolitical statistics that are the proper products of a government statistical agency. One complication, of course, is that these same individuals don't want to choose, or rather, like the National War Labor Board, they don't want to be placed in the position of having to make a contentious choice. As Senator Alan K. Simpson (R-Wyoming) put it glumly at the end of 1995 hearings on the CPI before the Senate Finance Committee, "Where we have to go politically, no one wants to go politically."[84]

That complication takes on greater urgency if one believes that the framing of a statistical calculation—the theory or methodological principle that justifies it—can shape the subsequent political choice (or inaction). Union officials raised this point during the Second World War, arguing that there was a disjuncture between the bureau's official description of its index and the underlying reality. "You persist in calling your index a cost-of-living index," George Meany complained in 1943, "and then when you discuss it, you insist on discussing it as an index of prices."[85] The core problem behind the wartime controversy was the ambiguity of the phrase "cost of

[83] Wickens to Lubin, Nov. 18, 1942, pp. 1–2, Cost of Living Materials, box 17, GCS 1934–50, BLS.

[84] U.S. Senate, Committee on Finance, *Consumer Price Index*, 103.

[85] *Verbatim Transcript of Meetings: The President's Committee on the Cost of Living* (unpublished transcript housed in Langdell Law Library, Harvard University), Nov. 23, 1943, p. 26.

living." Though many Americans could agree that the rising cost of living should provide an upper limit for wage increases, they often had very different ideas about what that should mean in practice. Naturally, defining this upper limit was not, and could not be, merely a technical issue. But by labeling their calculation a "cost-of-living index," BLS economists provided convenient grounds for the NWLB to sidestep the difficult political problems surrounding wartime wage adjustments.

Turning to the present, it should be obvious why Congress has shown little interest in adopting wage indexation for OASDI or other programs: the bulk of the political pressures run in the opposite direction, toward trimming federal expenditures and increasing revenues. Income adjustments that allow beneficiaries to meet the rising "cost of living" are acceptable; boosts above that level, which are construed as raising beneficiaries' "standards of living," are not. Such consensus may seem to imply a broad political agreement about the proper basis for income adjustment. But, just as in the Second World War, superficial consensus may mask a far more fragmented set of pragmatic objectives.

To be sure, most politicians and bureaucrats from the late 1960s and 1970s did not expect indexation per se to address distributional equity. The OEO made a deliberate choice to avoid adding relative dimensions to the poverty thresholds, and although left-wing advocates and unions wanted OASDI payments to rise with "our increased ability to produce a greater volume of goods and services," most proposals distinguished these increases from the effects of indexation. (Walter Reuther, for example, suggested combining indexation with what he called an "improvement factor"—just as in the GM-UAW contracts—which would compensate for rising productivity.)

Still, no one suggested that a constant-utility index would be the proper basis for federal indexation. If anything, most participants seem to have had some version of a constant-goods index in mind. Indeed, the basis for the poverty thresholds is a rigid set of goods—the Department of Agriculture's 1962 economy food plan—which remains unchanged year after year. Likewise, Reuther's use of labor contracts as a model for indexation implied his endorsement of the standard union view: the CPI should be a constant-goods index. None of these advocates ever addressed the theoretical and operational problems raised by using the constant-goods framework, nor did they explicitly consider what constituted a constant standard of living over time. In short, it would be most accurate to say that few participants in the 1970s debates had a clear idea of the conceptual basis for indexation or for the CPI. (The representative for the AARP, for example, apparently thought that indexation for the "cost of living" would include boosts from "national productivity.")[86]

More generally, as we have seen over the course of this book, the phrase "cost of living" can encompass a range of different meanings. At its heart, the desire to adjust incomes (temporarily or partially) to meet the changing cost of living has been a desire to make a fair adjustment to income in response to a changing economic environment. Naturally, there can be no objective, politically neutral answer to such a question. Moreover, points of consensus and dissension can only be revealed once discussions move from an abstract level to concrete terms. Should tax brackets fall (leading to higher tax payments) as the picture quality of televisions improves? Should the introduction of novel (and beneficial) medical procedures cause cuts in Social Security payments? Do the poverty thresholds really define the same level of economic welfare today as they did in 1965?

Discussing these questions would be difficult. I suspect that responses would tend to reveal the need for a systematic reform in programs such as OASDI and the need to confront inequality overtly rather than covertly. Consequently, the resulting conversations could founder on, or further develop, the fractures and weaknesses of our existing political structure. But they would have the virtue of being honest and conscientious about what we are doing. Unfortunately, when price index theorists insist that an ordinalist, constant-utility index is the only "true" form of a cost-of-living index, they thereby bind indexation to such a concept, especially when (as in the current fiscal environment) adopting the constant-utility approach would tend to bypass difficult political problems. In turn, this forestalls further public conversation about the different possible interpretations of the "change in the cost of living" and thereby inhibits a conscious political choice about which interpretation should govern indexation of different federal programs.

Quantitative economists and government statisticians have an understandable desire to eliminate normative or subjective elements from their calculations. Of course, they also want their work to have relevance for policy decisions. And herein lies the problem. The very strategies designed to avoid normative judgments necessarily require defining politically salient

---

[86] On the desire to raise OASI benefits alongside economic growth, see U.S. House, Committee on Ways and Means, *Social Security and Welfare Proposals*, 1779, 2214, 2238, 2422. The AARP representative declared that congressmen "who are willing to take social security adjustments out of politics and gear such adjustments to our ever-increasing national productivity should write a provision into the social security law this year to require automatic adjustments as the cost of living price index rises." Ibid., 2422.

concepts in highly limited ways which may not match the outcomes that would be achieved through deliberate political discussion. Concepts such as "standards of living," "the cost of living," or "welfare" have enormous political resonance and equally extensive ambiguity. To define those concepts is to make a political choice—irrespective of the motivations for the choice itself. I have no doubt that members of the 1996 Boskin commission, like many of their colleagues, were entirely sincere in their desire to focus on technical matters and to hand responsibility for political decisions to elected officials. I am less sure that the requisite boundaries can be drawn so neatly. Perhaps when the Boskin commission told Congress that the change in "minimum expenditure required to achieve the same level of well-being" was most likely 1.1 percentage points below the CPI, the political decision had already been made.[87]

[87] Boskin et al., *Toward a More Accurate Measure of the Cost of Living*, 20.

Epilogue: Governance and Economic Statistics

It is not open to serious question that for certain questions of applied Economics on the one hand, and interpretation of history on the other, the index number technique is of great practical utility. Given a willingness to make arbitrary assumptions with regard to the significance of certain price sums, it is not denied that conclusions which are important for practice may be reached. All that it is desired to emphasise is that such conclusions do not follow from the categories of pure theory, and that they must necessarily involve a *conventional* element depending either upon the assumption of a certain empirical constancy of data or upon arbitrary judgments of value with regard to the relative importance of particular prices and particular economic subjects.[1]

> —Lionel Robbins, *An Essay on the Nature & Significance of*
> *Economic Science*, 1932

Looking over the last century, we have seen the dominant form of cost-of-living statistics move from local, often normative, "special investigations" intended to galvanize public action toward national, diachronic, putatively objective data series used to monitor and manage American economic life. I have argued that this transformation was strongly correlated with a drive to rationalize American political economy, that is, to provide a rule-governed framework for assessing, justifying, and guiding the production and distribution of material resources, typically within a bureaucratic context. Rationalization (whether self-imposed or externally mandated) promised to restrain the arbitrary abuse of collective power and, if properly constructed, channel that power toward broader community benefit. For bureaucratic organizations, rationalization offered a way to simplify administration, to justify their actions (as logical, neutral, and apolitical), and to constrain conflict.

---

[1] Lionel Robbins, *An Essay on the Nature and Significance of Economic Science*, 2nd ed. (London: MacMillan, 1945), 63.

For the first two-thirds of the twentieth century, Americans turned to cost-of-living statistics primarily to promote labor reform or resolve labor conflicts. Accordingly, rationalization based on national statistics emerged only when conflicts were construed as national (rather than regional or local) and when political or economic pressures put a high premium on stabilizing otherwise turbulent situations. It therefore surged in dramatic (if often temporary) bursts when the federal government assumed greater control over labor relations during two world wars and to a lesser degree during the New Deal. By the 1950s, the presence of large industrial unions (predicated on New Deal labor policy) had prompted a privatized form of rationalized labor relations that drew heavily on national statistics, especially on the CPI. Yet this system gained little ground outside of unionized sectors, and as union growth reached a plateau and then waned, the salience of key techniques such as cost-of-living adjustment clauses likewise declined.

Meanwhile, though, the crucible of depression and war had also reshaped the functions of the federal government and thereby generated alternative and far more durable sources of demand for national cost-of-living statistics. The underconsumption arguments of the 1930s, later transmuted into Americanized Keynesianism, created a conceptual focus on aggregate consumer purchasing power. The apparent success of wartime mobilization and economic management produced both analytic tools (especially the national accounts system) and a conviction that the national economy could be controlled, or at least modulated, through the manipulation of macroeconomic variables. From this basis, aggregate consumer inflation developed into a central part of national politics and macroeconomic policy, a gauge whose fluctuations signaled the success or failure of the complex network of federal institutions responsible for guiding the American economy toward ever-greater growth.

The decades following the Second World War also produced a massive expansion of the federal welfare state, including the 1950 amendments to the Social Security Act and the ambitious anti-poverty efforts of the Great Society. The large financial sums and the number of people affected by these programs created both administrative burdens and serious political hazards, to which rationalization became a standard response. Drawing on the model of labor contracts, politicians and bureaucrats turned to the CPI to adjust benefits and parameters to account for changes in the cost of living, thereby (rhetorically) turning these tasks into apolitical adjustments. By the end of the twentieth century, federal indexation had swollen to extraordinary proportions, with changes in the CPI directly affecting 45 percent of federal revenues (via income tax brackets) and roughly 30 percent of federal expenditures (not to mention many other federal programs via indexed parameters such as the poverty thresholds). Naturally, the financial consequences of miscalculations were equally enormous: during Senate testimony, Dale Jorgenson estimated that just one alleged error in the CPI (its treatment of housing costs from 1968 through 1982) might account for over one-quarter of the federal deficit by the mid-1990s.[2] The ties between federal debt and the CPI were further strengthened in 1997, when the U.S. Treasury began issuing Treasury Inflation-Protected Securities (TIPS), in which both interest payments and principal are adjusted according to the CPI.

In general, I have argued that the initial push to design these rationalized systems and policy arguments came primarily from left-wing and moderate attempts to reduce income inequality and to boost the living conditions of poor and working-class Americans. Of course, employers and conservatives quickly responded to those efforts with sharp critiques, their own alternative rationalized systems, and occasionally their own statistics. In the end, judgments with political valences suffused administrative rules, bureaucratic action, and even the statistical knowledge upon which those rules and actions depended. Accordingly, rationalization could not evade the asymmetries of power, ideological beliefs, and fragmentation (social, political, and economic) that had stymied earlier reform projects. That did not mean that the efforts of left-wing and moderate Americans to pursue reform through rationalization were ineffective: one would be hard-pressed to argue that the average American wage-earner today is not in better economic shape (in terms of income, working conditions, and economic security) than a counterpart from a century ago. But it did mean that rationalization could not be a source of radical transformation and that serious inequities in wealth and power would continue to characterize American economic life.

Whether and how those inequities can be addressed are pressing but immensely difficult questions, and I will not pretend to be able to treat them here. My focus is a more constrained, but still important, topic: the function, or rather malfunction, of economic statistics in rationalized governance in the United States today.

The basic premise of rationalized administration is that once a political body has identified an objective that enjoys widespread support (adjusting income payments to meet the rising cost of living), it can safely hand responsibility for enacting that objective to a technically skilled bureaucracy. Moreover, the same data that guide administrative policy can also

---

[2] U.S. Senate, Committee on Finance, *Consumer Price Index: Hearings before the Committee on Finance*, 104th Cong., 1st sess., March 13, April 6, and June 6, 1995, 2, 40.

gauge its success: the work of a government that selects economic growth as its goal and high consumer inflation as its nemesis can be publicly judged through its own official statistics. Rationalization thereby purports to make consolidated government power safe for a democracy: elected representatives can devise the objectives; career civil servants or political appointees can carry out those tasks while exercising merely technical judgments; and the public will have a transparent system to monitor the outcomes.

As we have seen, a crucial support for this vision of rational governance—the assumption that statistical calculations are straightforward, apolitical facts—cannot be sustained. Insofar as economic statistics are going to be politically relevant, they must draw on the common idiom of political discussion: growth, unemployment, cost of living, standard of living, productivity, and so forth. Yet these are nebulous phrases whose ambiguities only become clear when we seek to translate them into operational terms. Making the right methodological choices then requires defining the goals of our calculations, that is, what we are trying to accomplish by gathering this information. We can start by saying we wish to compensate seniors for the rising cost of living, but when we are confronted with the operational problems of pricing medical care and accounting for specific quality changes, we must further refine our objectives: what kinds of changes will and will not prompt higher (or lower) benefit payments?[3] These are judgments with political valences, and though statisticians and economists assiduously try to find other grounds for making such decisions, the political consequences of their choices cannot be evaded. Accordingly, politically important judgments saturate the process of statistical calculation down to a highly detailed methodological level. The strict separation of the political and the technical that is typically used to justify rationalized governance does not exist.

Nonetheless, unless Americans are willing to forgo macroeconomic planning, abandon federal attempts to reduce poverty, and dismantle social insurance, then federal bureaucracies will continue to exercise substantial control over American political economy, and national statistics will remain powerful elements in political life. Rule-governed administration of federal programs based on statistical calculations is not going away, and official statistics will continue to be central tools for guiding and judging federal economic policy. That reality raises an important question: Can we construct a new vision of "rationalized" governance, one that creates space for political

---

[3] For a similar (and more rigorously formulated) view, including an application to the problem of quality change in the CPI, see Julian Reiss, *Error in Economics: Towards a More Evidence-Based Methodology* (New York: Routledge, 2008).

discussion in the production of economic statistics but nevertheless serves to constrain the operations of federal bureaucracies (toward goals that have been defined by political negotiation) and provides a semi-independent check on the outcomes of the policies set by ruling parties?[4]

* * *

Addressing this question requires re-imagining some of the basic concepts that formed the traditional foundation of rationalized governance, especially the hoary concept of objectivity. What follows is a preliminary effort in that direction. My proposal rests on three legs that, taken together, provide a perspective from which we can construct a more effective way to allow economic statistics to serve a political purpose without being "politicized." With that philosophical groundwork in place, I suggest some pragmatic institutional changes based on this framework.

The first conceptual step requires adopting a weaker notion of objectivity, namely objectivity as full community consensus.[5] There is no pretense to transcendent knowledge under this definition, nor claim to a "view from nowhere"; instead, a statement or procedure counts as objective insofar as any suitably informed community member would assent to its validity.[6] In our case (official government statistics), the relevant community is not comprised by professional economists and statisticians but rather by the citizens of the particular political entity: city, state, nation, and so on. It is political, rather than professional, objectivity which we seek. This criterion is more difficult than achieving merely professional assent in some respects: we must persuade all citizens, not just an elite few. But it also undercuts the typical scientific claim to universal validity by emphasizing political borders: there is no requirement that an economist in Sweden must approve the Canadian statistical system.[7]

---

[4] This task is one subset of the larger problems arising from what Stephen Turner has identified as "the new politics of expertise" in contemporary democracies. Turner, *Liberal Democracy 3.0: Civil Society in an Age of Experts* (London: Sage Publications, 2003), 4–5.

[5] My views on objectivity and statistics build on the work of Ted Porter, though his emphasis is on professional consensus as formalized through rules: Theodore M. Porter, *Trust in Numbers: The Pursuit of Objectivity in Science and Public Life* (Princeton: Princeton University Press, 1995).

[6] The skeptic will already have questions about the ambiguity in this definition—e.g., what counts as "suitably informed"? Fair enough; bear with me. As discussed below, this definition creates an ideal that will probably never be reached; being overly concerned about precision here is of doubtful utility.

[7] Of course, such a step could threaten the statistical compatibility necessary for international comparisons, but only if one assumes that statistics for domestic policies and analysis must be the same as those for comparative international studies. The Harmonised

The second step requires differentiating between *apolitical* and *nonpartisan*. Statistical calculation cannot be apolitical—that is, free from political judgment. But it conceivably can be nonpartisan, insofar as all citizens with a stake in the outcome of a calculation accept its procedural validity as a practical matter. Nonpartisan (in my terminology) is thus a weaker criterion than objective: We have shifted from all citizens to relevant stakeholders and added the qualifier, "as a practical matter." The latter implies that a stakeholder may disagree with certain aspects of a calculation but, recognizing the impossibility of full consensus in the short term, is nevertheless willing to accept its validity.

Although we have weakened the constraints often placed on economic statistics (viz., that they be apolitical and subject to universal norms), these criteria are nonetheless stiff. The first (objectivity as consensus) is probably unachievable except in the most trivial instances. The second (nonpartisan) sounds more reasonable until one realizes that the pragmatic acceptance of most government economic statistics arises either through ignorance of details and consequences, or through impotence to affect the situation. We have not, in short, realized the goal of nonpartisan statistics merely because there are not weekly protests over the calculation of the Consumer Price Index.

Replacing one impossible goal (apolitical neutrality) with a weaker but still unreachable objective is not especially helpful. To remedy this situation, though, we can borrow the notion of an "epistemic virtue" from Lorraine Daston and Peter Galison for the third step. Combining "epistemic" and "virtue" may sound peculiar, but it means exactly what one would expect: a virtue that is applied in the realm of epistemology. In Daston and Galison's words, epistemic virtues "are norms that are internalized and enforced by appeal to ethical values, as well as to pragmatic efficacy in securing knowledge."[8] For my third step, I propose that we consider objectivity and nonpartisanship as epistemic virtues for the production of economic statistics.

Thinking about objectivity and nonpartisanship in these terms brings several benefits. First, it frees us from the onerous burden of setting standards that must be achievable on a regular basis: A virtue can be an object of pursuit even when it is not caught. Second, it prods us to consider objectivity

Indices of Consumer Prices (calculated by all members of the European Union alongside their national price indexes) provide a model for distinct international and domestic economic statistics.

[8] Lorraine Daston and Peter Galison, *Objectivity* (Cambridge: MIT Press, 2007), 40–41. My description of objectivity here, however, is not the same as Daston and Galison's version.

and nonpartisanship as habits and traits that can be deliberately cultivated, that can be partially formed through education, and that can be reinforced through institutional structures and carefully designed procedures.[9] Finally, characterizing objectivity and nonpartisanship as virtues frees us from the neurotic attitude toward statistics and politics that too often manifests itself. Liberated from the demand that state statistics *must* be objective, we are free to admit that political judgments inevitably occur, to search out where those judgments exist, and to encourage dialogue and debate. Guided by the premise that statistics *ought* to be objective, ought to be judged valid by all members of the community, we are handed a mandate to seek out stakeholders, to engage with opposing views, and to recognize the legitimacy of dissent founded on different values.

What would such a perspective bring in practice to the creation of government economic statistics? The potential ramifications are broad,[10] but here I will concentrate on the narrower question of institutional structures that are directly involved in constructing federal labor statistics.

First, the BLS should set (political) objectivity as an ideal goal and pragmatic nonpartisanship as a working target. To a large extent, this matches long-standing agency tradition; having spent many years reading through BLS archival materials, I can testify to the seriousness with which the agency has guarded its reputation for avoiding political manipulation. Nevertheless, the definitions given above would change agency directives in subtle ways. Pursuing objectivity would not mean pursuing a (perhaps mythical) universal professional consensus about the basis for a "true cost-of-living

---

[9]   This line of thought, of course, draws much from Michel Foucault, although it is almost Foucault's governmentality in reverse: Where Foucault examined how states shape their subjects into self-regulating citizens in order to make liberal government possible, this approach asks citizens to consider how to shape and cultivate self-disciplined government officials. Michel Foucault et al., *The Foucault Effect: Studies in Governmentality* (Chicago: University of Chicago Press, 1991). Numerous studies in political science and public policy analysis have explored institutional and procedural influences on knowledge creation for public policy, e.g., Judith Eleanor Innes, *Knowledge and Public Policy: The Search for Meaningful Indicators* (New Brunswick: Transaction Publishers, 1990); Sheila Jasanoff, *The Fifth Branch: Science Advisors as Policymakers* (Cambridge: Harvard University Press, 1990); Daniel Lee Kleinman, ed., *Science, Technology, and Democracy* (Albany: State University of New York Press, 2000).

[10] Consider training in econometrics or the study of economic statistics, for example. Rather than concentrating solely on quantitative techniques and economic theory, the view outlined above would push students to analyze the assumptions and conceptual foundations of statistical calculations from an avowedly political viewpoint. The goal here would not be to train partisan statisticians but to train experts skilled in mathematical techniques and economic analysis who are also attuned to recognizing the spaces where judgments with political valences enter into statistical calculation.

index" (though it would not require discarding theory either). Instead, it would mean pursuing a situation where all members of the relevant society would accept the validity of a given calculation. Nonpartisanship, based on compromise and consensus, would be distinguished from supposedly apolitical, technical neutrality, which emphasizes the dominance of theory but precludes considering statistics in light of their applications and the political judgments that necessarily accompany such an analysis.

Second, the pursuit of (political) objectivity requires expanding the bureau's work in educating the public about its statistical series. The bureau does an excellent job documenting the methods that it uses. It is less successful in thoroughly explaining the conceptual foundations of its statistics, the assumptions that are involved, and the potential ramifications of those assumptions.[11] In particular, the pursuit of (political) objectivity would push the bureau to address how its statistics fit with existing applications (especially within the federal government), what consequences are entailed by different methodological choices, and what objections have been raised. BLS staff themselves need not be responsible for developing these analyses, but the bureau should be responsible for collating this information and making it available alongside its own explication of current methods. Historically, the BLS has been reluctant to publicize overtly political criticism and analysis of its work. Such reluctance is understandable under the existing, rationalized framework for federal statistics, for it highlights the very kind of political valences to statistical calculation that the bureau wishes to avoid. Yet, in my view, that attitude is a mistake. Not only does it deny working reality, but it tends to breed frustration instead of defusing it. I suspect, for example, that union hostility during the Second World War would have been greatly reduced had the BLS published a short but frank statement about the limits of the index with every monthly news release (as it did from July 1944 onward; Chapter 6), especially if that statement had quoted some of the skeptical comments from the 1943 American Statistical Association committee about the relevance of the index for wage adjustment.

The third task is by far the most complicated: devising an institutional process by which political discussion can become an integral part of the creation of economic statistics. The temptation here is to revert to the

---

[11] Consider the current (2007) BLS *Handbook of Methods*, which describes a cost-of-living index as answering the question, "What is the cost, at this month's market prices, of achieving the standard of living actually attained in the base period?" Then, without qualifying this concept, it reports that economists usually view a Laspeyres index such as the CPI as an "upper bound" to a cost-of-living index.

traditional, rationalized model, in which politicians are responsible for hashing out broad goals and technicians are left to handle the details. As I have argued, though, that model is insufficient: it is only through discussion of methodological details that the ambiguities in broader concepts (e.g., maintaining a constant standard of living over time) can be differentiated. Choice between these methodological options then requires reconsidering the objectives of statistical applications. Politicians may agree that tax brackets should rise alongside the cost of living, but do they want tax brackets to fall just because cell phones get smaller? That outcome might be implied by neoclassical price index theory, but it cannot be inferred from the original congressional debates over indexation.

Political discussions, therefore, must extend down into the depths of statistical methodology. Moreover, there is no reason to expect that the outcome of any given discussion will remain fixed over time. Political consensus can shift, and theoretical developments may yield new refinements or previously unrecognized problems. The BLS therefore requires a permanent institutional process through which political judgments can be incorporated into both basic conceptual frameworks for its statistics and low-level methodological decisions.

The simplest option would be to treat the BLS as a policy agency, subject to the high rates of political appointments that typically accompany such a designation. That change would be a serious mistake, however. First, since the executive branch has primary control over political appointments, treating the BLS as a policy agency would lead to strong ideological imbalances that would fluctuate with control of the White House. Rather than fostering broad political discussion and compromise, the bureau would slip back and forth between alternative views. Second, this instability itself runs counter to the needs of statistical agencies. There is a vast amount of tacit knowledge—informal know-how learned through experience—required to produce valuable statistics on a broad scale and in a timely manner. Constant churning of high-level staff, and especially the repeated introduction of economists unfamiliar with federal statistical work, would handicap the bureau. Moreover, the continuity of the bureau's data series themselves could suffer serious blows if the agency faced radical changes each electoral cycle. Institutional stability is a basic requirement for the production of reliable, national data series.

If the BLS itself cannot provide the forum for balanced political discussion of its methodology, then that forum must come from outside, that is, from a committee. Committees have a deserved reputation for serving as paper-generating alternatives to real action; in that respect, creating a committee to handle political discussions about BLS statistics may seem tantamount to making them innocuous and ineffectual. Nevertheless, there are ways to structure committee systems to minimize these dangers. First, the advisory committee must be a permanent body so that its critical voice does not disappear (after a great fanfare surrounding a single report) but continues to be an ongoing presence for the BLS and the public. Second, unlike the bureau's old advisory committees, LRAC and BRAC, there should be no pretense that the committee is merely a technical body that avoids using political judgments when making its recommendations. (In this way, the committee can avoid some of the problems that repeatedly constrained LRAC by forcing it to treat its recommendations as if they were simply technical arguments about how to measure inflation properly; Chapters 7 and 9). Finally, the membership must be adaptable to changes in the political economy of statistical calculation (again, unlike LRAC and BRAC, which were locked in a static structure that did not reflect the uses of BLS statistics from the 1960s on).

I suggest forming an overarching Labor Statistics Advisory Committee with specialized subcommittees that would gather representatives of those who use BLS statistics and who are affected by them to critique the bureau's methods, to offer alternatives, and to advise the bureau in its decisions. (The time is ripe for such a change, since the BLS disbanded LRAC and BRAC in the fall of 2007, declaring its intention to replace them with an as—of yet unannounced structure.)[12] The BLS should not be bound by Advisory Committee recommendations, which would largely replicate the problems that might be caused by turning the BLS itself into a policy agency. Instead, the committee would provide an official forum for criticism, and, in light of the bureau's goals of objectivity and nonpartisanship, it would continually press the agency to take criticism seriously, to seek compromises where possible, to develop more persuasive rationales, and to open itself to change.

There is, on the surface, a potential pitfall here. If statistical calculations are inherently political, and if the Advisory Committee is strictly "advisory," then by implication the BLS has control over political decisions. How can such control be handed to an agency not subject to typical political appointment procedures? To ease this dilemma, we must return to the bureau's working goal of nonpartisanship, a standard that must continue to be inculcated within the bureau's working culture (as it already has been) and to which it can be held. In practice, nonpartisanship means

---

[12] Larry Swisher, "Economic Statistics: BLS's Business, Labor Advisory Panels Expire Pending DOL Restructuring Plan," *NABE News*, no. 189 (2007).

seeking compromise, striving to avoid favoritism, looking for consensus, and working for balance. Official rhetoric to the contrary, such an attitude (rather than apolitical neutrality) has always characterized the bureau at its best, and it served the BLS especially well under Ewan Clague in the 1950s, when the bureau faced two extremely "interested" advisory groups. The short answer, in other words, is that the BLS can be politic without being politicized. Meanwhile, critics of bureau decisions are free to air their complaints publicly (putting additional pressure on the bureau) and through the Advisory Committee; if the committee tends strongly in one direction, it will become harder and harder for the BLS to resist a change while maintaining a reputation for nonpartisan action.

The essential role of the Advisory Committee as a conduit for broader public views and representation brings us to the most difficult question: membership. It is obviously impossible for the committee to represent all views in a diverse nation such as the United States. Moreover, membership is further limited by the expertise required to handle technical discussions about statistics and economic theory. Creating space for political judgments in economic statistics does not mean eliminating expertise; these are complex tasks, and indeed it is only sustained attempts to wrestle with concepts such as the "change in the national cost of living" that have revealed the potential contradictions and ambiguities inherent in seemingly simple ideas. What we need, therefore, is a means to gather a group of experts who are roughly representative of the political balance in the United States.

My suggestion is to build off of existing democratic structures: allot a small number of slots for assignment by the White House and a larger number by the Democratic and Republican members of the Joint Economic Committee, respectively. In turn, Advisory Committee members would be understood to represent specific user groups or political perspectives. Like the BLS, the committee should set nonpartisanship as a working target, which means striving for unanimous recommendations whenever possible but also accepting and acknowledging dissent as it occurs. Because of that goal, having lengthier tenures for members would be an advantage, giving the members time to overcome distrust, to learn to work together, and perhaps even to learn from one another.

The influence of the Labor Statistics Advisory Committee should not be diluted by trying to balance it against supposedly apolitical, technical committees. Accordingly, the BLS should end its involvement with the Federal Economic Statistics Advisory Committee (FESAC) and instead expand funding and support for its internal research divisions. FESAC—which consists primarily of academic economists and statisticians convened to advise the BLS, the Bureau of Economic Analysis, and the Bureau of the Census—is predicated precisely on the view that I have rejected here, namely that the best way to create "objective" statistics is to ensure that they mesh with theory and to avoid considering existing statistics in light of their applications or the political judgments that such consideration necessarily entails. Of course, the BLS needs to retain contact with ongoing research and analysis, and of course it should face critiques and gather advice from prominent academic professionals. Yet the proper forums for that contact are through ad hoc commissions that aim primarily to collect and summarize scholarly research and through the bureau's research divisions (currently, the BLS has five, covering different fields within labor statistics). The 2002 review of the CPI by the National Academy of Sciences, despite its weakness as an operational guide for the CPI, provides an excellent example of how a professional committee can summarize points of consensus and dissension within the academic community.[13] Meanwhile, the research divisions should serve two functions: (1) being a regular conduit to the academic community (taking advice but also continuing to publish research on BLS methods), and (2) pursuing research and exploring conceptual questions proposed by the Advisory Committee.

* * *

The recommendations above have two goals. First, they are intended to weaken the bureau's reliance on economic theory as a proxy for "objectivity" and impartial analysis, since I am not persuaded that theory can serve that purpose. The adequacy of theory can only be judged in light of the application for a statistical calculation, and making that judgment is a political decision. Ideally, the pressures produced by the decision-making process will push Congress to recognize that key statistics such as the CPI are serving multiple, sometimes conflicting objectives (income adjustment, deflating macroeconomic statistics) which would be better served by individualized statistical measures. Second, the recommendations treat nonpartisanship in pragmatic terms and aim to find institutional structures that can achieve that goal. I do not pretend that the proposals above are perfect; there may be far better ways to achieve what I have in mind. Nor do I believe that any such restructuring will suddenly eliminate all problems and leave everyone

---

[13] Charles L. Schultze and Christopher Mackie, eds., *At What Price? Conceptualizing and Measuring Cost-of-Living and Price Indexes* (Washington, D.C.: National Academy Press, 2002).

pleased with the outcomes. On the contrary, I expect that they will produce frustration: headaches for BLS staff members who will need to face contentious decisions while monitored by interested parties and frustration for Advisory Committee members who find their perspectives outvoted or overlooked by the bureau. In short, they will produce politics.

The advantage of this approach is that it brings to the surface the judgments that are in fact embedded in the calculation of economic statistics and asks us to consider the political ramifications of those choices. It does not eliminate the asymmetries of power that will continue to function (just as they did for BRAC and LRAC in the 1950s); it does not make the hard questions any easier; it does not provide a solution to political deadlocks; and it does not force Americans to deal with inequality or to adopt Amartya Sen's capabilities approach to defining a standard of living (though I think that would be a more appropriate basis for income adjustment). But it does ask us to think more consciously about the objectives behind our use of economic statistics and about the appropriateness of our choices. The limitations of rationalization are many. The strength of setting objectivity and nonpartisanship as goals, however, is not that they are easily reached but that they press us to listen to dissent and to recognize inadequacies. If rationalized governance is an inevitable accompaniment to contemporary political economy (and as long as we cling to both liberalism and collective economic organization, I am convinced that it will be), then we must find some way to grapple with its demands more effectively and forthrightly.

Technical Appendix: A Brief Primer on Cost-of-Living Indexes

COST-OF-LIVING INDEXES: A PRELIMINARY DEFINITION

The phrase "cost-of-living index" was used in many different ways during the twentieth century. For most economists, however, a cost-of-living index was a ratio that compared the cost of obtaining a given standard of living in two different places or time periods. Thus, a cost-of-living index comparing 1910 to 1900 would look like this:

$$\text{Cost-of-living index}_{(1900\text{-}1910)} = \frac{\text{Cost of a given standard of living in 1910}}{\text{Cost of same standard of living in 1900}}$$

Most cost-of-living indexes are used to make comparisons over time and are typically produced as data series, in which the denominator remains constant (showing the cost of a particular standard in the initial, *base period*) while the numerator is updated at regular intervals:

$$\text{Cost-of-living index}_{(\text{base period--present})}$$
$$= \frac{\text{Cost of given standard of living (currently)}}{\text{Cost of same standard of living (in base period)}}$$

Traditionally, cost-of-living indexes are expressed as percentages (calculated by multiplying the cost-ratio by one hundred). Thus, if a particular standard of living could be purchased for the same amount of money in both 1900 and 1910, the index would be 100; if the cost rose by 30 percent, the index would be 130; by 40 percent, 140; and so forth.

DEFINING THE "STANDARD OF LIVING": CONSTANT-GOODS AND CONSTANT-UTILITY INDEXES

Obviously, the tricky part of calculating a cost-of-living index is deciding how to define a common "standard of living" in two different situations (e.g., 1900 and 1910). The oldest approach used a fixed collection of goods and services, known as the *market basket*. In the main text, I have labeled this a "constant-goods index":

$$\text{Constant-goods index}_{(\text{base period–present})}$$
$$= \frac{\text{Cost of specified market basket (currently)}}{\text{Cost of same market basket (in base period)}}$$

The goods and services comprising the market basket might be defined on an a priori, theoretical basis (e.g., a minimum adequate market basket for a family of five), but more typically the basket was based to some degree on the actual, average expenditures of a particular social group, such as urban, working-class families.

The constant-goods approach created certain practical problems (for example, consumer goods change over time: how should the index be altered to reflect these changes?). But it also faced theoretical critiques, most notably from neoclassical economists. The latter argued that a standard of living was defined not by goods and services per se, but by the "utility," "satisfaction," or "welfare" brought to the individual through those purchases. A cost-of-living index, therefore, ought to track the minimum cost of obtaining a fixed level of "utility." In the manuscript, I have labeled this a "constant-utility index":

$$\text{Constant-utility index}$$
$$= \frac{\text{Cost of obtaining a fixed level of "utility" (currently)}}{\text{Cost of obtaining the same level of utility (in base period)}}$$

A constant-utility approach provides a more theoretically consistent method for handling problems such as changing consumer markets: in each situation, one should select the most inexpensive set of goods and services that provides the same level of welfare as the initial market basket. But if the theory is more flexible, the practical problems are no less daunting: how can you compare the "satisfaction" produced by different goods and services in different contexts? What, in fact, does "utility" mean?

Today, driven primarily by the dominance of neoclassical economics, the "constant-goods" approach is commonly called a "cost-of-goods index," while the phrase "cost-of-living index" usually refers to the constant-utility ideal. In the past, however, "cost-of-living index" had a much broader meaning; one goal of the book is to explain how this concept became tied so tightly to the constant-utility approach.

PRACTICAL CALCULATION: COST-OF-LIVING INDEXES AS PRICE INDEXES

Historically, cost-of-living indexes have been classified as a special form of a "price index"; indeed, for much of the twentieth century, the phrase "cost-of-living index" was synonymous with "retail price index"—that is, a price index focused on consumer goods and services. The other major form of a price index was a "wholesale price index" (today frequently known as a "producer price index"), which tracked the prices of commodities (often, but not always, raw materials) that were purchased by businesses for further processing or sale rather than by end consumers.

Most early price indexes were wholesale price indexes, created first by commercial periodicals in the mid- to late nineteenth century and followed several decades later by official government versions. The basic components of these statistics were smaller ratios (known as *price relatives*) that each showed the price change in a specific commodity over a given period. For example, if p_{iron}^{1915} represents the average price of iron in 1915, the price relative for iron over the period 1900–1915 would be:

$$\frac{p_{iron}^{1915}}{p_{iron}^{1900}}$$

To calculate an overall index, economists created an average of the price relatives for a set of relevant commodities. Continuing our example, we can calculate a price index for iron, wheat, and corn over the period 1900–1915 as follows:

$$\text{Price Index}_{1900-1915} = \left(\frac{p_{iron}^{1915}}{p_{iron}^{1900}} + \frac{p_{wheat}^{1915}}{p_{wheat}^{1900}} + \frac{p_{corn}^{1915}}{p_{corn}^{1900}} \right) \times \frac{1}{3}$$

In this calculation, the price relatives are "unweighted"; that is, each has a similar potential to influence the overall result. By contrast, many economists recommended *weighting* the price relatives when combining them into an average, so that the price changes of commodities with greater impact on the economy would have a proportionally greater effect on the overall index:

$$\text{Weighted Price Index}_{1900-1915} = w_{iron} \times \frac{P_{iron}^{1915}}{P_{iron}^{1900}} + w_{wheat} \times \frac{P_{wheat}^{1915}}{P_{wheat}^{1900}} + w_{corn} \times \frac{P_{corn}^{1915}}{P_{corn}^{1900}}$$

where w_{iron} is the weight used for the price relative of iron, and so forth. (Note that rather than dividing the sum of the price relatives by the number of commodities—as was done for the unweighted price index above—we can now simply adjust the weights to account for the number of elements in our average.) Typically these weights were based on the proportional expenditure on each commodity in a given year (i.e., the expenditure on a given commodity divided by the total expenditure on all commodities in the index). Thus, if 50 percent of the money in our hypothetical economy of iron, wheat, and corn was spent on wheat, the price relative for wheat would have a weight of 0.5 in the overall index.

A retail price index would have followed the same form, with the price relatives drawn from key consumer goods and services while the weights were derived from the expenditures of a specific social group (typically urban, working-class families). On an abstract level, keeping the weights constant was like using a fixed market basket; in fact, if the weights were derived from proportional expenditure in the base year of the index, the calculation was exactly equivalent to a constant-goods index with a base-period market basket.[1] This connection explains why "retail price index" and "cost-of-living index" were used interchangeably by many statisticians through much of the twentieth century. For the reader, the essential point

---

[1] In mathematical terms:

Weighted average of price relatives $= \sum w_n \frac{p^t}{p^0}$, where w_n is the weight for the nth price relative

Constant-goods index $= \frac{\sum q_n p_n^t}{\sum q_n p_n^0}$, where q_n is the quantity of the nth item With the weights

equal to the proportionate expenditure on each item at base period prices, these two forms become equivalent:

$$Index = \sum_{n=1}^{N} w_n \frac{p_n^t}{p_n^0} = \sum_{n=1}^{N} \left(\frac{q_n p_n^0}{\sum_{n=1}^{N} q_n p_n^0} \right) \frac{p_n^t}{p_n^0} = \frac{\sum_{n=1}^{N} q_n p_n^t}{\sum_{n=1}^{N} q_n p_n^0}$$

to remember is that the market basket used in a cost-of-living index was defined by the list of goods priced for the index and by the weights assigned their price relatives. Within this framework, maintaining a constant set of weights was equivalent to using a fixed market basket; to change the weights was (in effect) to introduce a new market basket.

Index